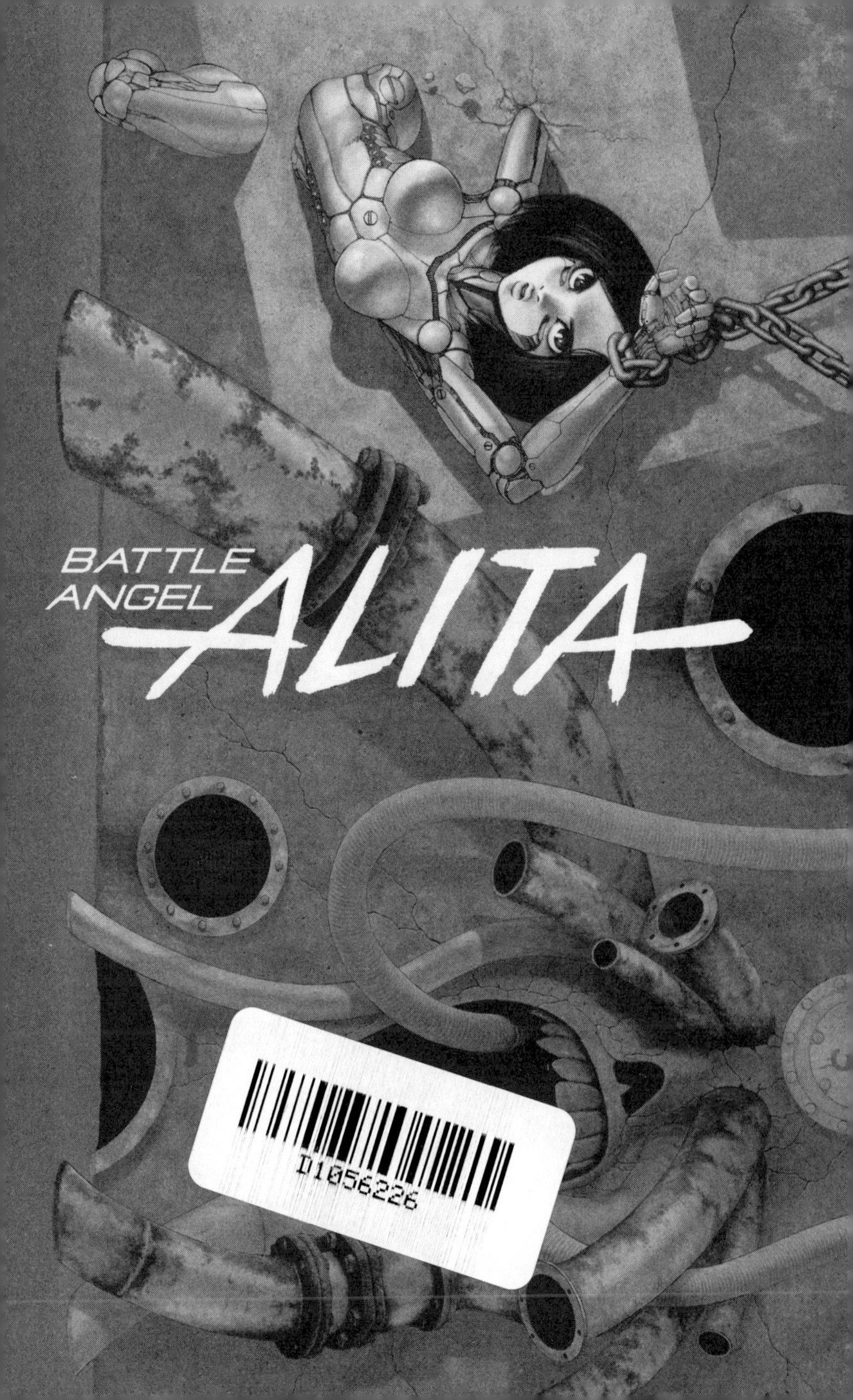
BATTLE
ANGEL
ALITA

C O N T E N T S

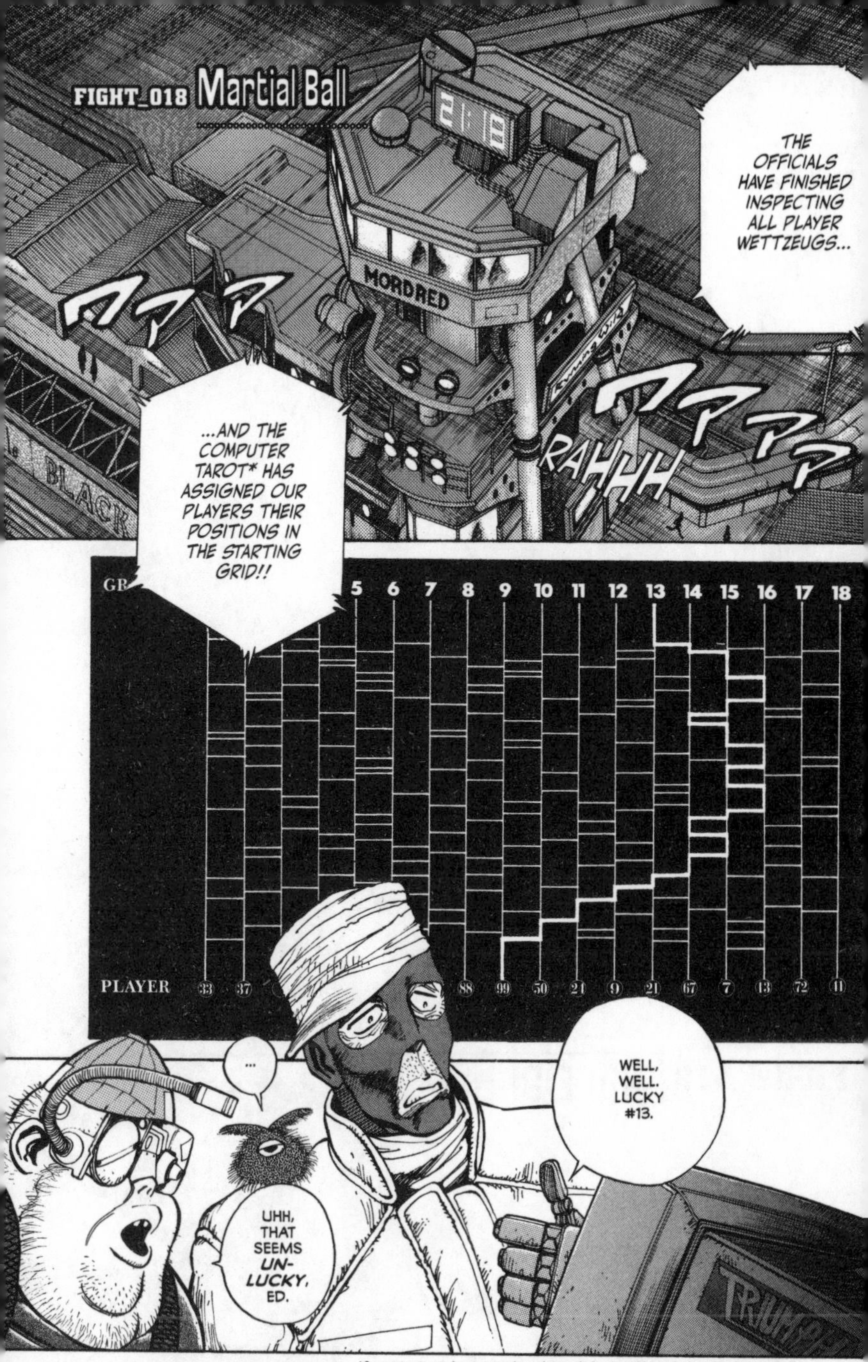
FIGHT_018 Martial Ball
21:18
THE OFFICIALS HAVE FINISHED INSPECTING ALL PLAYER WETTZEUGS...
RAHHH
MORDRED
...AND THE COMPUTER TAROT* HAS ASSIGNED OUR PLAYERS THEIR POSITIONS IN THE STARTING GRID!!
5 6 7 8 9 10 11 12 13 14 15 16 17 18
PLAYER
33 37 88 99 50 21 9 21 67 7 13 72 11
WELL, WELL. LUCKY #13.
...
UHH, THAT SEEMS UN-LUCKY, ED.

***Computer tarot:** A computer draws lots to derive the grid (starting) position in motorball. The higher one's point total, the higher the placement priority.

FIGHT_018 Martial Ball

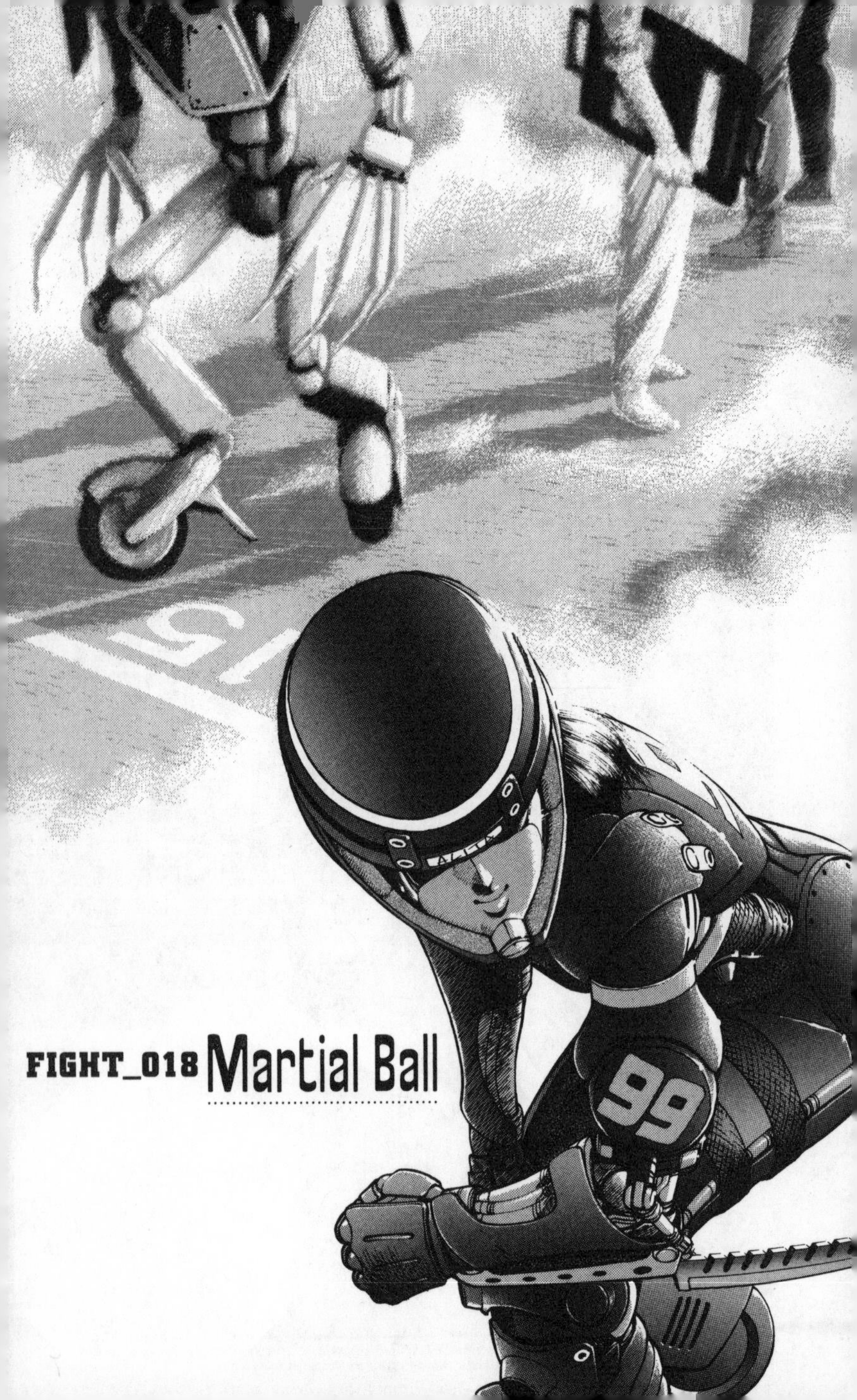
99

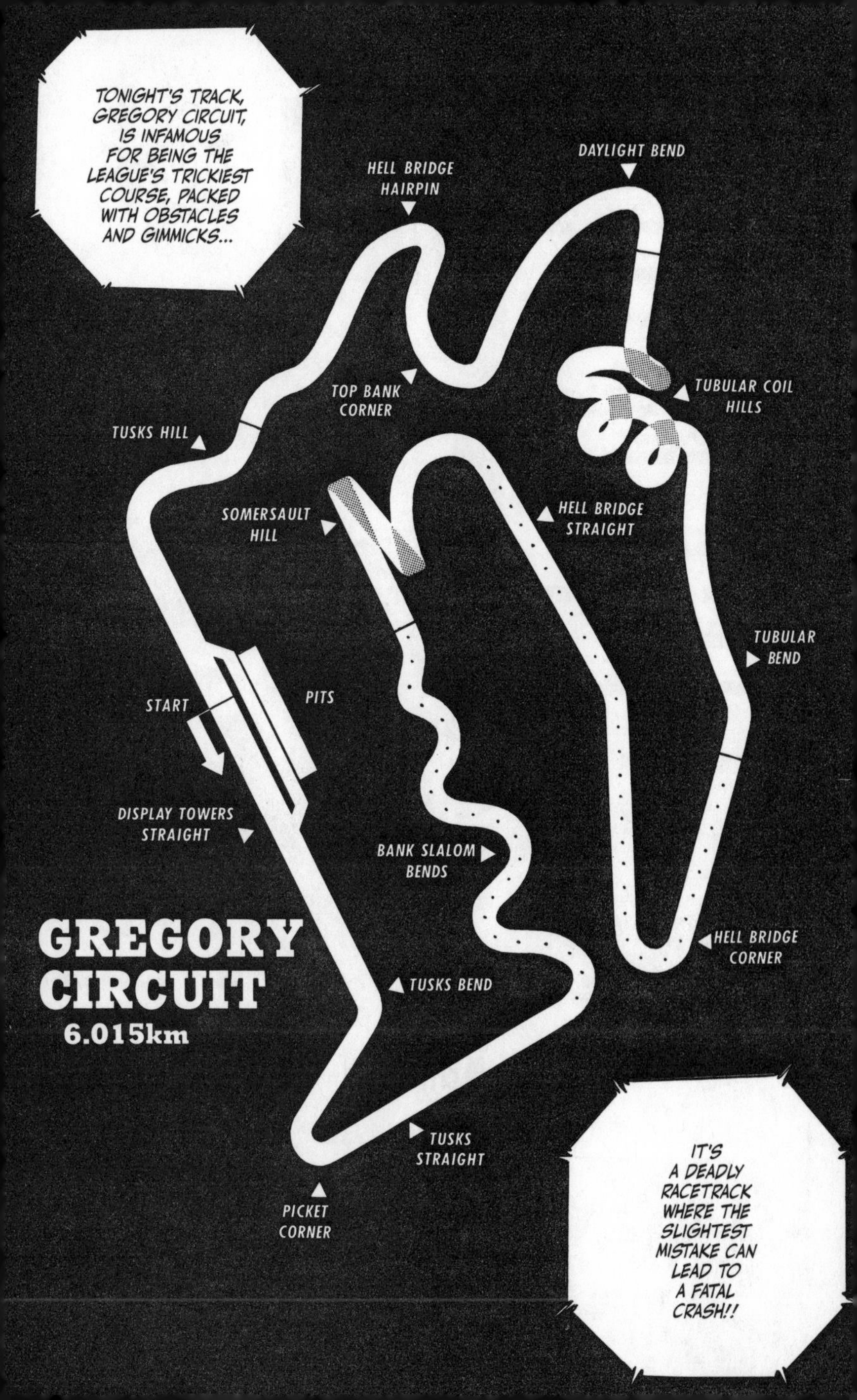
TONIGHT'S TRACK, GREGORY CIRCUIT, IS INFAMOUS FOR BEING THE LEAGUE'S TRICKIEST COURSE, PACKED WITH OBSTACLES AND GIMMICKS...
DAYLIGHT BEND
HELL BRIDGE HAIRPIN
TUBULAR COIL HILLS
TOP BANK CORNER
TUSKS HILL
HELL BRIDGE STRAIGHT
SOMERSAULT HILL
TUBULAR BEND
PITS
START
DISPLAY TOWERS STRAIGHT
BANK SLALOM BENDS
HELL BRIDGE CORNER
GREGORY CIRCUIT
6.015km
TUSKS BEND
TUSKS STRAIGHT
PICKET CORNER
IT'S A DEADLY RACETRACK WHERE THE SLIGHTEST MISTAKE CAN LEAD TO A FATAL CRASH!!

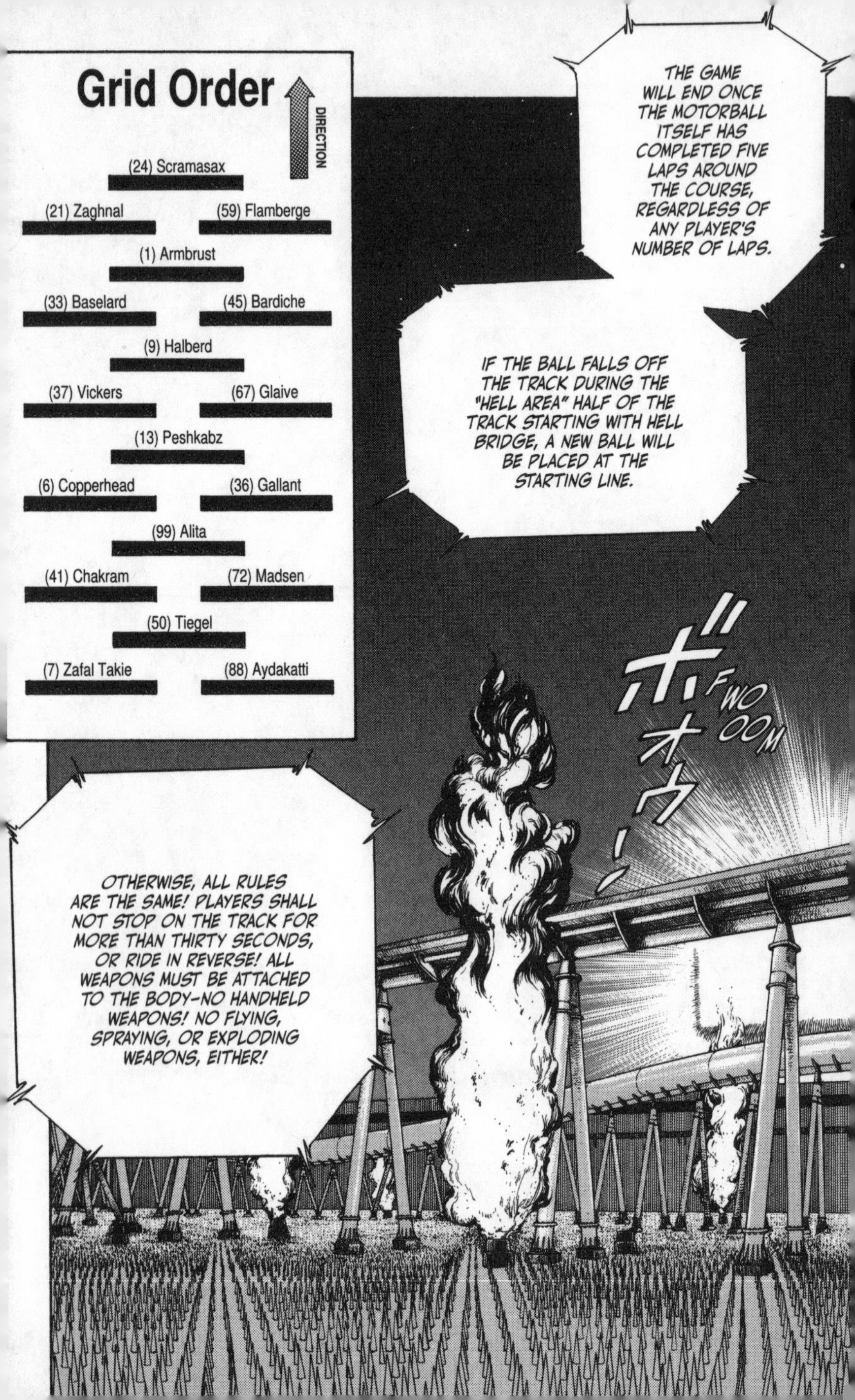
THE GAME WILL END ONCE THE MOTORBALL ITSELF HAS COMPLETED FIVE LAPS AROUND THE COURSE, REGARDLESS OF ANY PLAYER'S NUMBER OF LAPS.
IF THE BALL FALLS OFF THE TRACK DURING THE "HELL AREA" HALF OF THE TRACK STARTING WITH HELL BRIDGE, A NEW BALL WILL BE PLACED AT THE STARTING LINE.
ボオウ!!
FWOOOM
Grid Order
DIRECTION
(24) Scramasax
(21) Zaghnal
(59) Flamberge
(1) Armbrust
(33) Baselard
(45) Bardiche
(9) Halberd
(37) Vickers
(67) Glaive
(13) Peshkabz
(6) Copperhead
(36) Gallant
(99) Alita
(41) Chakram
(72) Madsen
(50) Tiegel
(7) Zafal Takie
(88) Aydakatti
OTHERWISE, ALL RULES ARE THE SAME! PLAYERS SHALL NOT STOP ON THE TRACK FOR MORE THAN THIRTY SECONDS, OR RIDE IN REVERSE! ALL WEAPONS MUST BE ATTACHED TO THE BODY—NO HANDHELD WEAPONS! NO FLYING, SPRAYING, OR EXPLODING WEAPONS, EITHER!

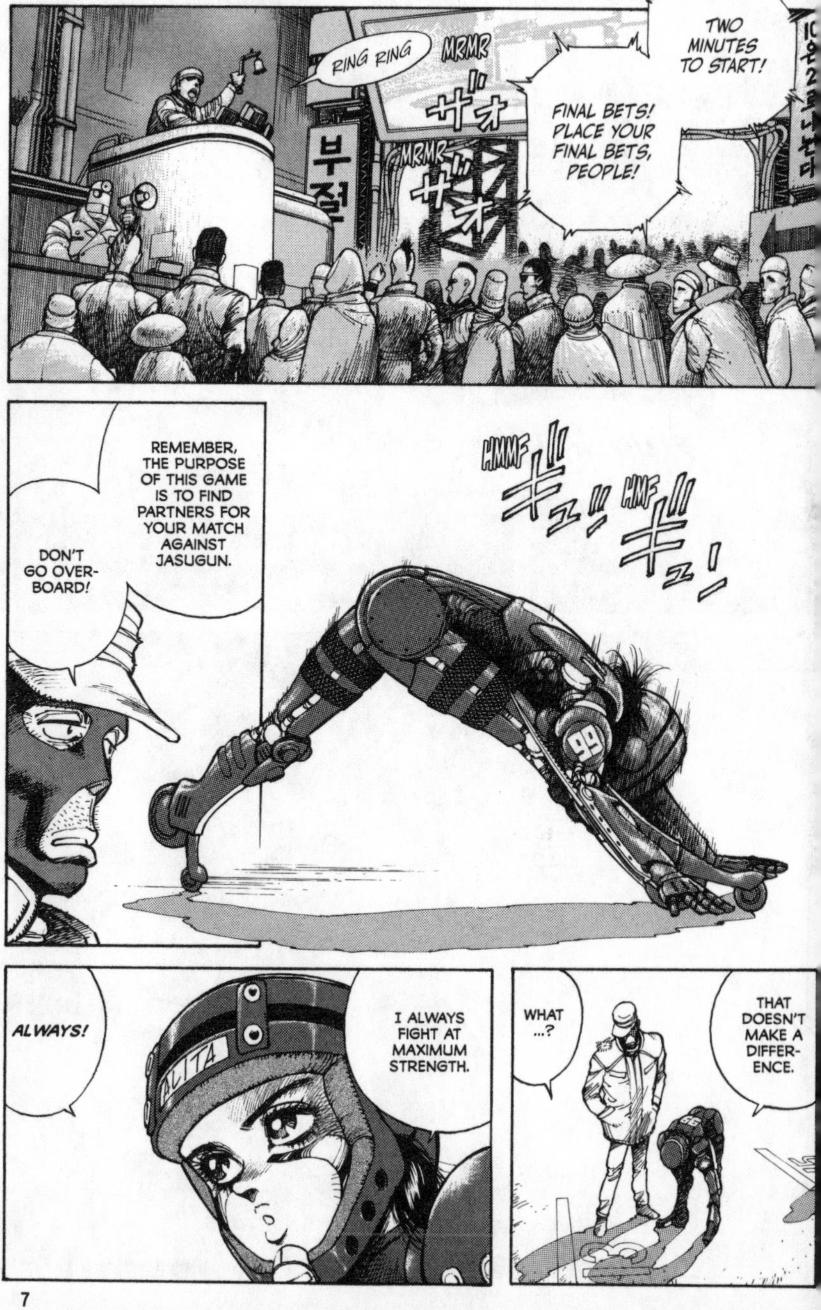
TWO MINUTES TO START!
FINAL BETS! PLACE YOUR FINAL BETS, PEOPLE!
MRMR
ザオ
MRMR
ザオ
RING RING
부절
REMEMBER, THE PURPOSE OF THIS GAME IS TO FIND PARTNERS FOR YOUR MATCH AGAINST JASUGUN.
DON'T GO OVER-BOARD!
HMMF
ギュ!!
HMF
ギュ!
THAT DOESN'T MAKE A DIFFER-ENCE.
WHAT ...?
I ALWAYS FIGHT AT MAXIMUM STRENGTH.
ALWAYS!
ALITA

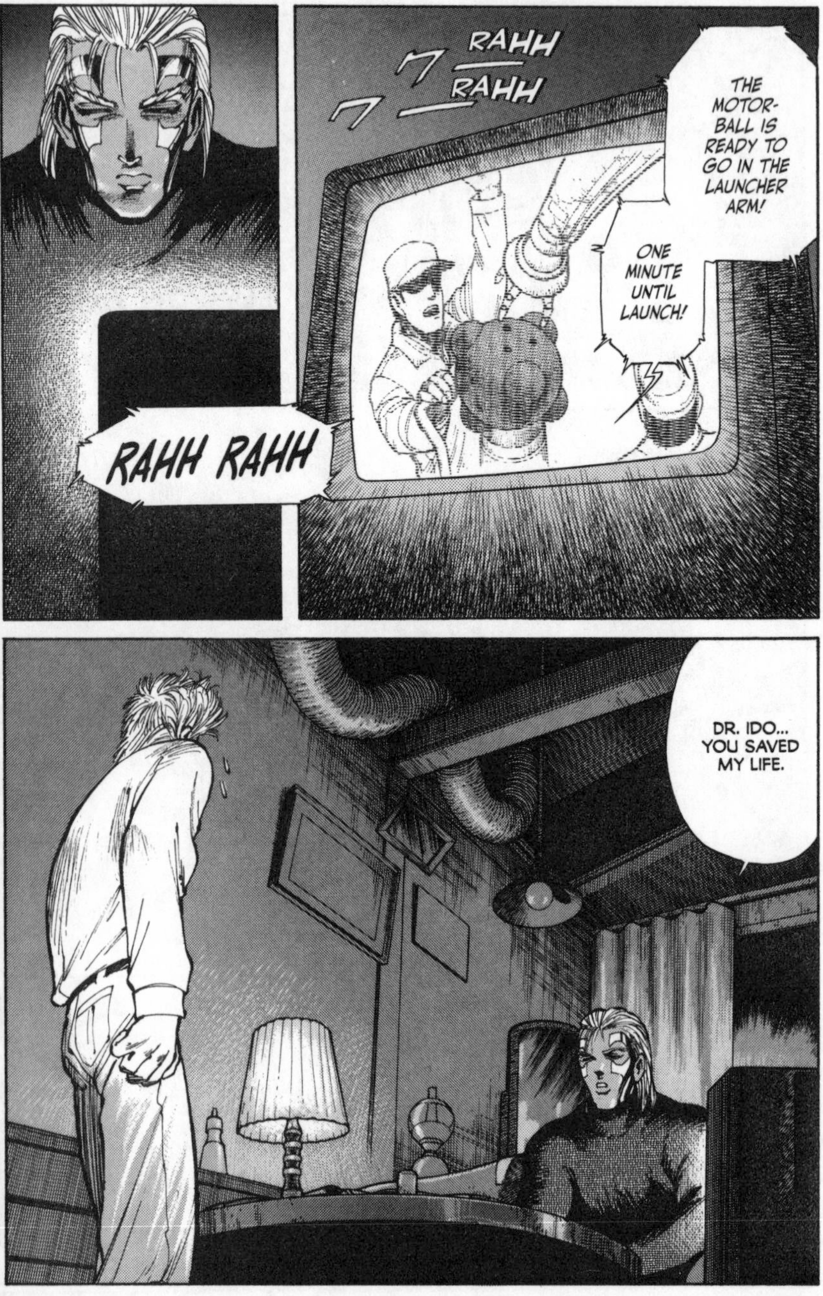
THE MOTOR-BALL IS READY TO GO IN THE LAUNCHER ARM!
ONE MINUTE UNTIL LAUNCH!
RAHH
RAHH
RAHH RAHH
DR. IDO... YOU SAVED MY LIFE.

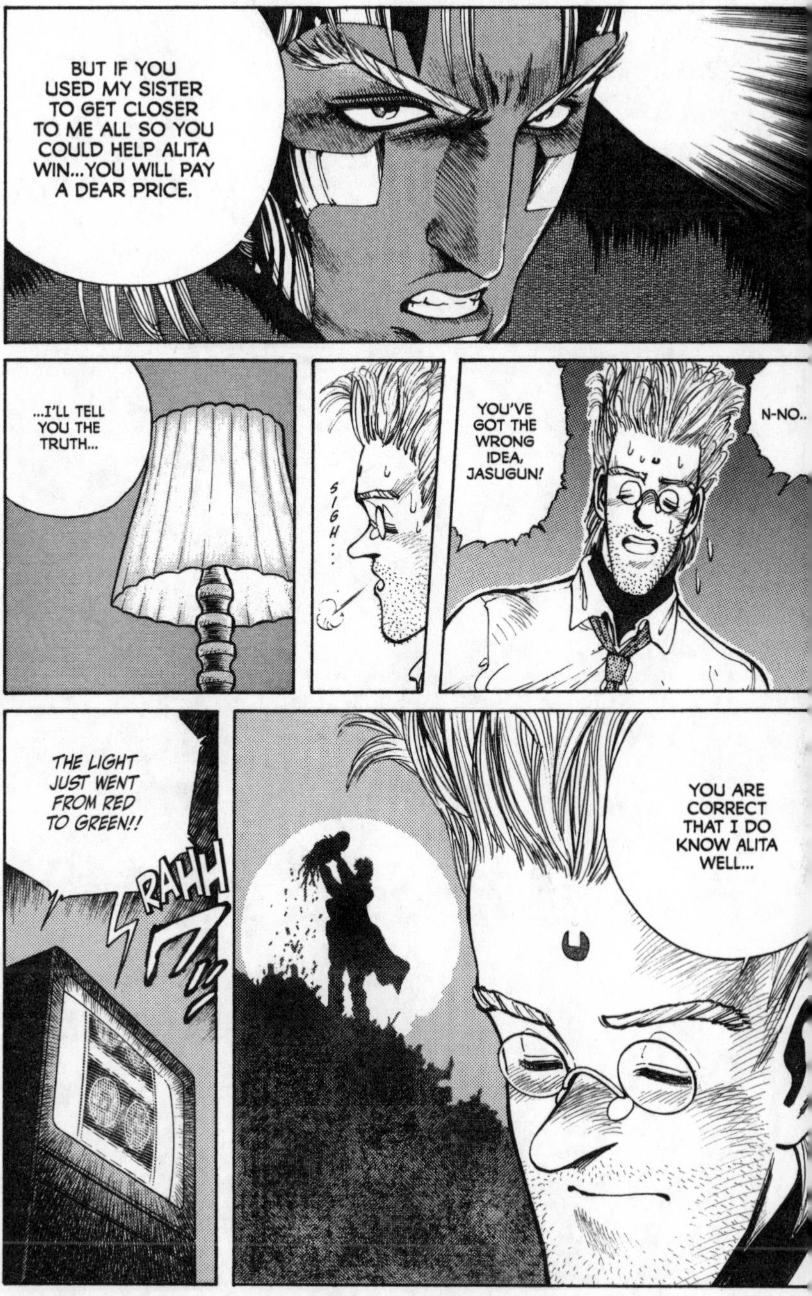
BUT IF YOU USED MY SISTER TO GET CLOSER TO ME ALL SO YOU COULD HELP ALITA WIN...YOU WILL PAY A DEAR PRICE.
N-NO..
YOU'VE GOT THE WRONG IDEA, JASUGUN!
SIGH...
...I'LL TELL YOU THE TRUTH...
YOU ARE CORRECT THAT I DO KNOW ALITA WELL...
THE LIGHT JUST WENT FROM RED TO GREEN!!
RAHH

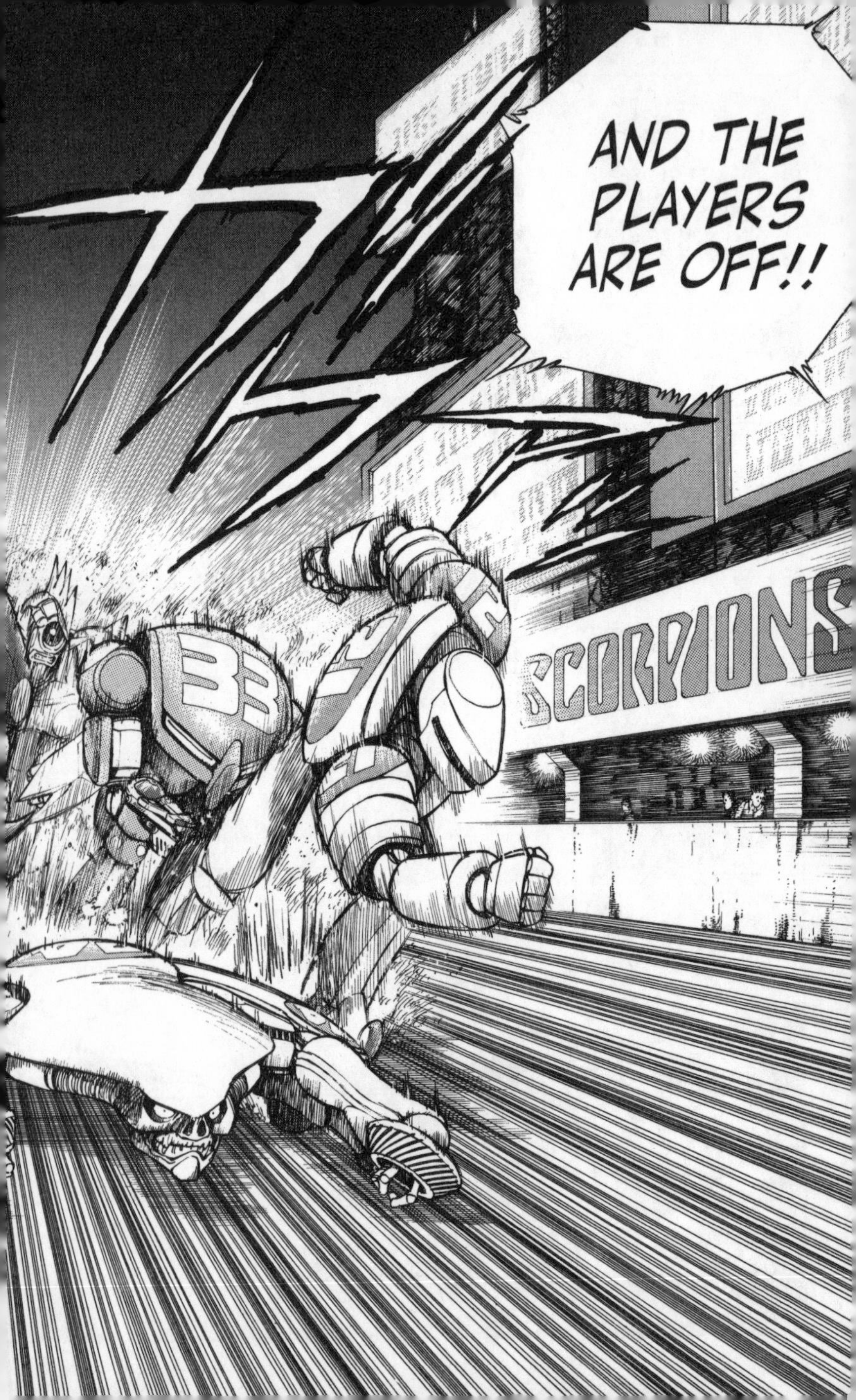
AND THE PLAYERS ARE OFF!!
SCORPIONS

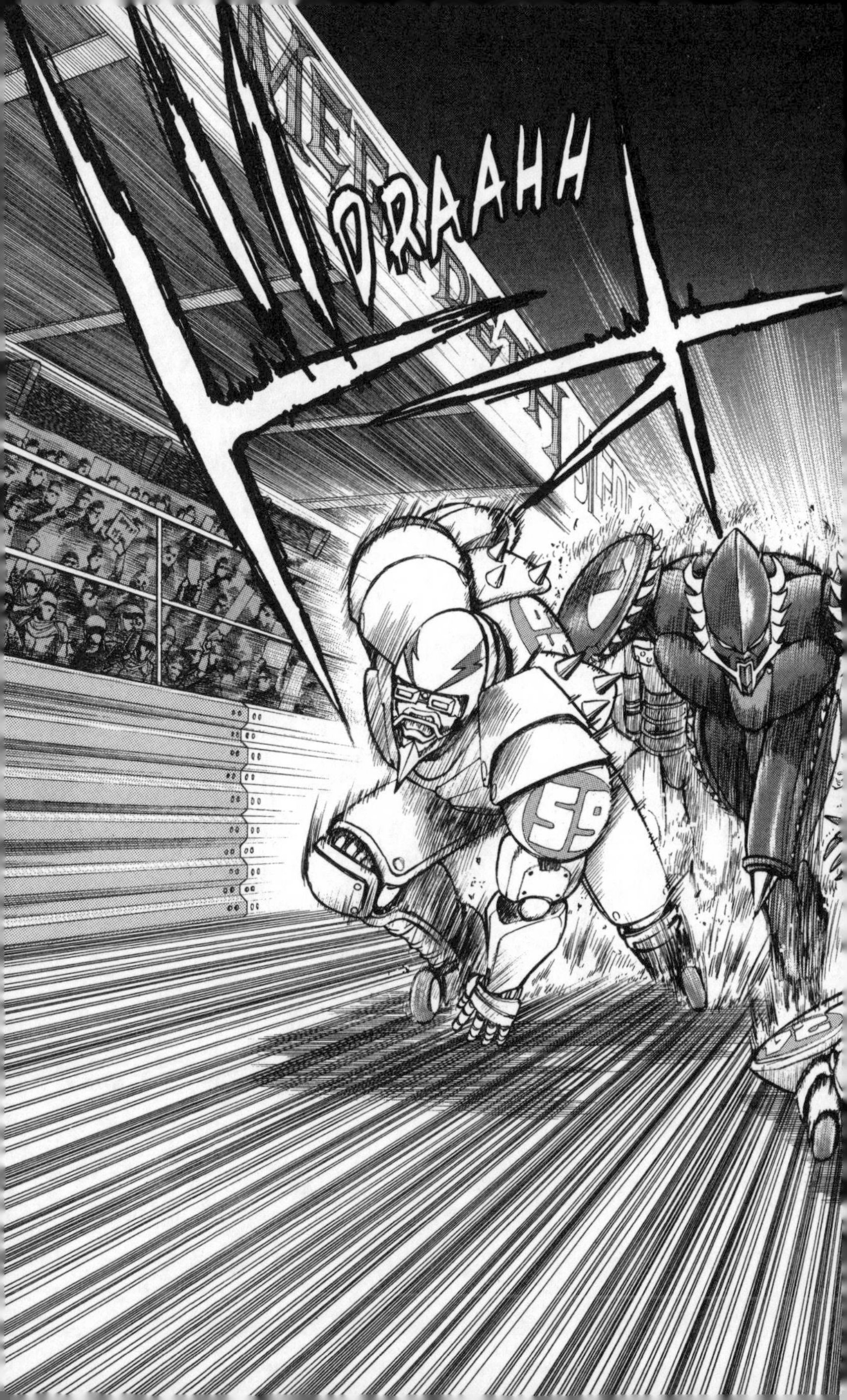
DRAAHH

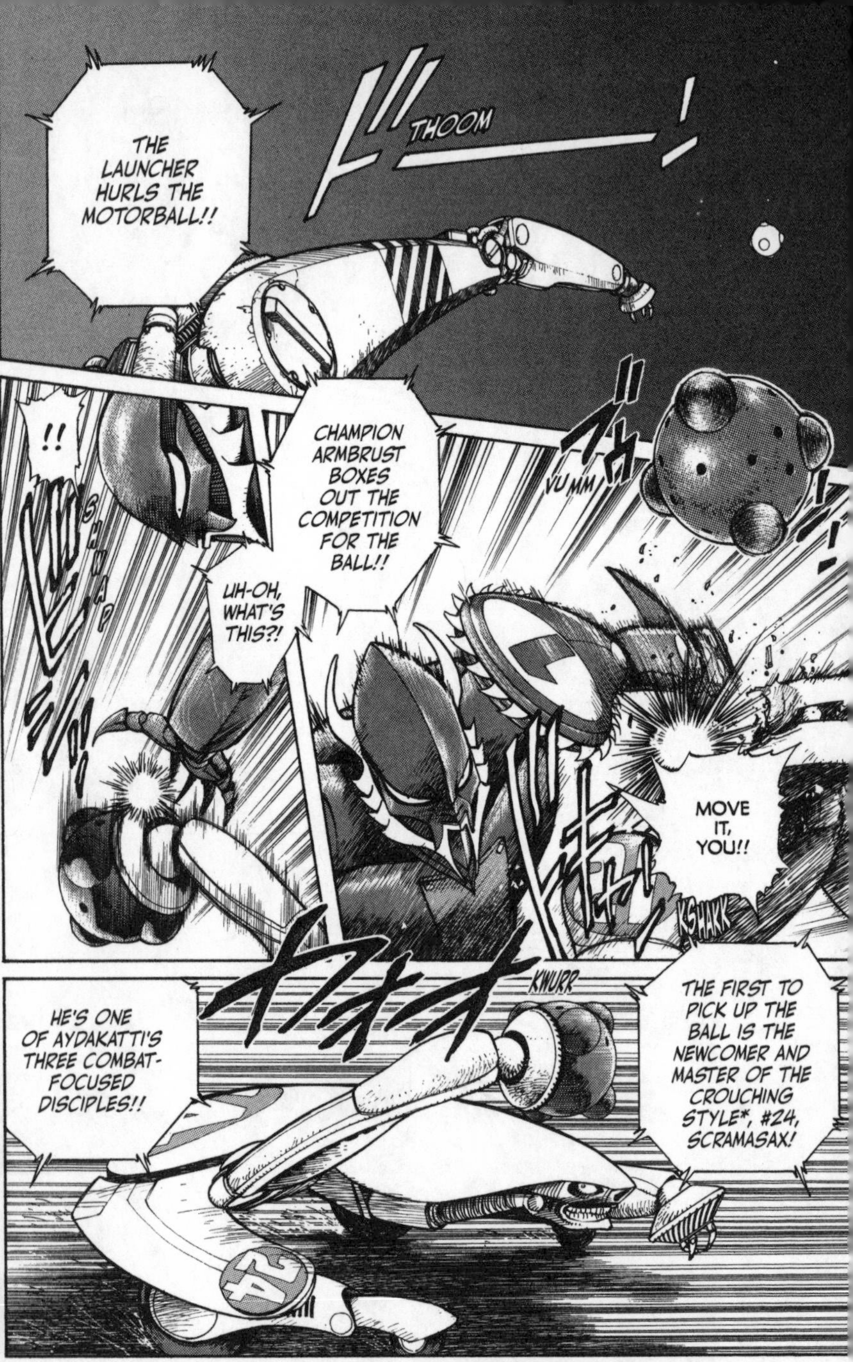
THE LAUNCHER HURLS THE MOTORBALL!!
THOOM
VUMM
CHAMPION ARMBRUST BOXES OUT THE COMPETITION FOR THE BALL!!
!!
MOVE IT, YOU!!
UH-OH, WHAT'S THIS?!
KSHAKK
SHWAP
THE FIRST TO PICK UP THE BALL IS THE NEWCOMER AND MASTER OF THE CROUCHING STYLE*, #24, SCRAMASAX!
KWURR
HE'S ONE OF AYDAKATTI'S THREE COMBAT-FOCUSED DISCIPLES!!

***Crouching Style:** A Wettzeug design that cuts down on wind resistance and increases downforce. As long as you have one pair each of arms and legs, it's not against regulations.

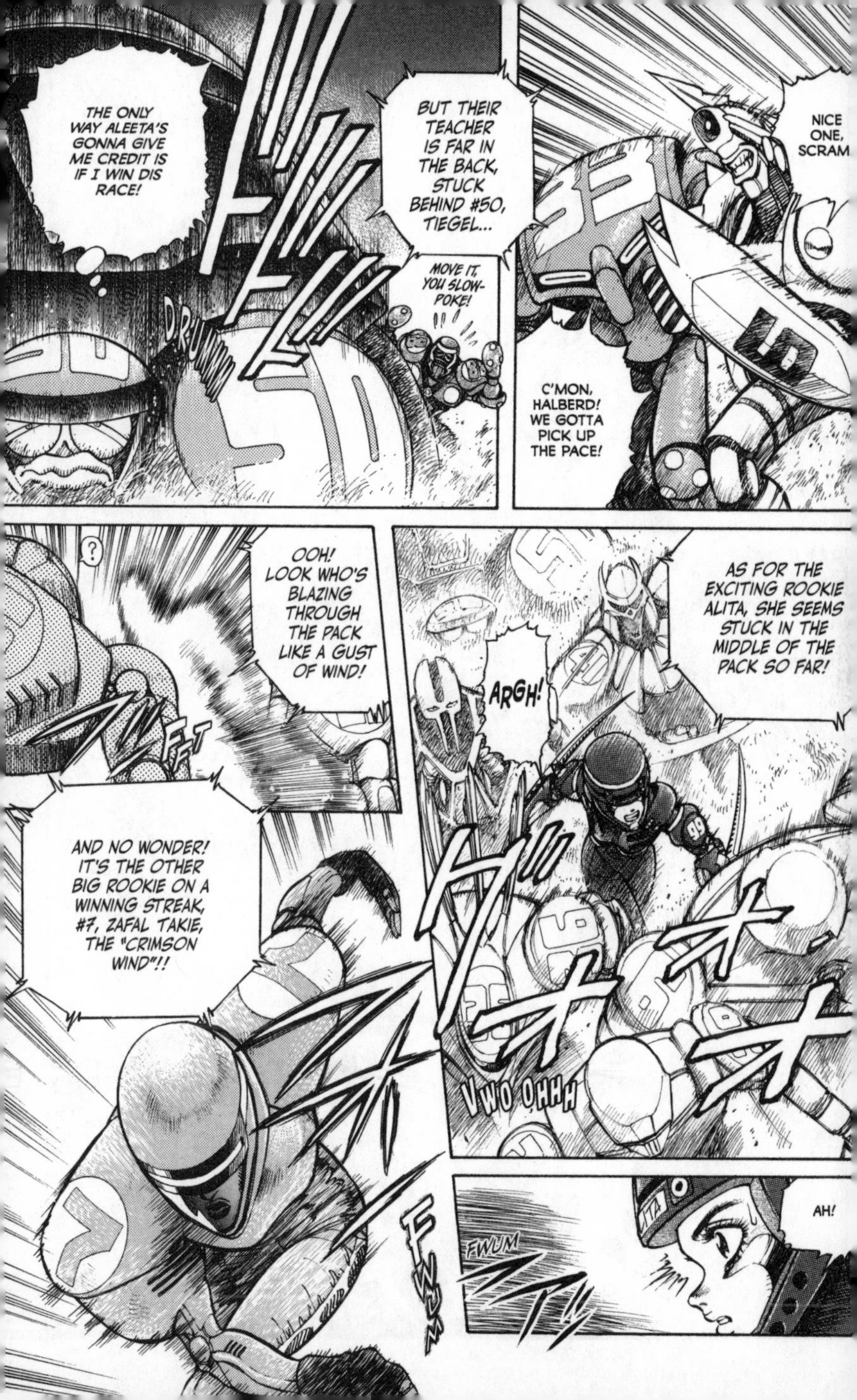
NICE ONE, SCRAM
C'MON, HALBERD! WE GOTTA PICK UP THE PACE!
BUT THEIR TEACHER IS FAR IN THE BACK, STUCK BEHIND #50, TIEGEL...
MOVE IT, YOU SLOW-POKE!
THE ONLY WAY ALEETA'S GONNA GIVE ME CREDIT IS IF I WIN DIS RACE!
DRUNNN
AS FOR THE EXCITING ROOKIE ALITA, SHE SEEMS STUCK IN THE MIDDLE OF THE PACK SO FAR!
ARGH!
VWO OHHH
?
OOH! LOOK WHO'S BLAZING THROUGH THE PACK LIKE A GUST OF WIND!
FFFT
AND NO WONDER! IT'S THE OTHER BIG ROOKIE ON A WINNING STREAK, #7, ZAFAL TAKIE, THE "CRIMSON WIND"!!
AH!
FWUM
FWUM

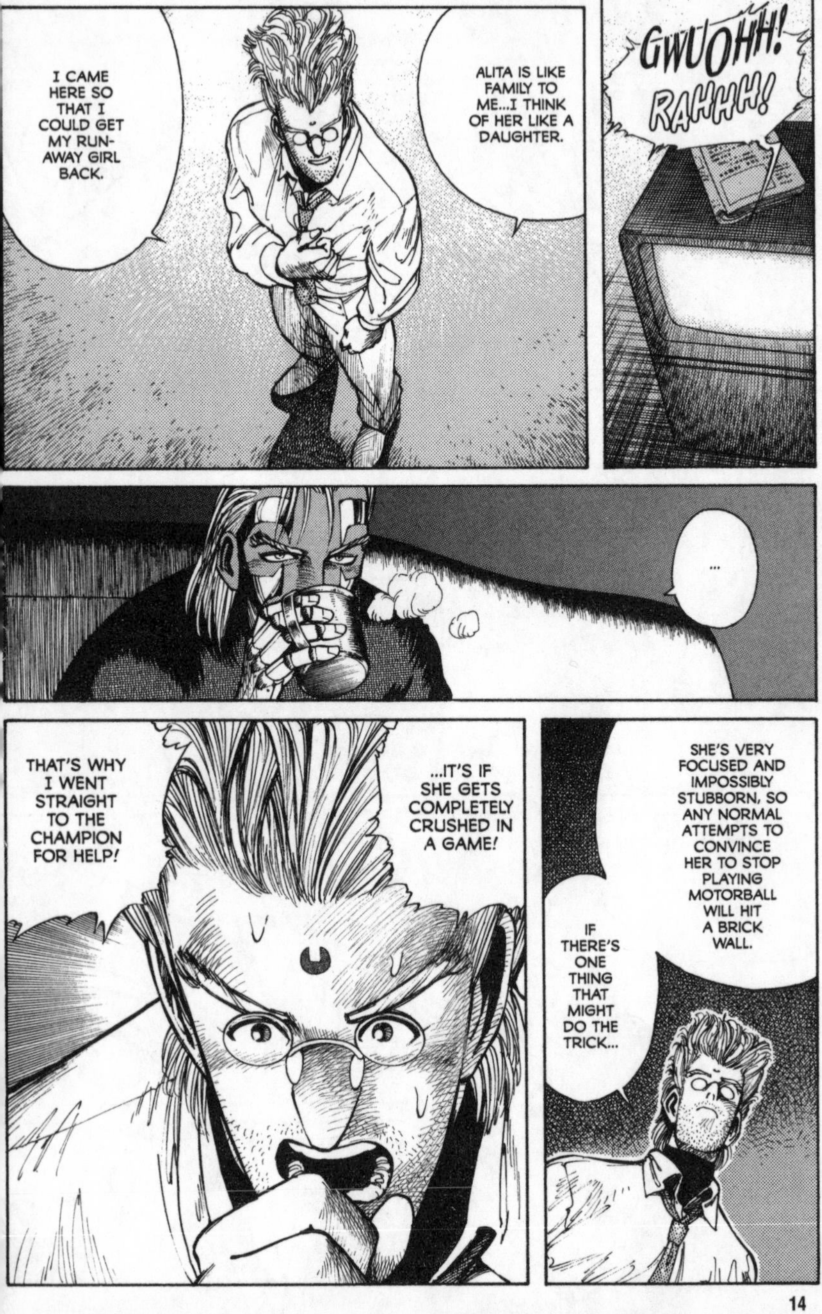
GWUOHH! RAHHH!
ALITA IS LIKE FAMILY TO ME...I THINK OF HER LIKE A DAUGHTER.
I CAME HERE SO THAT I COULD GET MY RUN-AWAY GIRL BACK.
...
SHE'S VERY FOCUSED AND IMPOSSIBLY STUBBORN, SO ANY NORMAL ATTEMPTS TO CONVINCE HER TO STOP PLAYING MOTORBALL WILL HIT A BRICK WALL.
IF THERE'S ONE THING THAT MIGHT DO THE TRICK...
...IT'S IF SHE GETS COMPLETELY CRUSHED IN A GAME!
THAT'S WHY I WENT STRAIGHT TO THE CHAMPION FOR HELP!

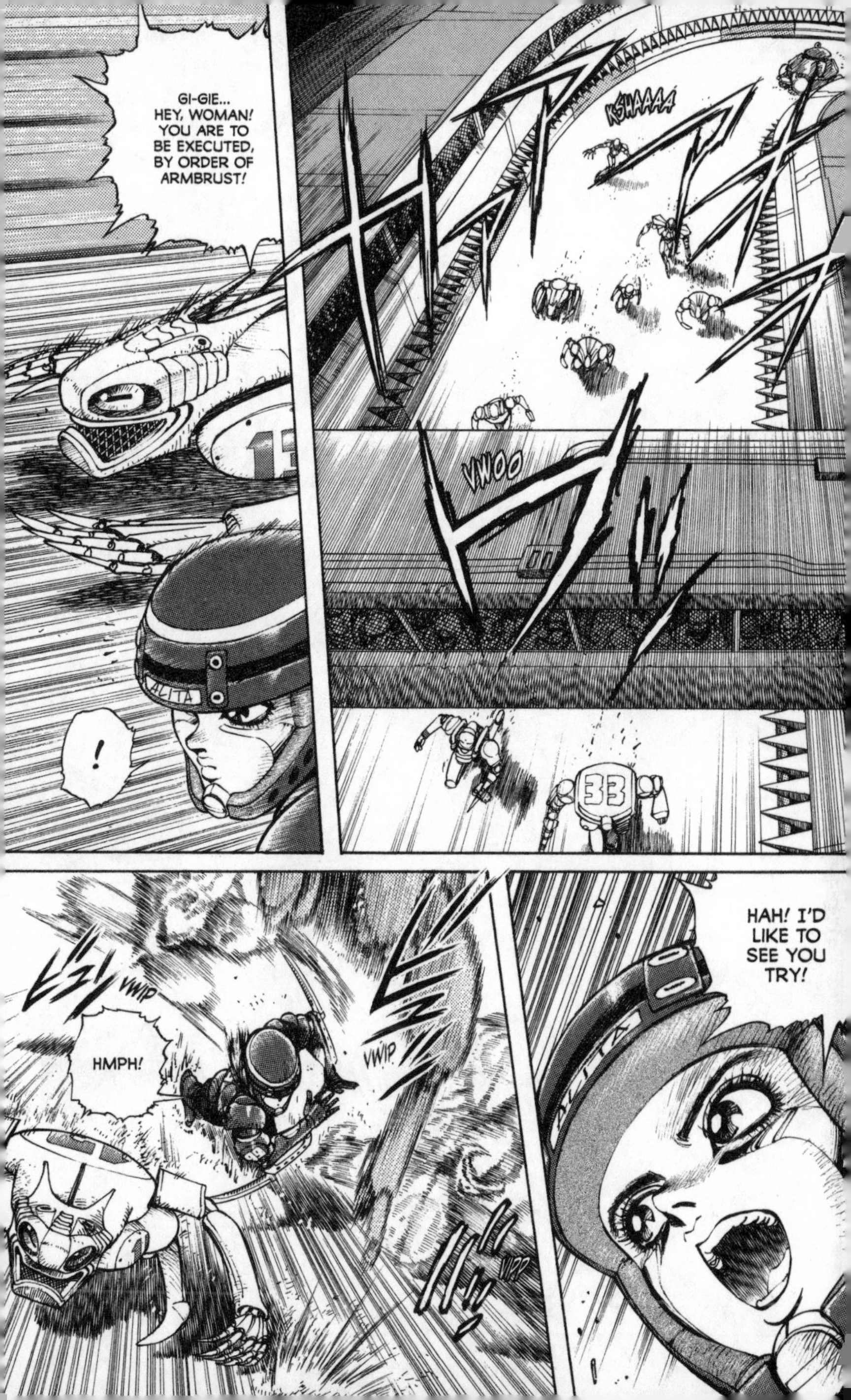
KSHAAAA
VWOO
GI-GIE... HEY, WOMAN! YOU ARE TO BE EXECUTED, BY ORDER OF ARMBRUST!
!
HAH! I'D LIKE TO SEE YOU TRY!
VWIP
HMPH!
VWIP
VIPP

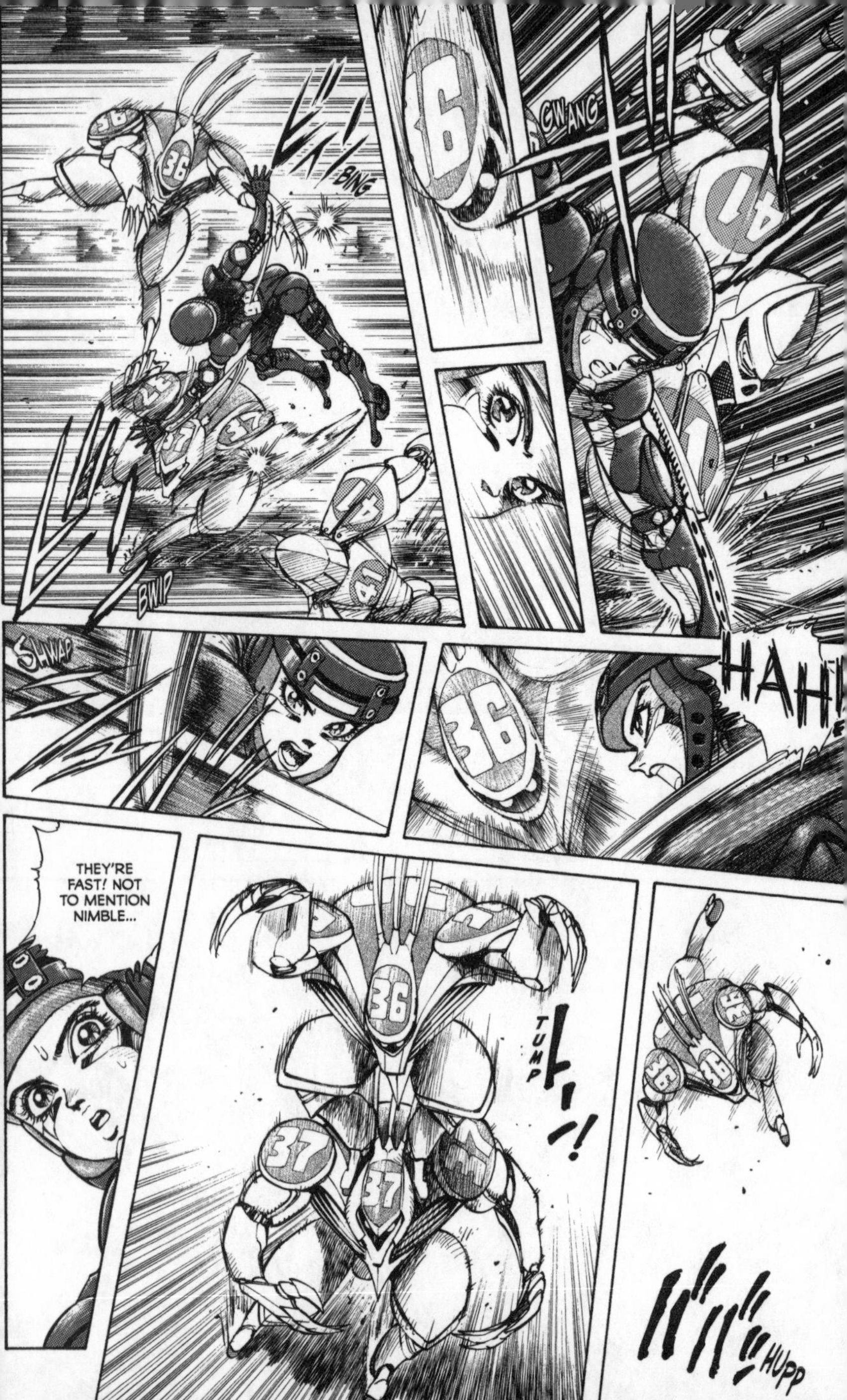
GWANG
BING
BWIP
HAH!
SHWAP
HUPP
TUMP
THEY'RE FAST! NOT TO MENTION NIMBLE...

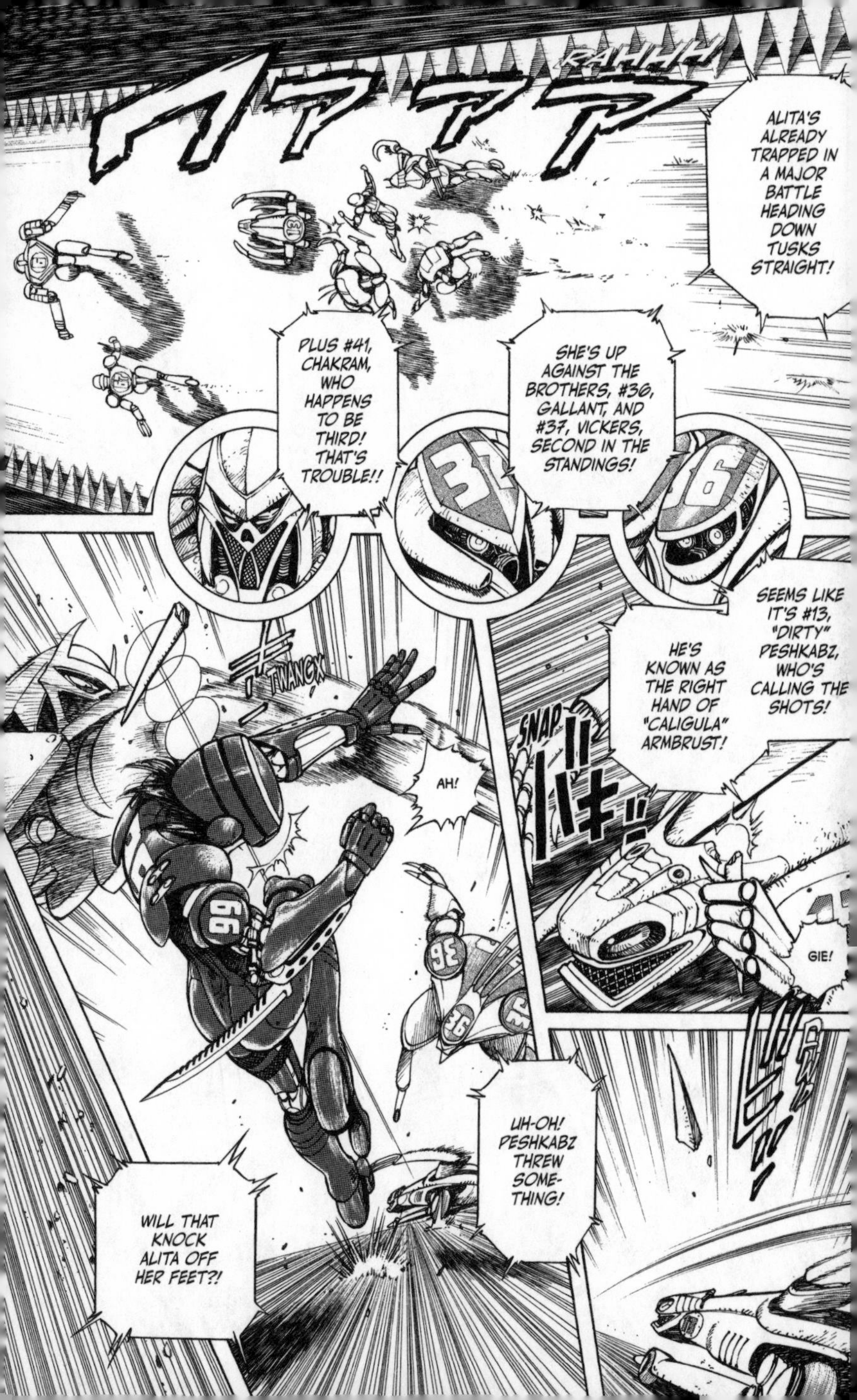
RAHHH
ALITA'S ALREADY TRAPPED IN A MAJOR BATTLE HEADING DOWN TUSKS STRAIGHT!
SHE'S UP AGAINST THE BROTHERS, #36, GALLANT, AND #37, VICKERS, SECOND IN THE STANDINGS!
PLUS #41, CHAKRAM, WHO HAPPENS TO BE THIRD! THAT'S TROUBLE!!
SEEMS LIKE IT'S #13, "DIRTY" PESHKABZ, WHO'S CALLING THE SHOTS!
HE'S KNOWN AS THE RIGHT HAND OF "CALIGULA" ARMBRUST!
SNAP
GIE!
UH-OH! PESHKABZ THREW SOME-THING!
TWANG
AH!
WILL THAT KNOCK ALITA OFF HER FEET?!

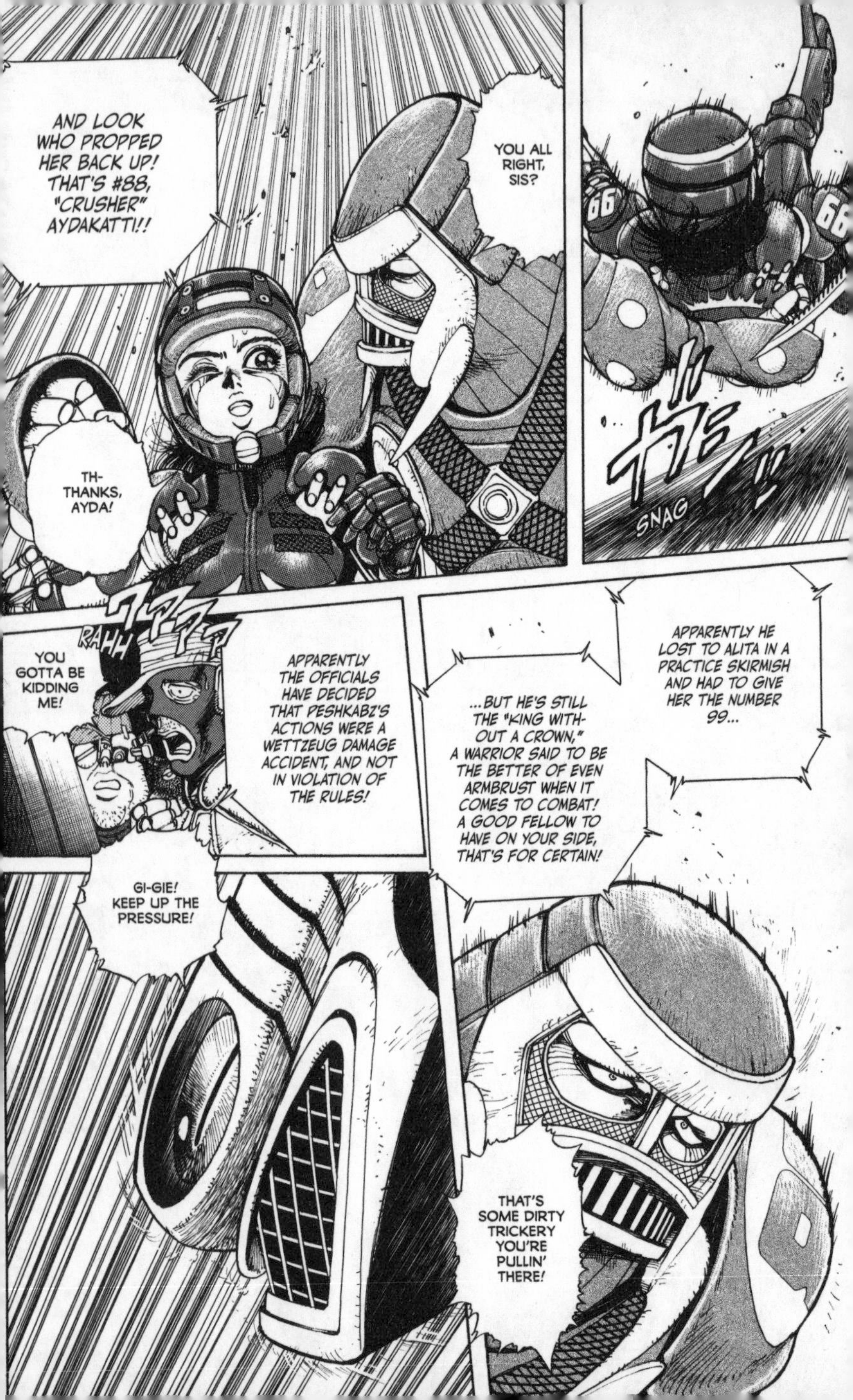
SNAG
YOU ALL RIGHT, SIS?
AND LOOK WHO PROPPED HER BACK UP! THAT'S #88, "CRUSHER" AYDAKATTI!!
TH-THANKS, AYDA!
APPARENTLY HE LOST TO ALITA IN A PRACTICE SKIRMISH AND HAD TO GIVE HER THE NUMBER 99...
...BUT HE'S STILL THE "KING WITH-OUT A CROWN," A WARRIOR SAID TO BE THE BETTER OF EVEN ARMBRUST WHEN IT COMES TO COMBAT! A GOOD FELLOW TO HAVE ON YOUR SIDE, THAT'S FOR CERTAIN!
APPARENTLY THE OFFICIALS HAVE DECIDED THAT PESHKABZ'S ACTIONS WERE A WETTZEUG DAMAGE ACCIDENT, AND NOT IN VIOLATION OF THE RULES!
RAHH
YOU GOTTA BE KIDDING ME!
THAT'S SOME DIRTY TRICKERY YOU'RE PULLIN' THERE!
GI-GIE! KEEP UP THE PRESSURE!

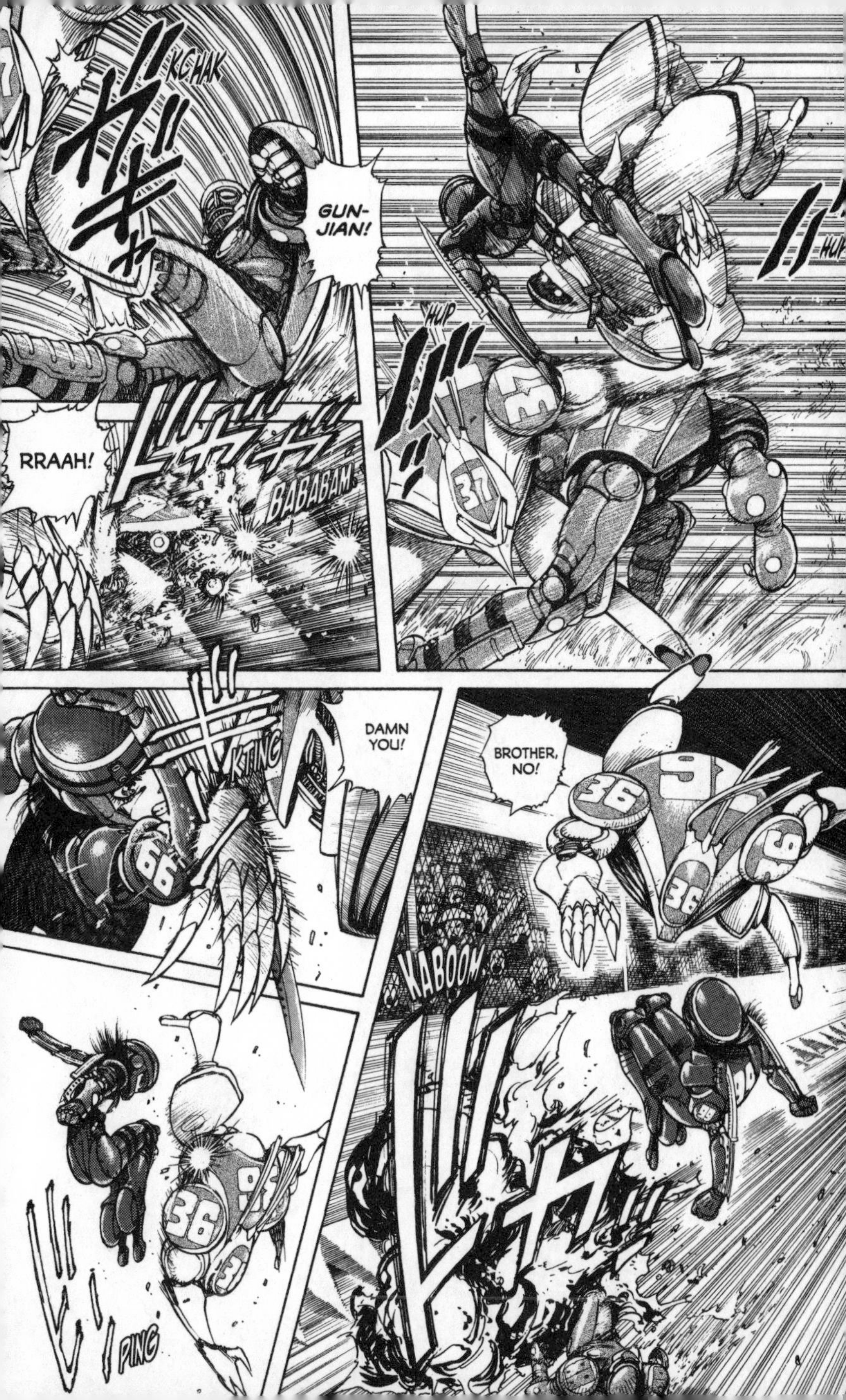
HUP
HUP
KCHAK
GUN-JIAN!
RRAAH!
BABABAM
BROTHER, NO!
KABOOM
DAMN YOU!
KTING
PING

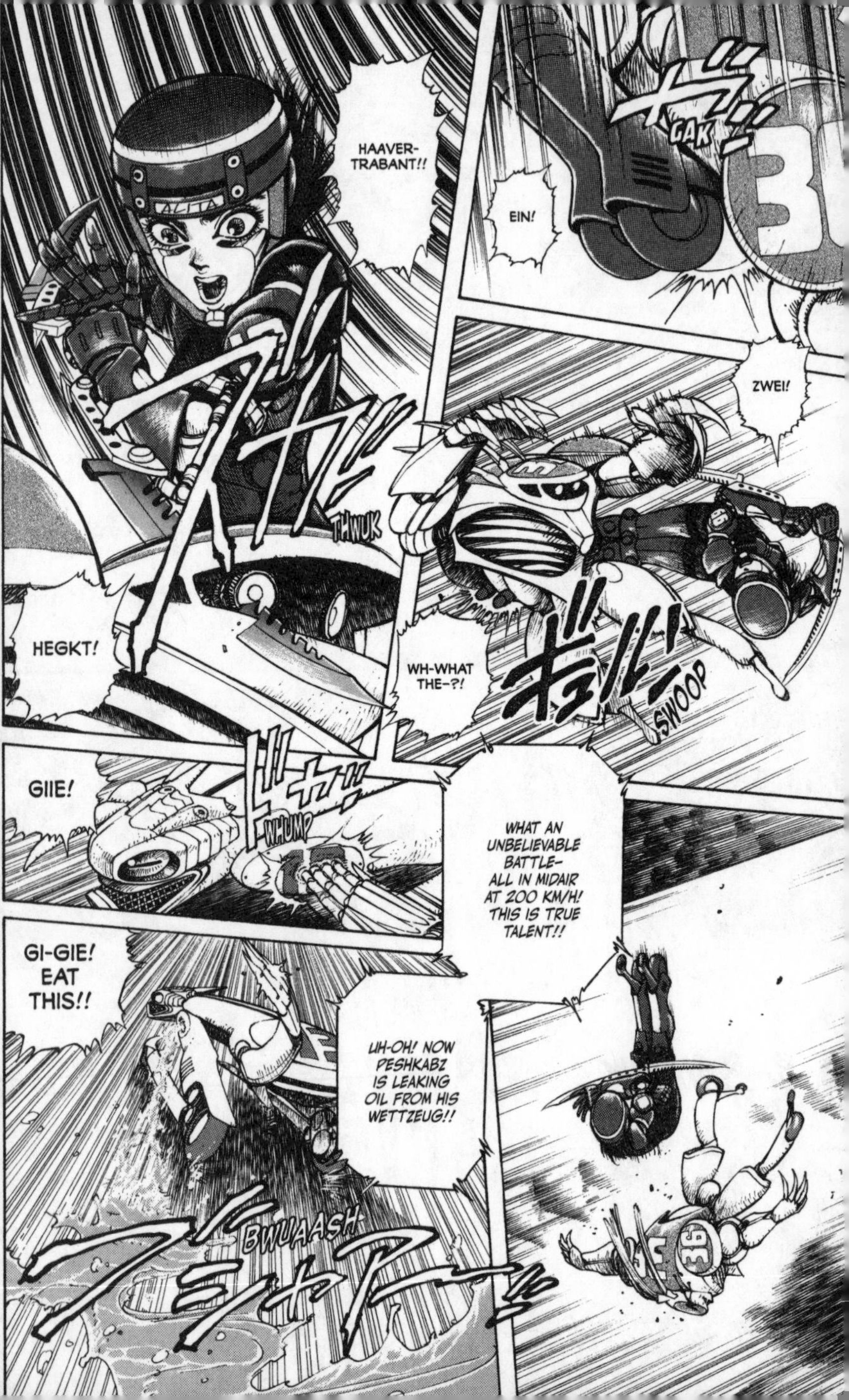

GAK
EIN!
ZWEI!
WH-WHAT THE-?!
SWOOP
HAAVER-TRABANT!!
THWUK
HEGKT!
WHAT AN UNBELIEVABLE BATTLE- ALL IN MIDAIR AT 200 KM/H! THIS IS TRUE TALENT!!
WHUMP
GIIE!
UH-OH! NOW PESHKABZ IS LEAKING OIL FROM HIS WETTZEUG!!
GI-GIE! EAT THIS!!
BWUAASH

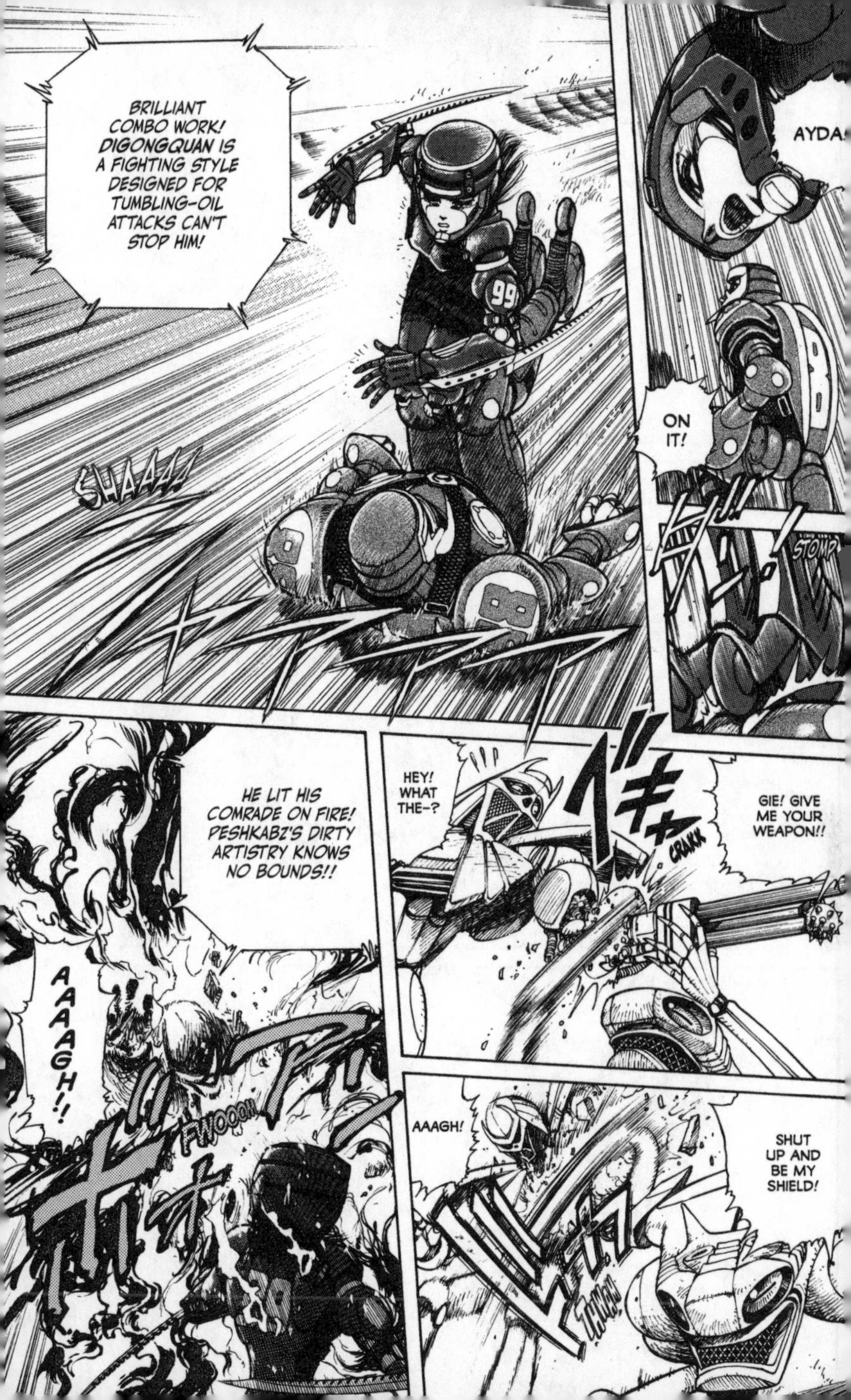
AYDA!
ON IT!
STOMP
BRILLIANT COMBO WORK! DIGONGQUAN IS A FIGHTING STYLE DESIGNED FOR TUMBLING-OIL ATTACKS CAN'T STOP HIM!
SHAAAA
HEY! WHAT THE-?
GIE! GIVE ME YOUR WEAPON!!
CRAKK
AAAGH!
SHUT UP AND BE MY SHIELD!
HE LIT HIS COMRADE ON FIRE! PESHKABZ'S DIRTY ARTISTRY KNOWS NO BOUNDS!!
AAAAAGH!!
FWOOOH

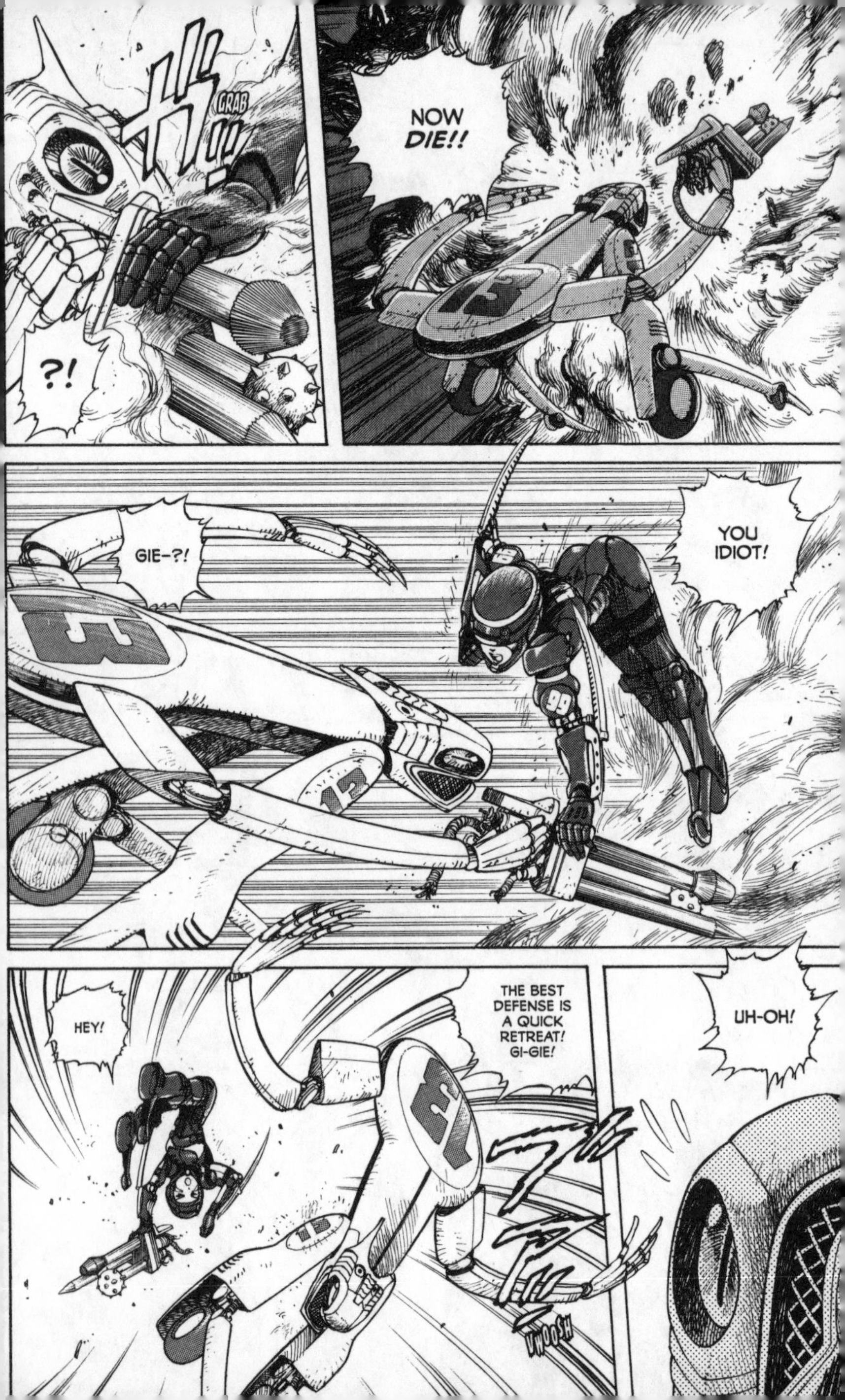
NOW DIE!!
GRAB
?!
YOU IDIOT!
GIE-?!
UH-OH!
THE BEST DEFENSE IS A QUICK RETREAT! GI-GIE!
HEY!
WHOOSH

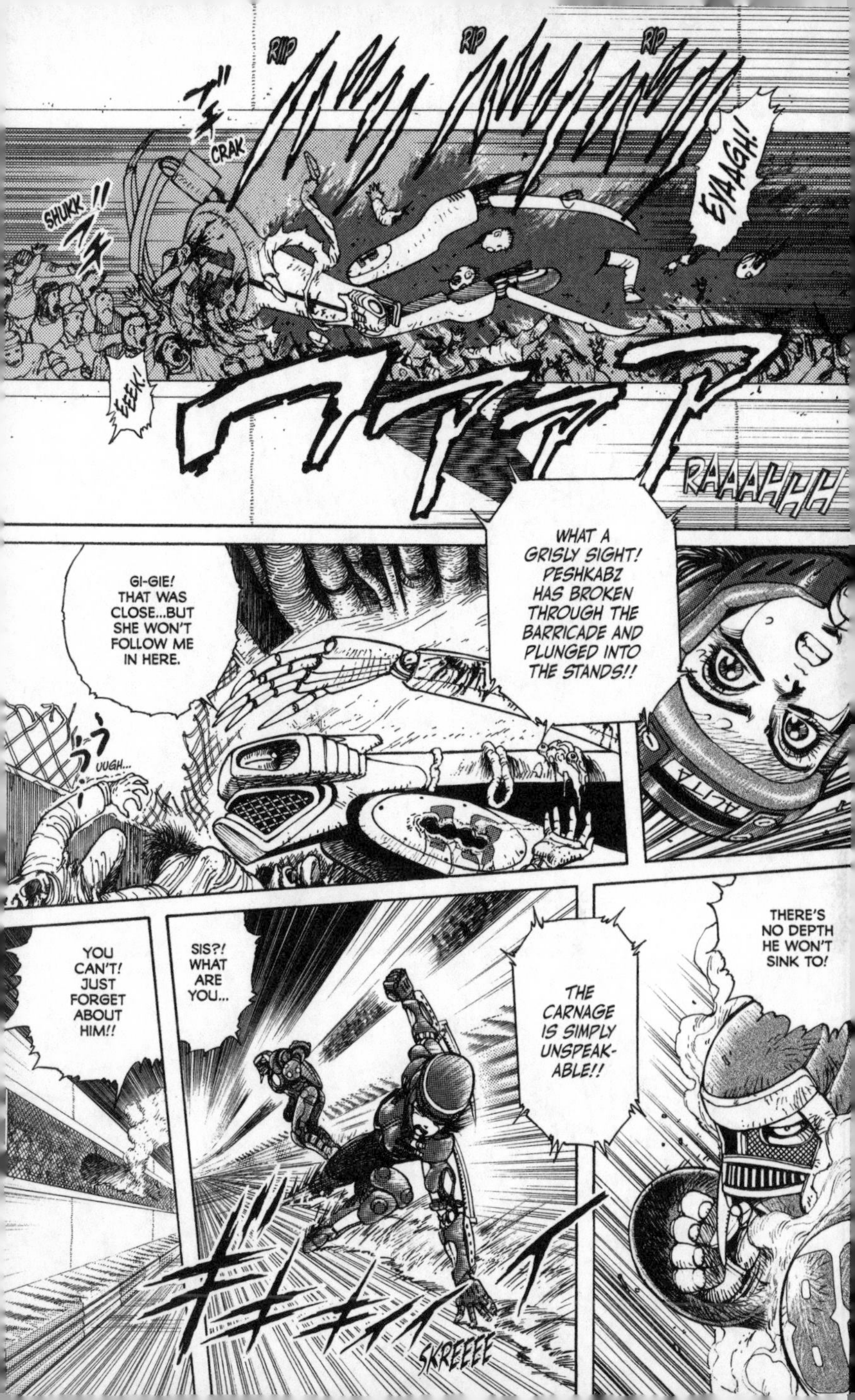
EYAAGH!
RIP
RIP
RIP
CRAK
SHUKK!!
EEEK!
RAAAHHH
WHAT A GRISLY SIGHT! PESHKABZ HAS BROKEN THROUGH THE BARRICADE AND PLUNGED INTO THE STANDS!!
ALITA
GI-GIE! THAT WAS CLOSE...BUT SHE WON'T FOLLOW ME IN HERE.
UUGH...
THERE'S NO DEPTH HE WON'T SINK TO!
THE CARNAGE IS SIMPLY UNSPEAK-ABLE!!
SIS?! WHAT ARE YOU...
SKREEEE
YOU CAN'T! JUST FORGET ABOUT HIM!!

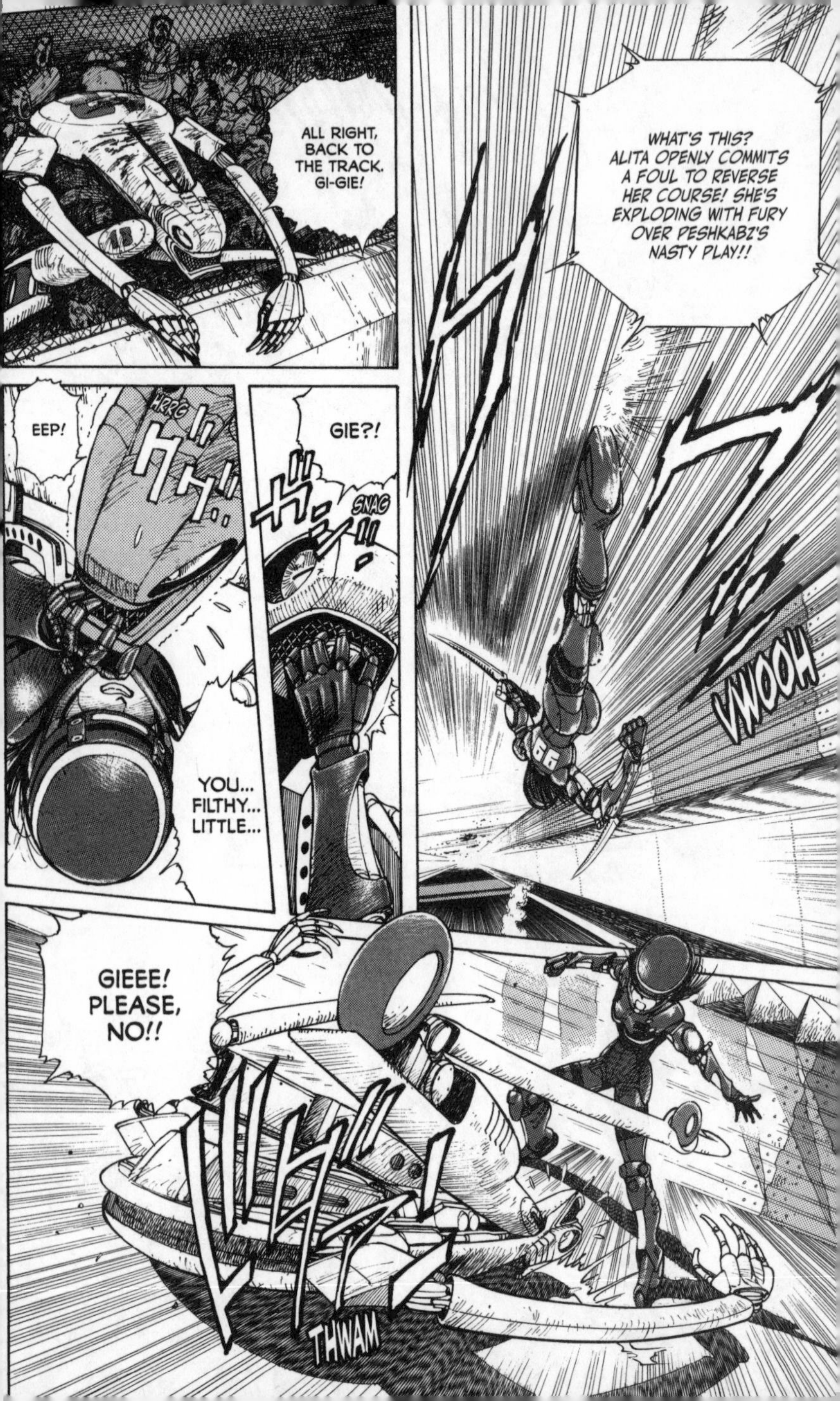
WHAT'S THIS? ALITA OPENLY COMMITS A FOUL TO REVERSE HER COURSE! SHE'S EXPLODING WITH FURY OVER PESHKABZ'S NASTY PLAY!!
VWOOH
ALL RIGHT, BACK TO THE TRACK. GI-GIE!
GIE?!
SNAG
EEP!
HRRG
YOU... FILTHY... LITTLE...
GIEEE! PLEASE, NO!!
THWAM

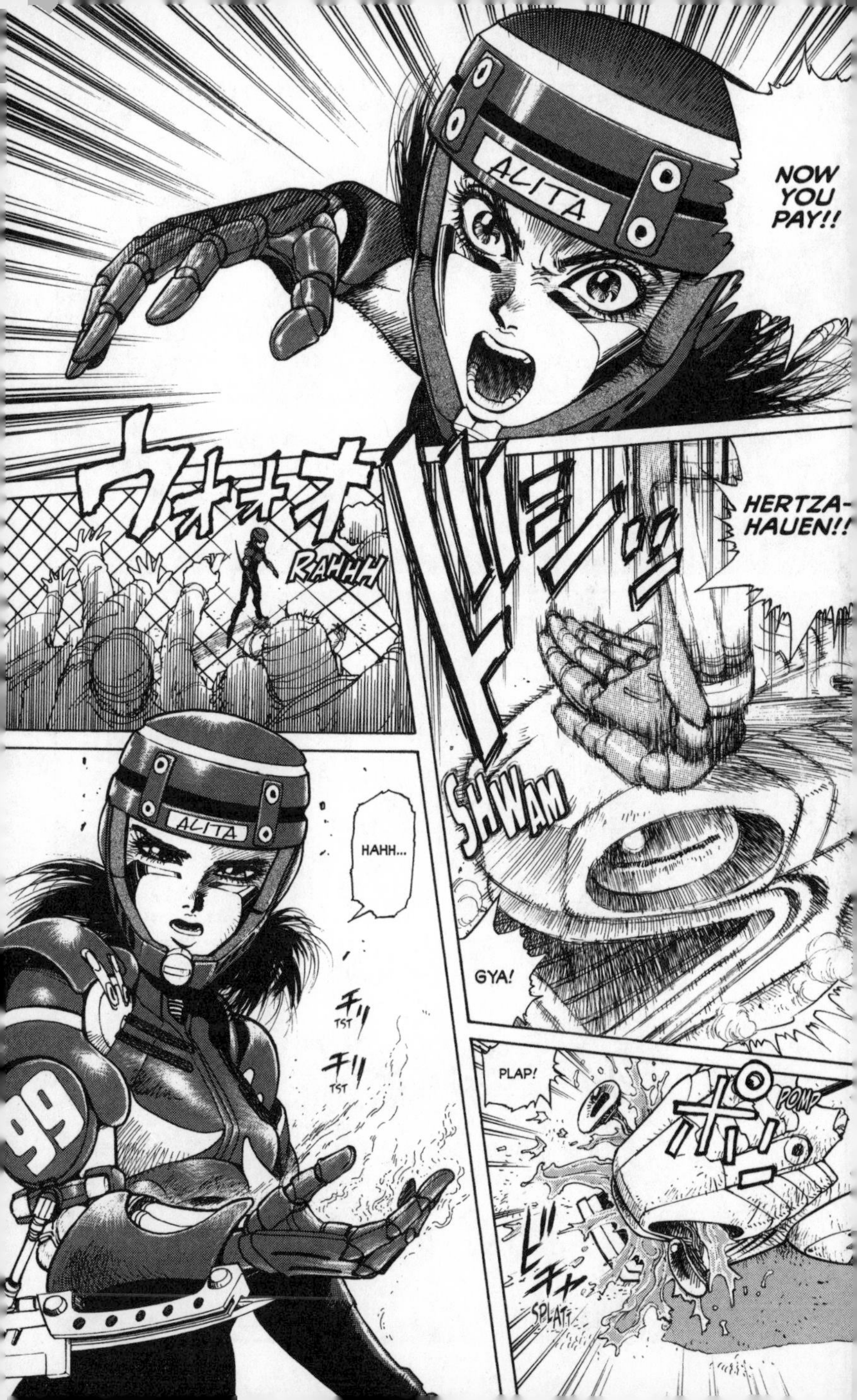
NOW YOU PAY!!
HERTZA-HAUEN!!
SHWAM
GYA!
RAHHH
PLAP!
POMP
SPLAT
HAHH...
TST
TST

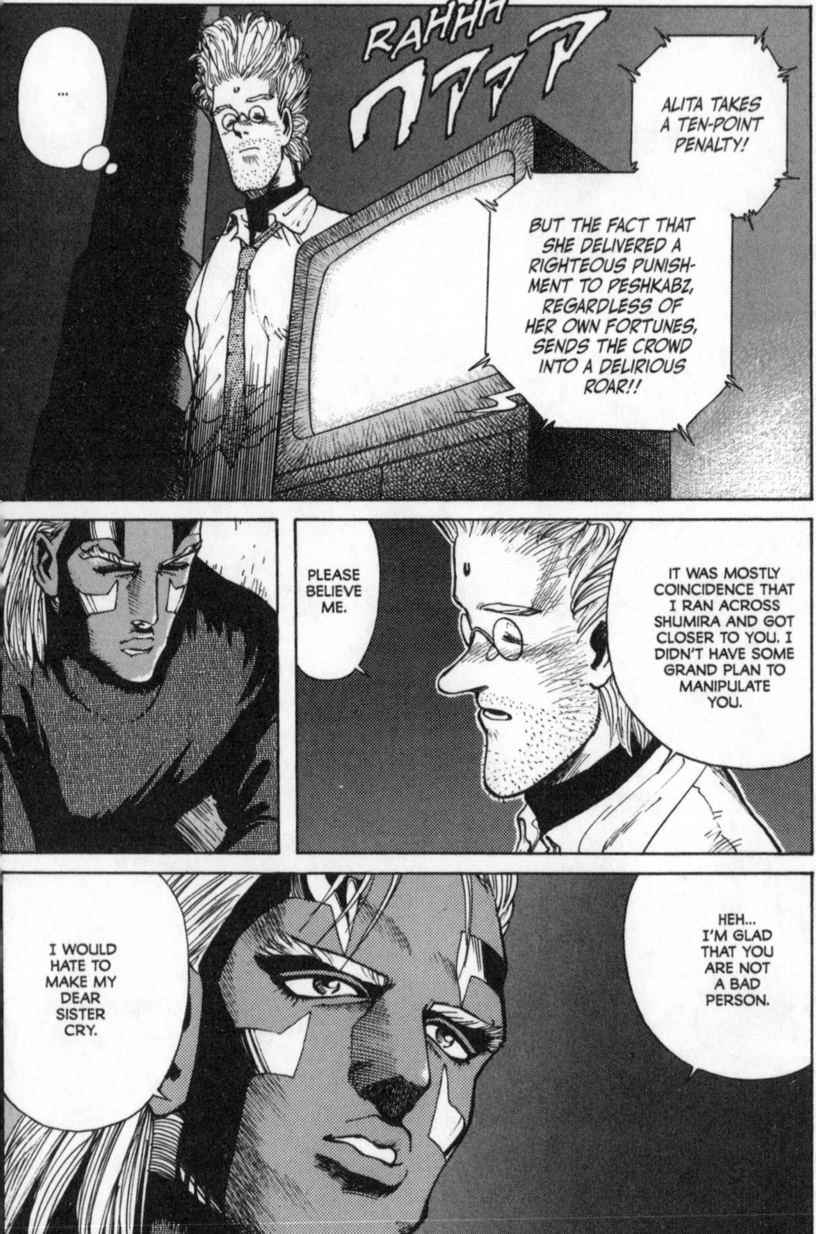
ALITA TAKES A TEN-POINT PENALTY!
BUT THE FACT THAT SHE DELIVERED A RIGHTEOUS PUNISHMENT TO PESHKABZ, REGARDLESS OF HER OWN FORTUNES, SENDS THE CROWD INTO A DELIRIOUS ROAR!!
RAHHH
ウァァア
...
IT WAS MOSTLY COINCIDENCE THAT I RAN ACROSS SHUMIRA AND GOT CLOSER TO YOU. I DIDN'T HAVE SOME GRAND PLAN TO MANIPULATE YOU.
PLEASE BELIEVE ME.
HEH... I'M GLAD THAT YOU ARE NOT A BAD PERSON.
I WOULD HATE TO MAKE MY DEAR SISTER CRY.

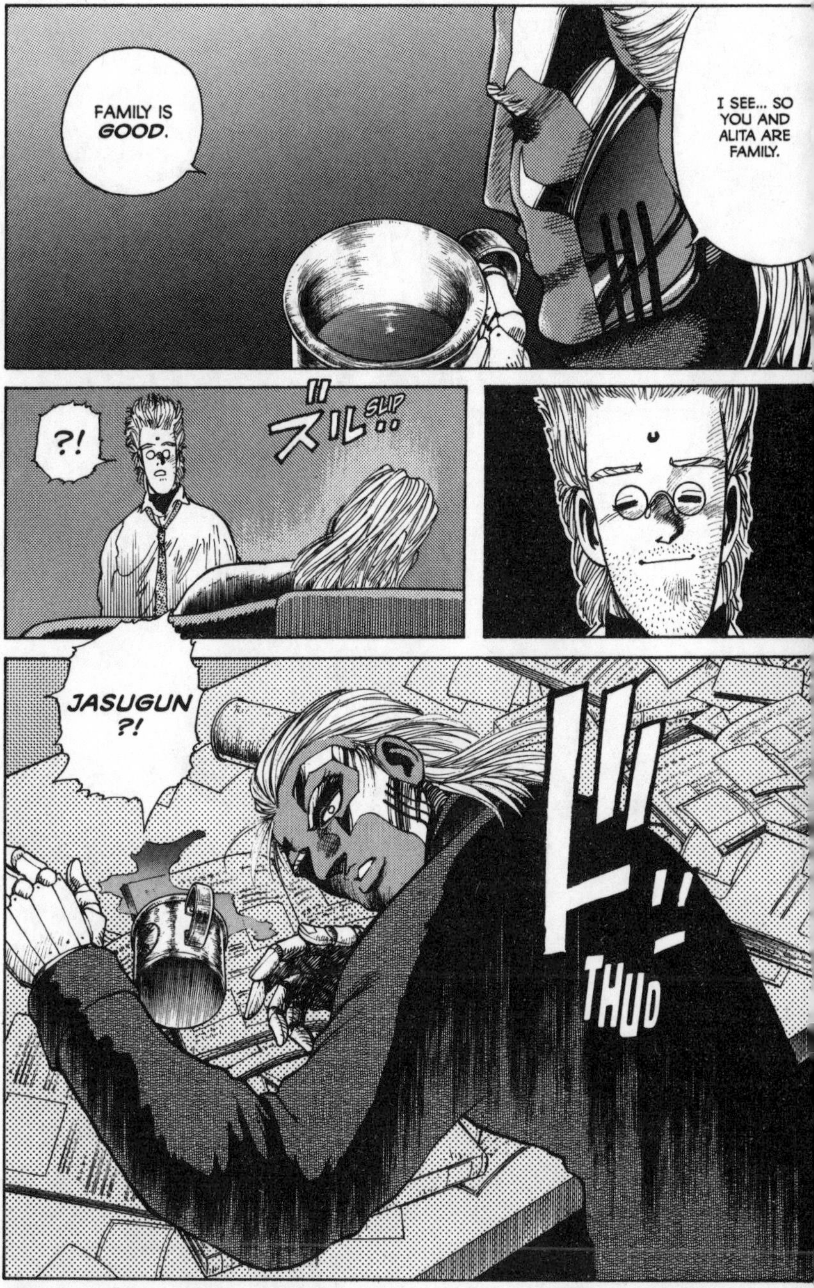
I SEE... SO YOU AND ALITA ARE FAMILY.
FAMILY IS GOOD.
ズル SLIP
?!
ドッ THUD
JASUGUN ?!

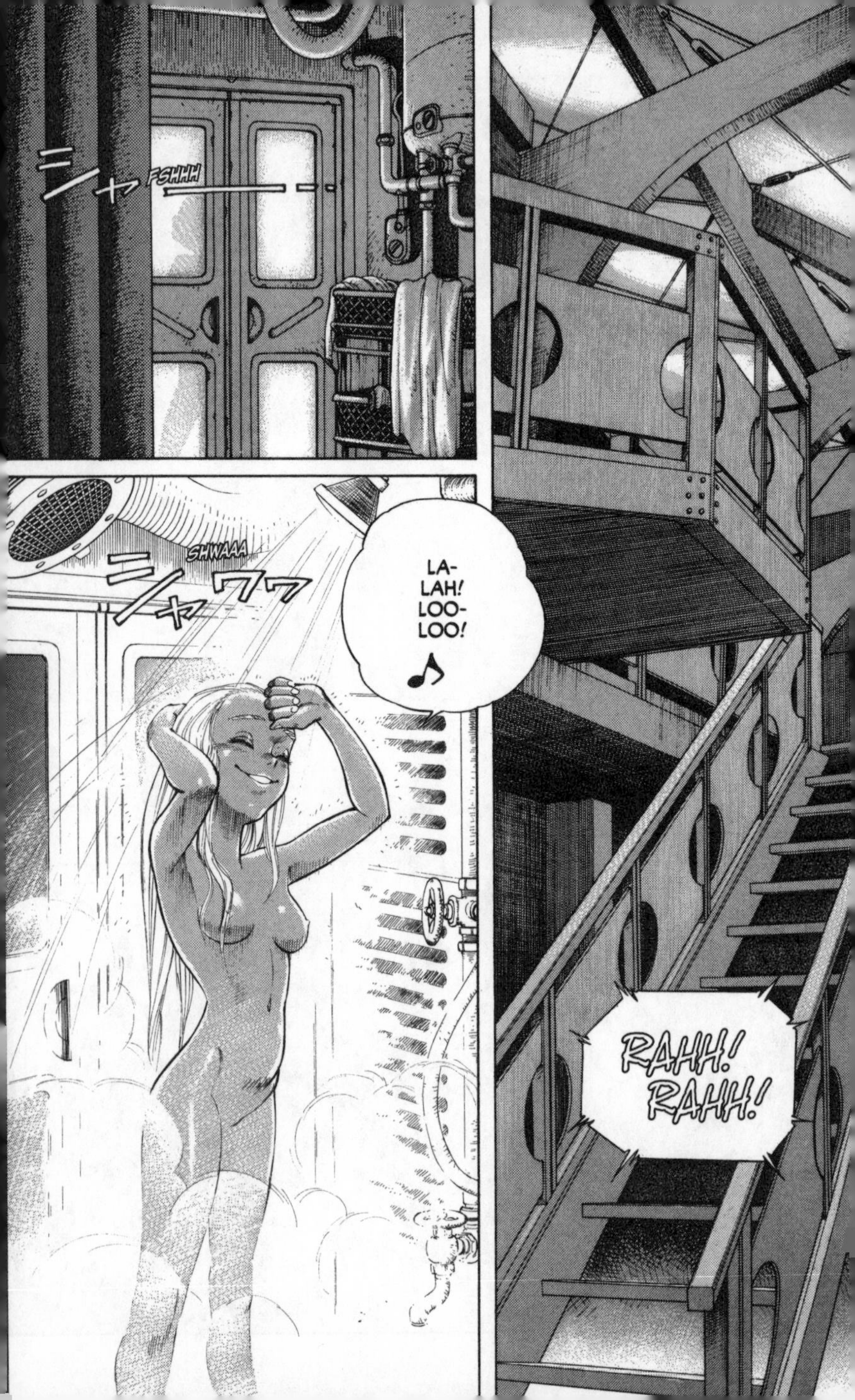
RAHH! RAHH!
シャー
FSHHH
SHWAAA
シャワワ
LA-LAH! LOO-LOO! ♪

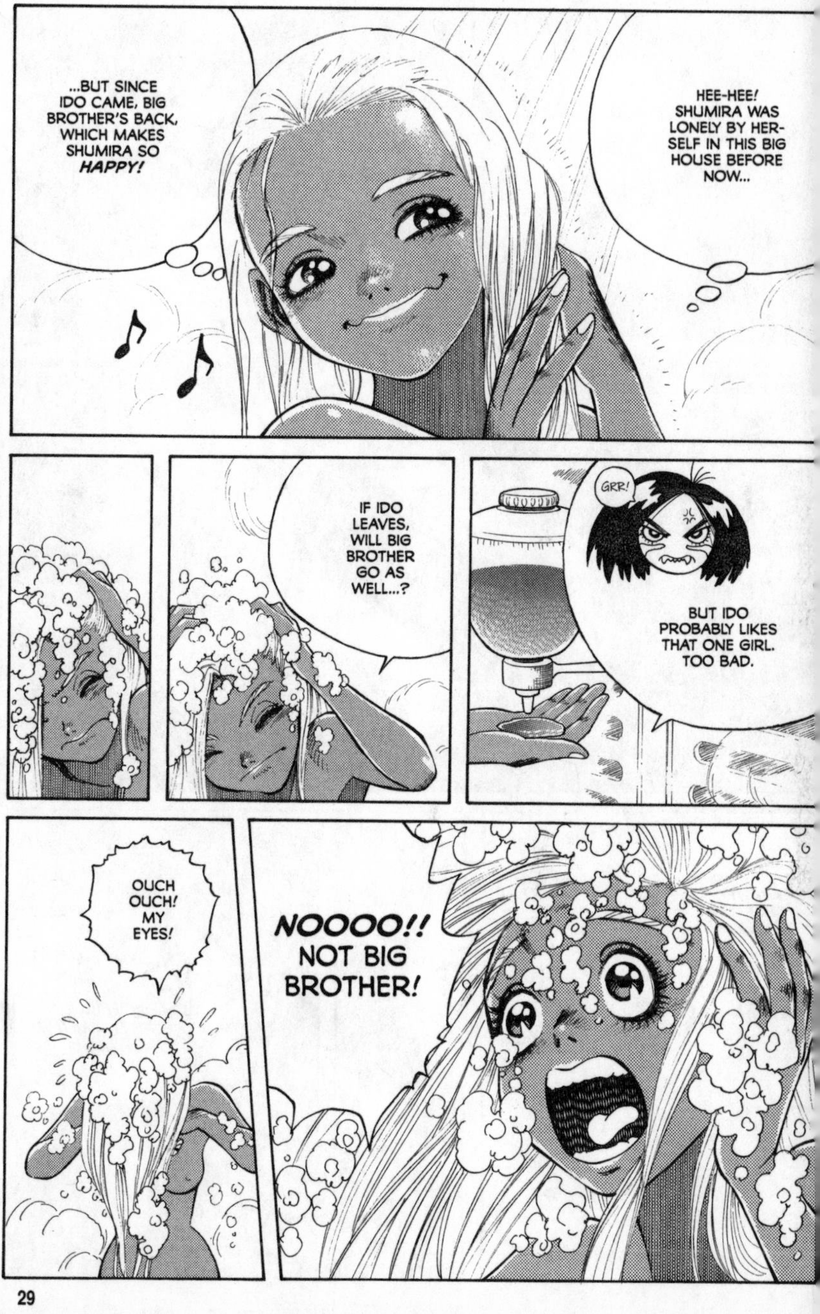
HEE-HEE! SHUMIRA WAS LONELY BY HER-SELF IN THIS BIG HOUSE BEFORE NOW...
...BUT SINCE IDO CAME, BIG BROTHER'S BACK, WHICH MAKES SHUMIRA SO *HAPPY!*
GRR!
BUT IDO PROBABLY LIKES THAT ONE GIRL. TOO BAD.
IF IDO LEAVES, WILL BIG BROTHER GO AS WELL...?
NOOOO!! NOT BIG BROTHER!
OUCH OUCH! MY EYES!

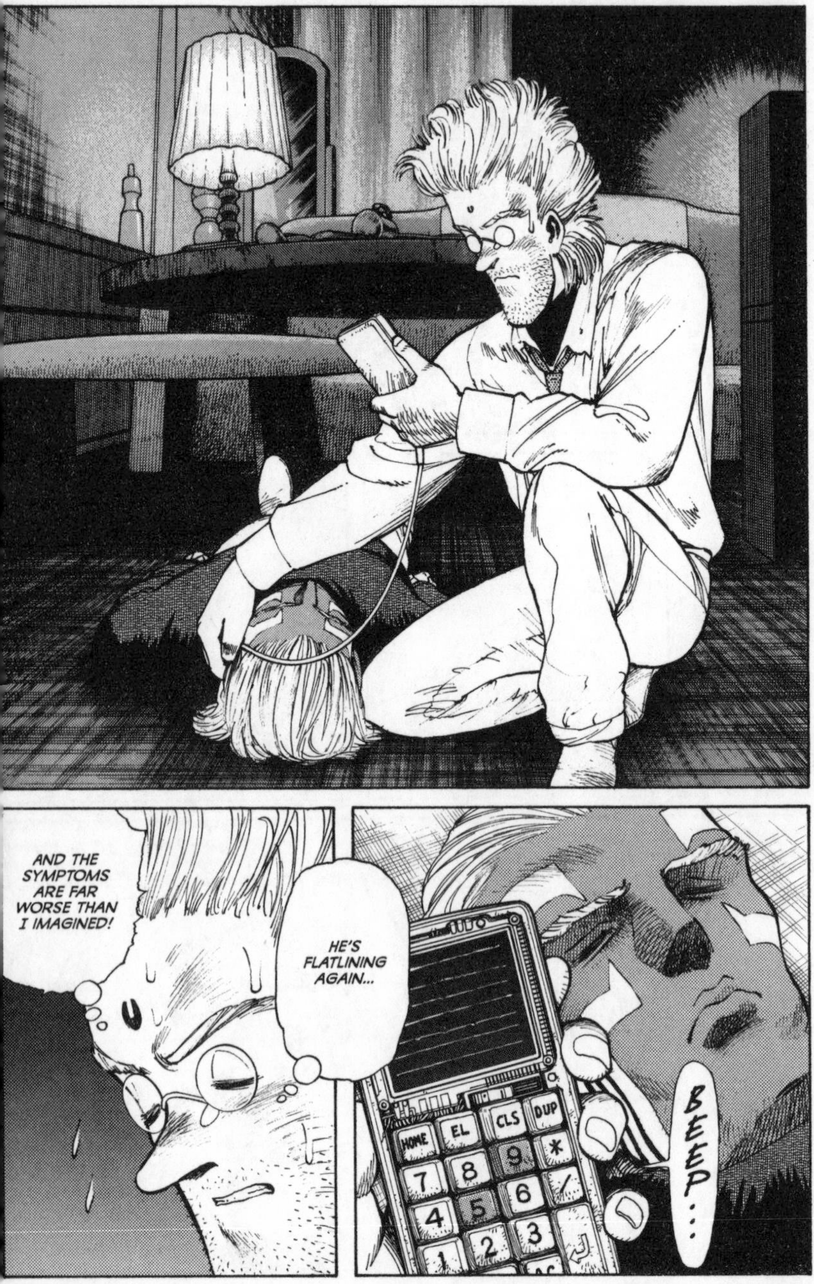
BEEP...
HOME EL CLS DUP
HE'S FLATLINING AGAIN...
AND THE SYMPTOMS ARE FAR WORSE THAN I IMAGINED!

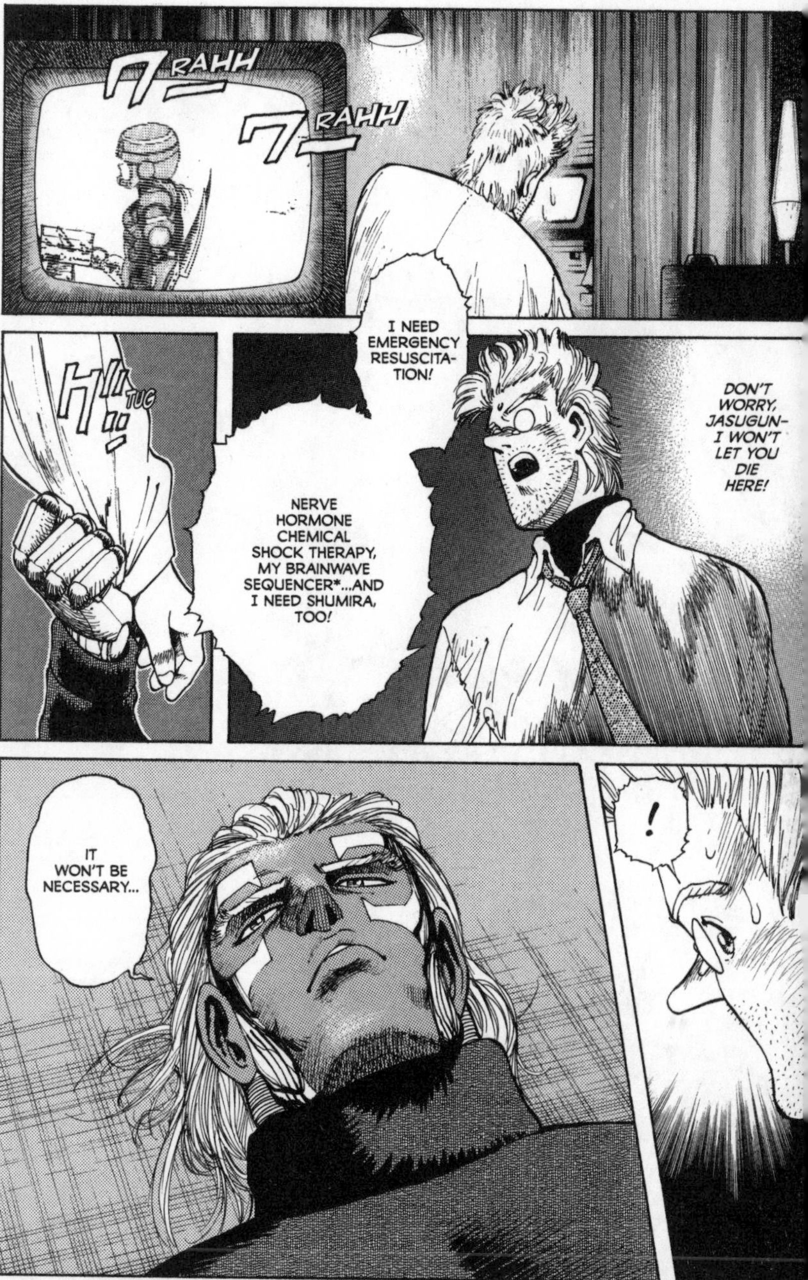
RAHH
RAHH
DON'T WORRY, JASUGUN– I WON'T LET YOU DIE HERE!
I NEED EMERGENCY RESUSCITATION!
NERVE HORMONE CHEMICAL SHOCK THERAPY, MY BRAINWAVE SEQUENCER*...AND I NEED SHUMIRA, TOO!
TUG
!
IT WON'T BE NECESSARY...

***Brainwave sequencer:** A device that takes the parameters of a sampled brainwave pattern and can alter and set them at will. It's a homemade module of Ido's own design.

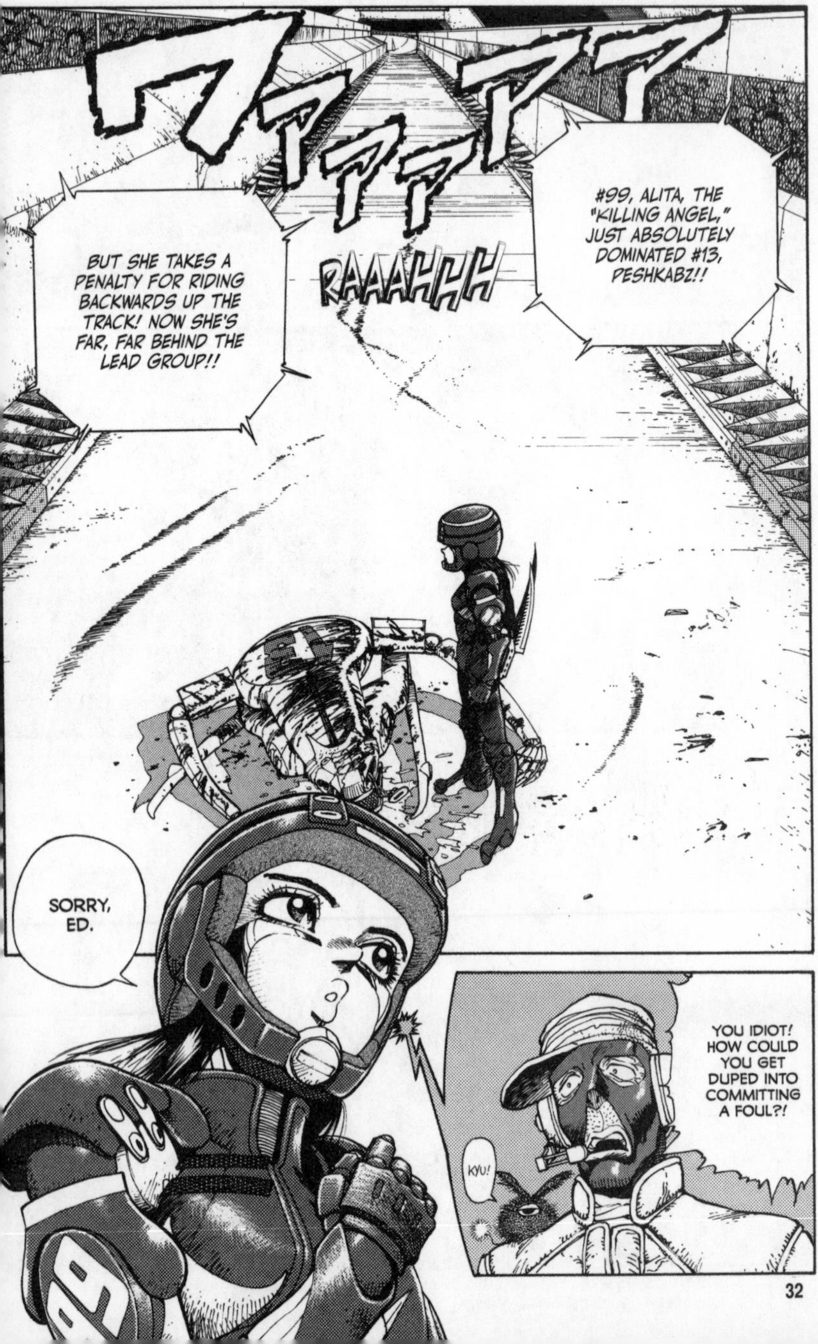
RAAAHHH
#99, ALITA, THE "KILLING ANGEL," JUST ABSOLUTELY DOMINATED #13, PESHKABZ!!
BUT SHE TAKES A PENALTY FOR RIDING BACKWARDS UP THE TRACK! NOW SHE'S FAR, FAR BEHIND THE LEAD GROUP!!
YOU IDIOT! HOW COULD YOU GET DUPED INTO COMMITTING A FOUL?!
KYU!
SORRY, ED.

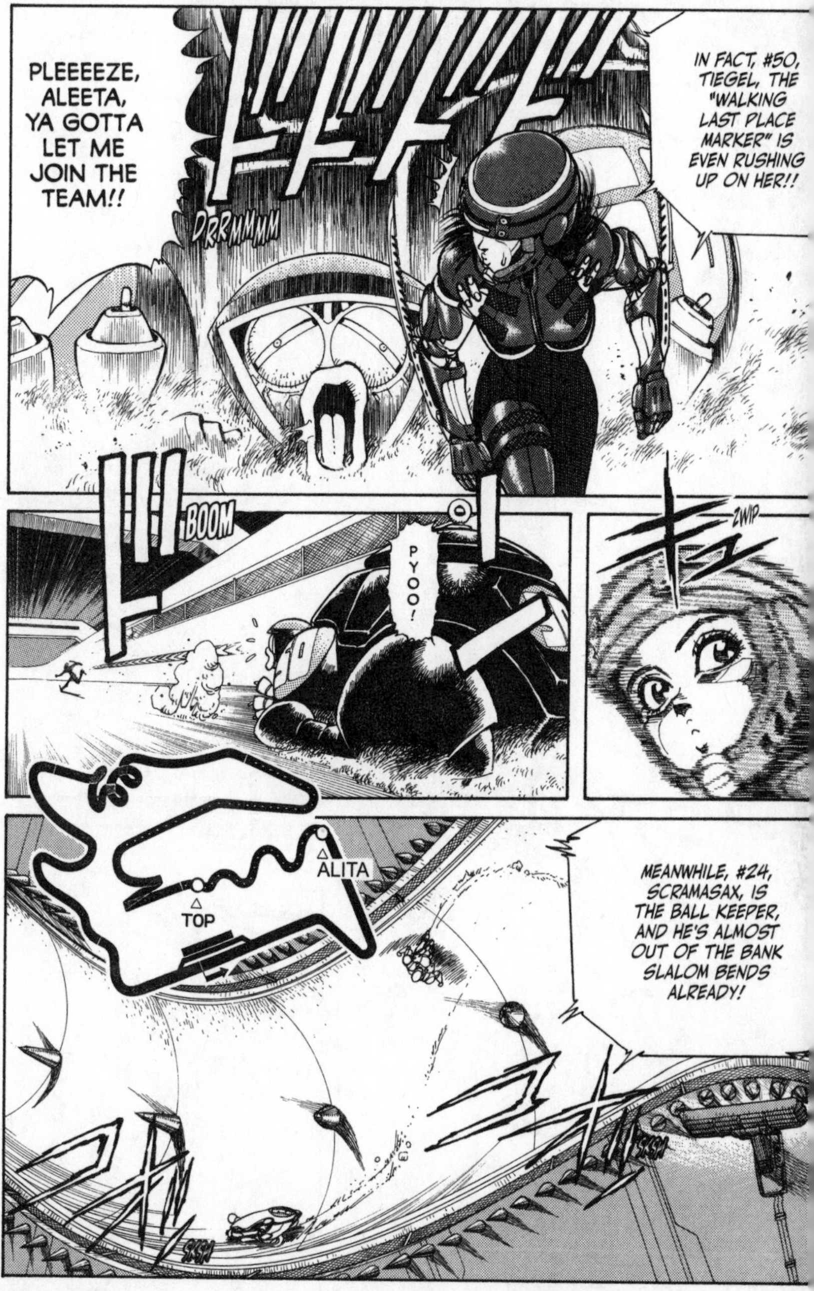
IN FACT, #50, TIEGEL, THE "WALKING LAST PLACE MARKER" IS EVEN RUSHING UP ON HER!!
PLEEEEZE, ALEETA, YA GOTTA LET ME JOIN THE TEAM!!
DRRMMMM
ZWIP
BOOM
PYOO!
MEANWHILE, #24, SCRAMASAX, IS THE BALL KEEPER, AND HE'S ALMOST OUT OF THE BANK SLALOM BENDS ALREADY!
ALITA
TOP
SKSH
SKSH

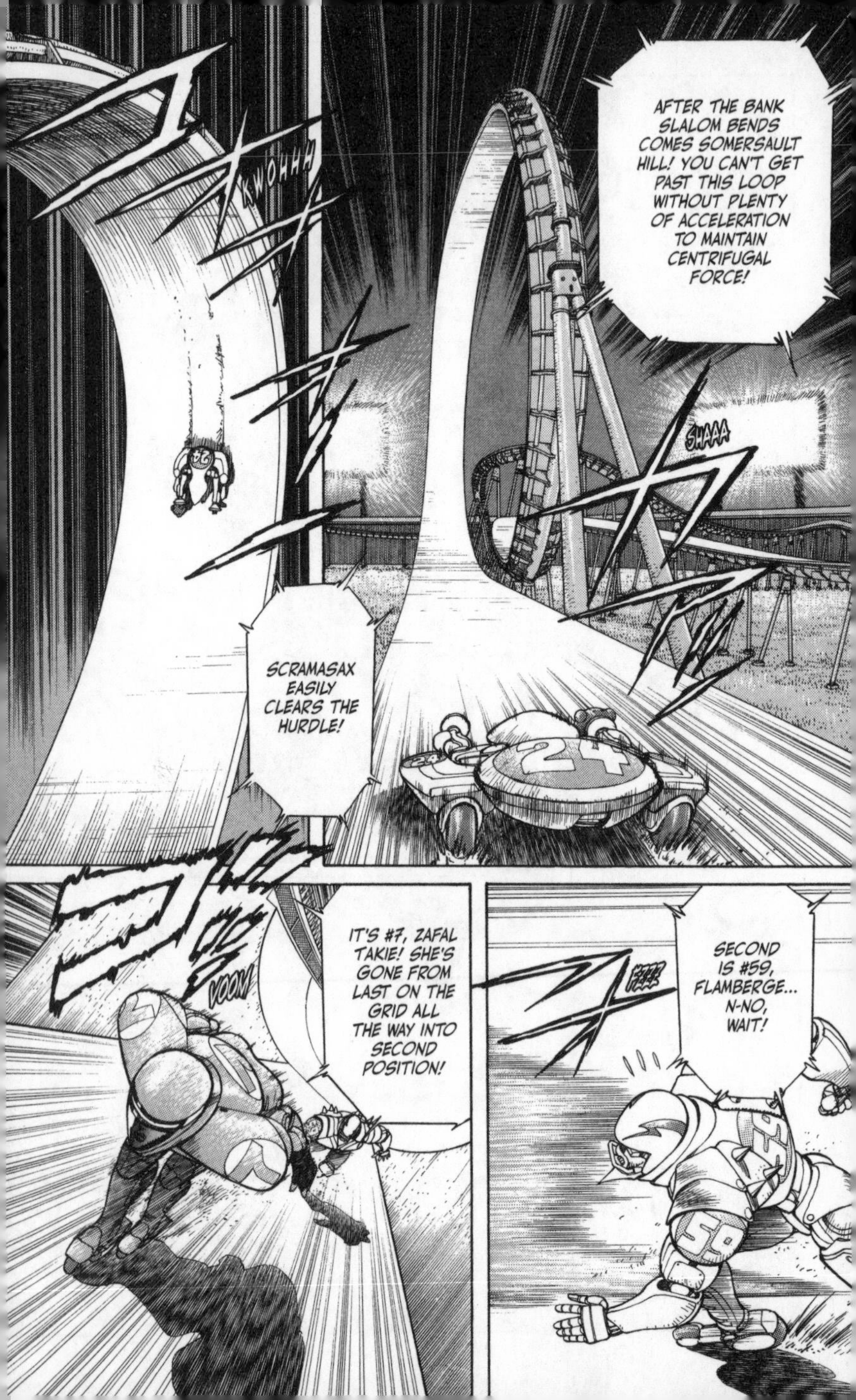
AFTER THE BANK SLALOM BENDS COMES SOMERSAULT HILL! YOU CAN'T GET PAST THIS LOOP WITHOUT PLENTY OF ACCELERATION TO MAINTAIN CENTRIFUGAL FORCE!
SHAAA
KWOHHH
SCRAMASAX EASILY CLEARS THE HURDLE!
SECOND IS #59, FLAMBERGE... N-NO, WAIT!
IT'S #7, ZAFAL TAKIE! SHE'S GONE FROM LAST ON THE GRID ALL THE WAY INTO SECOND POSITION!
VOOM

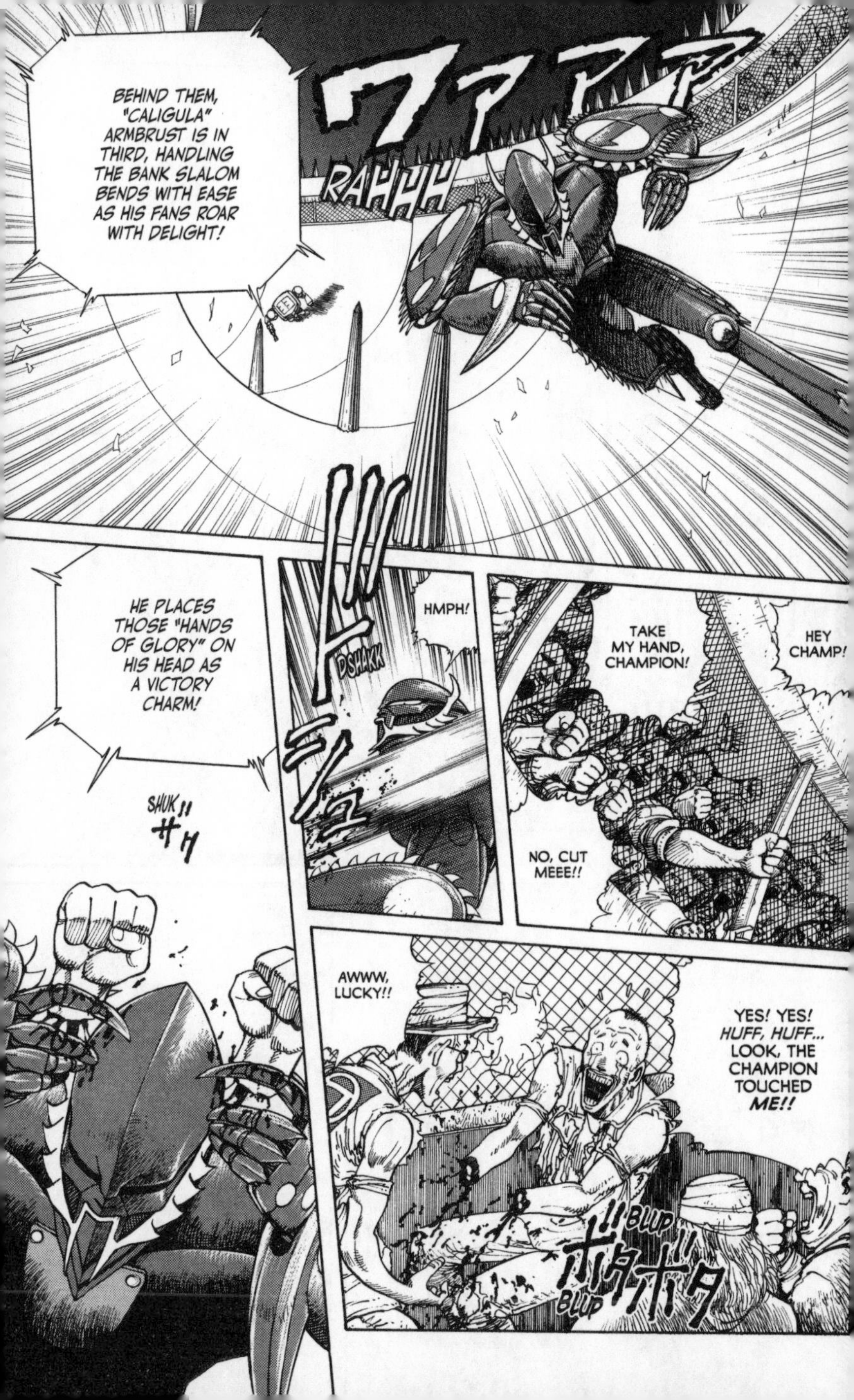
RAHHH
BEHIND THEM, "CALIGULA" ARMBRUST IS IN THIRD, HANDLING THE BANK SLALOM BENDS WITH EASE AS HIS FANS ROAR WITH DELIGHT!
HEY CHAMP!
TAKE MY HAND, CHAMPION!
NO, CUT MEEE!!
HMPH!
DSHAKK
YES! YES! HUFF, HUFF... LOOK, THE CHAMPION TOUCHED ME!!
AWWW, LUCKY!!
BLUP
BLUP
HE PLACES THOSE "HANDS OF GLORY" ON HIS HEAD AS A VICTORY CHARM!
SHUK!!

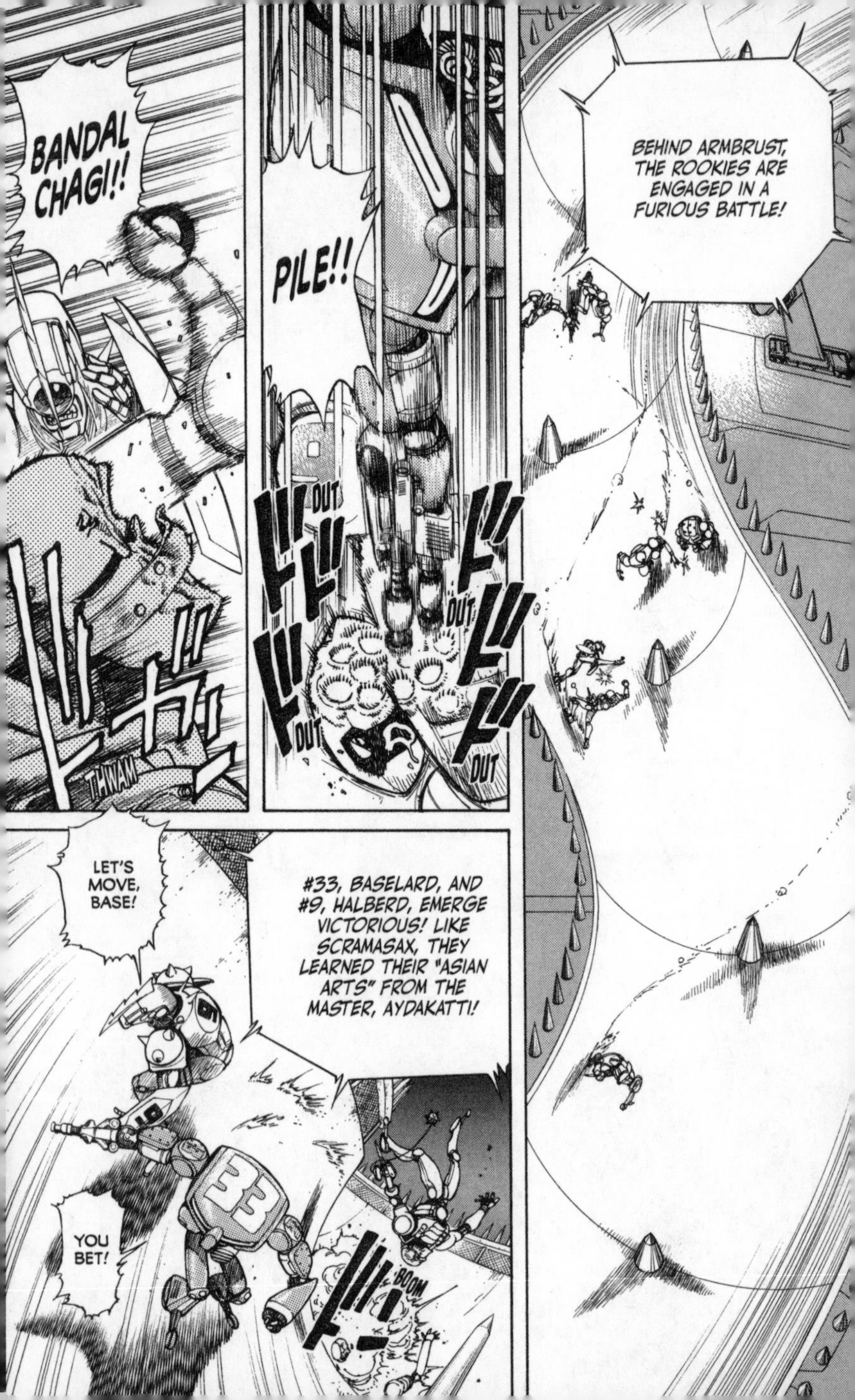
BEHIND ARMBRUST, THE ROOKIES ARE ENGAGED IN A FURIOUS BATTLE!
PILE!!
DUT
DUT
DUT
DUT
BANDAL CHAGI!!
THWAM
#33, BASELARD, AND #9, HALBERD, EMERGE VICTORIOUS! LIKE SCRAMASAX, THEY LEARNED THEIR "ASIAN ARTS" FROM THE MASTER, AYDAKATTI!
LET'S MOVE, BASE!
YOU BET!
BOOM

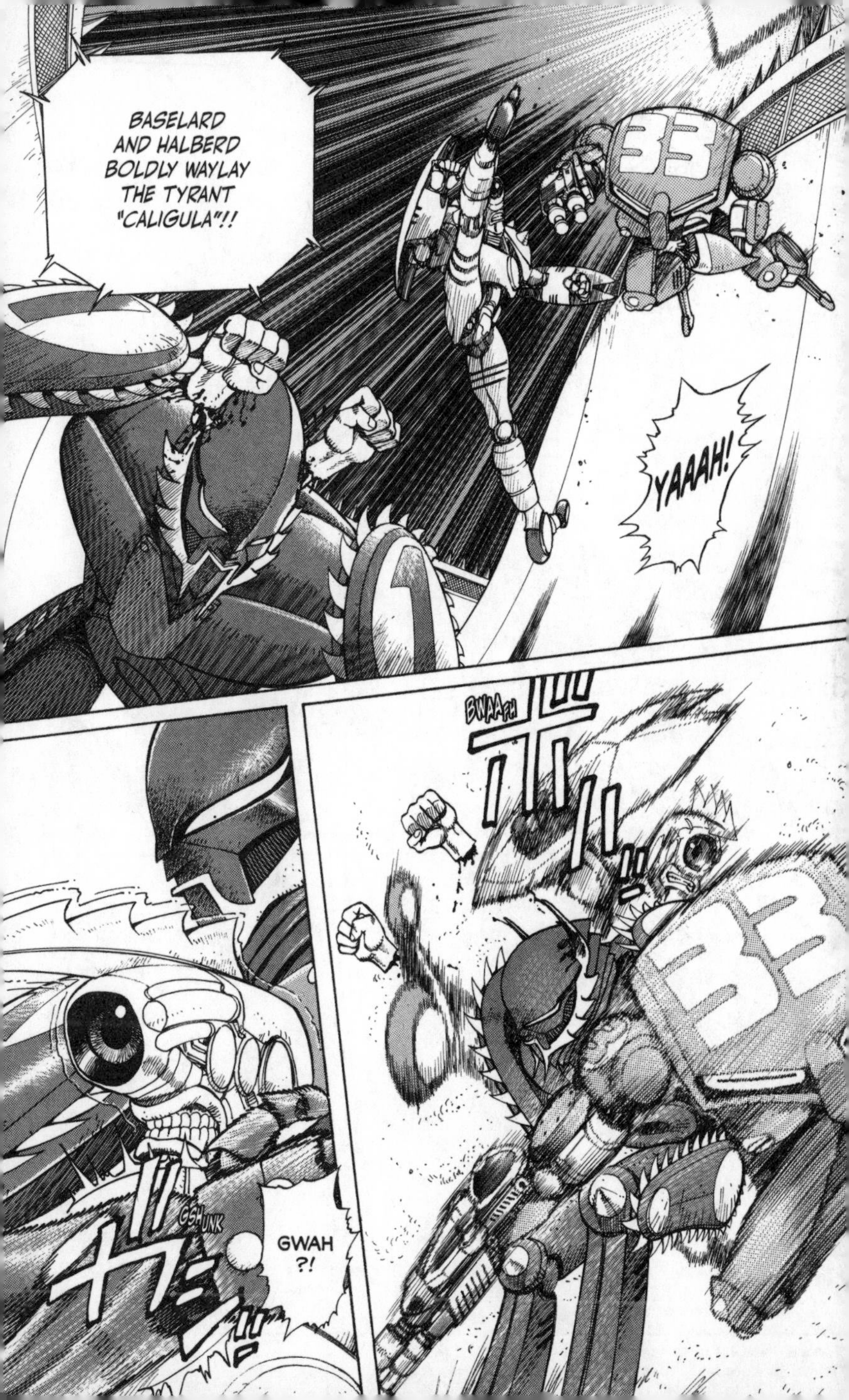
BASELARD AND HALBERD BOLDLY WAYLAY THE TYRANT "CALIGULA"!!
YAAAH!
BWAAPH
GSHUNK
GWAH ?!

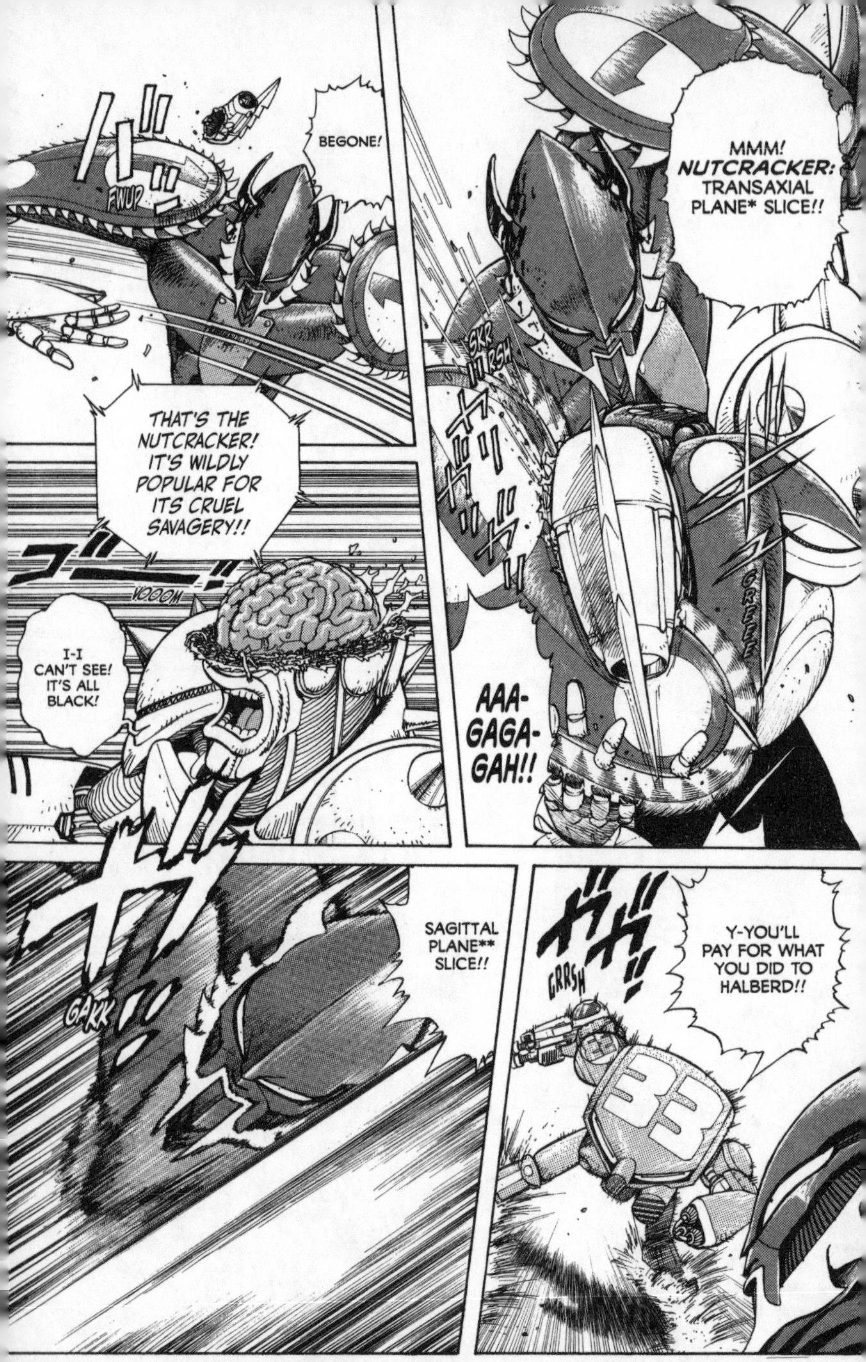
MMM! NUTCRACKER: TRANSAXIAL PLANE* SLICE!!
SKR RSH
GREEE
AAA-GAGA-GAH!!
BEGONE!
FWUP
THAT'S THE NUTCRACKER! IT'S WILDLY POPULAR FOR ITS CRUEL SAVAGERY!!
VOOOM
I-I CAN'T SEE! IT'S ALL BLACK!
Y-YOU'LL PAY FOR WHAT YOU DID TO HALBERD!!
GRRSH
SAGITTAL PLANE** SLICE!!
GAKK

***Transaxial Plane:** The medical term for the horizontal cross-section of the body.
****Sagittal Plane:** The term for the vertical plane that divides the body into left and right.

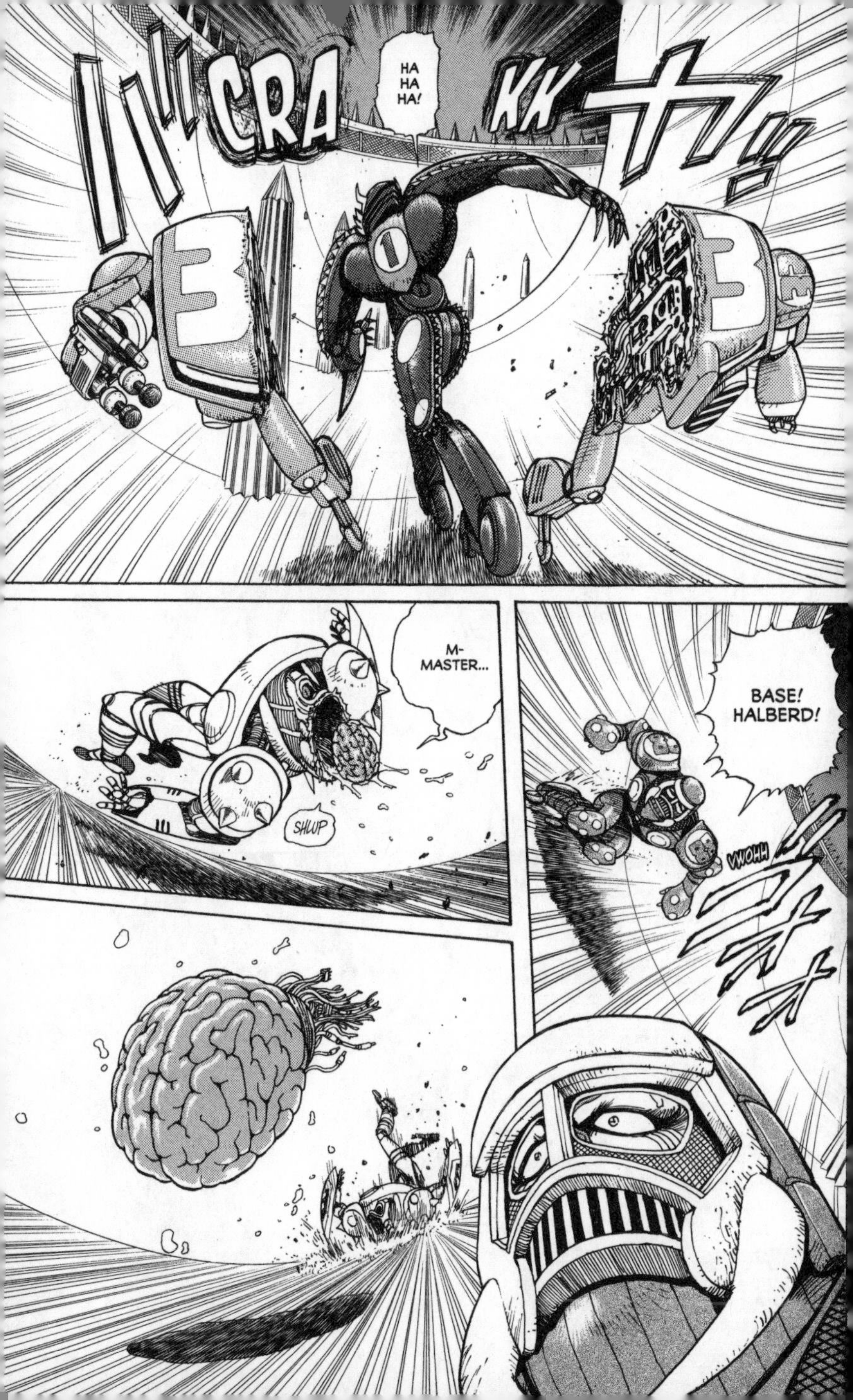
HA HA HA!
CRAKK
BASE! HALBERD!
VWOHH
M-MASTER...
SHLUP

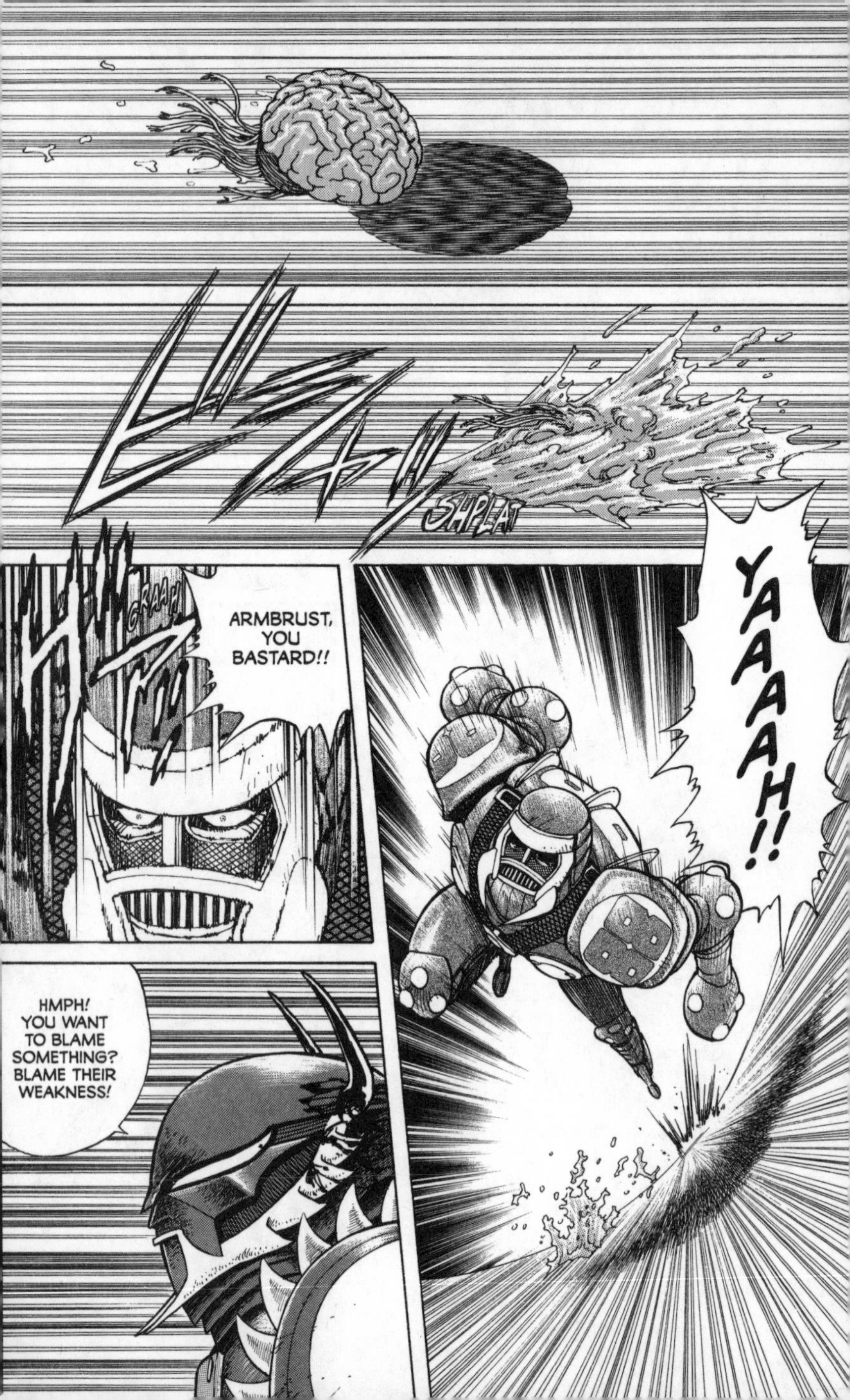
SHPLAT
YAAAAH!!
ARMBRUST, YOU BASTARD!!
HMPH! YOU WANT TO BLAME SOMETHING? BLAME THEIR WEAKNESS!

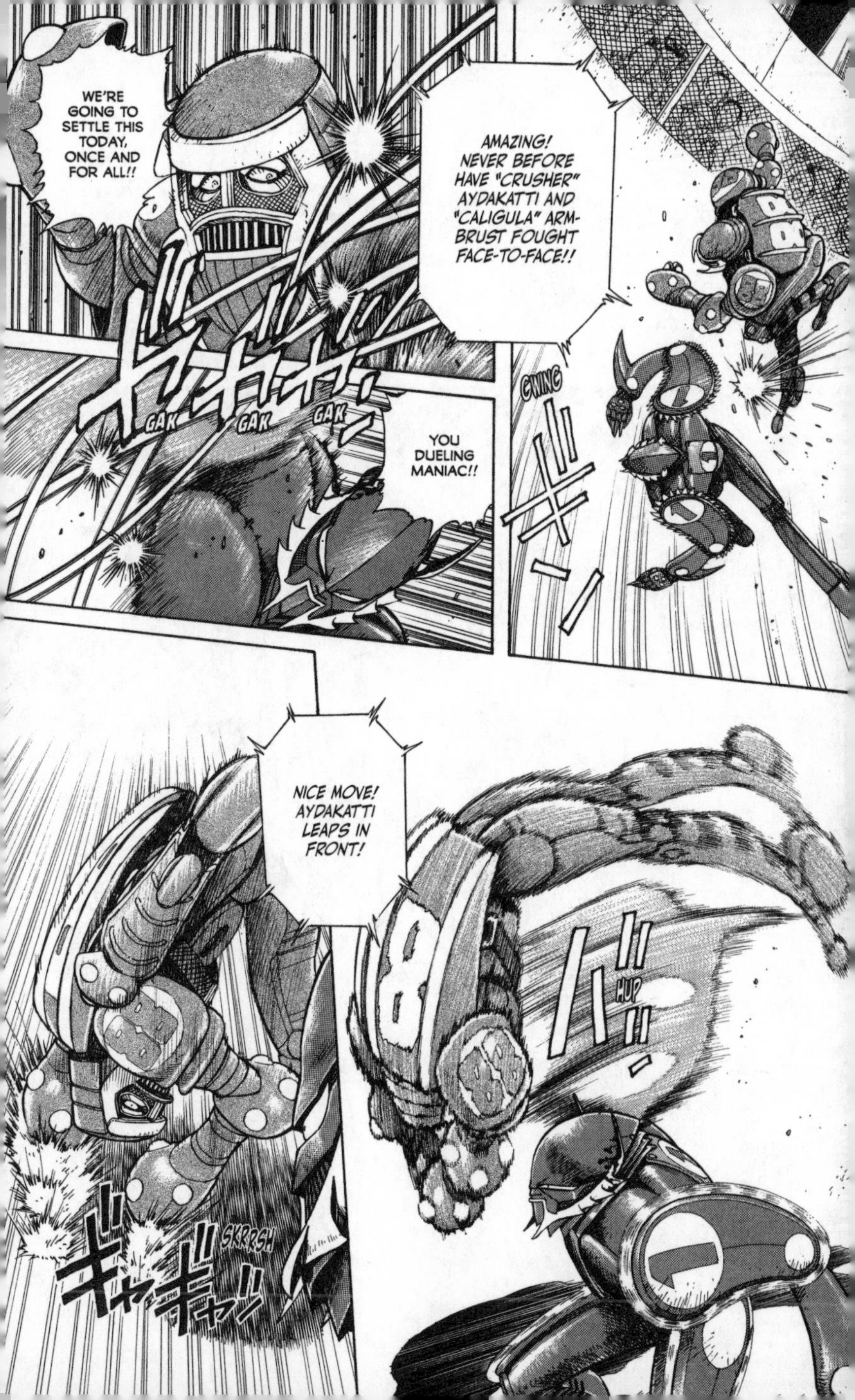
AMAZING! NEVER BEFORE HAVE "CRUSHER" AYDAKATTI AND "CALIGULA" ARMBRUST FOUGHT FACE-TO-FACE!!
WE'RE GOING TO SETTLE THIS TODAY, ONCE AND FOR ALL!!
CWING
GAK GAK GAK
YOU DUELING MANIAC!!
NICE MOVE! AYDAKATTI LEAPS IN FRONT!
HUP
SKRRSH

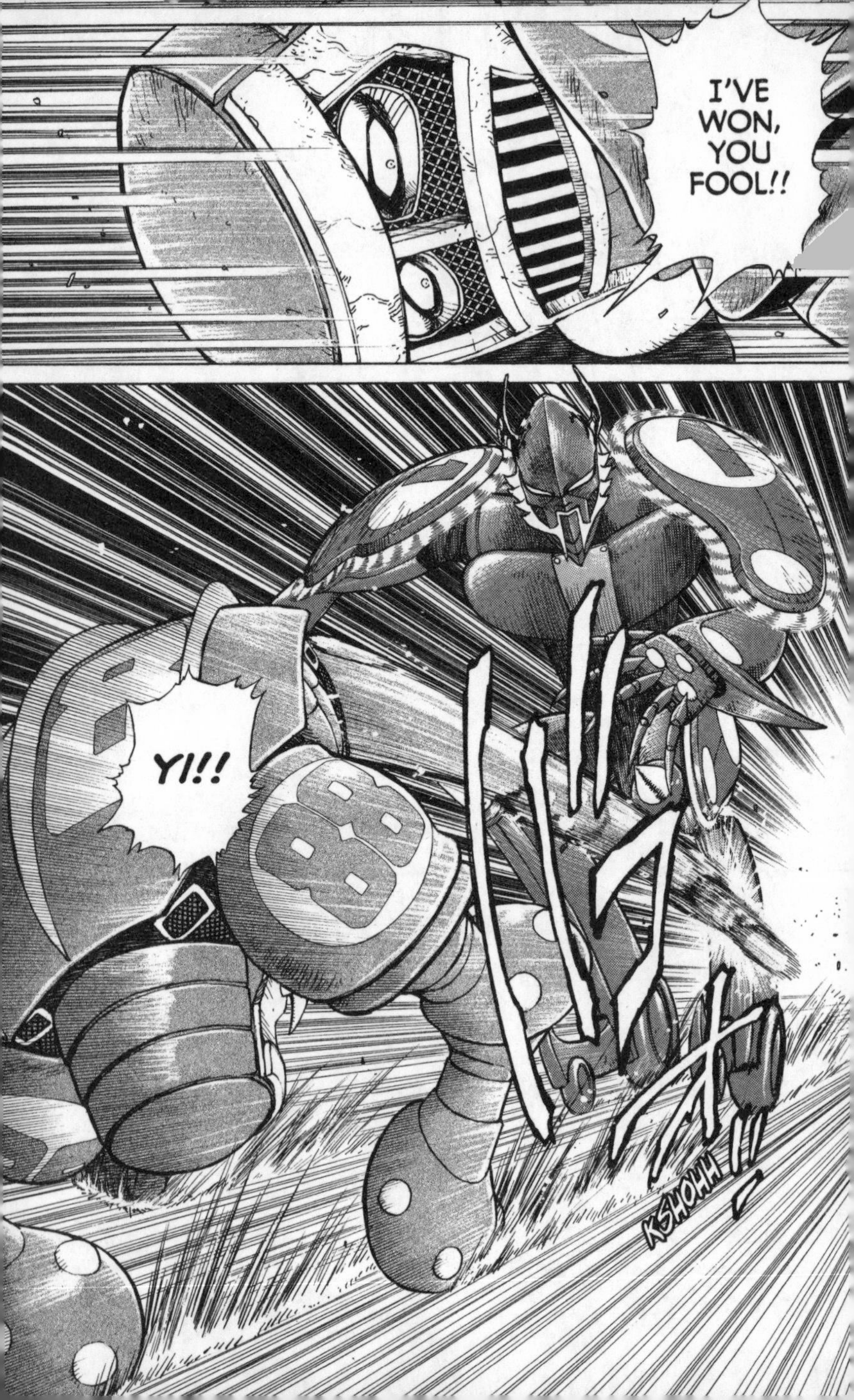
I'VE WON, YOU FOOL!!
YI!!
KSHOHH!!

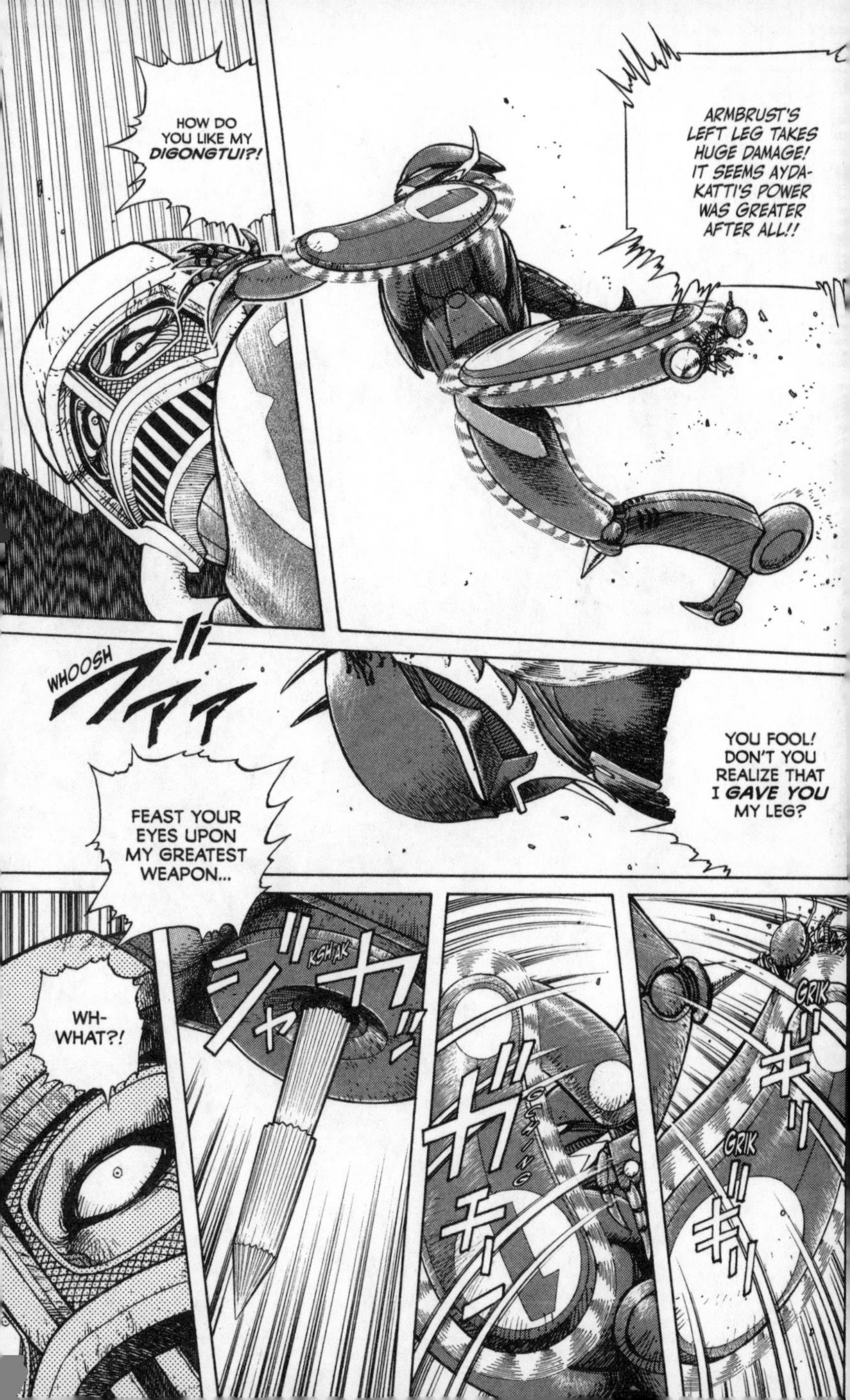
ARMBRUST'S LEFT LEG TAKES HUGE DAMAGE! IT SEEMS AYDA-KATTI'S POWER WAS GREATER AFTER ALL!!
HOW DO YOU LIKE MY *DIGONGTUI?!*
YOU FOOL! DON'T YOU REALIZE THAT I **GAVE YOU** MY LEG?
WHOOSH
FEAST YOUR EYES UPON MY GREATEST WEAPON...
GRIK
GRIK
KSHAK
WH- WHAT?!

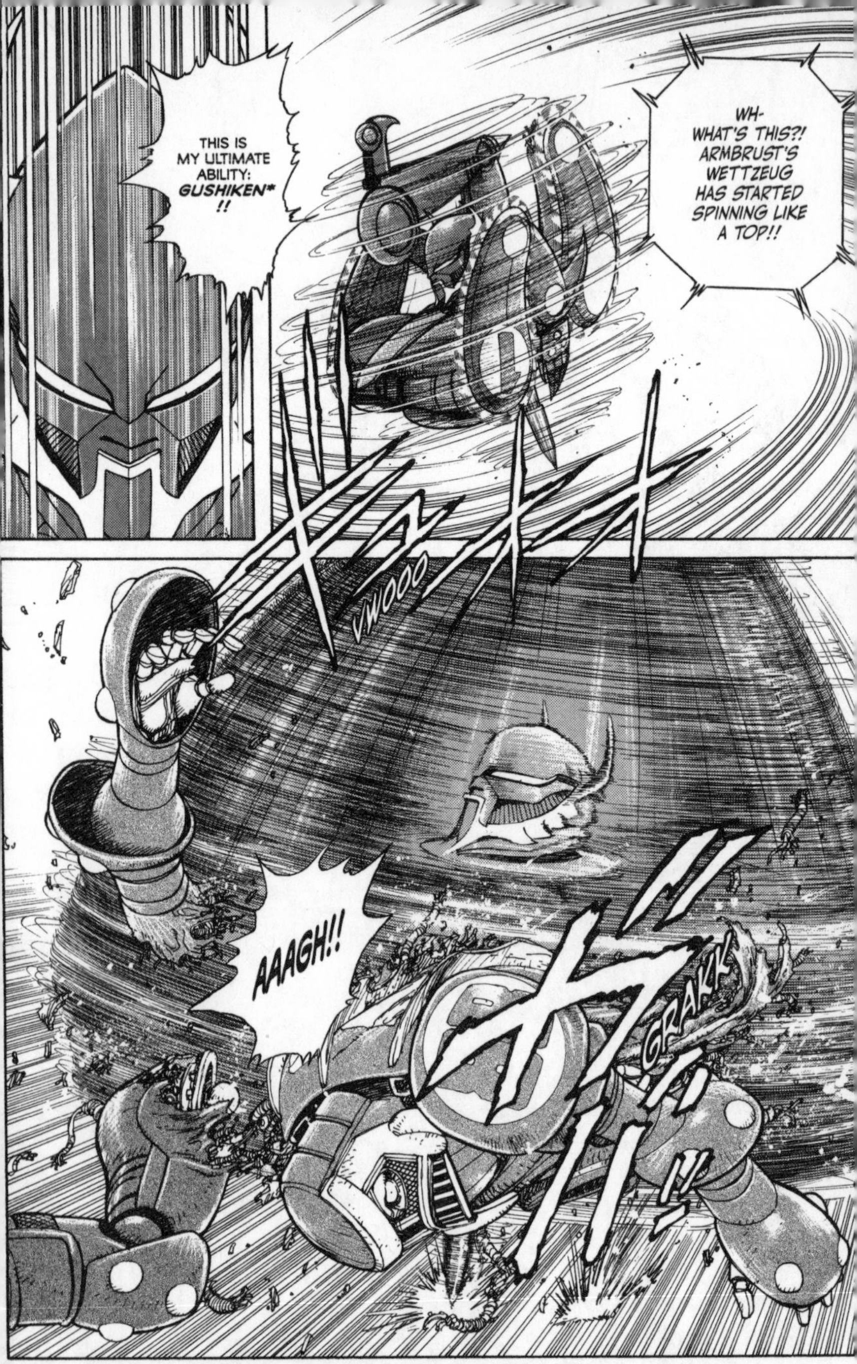
WH- WHAT'S THIS?! ARMBRUST'S WETTZEUG HAS STARTED SPINNING LIKE A TOP!!
THIS IS MY ULTIMATE ABILITY: GUSHIKEN* !!
VWOOO
GRAKK
AAAGH!!

*__Gushiken:__ A legendary ancient fighting art of the Ryukyu Islands. Even today, there are festivals in Taiwan that utilize giant spinning tops, and it is thought that the concept was turned into this fighting style.

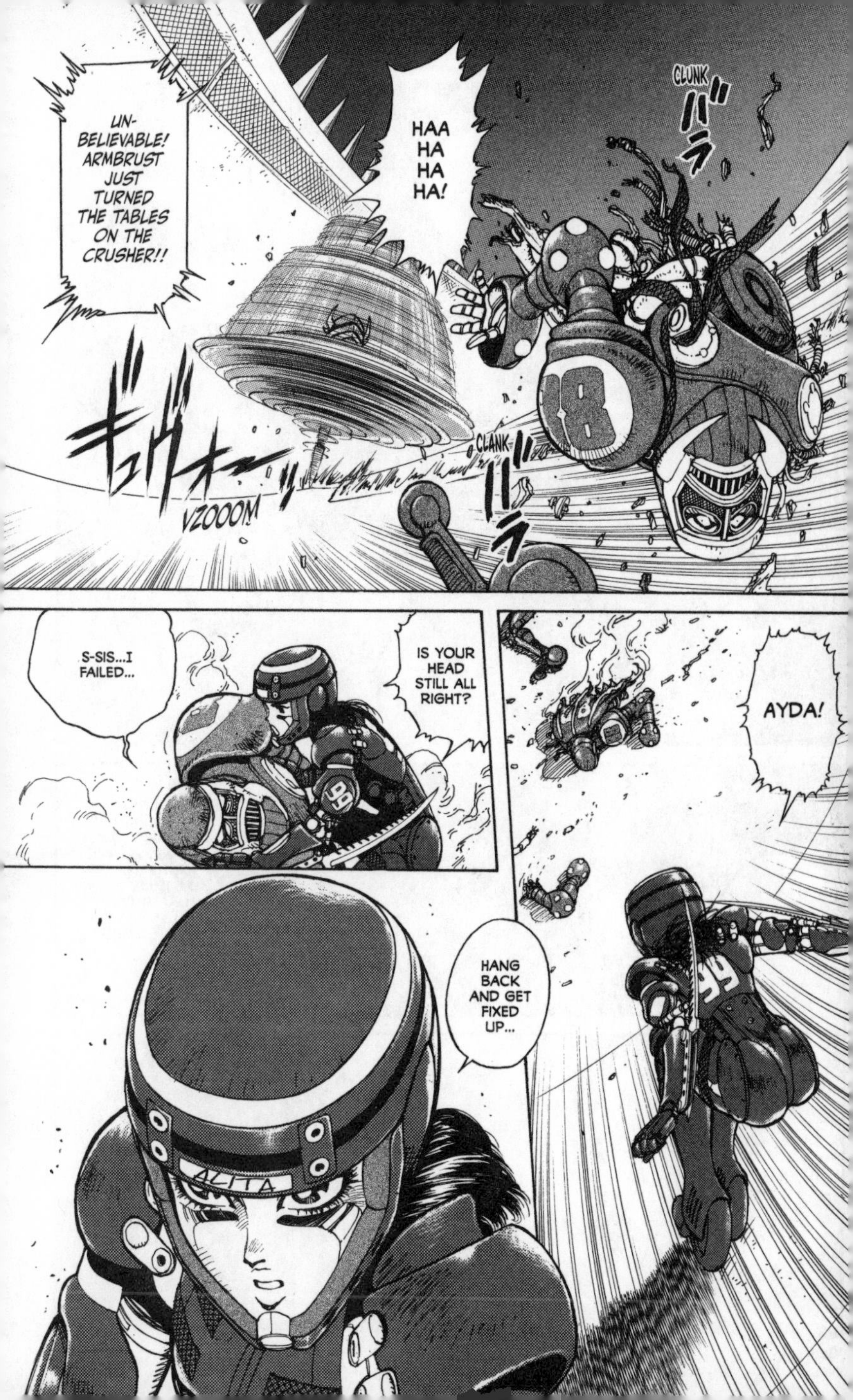
CLUNK
バラ
HAA HA HA HA!
UN-BELIEVABLE! ARMBRUST JUST TURNED THE TABLES ON THE CRUSHER!!
CLANK
バラ
ギュヴオーッ
VZOOOM
AYDA!
IS YOUR HEAD STILL ALL RIGHT?
S-SIS...I FAILED...
HANG BACK AND GET FIXED UP...

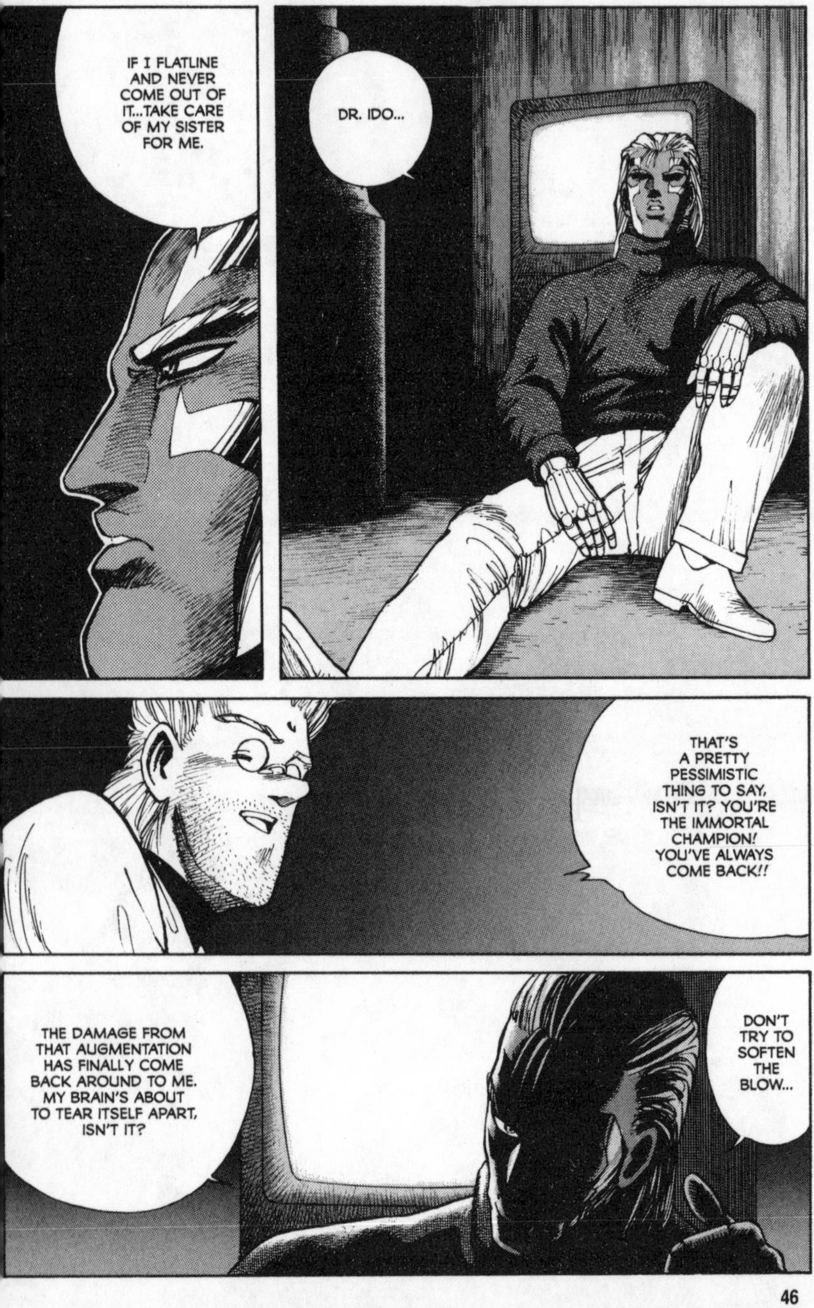
DR. IDO...
IF I FLATLINE AND NEVER COME OUT OF IT...TAKE CARE OF MY SISTER FOR ME.
THAT'S A PRETTY PESSIMISTIC THING TO SAY, ISN'T IT? YOU'RE THE IMMORTAL CHAMPION! YOU'VE ALWAYS COME BACK!!
DON'T TRY TO SOFTEN THE BLOW...
THE DAMAGE FROM THAT AUGMENTATION HAS FINALLY COME BACK AROUND TO ME. MY BRAIN'S ABOUT TO TEAR ITSELF APART, ISN'T IT?

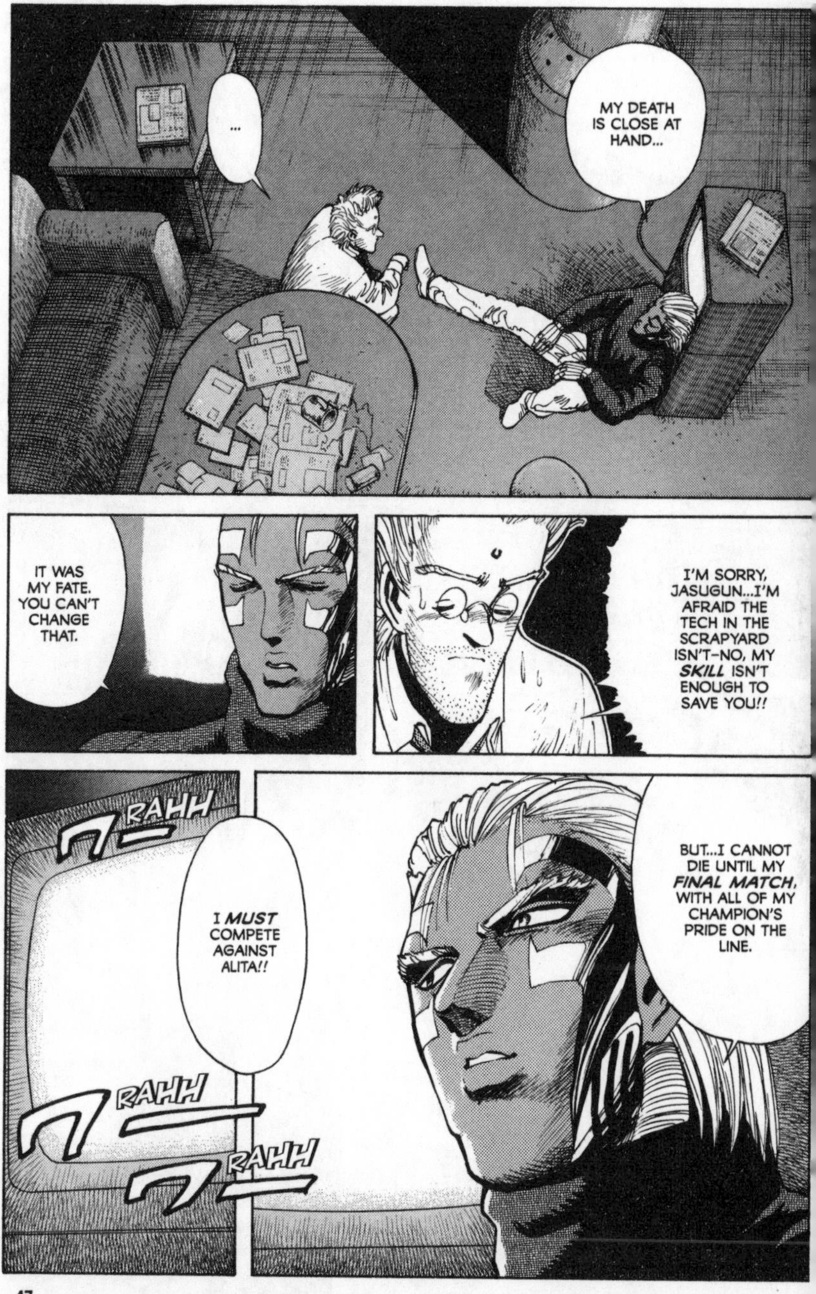
MY DEATH IS CLOSE AT HAND...
...
I'M SORRY, JASUGUN...I'M AFRAID THE TECH IN THE SCRAPYARD ISN'T–NO, MY *SKILL* ISN'T ENOUGH TO SAVE YOU!!
IT WAS MY FATE. YOU CAN'T CHANGE THAT.
BUT...I CANNOT DIE UNTIL MY *FINAL MATCH*, WITH ALL OF MY CHAMPION'S PRIDE ON THE LINE.
I *MUST* COMPETE AGAINST ALITA!!
RAHH
RAHH
RAHH

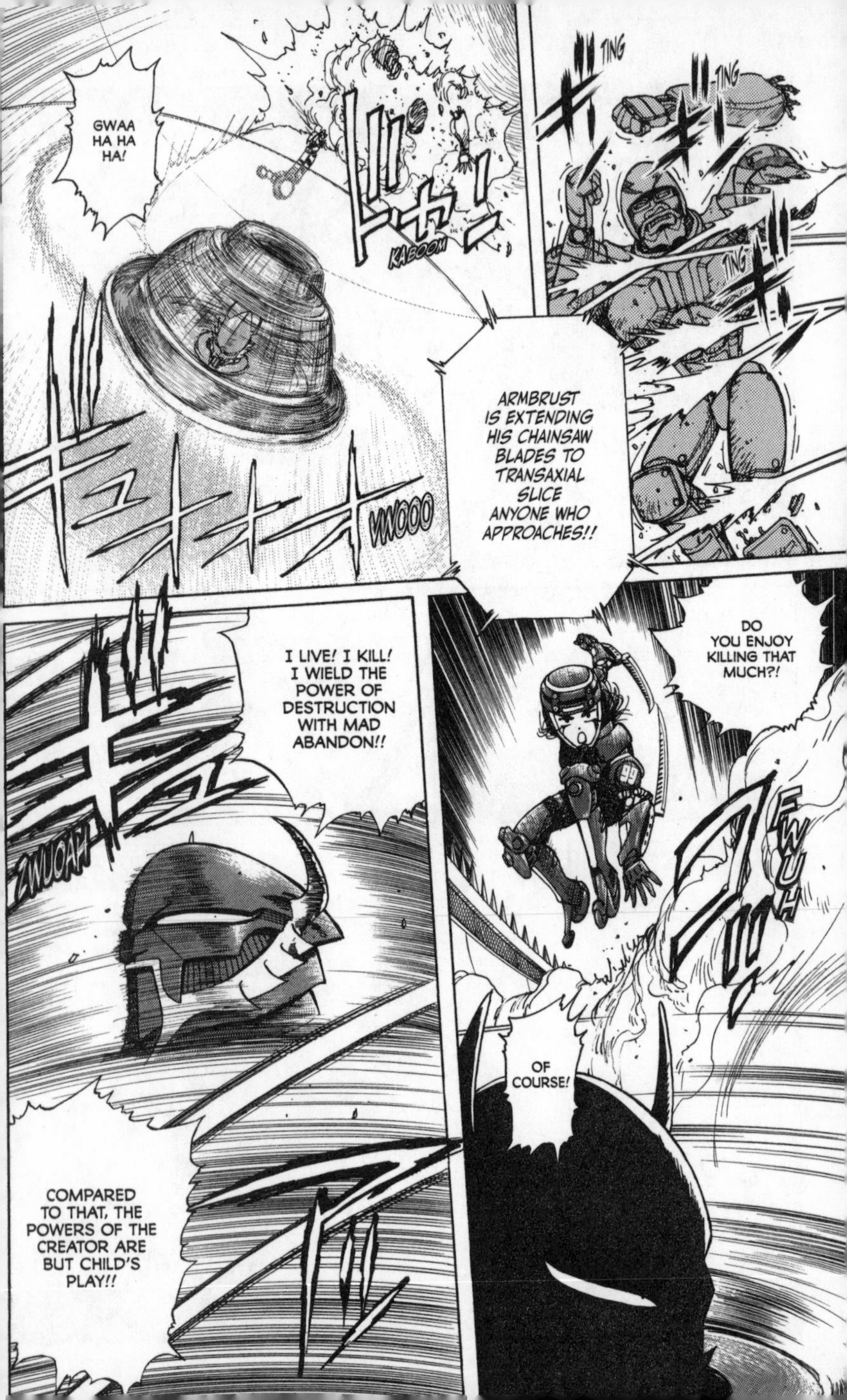
TING
TING
TING
ARMBRUST IS EXTENDING HIS CHAINSAW BLADES TO TRANSAXIAL SLICE ANYONE WHO APPROACHES!!
GWAA HA HA HA!
KABOOM
VWOOO
DO YOU ENJOY KILLING THAT MUCH?!
FWUH
OF COURSE!
I LIVE! I KILL! I WIELD THE POWER OF DESTRUCTION WITH MAD ABANDON!!
ZWUOAH
COMPARED TO THAT, THE POWERS OF THE CREATOR ARE BUT CHILD'S PLAY!!

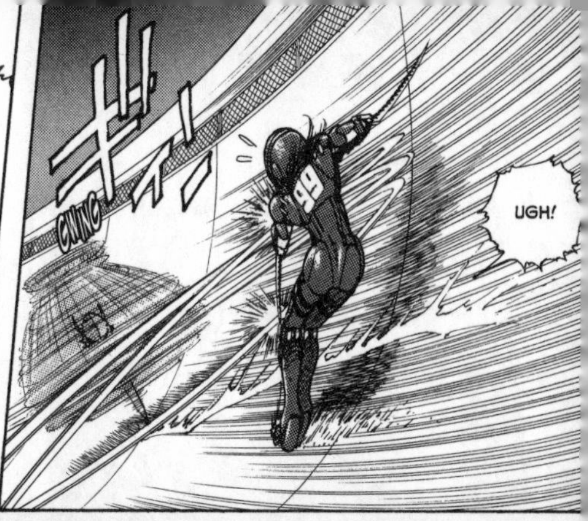
GWING
UGH!

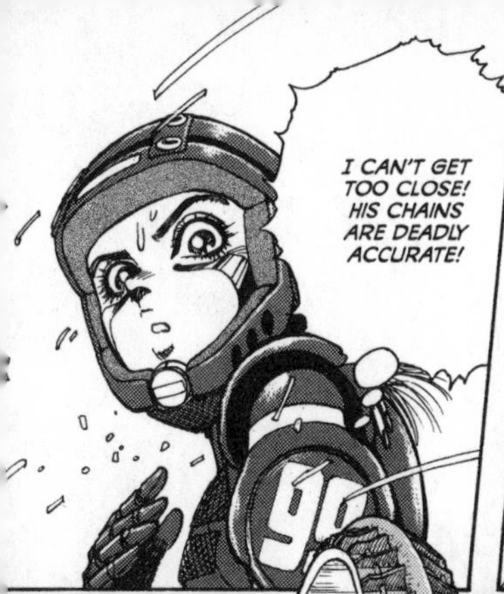
I CAN'T GET TOO CLOSE! HIS CHAINS ARE DEADLY ACCURATE!

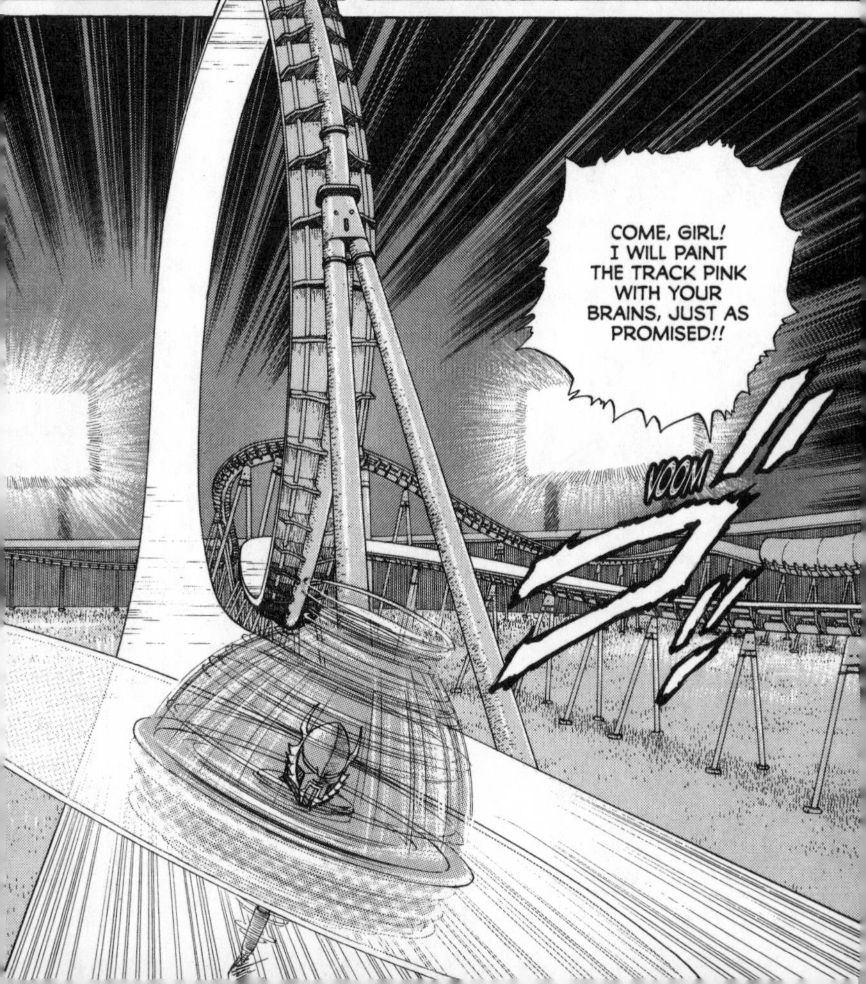
COME, GIRL! I WILL PAINT THE TRACK PINK WITH YOUR BRAINS, JUST AS PROMISED!!
VOOM

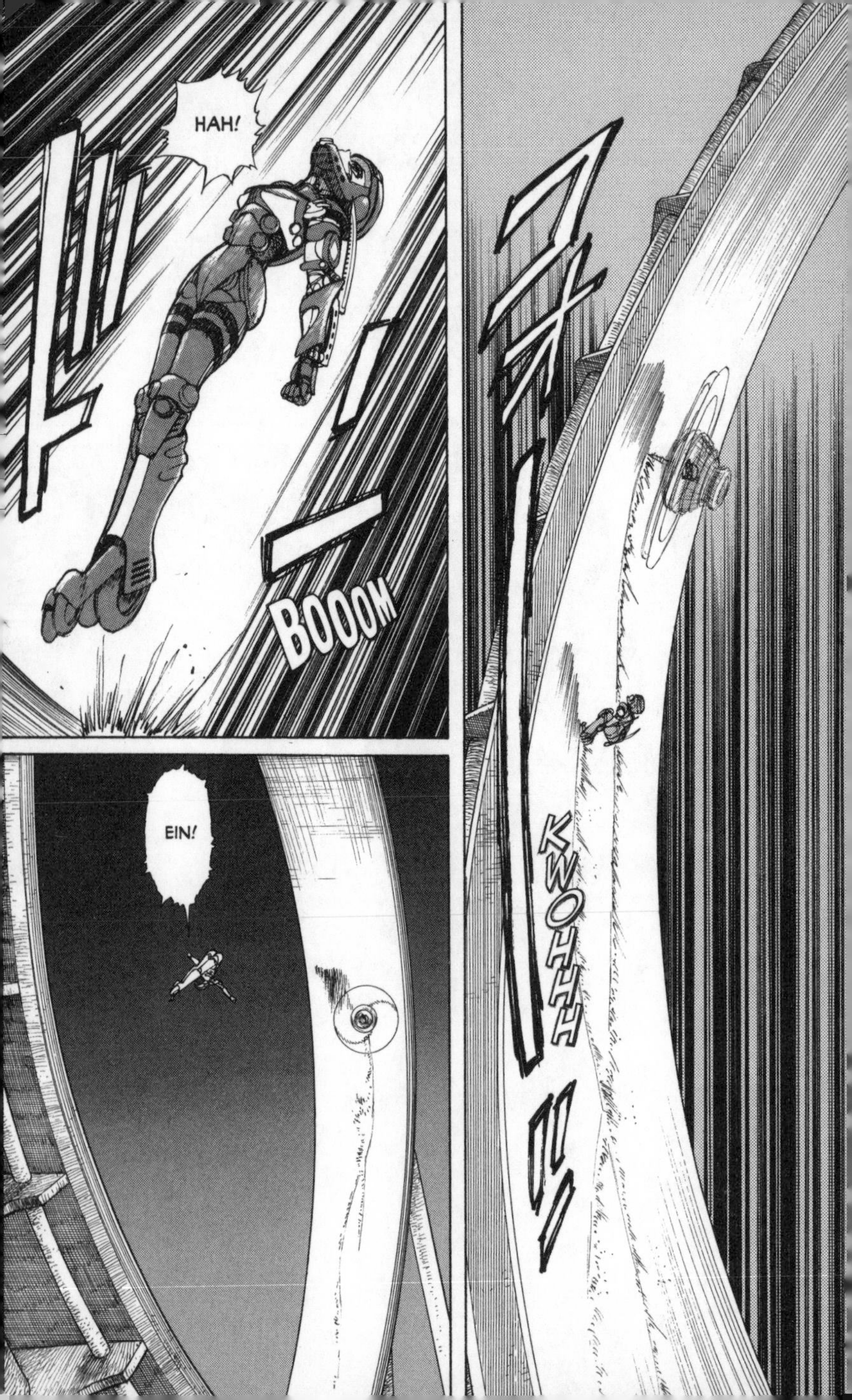
KWOHHH
HAH!
BOOOM
EIN!

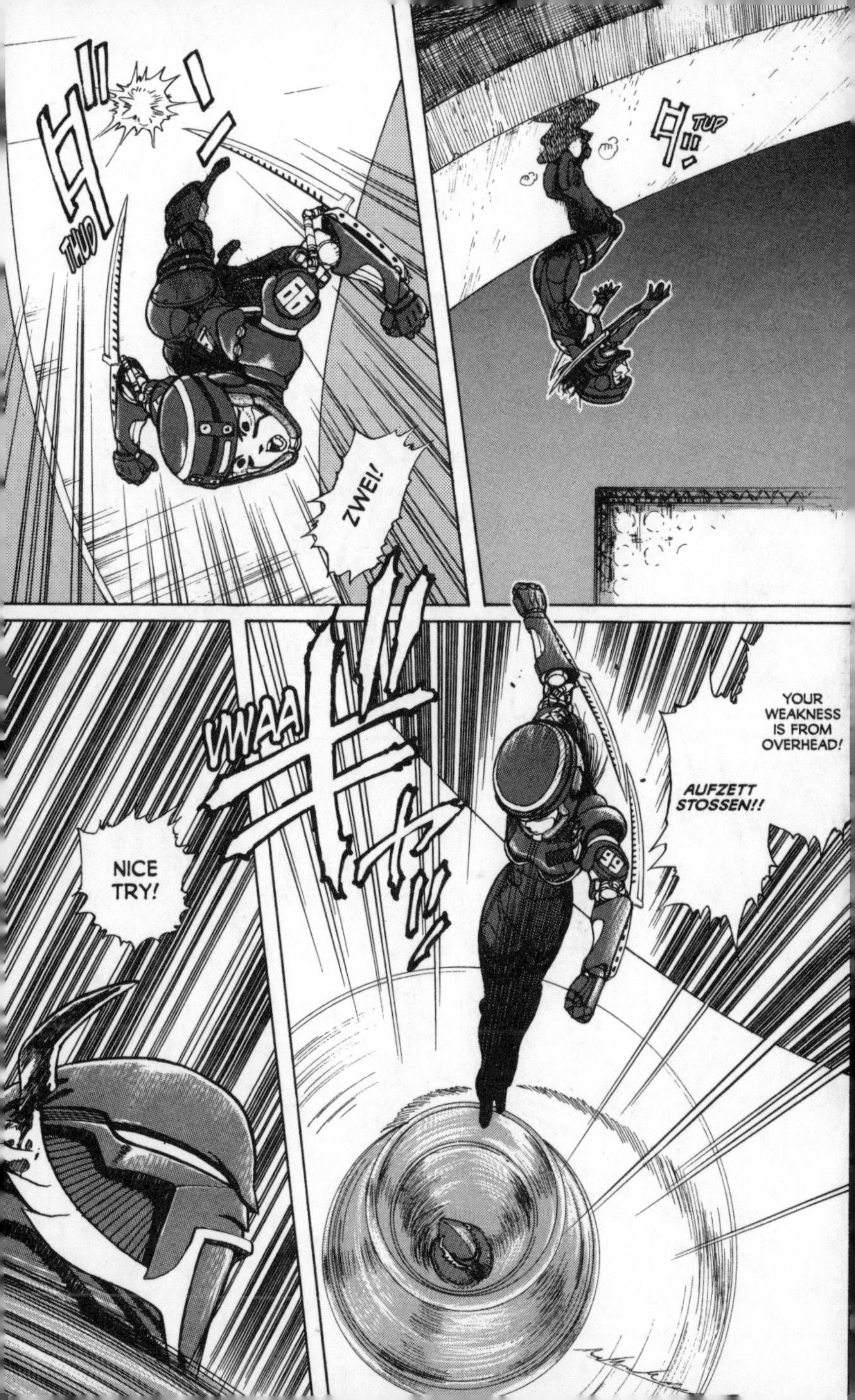
TUP
THUD
ZWEI!
YOUR WEAKNESS IS FROM OVERHEAD!
AUFZETT STOSSEN!!
VWAA
NICE TRY!

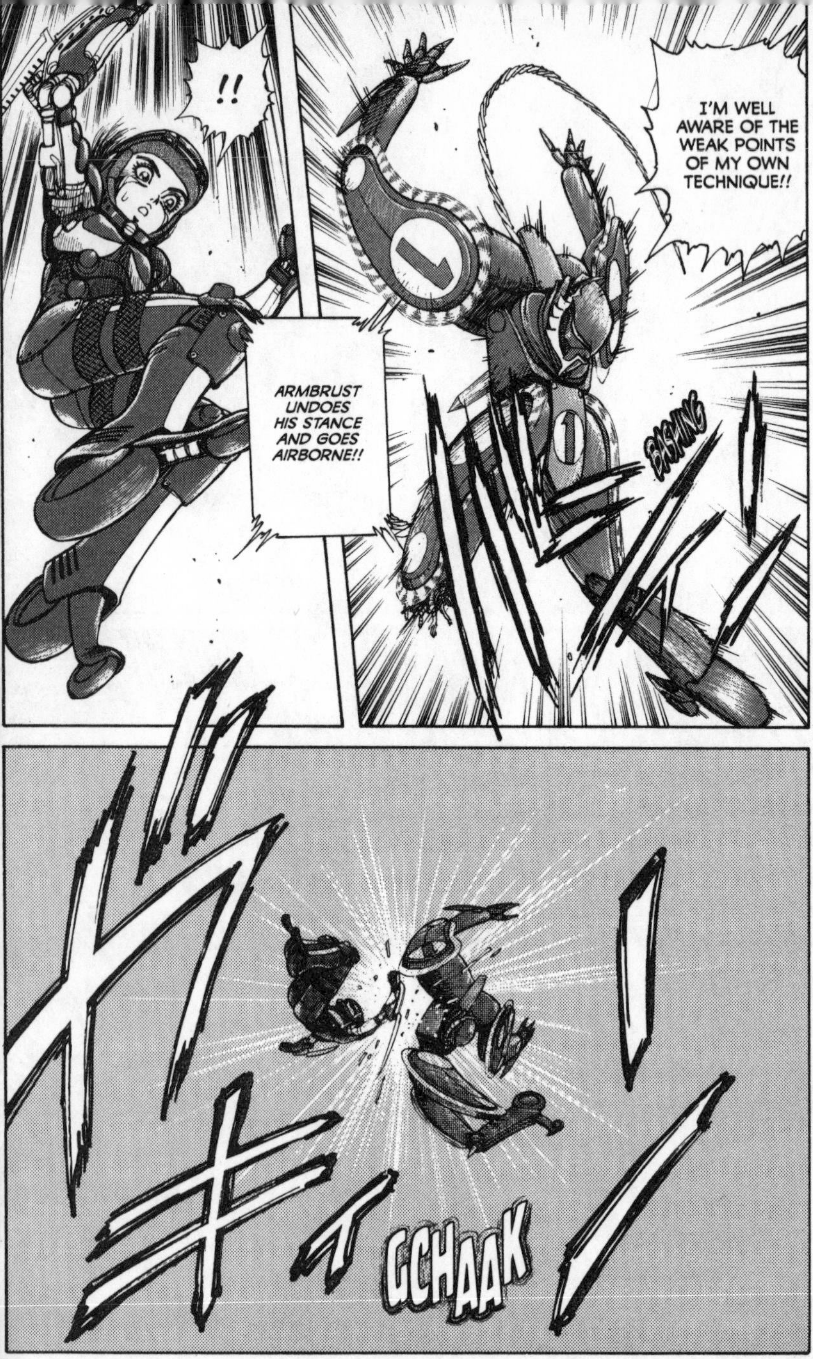
I'M WELL AWARE OF THE WEAK POINTS OF MY OWN TECHNIQUE!!
BASHING
ARMBRUST UNDOES HIS STANCE AND GOES AIRBORNE!!
!!
GCHAAK

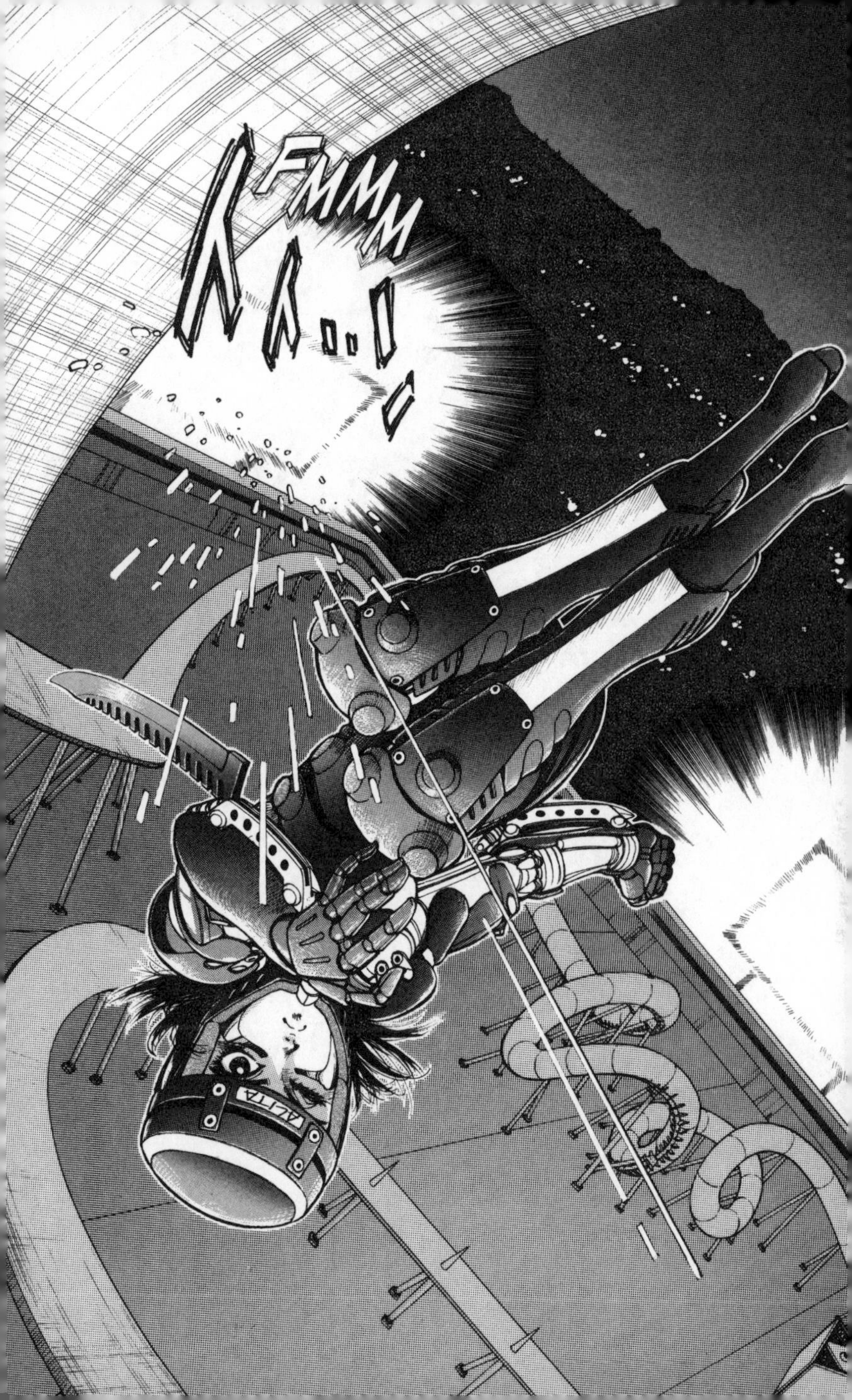
FMMM
ALITA

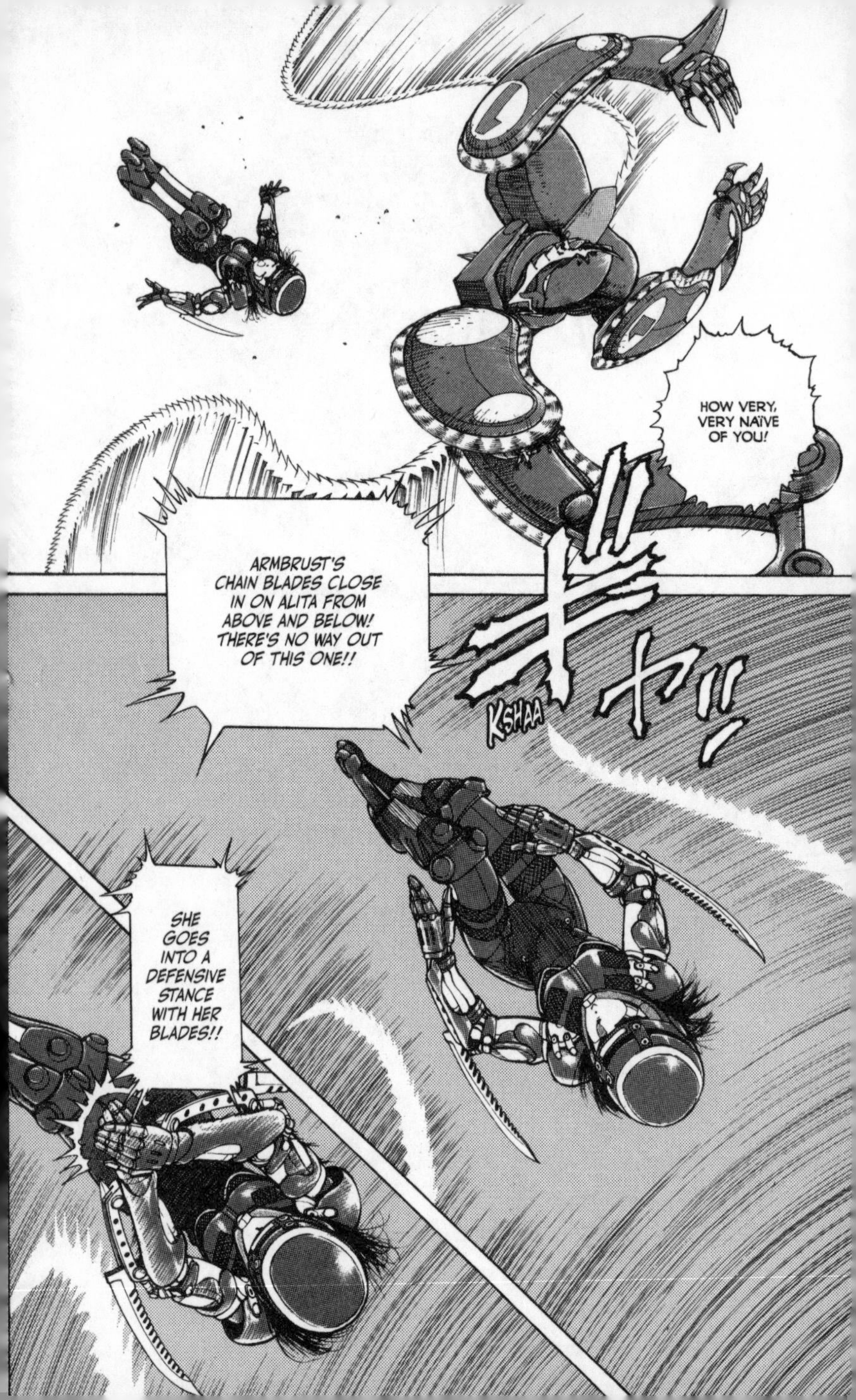
HOW VERY, VERY NAÏVE OF YOU!
ARMBRUST'S CHAIN BLADES CLOSE IN ON ALITA FROM ABOVE AND BELOW! THERE'S NO WAY OUT OF THIS ONE!!
KSHAA
SHE GOES INTO A DEFENSIVE STANCE WITH HER BLADES!!

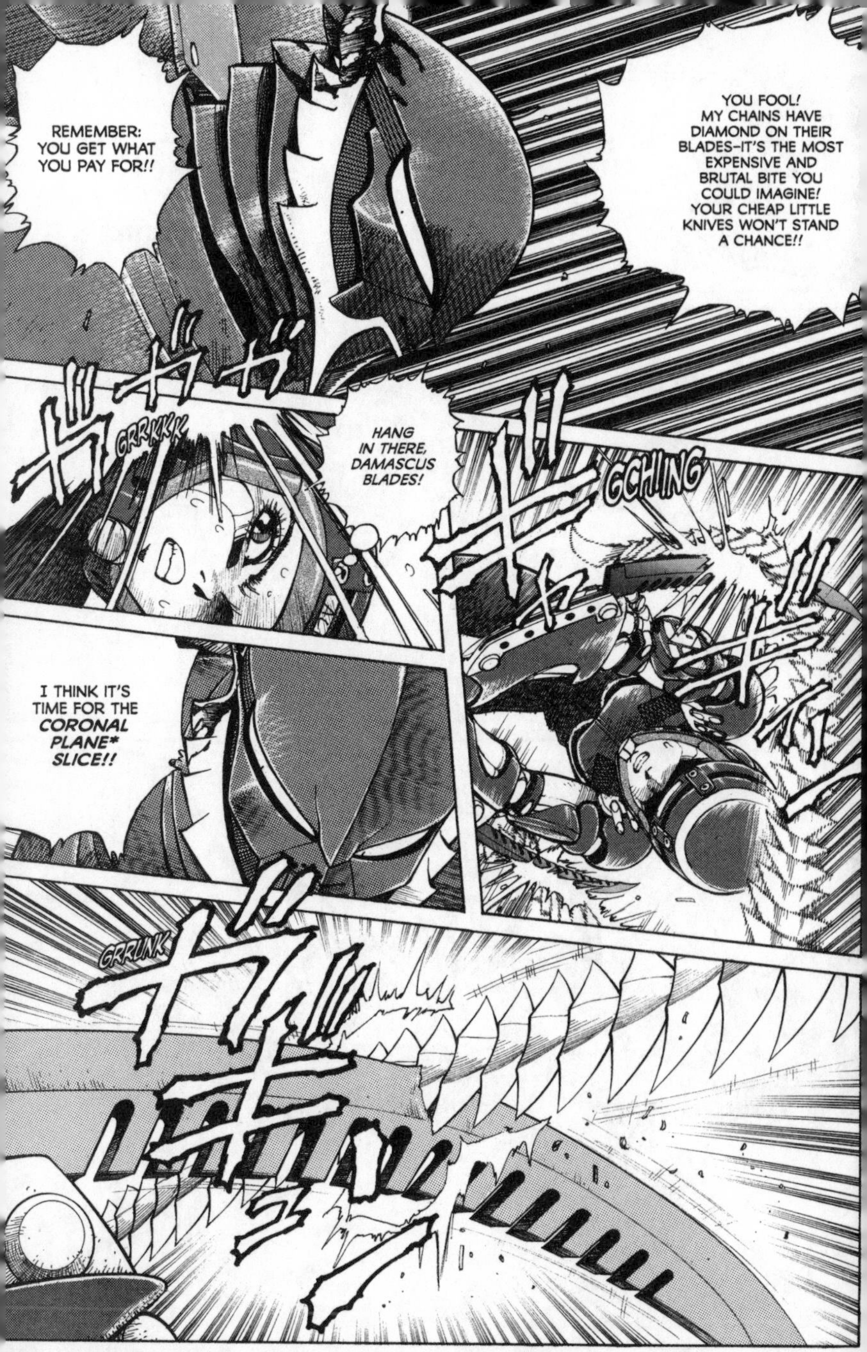
YOU FOOL! MY CHAINS HAVE DIAMOND ON THEIR BLADES–IT'S THE MOST EXPENSIVE AND BRUTAL BITE YOU COULD IMAGINE! YOUR CHEAP LITTLE KNIVES WON'T STAND A CHANCE!!
REMEMBER: YOU GET WHAT YOU PAY FOR!!
GCHING
HANG IN THERE, DAMASCUS BLADES!
GRRKKK
I THINK IT'S TIME FOR THE *CORONAL PLANE* SLICE!!*
GRRUNK

***Coronal Plane:** The plane that divides the body into front and back halves.

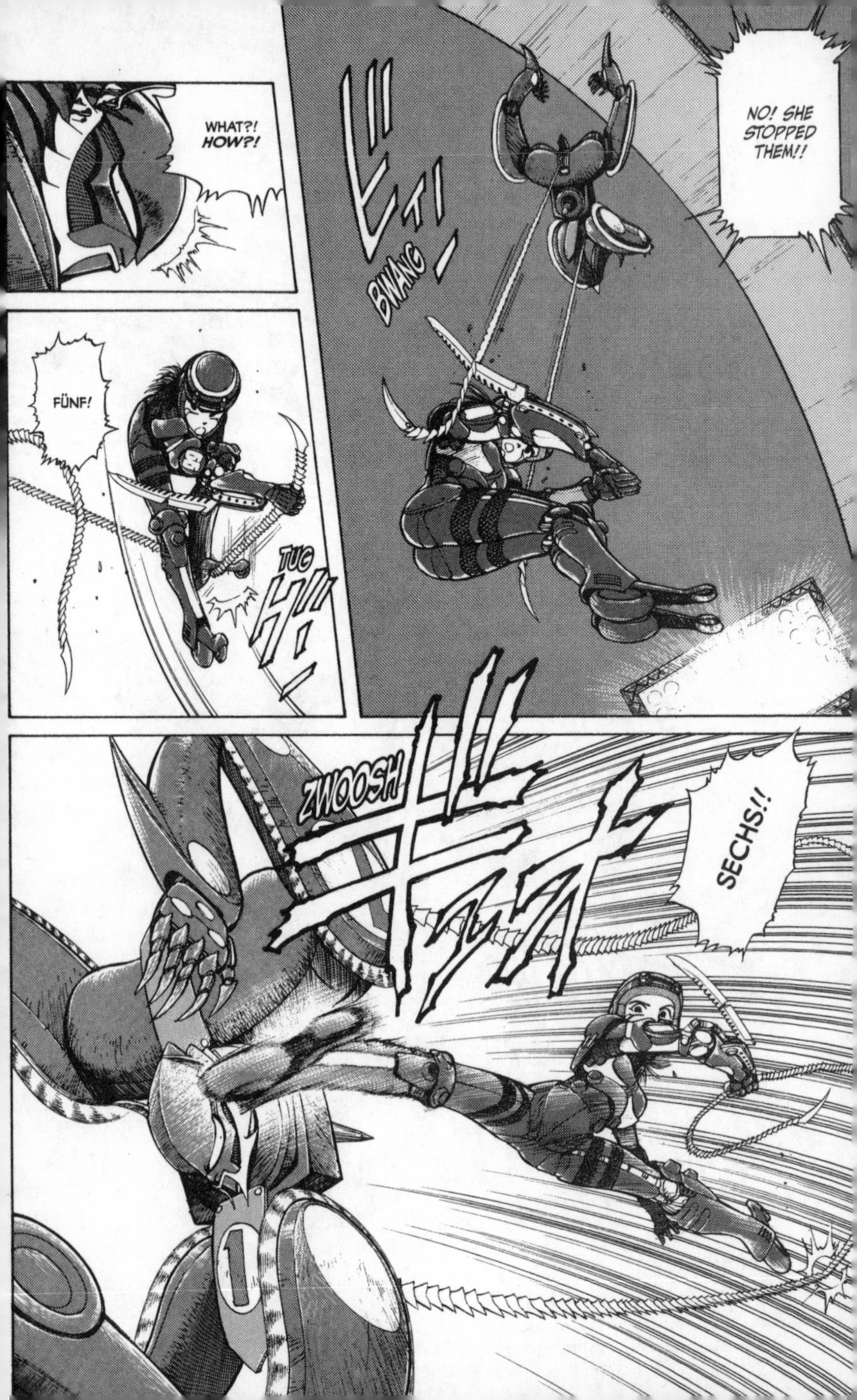
NO! SHE STOPPED THEM!!
BWANG
WHAT?! HOW?!
FÜNF!
TUG
ZWOOSH
SECHS!!

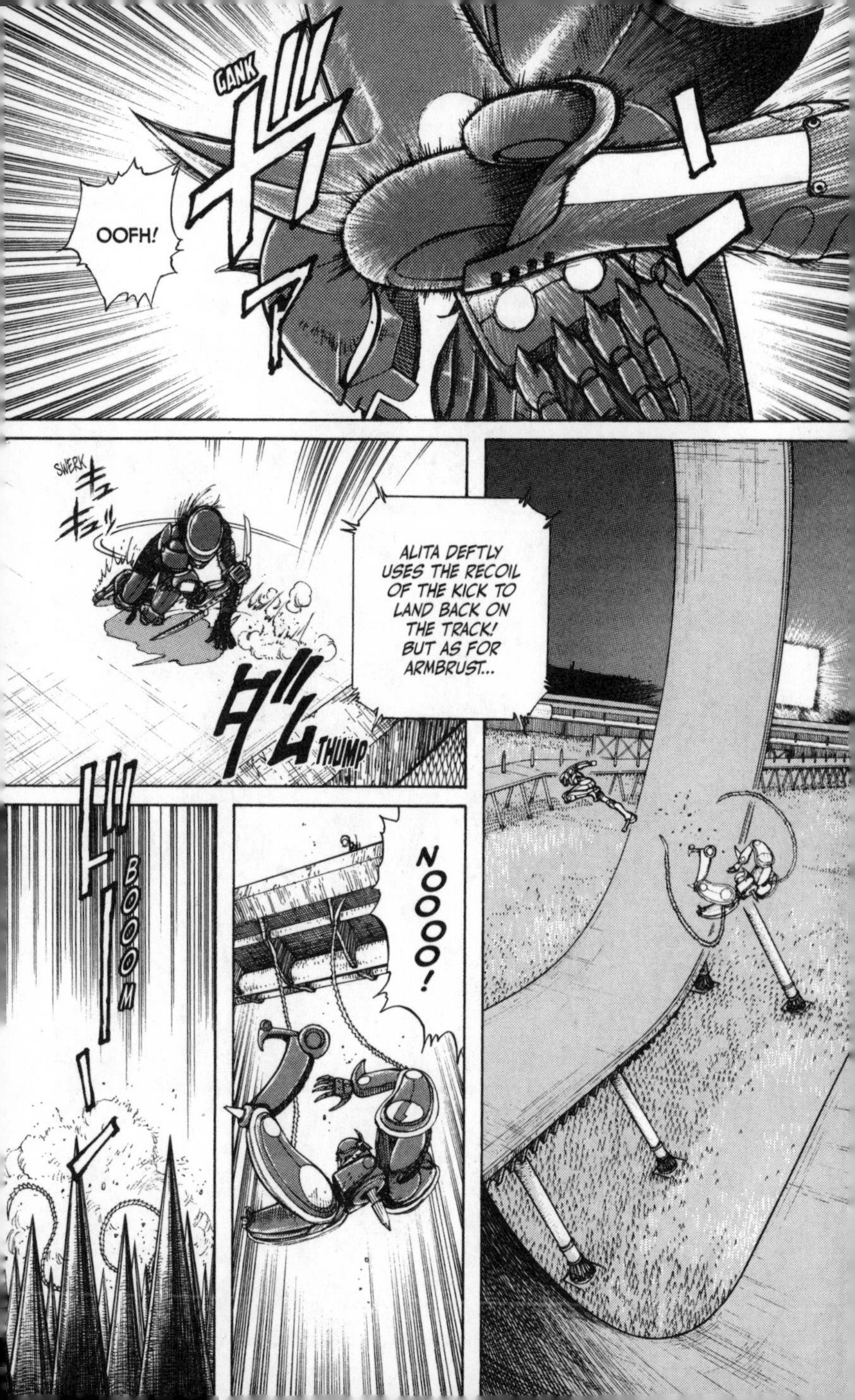
GANK
OOFH!
ALITA DEFTLY USES THE RECOIL OF THE KICK TO LAND BACK ON THE TRACK! BUT AS FOR ARMBRUST...
SWERK
THUMP
NOOOOO!
BOOOOM

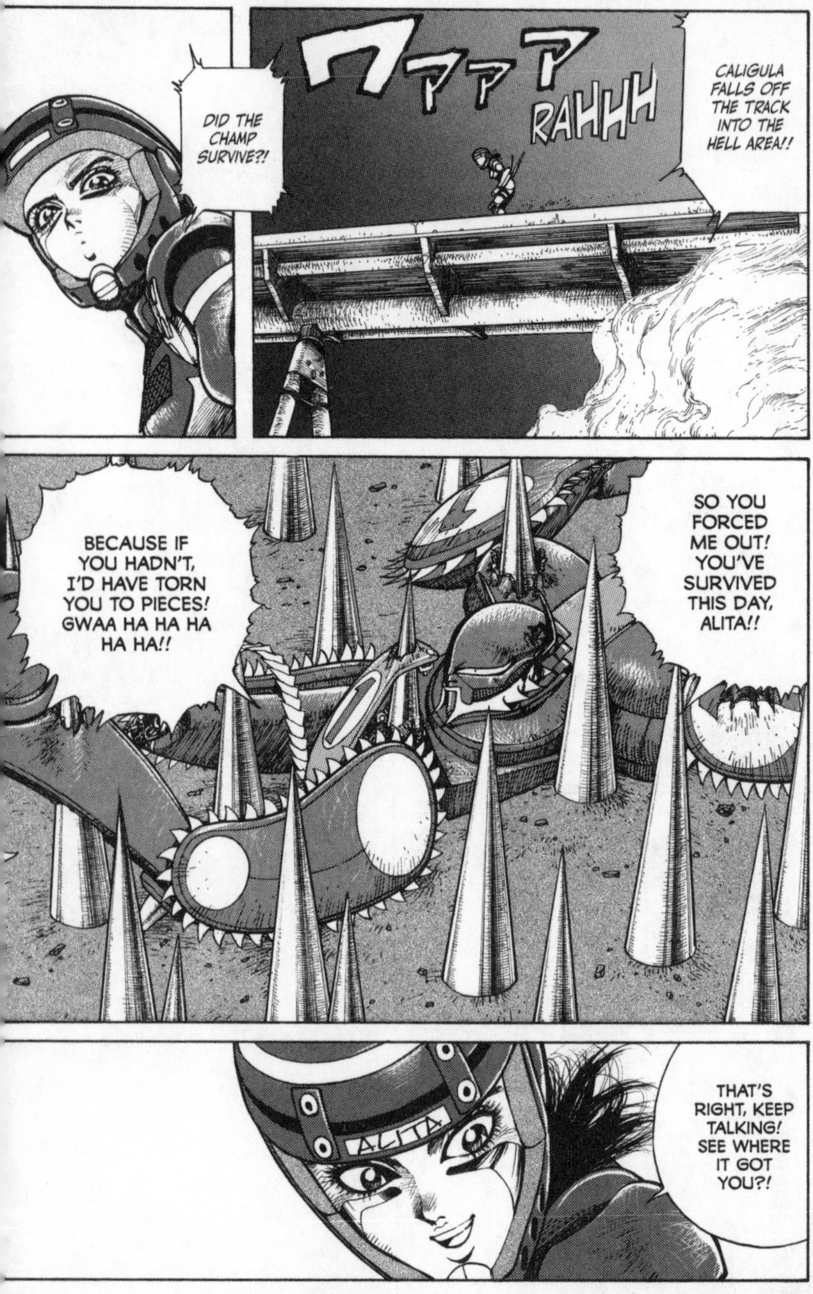
CALIGULA FALLS OFF THE TRACK INTO THE HELL AREA!!
ワァァァ
RAHHH
DID THE CHAMP SURVIVE?!
SO YOU FORCED ME OUT! YOU'VE SURVIVED THIS DAY, ALITA!!
BECAUSE IF YOU HADN'T, I'D HAVE TORN YOU TO PIECES! GWAA HA HA HA HA HA!!
ALITA
THAT'S RIGHT, KEEP TALKING! SEE WHERE IT GOT YOU?!

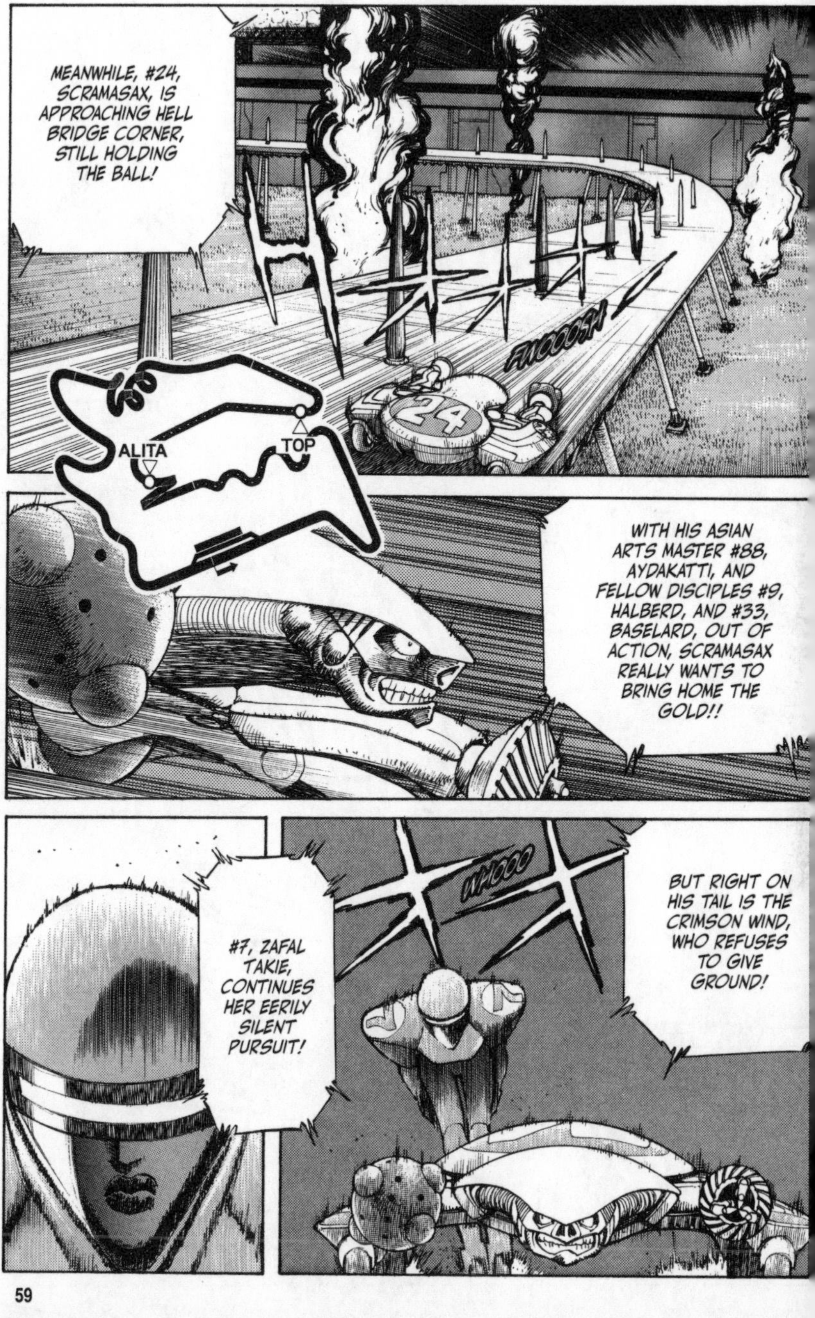
MEANWHILE, #24, SCRAMASAX, IS APPROACHING HELL BRIDGE CORNER, STILL HOLDING THE BALL!
FWOOOSH
ALITA
TOP
WITH HIS ASIAN ARTS MASTER #88, AYDAKATTI, AND FELLOW DISCIPLES #9, HALBERD, AND #33, BASELARD, OUT OF ACTION, SCRAMASAX REALLY WANTS TO BRING HOME THE GOLD!!
BUT RIGHT ON HIS TAIL IS THE CRIMSON WIND, WHO REFUSES TO GIVE GROUND!
WHOOO
#7, ZAFAL TAKIE, CONTINUES HER EERILY SILENT PURSUIT!

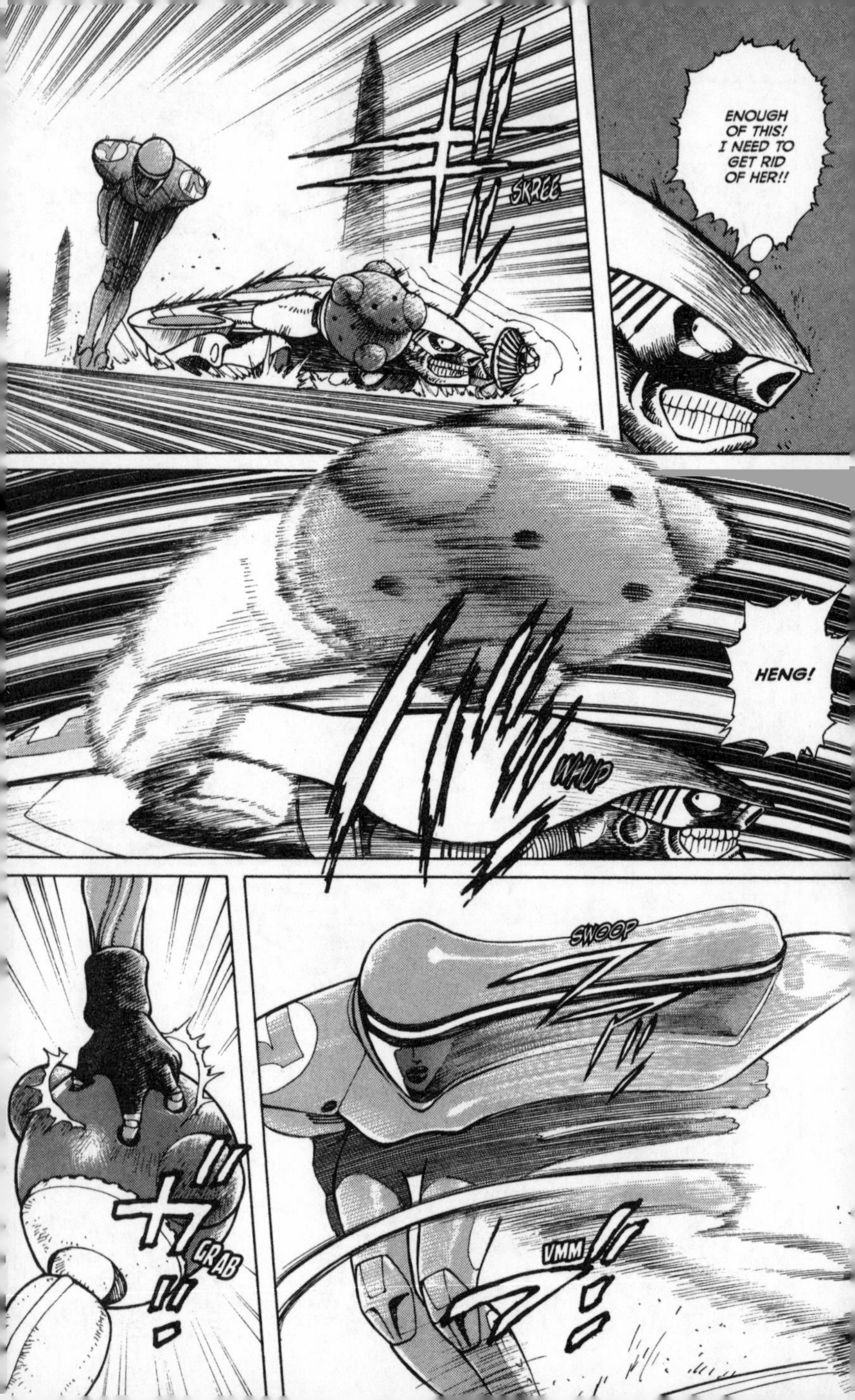
ENOUGH OF THIS! I NEED TO GET RID OF HER!!
SKREE
HENG!
WHUP
SWOOP
VMM
GRAB

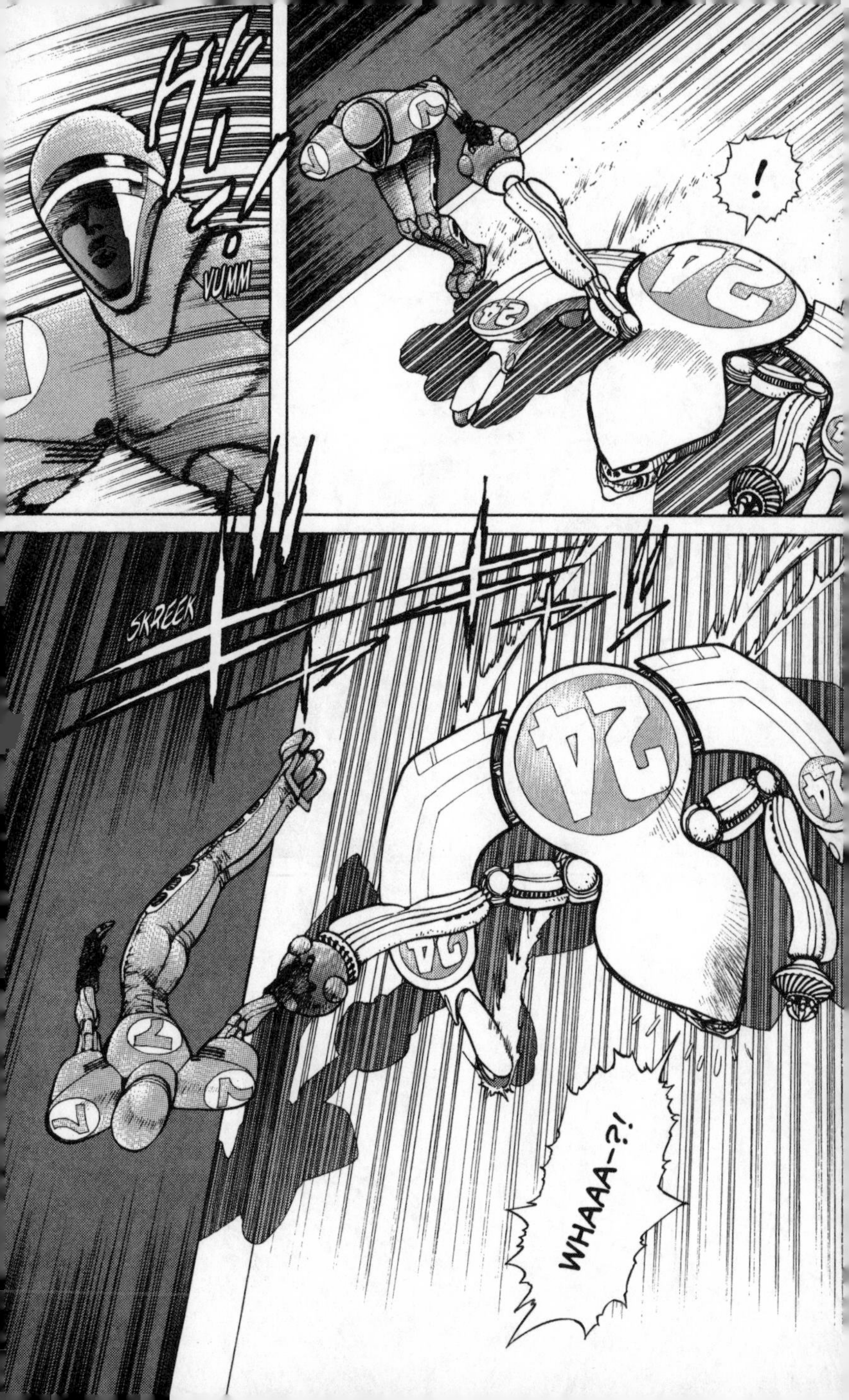
!
VUMM
SKREEK
WHAAA-?!

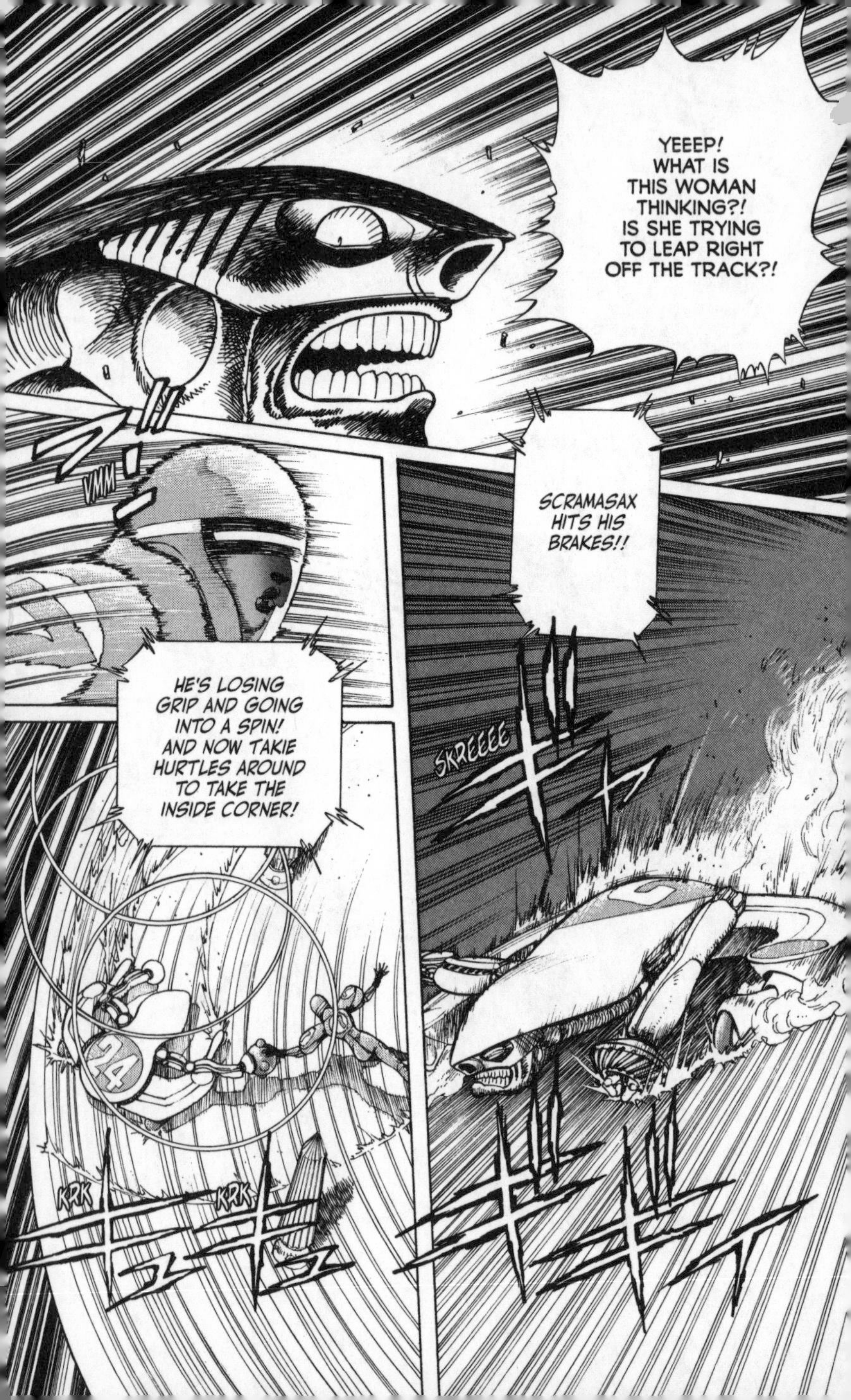
YEEEP! WHAT IS THIS WOMAN THINKING?! IS SHE TRYING TO LEAP RIGHT OFF THE TRACK?!
SCRAMASAX HITS HIS BRAKES!!
SKREEEE
VMM
HE'S LOSING GRIP AND GOING INTO A SPIN! AND NOW TAKIE HURTLES AROUND TO TAKE THE INSIDE CORNER!
KRK
KRK

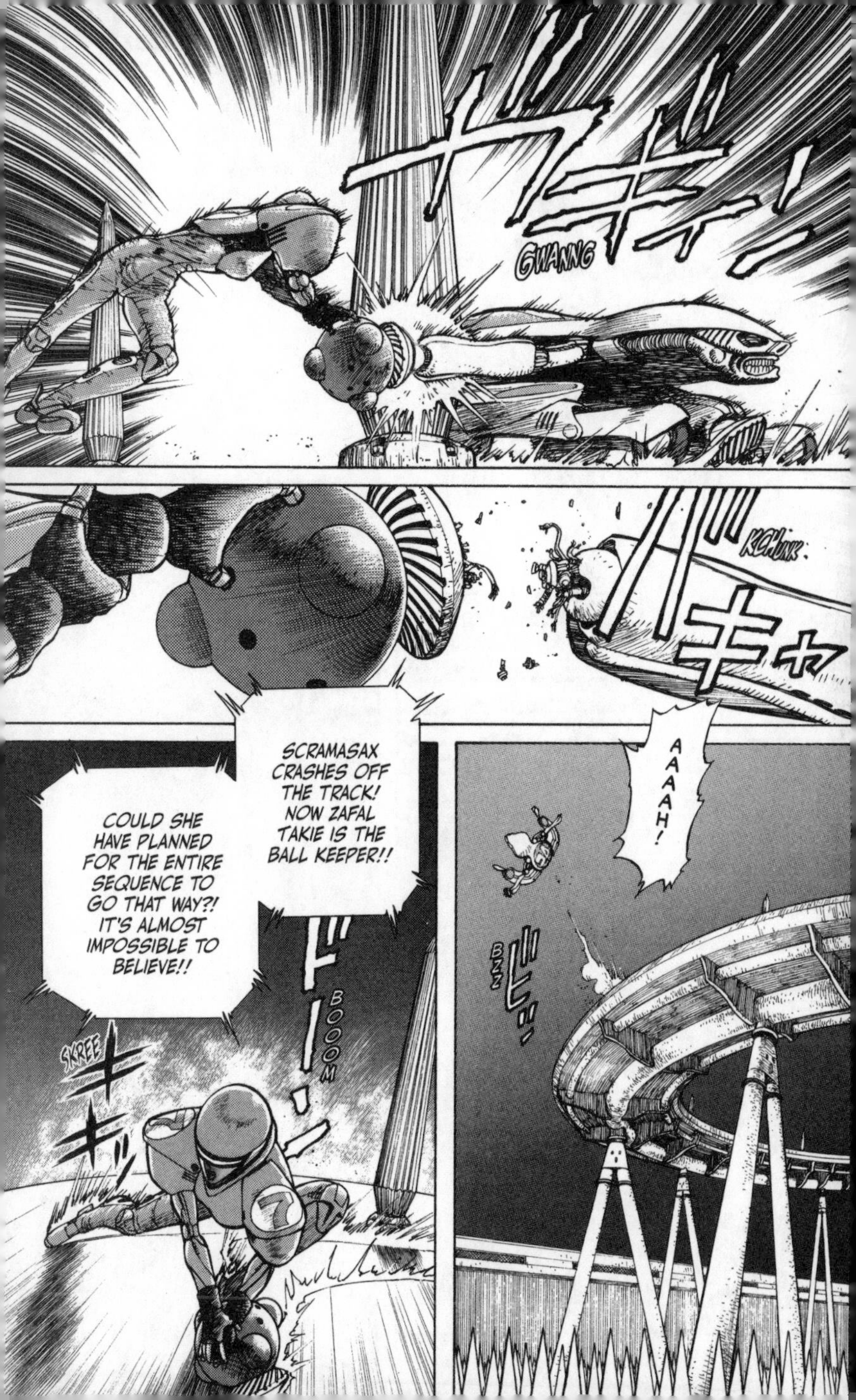
GWANNG
KCHUNK
AAAAAH!
BZZ
SCRAMASAX CRASHES OFF THE TRACK! NOW ZAFAL TAKIE IS THE BALL KEEPER!!
COULD SHE HAVE PLANNED FOR THE ENTIRE SEQUENCE TO GO THAT WAY?! IT'S ALMOST IMPOSSIBLE TO BELIEVE!!
BOOOOM
SKREE

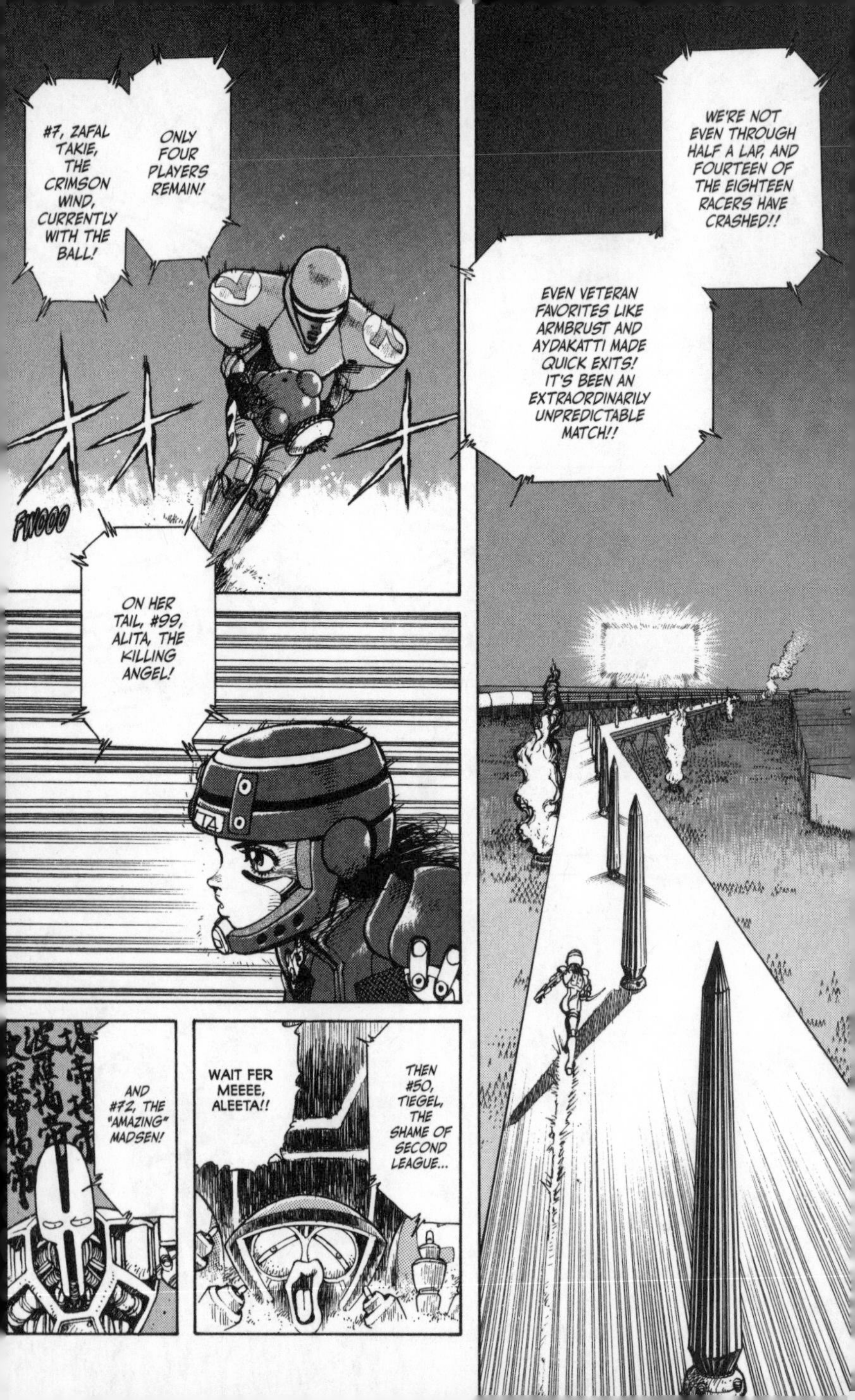
WE'RE NOT EVEN THROUGH HALF A LAP, AND FOURTEEN OF THE EIGHTEEN RACERS HAVE CRASHED!!
EVEN VETERAN FAVORITES LIKE ARMBRUST AND AYDAKATTI MADE QUICK EXITS! IT'S BEEN AN EXTRAORDINARILY UNPREDICTABLE MATCH!!
ONLY FOUR PLAYERS REMAIN!
#7, ZAFAL TAKIE, THE CRIMSON WIND, CURRENTLY WITH THE BALL!
FWOOO
ON HER TAIL, #99, ALITA, THE KILLING ANGEL!
THEN #50, TIEGEL, THE SHAME OF SECOND LEAGUE...
WAIT FER MEEEE, ALEETA!!
AND #72, THE "AMAZING" MADSEN!

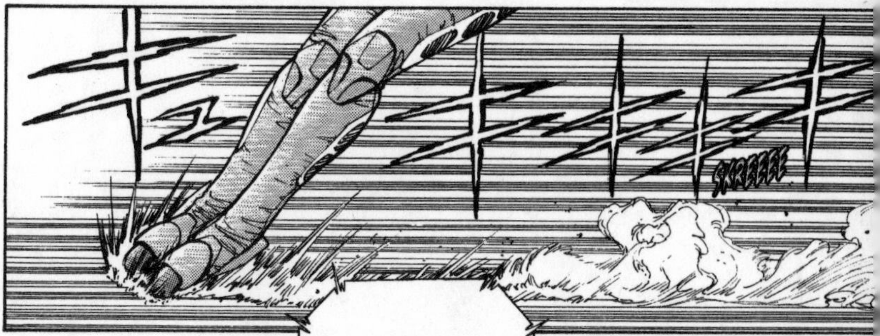
SKREEEEE

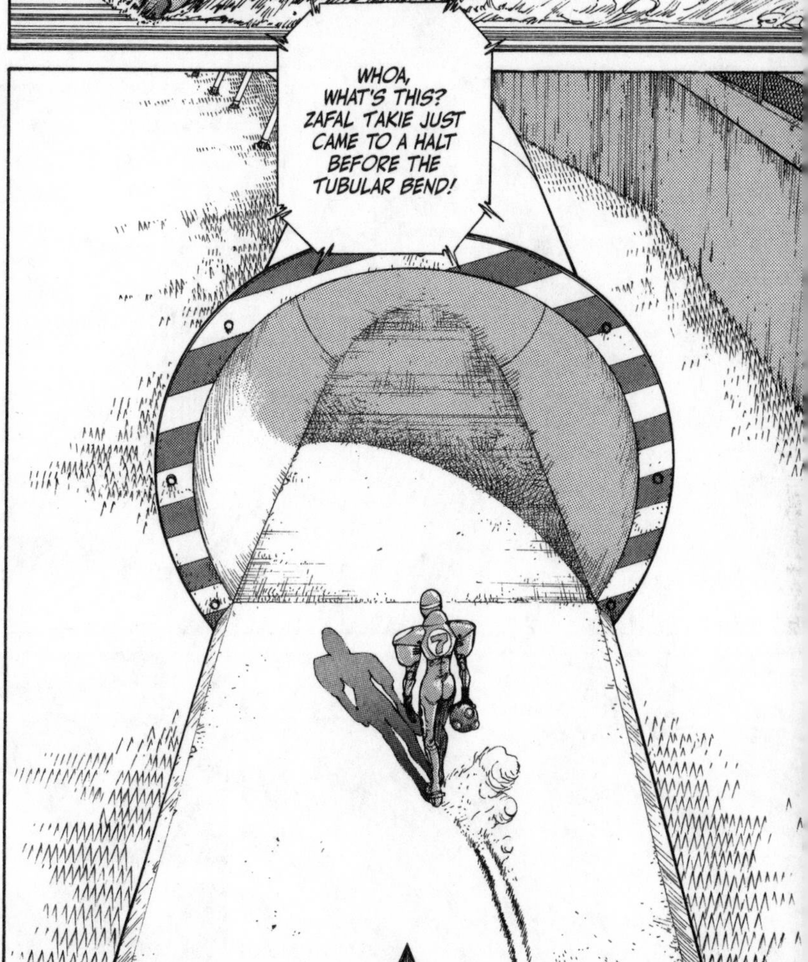
WHOA, WHAT'S THIS? ZAFAL TAKIE JUST CAME TO A HALT BEFORE THE TUBULAR BEND!

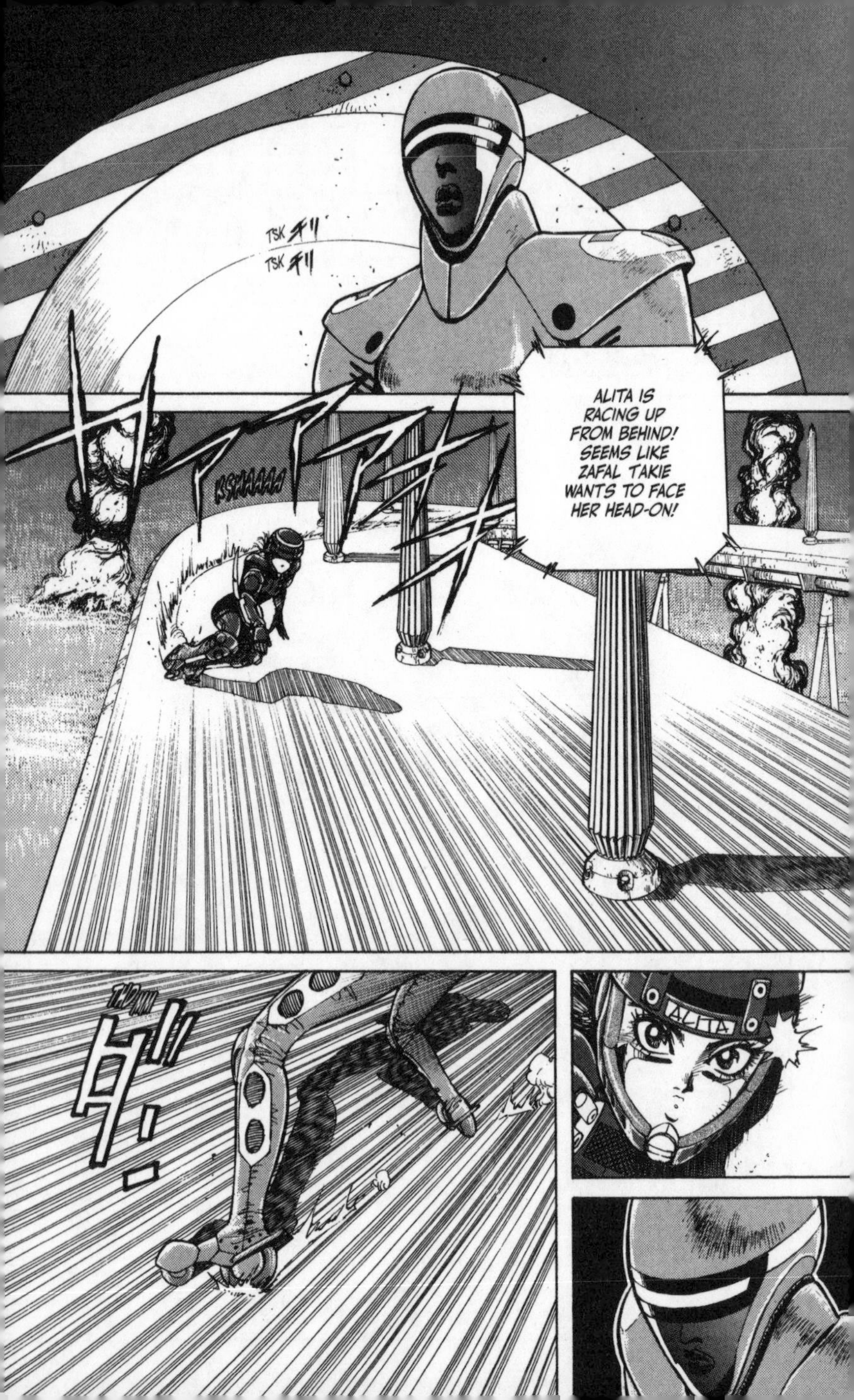
TSK チリ
TSK チリ
ISSHAAAA
ALITA IS RACING UP FROM BEHIND! SEEMS LIKE ZAFAL TAKIE WANTS TO FACE HER HEAD-ON!
THOMM

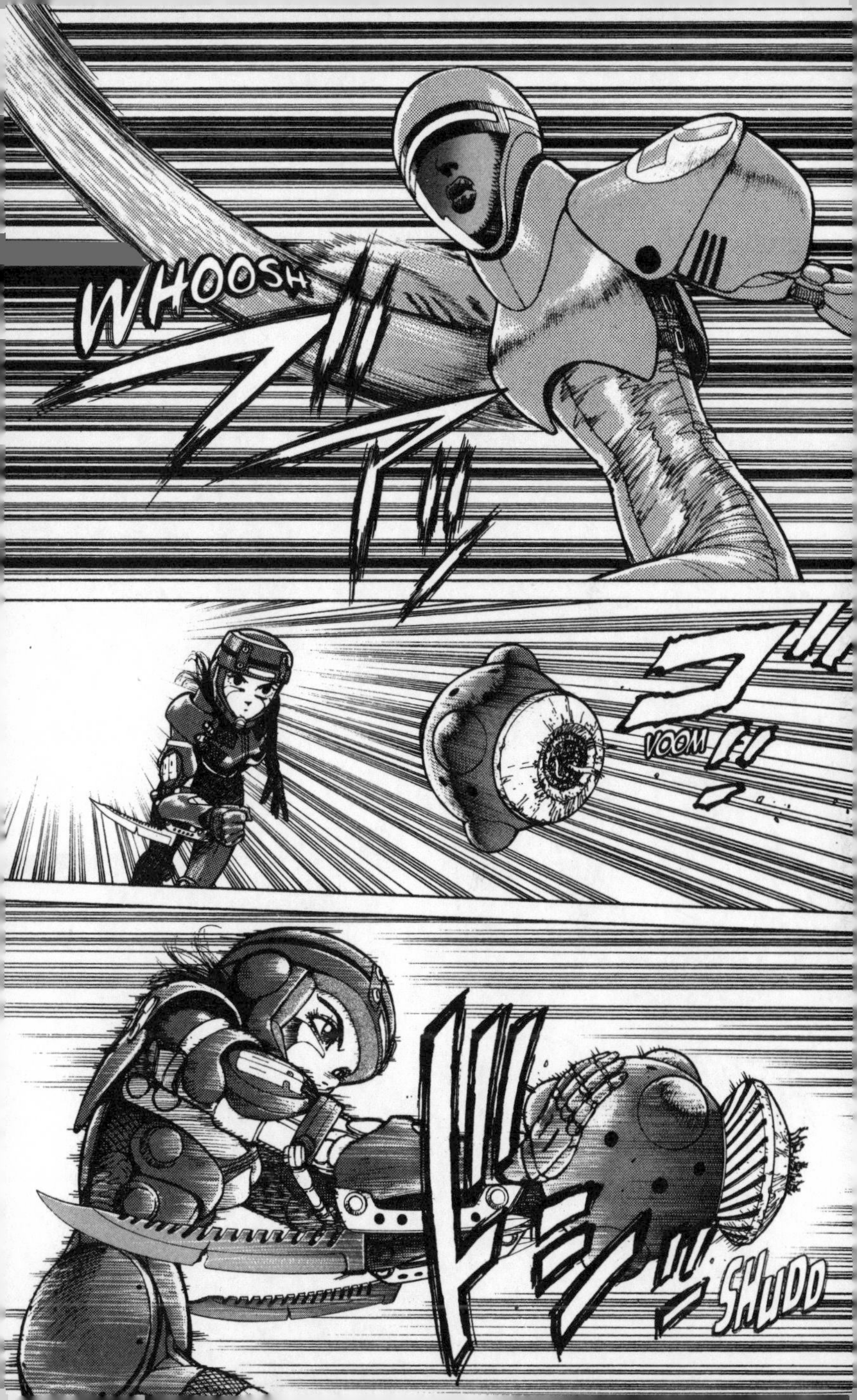
WHOOSH
VOOM
SHUDD

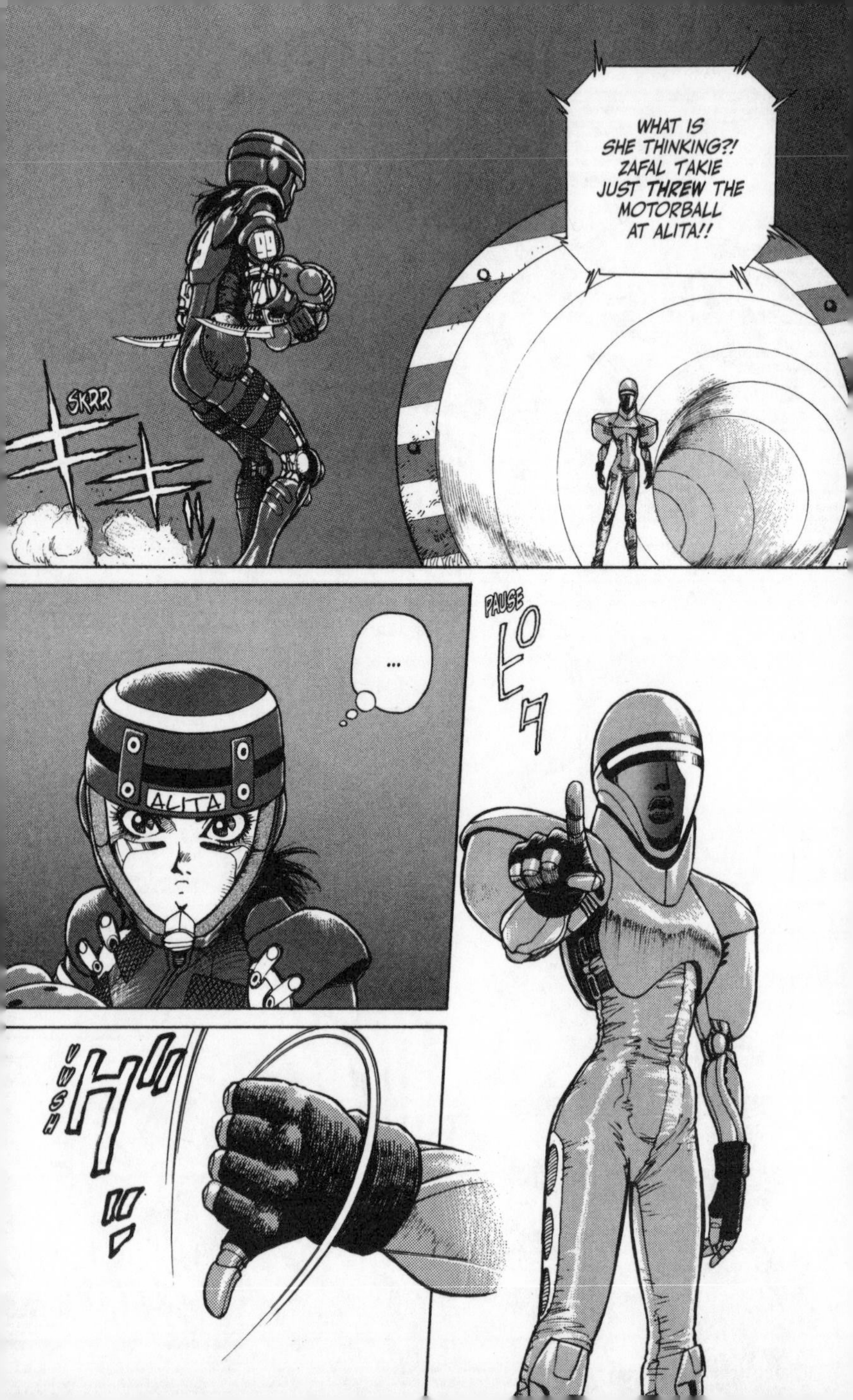
WHAT IS SHE THINKING?! ZAFAL TAKIE JUST THREW THE MOTORBALL AT ALITA!!
SKRR
PAUSE
...
ALITA
VWSH

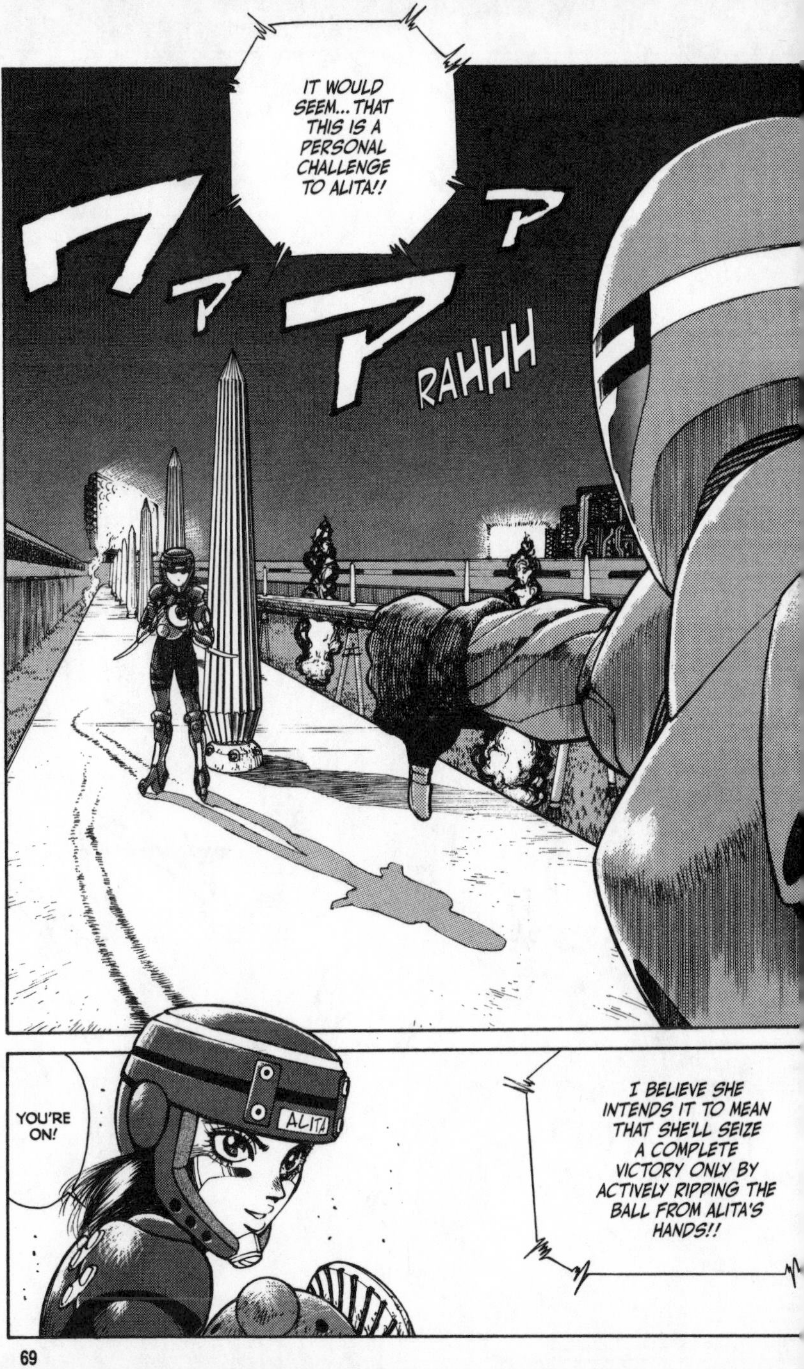
IT WOULD SEEM... THAT THIS IS A PERSONAL CHALLENGE TO ALITA!!
RAHHH
I BELIEVE SHE INTENDS IT TO MEAN THAT SHE'LL SEIZE A COMPLETE VICTORY ONLY BY ACTIVELY RIPPING THE BALL FROM ALITA'S HANDS!!
ALITA
YOU'RE ON!

THEY BOTH PLUNGE INTO TUBULAR BEND!

SKAAA

CAN YOU HEAR ME, ALITA?!

ED!

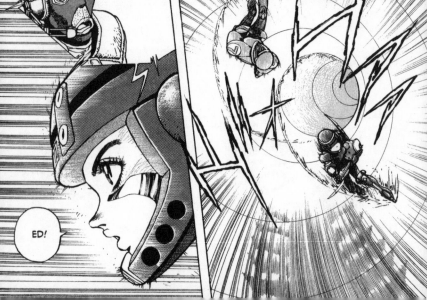

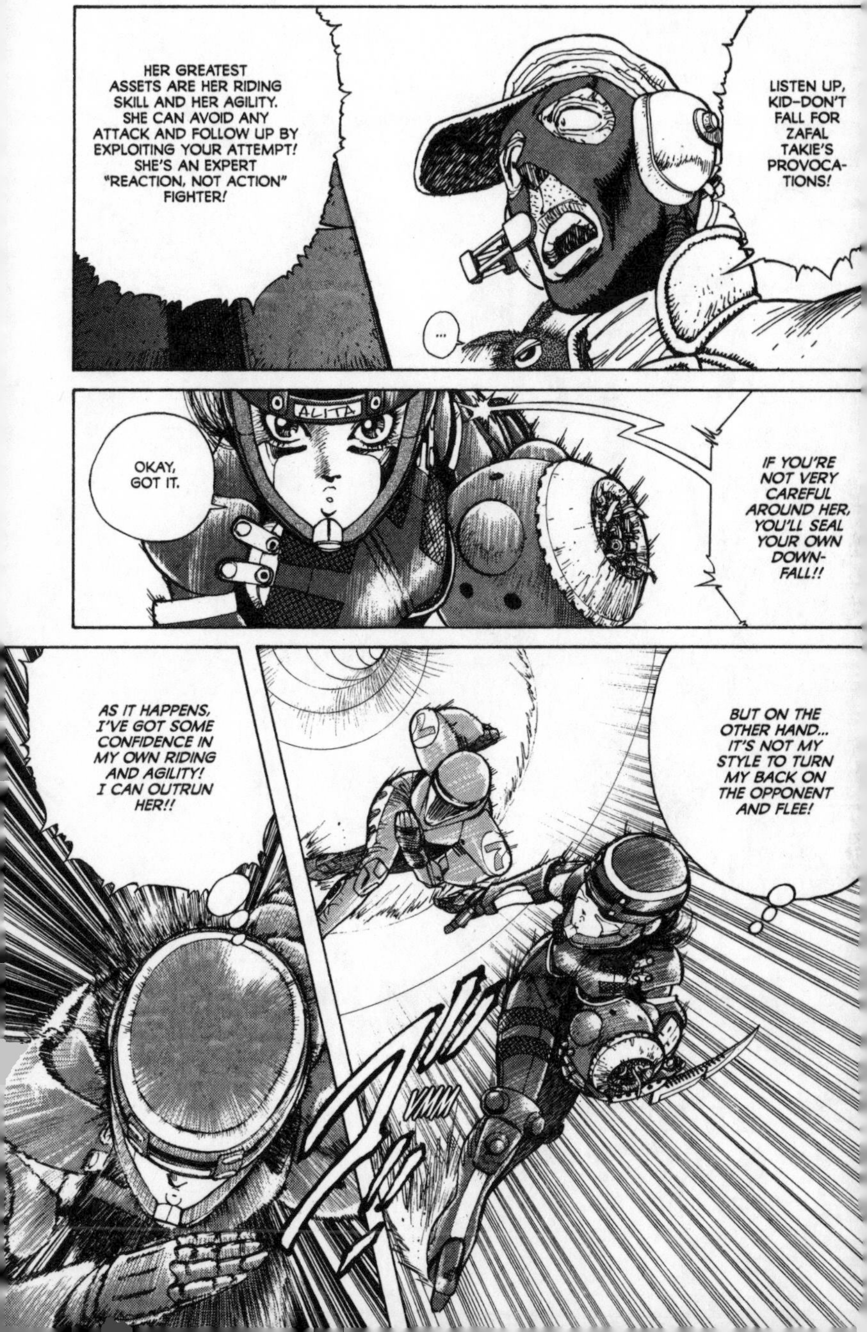
LISTEN UP, KID–DON'T FALL FOR ZAFAL TAKIE'S PROVOCA-TIONS!
HER GREATEST ASSETS ARE HER RIDING SKILL AND HER AGILITY. SHE CAN AVOID ANY ATTACK AND FOLLOW UP BY EXPLOITING YOUR ATTEMPT! SHE'S AN EXPERT "REACTION, NOT ACTION" FIGHTER!
...
IF YOU'RE NOT VERY CAREFUL AROUND HER, YOU'LL SEAL YOUR OWN DOWN-FALL!!
OKAY, GOT IT.
ALITA
BUT ON THE OTHER HAND... IT'S NOT MY STYLE TO TURN MY BACK ON THE OPPONENT AND FLEE!
AS IT HAPPENS, I'VE GOT SOME CONFIDENCE IN MY OWN RIDING AND AGILITY! I CAN OUTRUN HER!!

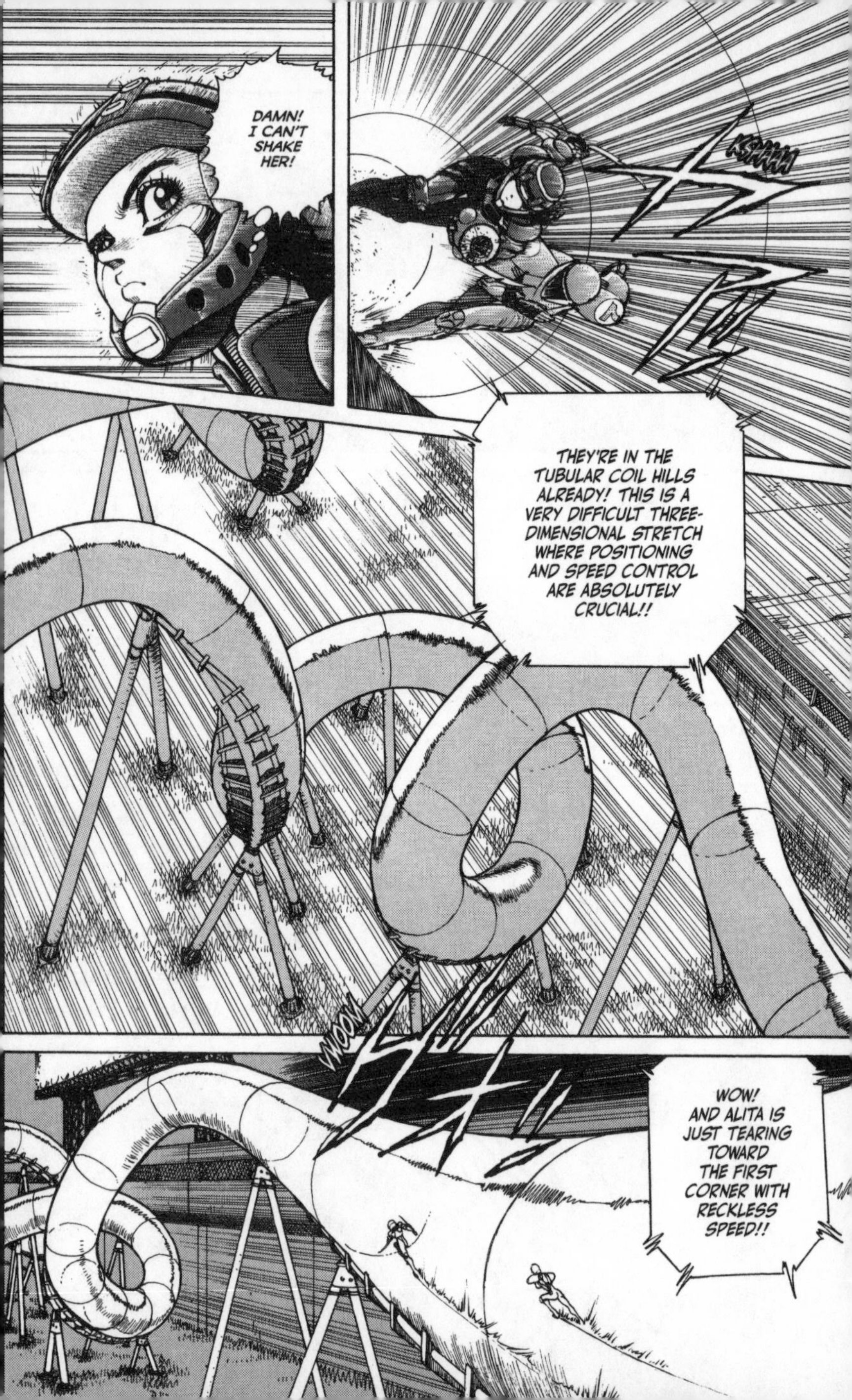
KSHAAA
DAMN! I CAN'T SHAKE HER!
THEY'RE IN THE TUBULAR COIL HILLS ALREADY! THIS IS A VERY DIFFICULT THREE-DIMENSIONAL STRETCH WHERE POSITIONING AND SPEED CONTROL ARE ABSOLUTELY CRUCIAL!!
WOOON
WOW! AND ALITA IS JUST TEARING TOWARD THE FIRST CORNER WITH RECKLESS SPEED!!

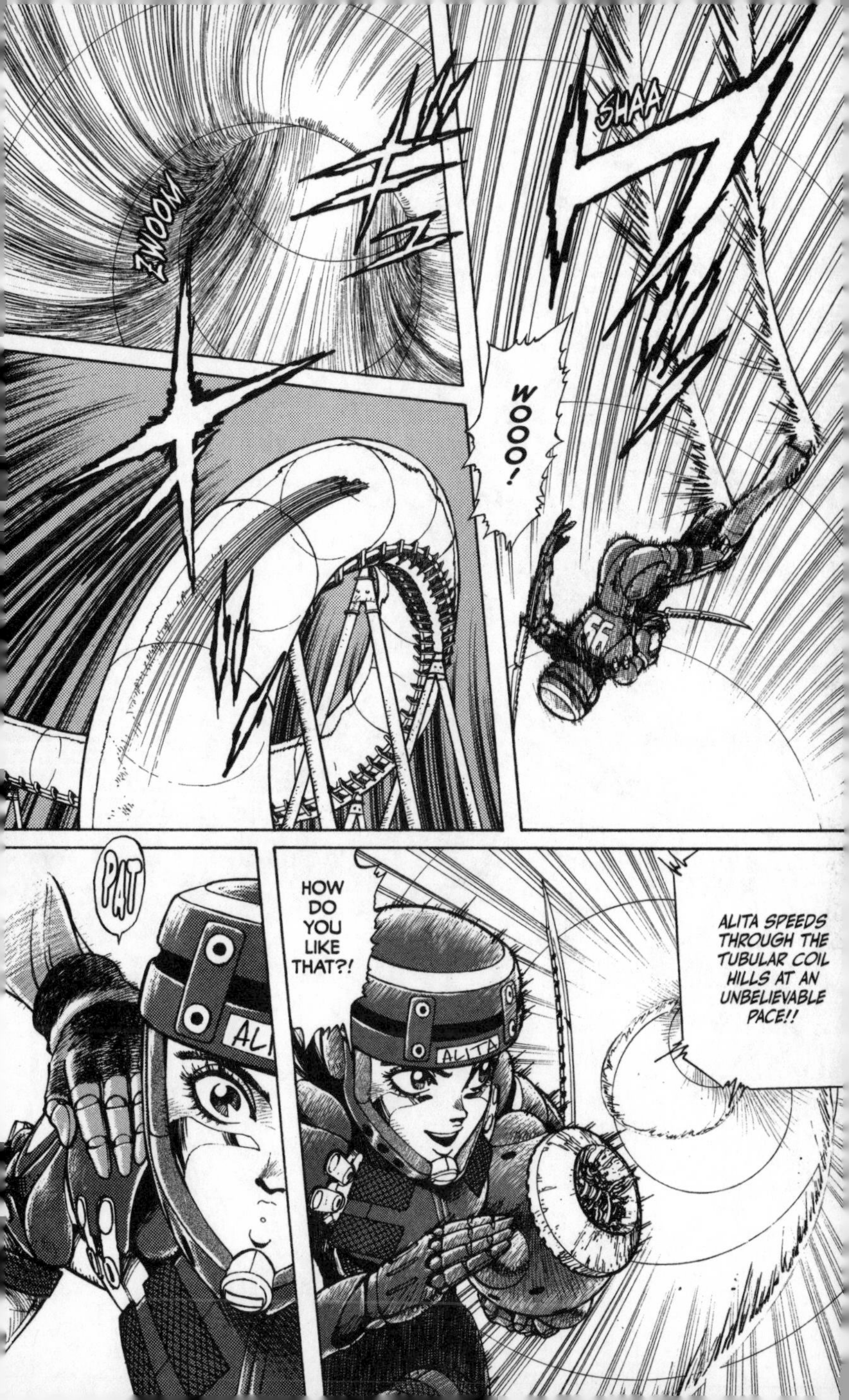
SHAA
WOOOO!
ZWOOM
ALITA SPEEDS THROUGH THE TUBULAR COIL HILLS AT AN UNBELIEVABLE PACE!!
HOW DO YOU LIKE THAT?!
PAT

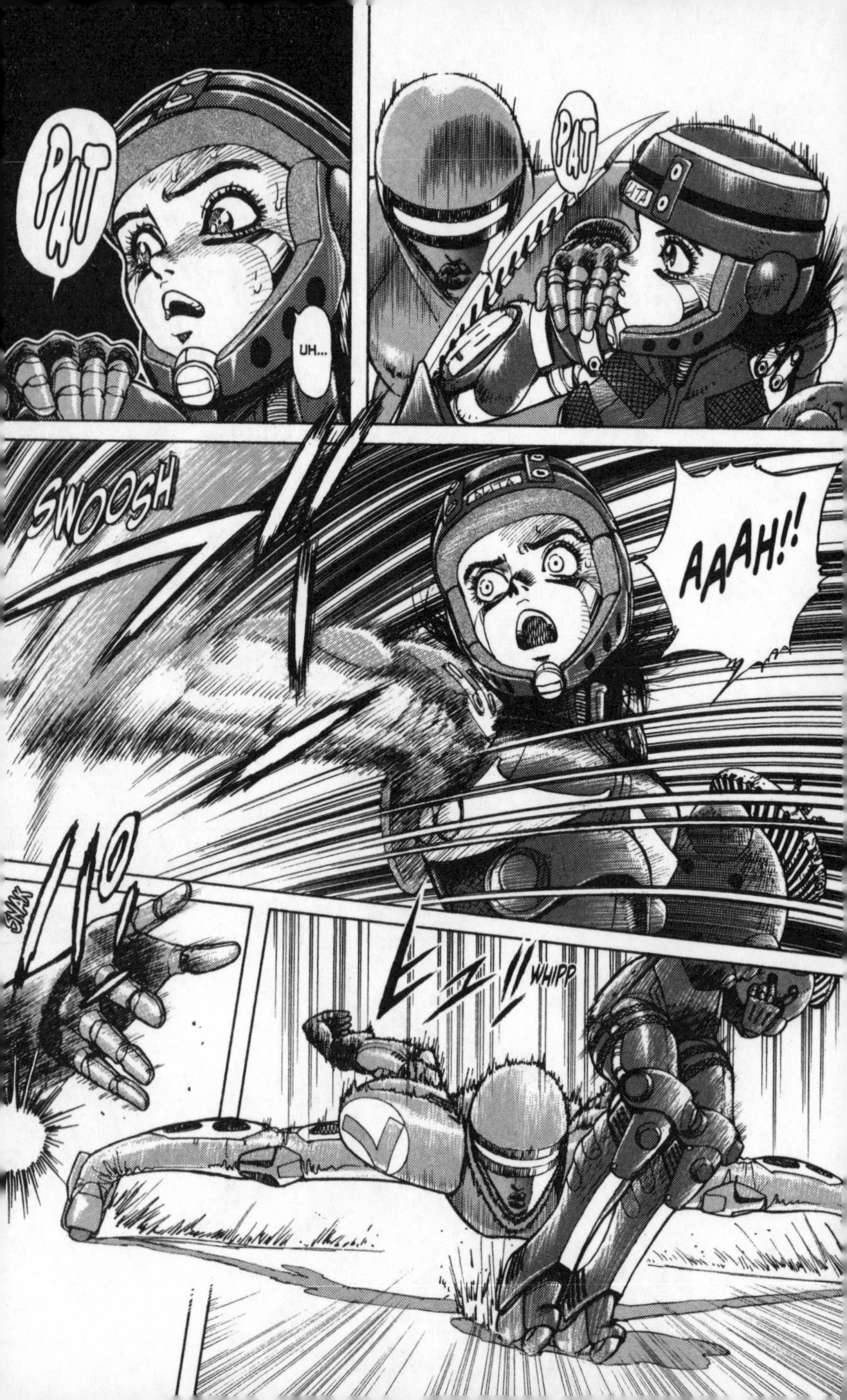
PAT
PAT
UH...
SWOOSH
AAAH!!
WHIPP
SNAK

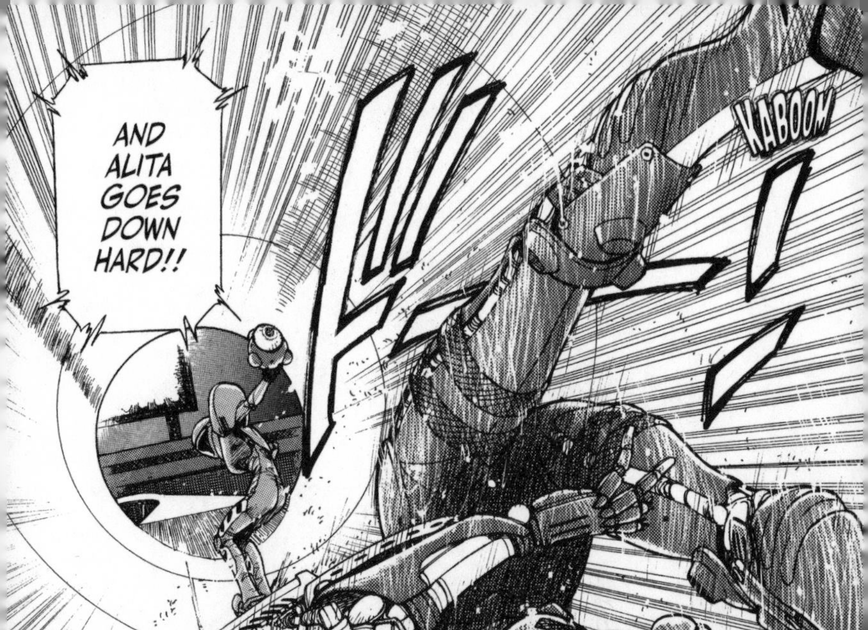
KABOOM
AND ALITA GOES DOWN HARD!!

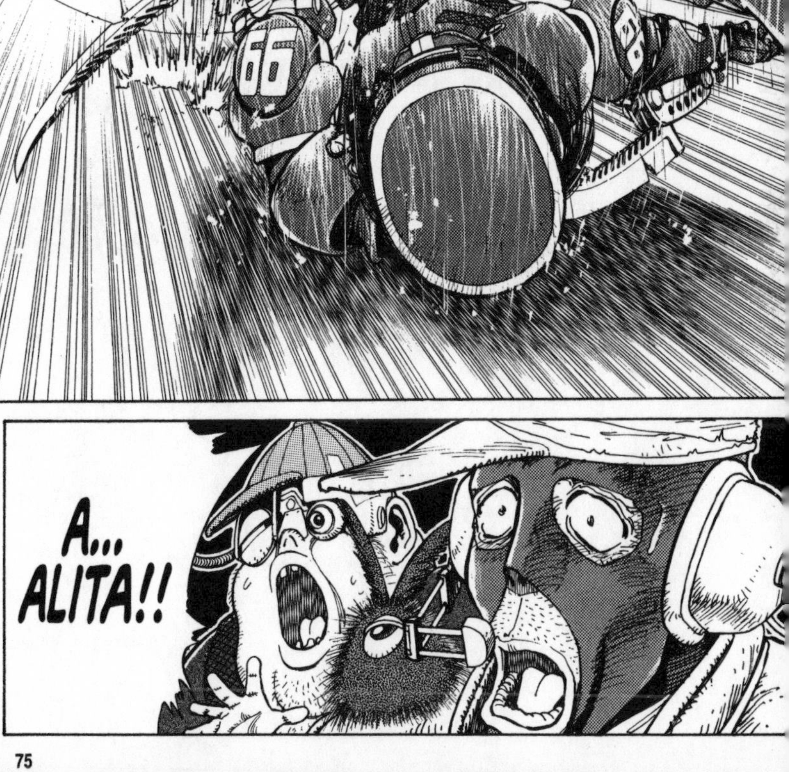
A... ALITA!!

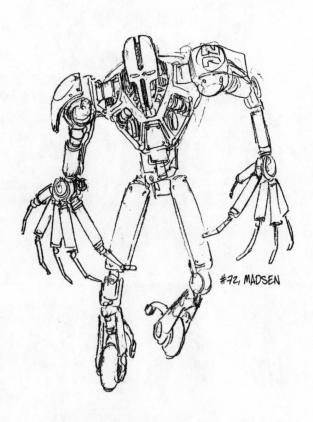

#72, MADSEN

FIGHT_019 Red Zone

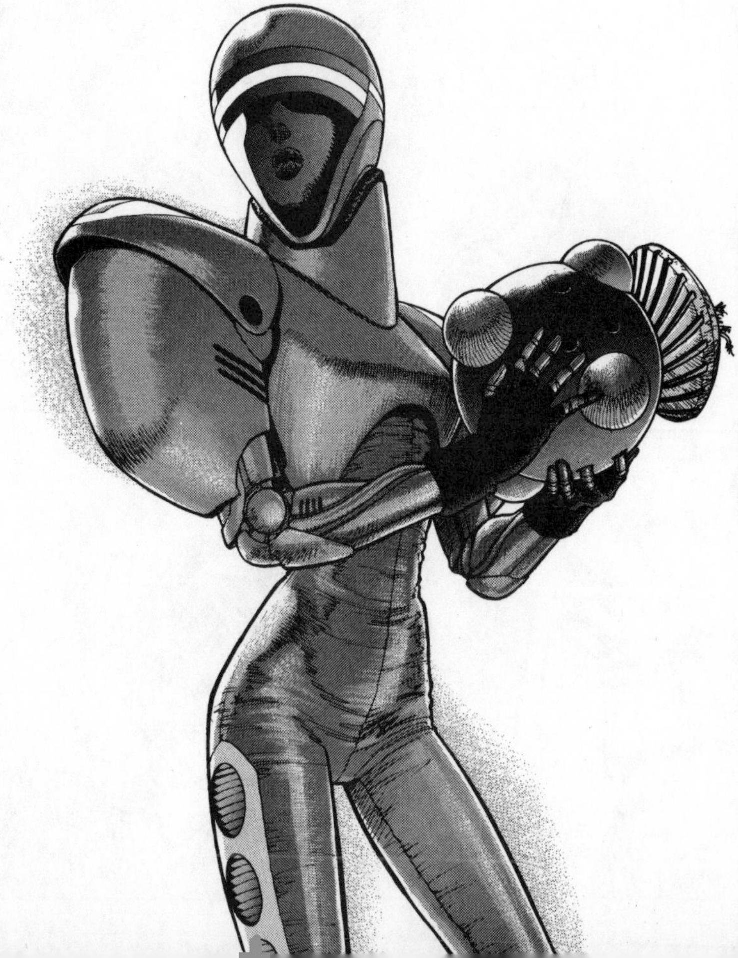

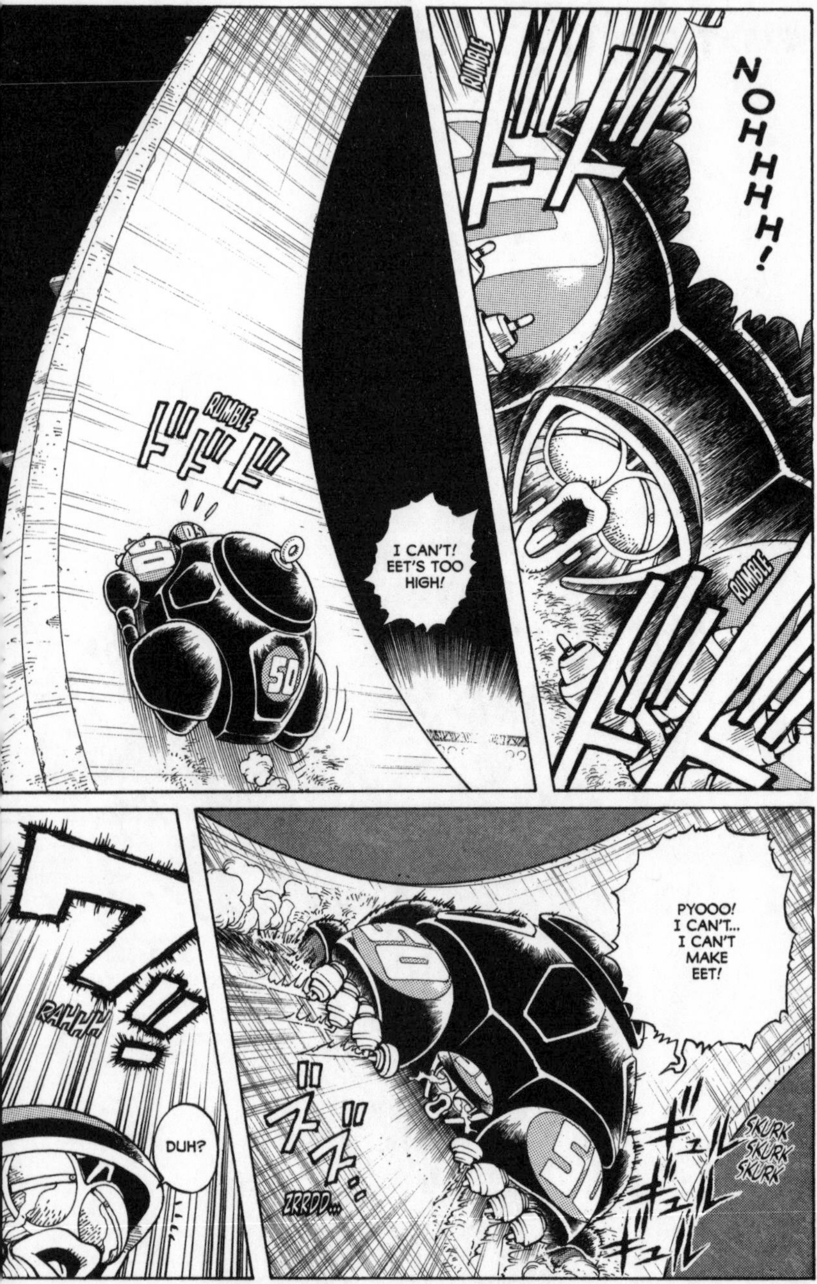

RUMBLE
NOHHHHH!
RUMBLE
RUMBLE
I CAN'T! EET'S TOO HIGH!
PYOOO! I CAN'T... I CAN'T MAKE EET!
SKURK SKURK SKURK
ZRRDD...
RAHHH
DUH?

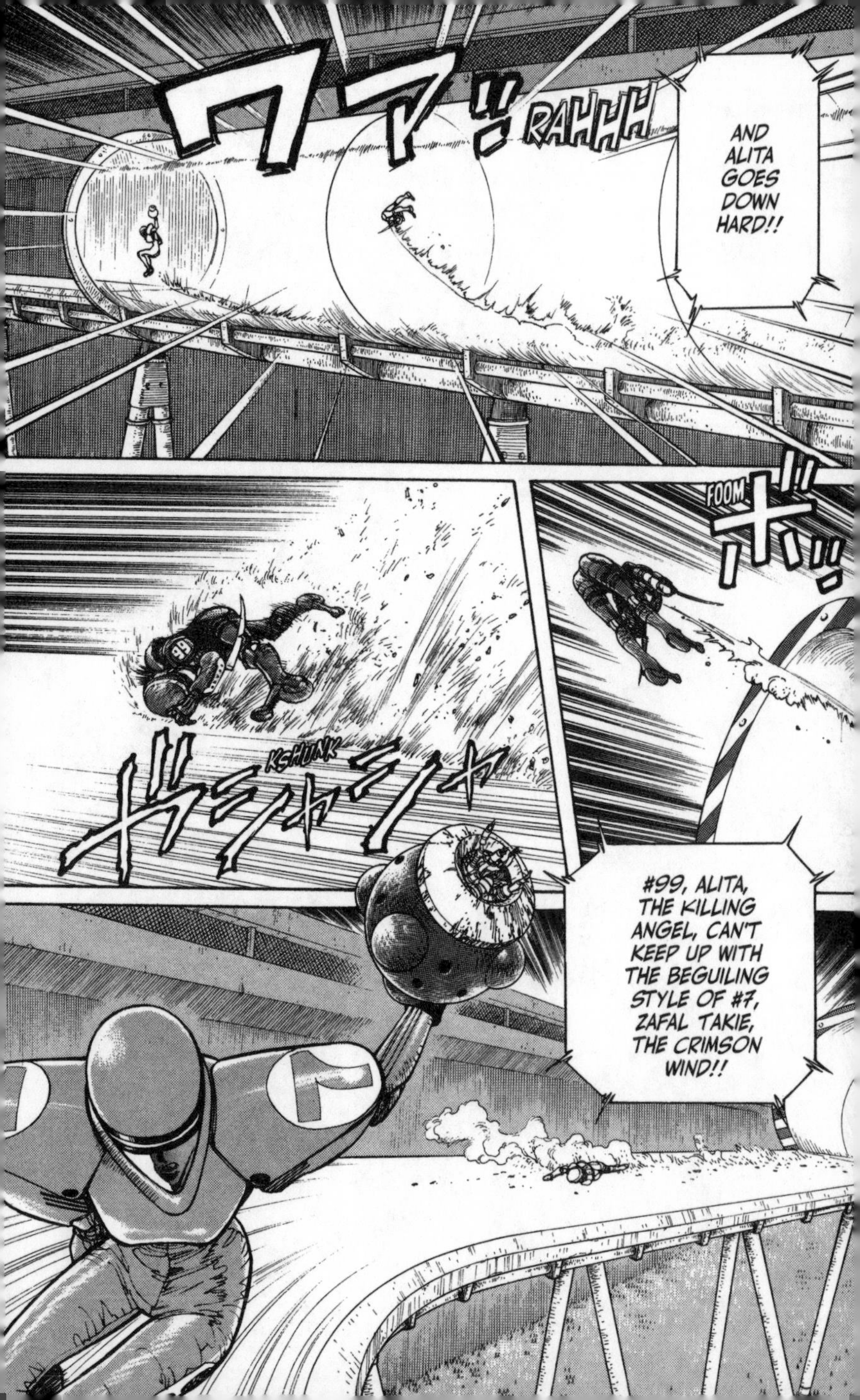
ワァ!!
RAHHH
AND ALITA GOES DOWN HARD!!
FOOM
ボッ!!
KSHUNK
ズシャシャッ
#99, ALITA, THE KILLING ANGEL, CAN'T KEEP UP WITH THE BEGUILING STYLE OF #7, ZAFAL TAKIE, THE CRIMSON WIND!!

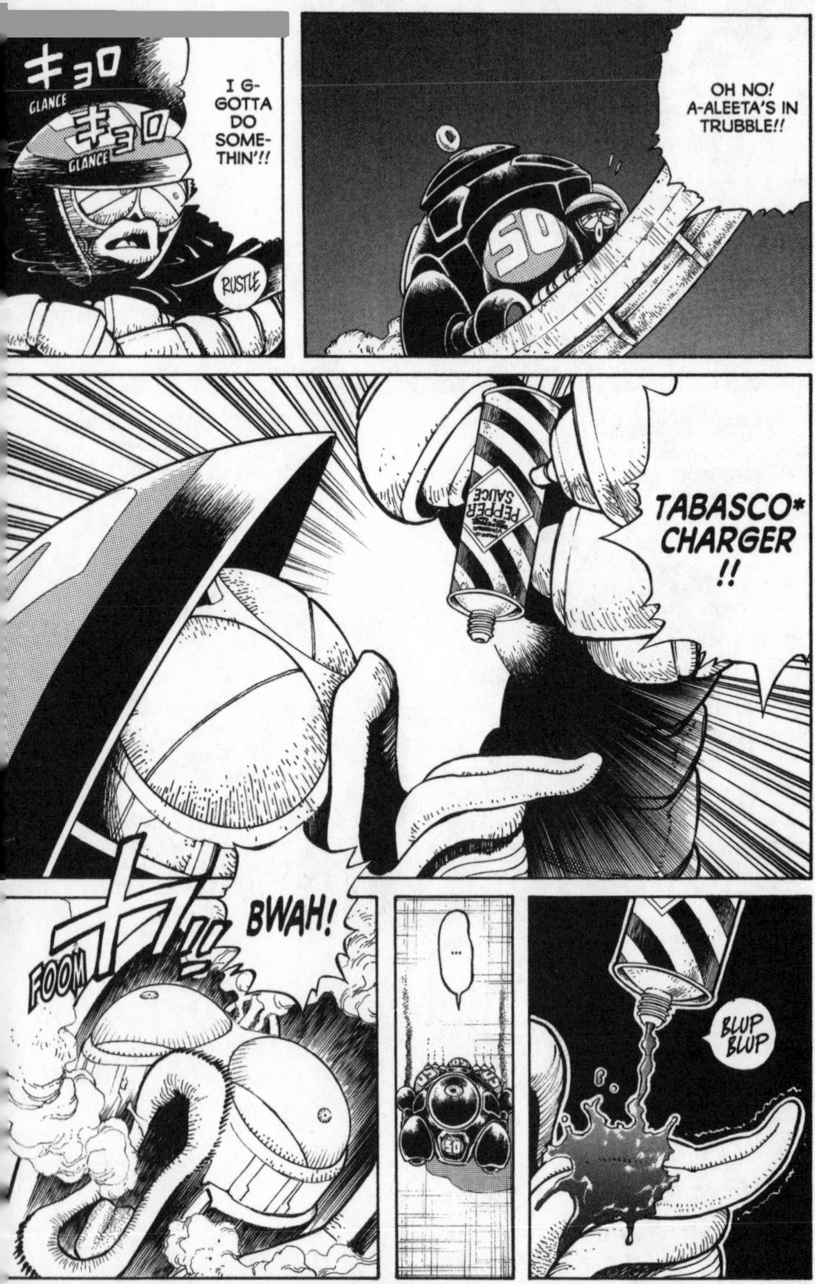
OH NO! A-ALEETA'S IN TRUBBLE!!
キョロ
GLANCE
キョロ
GLANCE
I G-GOTTA DO SOME-THIN'!!
RUSTLE
PEPPER SAUCE
TABASCO* CHARGER !!
BLUP BLUP
...
BWAH!
FOOM

Tabasco: A trademarked brand of pepper sauce invented by E. McIlhenny in 1868. The peppers are aged with salt, then distilled with vinegar.

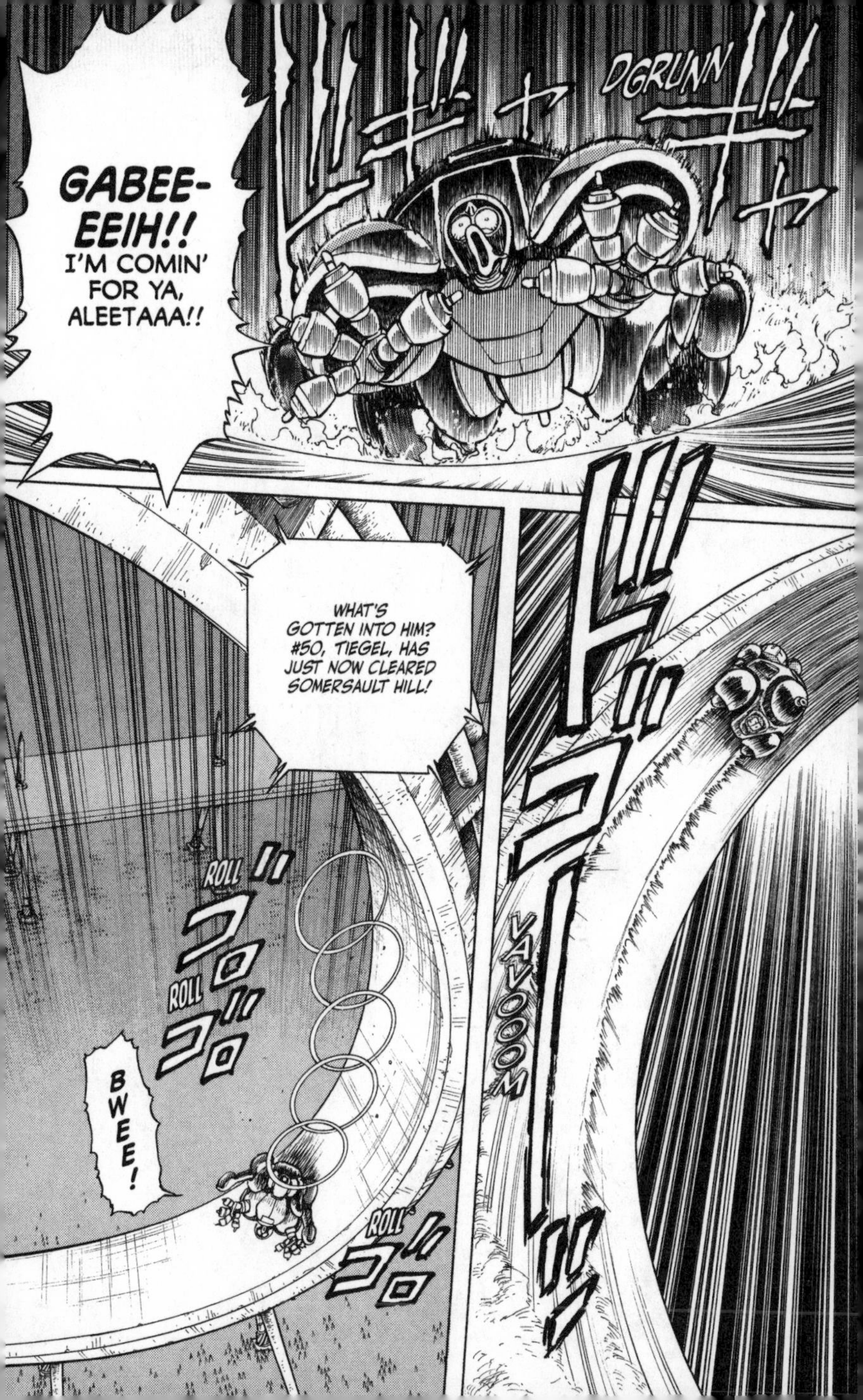
DGRUNN
GABEE-EEIH!! I'M COMIN' FOR YA, ALEETAAA!!
VAVOOOOM
WHAT'S GOTTEN INTO HIM? #50, TIEGEL, HAS JUST NOW CLEARED SOMERSAULT HILL!
ROLL
ROLL
ROLL
BWEEE!

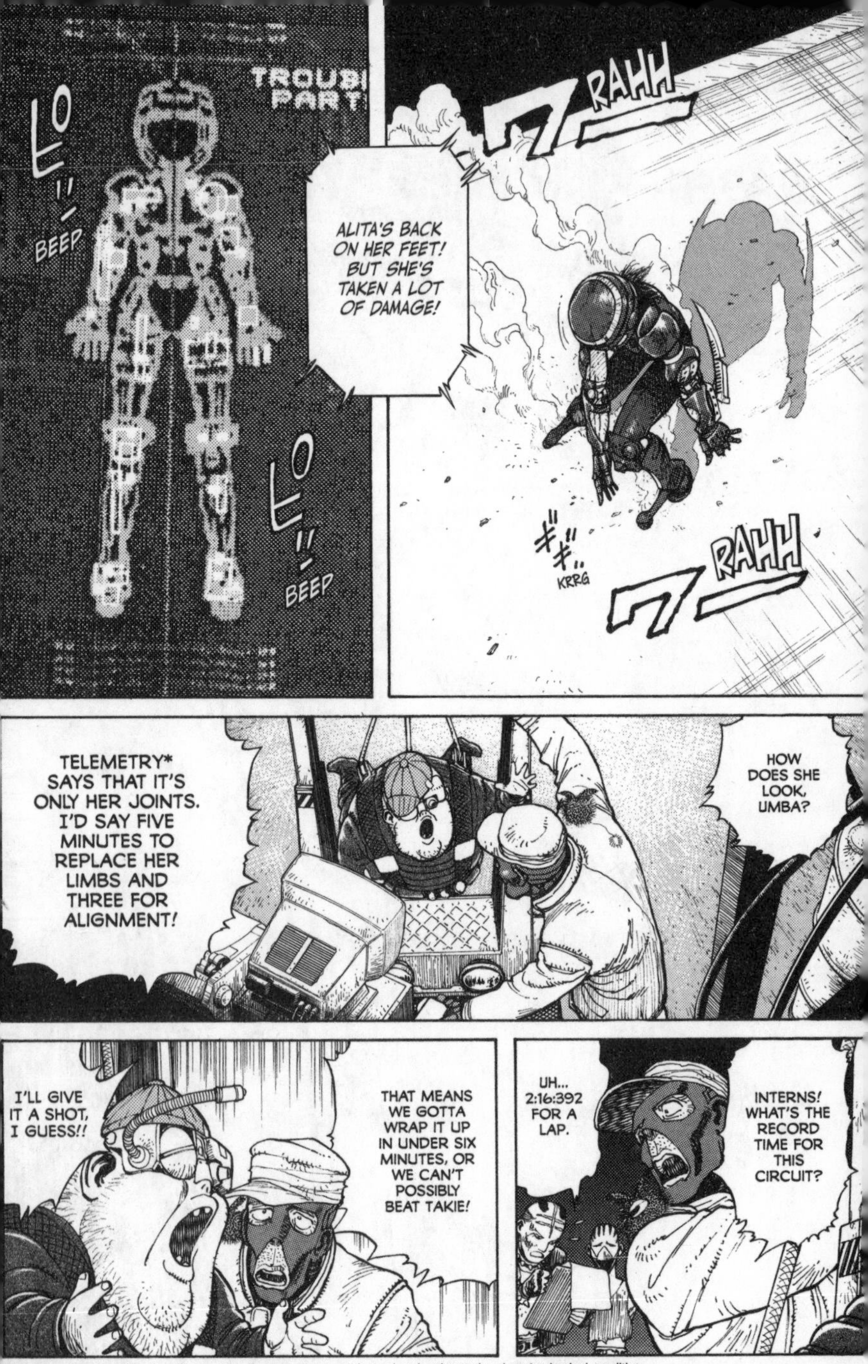
RAHH
ALITA'S BACK ON HER FEET! BUT SHE'S TAKEN A LOT OF DAMAGE!
KRRG
RAHH
TROUB
PART
BEEP
BEEP
HOW DOES SHE LOOK, UMBA?
TELEMETRY* SAYS THAT IT'S ONLY HER JOINTS. I'D SAY FIVE MINUTES TO REPLACE HER LIMBS AND THREE FOR ALIGNMENT!
INTERNS! WHAT'S THE RECORD TIME FOR THIS CIRCUIT?
UH... 2:16:392 FOR A LAP.
THAT MEANS WE GOTTA WRAP IT UP IN UNDER SIX MINUTES, OR WE CAN'T POSSIBLY BEAT TAKIE!
I'LL GIVE IT A SHOT, I GUESS!!

***Telemetry System:** A system that uses radio waves to remotely read and estimate the player's physical condition.

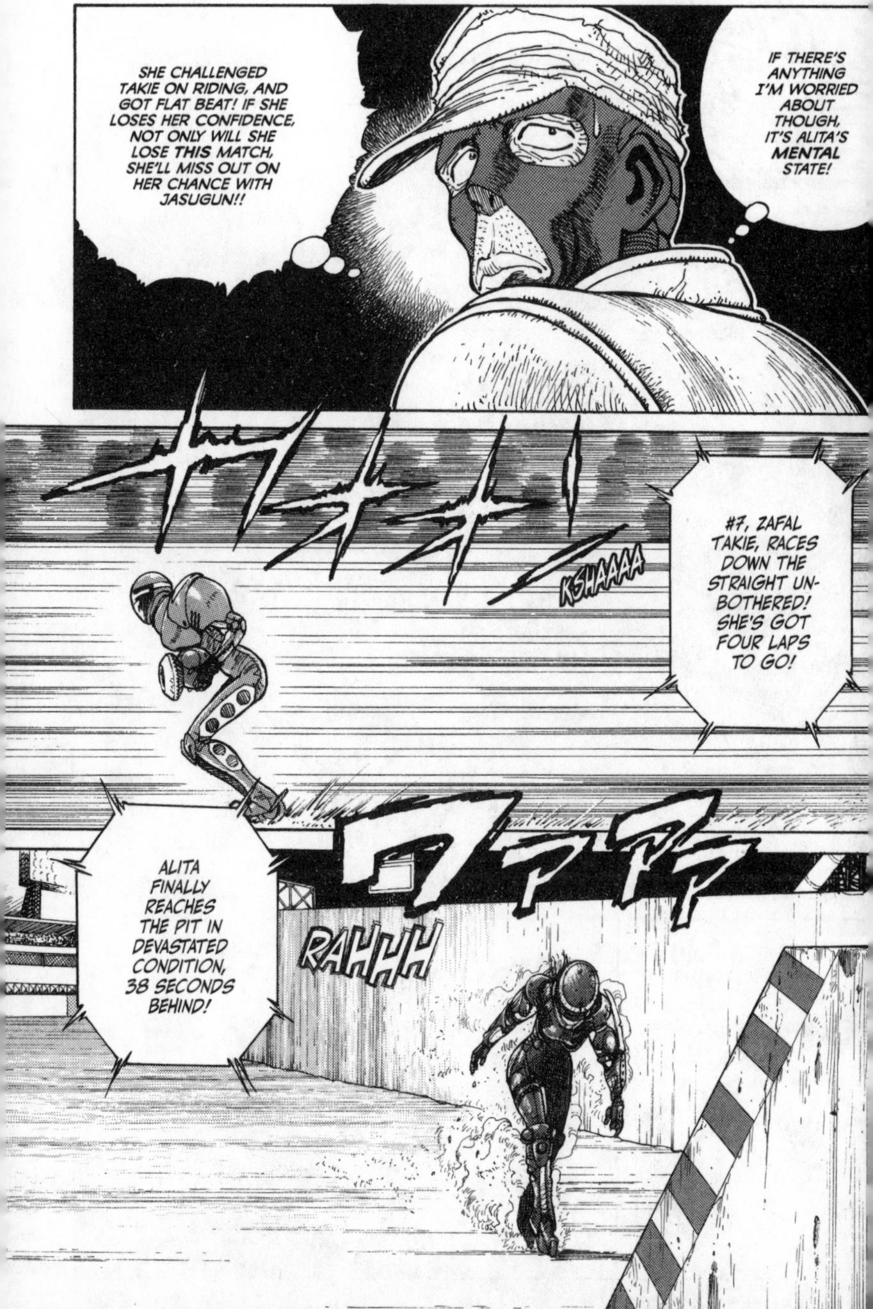
IF THERE'S ANYTHING I'M WORRIED ABOUT THOUGH, IT'S ALITA'S **MENTAL** STATE!
SHE CHALLENGED TAKIE ON RIDING, AND GOT FLAT BEAT! IF SHE LOSES HER CONFIDENCE, NOT ONLY WILL SHE LOSE **THIS** MATCH, SHE'LL MISS OUT ON HER CHANCE WITH JASUGUN!!
#7, ZAFAL TAKIE, RACES DOWN THE STRAIGHT UN-BOTHERED! SHE'S GOT FOUR LAPS TO GO!
KSHAAAA
RAHHH
ALITA FINALLY REACHES THE PIT IN DEVASTATED CONDITION, 38 SECONDS BEHIND!

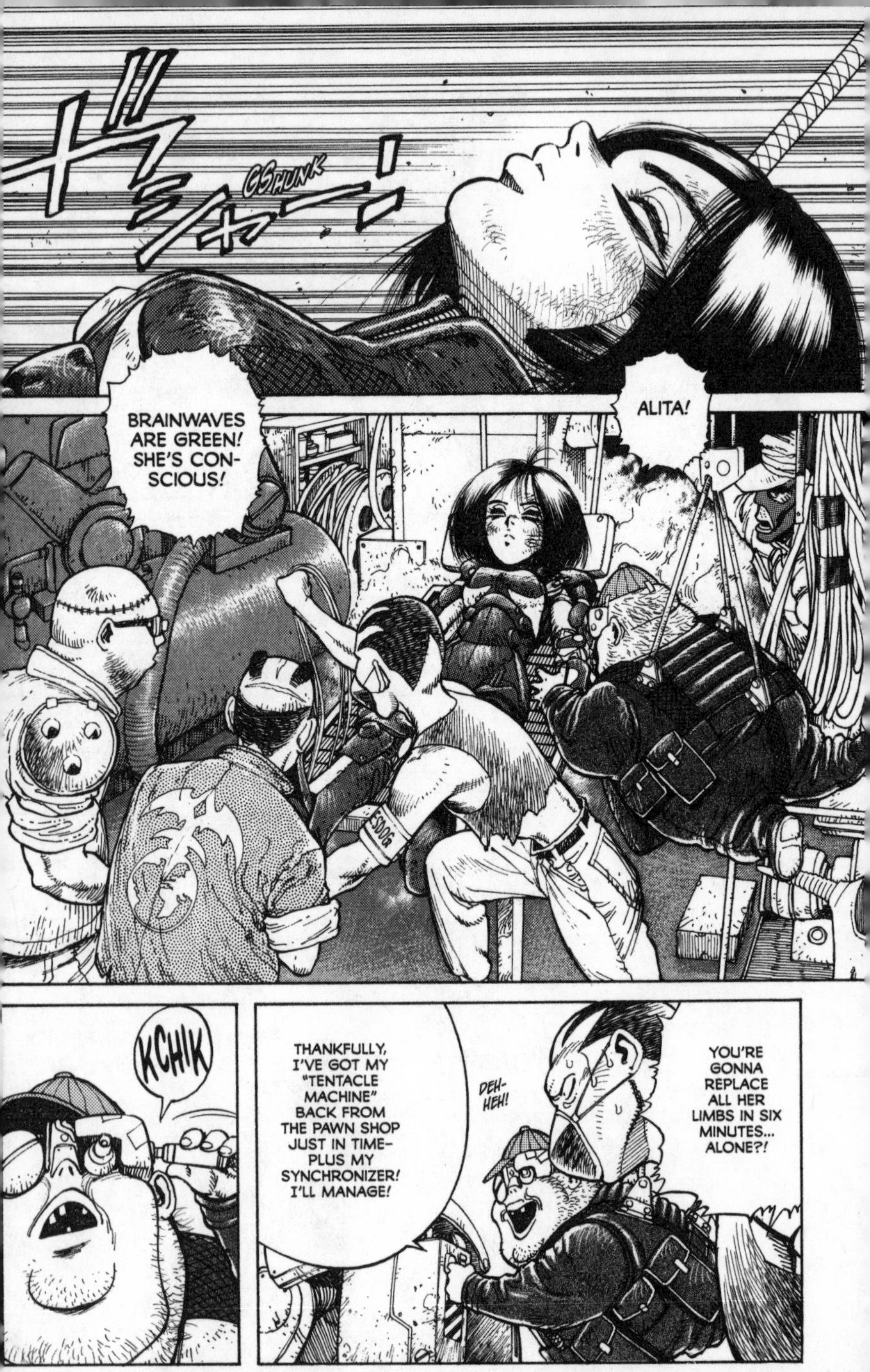
CSHUNK
ALITA!
BRAINWAVES ARE GREEN! SHE'S CONSCIOUS!
YOU'RE GONNA REPLACE ALL HER LIMBS IN SIX MINUTES... ALONE?!
DEH-HEH!
THANKFULLY, I'VE GOT MY "TENTACLE MACHINE" BACK FROM THE PAWN SHOP JUST IN TIME- PLUS MY SYNCHRONIZER! I'LL MANAGE!
KCHIK

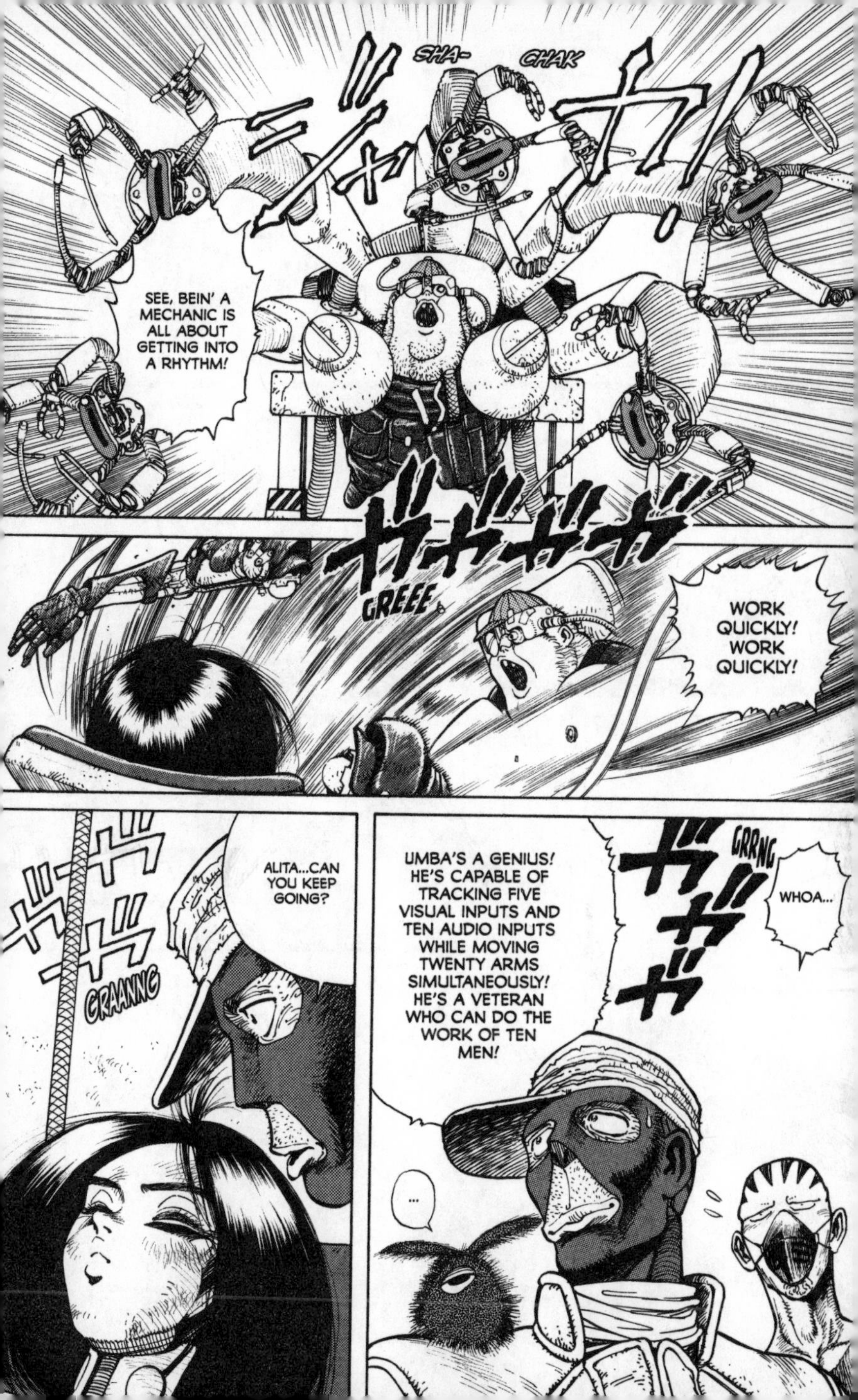
SHA-
CHAK
SEE, BEIN' A MECHANIC IS ALL ABOUT GETTING INTO A RHYTHM!
WORK QUICKLY! WORK QUICKLY!
GREEE
GRRRNG
WHOA...
UMBA'S A GENIUS! HE'S CAPABLE OF TRACKING FIVE VISUAL INPUTS AND TEN AUDIO INPUTS WHILE MOVING TWENTY ARMS SIMULTANEOUSLY! HE'S A VETERAN WHO CAN DO THE WORK OF TEN MEN!
...
ALITA...CAN YOU KEEP GOING?
CRAANNG

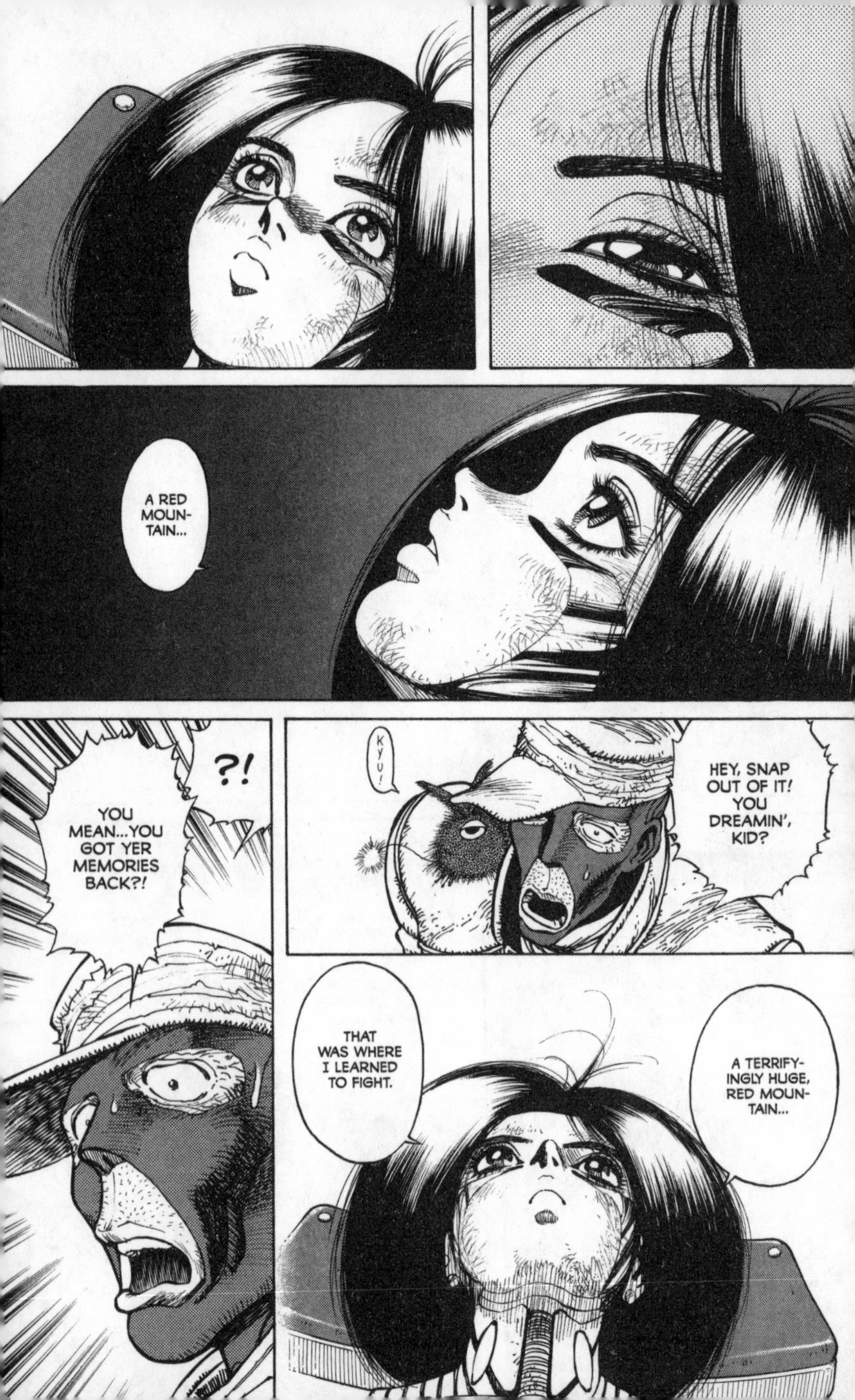
A RED MOUNTAIN...
KYU!
HEY, SNAP OUT OF IT! YOU DREAMIN', KID?
A TERRIFYINGLY HUGE, RED MOUNTAIN...
THAT WAS WHERE I LEARNED TO FIGHT.
?!
YOU MEAN...YOU GOT YER MEMORIES BACK?!

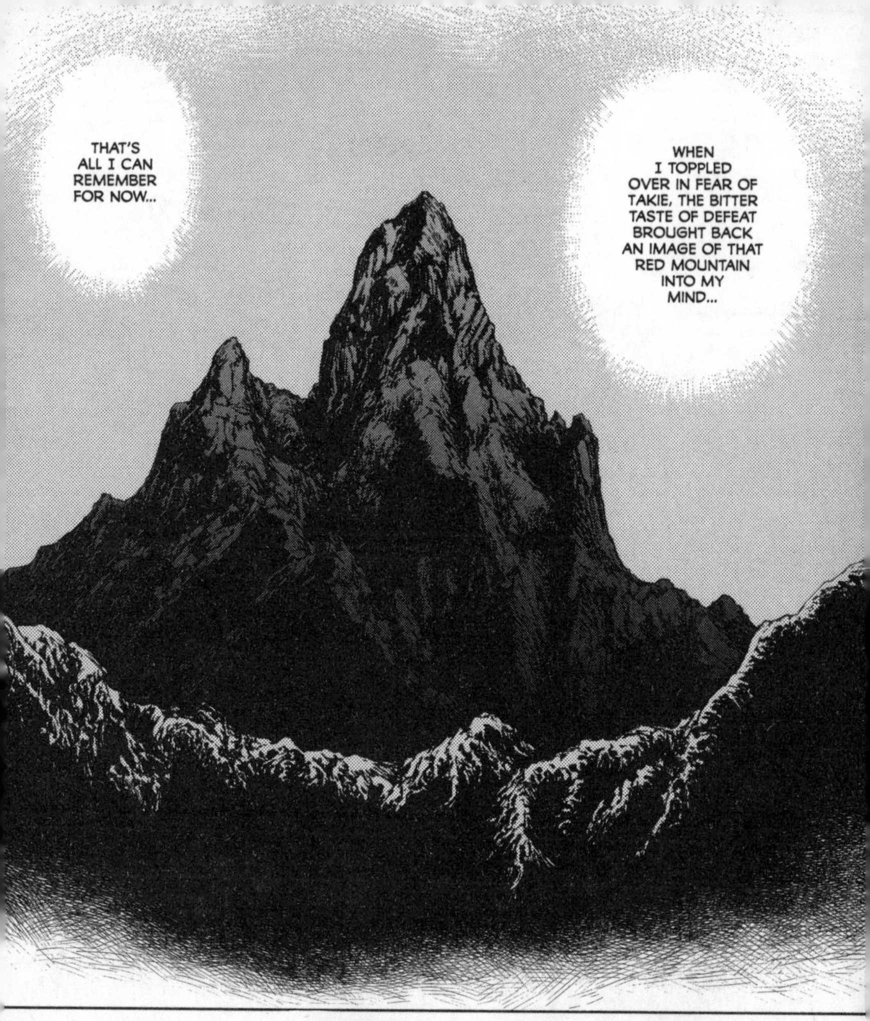
WHEN I TOPPLED OVER IN FEAR OF TAKIE, THE BITTER TASTE OF DEFEAT BROUGHT BACK AN IMAGE OF THAT RED MOUNTAIN INTO MY MIND...
THAT'S ALL I CAN REMEMBER FOR NOW...

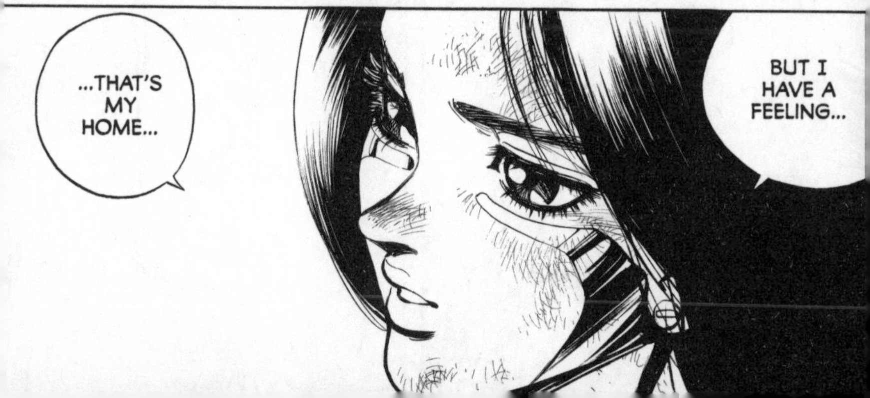
BUT I HAVE A FEELING...
...THAT'S MY HOME...

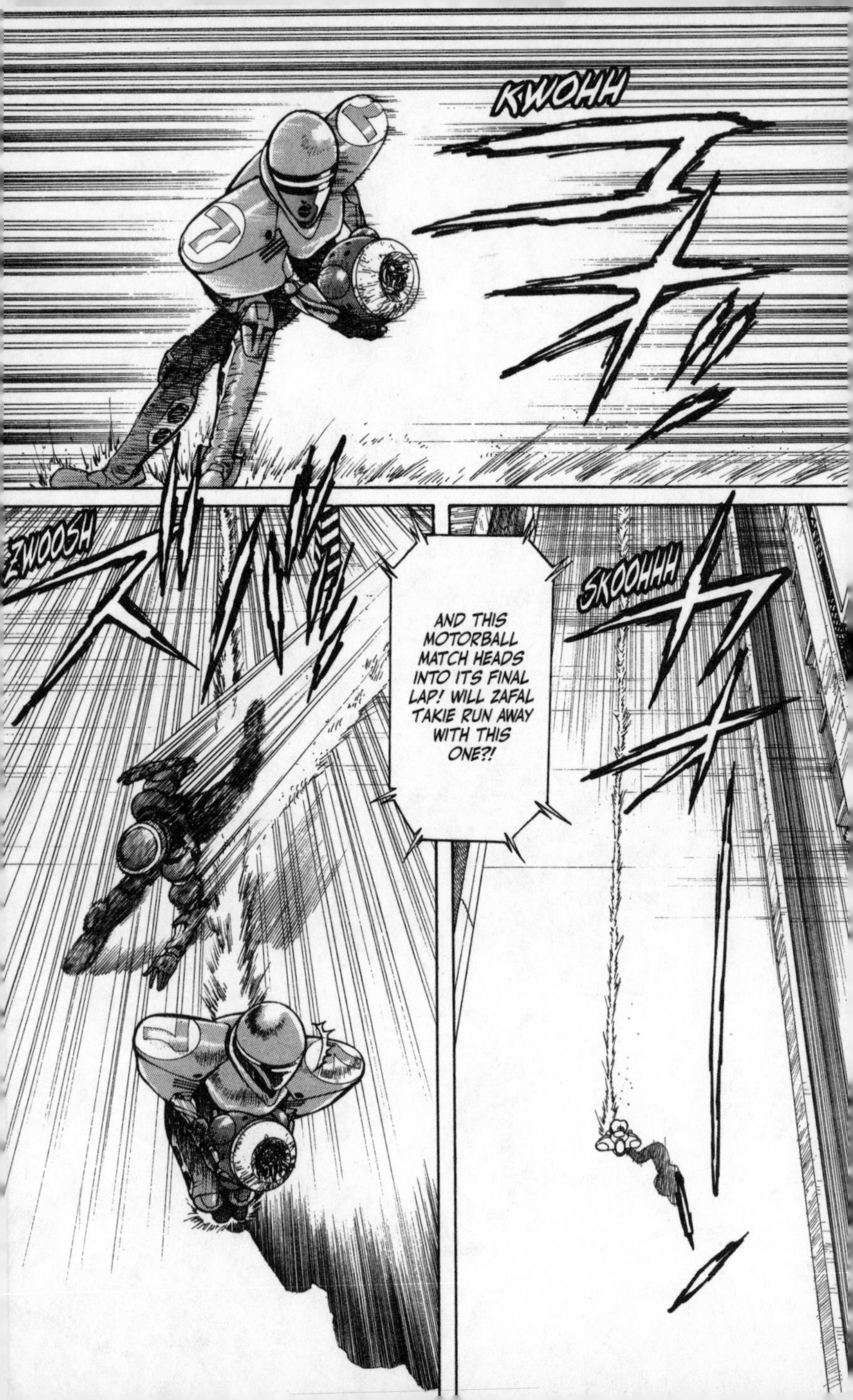
KWOHH
SKOOHHH
AND THIS MOTORBALL MATCH HEADS INTO ITS FINAL LAP! WILL ZAFAL TAKIE RUN AWAY WITH THIS ONE?!
ZWOOSH

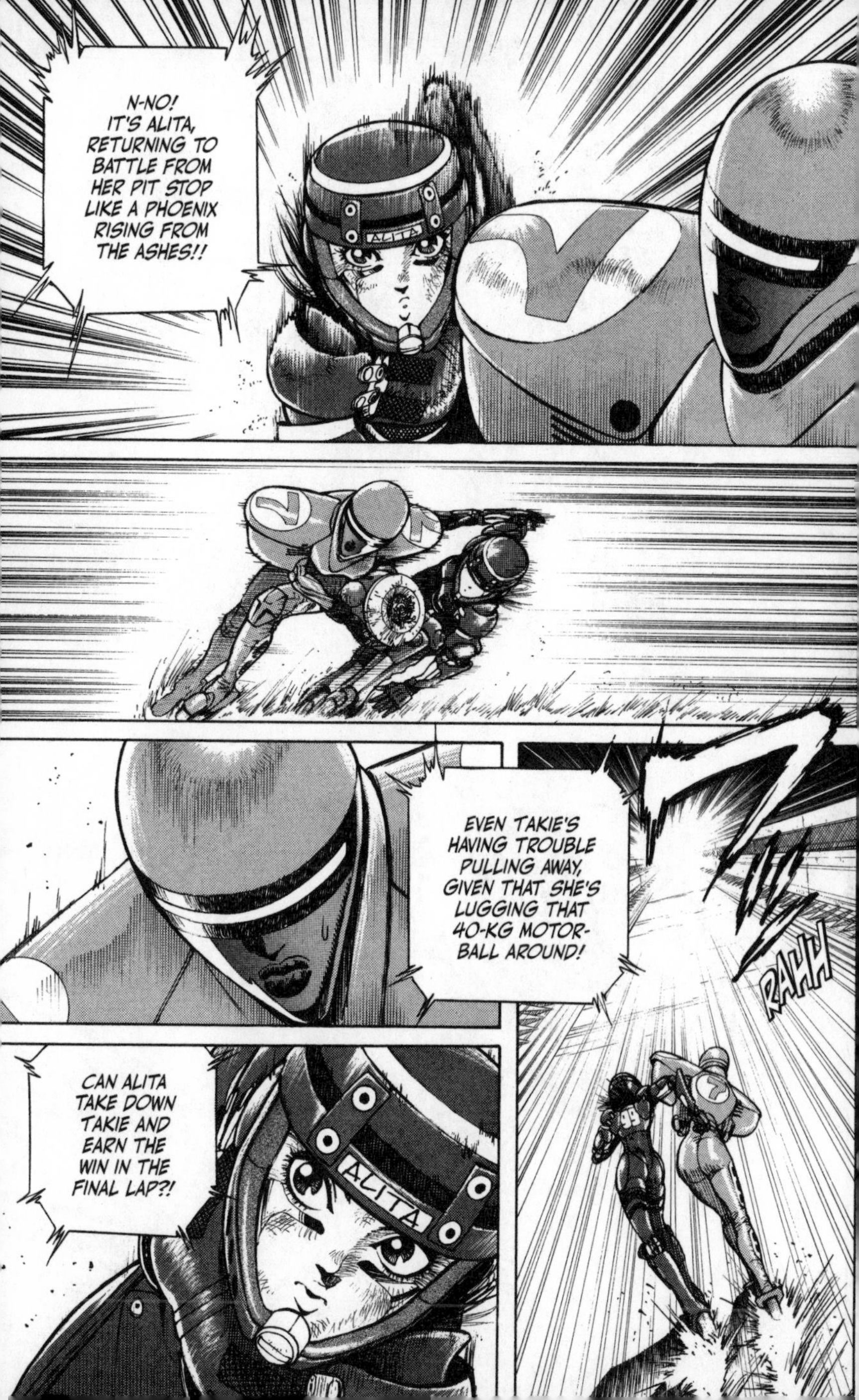
N-NO! IT'S ALITA, RETURNING TO BATTLE FROM HER PIT STOP LIKE A PHOENIX RISING FROM THE ASHES!!
RAHH
EVEN TAKIE'S HAVING TROUBLE PULLING AWAY, GIVEN THAT SHE'S LUGGING THAT 40-KG MOTOR-BALL AROUND!
CAN ALITA TAKE DOWN TAKIE AND EARN THE WIN IN THE FINAL LAP?!

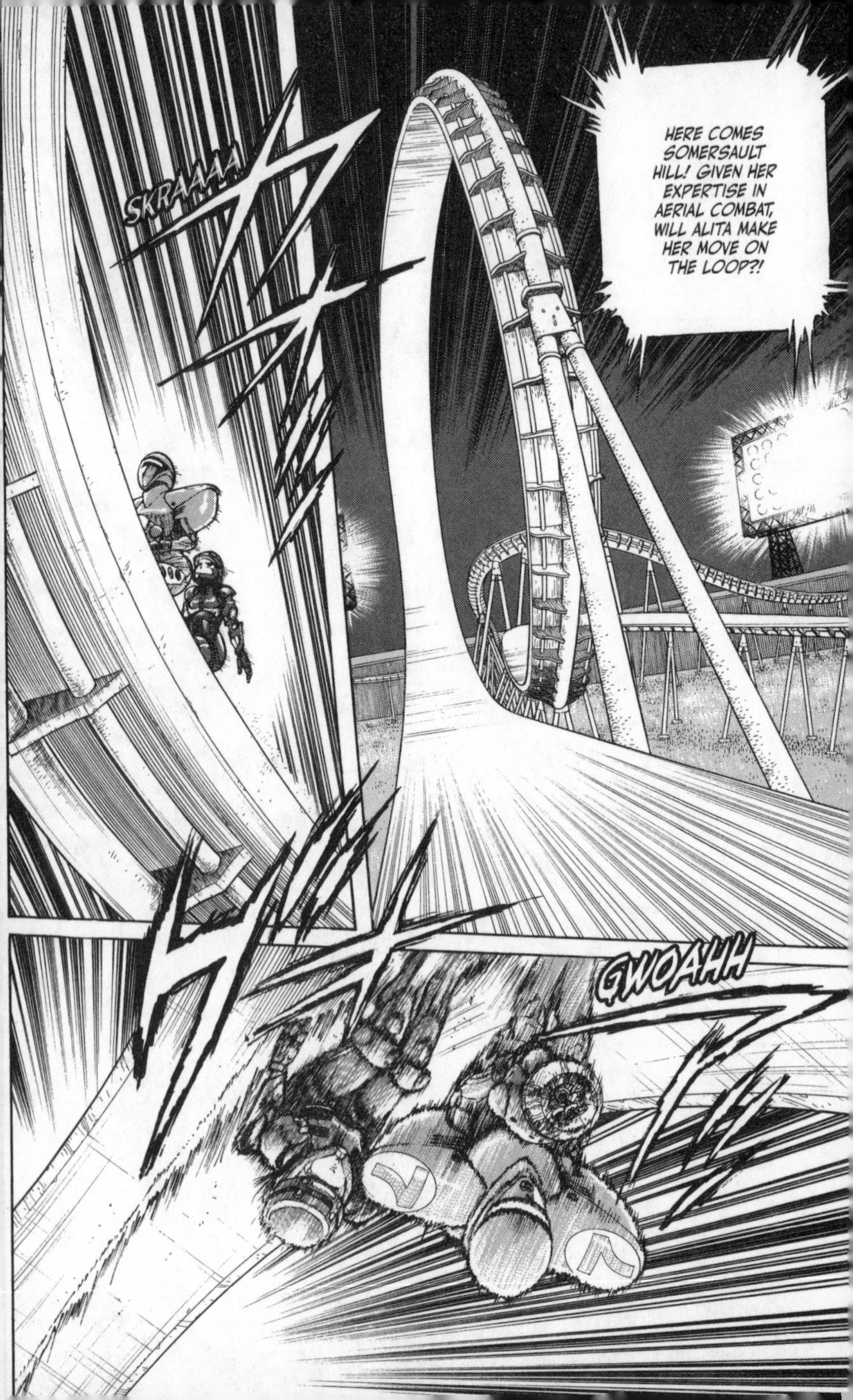
HERE COMES SOMERSAULT HILL! GIVEN HER EXPERTISE IN AERIAL COMBAT, WILL ALITA MAKE HER MOVE ON THE LOOP?!
SKRAAAA
GWOAHH

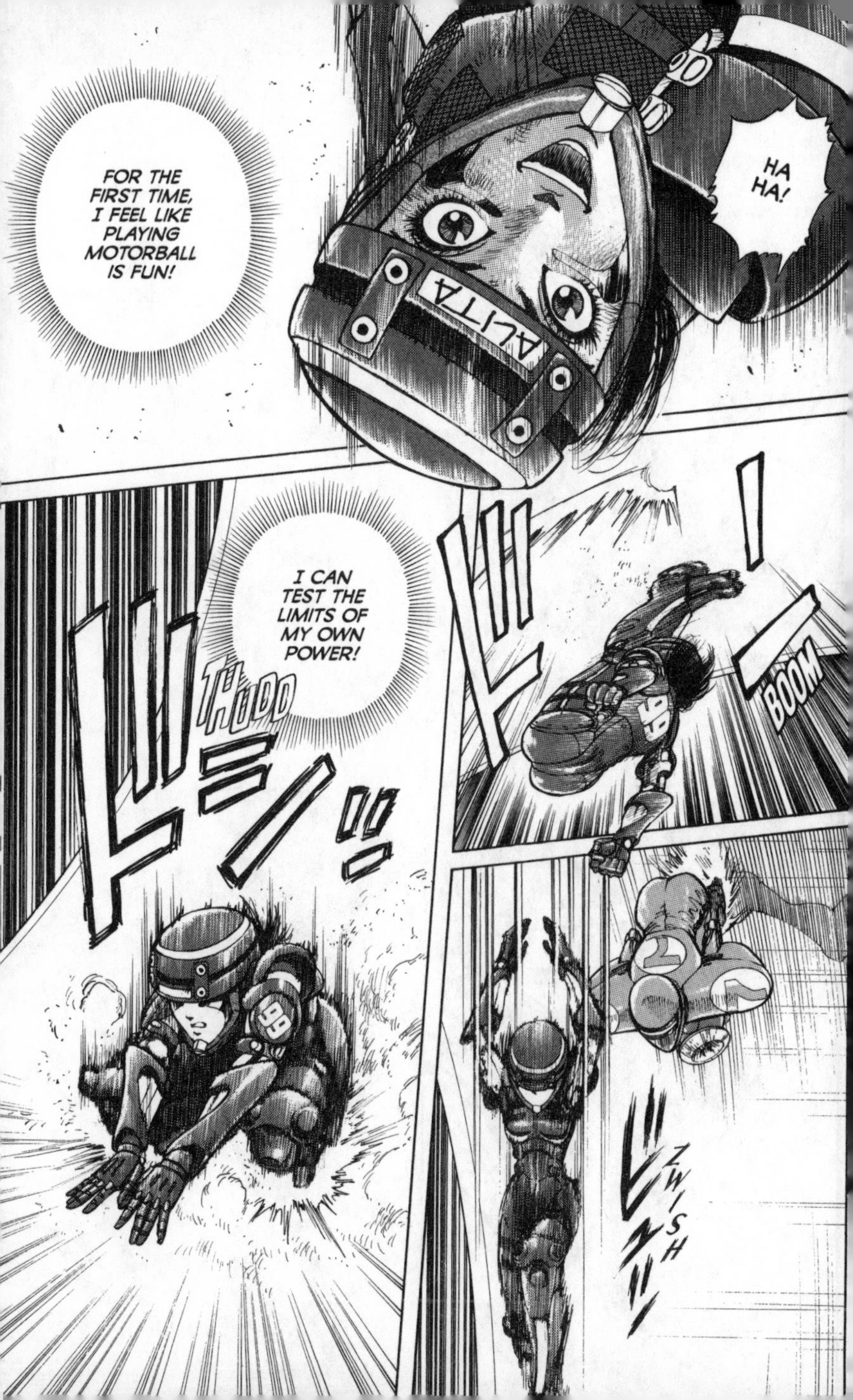
HA HA!
FOR THE FIRST TIME, I FEEL LIKE PLAYING MOTORBALL IS FUN!
BOOM
ZWISH
I CAN TEST THE LIMITS OF MY OWN POWER!
THUDD

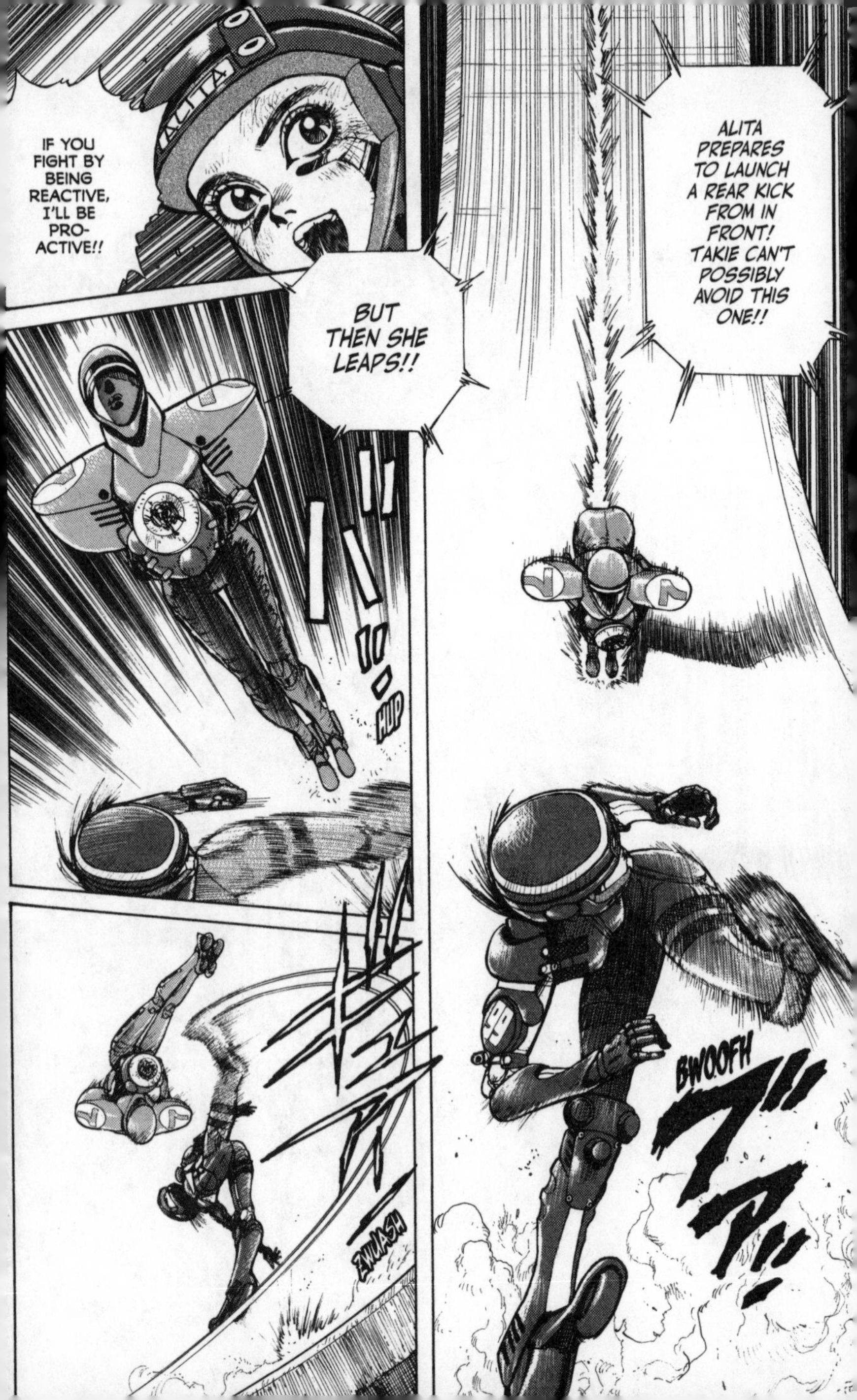
ALITA PREPARES TO LAUNCH A REAR KICK FROM IN FRONT! TAKIE CAN'T POSSIBLY AVOID THIS ONE!!
BWOOFH
IF YOU FIGHT BY BEING REACTIVE, I'LL BE PRO-ACTIVE!!
BUT THEN SHE LEAPS!!
HUP
ZWUASH

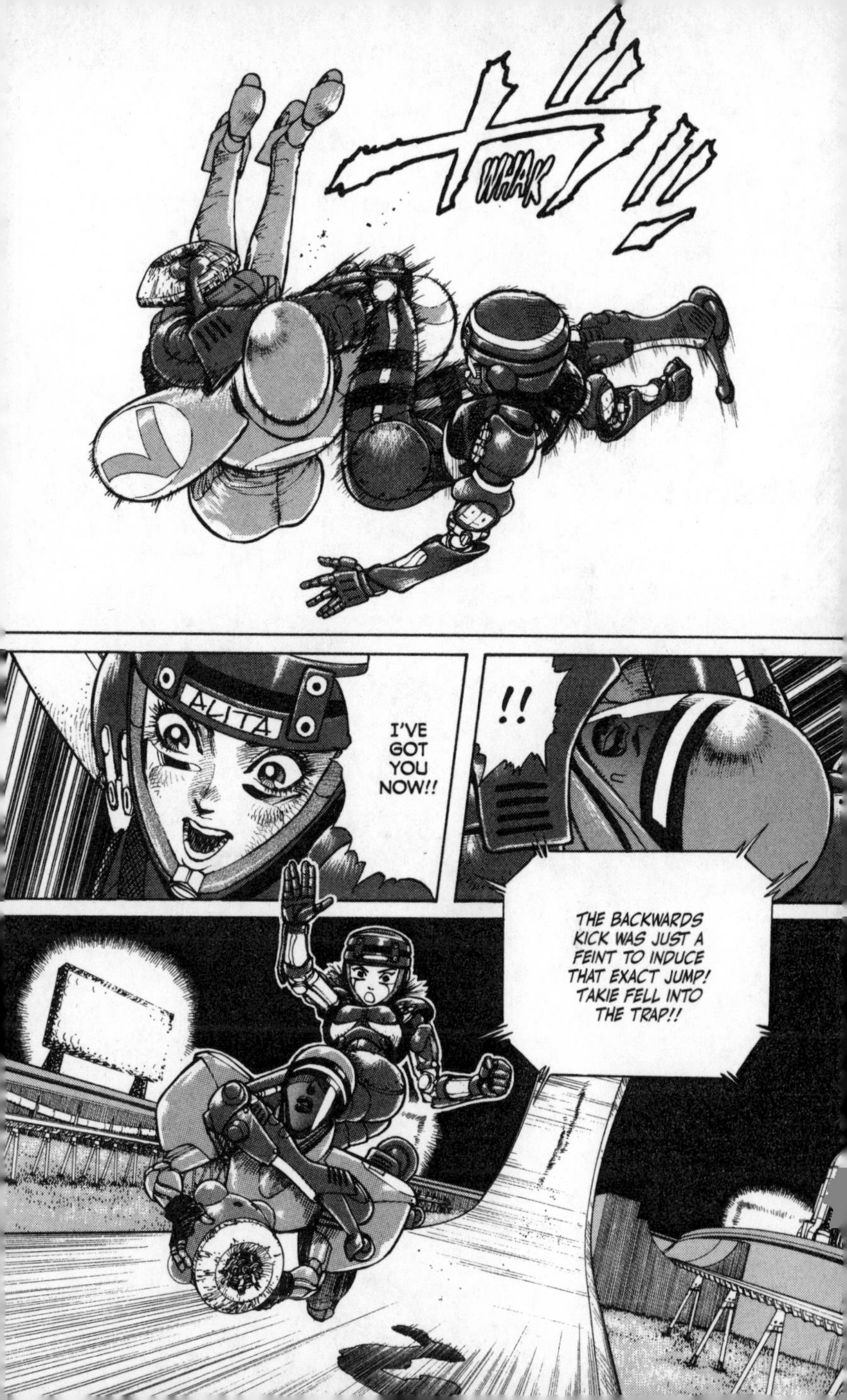
WHAK
!!
I'VE GOT YOU NOW!!
THE BACKWARDS KICK WAS JUST A FEINT TO INDUCE THAT EXACT JUMP! TAKIE FELL INTO THE TRAP!!

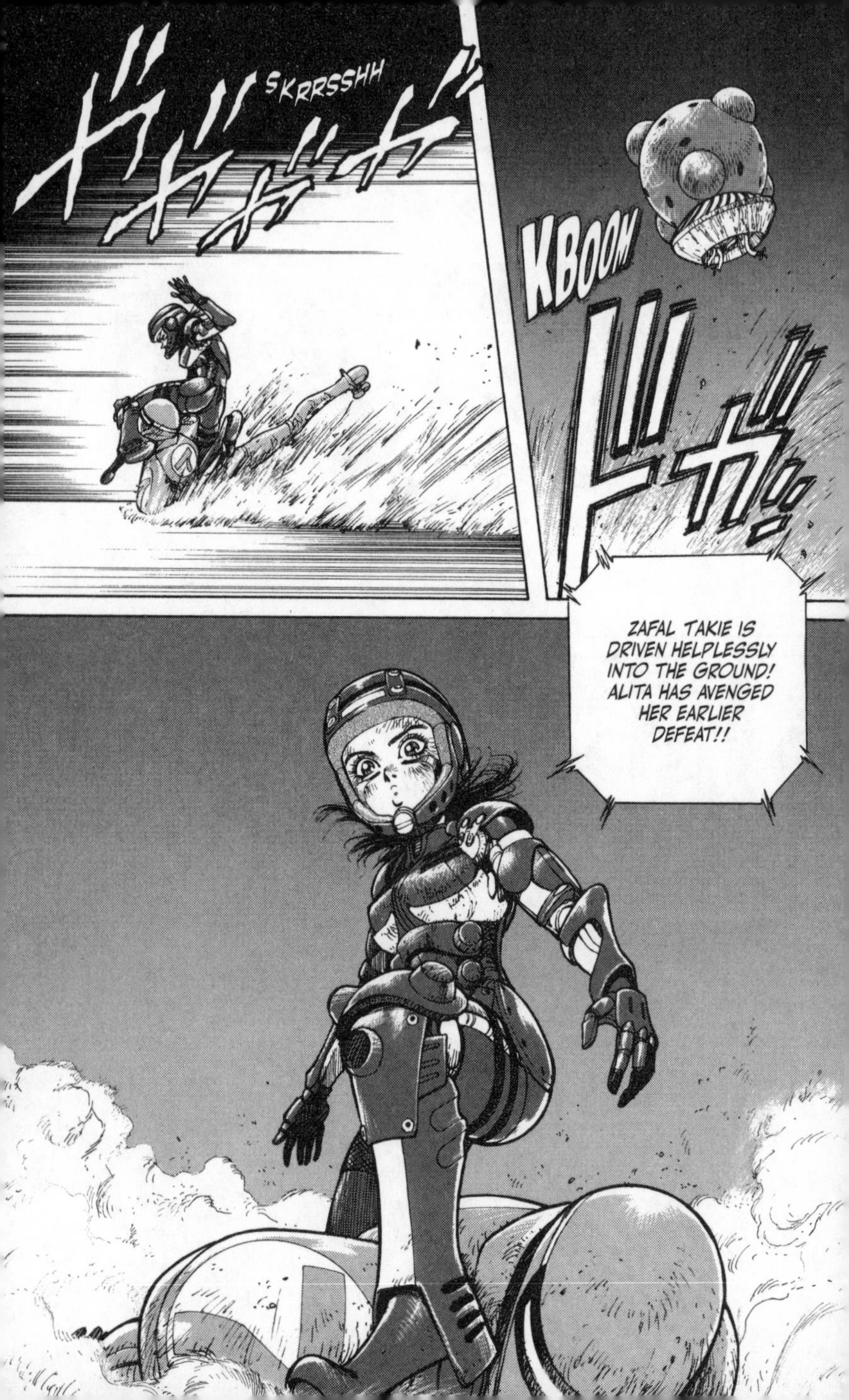
KBOOM
SKRRSSHH
ZAFAL TAKIE IS DRIVEN HELPLESSLY INTO THE GROUND! ALITA HAS AVENGED HER EARLIER DEFEAT!!

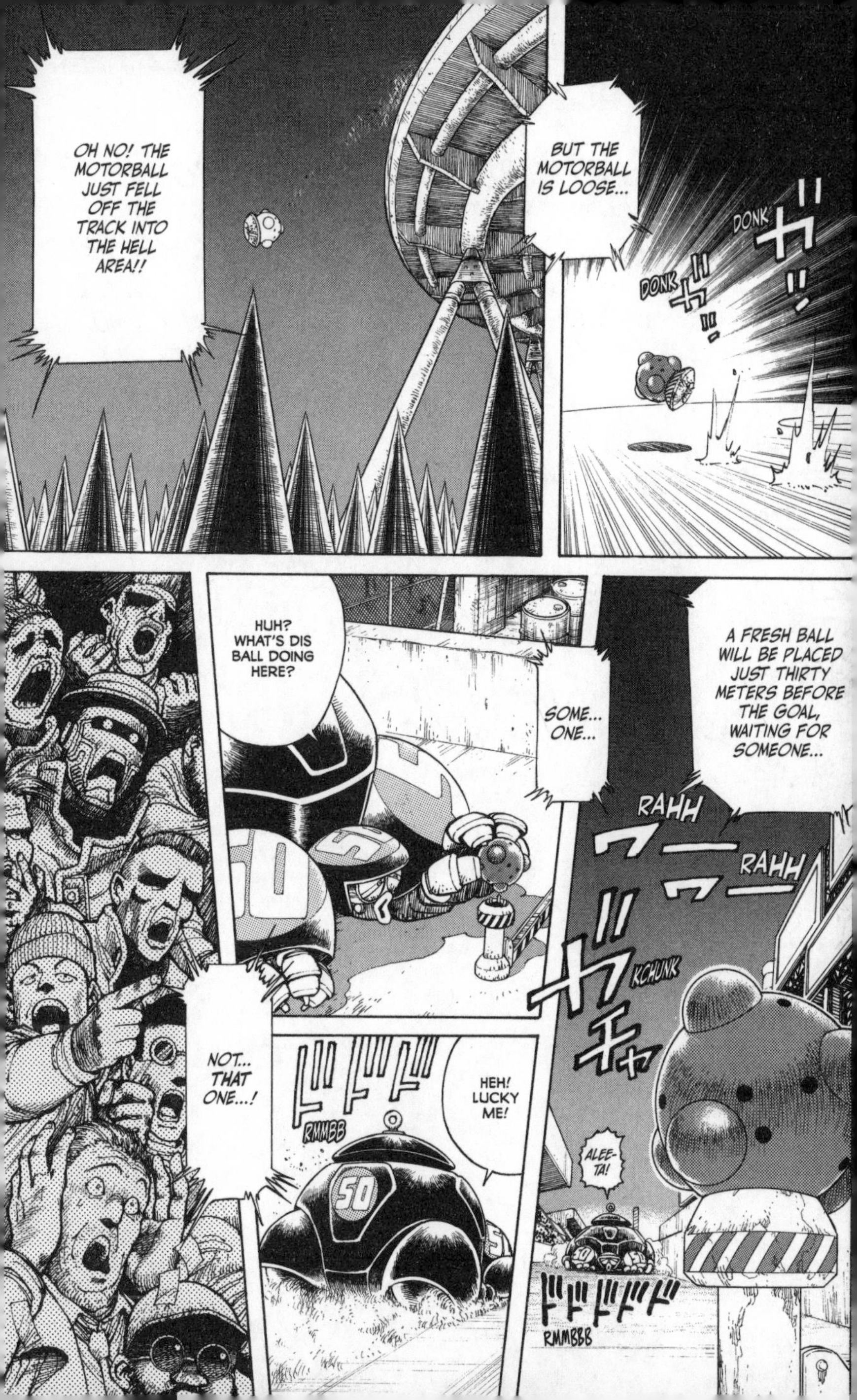
BUT THE MOTORBALL IS LOOSE...
DONK
DONK
OH NO! THE MOTORBALL JUST FELL OFF THE TRACK INTO THE HELL AREA!!
A FRESH BALL WILL BE PLACED JUST THIRTY METERS BEFORE THE GOAL, WAITING FOR SOMEONE...
RAHH
RAHH
KCHUNK
ALEE-TA!
RMMBBB
SOME... ONE...
HUH? WHAT'S DIS BALL DOING HERE?
HEH! LUCKY ME!
RMMBB
50
NOT... THAT ONE...!

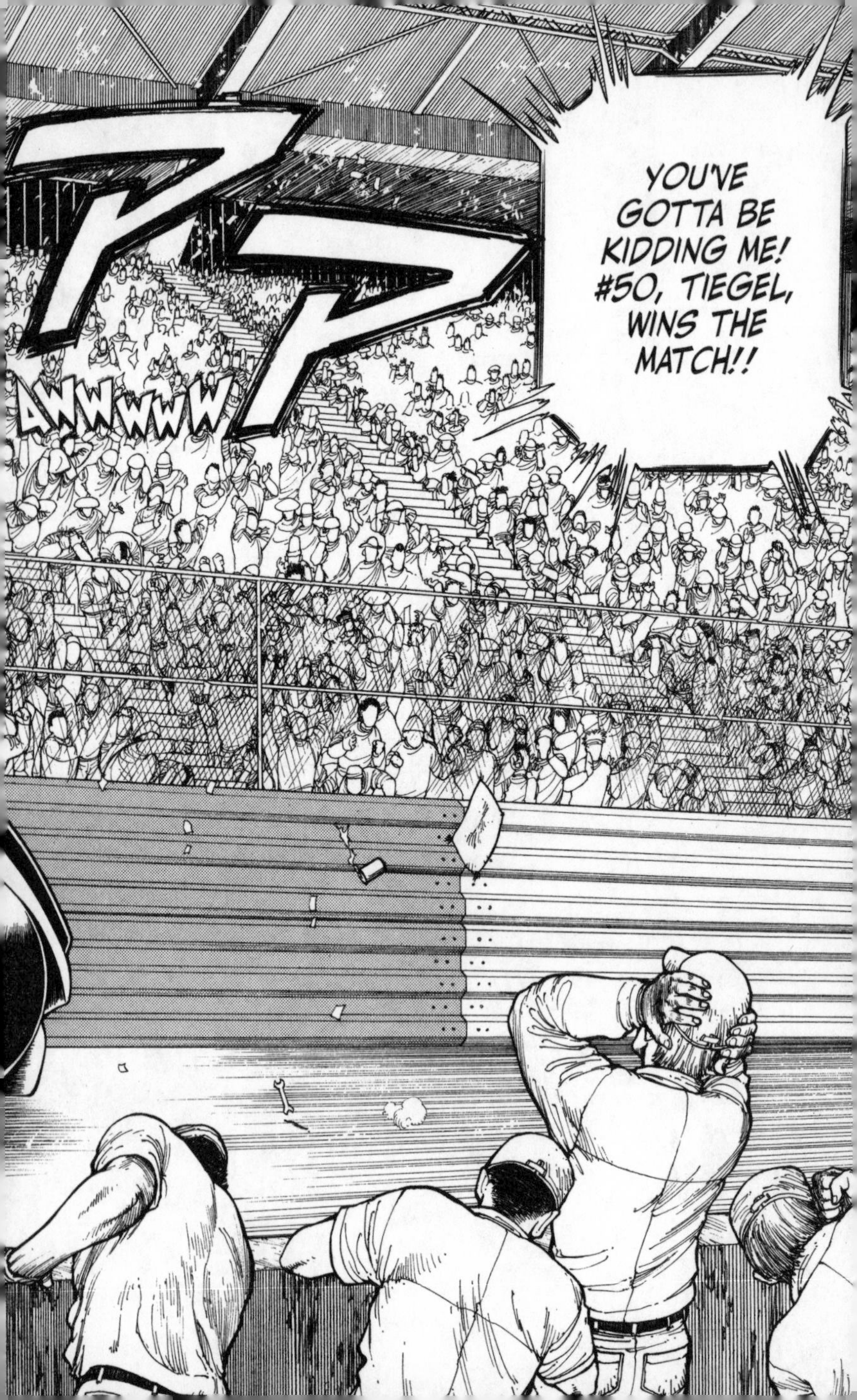

YOU'VE GOTTA BE KIDDING ME! #50, TIEGEL, WINS THE MATCH!!
AWWWWW

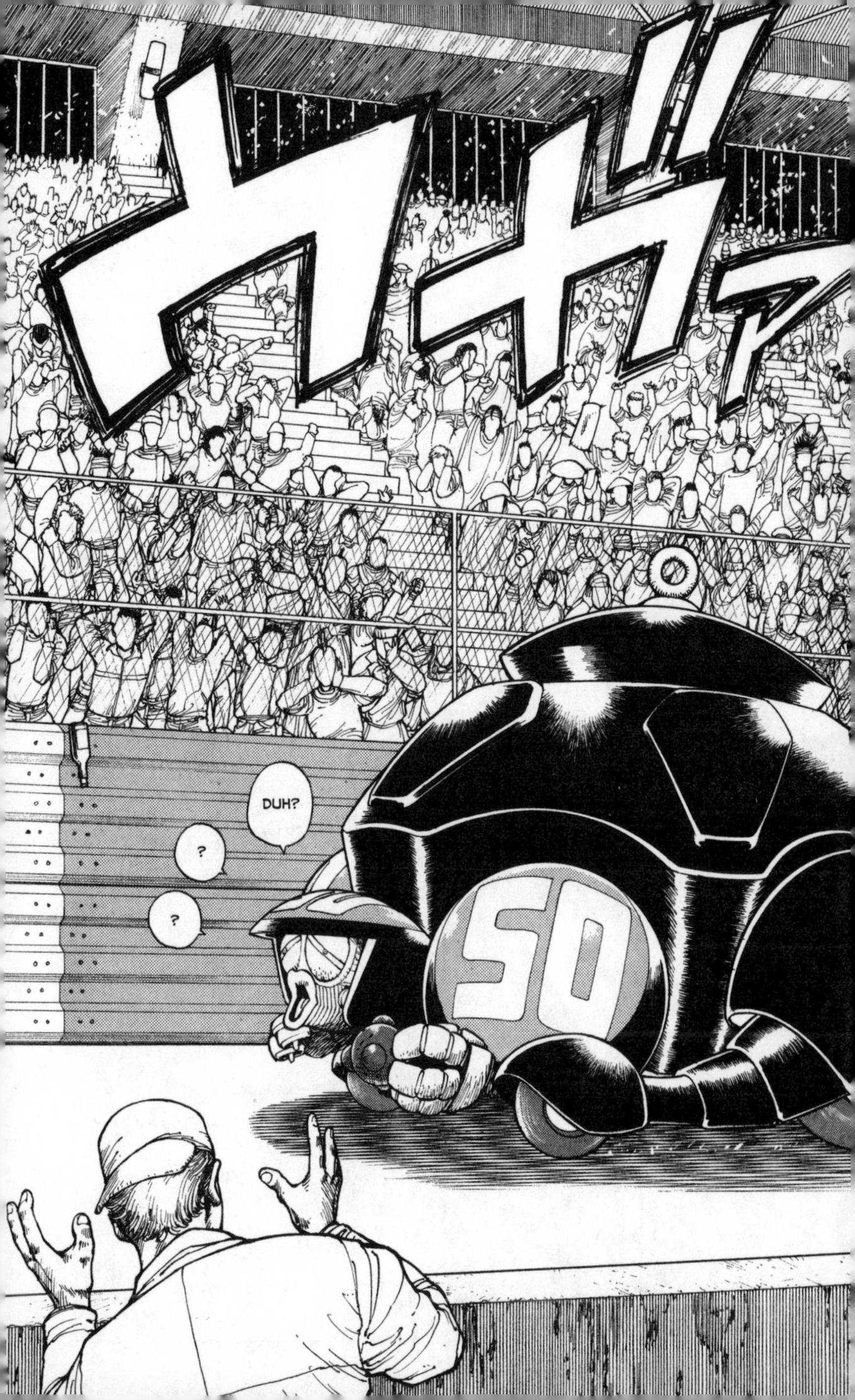
DUH?
?
?

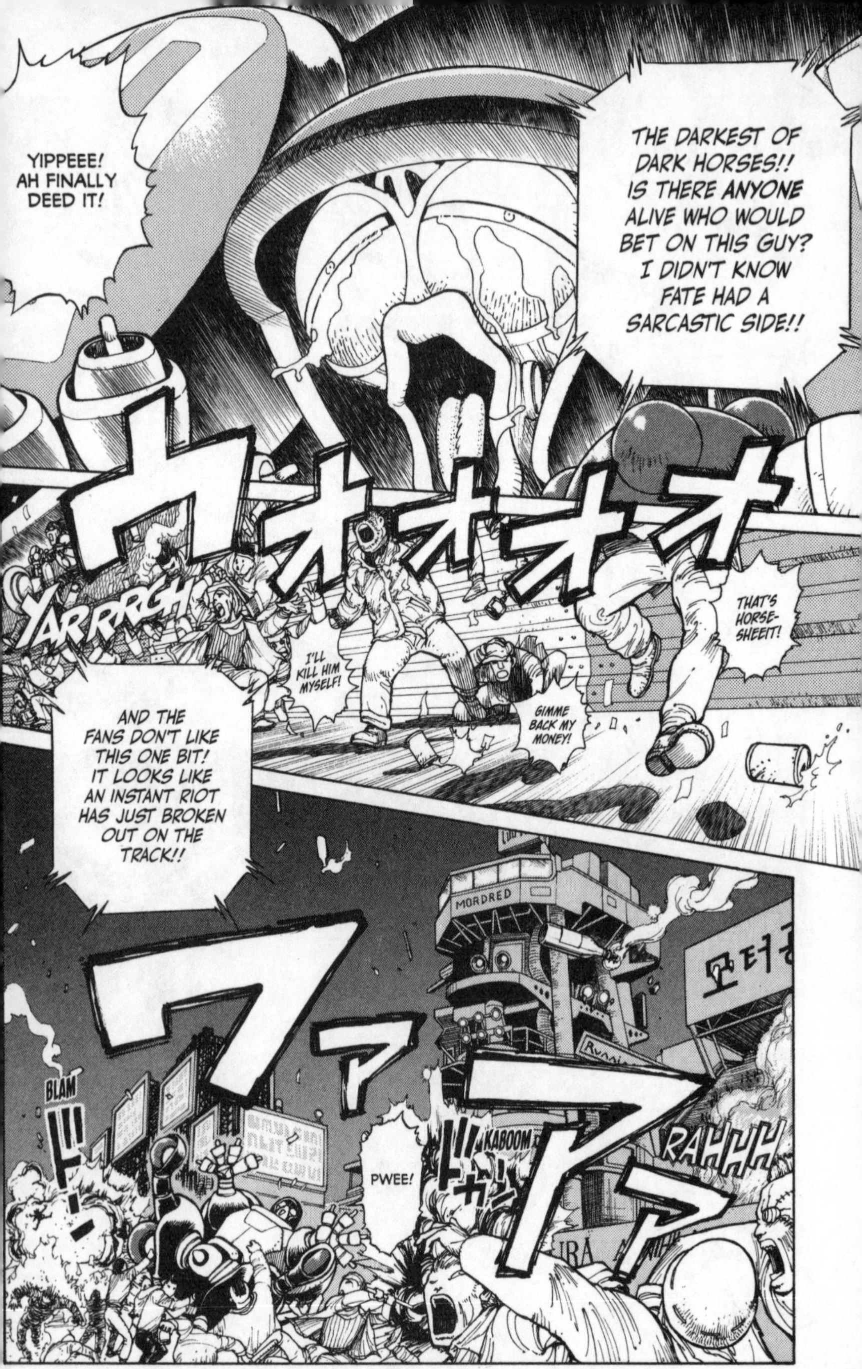
THE DARKEST OF DARK HORSES!! IS THERE ANYONE ALIVE WHO WOULD BET ON THIS GUY? I DIDN'T KNOW FATE HAD A SARCASTIC SIDE!!
YIPPEEE! AH FINALLY DEED IT!
ウオオオオ
YARRRGH
THAT'S HORSE-SHEEIT!
I'LL KILL HIM MYSELF!
GIMME BACK MY MONEY!
AND THE FANS DON'T LIKE THIS ONE BIT! IT LOOKS LIKE AN INSTANT RIOT HAS JUST BROKEN OUT ON THE TRACK!!
MORDRED
RAHHH
KABOOM
PWEE!
ファァアァ
BLAM

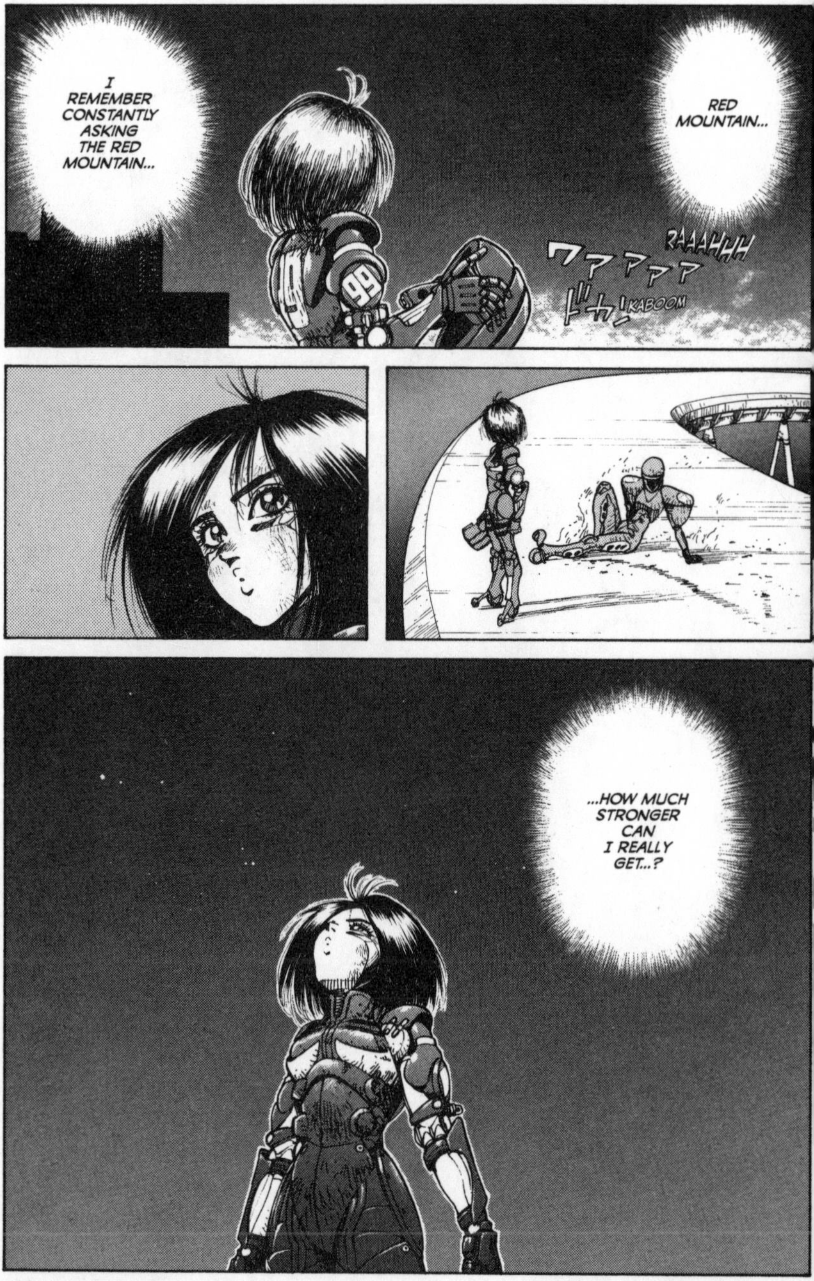
I REMEMBER CONSTANTLY ASKING THE RED MOUNTAIN...
RED MOUNTAIN...
ワァァァァ
RAAAHHH
ドカ!
KABOOM
...HOW MUCH STRONGER CAN I REALLY GET...?

FIGHT_020 Inheriting the Dream

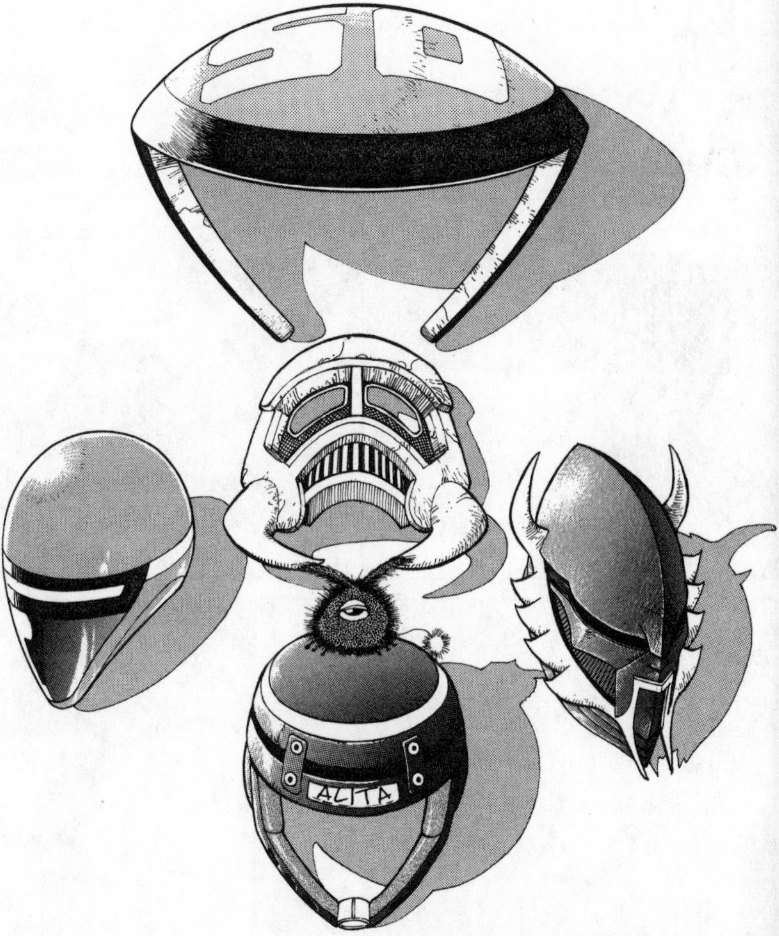
ALITA

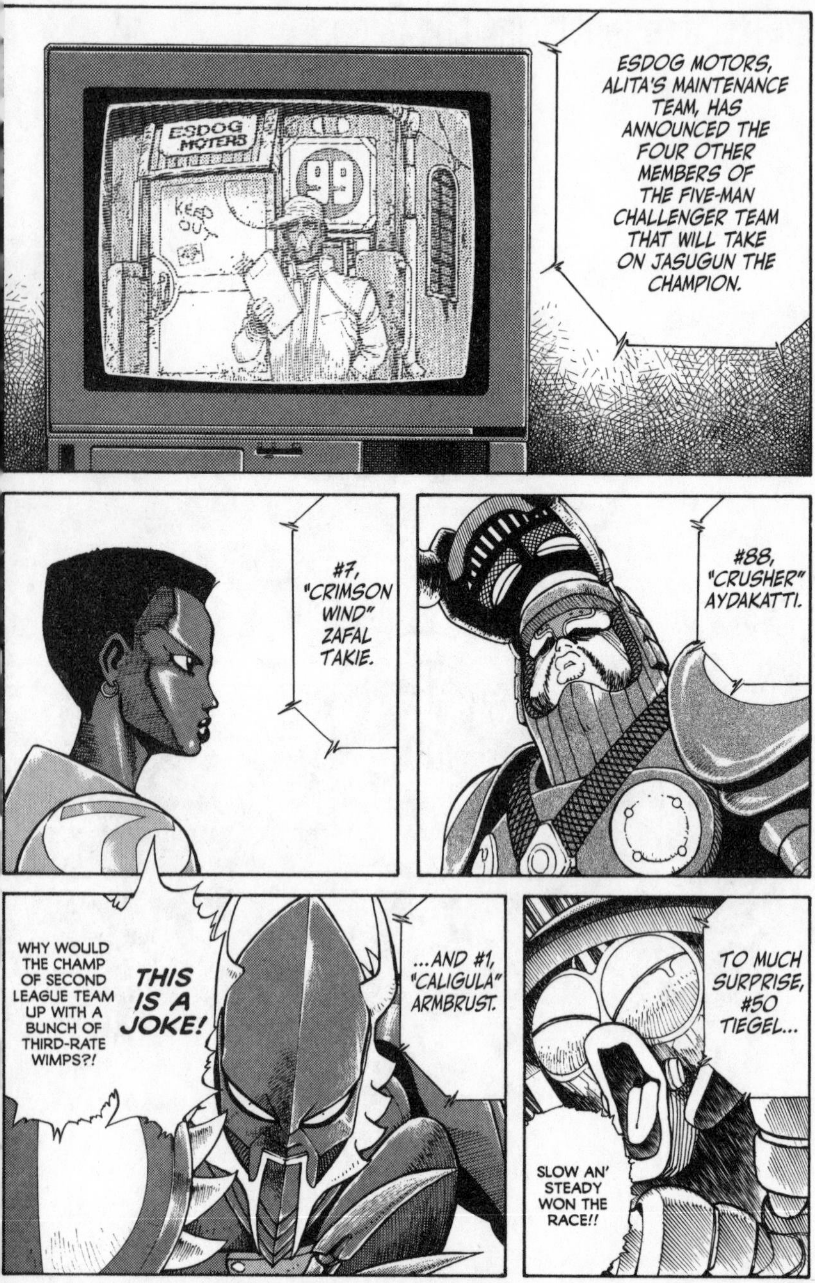
ESDOG MOTORS
99
KEEP OUT
ESDOG MOTORS, ALITA'S MAINTENANCE TEAM, HAS ANNOUNCED THE FOUR OTHER MEMBERS OF THE FIVE-MAN CHALLENGER TEAM THAT WILL TAKE ON JASUGUN THE CHAMPION.
#88, "CRUSHER" AYDAKATTI.
#7, "CRIMSON WIND" ZAFAL TAKIE.
TO MUCH SURPRISE, #50 TIEGEL...
SLOW AN' STEADY WON THE RACE!!
...AND #1, "CALIGULA" ARMBRUST.
THIS IS A JOKE!
WHY WOULD THE CHAMP OF SECOND LEAGUE TEAM UP WITH A BUNCH OF THIRD-RATE WIMPS?!

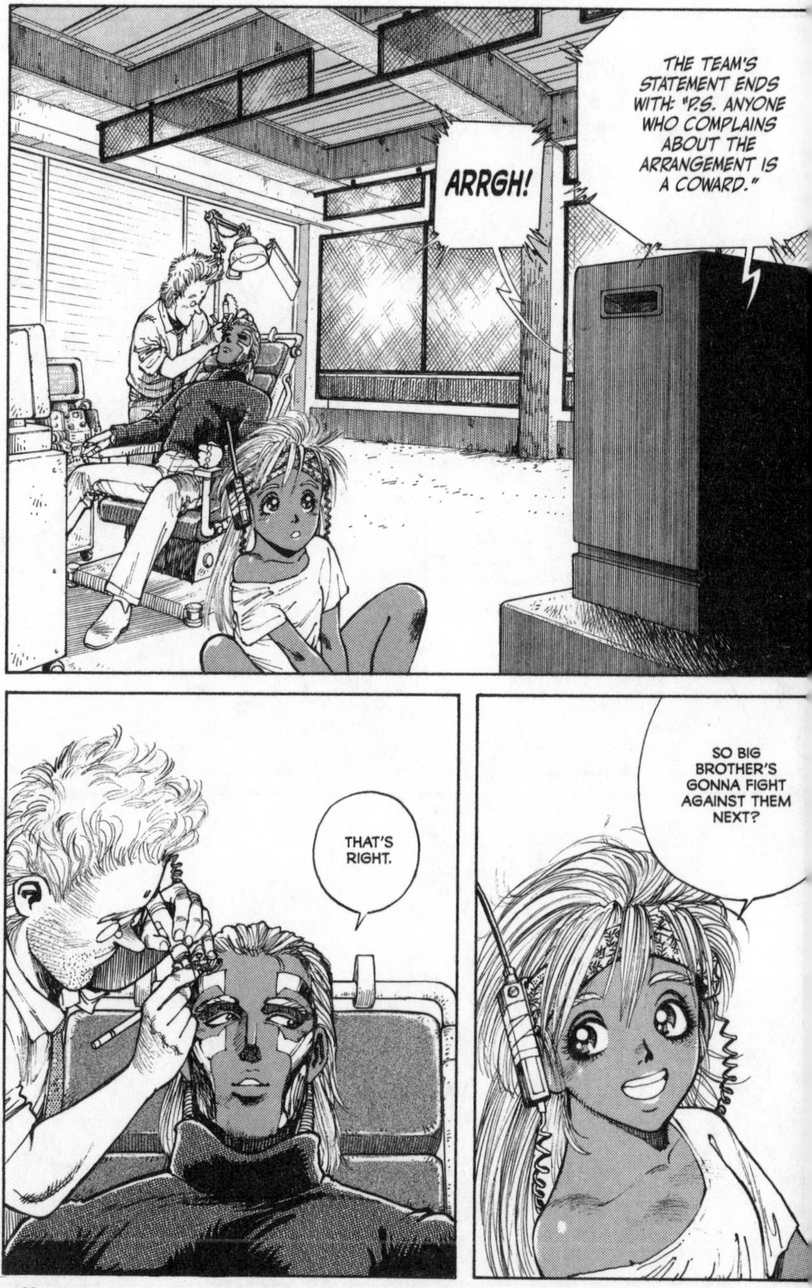
THE TEAM'S STATEMENT ENDS WITH: "P.S. ANYONE WHO COMPLAINS ABOUT THE ARRANGEMENT IS A COWARD."
ARRGH!
SO BIG BROTHER'S GONNA FIGHT AGAINST THEM NEXT?
THAT'S RIGHT.

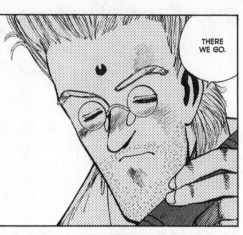

THERE WE GO.
I'VE SET IT UP SO THAT IF HE HAS ANOTHER FLATLINE SPASM, I CAN SEND SHUMIRA'S BRAIN-WAVES TO REVIVE HIM REMOTELY AT THE FLIP OF A SWITCH...
IT'S SHODDY WORK, BUT IT'S ALL THAT I CAN DO AT THE MOMENT.
BY THE WAY, JASUGUN, I'M CURIOUS...
WHAT IS IT?
THIS BRAIN AUGMENTATION SURGERY THAT LED TO YOUR FLATLINING EPISODES...
WHO PER-FORMED IT ON YOU?
...
I WAS INVOLVED IN A HUGE ACCIDENT JUST AFTER I REACHED THE MOTORBALL TOP LEAGUE AS AN UP-AND-COMING ROOKIE.

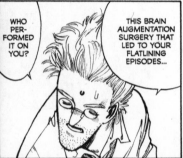

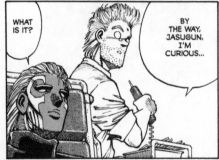

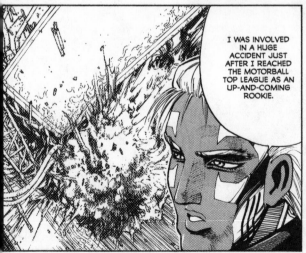

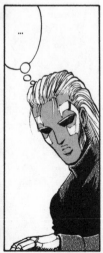

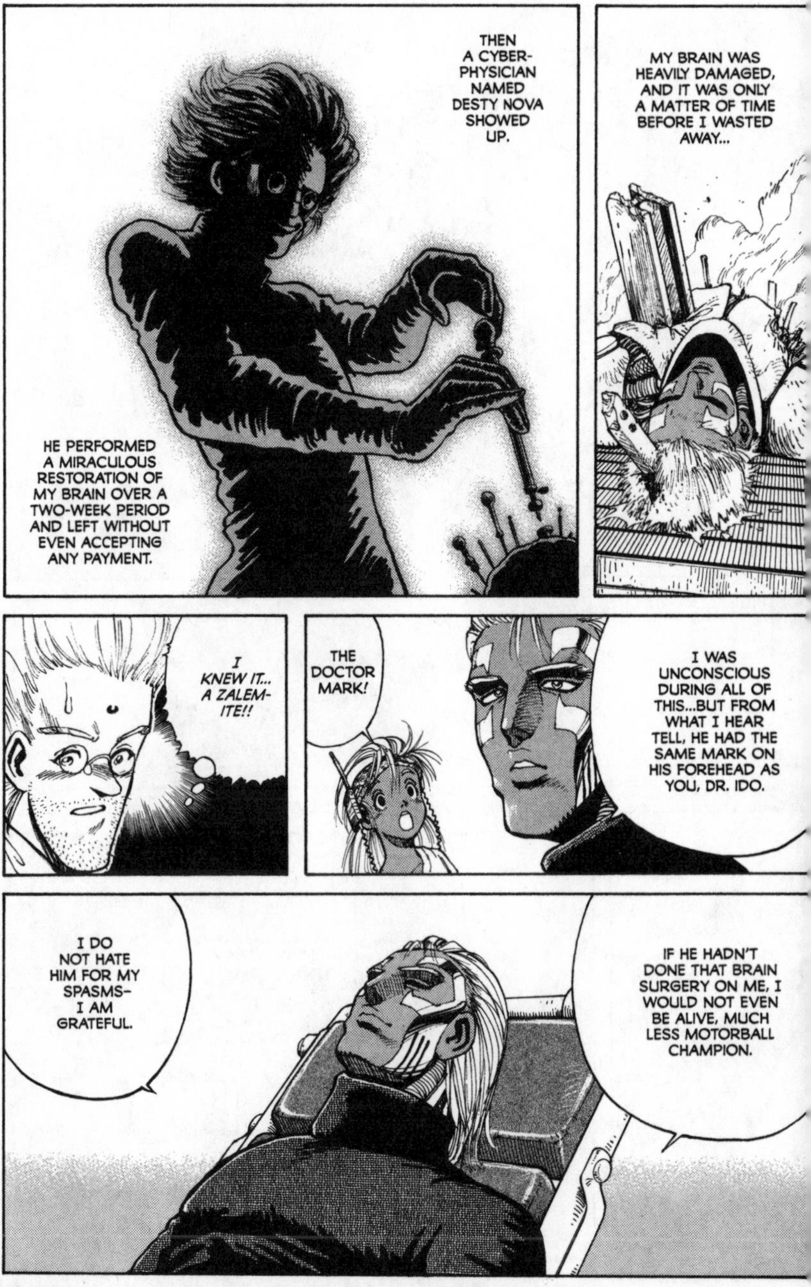
MY BRAIN WAS HEAVILY DAMAGED, AND IT WAS ONLY A MATTER OF TIME BEFORE I WASTED AWAY...
THEN A CYBER-PHYSICIAN NAMED DESTY NOVA SHOWED UP.
HE PERFORMED A MIRACULOUS RESTORATION OF MY BRAIN OVER A TWO-WEEK PERIOD AND LEFT WITHOUT EVEN ACCEPTING ANY PAYMENT.
I WAS UNCONSCIOUS DURING ALL OF THIS...BUT FROM WHAT I HEAR TELL, HE HAD THE SAME MARK ON HIS FOREHEAD AS YOU, DR. IDO.
THE DOCTOR MARK!
I KNEW IT... A ZALEM-ITE!!
IF HE HADN'T DONE THAT BRAIN SURGERY ON ME, I WOULD NOT EVEN BE ALIVE, MUCH LESS MOTORBALL CHAMPION.
I DO NOT HATE HIM FOR MY SPASMS– I AM GRATEFUL.

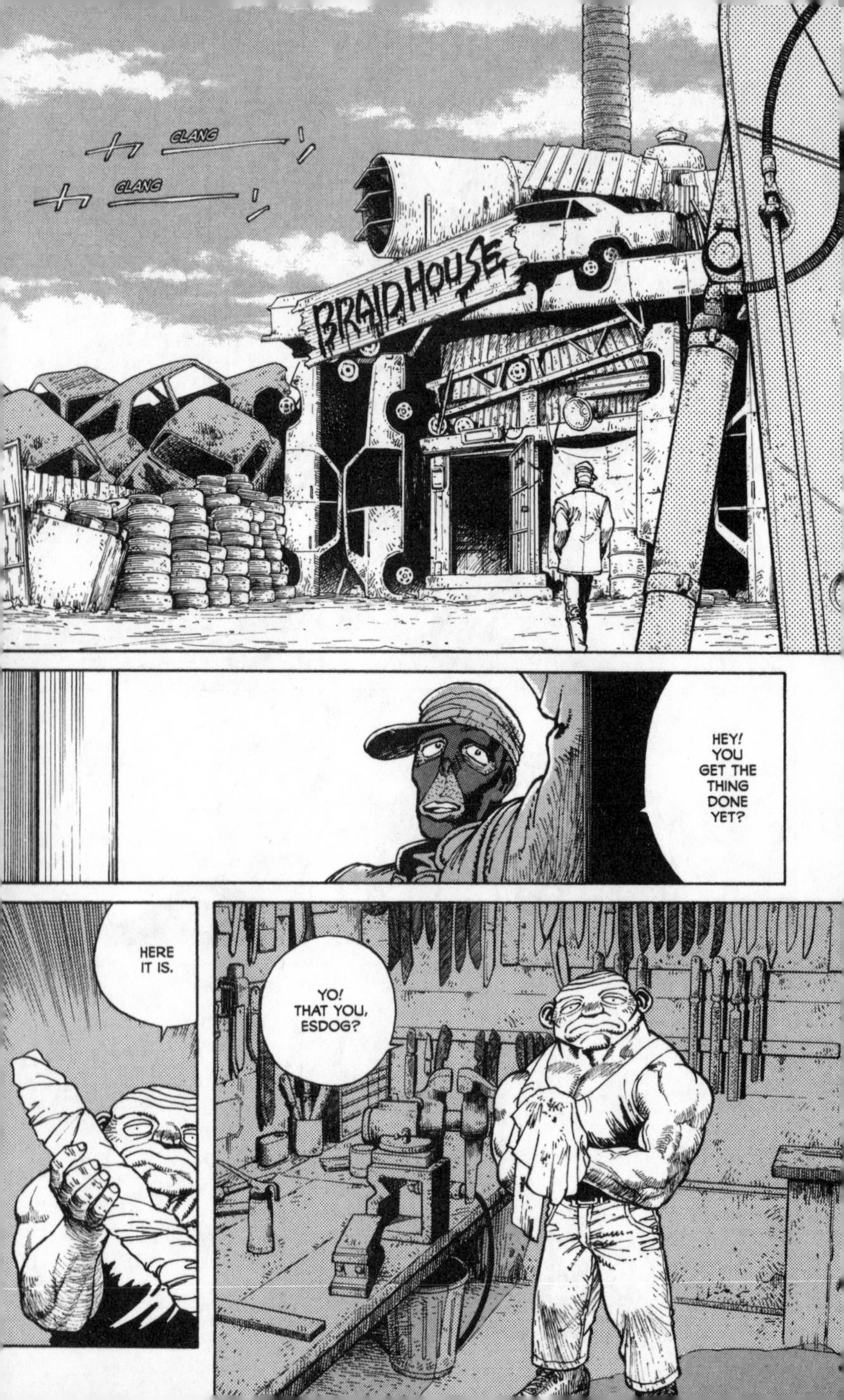
CLANG
CLANG
BRAID HOUSE
HEY! YOU GET THE THING DONE YET?
YO! THAT YOU, ESDOG?
HERE IT IS.

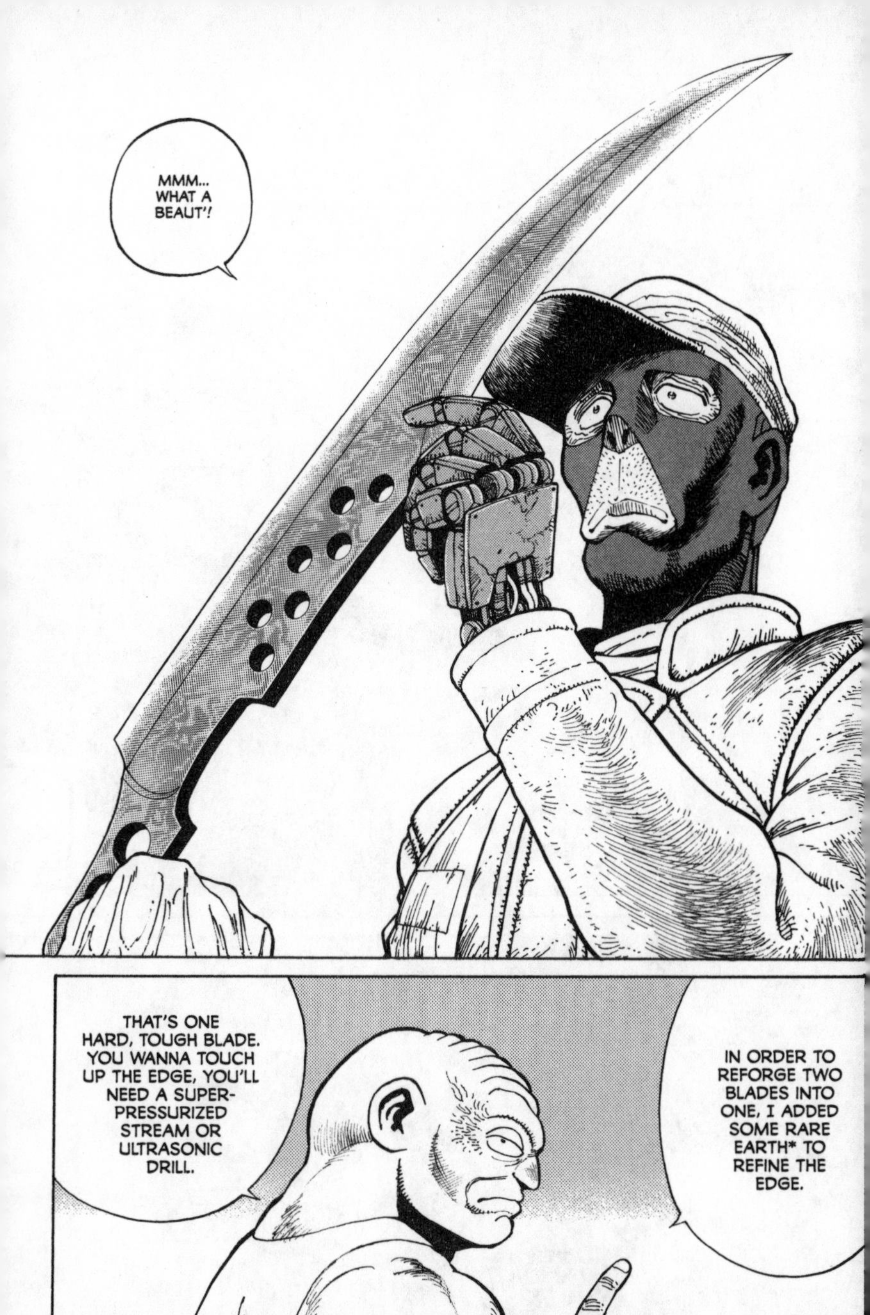
MMM... WHAT A BEAUT'!
IN ORDER TO REFORGE TWO BLADES INTO ONE, I ADDED SOME RARE EARTH* TO REFINE THE EDGE.
THAT'S ONE HARD, TOUGH BLADE. YOU WANNA TOUCH UP THE EDGE, YOU'LL NEED A SUPER-PRESSURIZED STREAM OR ULTRASONIC DRILL.

Rare earth: A category of earth elements, seventeen in total, including scandium, yttrium, and lanthanum.

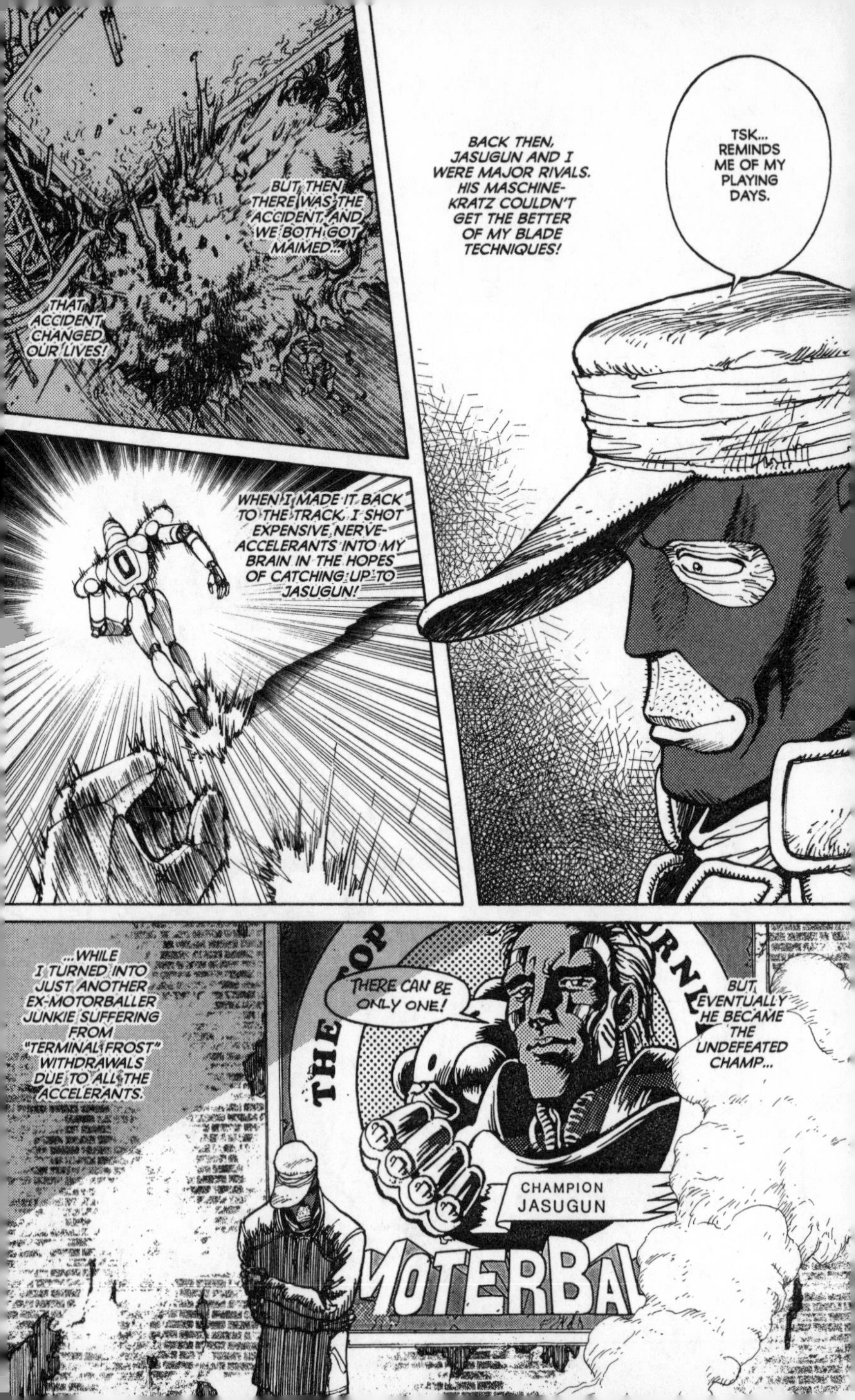
TSK... REMINDS ME OF MY PLAYING DAYS.
BACK THEN, JASUGUN AND I WERE MAJOR RIVALS. HIS MASCHINE-KRATZ COULDN'T GET THE BETTER OF MY BLADE TECHNIQUES!
BUT THEN THERE WAS THE ACCIDENT, AND WE BOTH GOT MAIMED...
THAT ACCIDENT CHANGED OUR LIVES!
WHEN I MADE IT BACK TO THE TRACK, I SHOT EXPENSIVE NERVE-ACCELERANTS INTO MY BRAIN IN THE HOPES OF CATCHING UP TO JASUGUN!
BUT EVENTUALLY HE BECAME THE UNDEFEATED CHAMP...
THERE CAN BE ONLY ONE!
CHAMPION JASUGUN
...WHILE I TURNED INTO JUST ANOTHER EX-MOTORBALLER JUNKIE SUFFERING FROM "TERMINAL FROST" WITHDRAWALS DUE TO ALL THE ACCELERANTS.

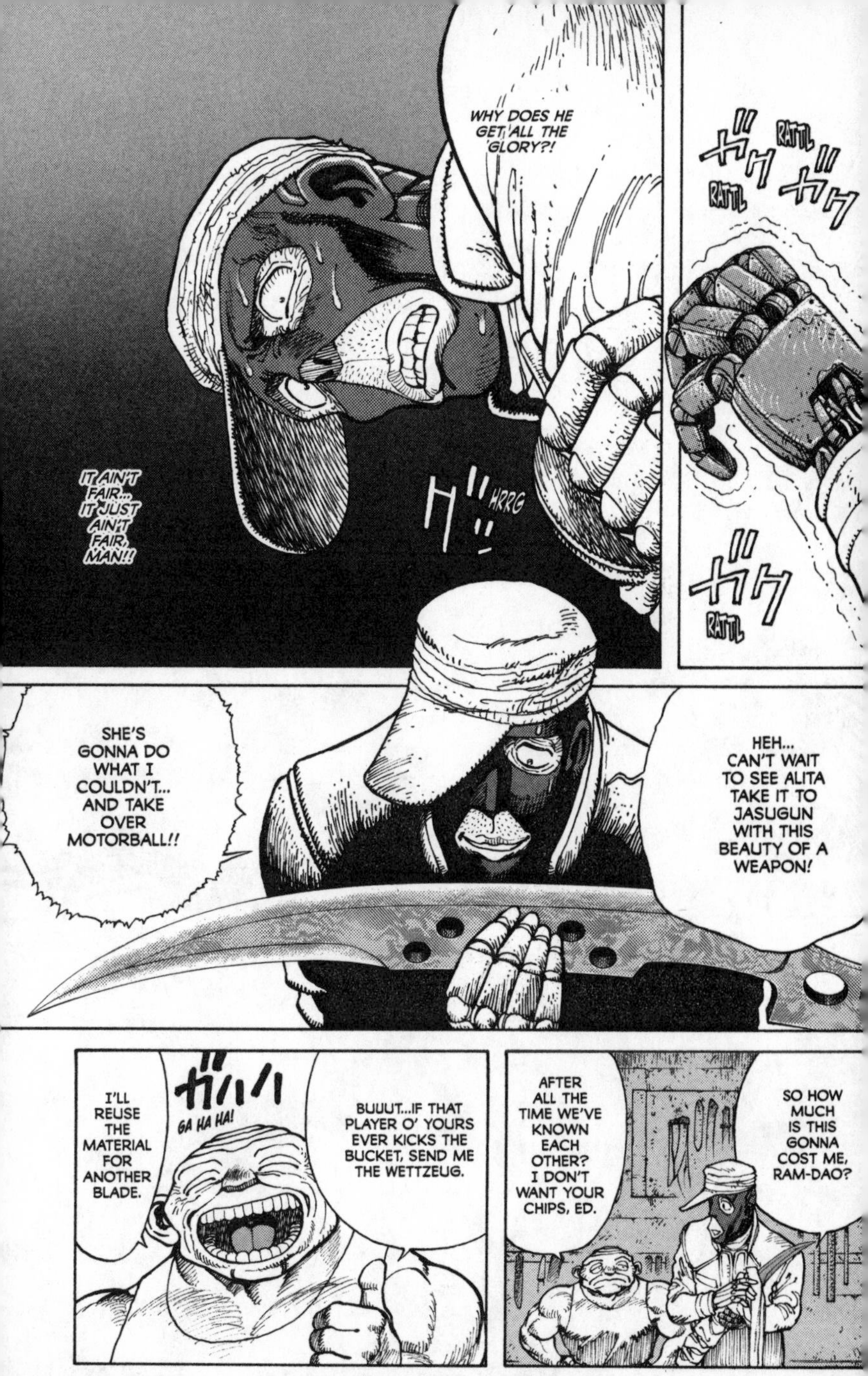
RATTL
RATTL
RATTL
WHY DOES HE GET ALL THE GLORY?!
HRRG
IT AIN'T FAIR... IT JUST AIN'T FAIR, MAN!!
HEH... CAN'T WAIT TO SEE ALITA TAKE IT TO JASUGUN WITH THIS BEAUTY OF A WEAPON!
SHE'S GONNA DO WHAT I COULDN'T... AND TAKE OVER MOTORBALL!!
SO HOW MUCH IS THIS GONNA COST ME, RAM-DAO?
AFTER ALL THE TIME WE'VE KNOWN EACH OTHER? I DON'T WANT YOUR CHIPS, ED.
BUUUT...IF THAT PLAYER O' YOURS EVER KICKS THE BUCKET, SEND ME THE WETTZEUG.
GA HA HA!
I'LL REUSE THE MATERIAL FOR ANOTHER BLADE.

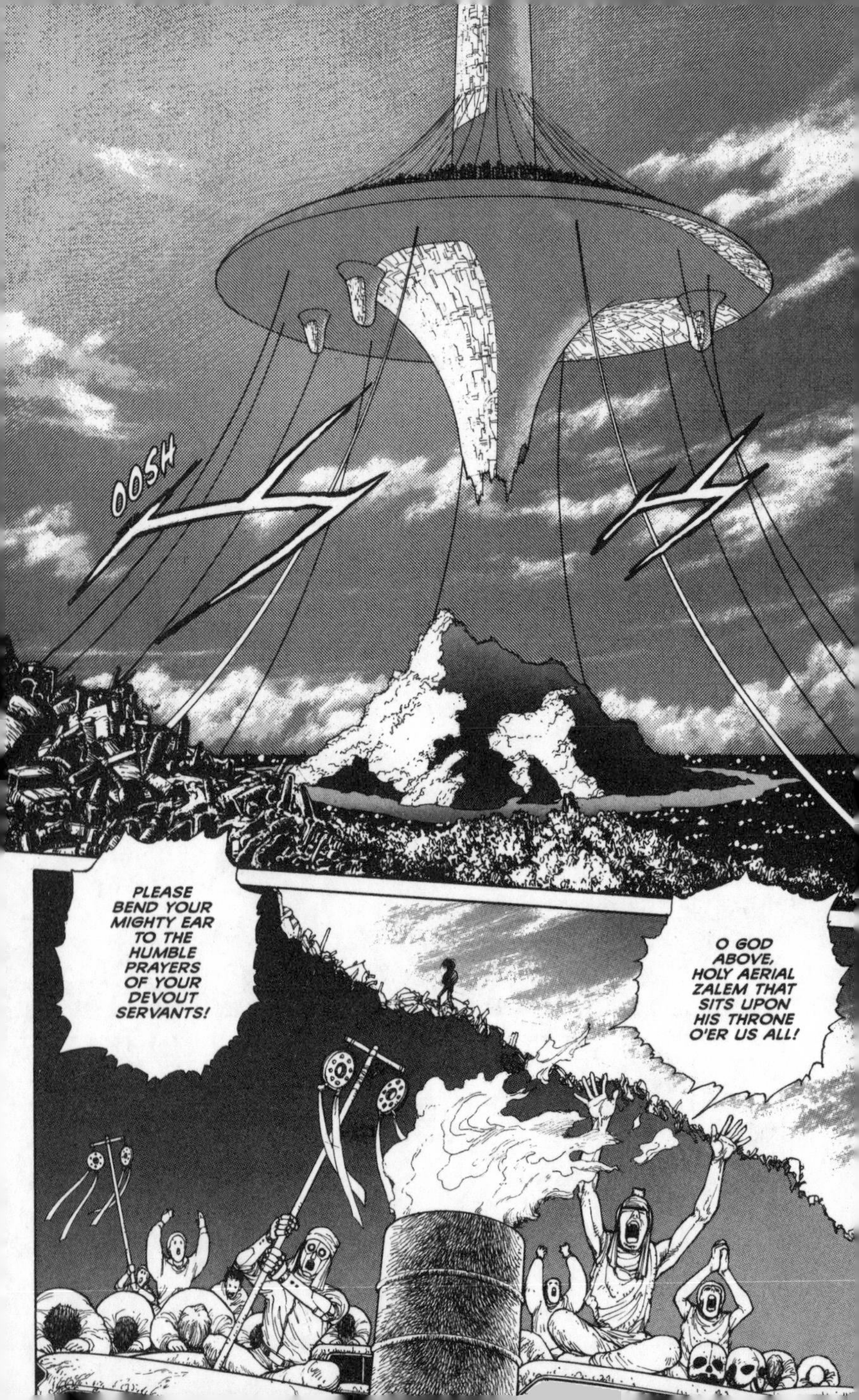
OOSH
O GOD ABOVE, HOLY AERIAL ZALEM THAT SITS UPON HIS THRONE O'ER US ALL!
PLEASE BEND YOUR MIGHTY EAR TO THE HUMBLE PRAYERS OF YOUR DEVOUT SERVANTS!

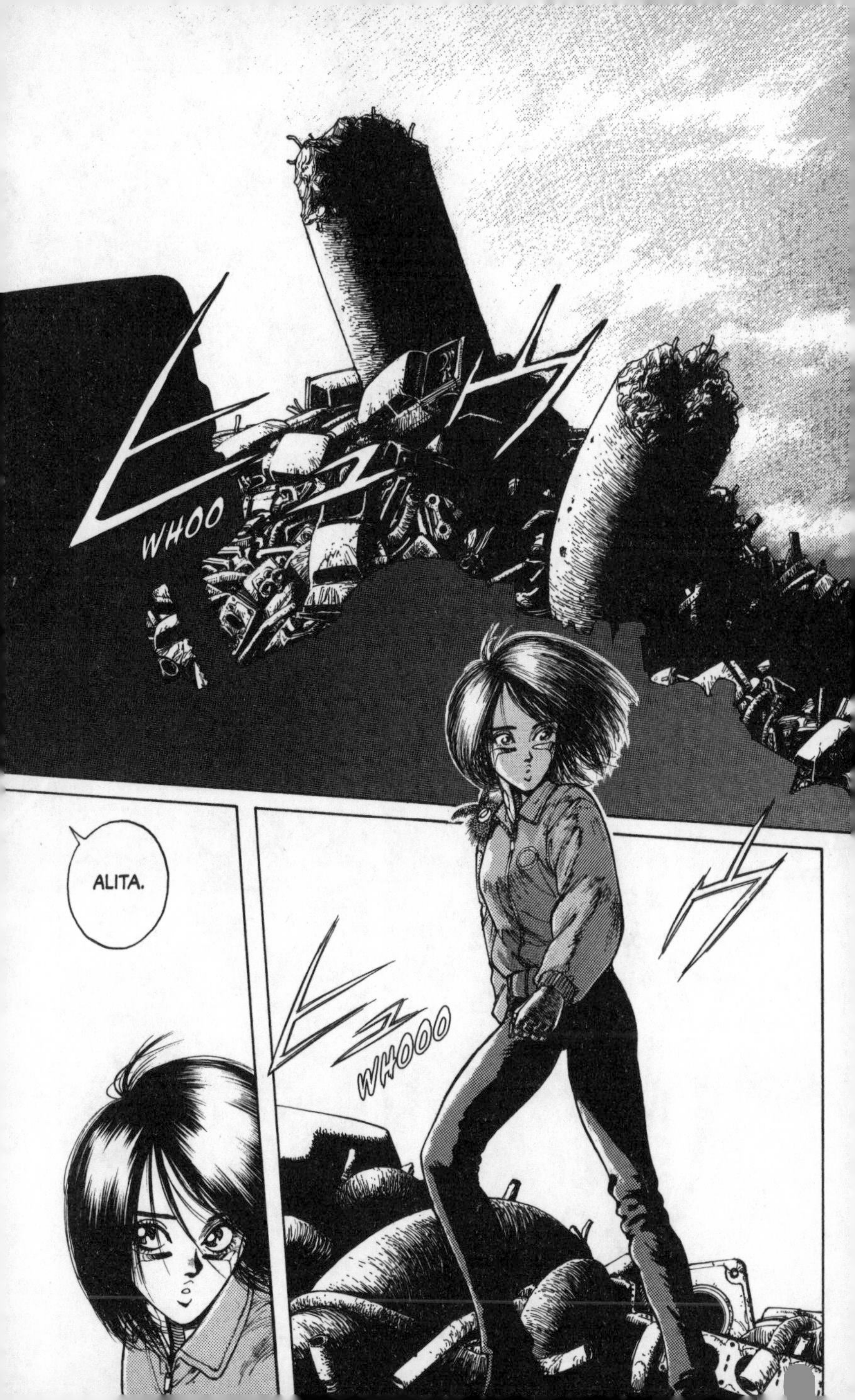
WHOO
WHOOO
ALITA.

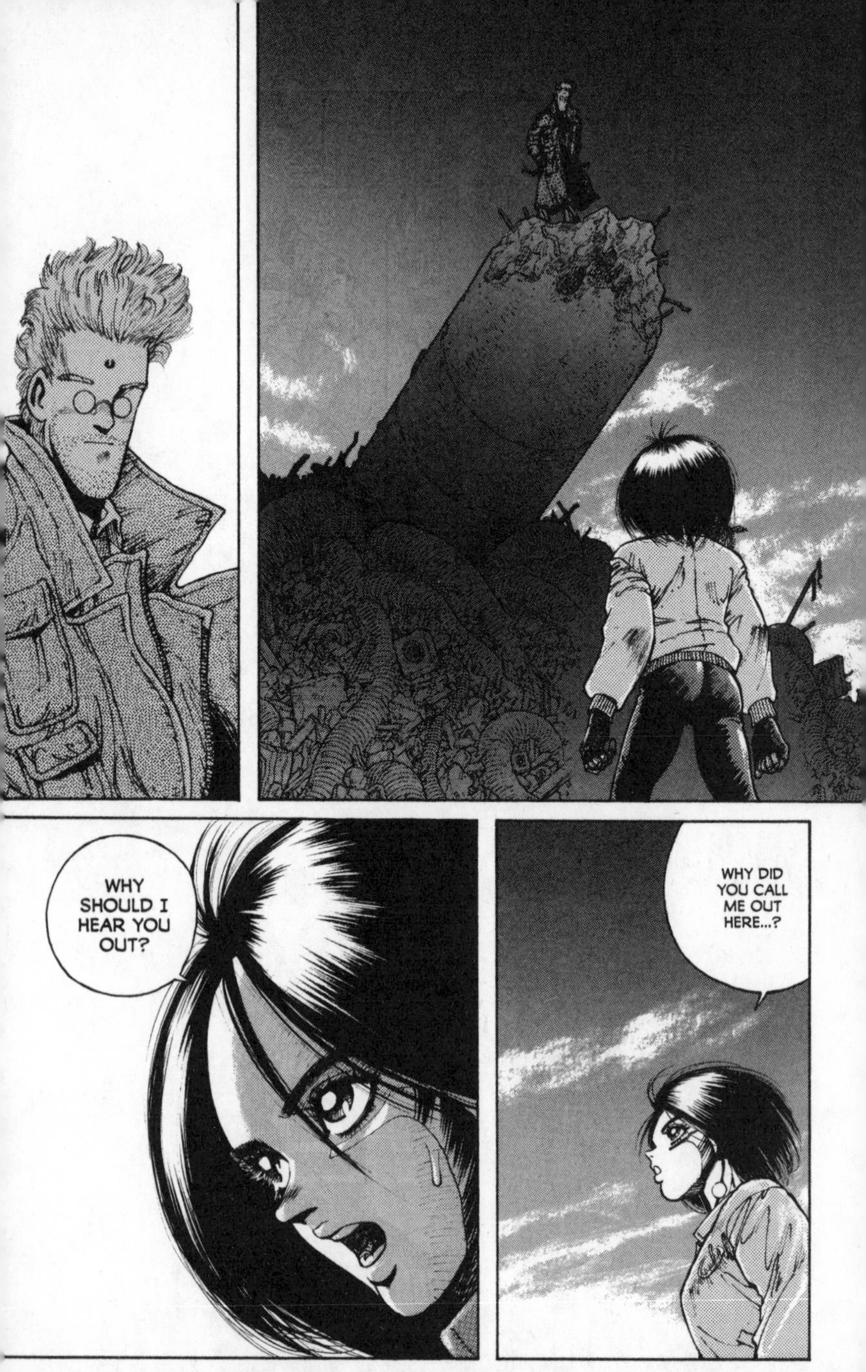
WHY DID YOU CALL ME OUT HERE...?
WHY SHOULD I HEAR YOU OUT?

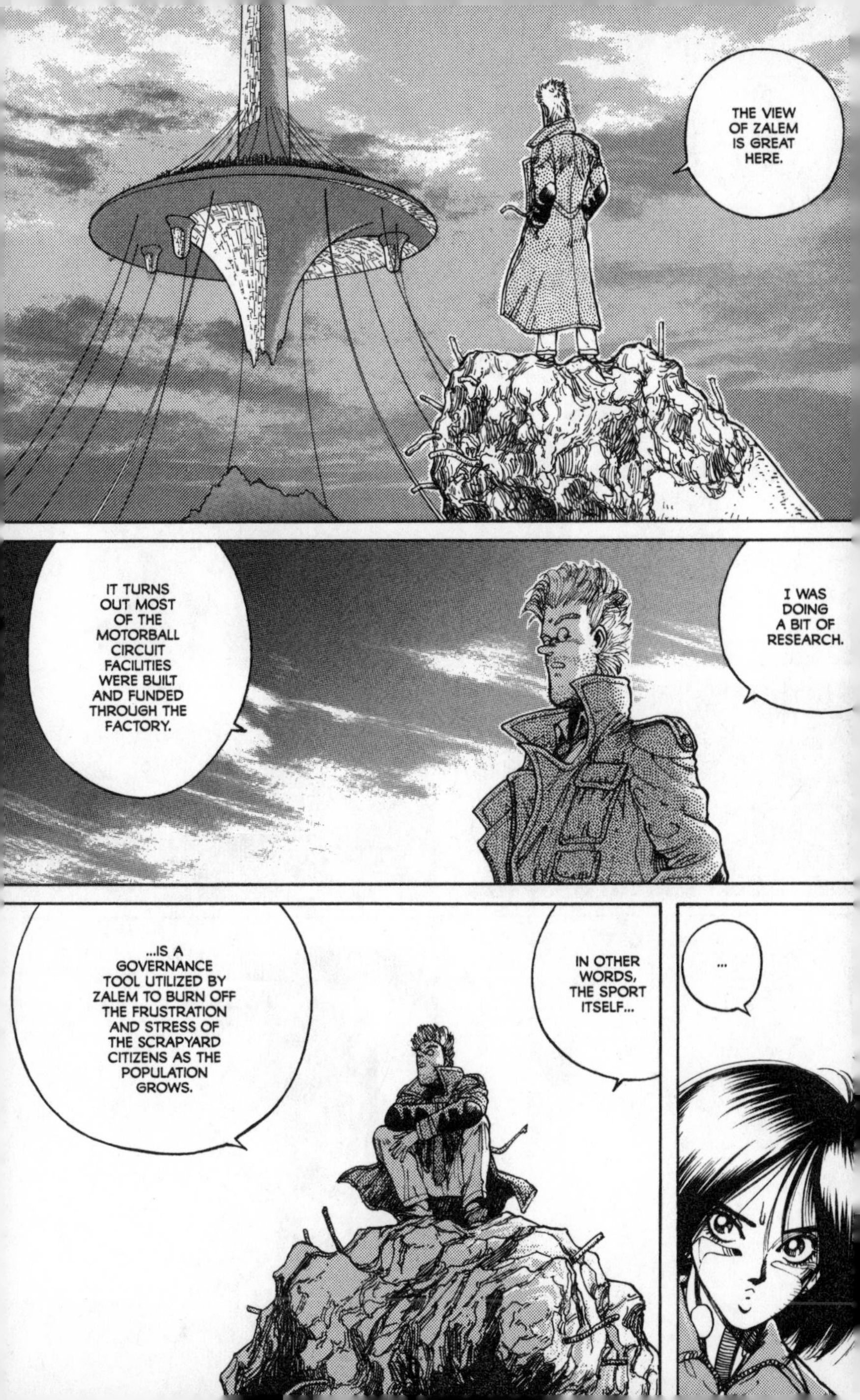
THE VIEW OF ZALEM IS GREAT HERE.
I WAS DOING A BIT OF RESEARCH.
IT TURNS OUT MOST OF THE MOTORBALL CIRCUIT FACILITIES WERE BUILT AND FUNDED THROUGH THE FACTORY.
...
IN OTHER WORDS, THE SPORT ITSELF...
...IS A GOVERNANCE TOOL UTILIZED BY ZALEM TO BURN OFF THE FRUSTRATION AND STRESS OF THE SCRAPYARD CITIZENS AS THE POPULATION GROWS.

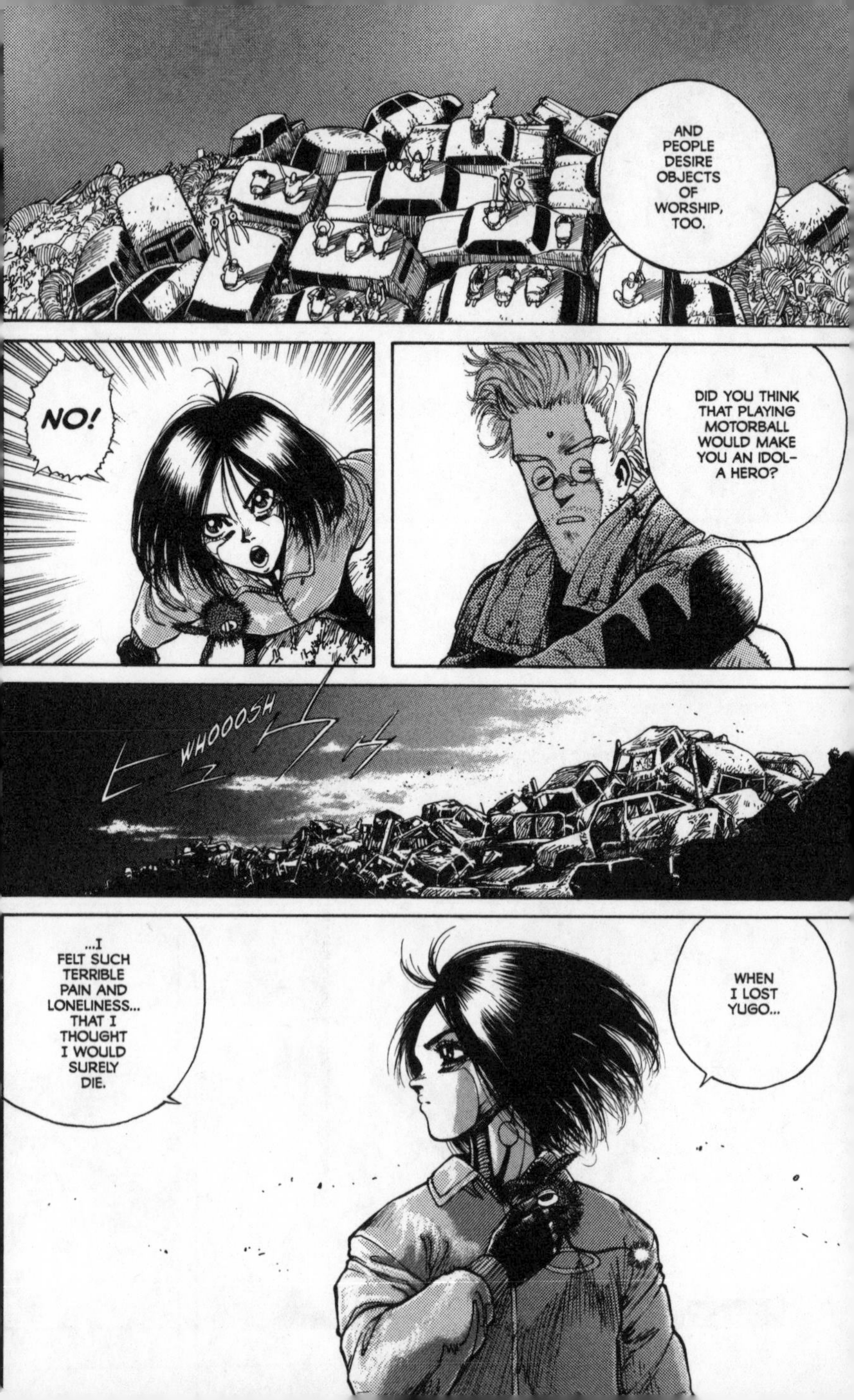
AND PEOPLE DESIRE OBJECTS OF WORSHIP, TOO.
DID YOU THINK THAT PLAYING MOTORBALL WOULD MAKE YOU AN IDOL– A HERO?
NO!
WHOOOSH
WHEN I LOST YUGO...
...I FELT SUCH TERRIBLE PAIN AND LONELINESS... THAT I THOUGHT I WOULD SURELY DIE.

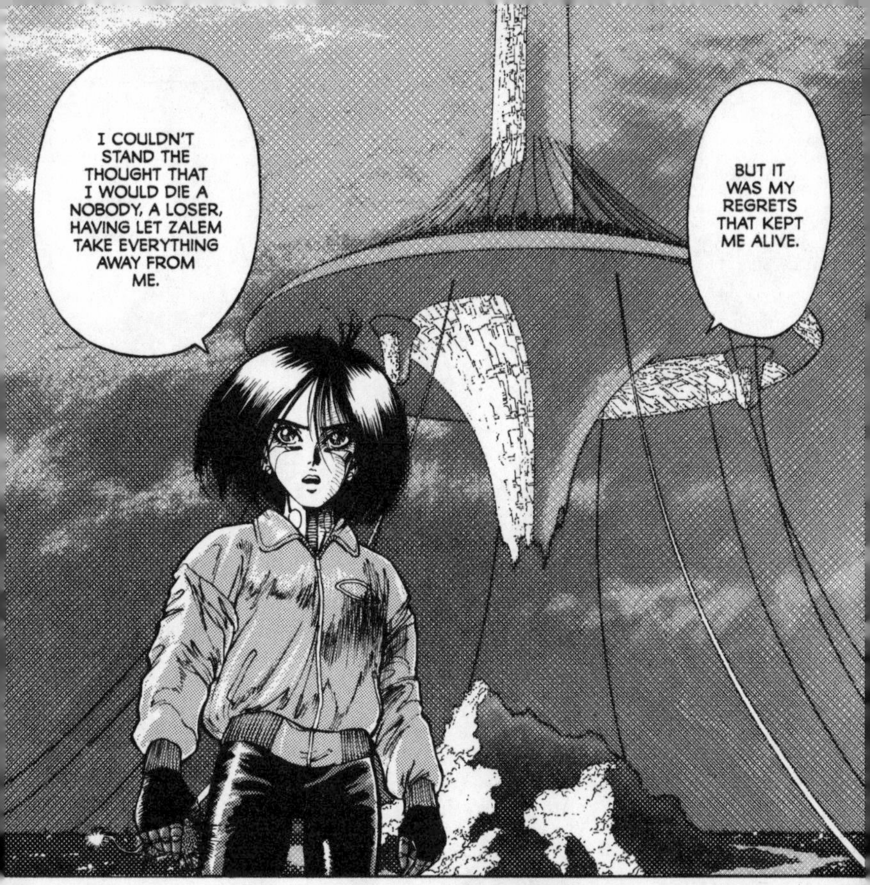
I COULDN'T STAND THE THOUGHT THAT I WOULD DIE A NOBODY, A LOSER, HAVING LET ZALEM TAKE EVERYTHING AWAY FROM ME.
BUT IT WAS MY REGRETS THAT KEPT ME ALIVE.

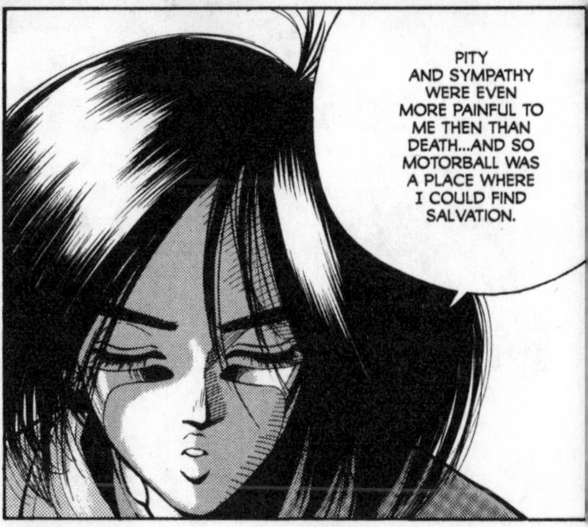
PITY AND SYMPATHY WERE EVEN MORE PAINFUL TO ME THEN THAN DEATH...AND SO MOTORBALL WAS A PLACE WHERE I COULD FIND SALVATION.

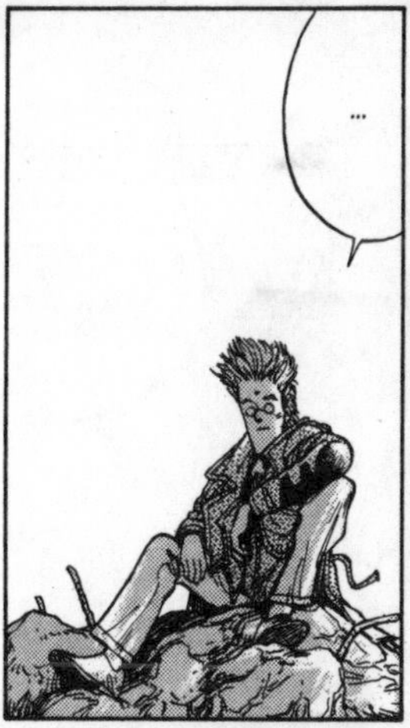
...

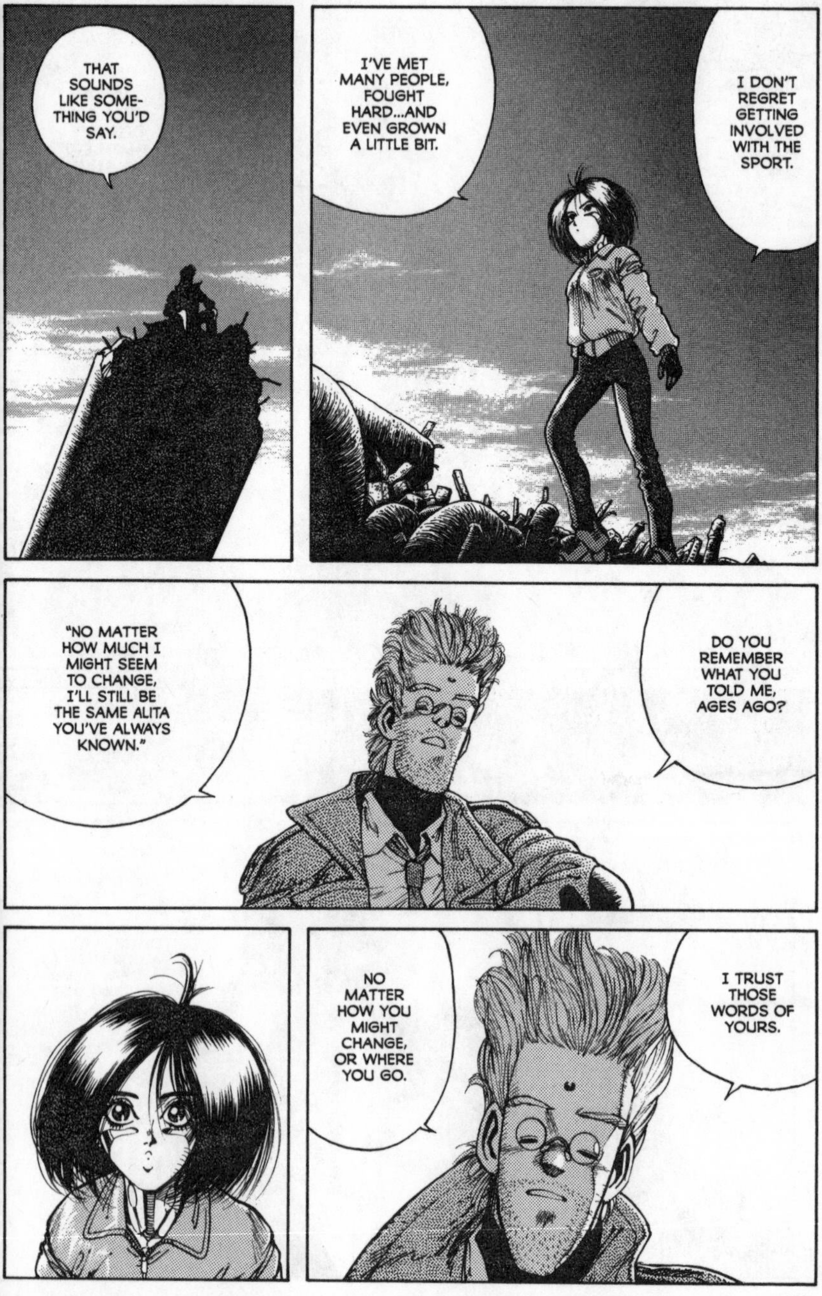
I DON'T REGRET GETTING INVOLVED WITH THE SPORT.
I'VE MET MANY PEOPLE, FOUGHT HARD...AND EVEN GROWN A LITTLE BIT.
THAT SOUNDS LIKE SOME-THING YOU'D SAY.
DO YOU REMEMBER WHAT YOU TOLD ME, AGES AGO?
"NO MATTER HOW MUCH I MIGHT SEEM TO CHANGE, I'LL STILL BE THE SAME ALITA YOU'VE ALWAYS KNOWN."
I TRUST THOSE WORDS OF YOURS.
NO MATTER HOW YOU MIGHT CHANGE, OR WHERE YOU GO.

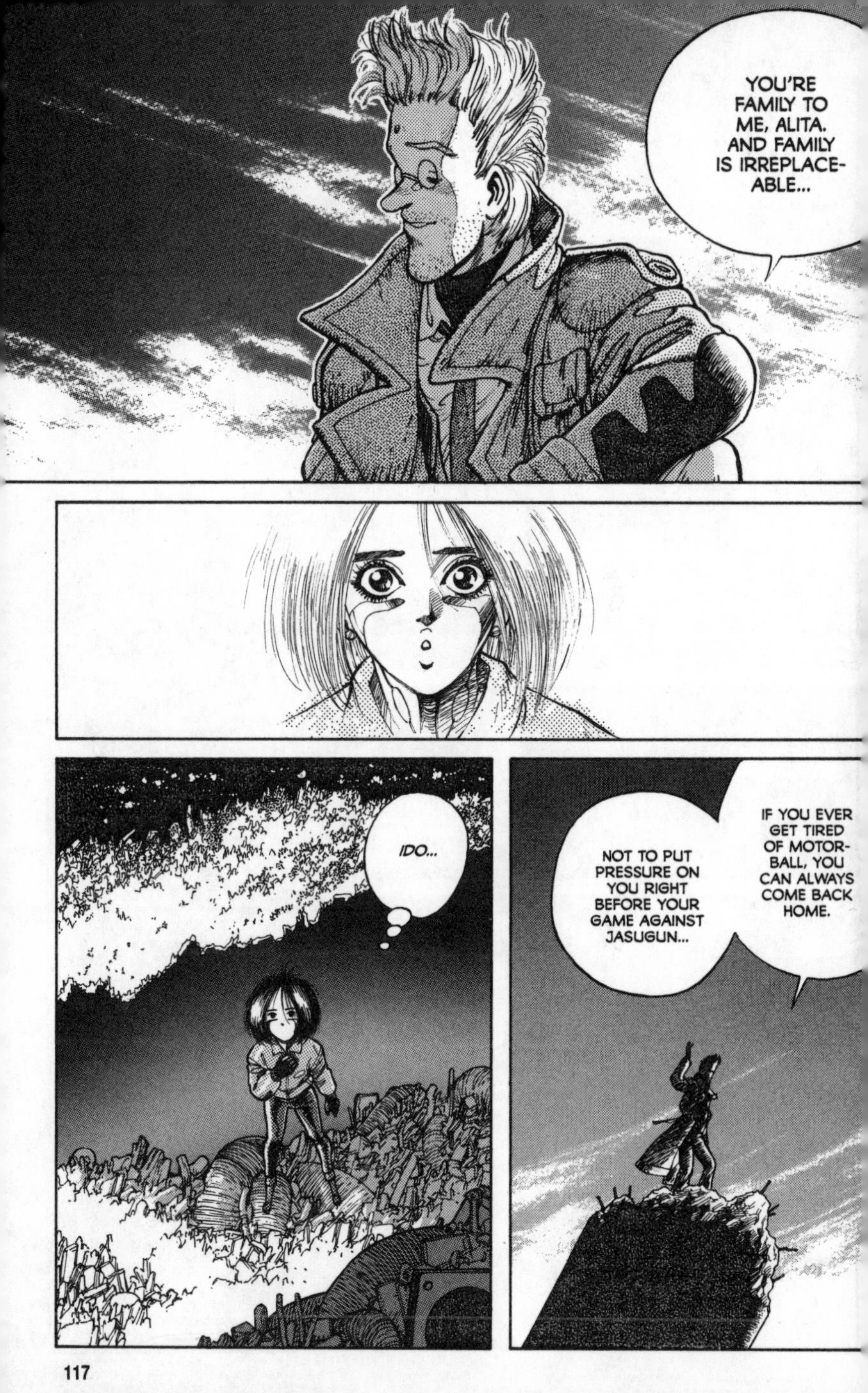
YOU'RE FAMILY TO ME, ALITA. AND FAMILY IS IRREPLACE-ABLE...
IF YOU EVER GET TIRED OF MOTOR-BALL, YOU CAN ALWAYS COME BACK HOME.
NOT TO PUT PRESSURE ON YOU RIGHT BEFORE YOUR GAME AGAINST JASUGUN...
IDO...

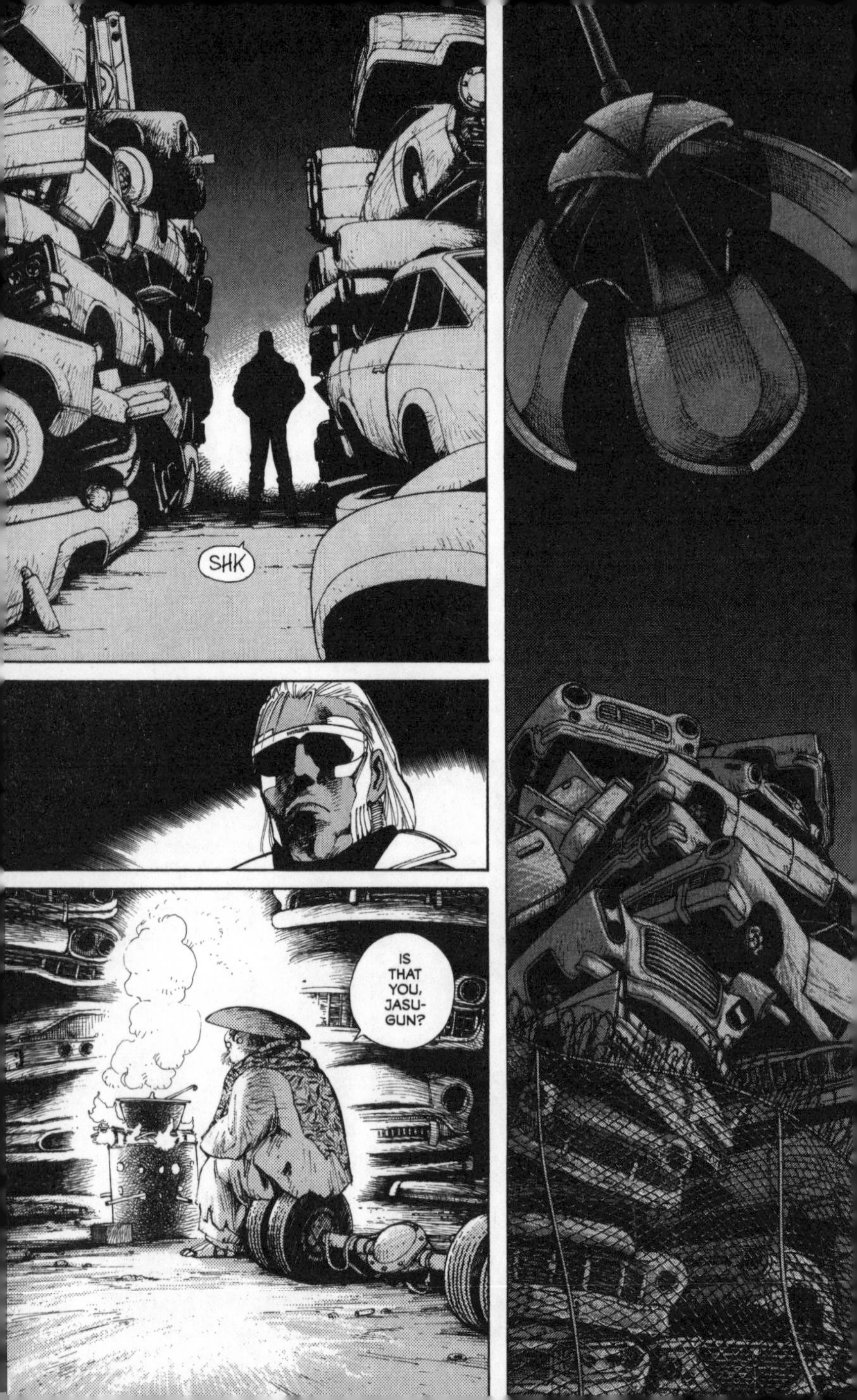
SHK
IS THAT YOU, JASU-GUN?

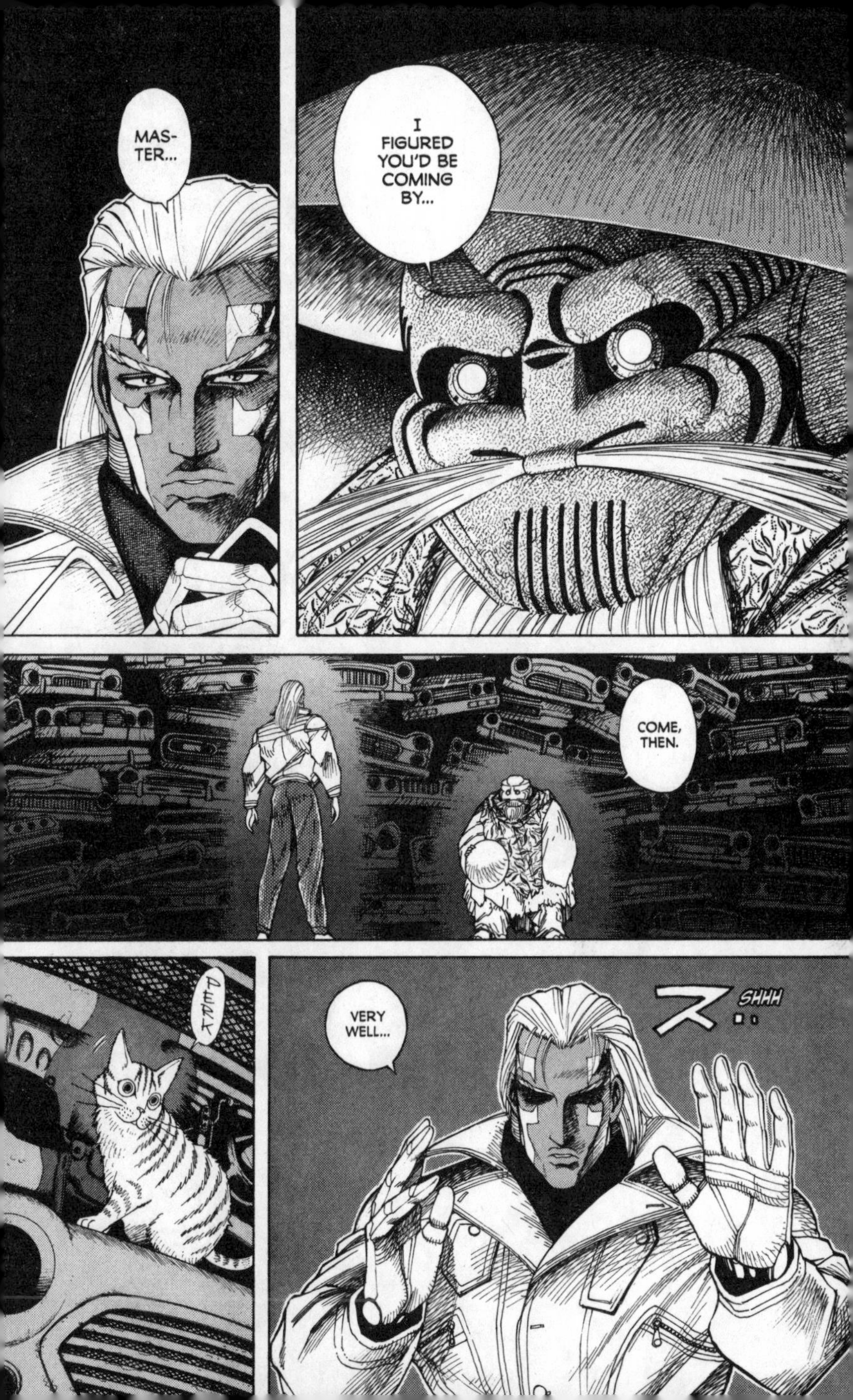
I FIGURED YOU'D BE COMING BY...
MAS-TER...
COME, THEN.
ス
SHHH
VERY WELL...
PERK

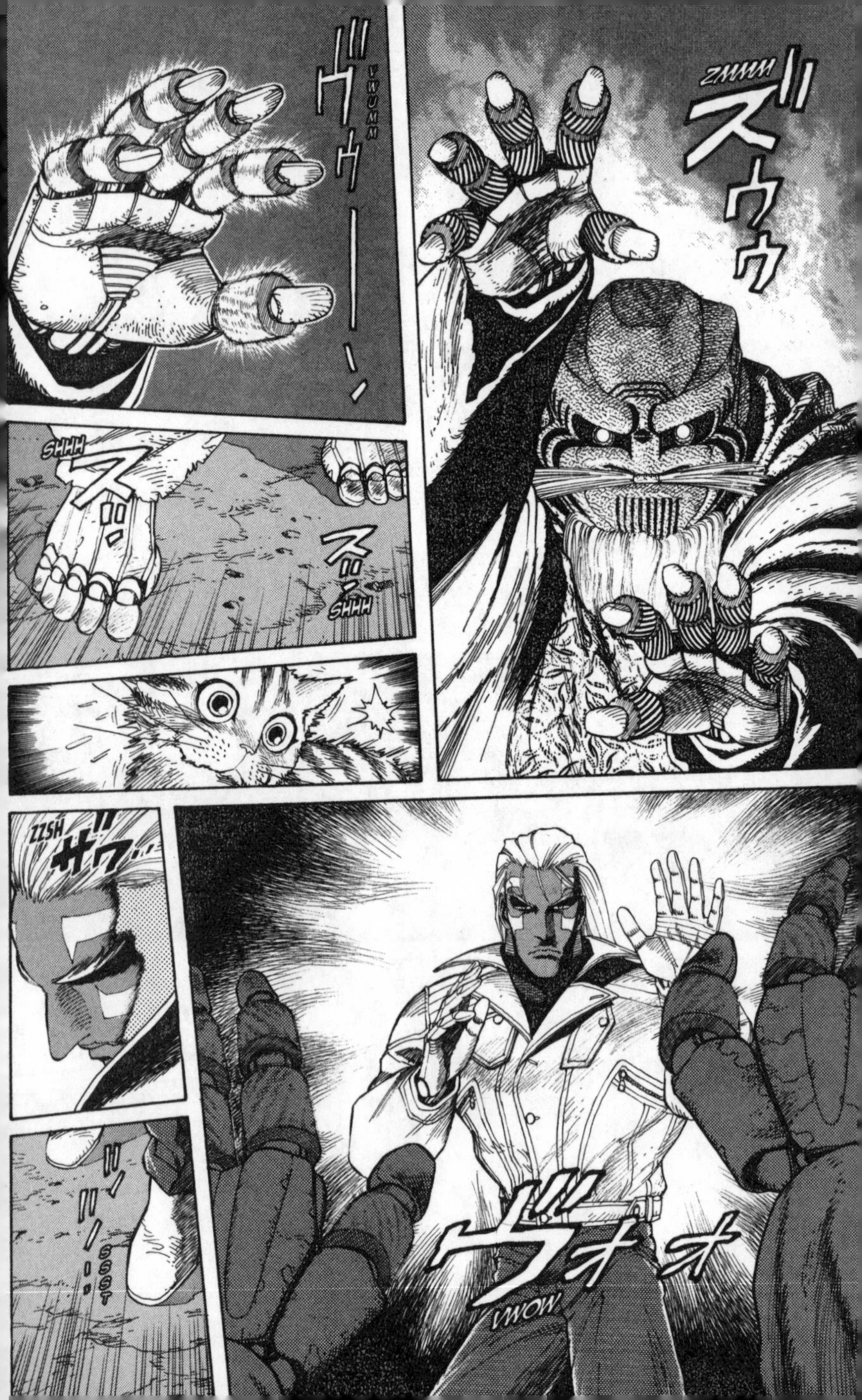
ZMMM
ズスウウ
VWUMM
ヴゥウー…
SHHH
ス
スッ
SHHH
VWOW
ヴォオオ
ZZSH
ザワ…
SSST

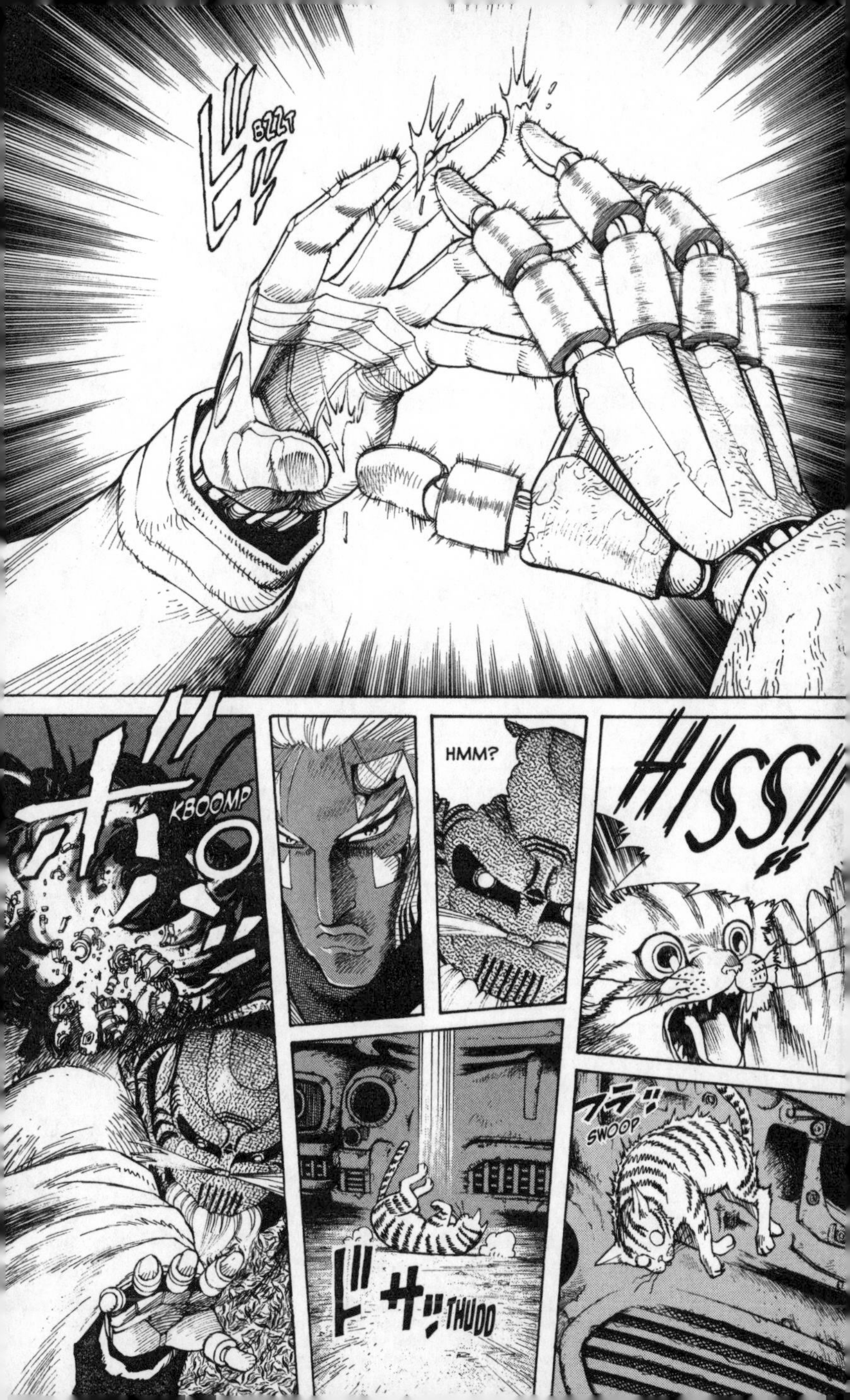

BZZT
HISS!!
HMM?
SWOOP
THUDD
KBOOMP

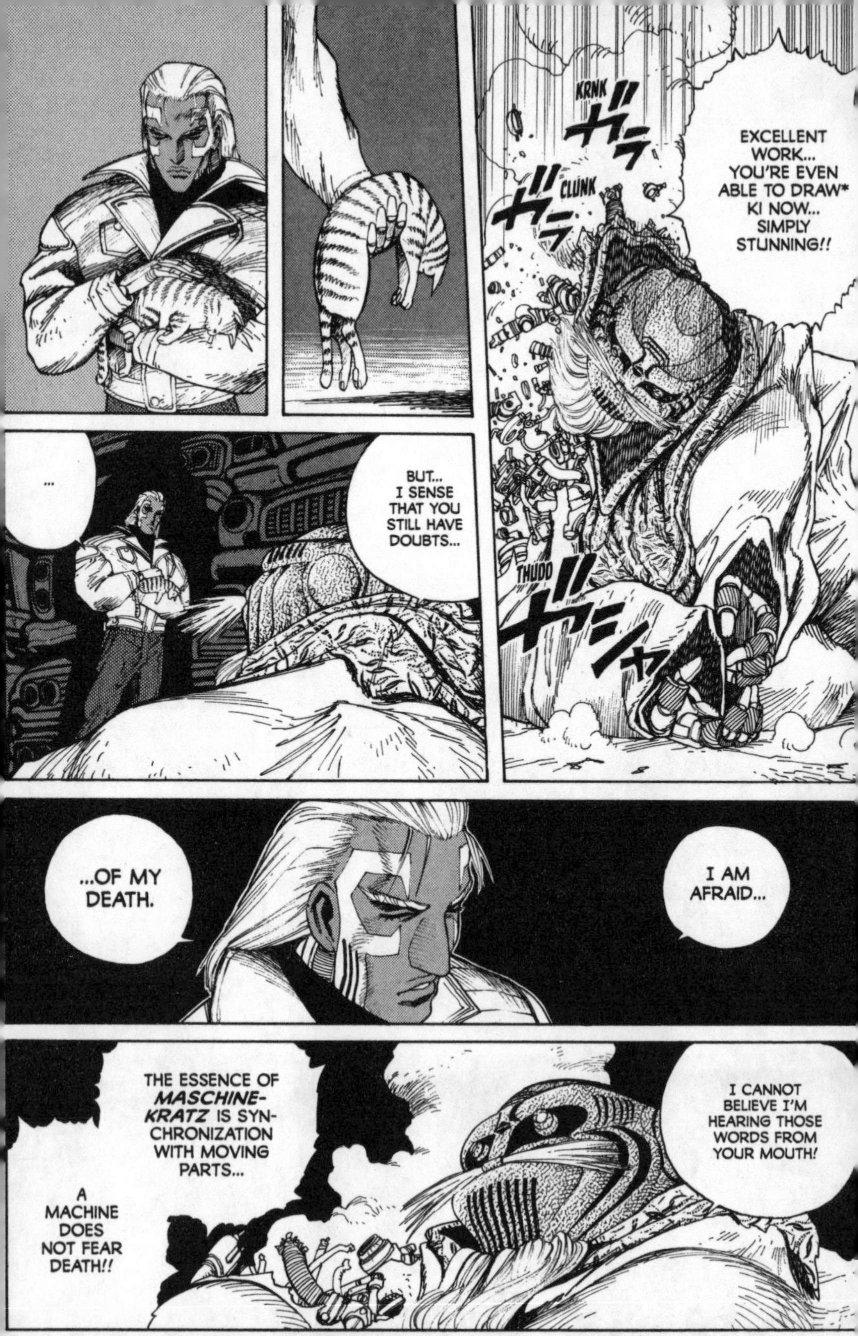
KRNK
CLUNK
EXCELLENT WORK... YOU'RE EVEN ABLE TO DRAW* KI NOW... SIMPLY STUNNING!!
THUDD
BUT... I SENSE THAT YOU STILL HAVE DOUBTS...
...
I AM AFRAID...
...OF MY DEATH.
I CANNOT BELIEVE I'M HEARING THOSE WORDS FROM YOUR MOUTH!
THE ESSENCE OF *MASCHINE-KRATZ* IS SYNCHRONIZATION WITH MOVING PARTS...
A MACHINE DOES NOT FEAR DEATH!!

***Draw:** A high-level "ki" counter attack. All waves have certain characteristics in common: rhythm (frequency), strength (amplitude), and structure (waveform). When two vibrating sources have frequencies that are very close but not identical, the two will gradually pull closer until they are on the same wavelength. When this resonance occurs, there is an exchange of energy between the two sources, and one of the two will absorb all the energy of the other. This is called "drawing" ki.

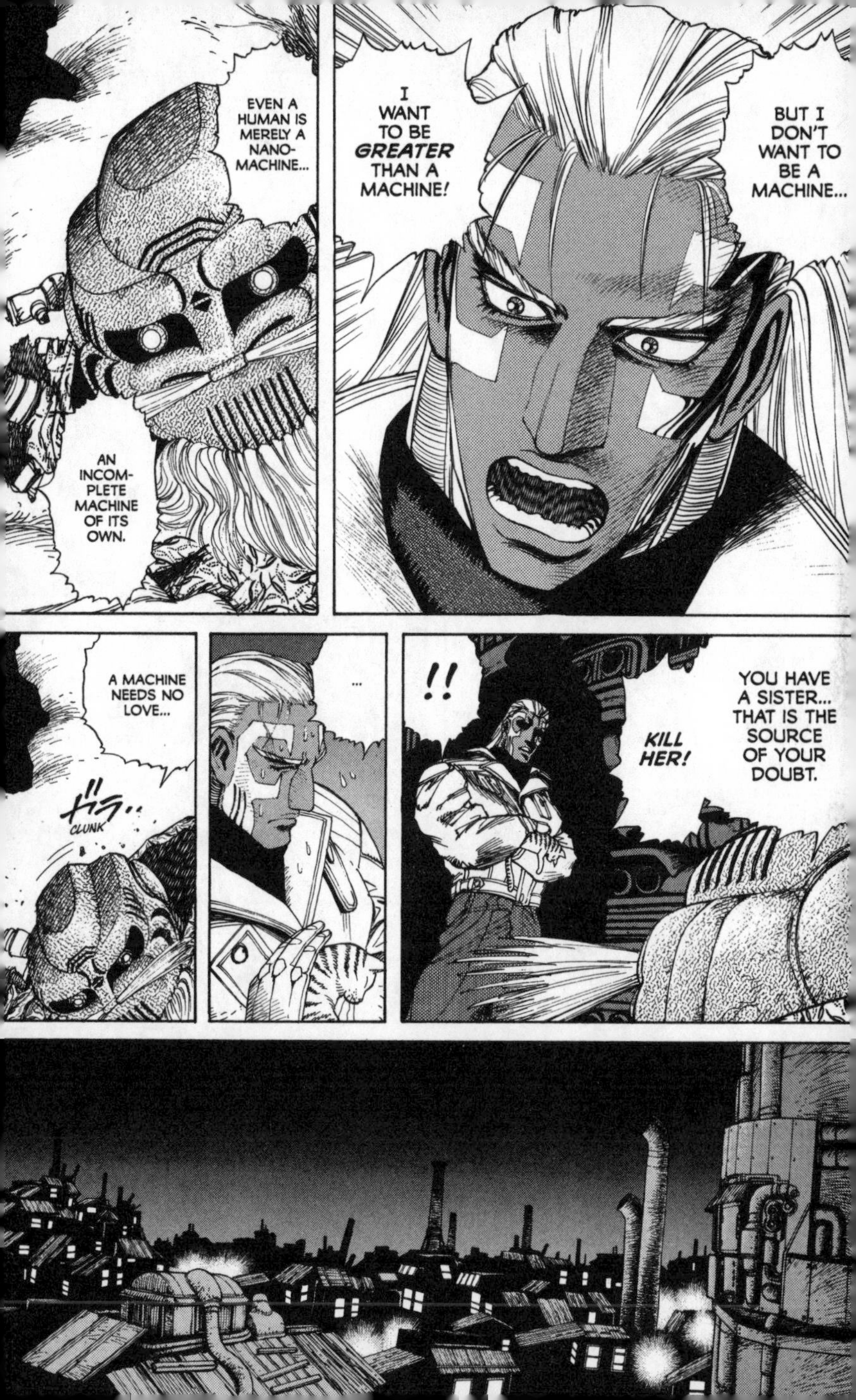

BUT I DON'T WANT TO BE A MACHINE...
I WANT TO BE ***GREATER*** THAN A MACHINE!
EVEN A HUMAN IS MERELY A NANO-MACHINE...
AN INCOMPLETE MACHINE OF ITS OWN.
YOU HAVE A SISTER... THAT IS THE SOURCE OF YOUR DOUBT.
KILL HER!
!!
...
A MACHINE NEEDS NO LOVE...
CLUNK

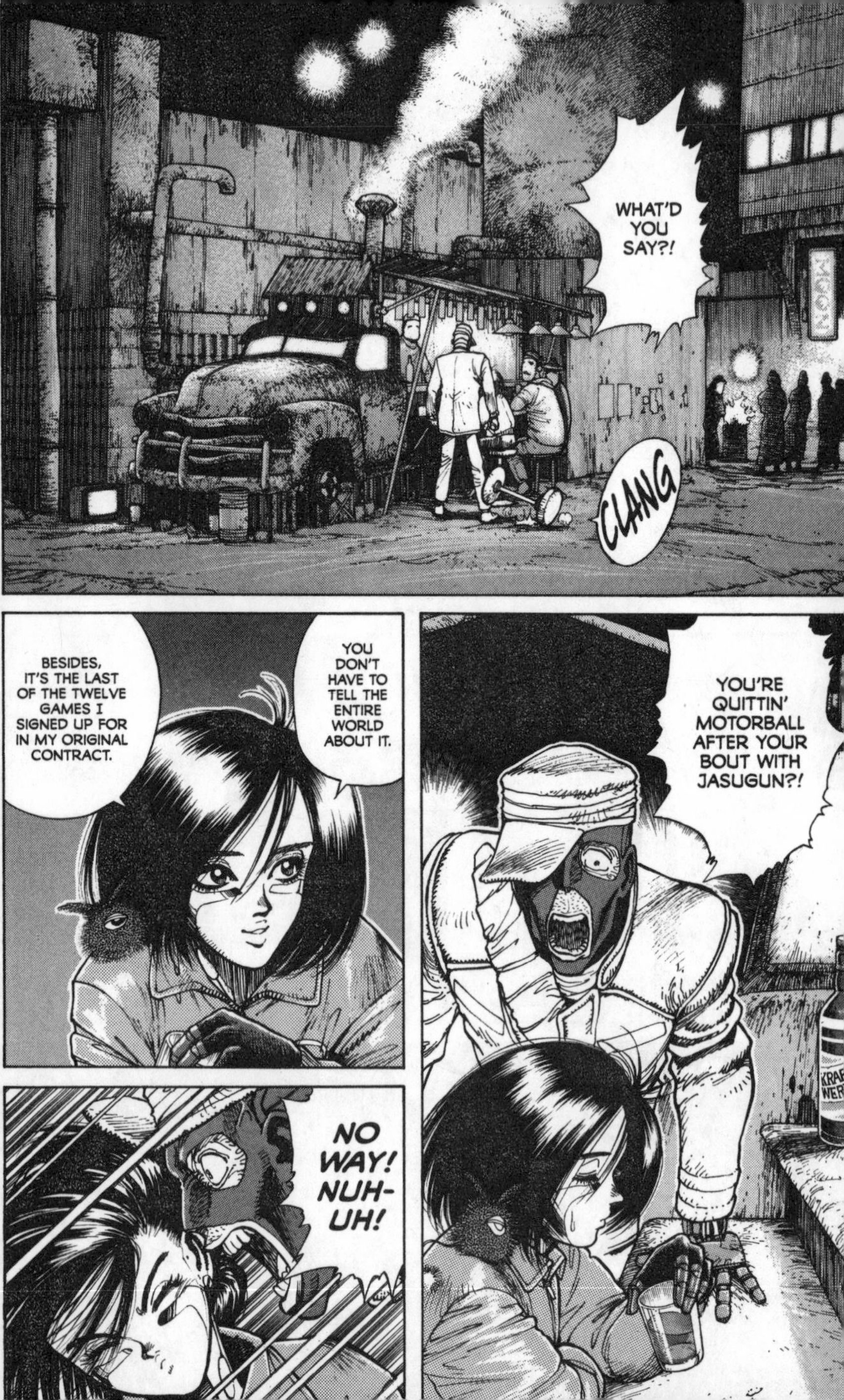
WHAT'D YOU SAY?!
MOON
CLANG
YOU'RE QUITTIN' MOTORBALL AFTER YOUR BOUT WITH JASUGUN?!
YOU DON'T HAVE TO TELL THE ENTIRE WORLD ABOUT IT.
BESIDES, IT'S THE LAST OF THE TWELVE GAMES I SIGNED UP FOR IN MY ORIGINAL CONTRACT.
NO WAY! NUH-UH!

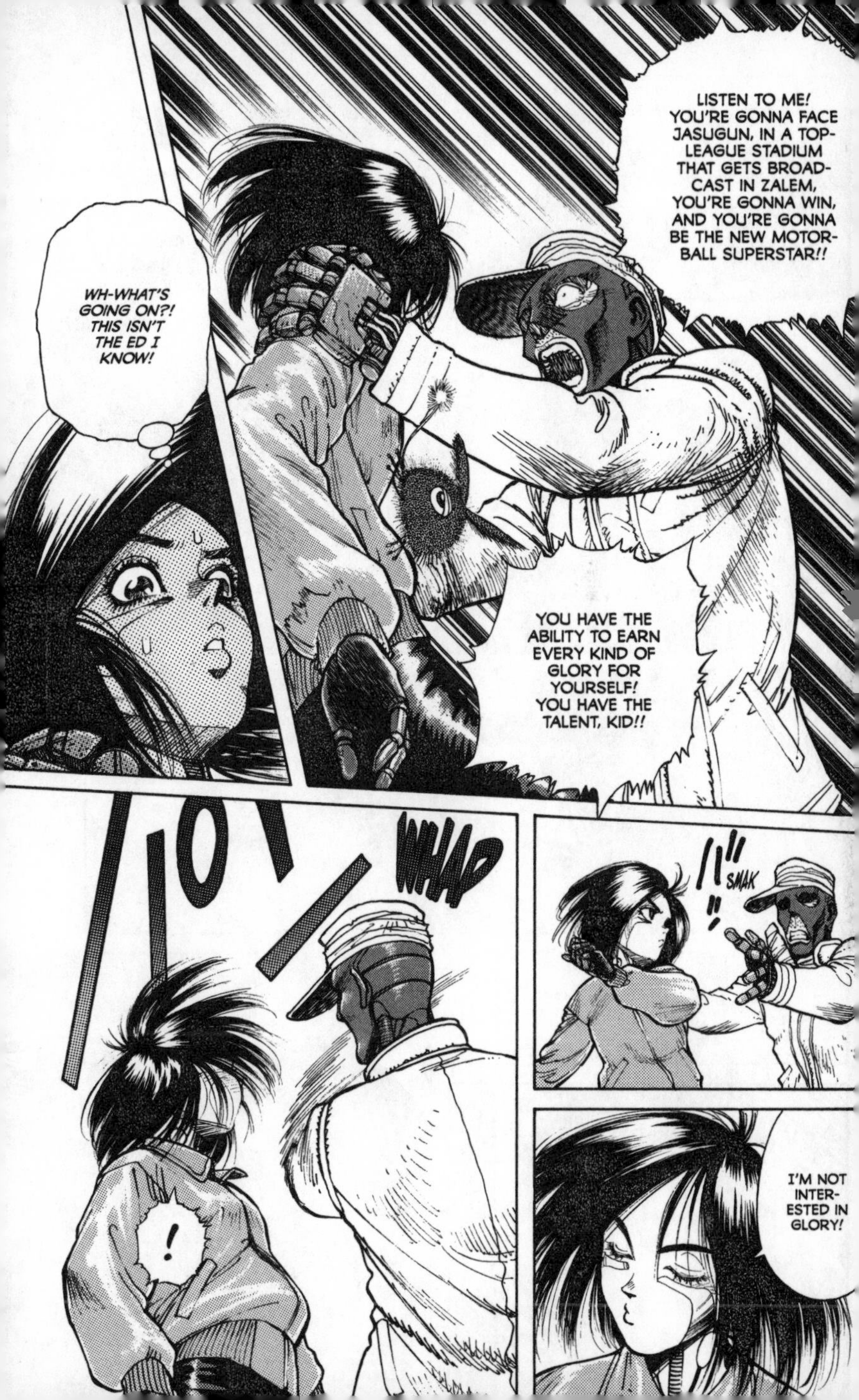

LISTEN TO ME! YOU'RE GONNA FACE JASUGUN, IN A TOP-LEAGUE STADIUM THAT GETS BROADCAST IN ZALEM, YOU'RE GONNA WIN, AND YOU'RE GONNA BE THE NEW MOTORBALL SUPERSTAR!!
YOU HAVE THE ABILITY TO EARN EVERY KIND OF GLORY FOR YOURSELF! YOU HAVE THE TALENT, KID!!
WH-WHAT'S GOING ON?! THIS ISN'T THE ED I KNOW!
SMAK
I'M NOT INTERESTED IN GLORY!
WHAP
!

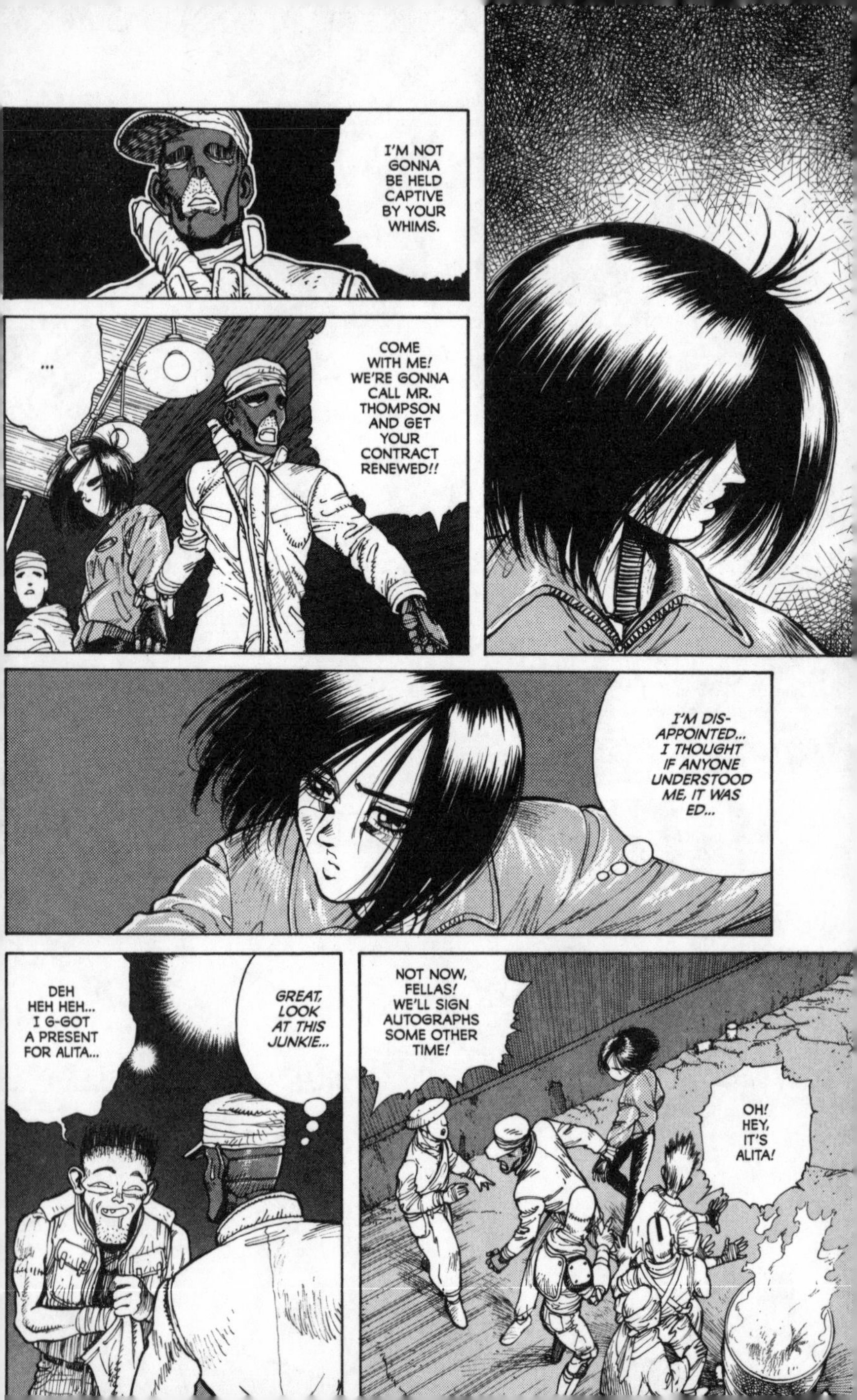
I'M NOT GONNA BE HELD CAPTIVE BY YOUR WHIMS.
COME WITH ME! WE'RE GONNA CALL MR. THOMPSON AND GET YOUR CONTRACT RENEWED!!
...
I'M DIS-APPOINTED... I THOUGHT IF ANYONE UNDERSTOOD ME, IT WAS ED...
NOT NOW, FELLAS! WE'LL SIGN AUTOGRAPHS SOME OTHER TIME!
OH! HEY, IT'S ALITA!
GREAT, LOOK AT THIS JUNKIE...
DEH HEH HEH... I G-GOT A PRESENT FOR ALITA...

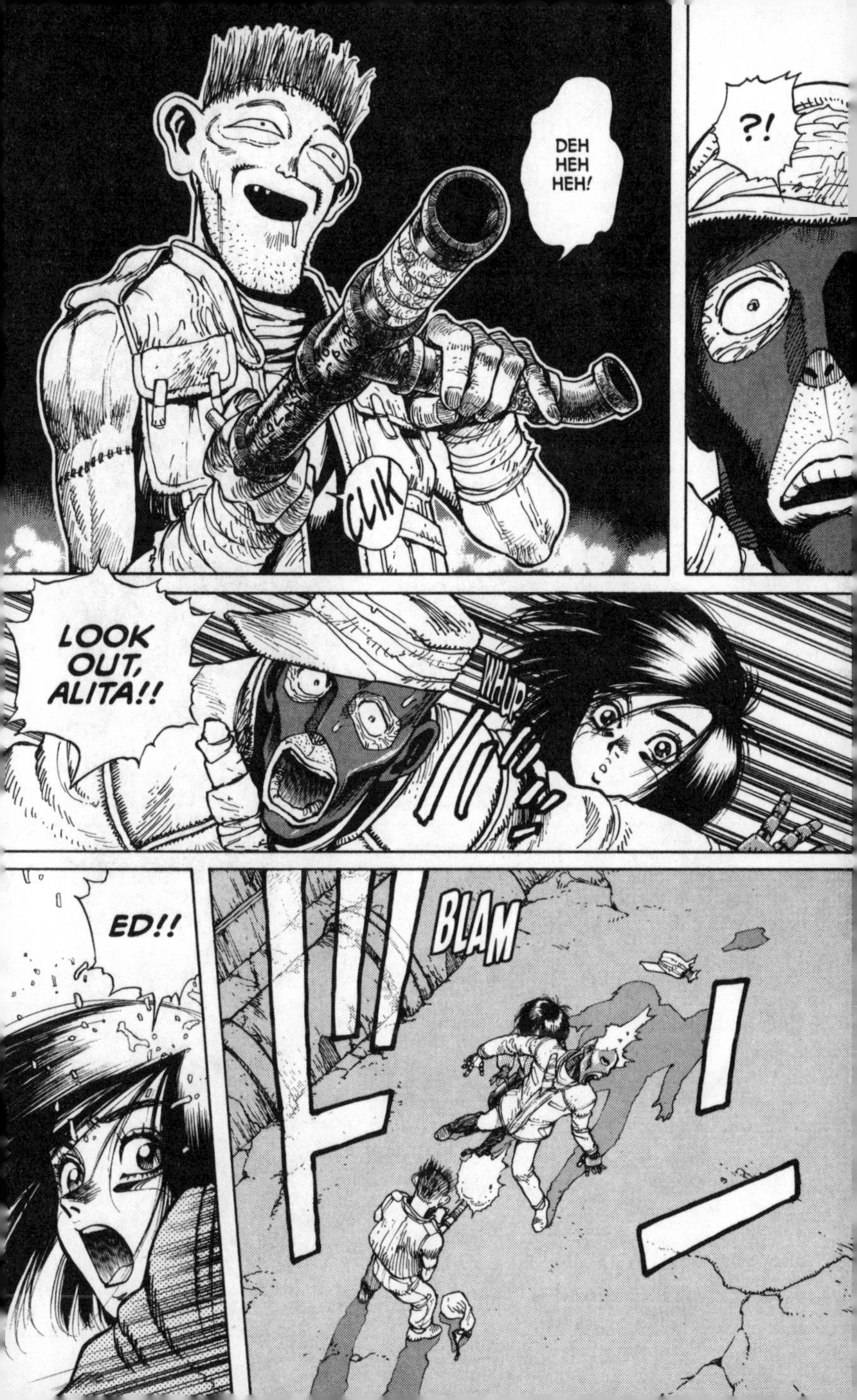
?!
DEH HEH HEH!
CLIK
WHUP
LOOK OUT, ALITA!!
BLAM
ED!!

HAH! I GOT 'IM! LUCKY ME, HONEYBEE, ENTROPY*...
BWA HAW HAW
SHAKK
PWEE!
I'LL BE DAMNED...IF I AIN'T THE UNLUCKIEST SON OF A BITCH...
HERE, ALITA...THIS BLADE IS... FOR YOU...

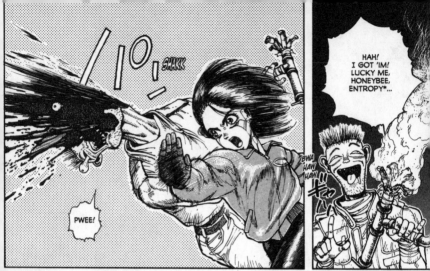

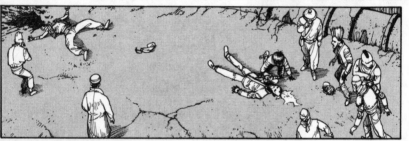

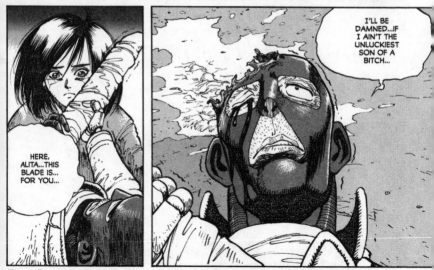

***Entropy:** The gradual transition of energy from order to disorder. Or in this case, a rhyme.

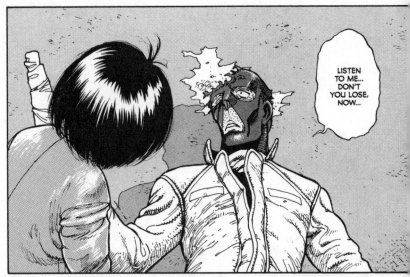

LISTEN TO ME... DON'T YOU LOSE, NOW...
AW DAMN, THERE GOES MY HAND...
カタ カタ カタ
RATTLE
RATTLE カタ
NEED MY... MED...
カタ カタ
RAT RATTL
カタカタ
RATTLE

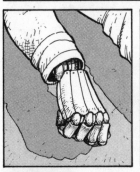

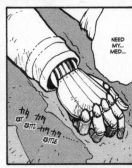

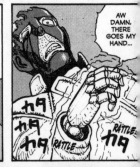

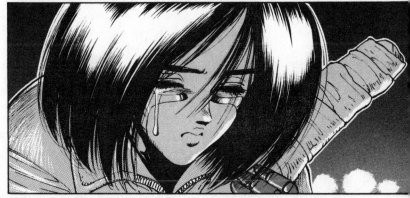

KIMJI
(SHORT FOR
KIMUJINA)

FIGHT_021 Outsider

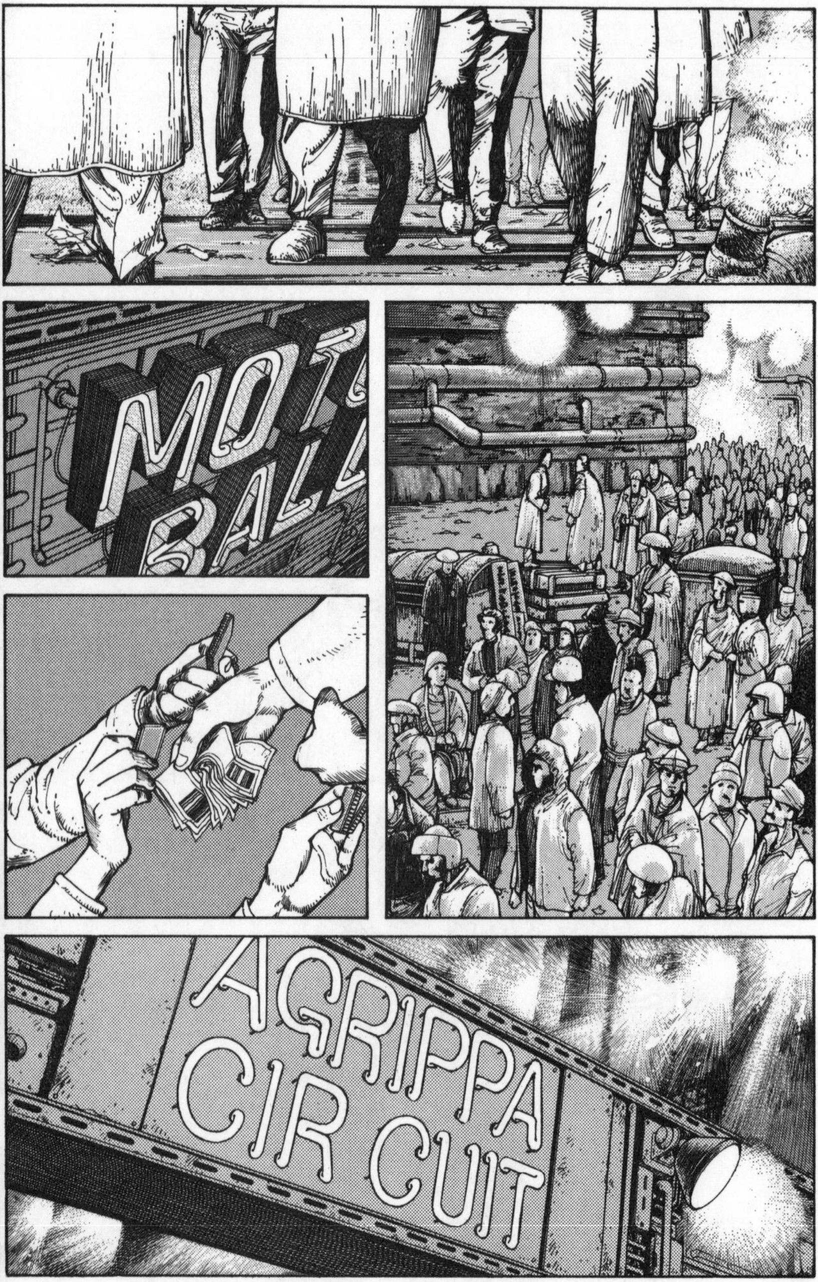
AGRIPPA
CIR CUIT

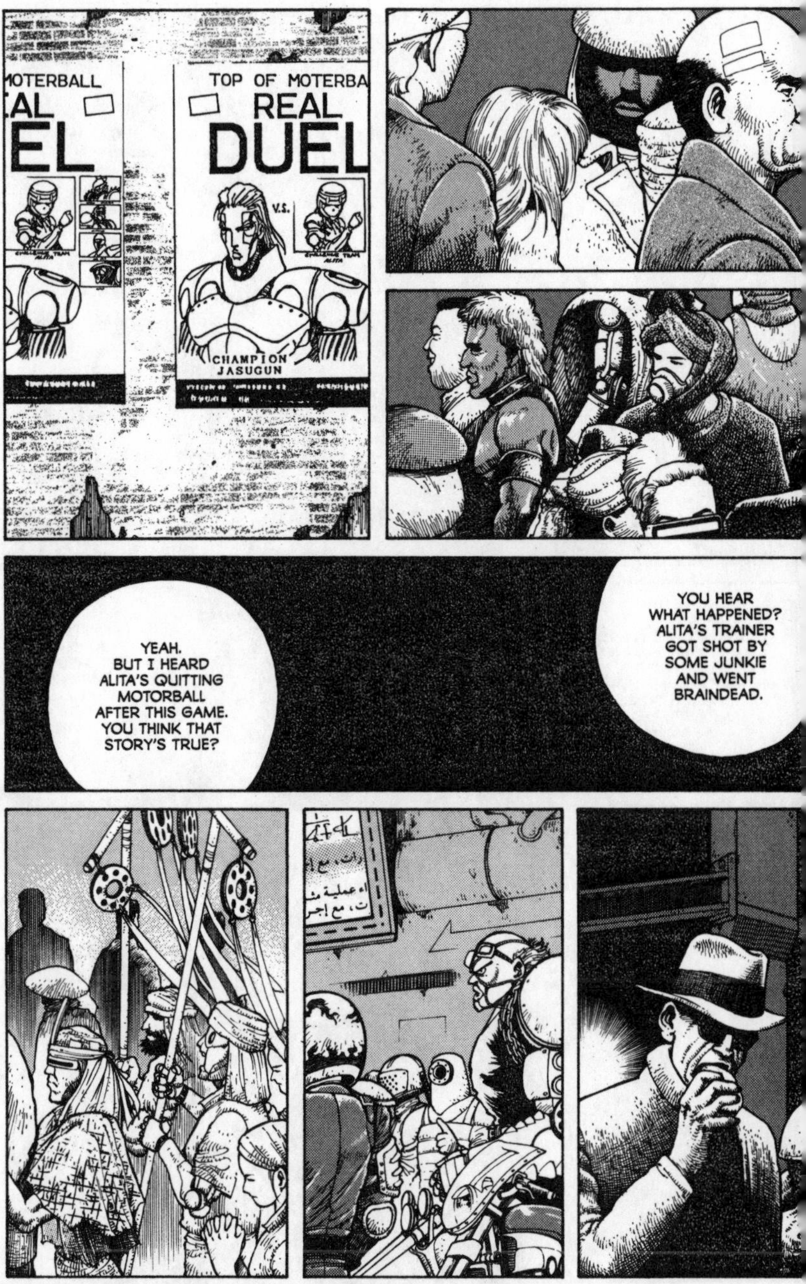
TOP OF MOTERBA
REAL
DUEL
V.S.
CHAMPION JASUGUN
YOU HEAR WHAT HAPPENED? ALITA'S TRAINER GOT SHOT BY SOME JUNKIE AND WENT BRAINDEAD.
YEAH. BUT I HEARD ALITA'S QUITTING MOTORBALL AFTER THIS GAME. YOU THINK THAT STORY'S TRUE?

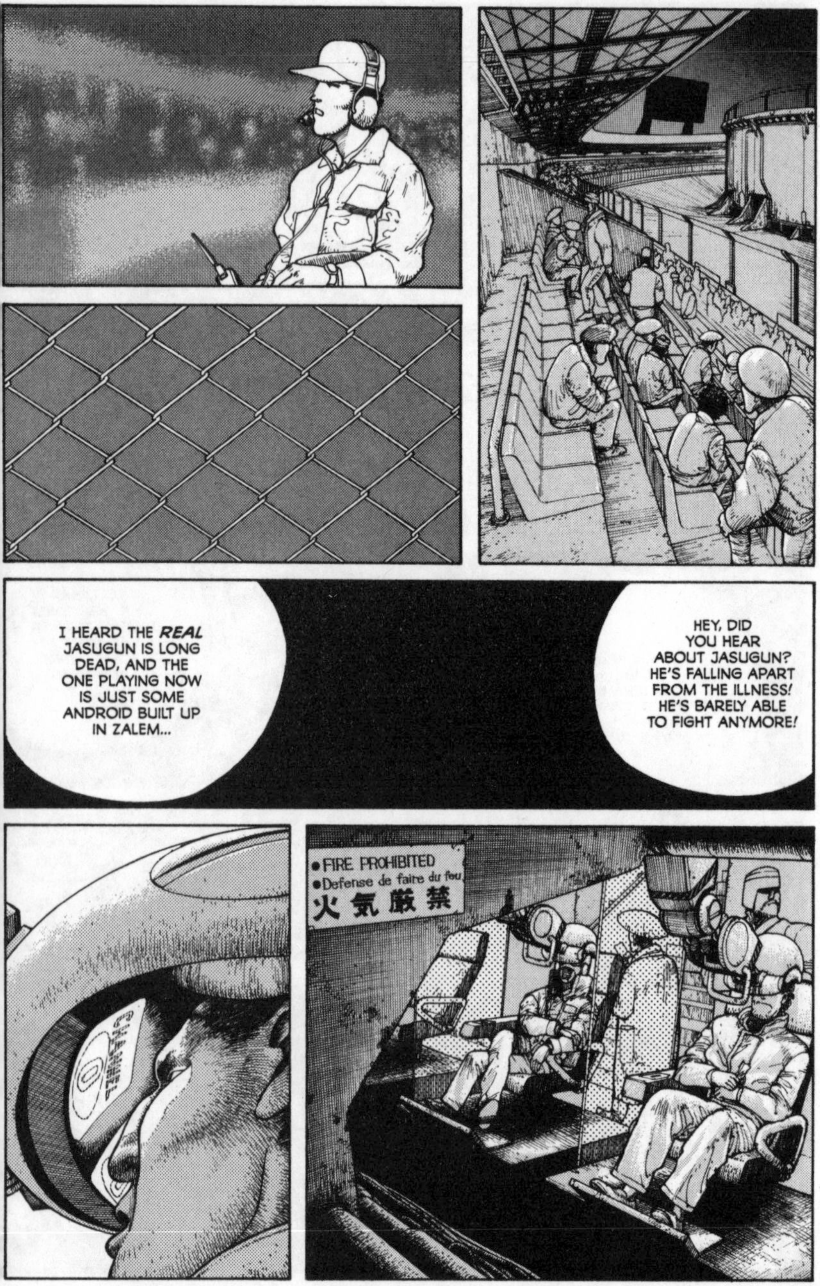
HEY, DID YOU HEAR ABOUT JASUGUN? HE'S FALLING APART FROM THE ILLNESS! HE'S BARELY ABLE TO FIGHT ANYMORE!
I HEARD THE ***REAL*** JASUGUN IS LONG DEAD, AND THE ONE PLAYING NOW IS JUST SOME ANDROID BUILT UP IN ZALEM...
●FIRE PROHIBITED
●Defense de faire du feu
火気厳禁

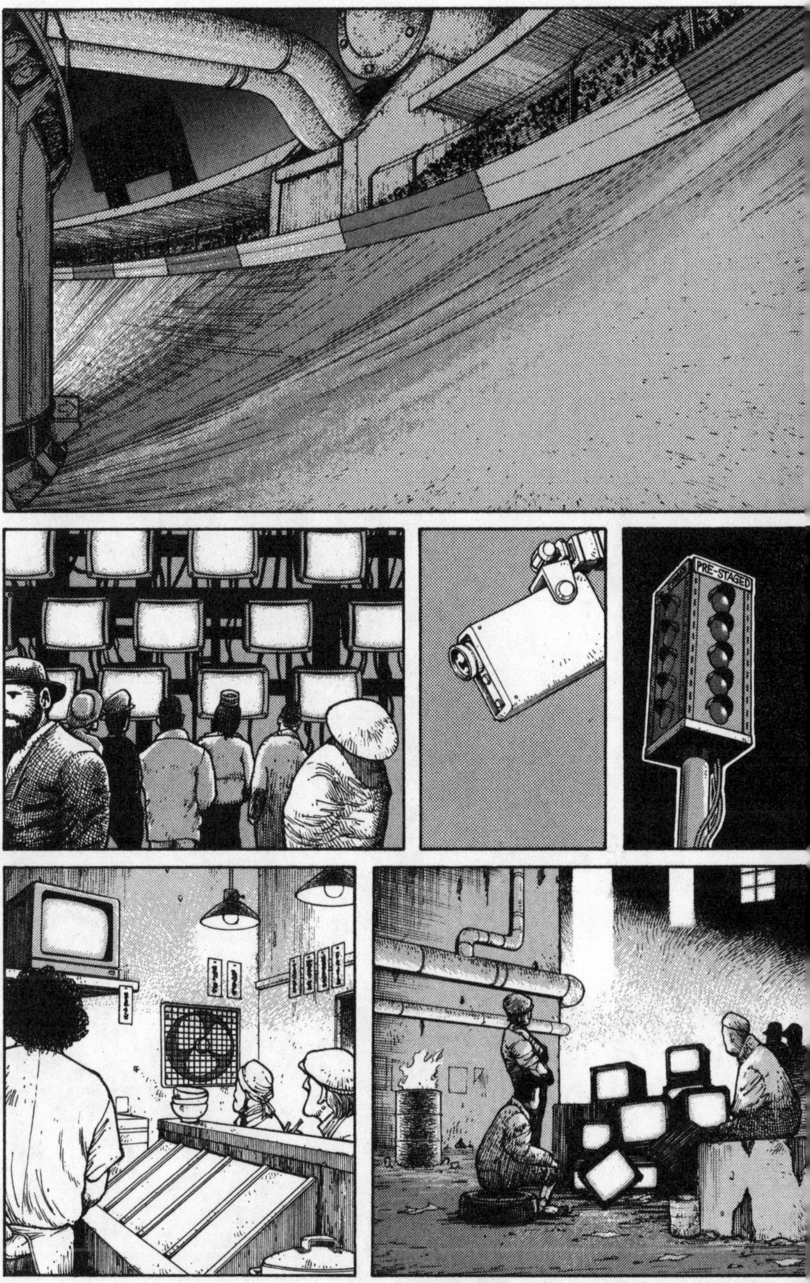
PRE-STAGED

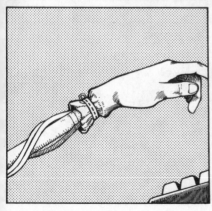

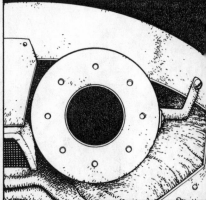

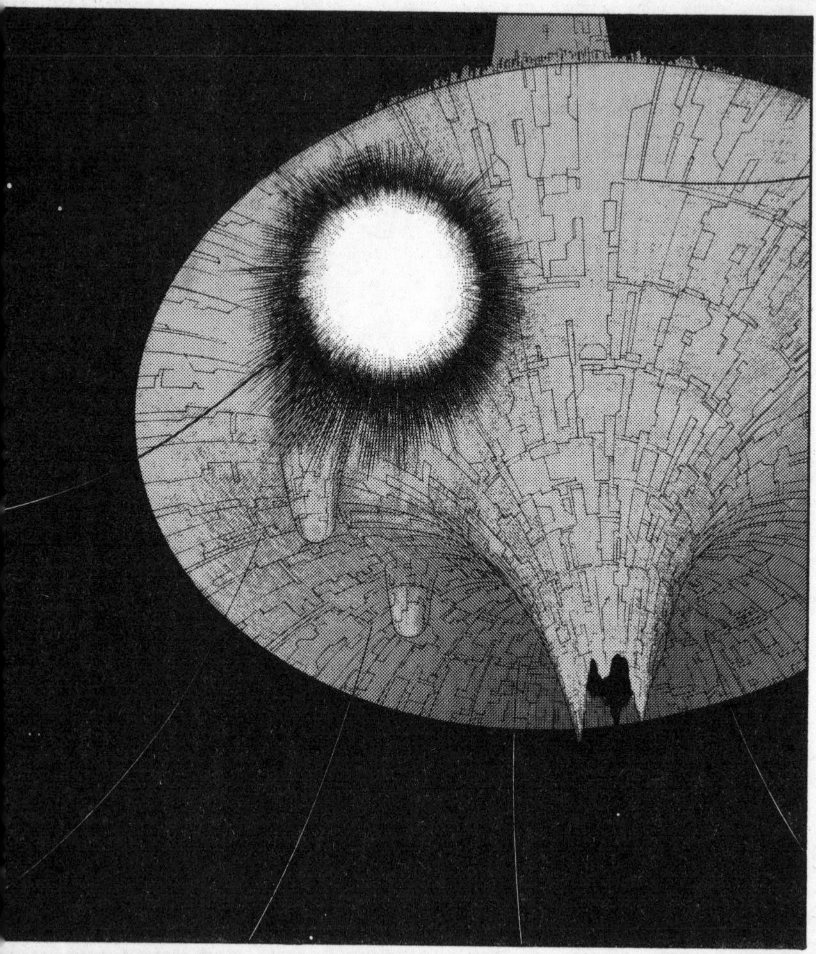

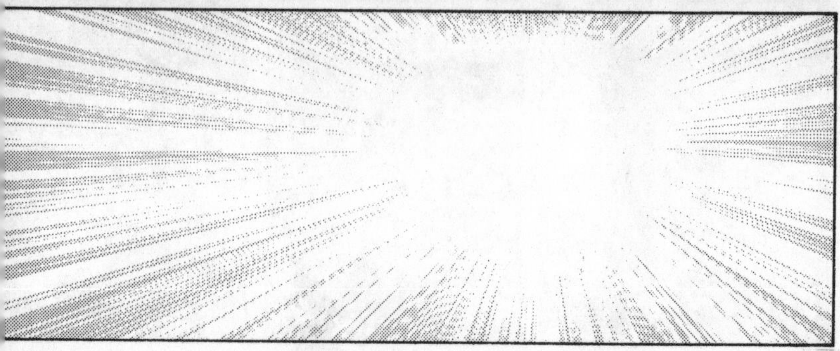

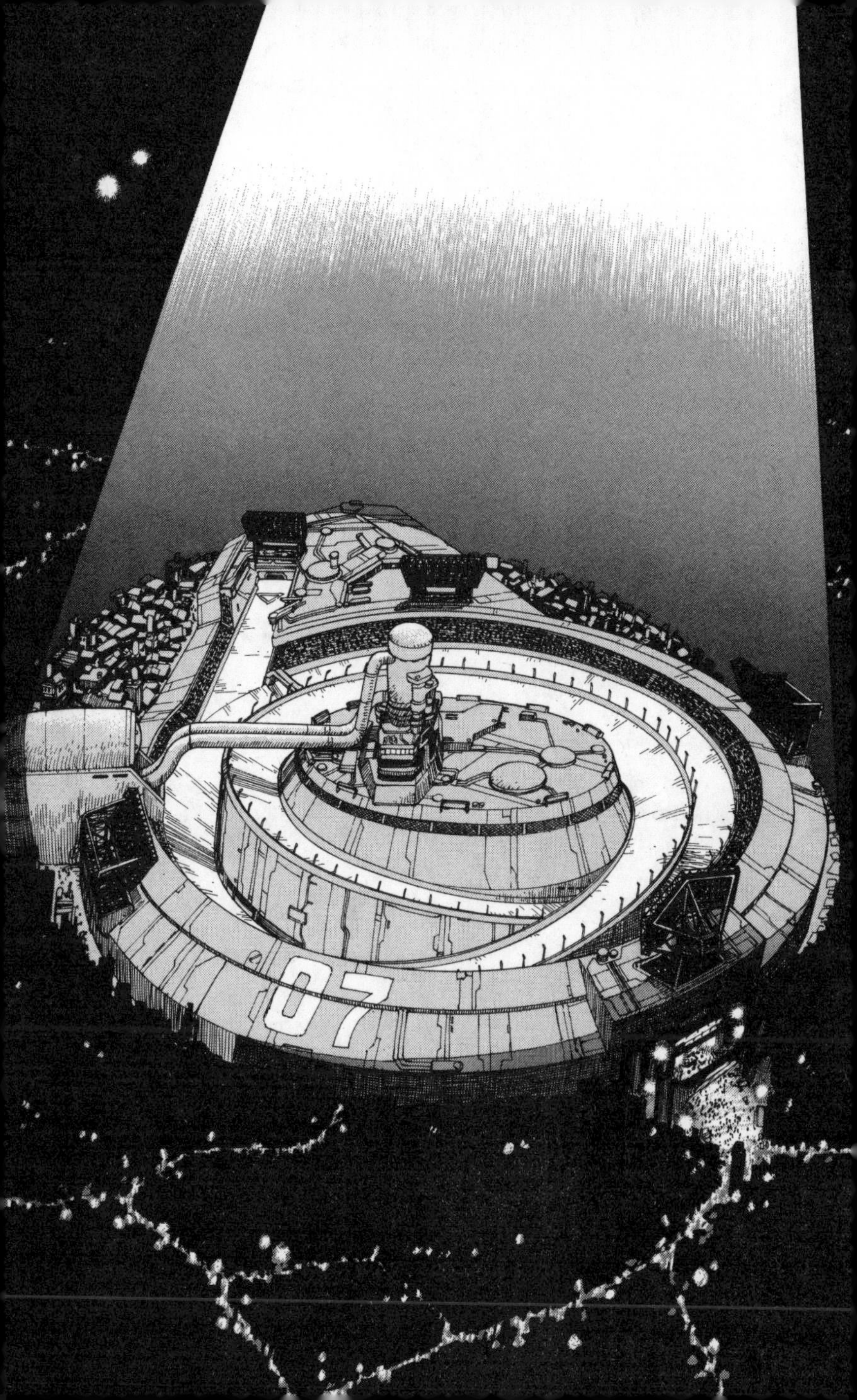
07

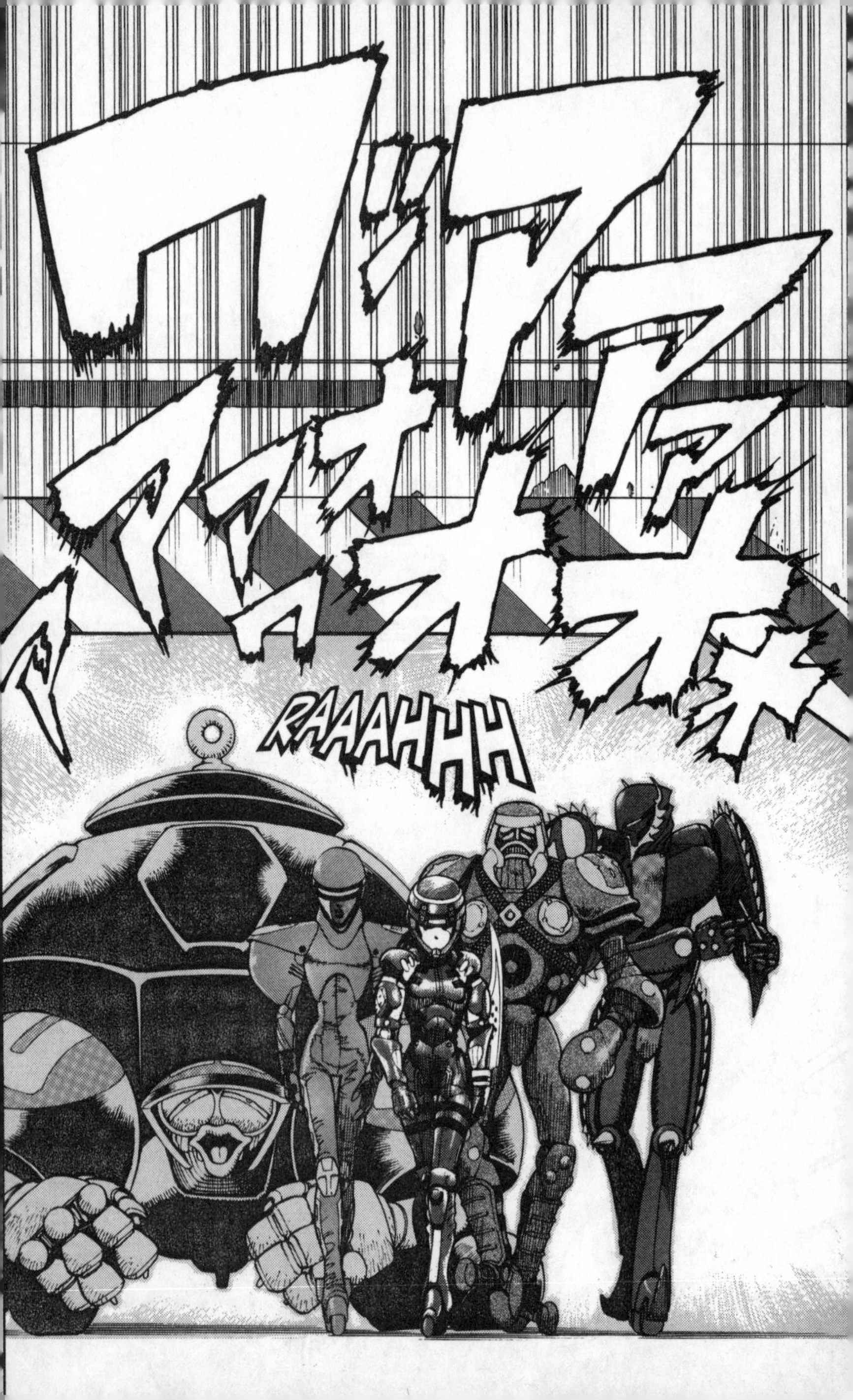
RAAAHHH

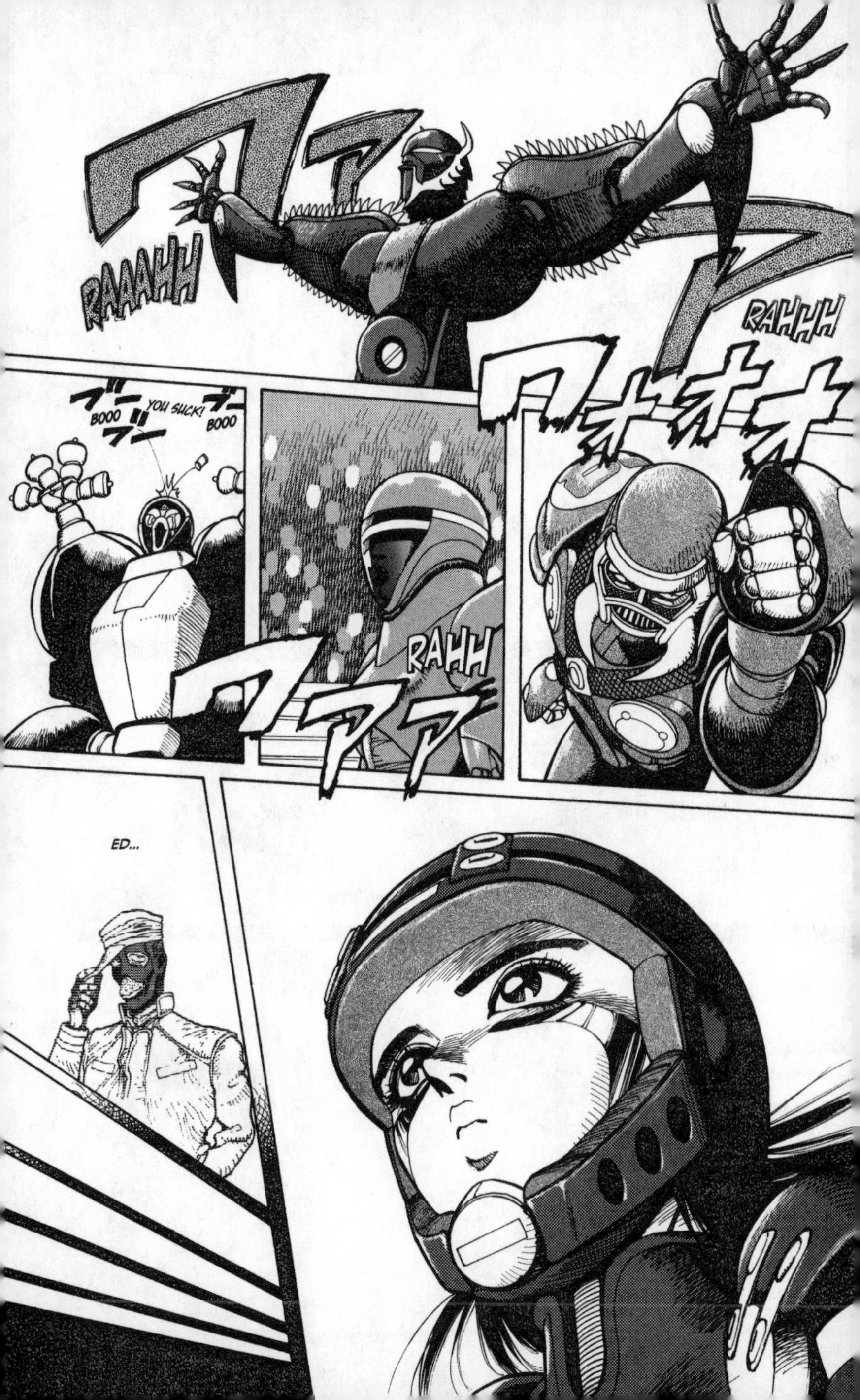
RAHHH
RAAAHH
RAHH
BOO
YOU SUCK!
BOO
ED...

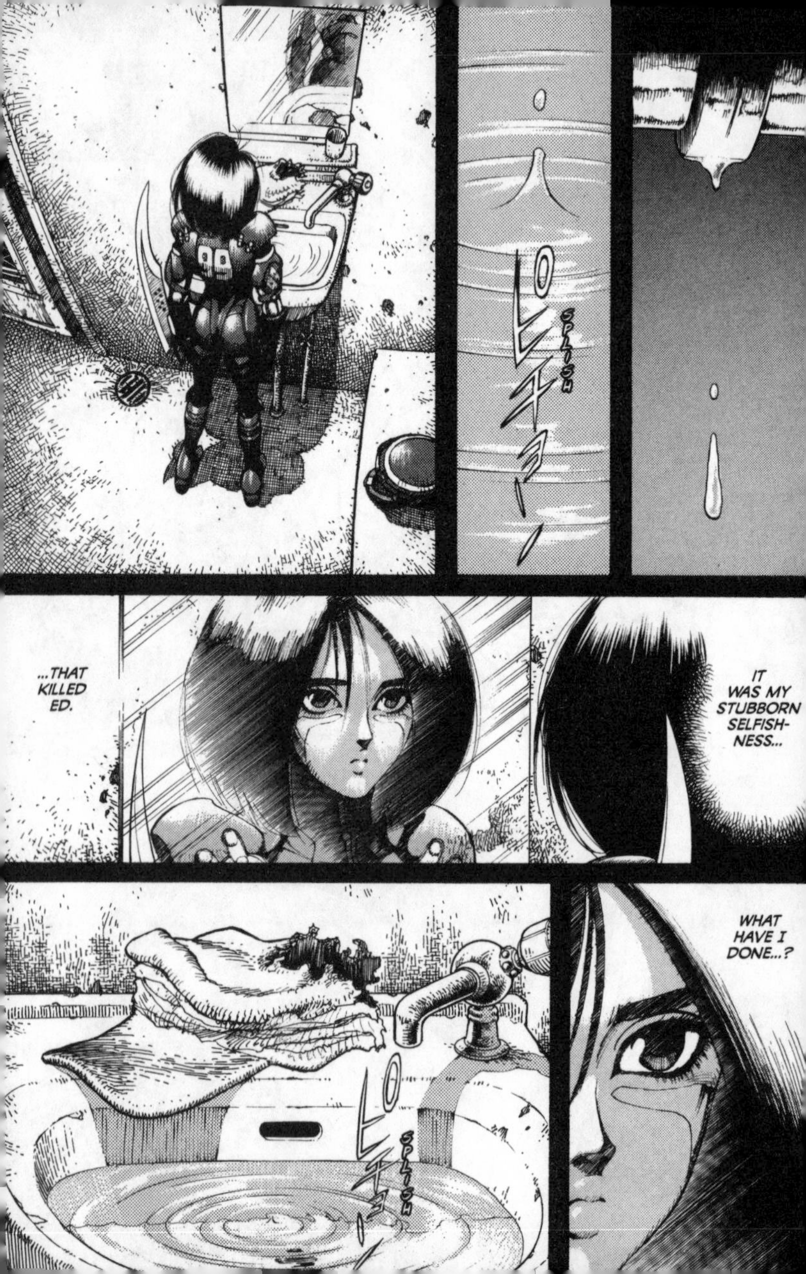
SPLISH
IT WAS MY STUBBORN SELFISHNESS...
...THAT KILLED ED.
WHAT HAVE I DONE...?
SPLISH

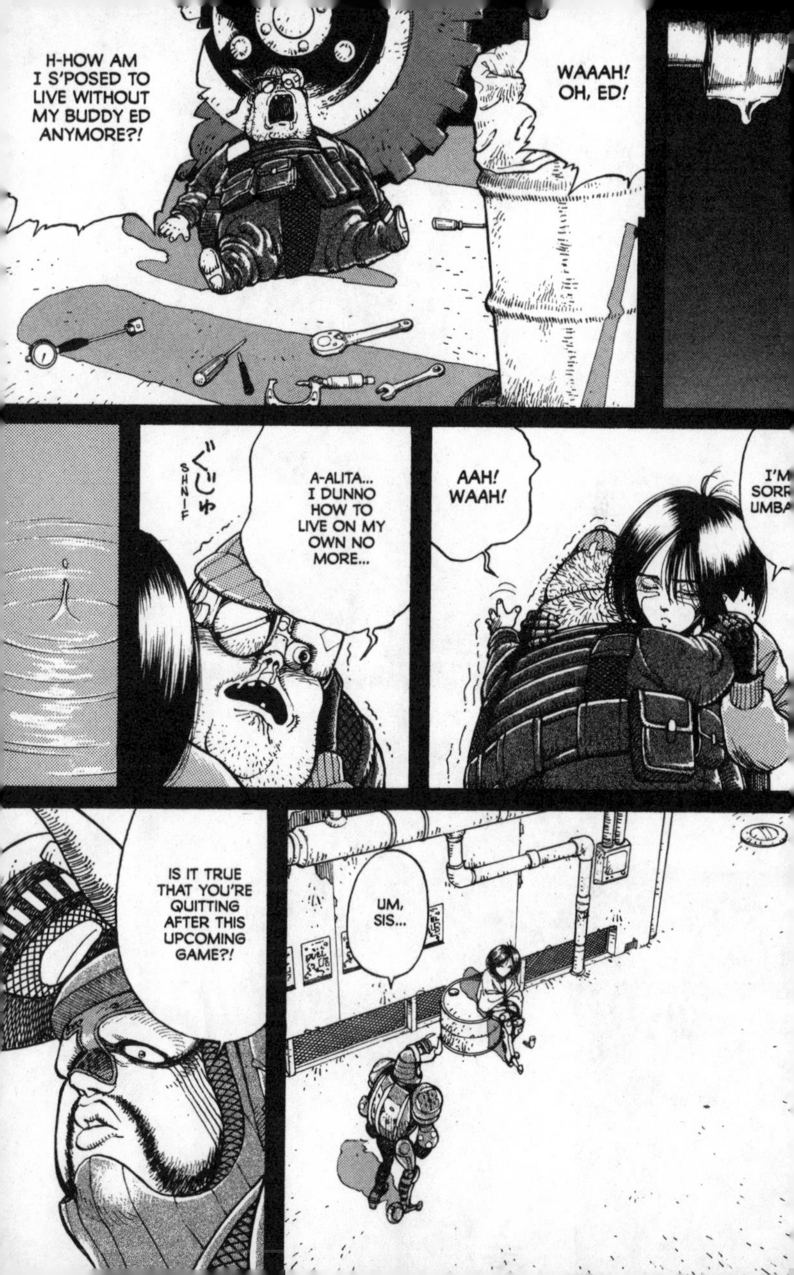
WAAAH! OH, ED!
H-HOW AM I S'POSED TO LIVE WITHOUT MY BUDDY ED ANYMORE?!
I'M SORR UMBA
AAH! WAAH!
ぐじゅ SHNIF
A-ALITA... I DUNNO HOW TO LIVE ON MY OWN NO MORE...
UM, SIS...
IS IT TRUE THAT YOU'RE QUITTING AFTER THIS UPCOMING GAME?!

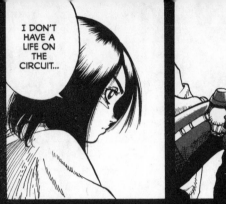

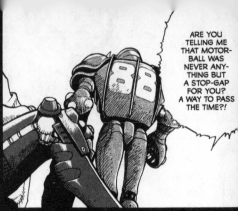

ARE YOU TELLING ME THAT MOTORBALL WAS NEVER ANYTHING BUT A STOP-GAP FOR YOU? A WAY TO PASS THE TIME?!
I DON'T HAVE A LIFE ON THE CIRCUIT...
NO. MOTORBALLERS GIVE THEIR LIVES TO THE CIRCUIT.
WE DO ANYTHING WE CAN TO DRAW THE ATTENTION OF THE CROWD. THAT MAKES MY FALLEN BROTHERS, THE HATED ARMBRUST, EVEN THAT SLOWPOKE TIEGEL, *ALL* FULLY-FLEDGED MOTORBALLERS!!
BUT YOU'RE DIFFERENT, SIS.
YOU'RE NOT A MOTORBALLER. NOT ONE OF US.
YOU'RE AN OUTSIDER.

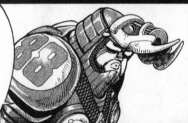

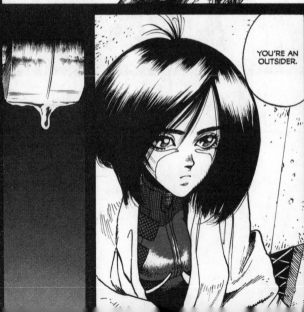

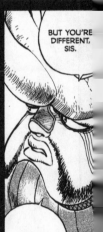

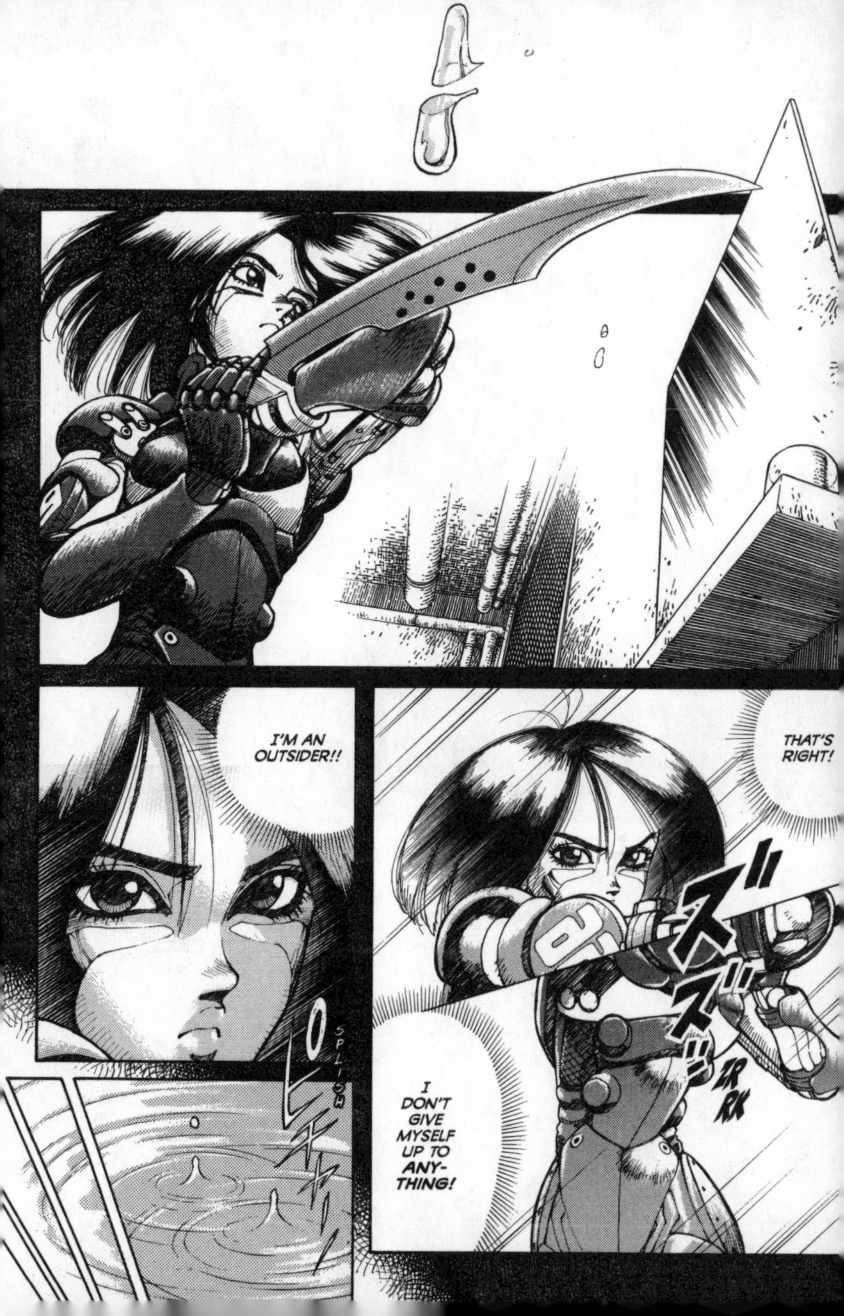
THAT'S RIGHT!
ZRRK
I DON'T GIVE MYSELF UP TO ANYTHING!
I'M AN OUTSIDER!!
SPLISH

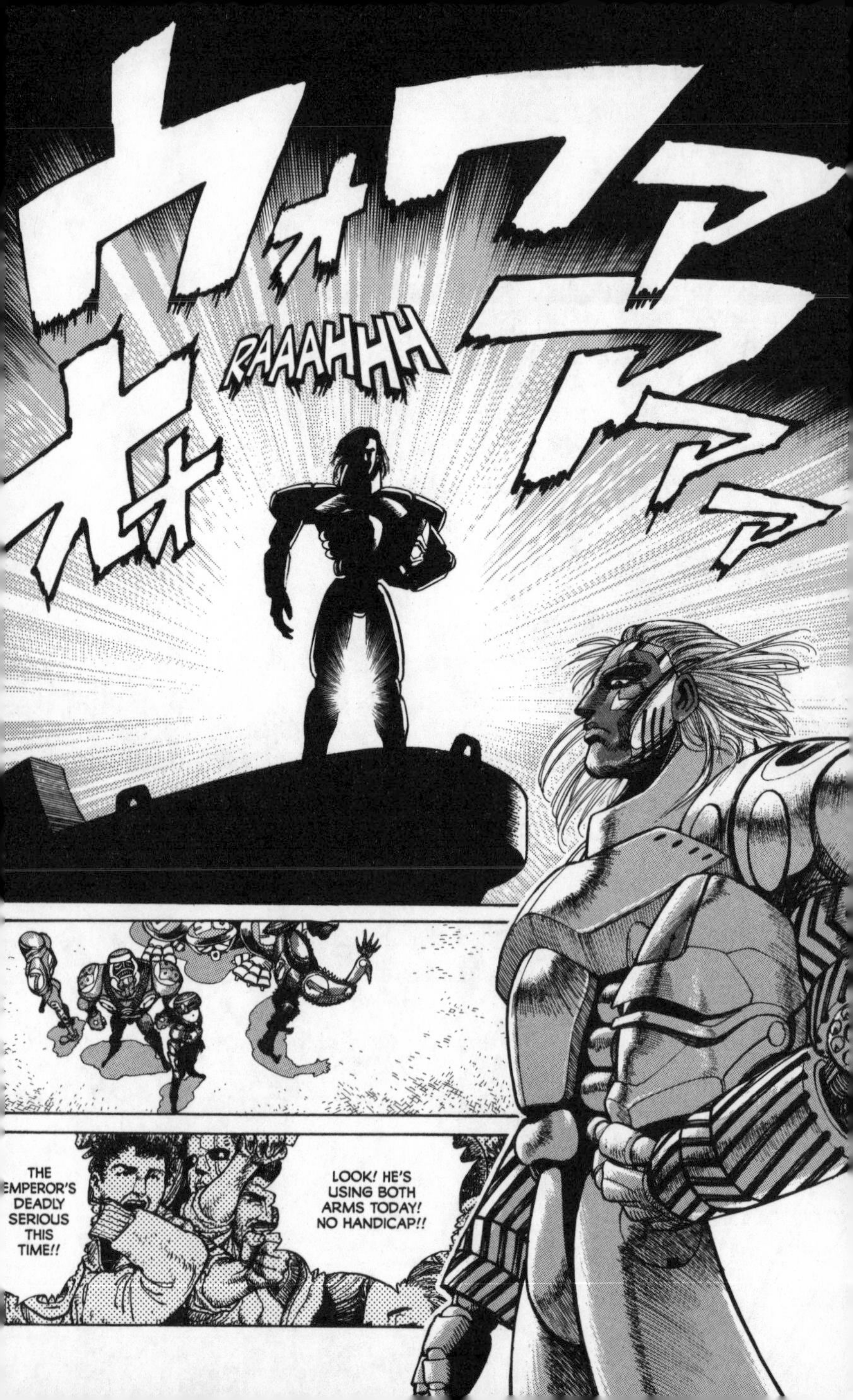
RAAAHHH
LOOK! HE'S USING BOTH ARMS TODAY! NO HANDICAP!!
THE EMPEROR'S DEADLY SERIOUS THIS TIME!!

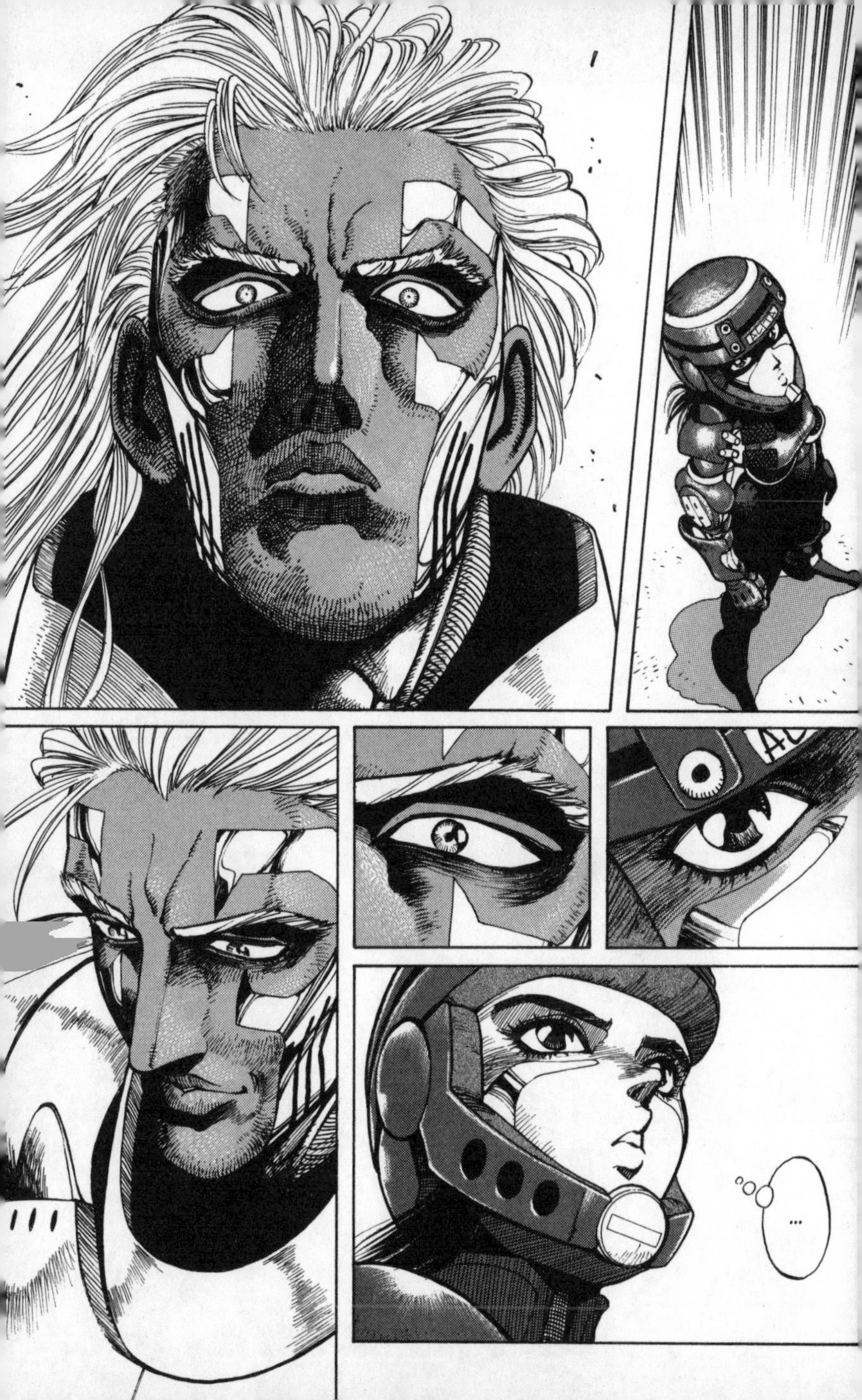
...

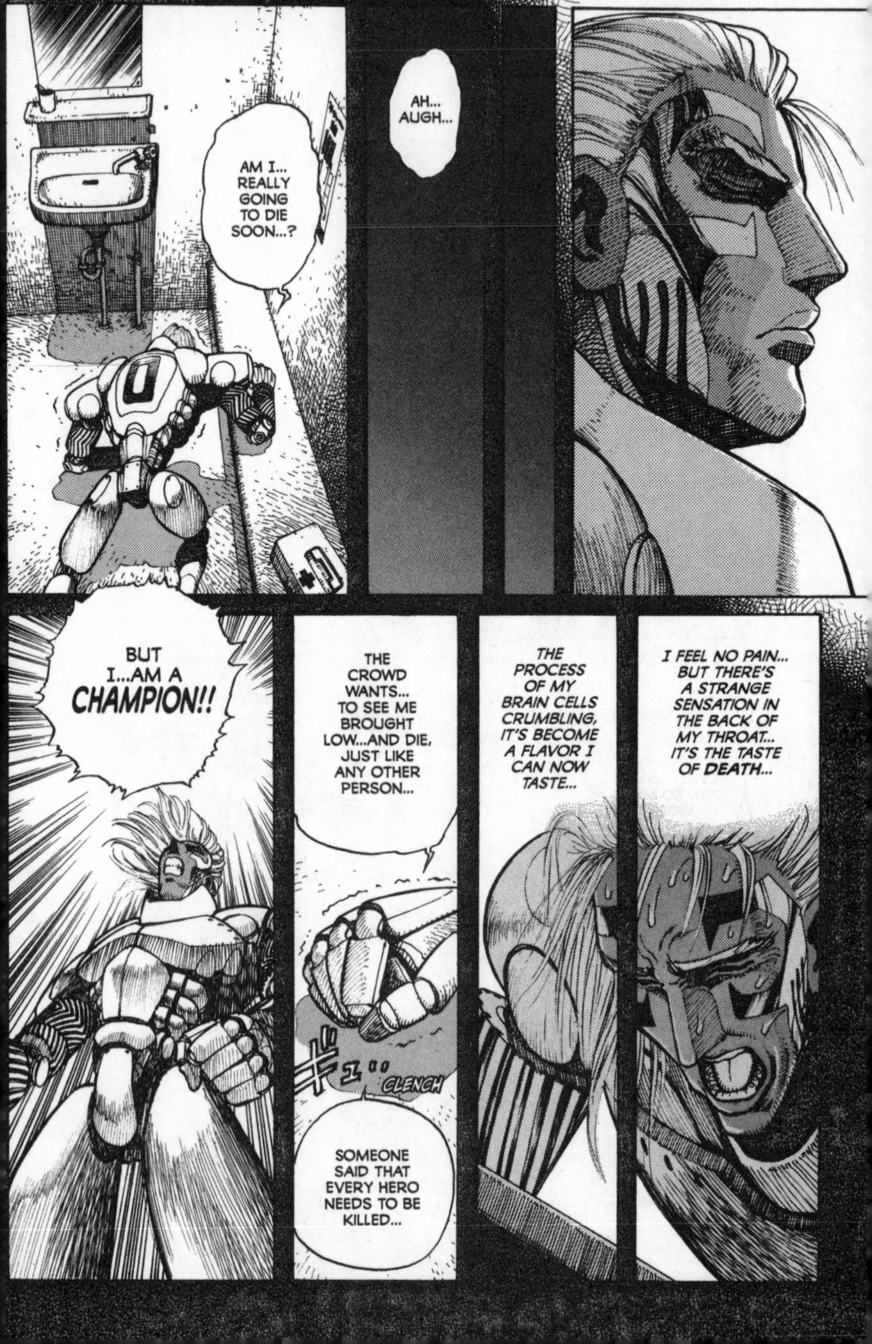
AH... AUGH...
AM I... REALLY GOING TO DIE SOON...?
I FEEL NO PAIN... BUT THERE'S A STRANGE SENSATION IN THE BACK OF MY THROAT... IT'S THE TASTE OF DEATH...
THE PROCESS OF MY BRAIN CELLS CRUMBLING, IT'S BECOME A FLAVOR I CAN NOW TASTE...
THE CROWD WANTS... TO SEE ME BROUGHT LOW...AND DIE, JUST LIKE ANY OTHER PERSON...
CLENCH
SOMEONE SAID THAT EVERY HERO NEEDS TO BE KILLED...
BUT I...AM A CHAMPION!!

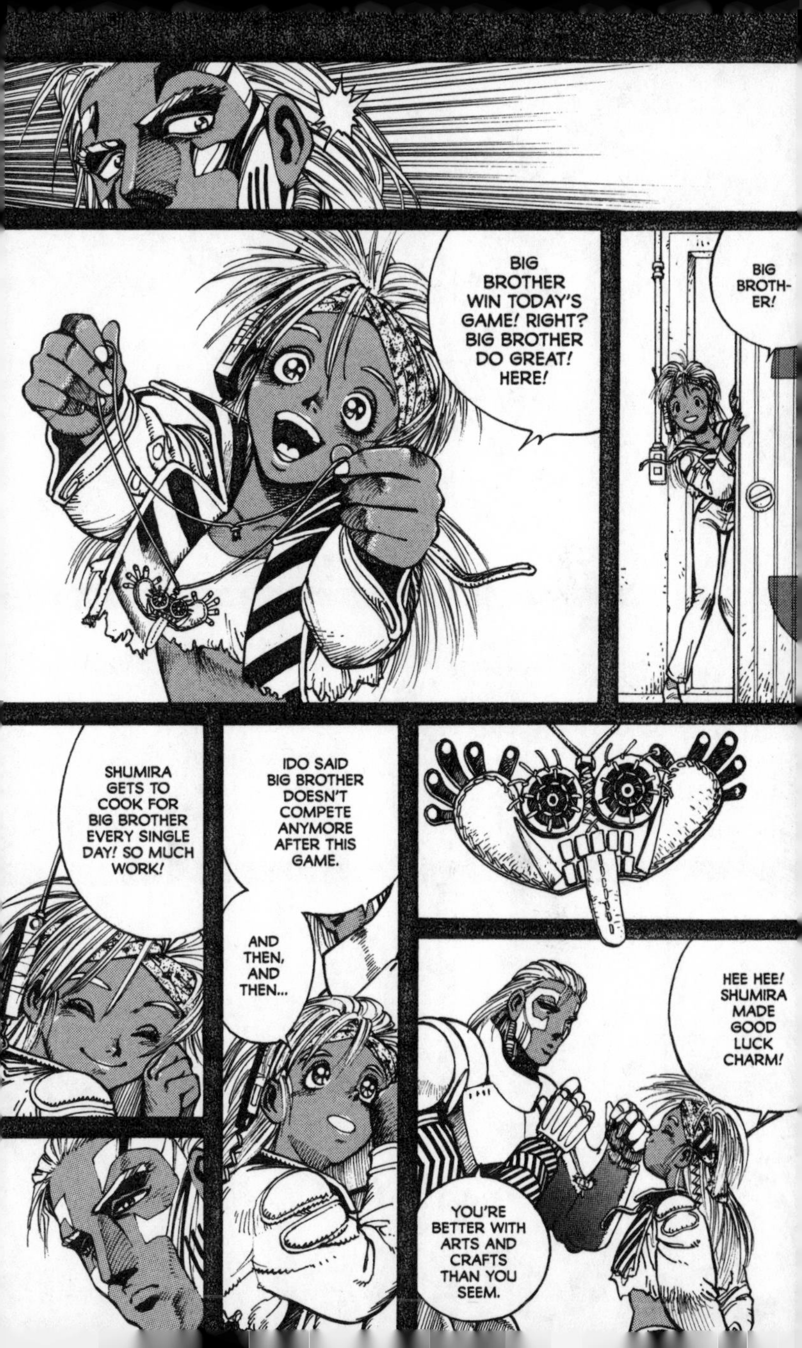
BIG BROTH-ER!
BIG BROTHER WIN TODAY'S GAME! RIGHT? BIG BROTHER DO GREAT! HERE!
HEE HEE! SHUMIRA MADE GOOD LUCK CHARM!
YOU'RE BETTER WITH ARTS AND CRAFTS THAN YOU SEEM.
IDO SAID BIG BROTHER DOESN'T COMPETE ANYMORE AFTER THIS GAME.
AND THEN, AND THEN...
SHUMIRA GETS TO COOK FOR BIG BROTHER EVERY SINGLE DAY! SO MUCH WORK!

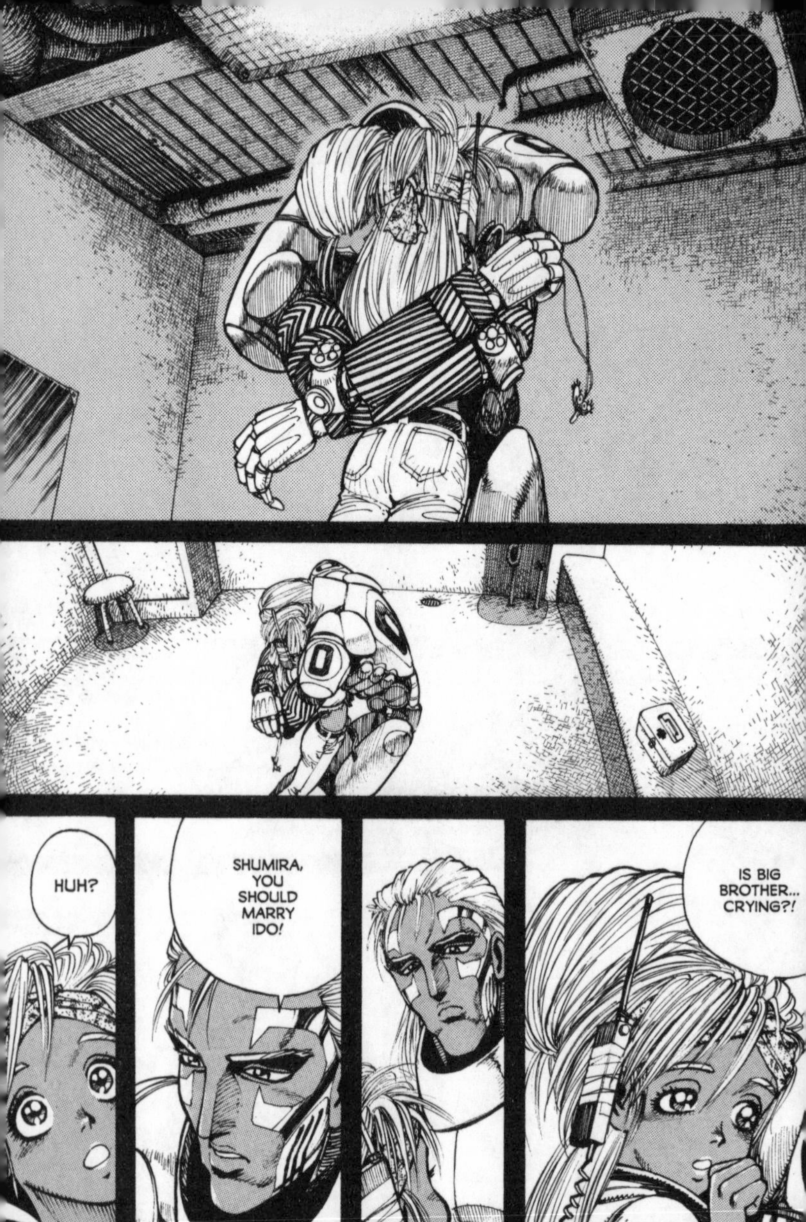
IS BIG BROTHER... CRYING?!
SHUMIRA, YOU SHOULD MARRY IDO!
HUH?

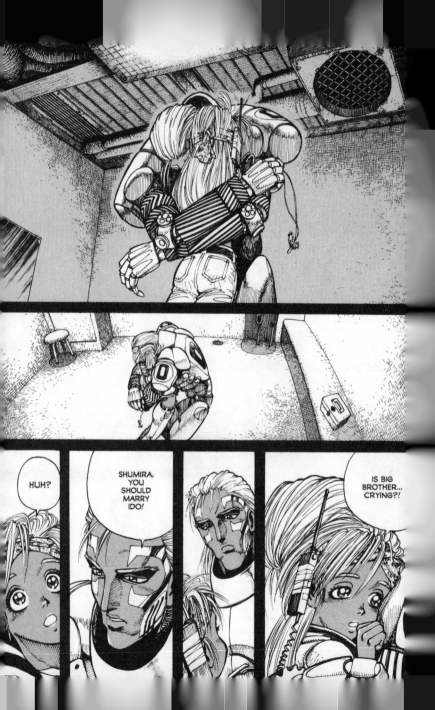

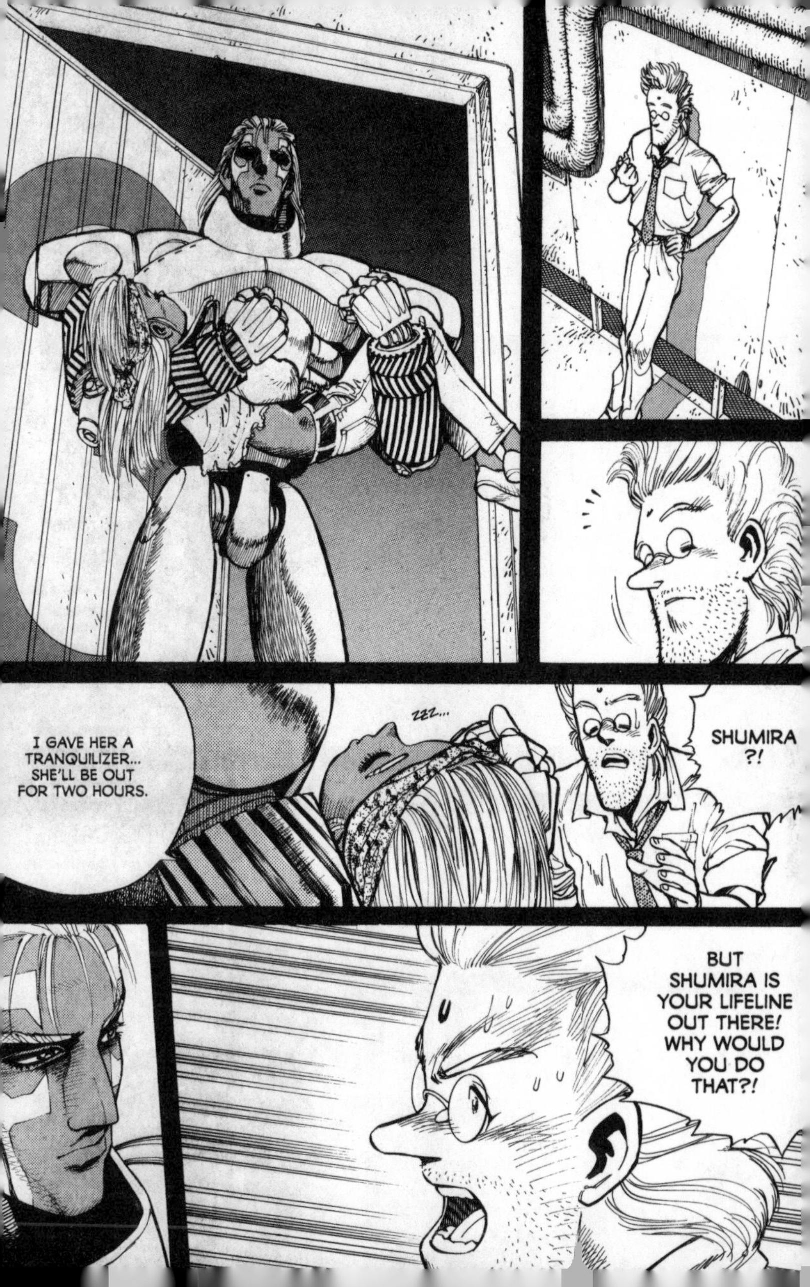
SHUMIRA ?!
ZZZ...
I GAVE HER A TRANQUILIZER... SHE'LL BE OUT FOR TWO HOURS.
BUT SHUMIRA IS YOUR LIFELINE OUT THERE! WHY WOULD YOU DO THAT?!

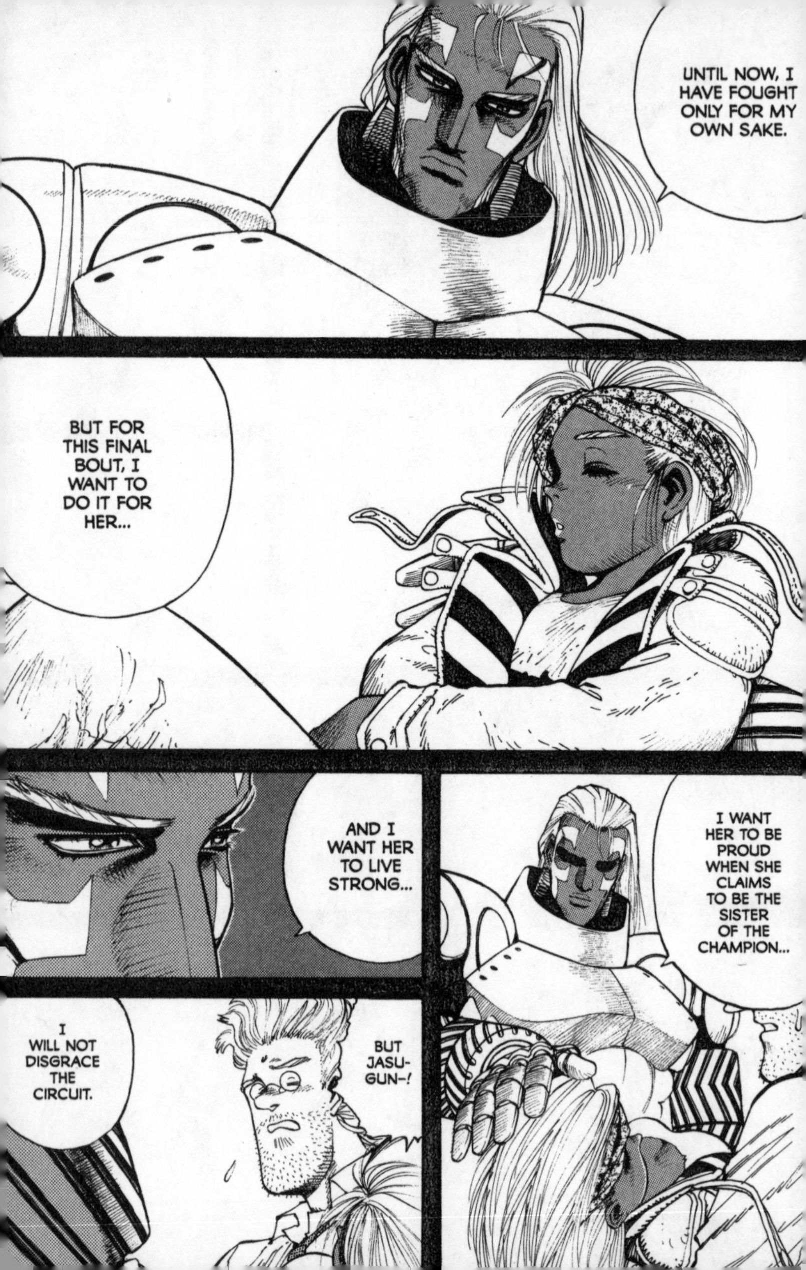
UNTIL NOW, I HAVE FOUGHT ONLY FOR MY OWN SAKE.
BUT FOR THIS FINAL BOUT, I WANT TO DO IT FOR HER...
I WANT HER TO BE PROUD WHEN SHE CLAIMS TO BE THE SISTER OF THE CHAMPION...
AND I WANT HER TO LIVE STRONG...
BUT JASU-GUN-!
I WILL NOT DISGRACE THE CIRCUIT.

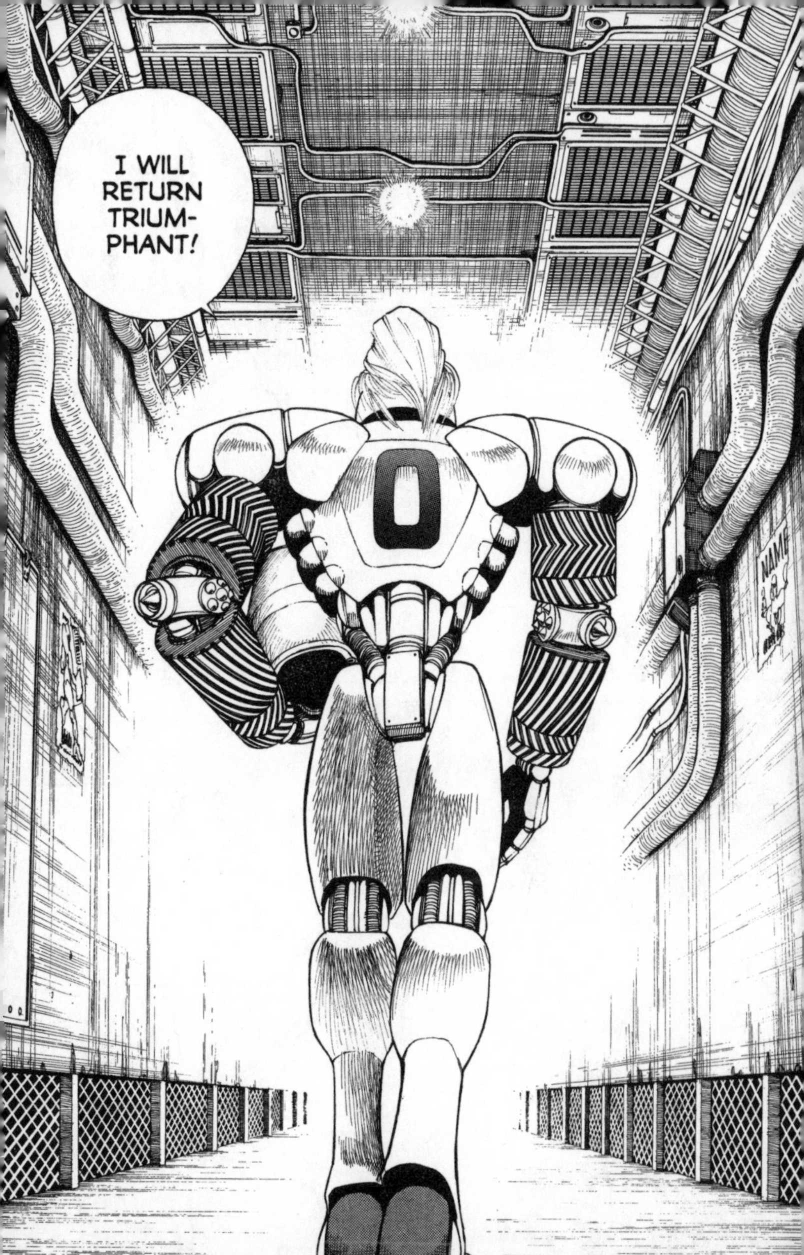
I WILL RETURN TRIUM-PHANT!

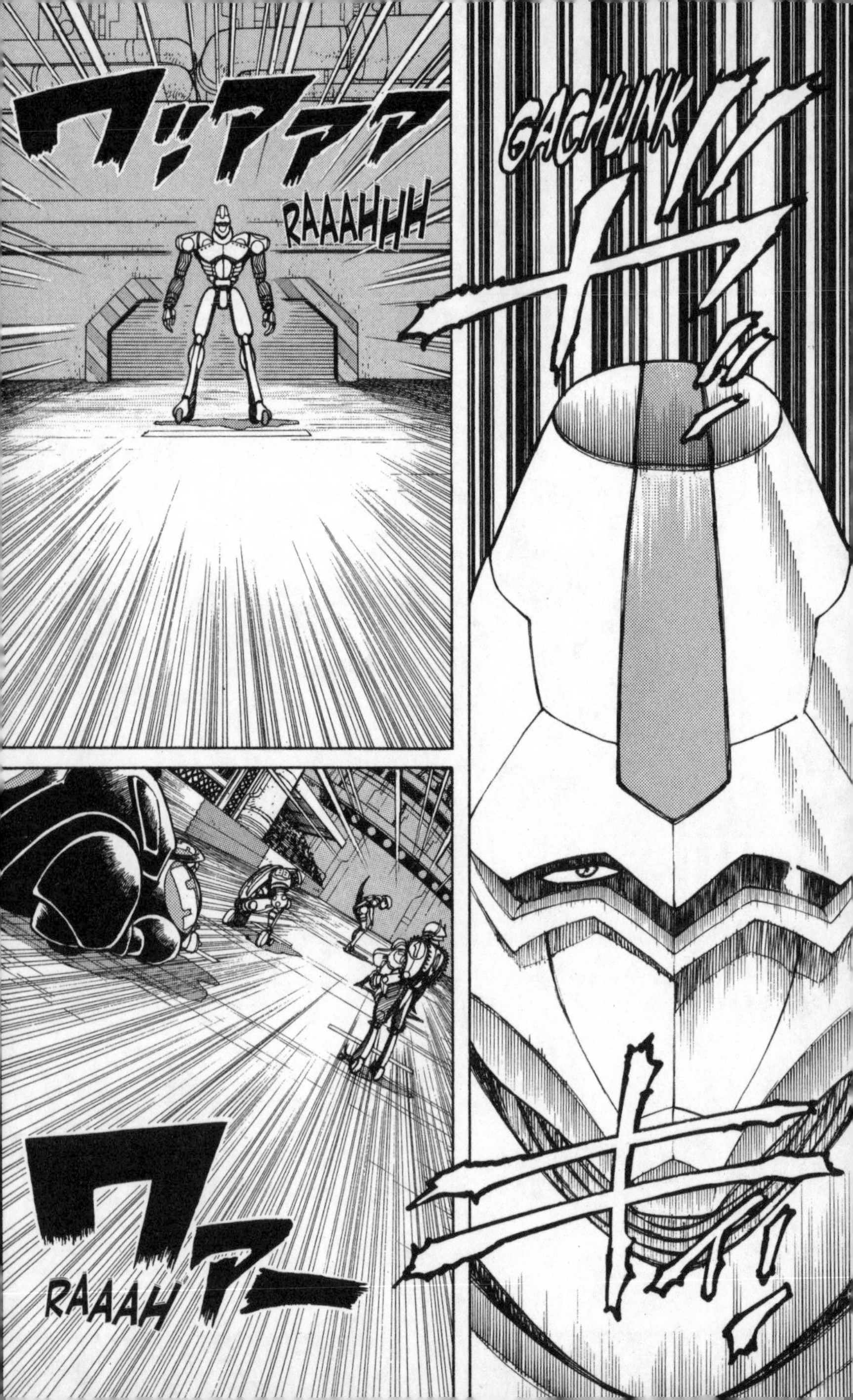
GACHUNK
RAAAHHH
RAAAH

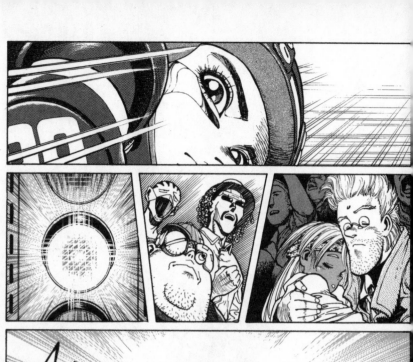

BOOOM

START!!

FIGHT_022 Ars Magna

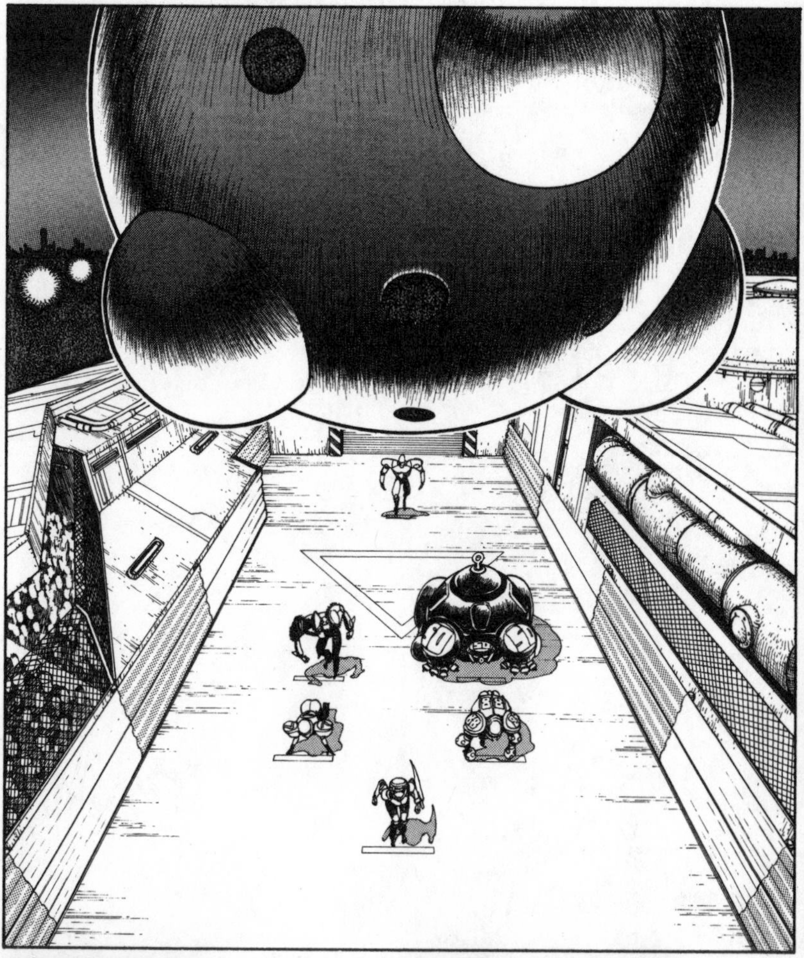

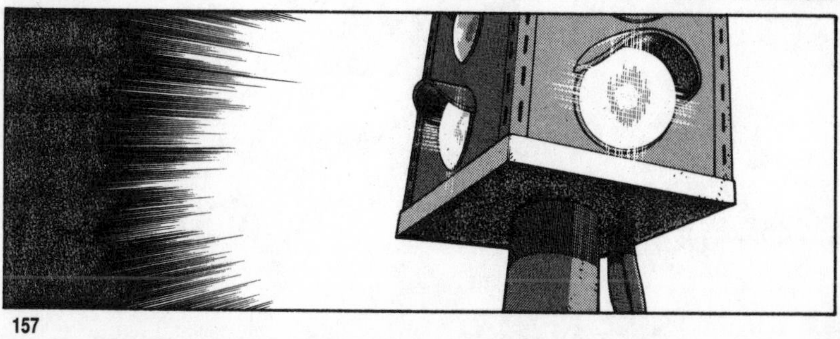

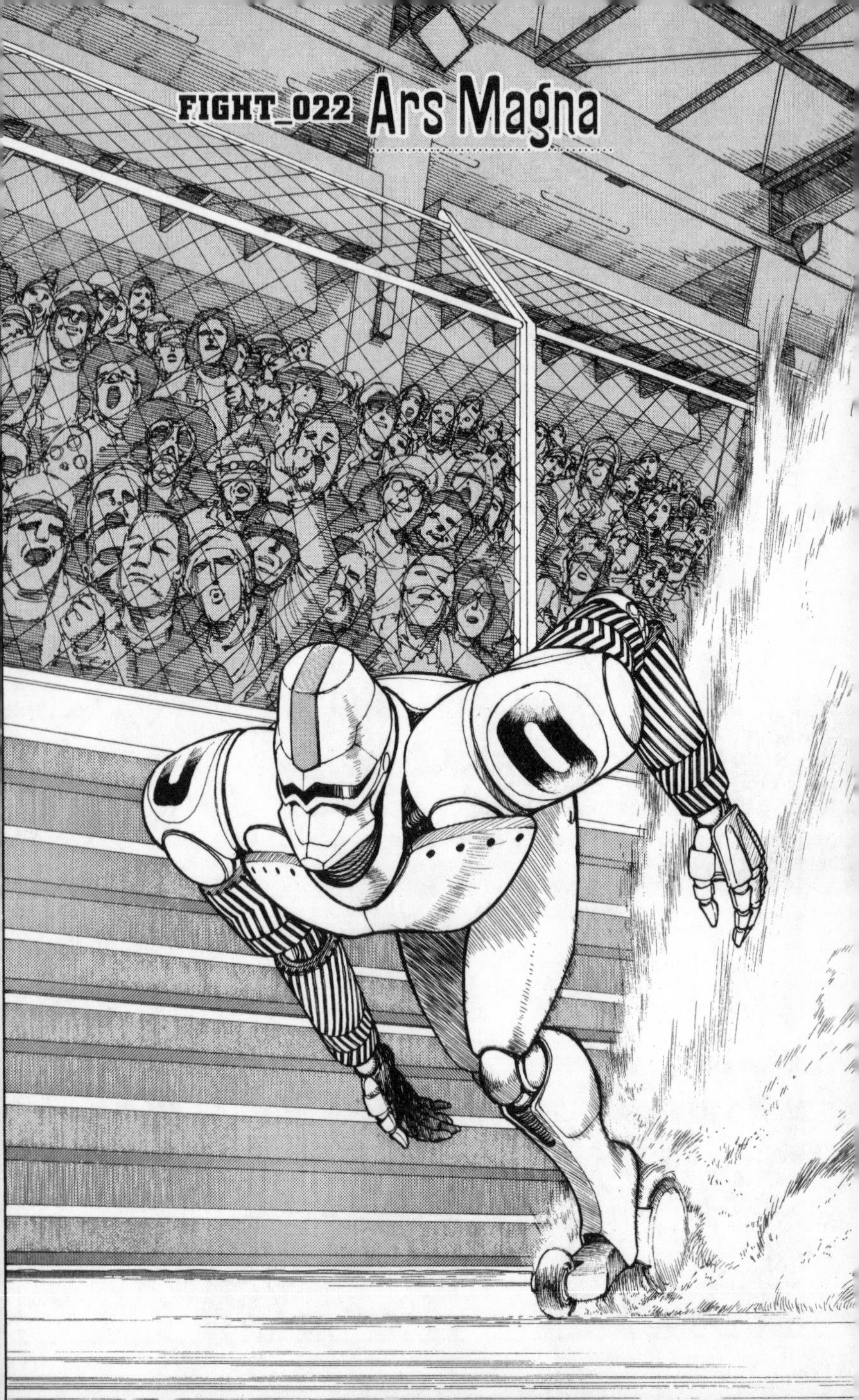
FIGHT_022 Ars Magna

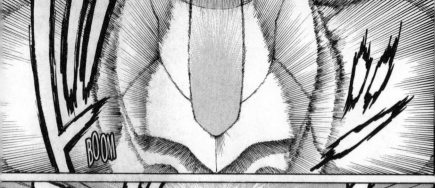

BOOM
VWOOSH
ARE YOU WATCHING THIS, ZALEM?!
CAN YOU SEE ME?!
THERE IS LITTLE TIME LEFT FOR ME.
BUT I WILL FIGHT UNTIL THE LAST SECOND–AS THE CHAMPION THAT I AM!

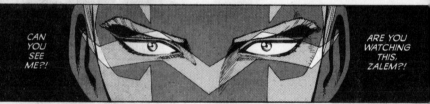

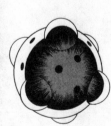

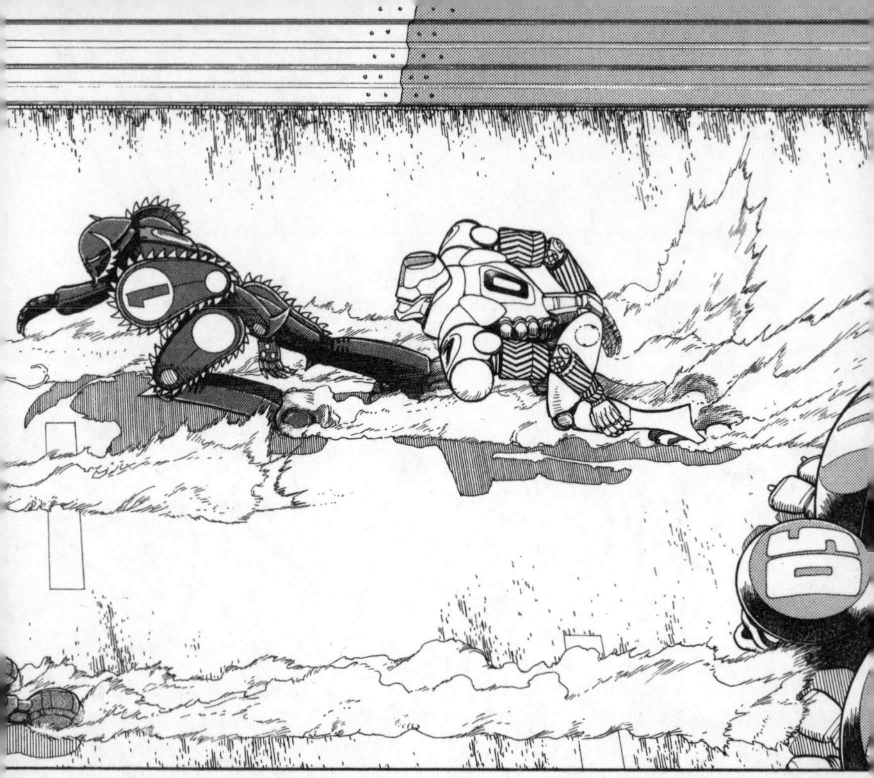

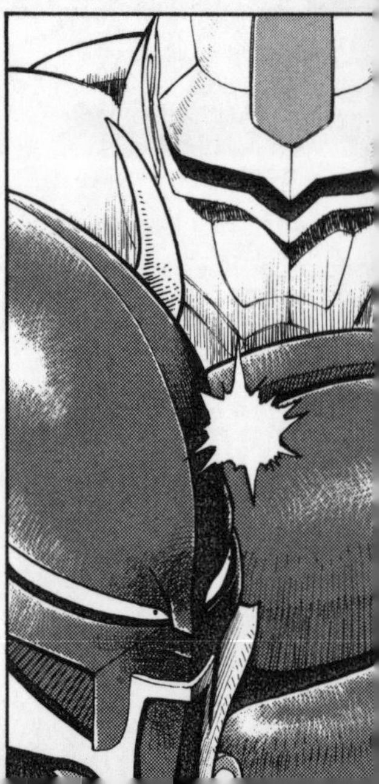

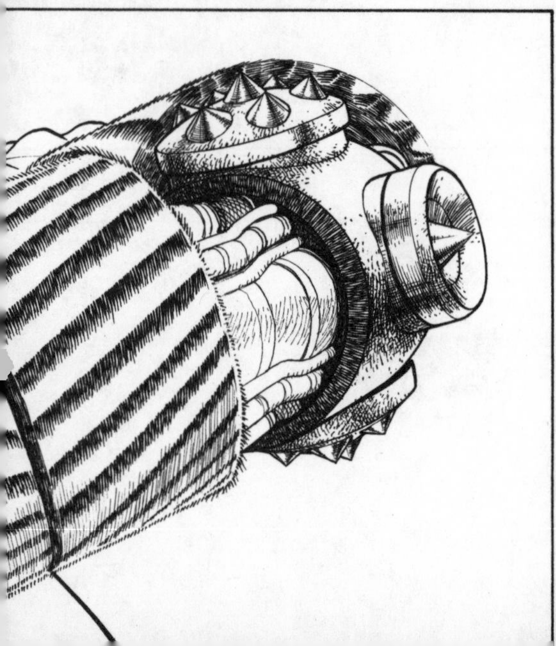

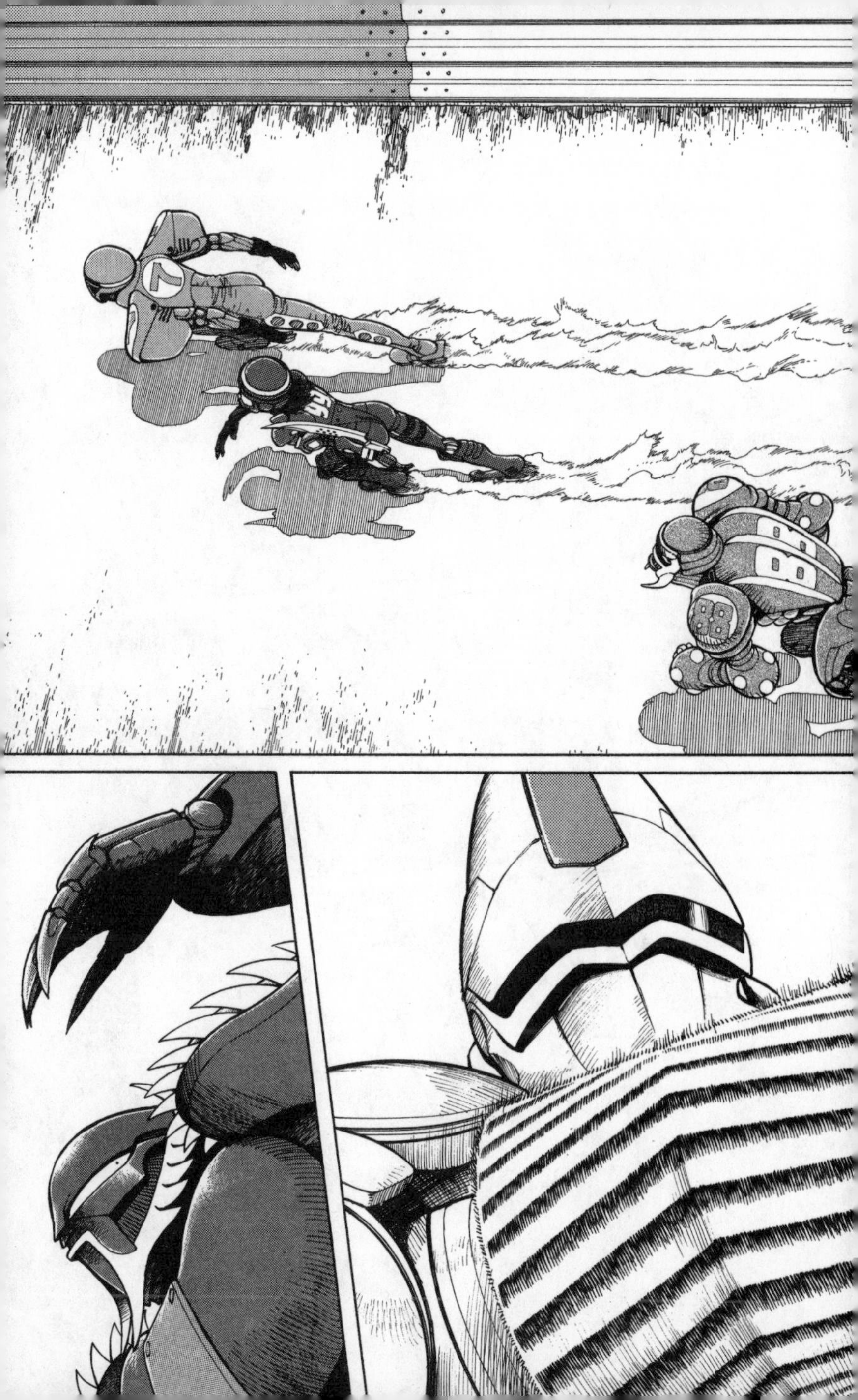

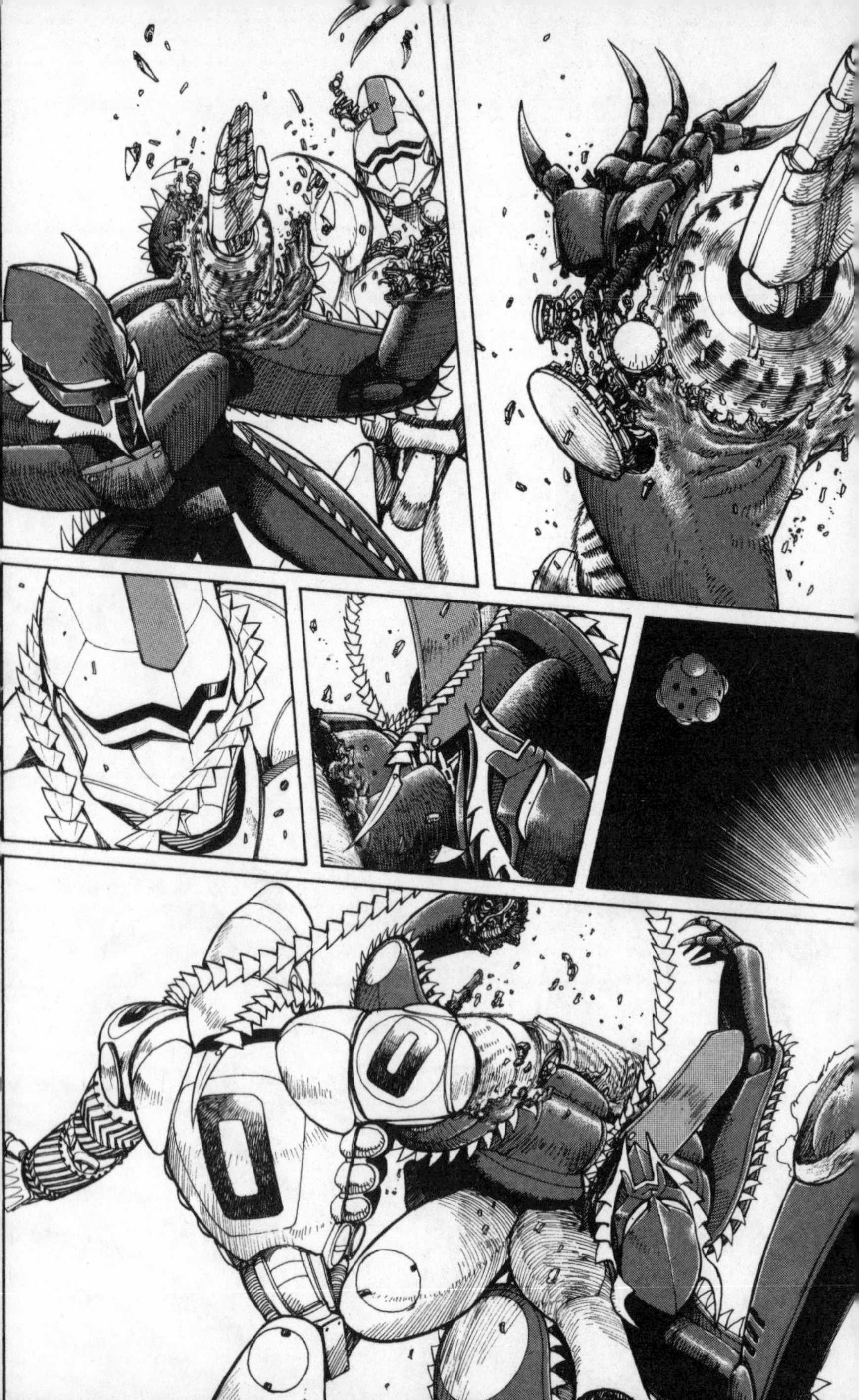

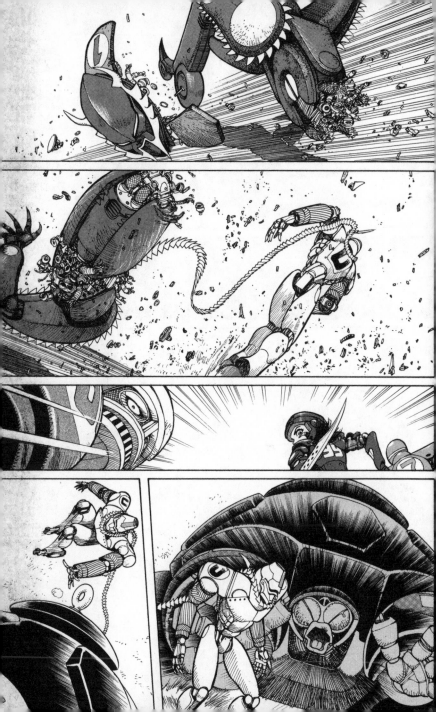

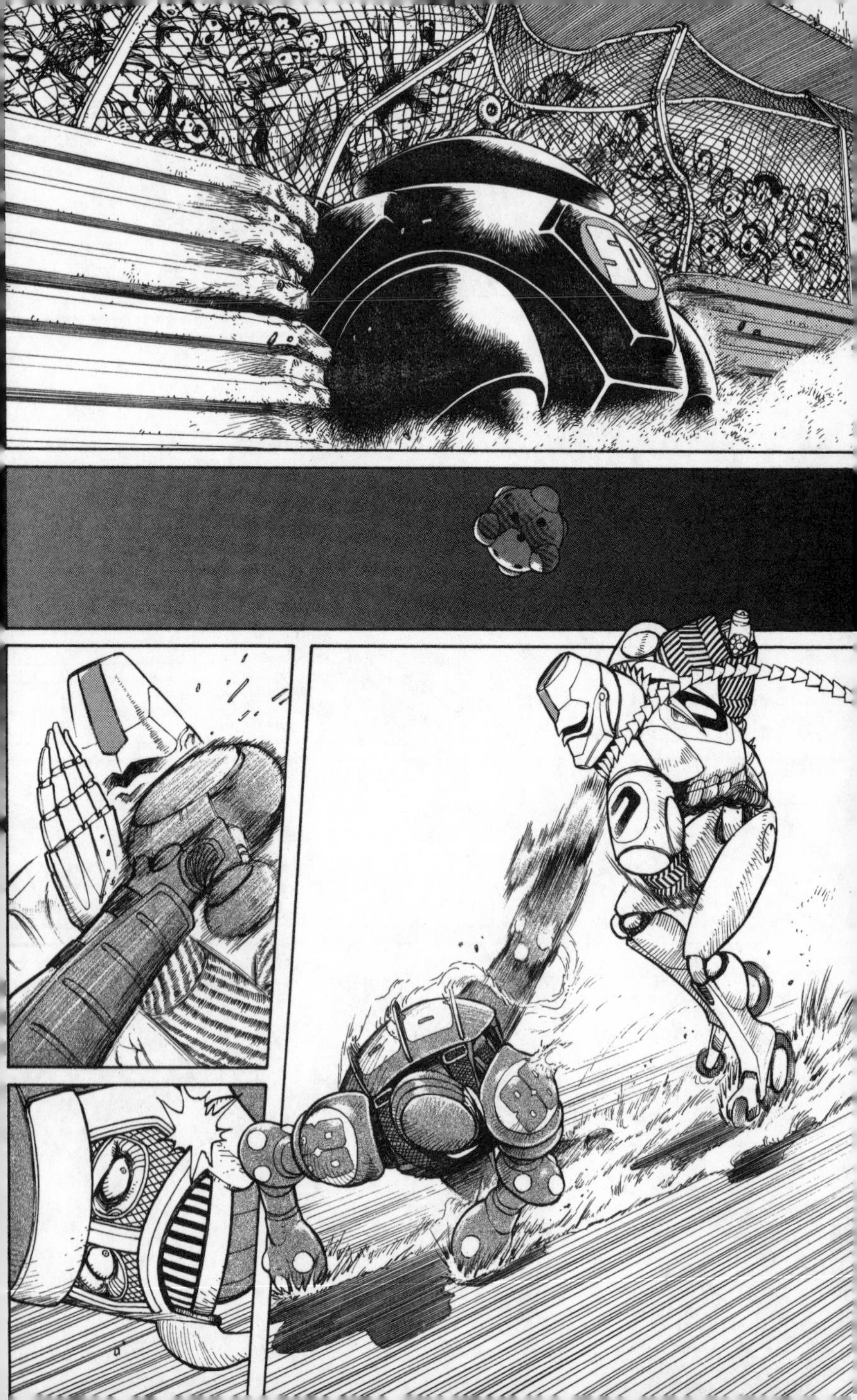

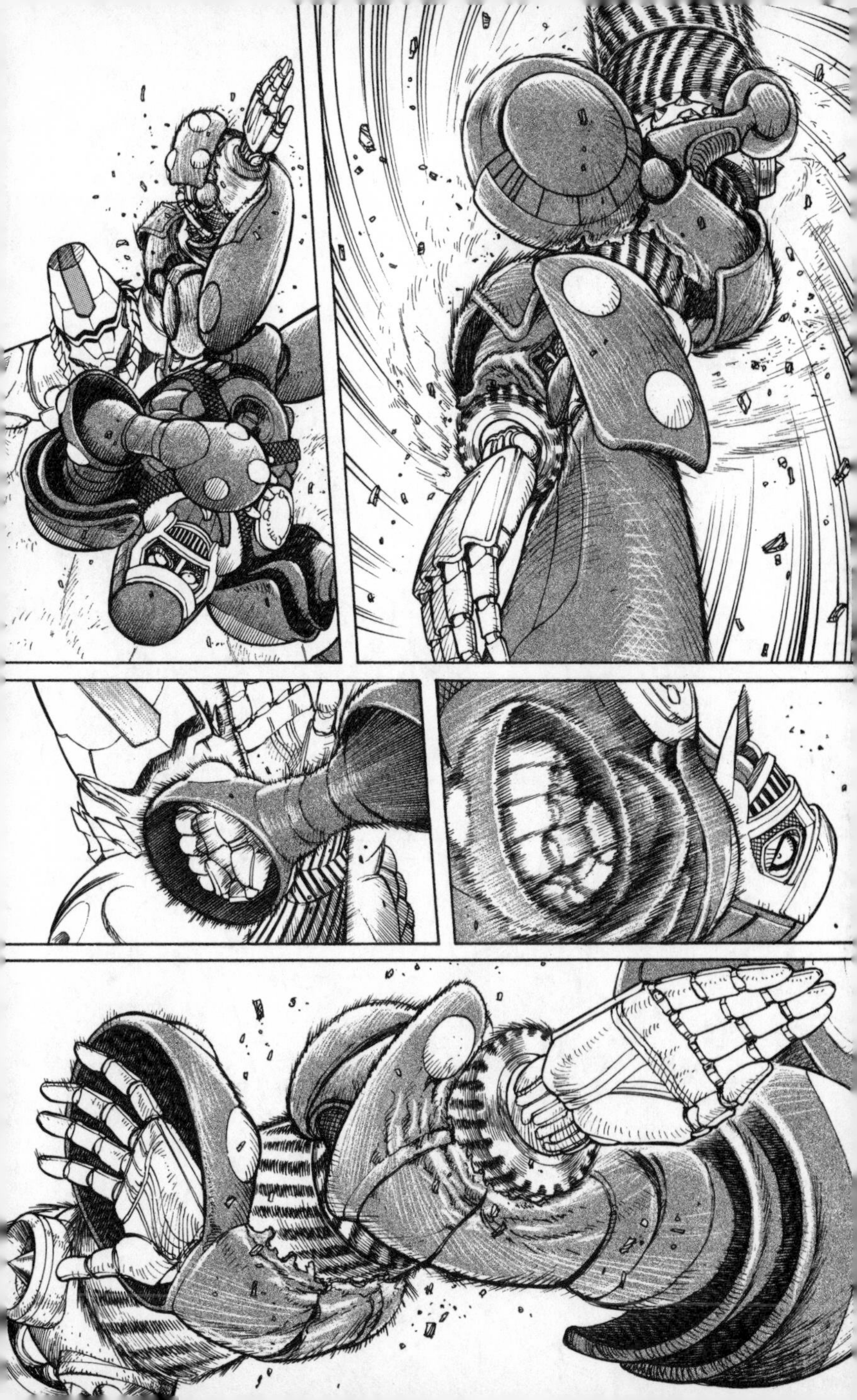

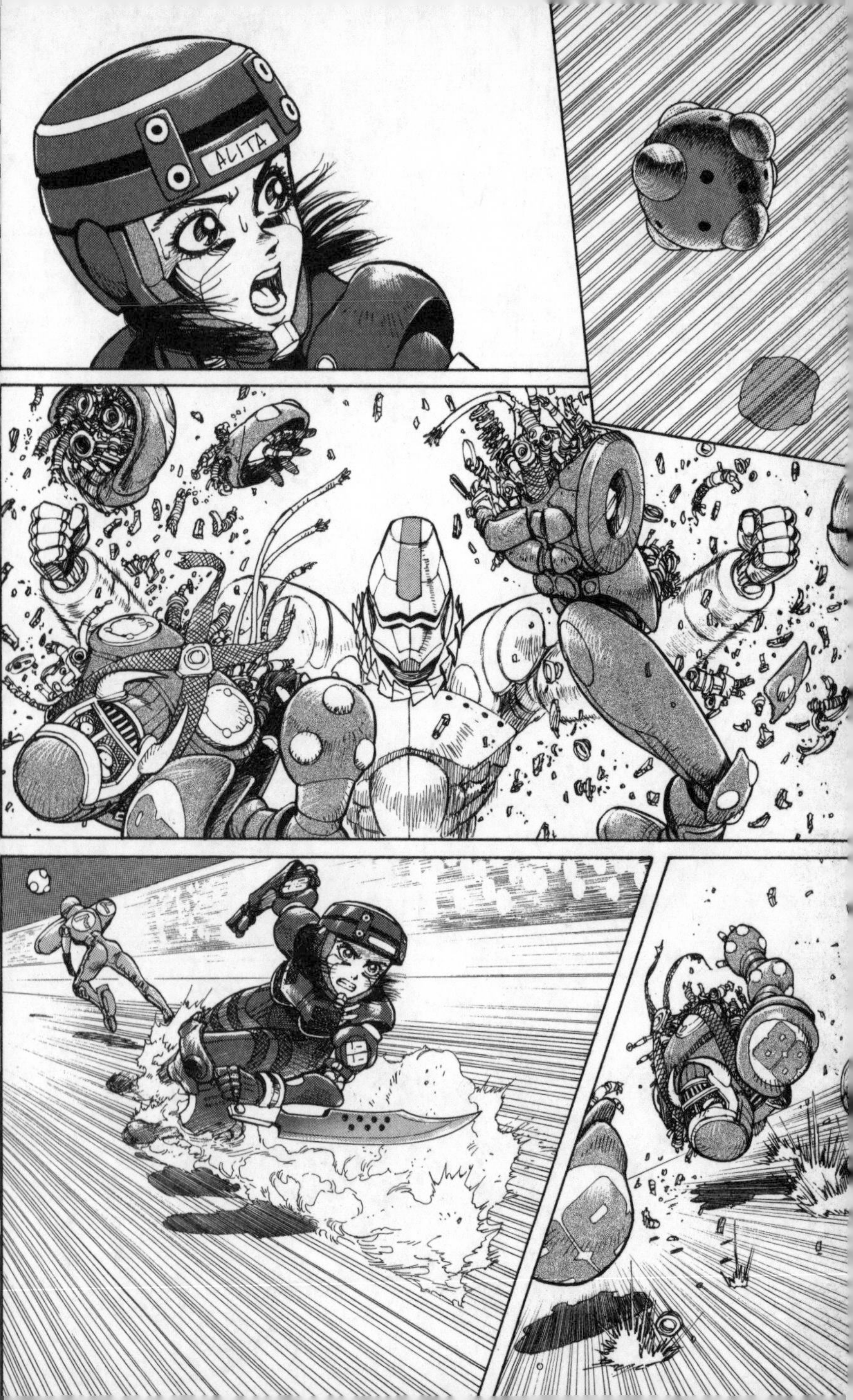
ALITA

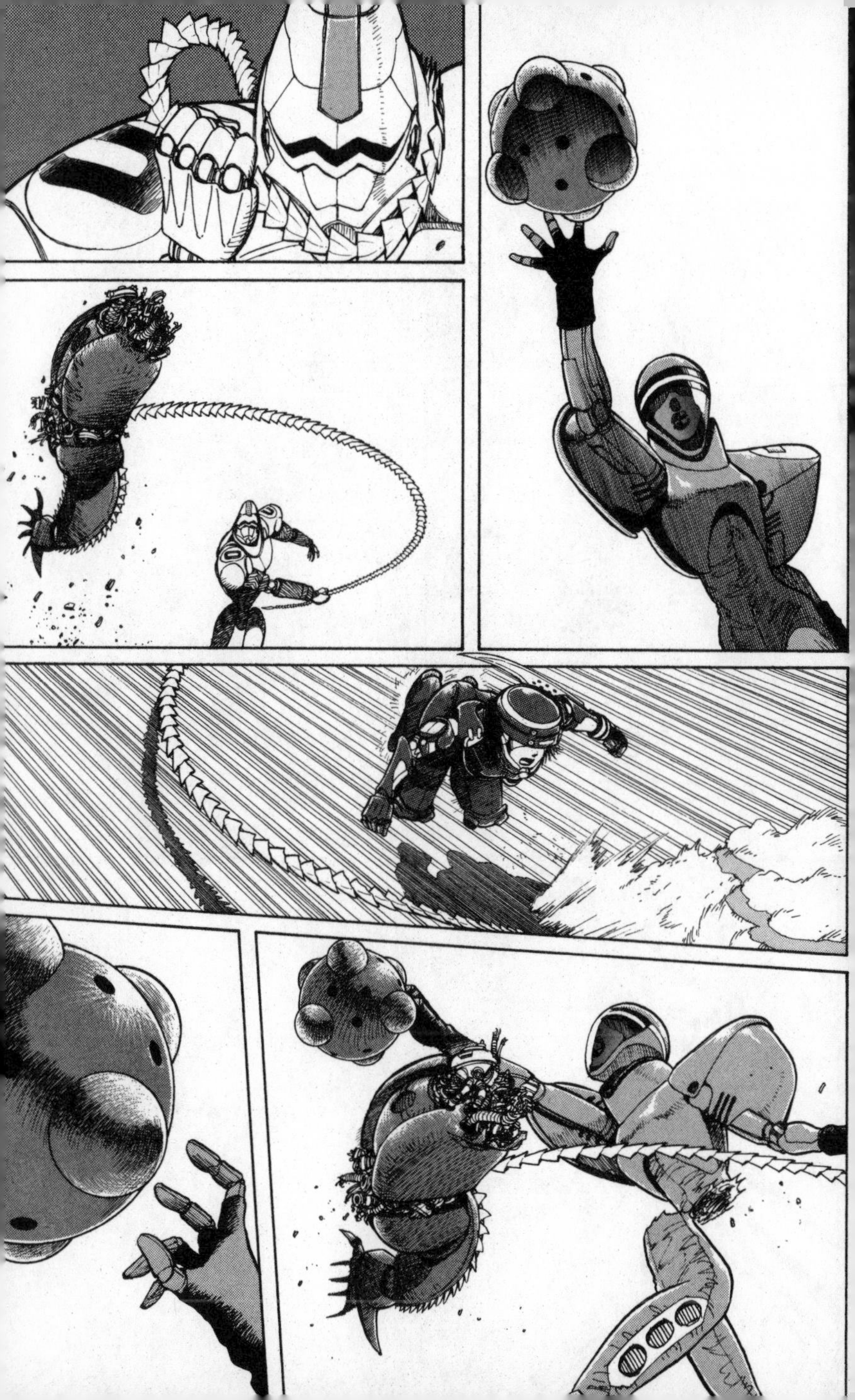

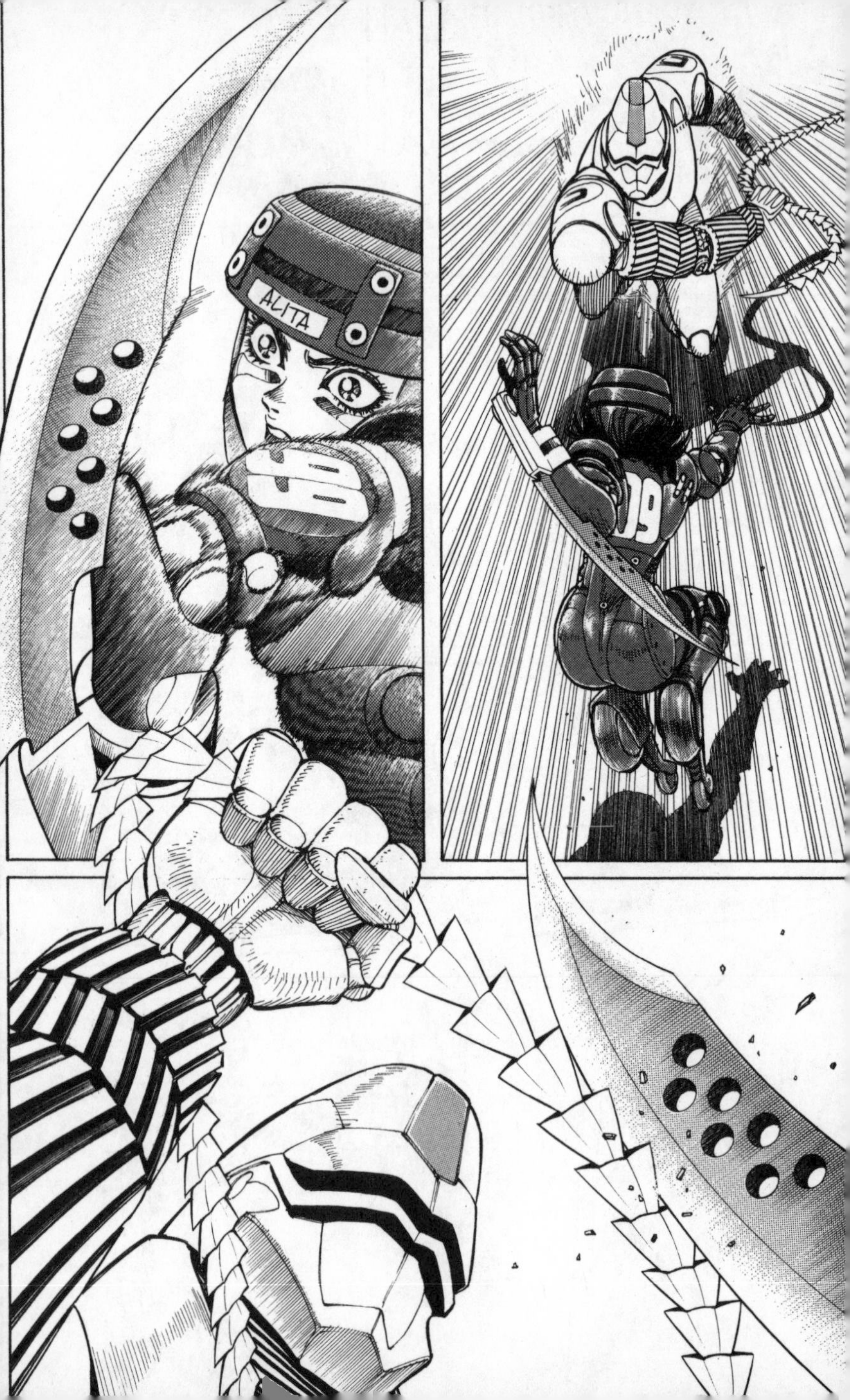
ALITA

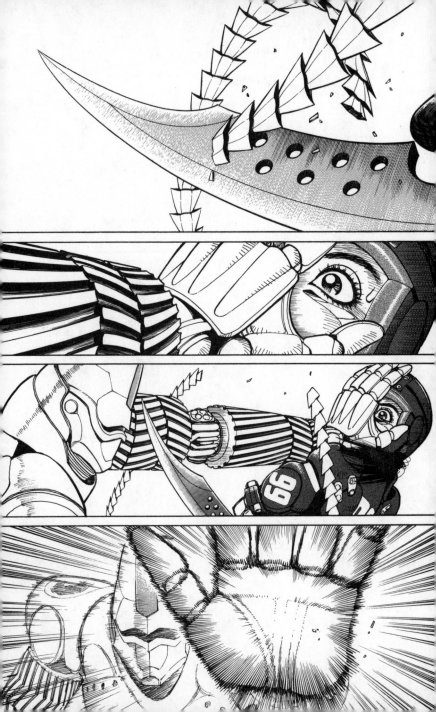

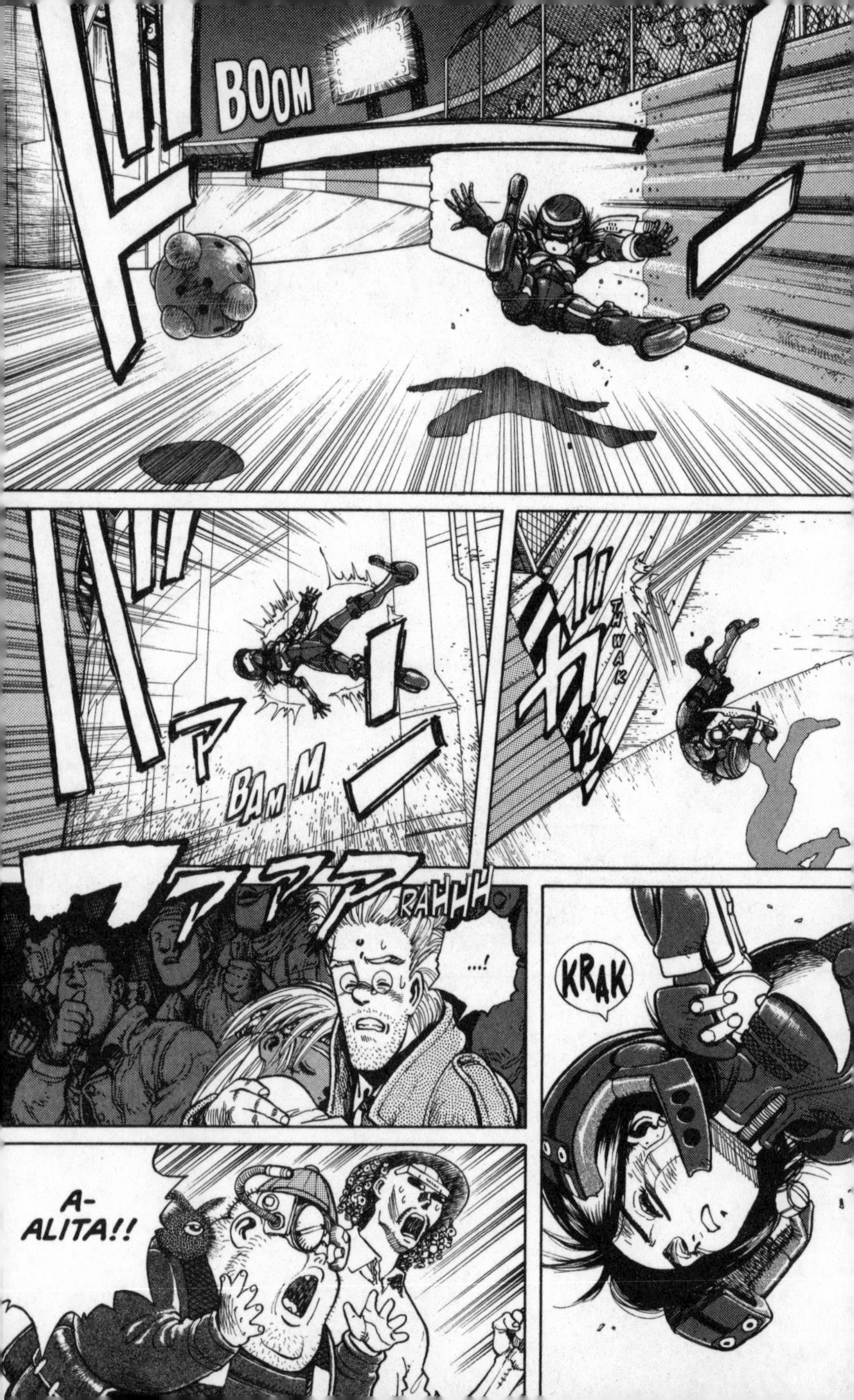
BOOM
THWAK
BAMM
KRAK
RAHHH
...!
A-
ALITA!!

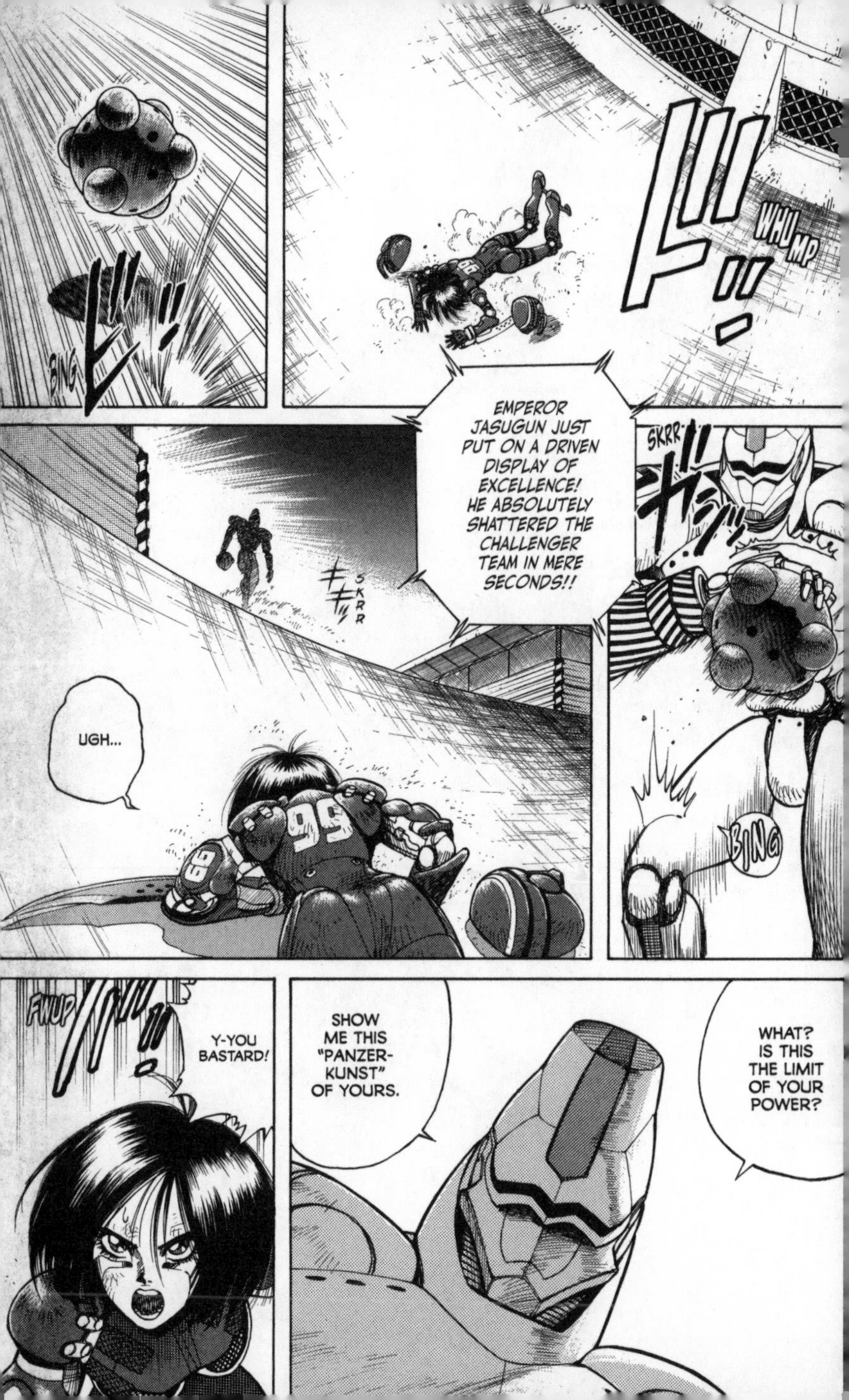
WHUMP
BING
SKRR
BING
EMPEROR JASUGUN JUST PUT ON A DRIVEN DISPLAY OF EXCELLENCE! HE ABSOLUTELY SHATTERED THE CHALLENGER TEAM IN MERE SECONDS!!
SKRR
UGH...
WHAT? IS THIS THE LIMIT OF YOUR POWER?
SHOW ME THIS "PANZER-KUNST" OF YOURS.
FWUP
Y-YOU BASTARD!

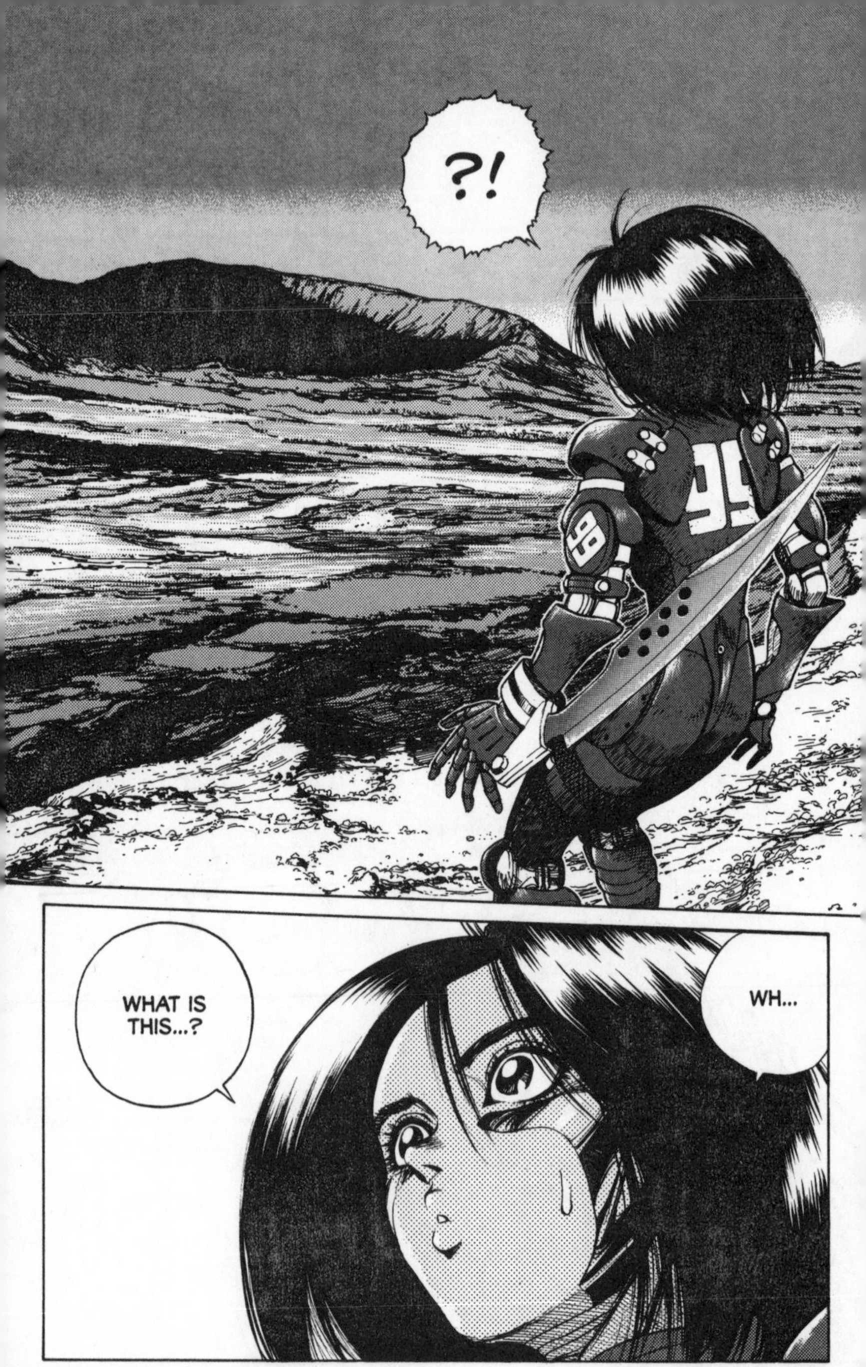
?!
WH...
WHAT IS THIS...?

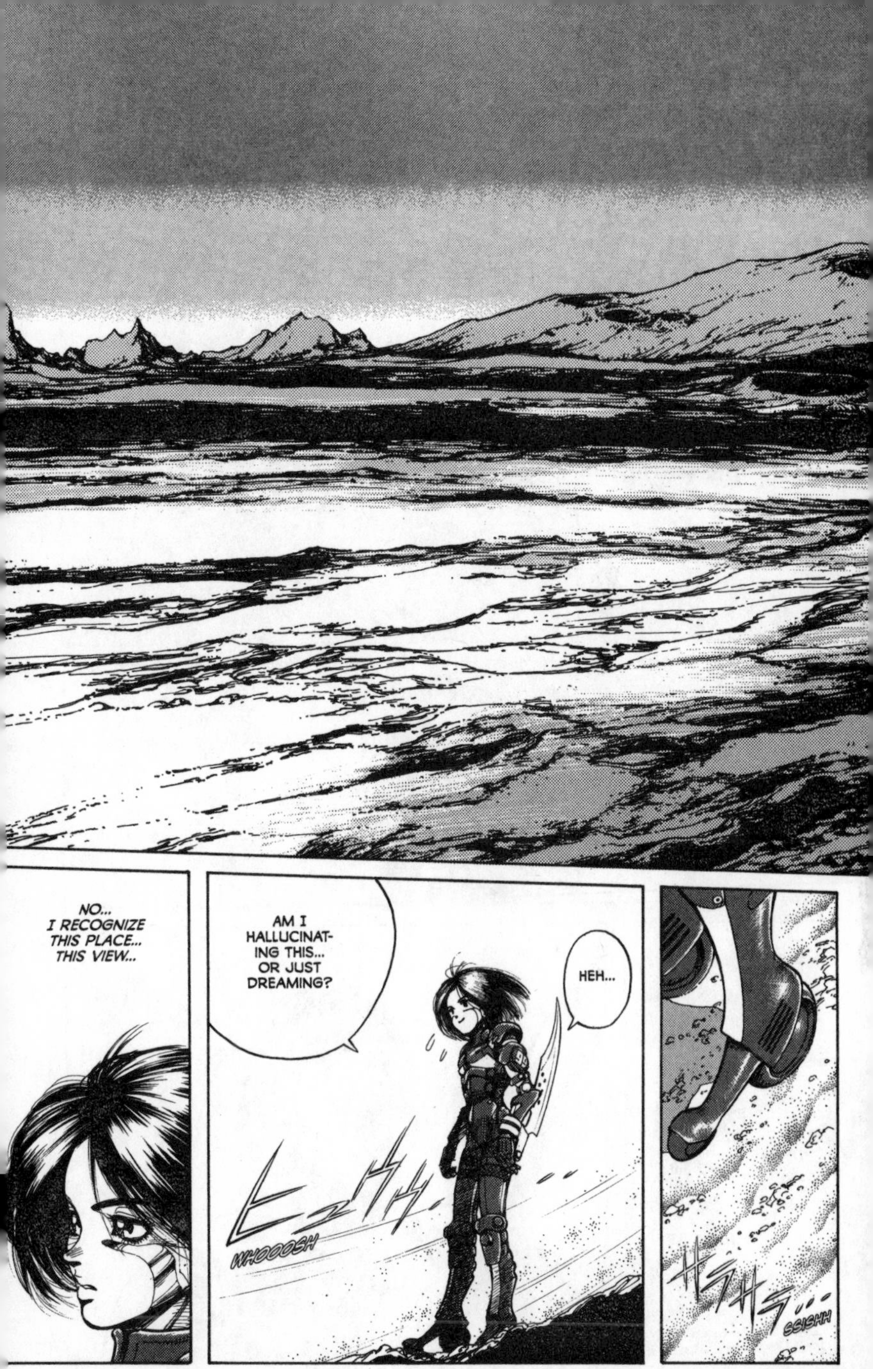
SSISHH
AM I HALLUCINATING THIS... OR JUST DREAMING?
HEH...
WHOOOSH
NO... I RECOGNIZE THIS PLACE... THIS VIEW...

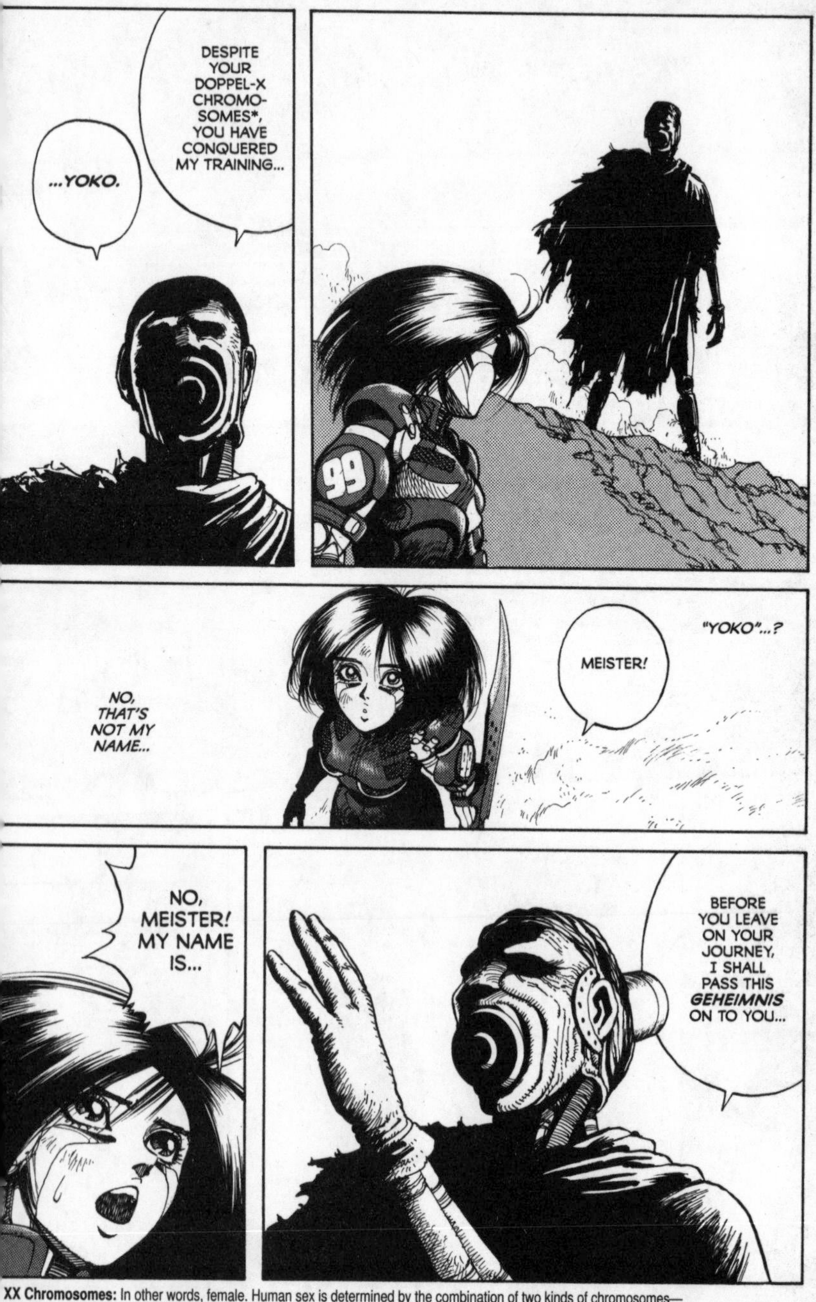
DESPITE YOUR DOPPEL-X CHROMOSOMES*, YOU HAVE CONQUERED MY TRAINING...
...YOKO.
"YOKO"...?
MEISTER!
NO, THAT'S NOT MY NAME...
BEFORE YOU LEAVE ON YOUR JOURNEY, I SHALL PASS THIS GEHEIMNIS ON TO YOU...
NO, MEISTER! MY NAME IS...

XX Chromosomes: In other words, female. Human sex is determined by the combination of two kinds of chromosomes—male chromosomes are XY (Doppel-X is the German way of saying "Double-X").

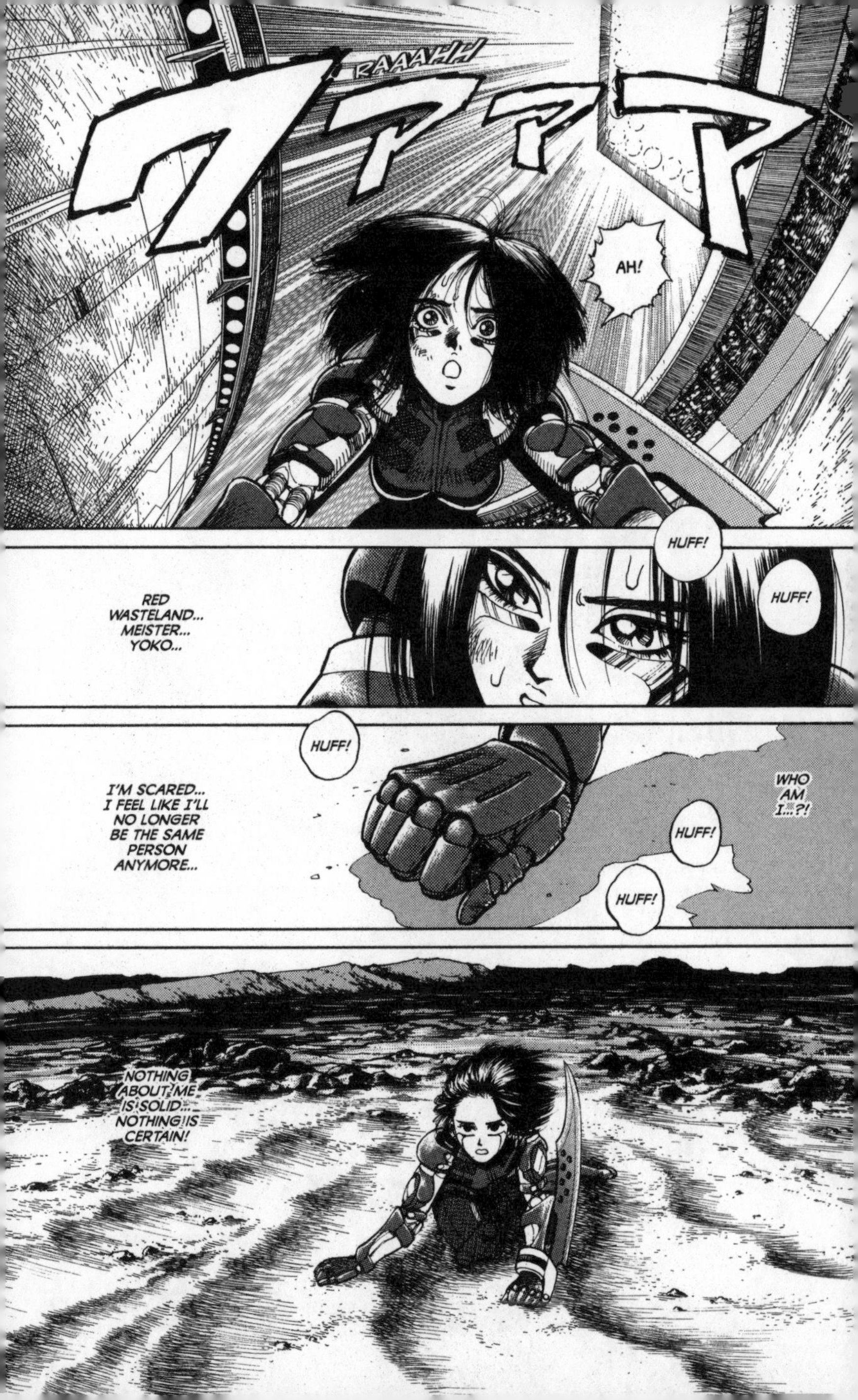
RAAAHH
AH!
HUFF!
HUFF!
RED WASTELAND... MEISTER... YOKO...
WHO AM I...?!
HUFF!
HUFF!
HUFF!
I'M SCARED... I FEEL LIKE I'LL NO LONGER BE THE SAME PERSON ANYMORE...
NOTHING ABOUT ME IS SOLID... NOTHING IS CERTAIN!

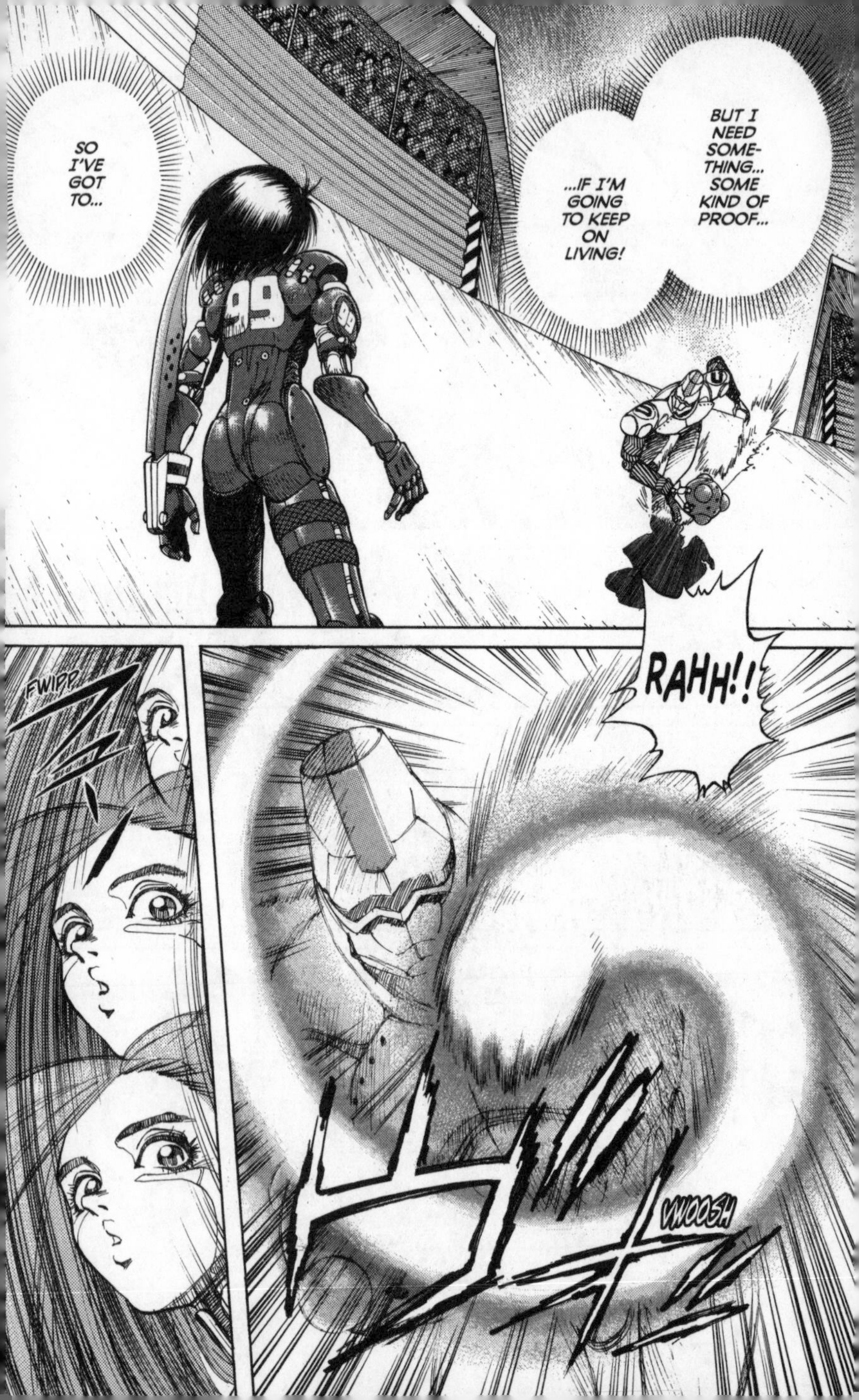
BUT I NEED SOME-THING... SOME KIND OF PROOF...
...IF I'M GOING TO KEEP ON LIVING!
SO I'VE GOT TO...
RAHH!!
VWOOSH
FWIPP

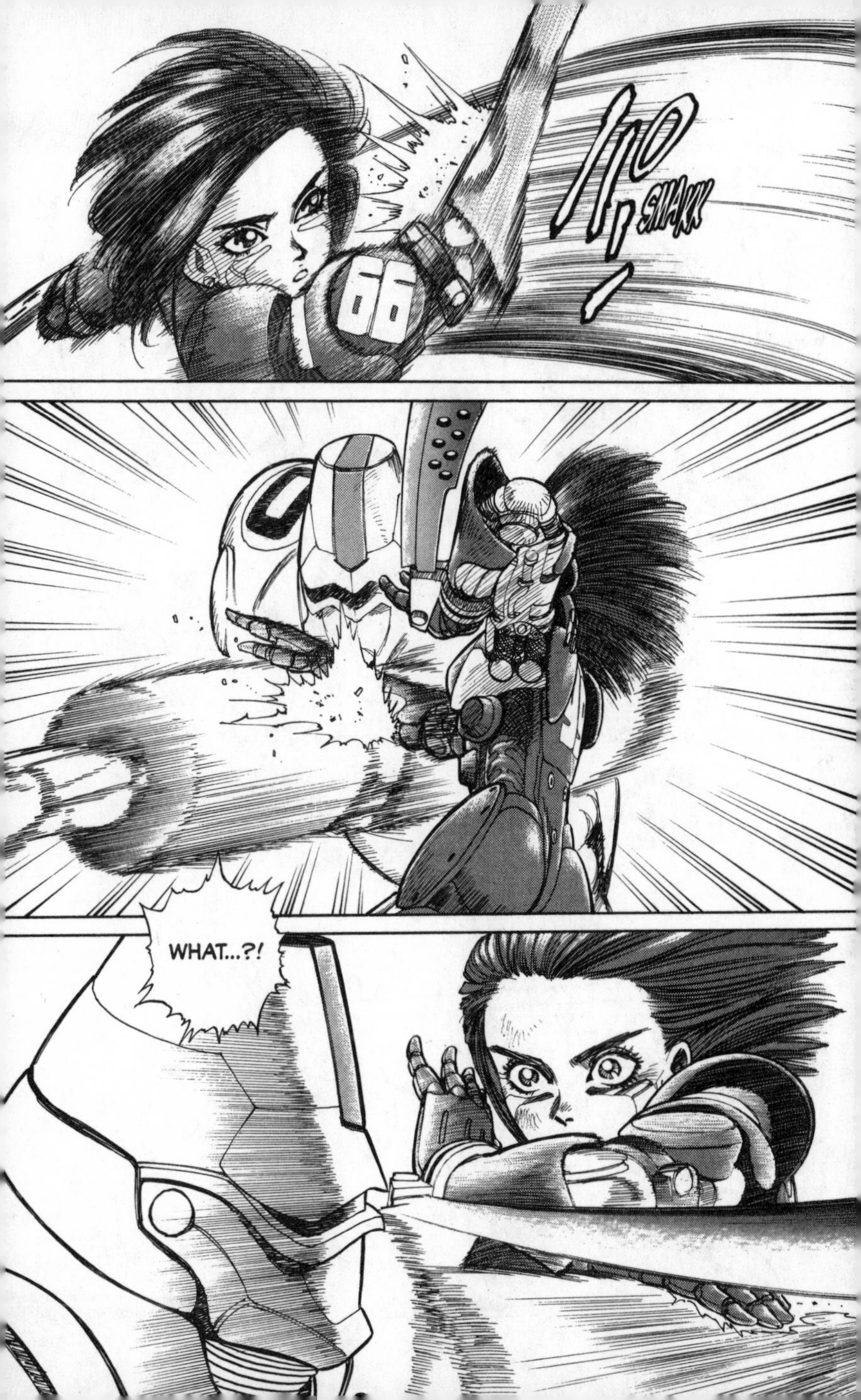
SHAKK
WHAT...?!

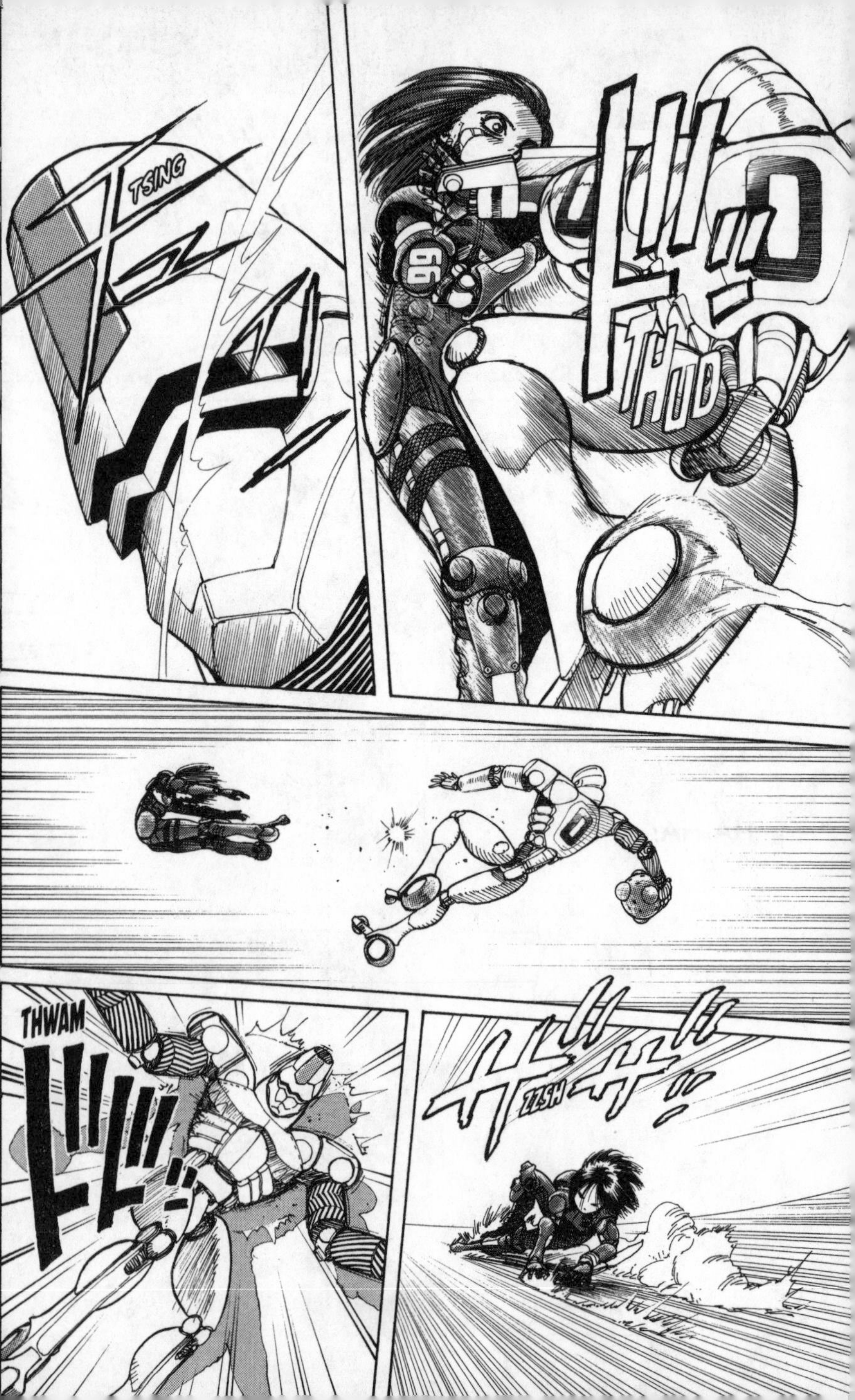
THUD
TSING
ZZSH
THWAM

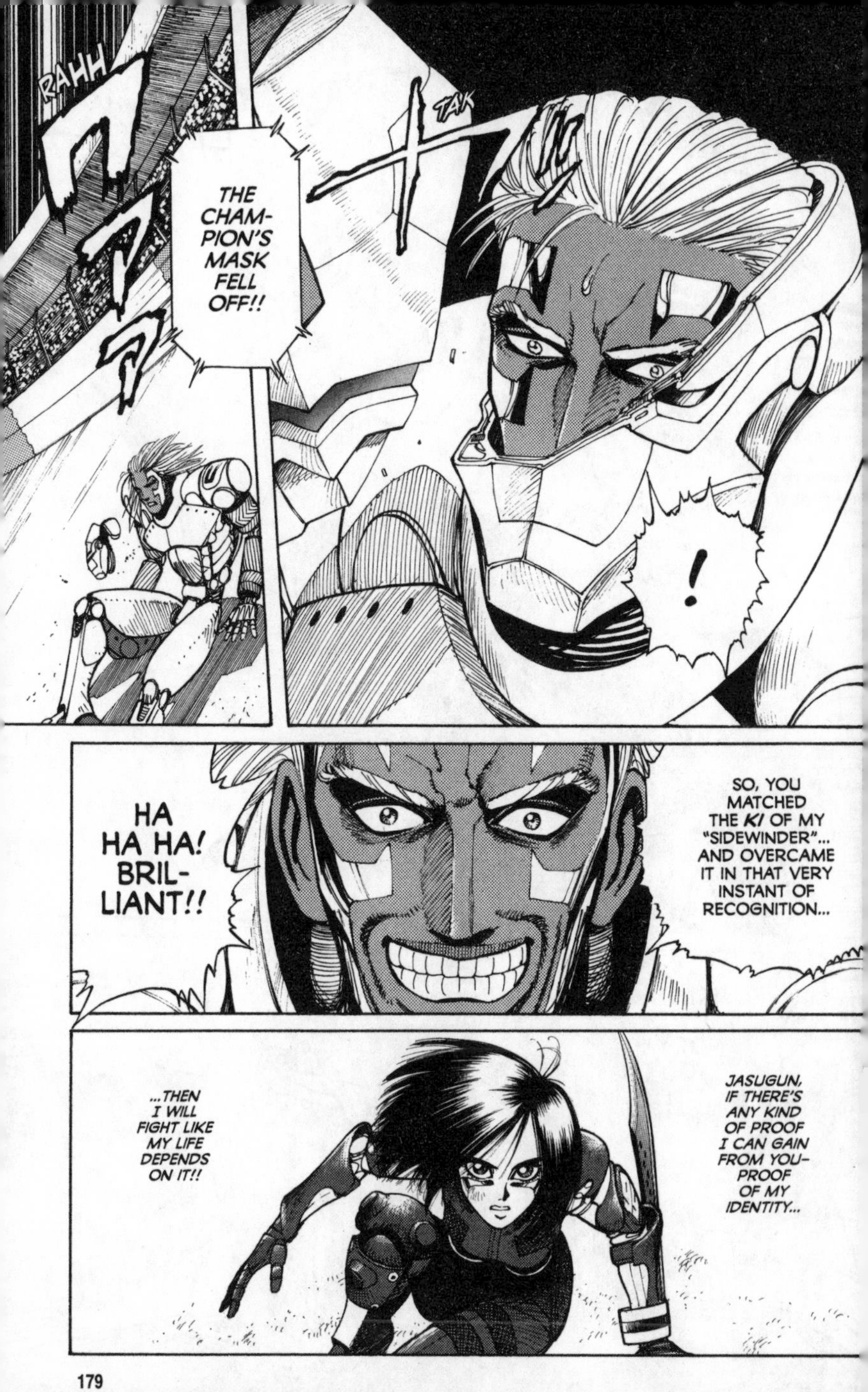
TAK
!
RAHH
THE CHAMPION'S MASK FELL OFF!!
SO, YOU MATCHED THE KI OF MY "SIDEWINDER"... AND OVERCAME IT IN THAT VERY INSTANT OF RECOGNITION...
HA HA HA! BRILLIANT!!
JASUGUN, IF THERE'S ANY KIND OF PROOF I CAN GAIN FROM YOU—PROOF OF MY IDENTITY...
...THEN I WILL FIGHT LIKE MY LIFE DEPENDS ON IT!!

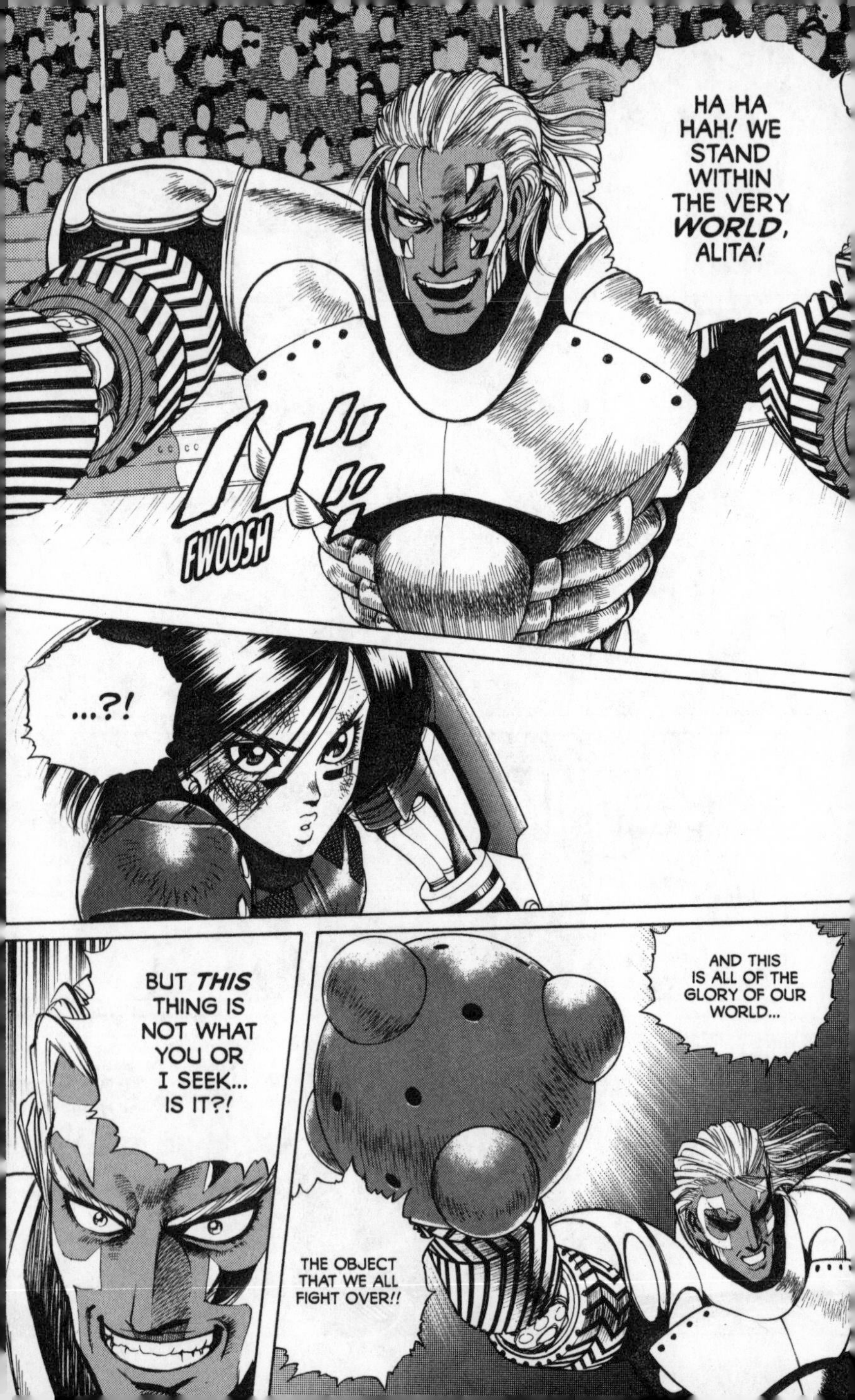
HA HA HAH! WE STAND WITHIN THE VERY WORLD, ALITA!
FWOOSH
...?!
AND THIS IS ALL OF THE GLORY OF OUR WORLD...
THE OBJECT THAT WE ALL FIGHT OVER!!
BUT THIS THING IS NOT WHAT YOU OR I SEEK... IS IT?!

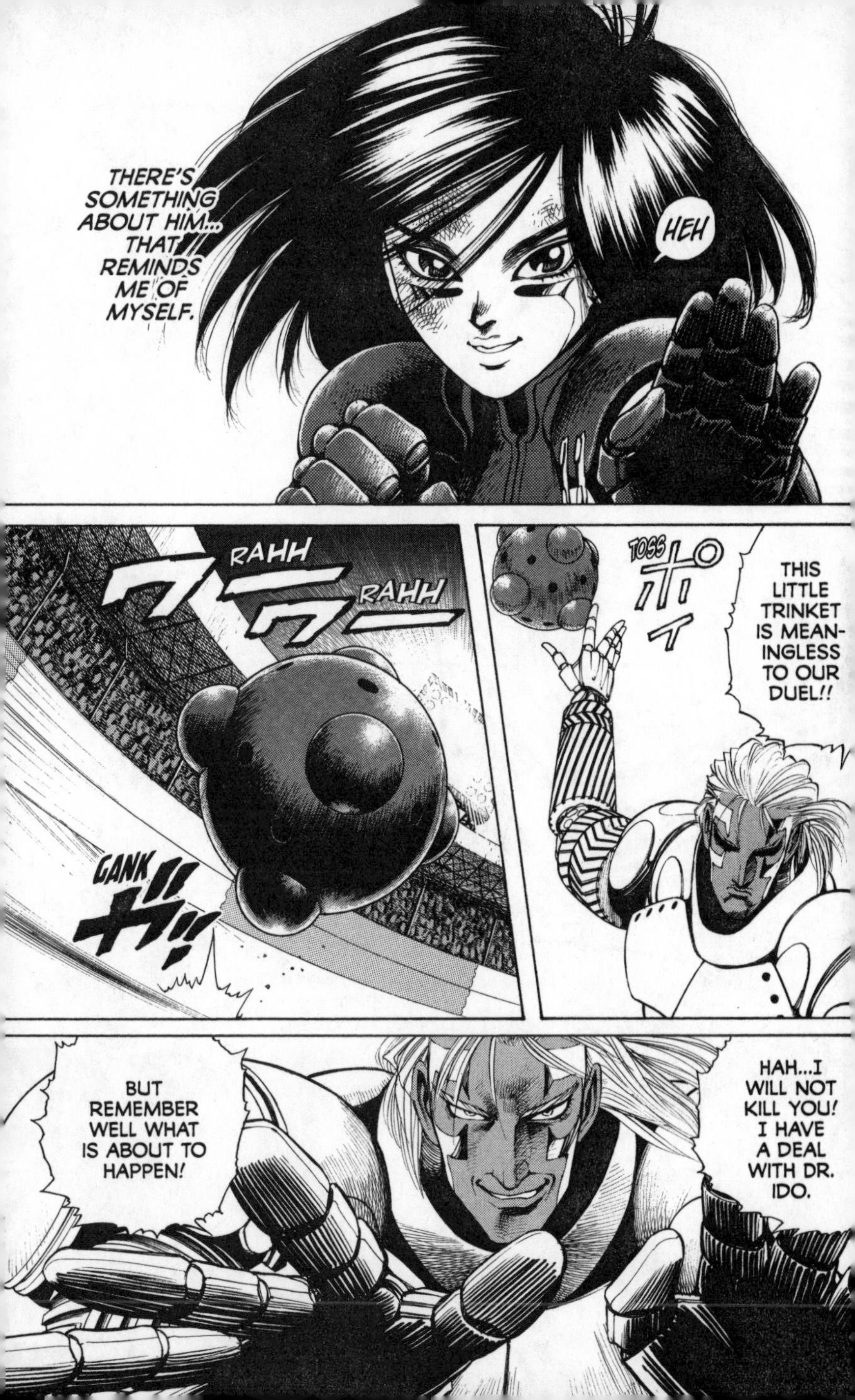
HEH
THERE'S SOMETHING ABOUT HIM... THAT REMINDS ME OF MYSELF.
TOSS
THIS LITTLE TRINKET IS MEAN-INGLESS TO OUR DUEL!!
RAHH
RAHH
GANK
HAH...I WILL NOT KILL YOU! I HAVE A DEAL WITH DR. IDO.
BUT REMEMBER WELL WHAT IS ABOUT TO HAPPEN!

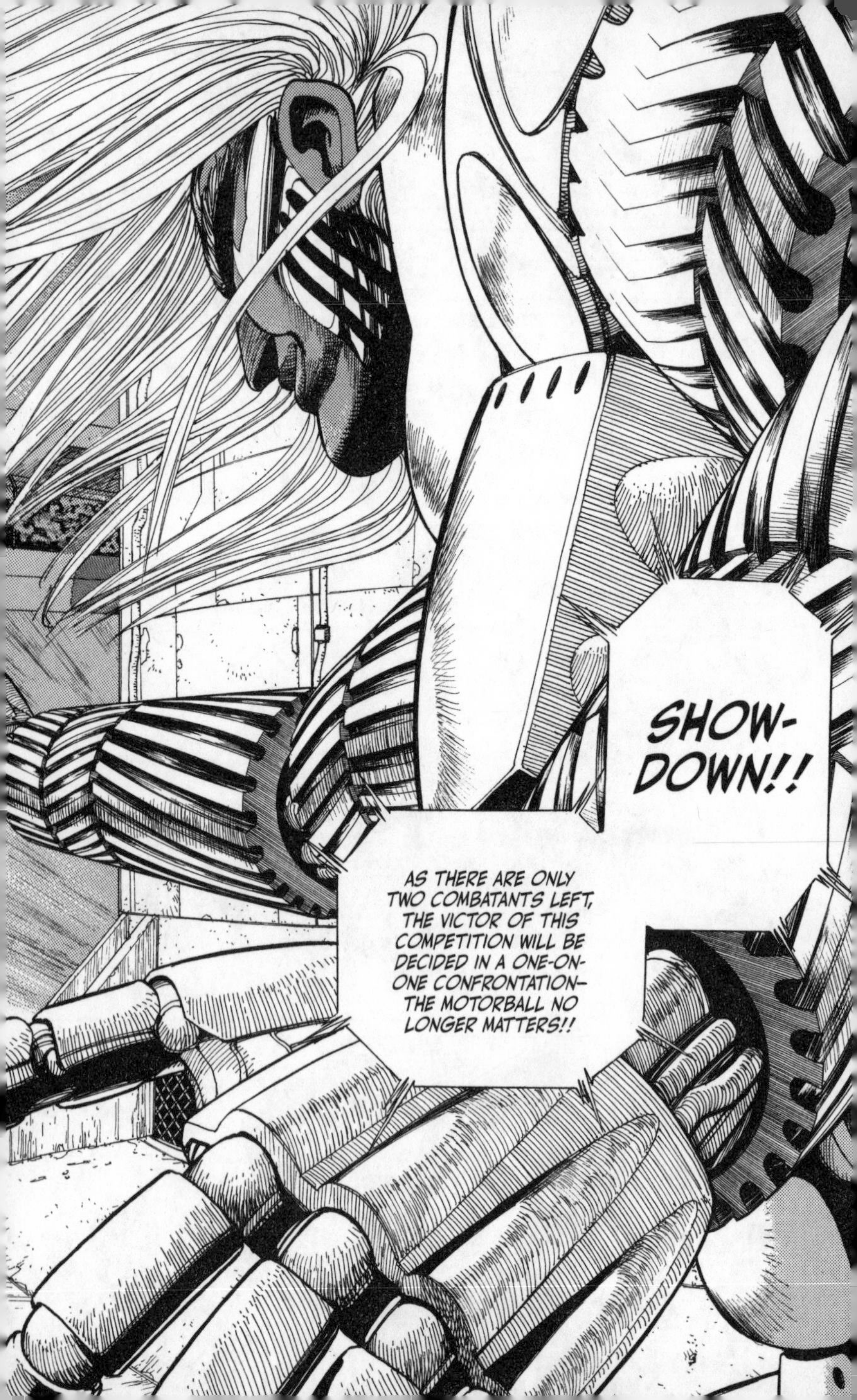
SHOW-DOWN!!
AS THERE ARE ONLY TWO COMBATANTS LEFT, THE VICTOR OF THIS COMPETITION WILL BE DECIDED IN A ONE-ON-ONE CONFRONTATION—THE MOTORBALL NO LONGER MATTERS!!

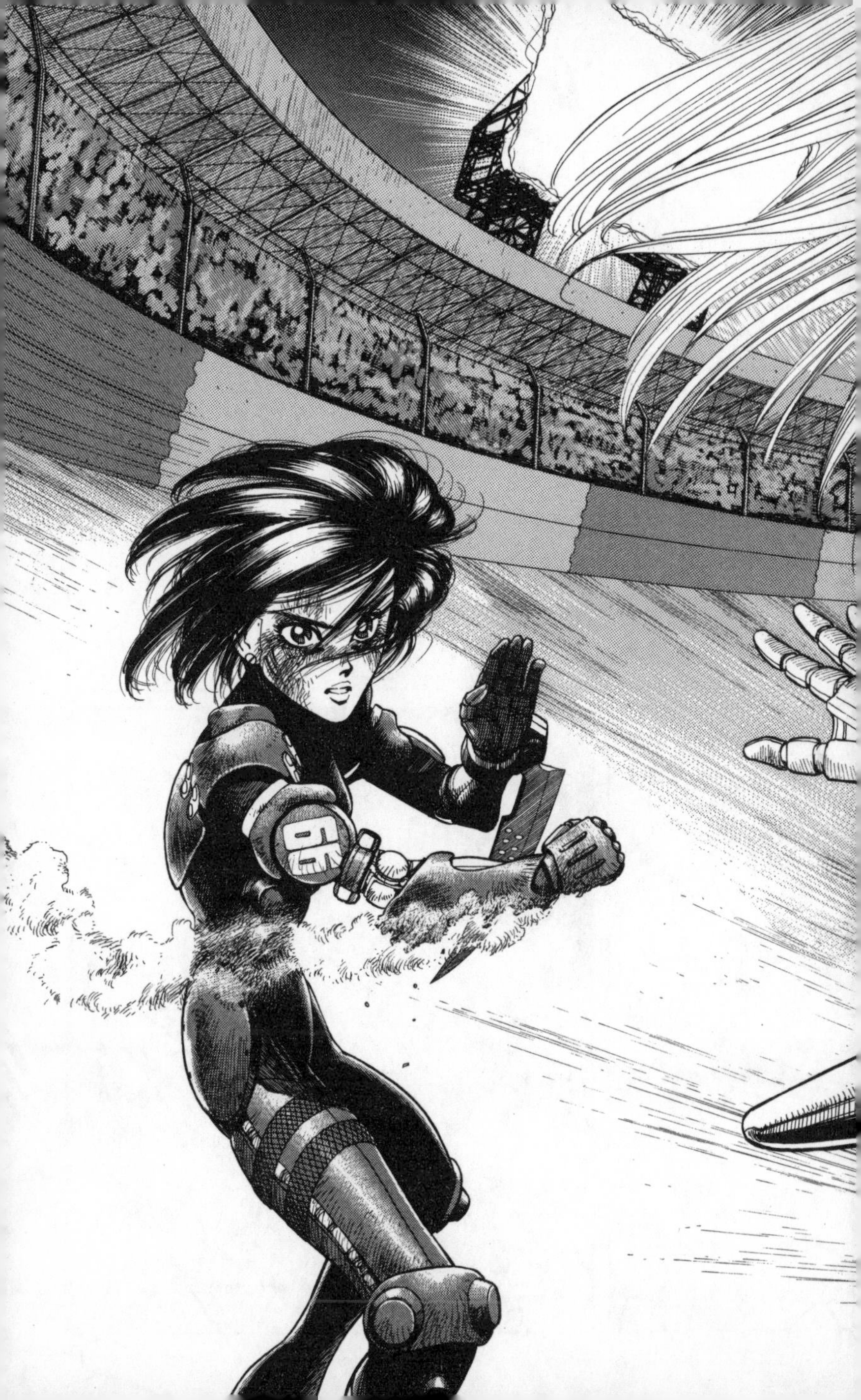

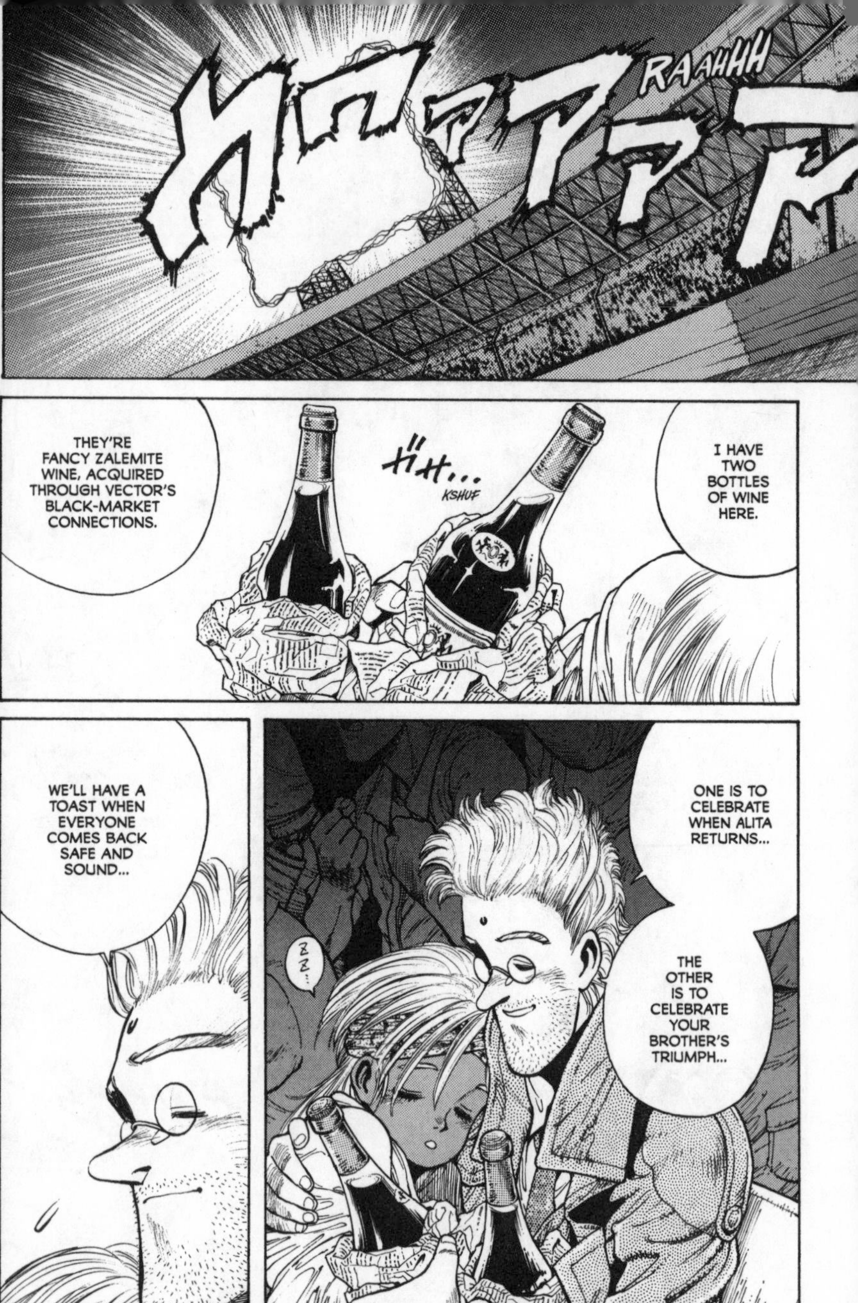
RAAHHH
I HAVE TWO BOTTLES OF WINE HERE.
KSHUF
THEY'RE FANCY ZALEMITE WINE, ACQUIRED THROUGH VECTOR'S BLACK-MARKET CONNECTIONS.
ONE IS TO CELEBRATE WHEN ALITA RETURNS...
THE OTHER IS TO CELEBRATE YOUR BROTHER'S TRIUMPH...
WE'LL HAVE A TOAST WHEN EVERYONE COMES BACK SAFE AND SOUND...

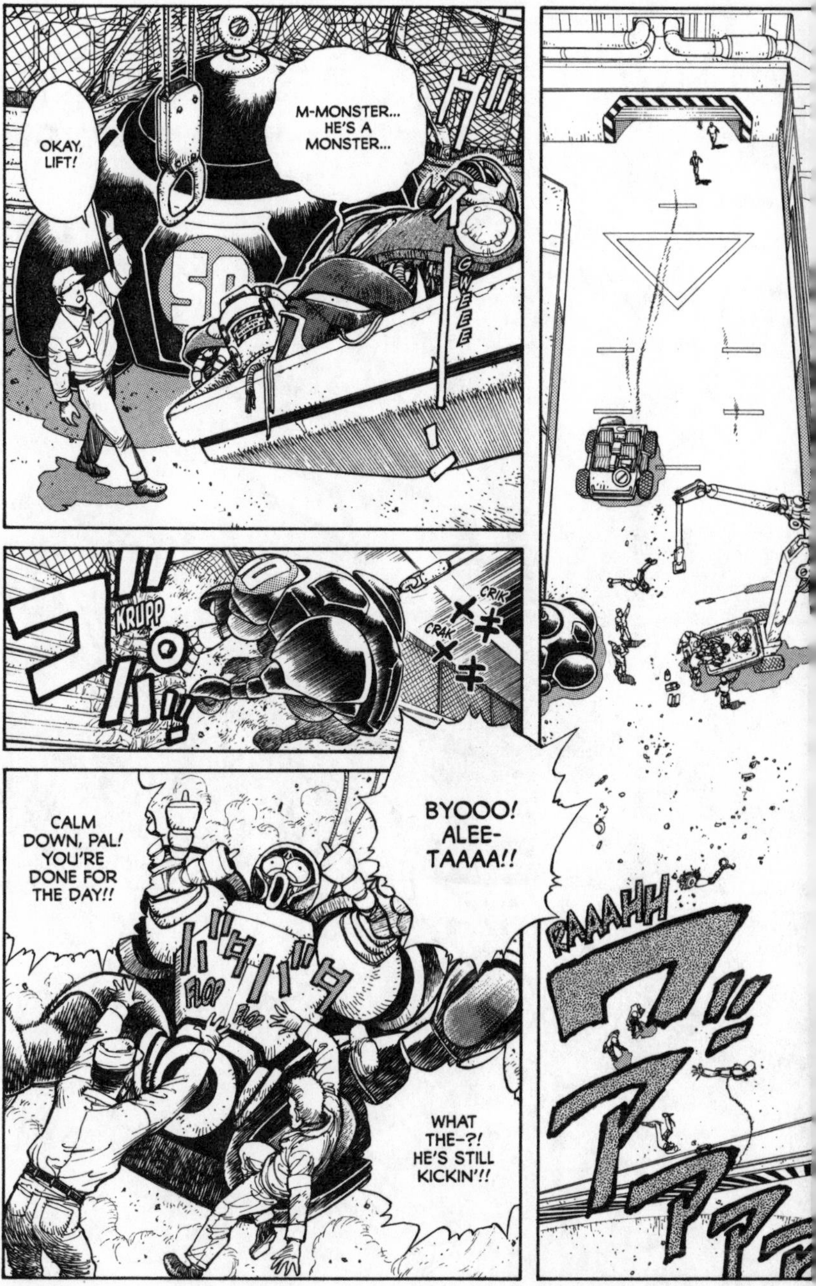
RAAAHH
M-MONSTER... HE'S A MONSTER...
OKAY, LIFT!
GWEEE
CRIK
CRAK
KRUPP
BYOOO! ALEE-TAAAA!!
CALM DOWN, PAL! YOU'RE DONE FOR THE DAY!!
FLOP
FLOP
WHAT THE-?! HE'S STILL KICKIN'!!

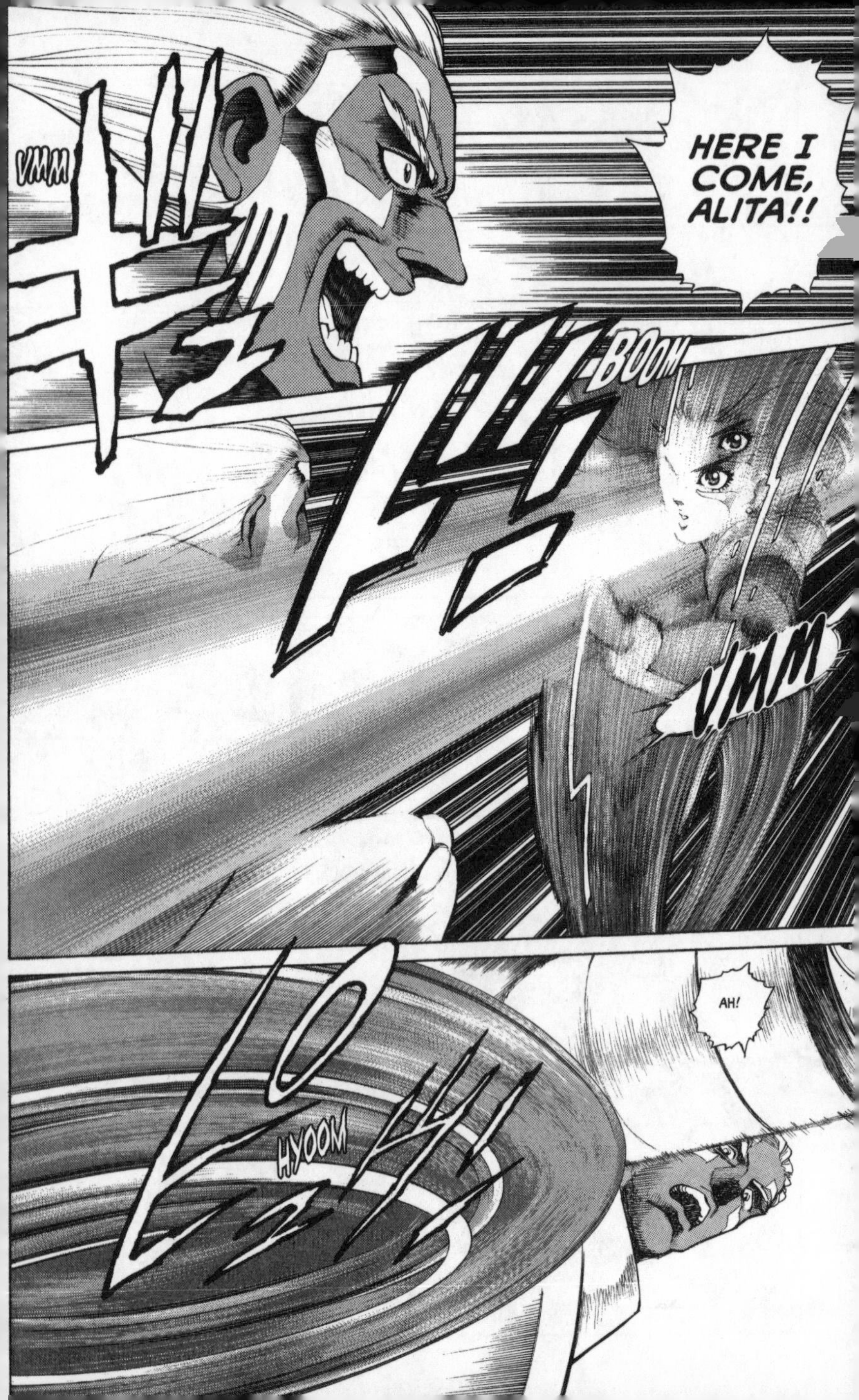
HERE I COME, ALITA!!
VMM
BOOM
VMM
AH!
HYOOM

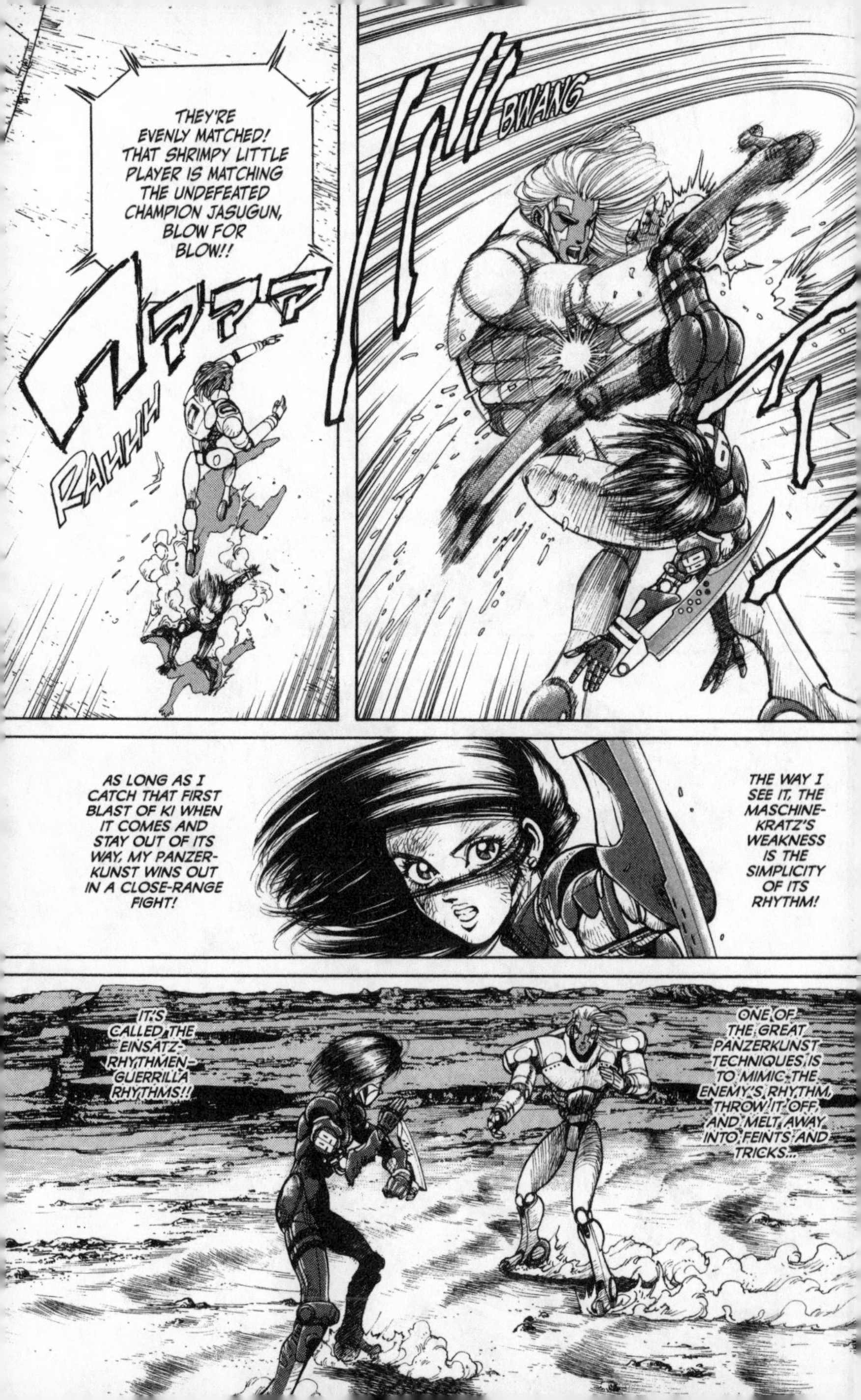
BWANG
THEY'RE EVENLY MATCHED! THAT SHRIMPY LITTLE PLAYER IS MATCHING THE UNDEFEATED CHAMPION JASUGUN, BLOW FOR BLOW!!
RAHHH
THE WAY I SEE IT, THE MASCHINE-KRATZ'S WEAKNESS IS THE SIMPLICITY OF ITS RHYTHM!
AS LONG AS I CATCH THAT FIRST BLAST OF KI WHEN IT COMES AND STAY OUT OF ITS WAY, MY PANZER-KUNST WINS OUT IN A CLOSE-RANGE FIGHT!
ONE OF THE GREAT PANZERKUNST TECHNIQUES IS TO MIMIC THE ENEMY'S RHYTHM, THROW IT OFF, AND MELT AWAY INTO FEINTS AND TRICKS...
IT'S CALLED THE EINSATZ-RHYTHMEN-GUERRILLA RHYTHMS!!

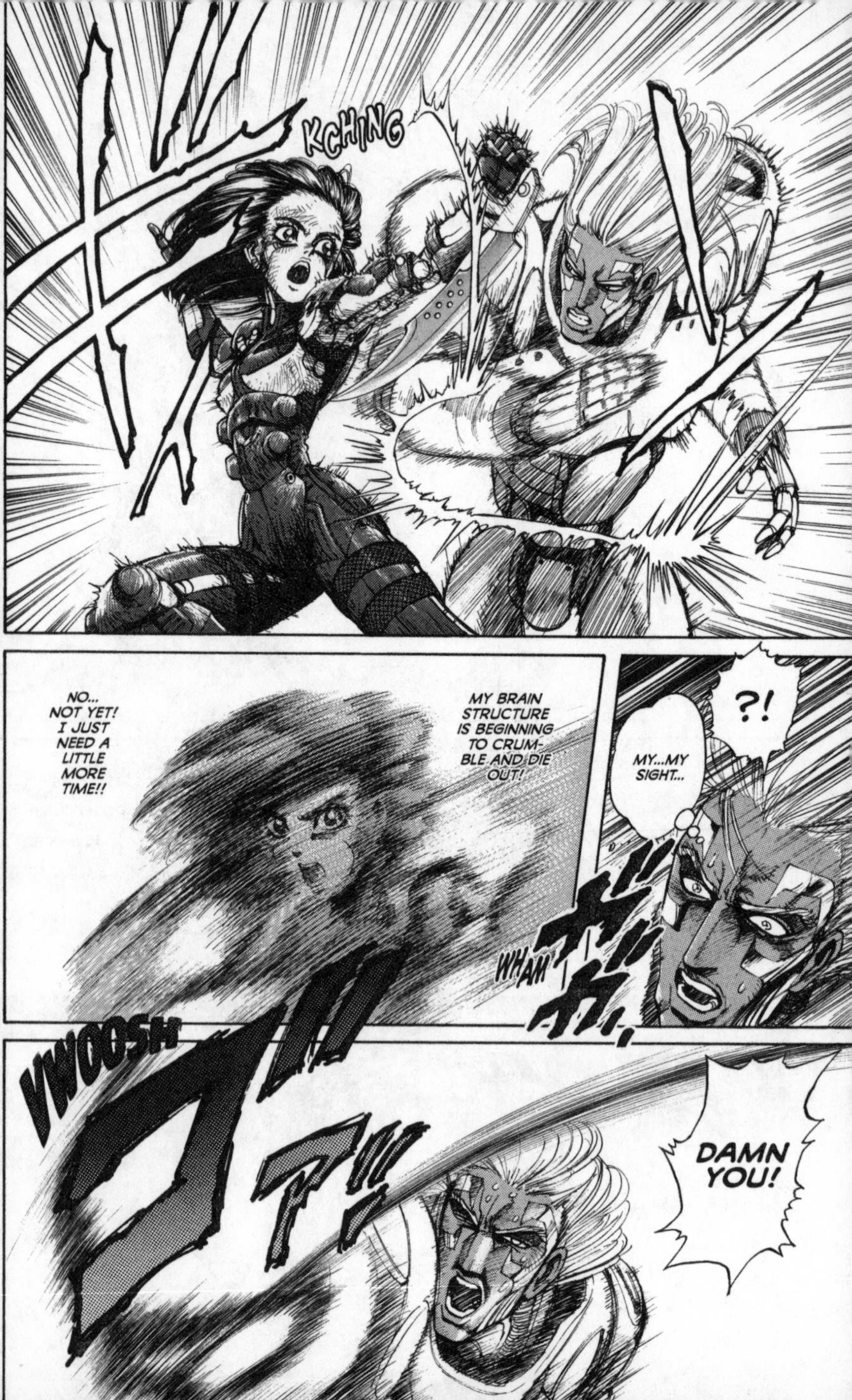
KCHING
?!
MY...MY SIGHT...
WHAM
MY BRAIN STRUCTURE IS BEGINNING TO CRUM-BLE AND DIE OUT!
NO... NOT YET! I JUST NEED A LITTLE MORE TIME!!
DAMN YOU!
VWOOSH

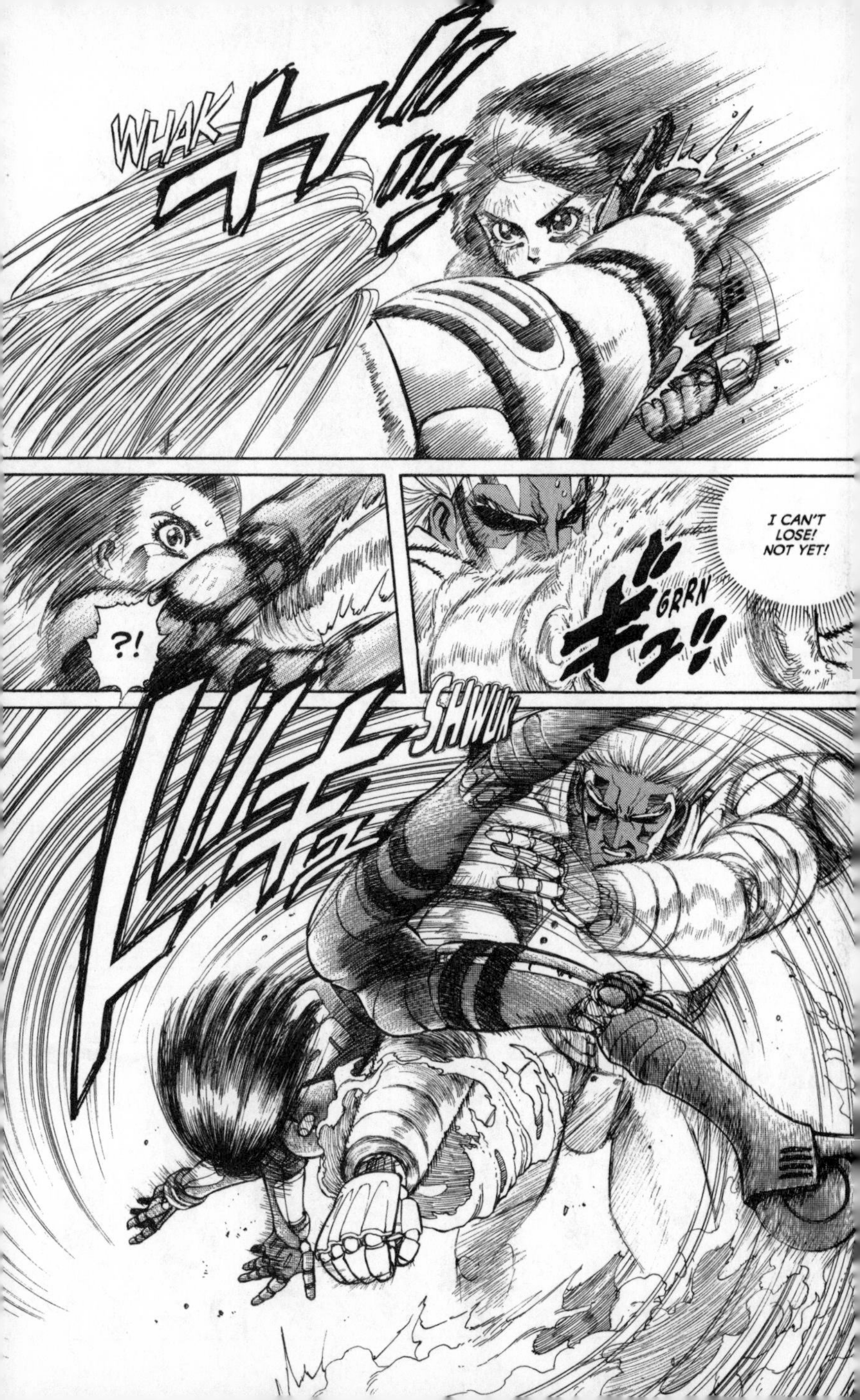
WHAK
I CAN'T LOSE! NOT YET!
GRRN
?!
SHWUK

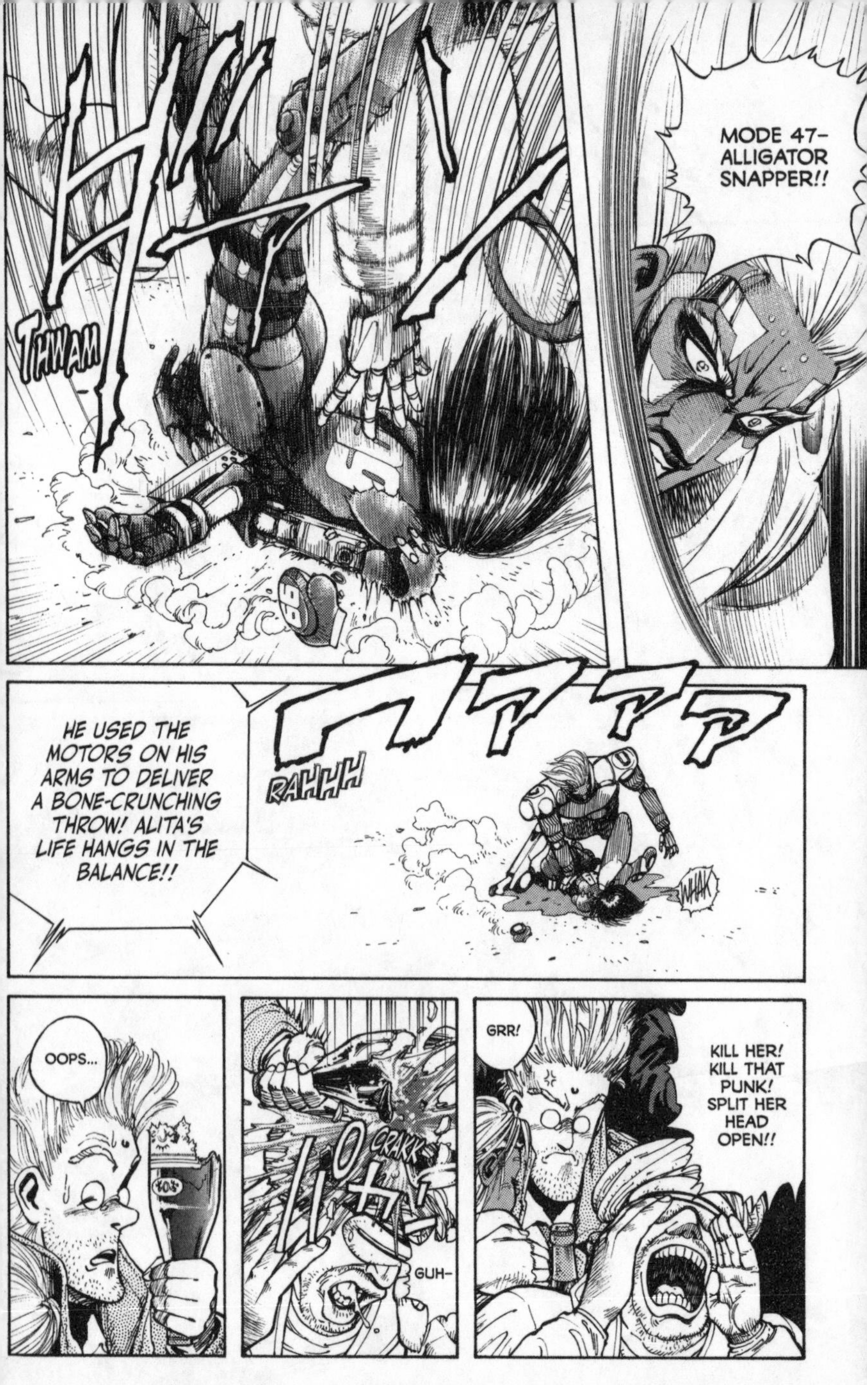
MODE 47–
ALLIGATOR
SNAPPER!!
THWAM
RAHHH
WHAK
HE USED THE MOTORS ON HIS ARMS TO DELIVER A BONE-CRUNCHING THROW! ALITA'S LIFE HANGS IN THE BALANCE!!
GRR!
KILL HER! KILL THAT PUNK! SPLIT HER HEAD OPEN!!
CRAKK
GUH–
OOPS...

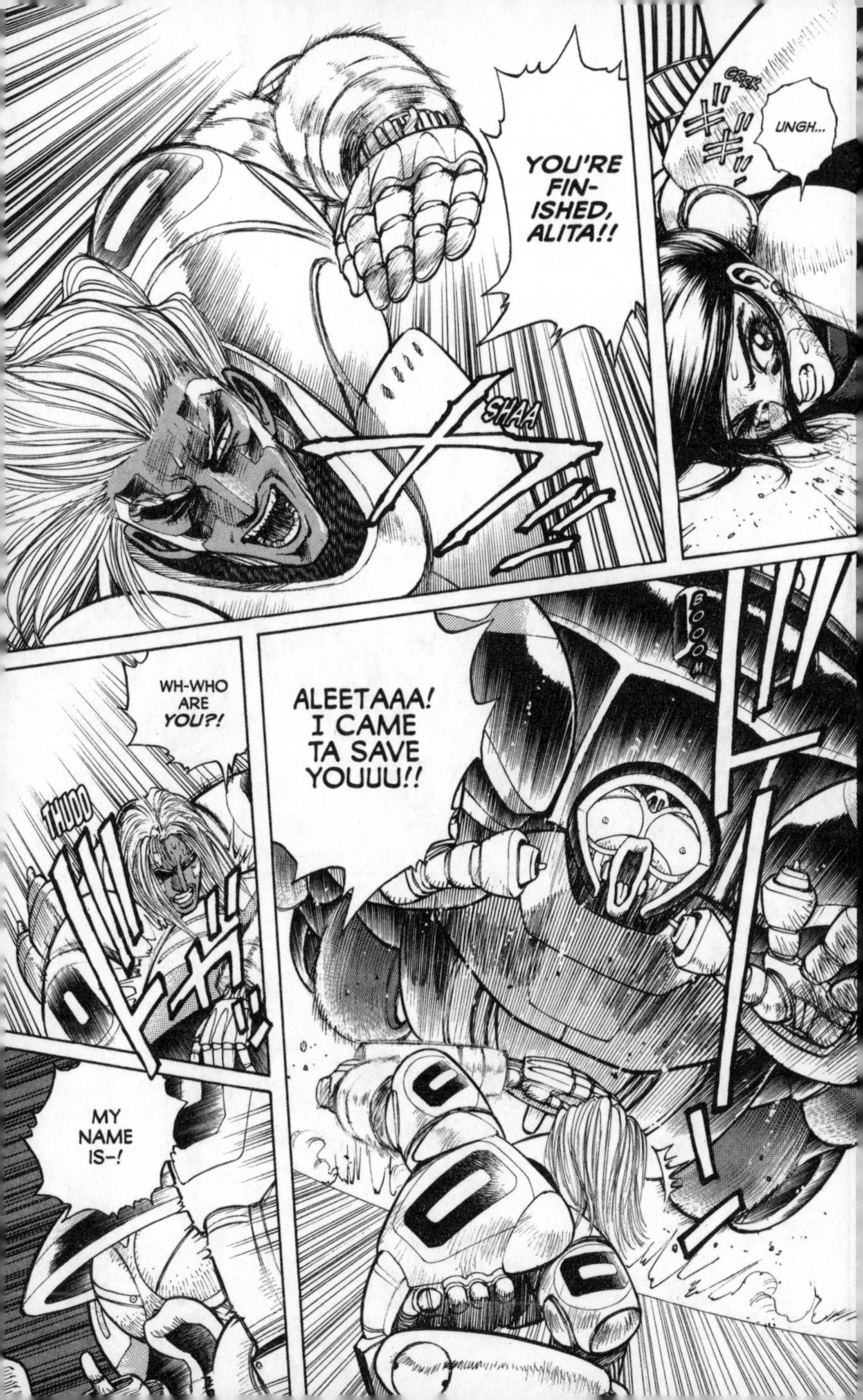

CRRK
UNGH...
YOU'RE FIN-ISHED, ALITA!!
SHAA
BOOOM
ALEETAAA! I CAME TA SAVE YOUUU!!
WH-WHO ARE YOU?!
THUDD
MY NAME IS–!

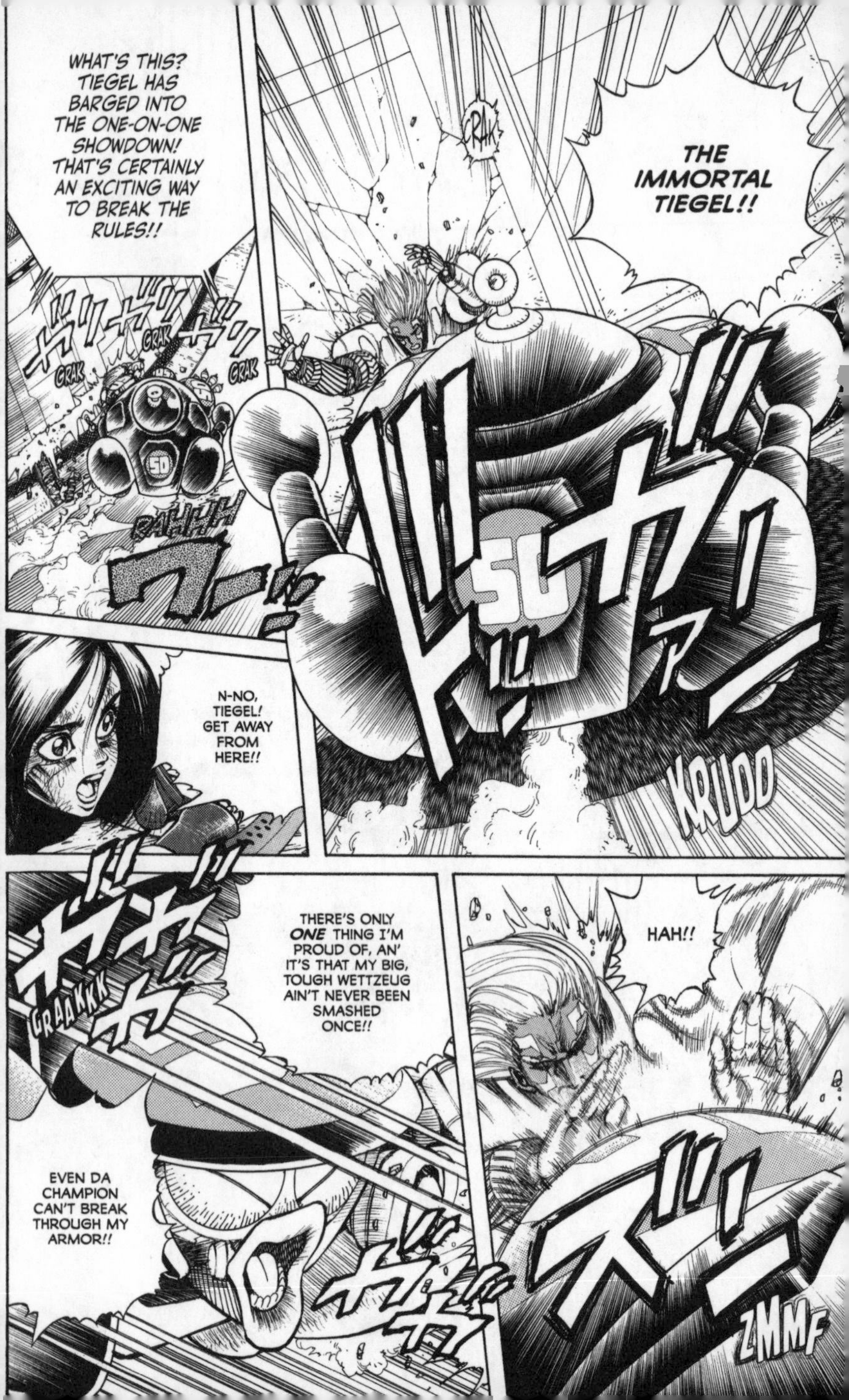
CRAK
THE IMMORTAL TIEGEL!!
KRUDD
WHAT'S THIS? TIEGEL HAS BARGED INTO THE ONE-ON-ONE SHOWDOWN! THAT'S CERTAINLY AN EXCITING WAY TO BREAK THE RULES!!
CRAK
CRAK
CRAK
RAHHHH
N-NO, TIEGEL! GET AWAY FROM HERE!!
HAH!!
ZMMF
GRAAKKK
THERE'S ONLY ***ONE*** THING I'M PROUD OF, AN' IT'S THAT MY BIG, TOUGH WETTZEUG AIN'T NEVER BEEN SMASHED ONCE!!
EVEN DA CHAMPION CAN'T BREAK THROUGH MY ARMOR!!

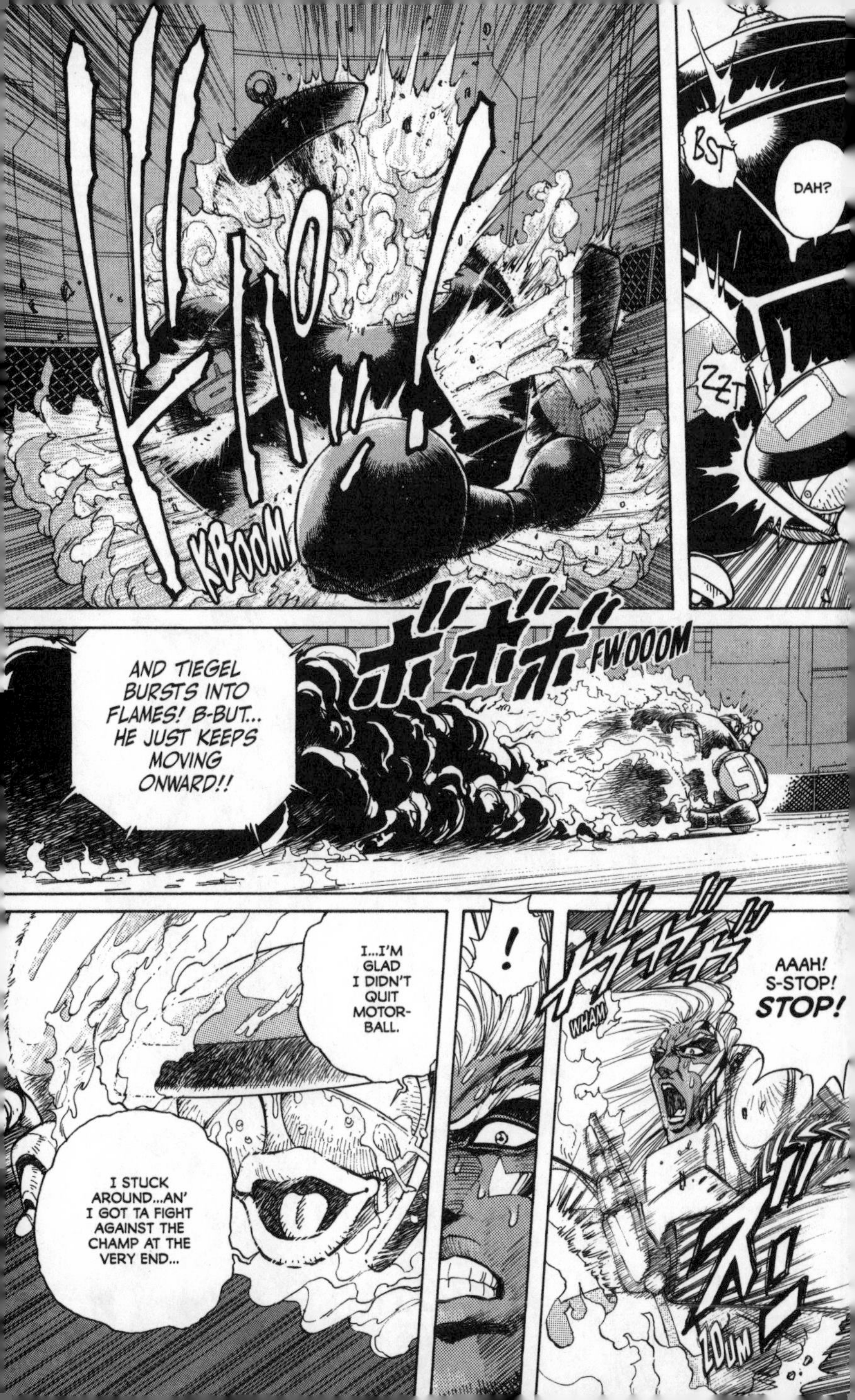
BST
DAH?
ZZZT
KBOOM
AND TIEGEL BURSTS INTO FLAMES! B-BUT... HE JUST KEEPS MOVING ONWARD!!
FWOOOM
WHAM
AAAH! S-STOP! **STOP!**
ZOOM
!
I...I'M GLAD I DIDN'T QUIT MOTOR-BALL.
I STUCK AROUND...AN' I GOT TA FIGHT AGAINST THE CHAMP AT THE VERY END...

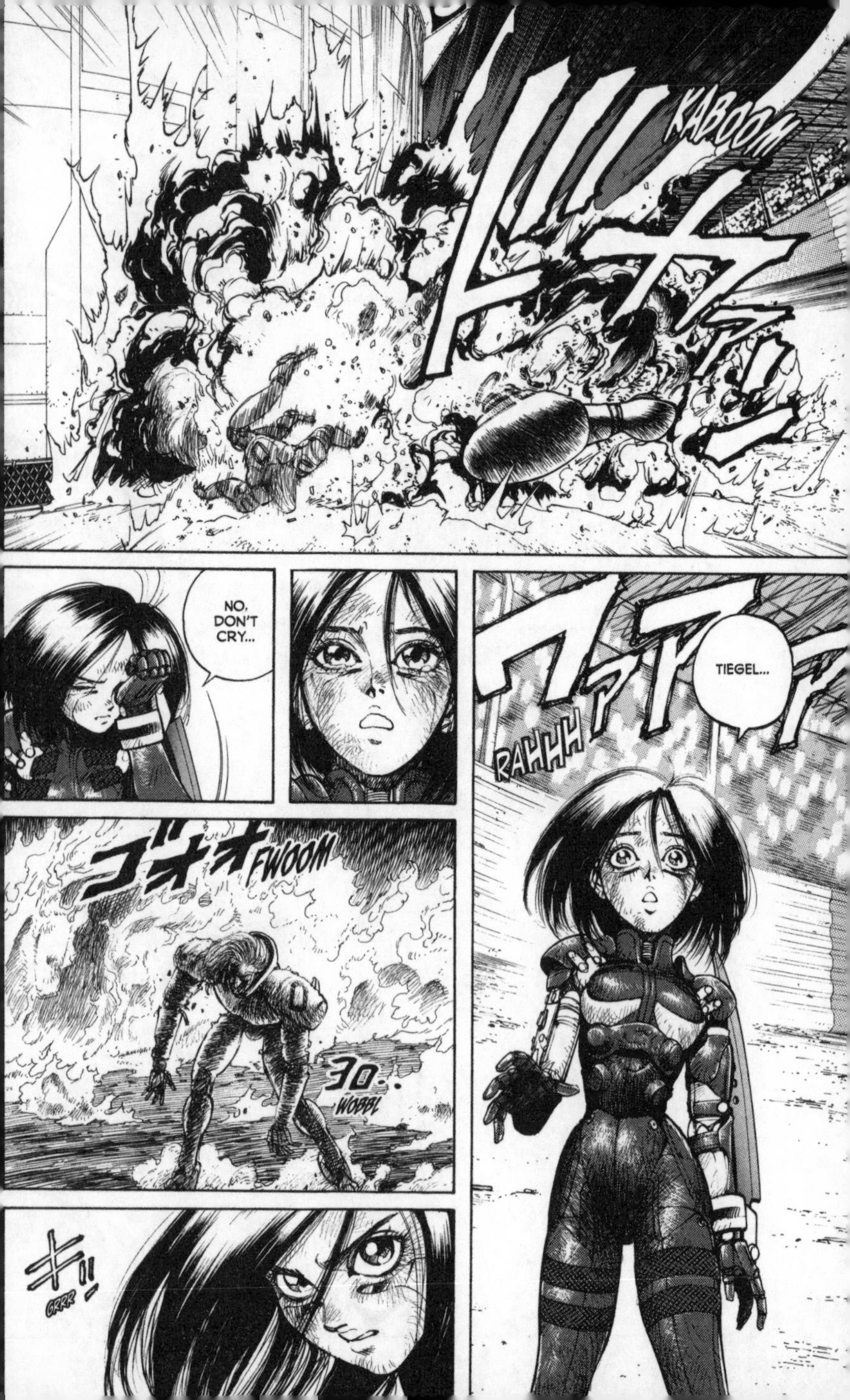
KABOOM
RAHHH
TIEGEL...
NO, DON'T CRY...
FWOOM
WOBBL
GRRR

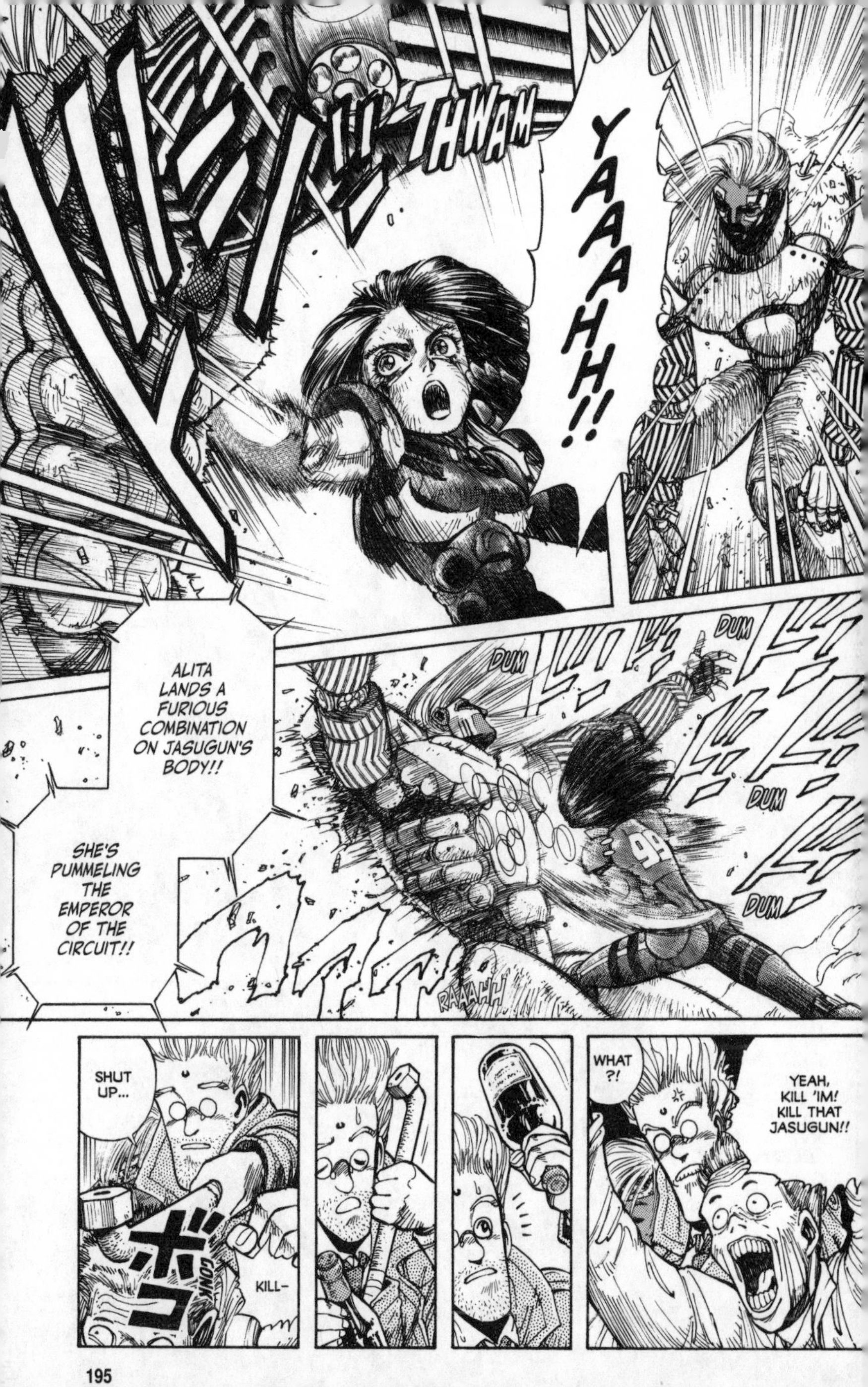
YAAAAHH!!
THWAM
DUM
DUM
DUM
DUM
ALITA LANDS A FURIOUS COMBINATION ON JASUGUN'S BODY!!
SHE'S PUMMELING THE EMPEROR OF THE CIRCUIT!!
RAAAHH
YEAH, KILL 'IM! KILL THAT JASUGUN!!
WHAT ?!
SHUT UP...
GONK
KILL-

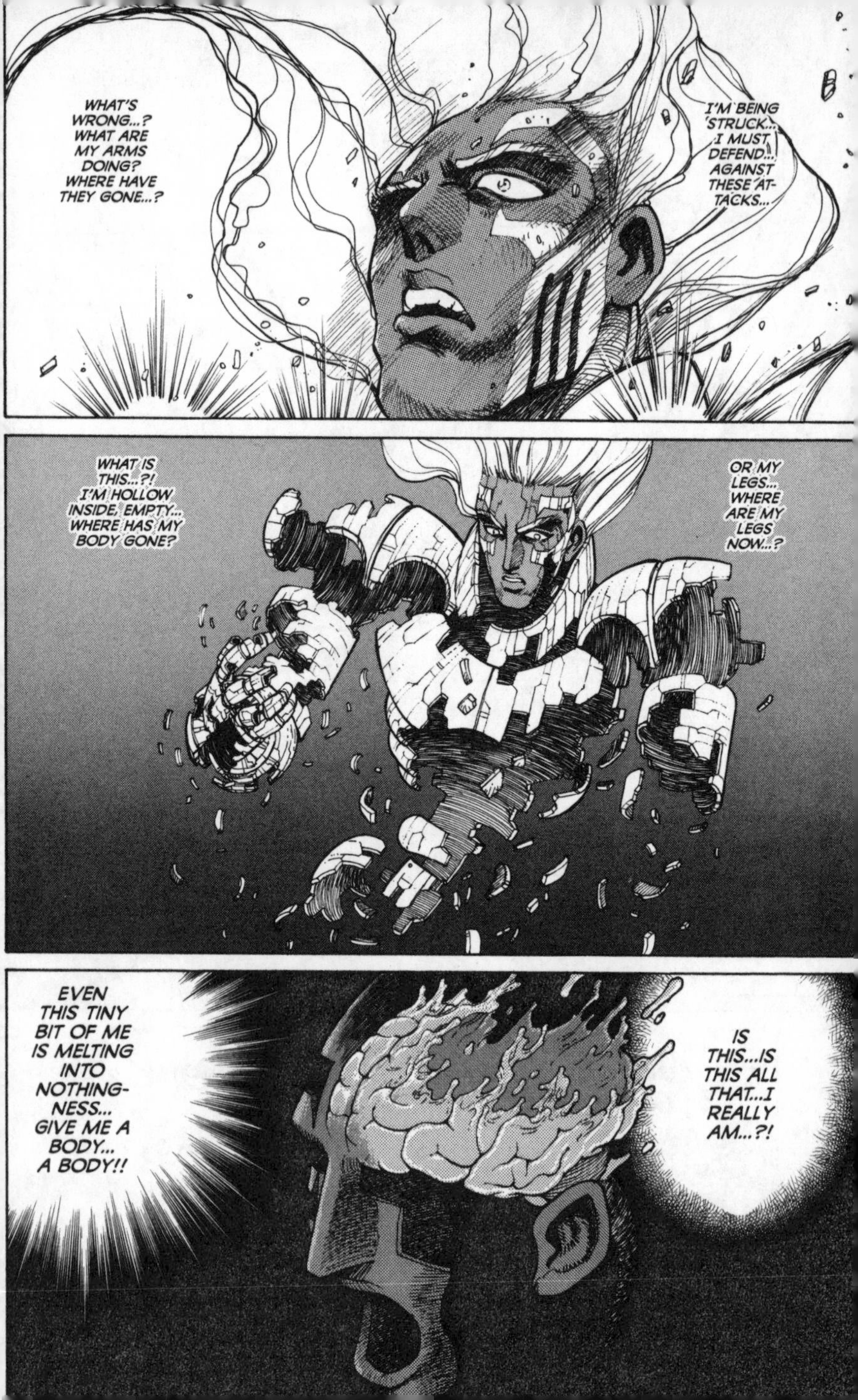
I'M BEING STRUCK... I MUST DEFEND... AGAINST THESE AT-TACKS...
WHAT'S WRONG...? WHAT ARE MY ARMS DOING? WHERE HAVE THEY GONE...?
OR MY LEGS... WHERE ARE MY LEGS NOW...?
WHAT IS THIS...?! I'M HOLLOW INSIDE, EMPTY... WHERE HAS MY BODY GONE?
IS THIS...IS THIS ALL THAT...I REALLY AM...?!
EVEN THIS TINY BIT OF ME IS MELTING INTO NOTHING-NESS... GIVE ME A BODY... A BODY!!

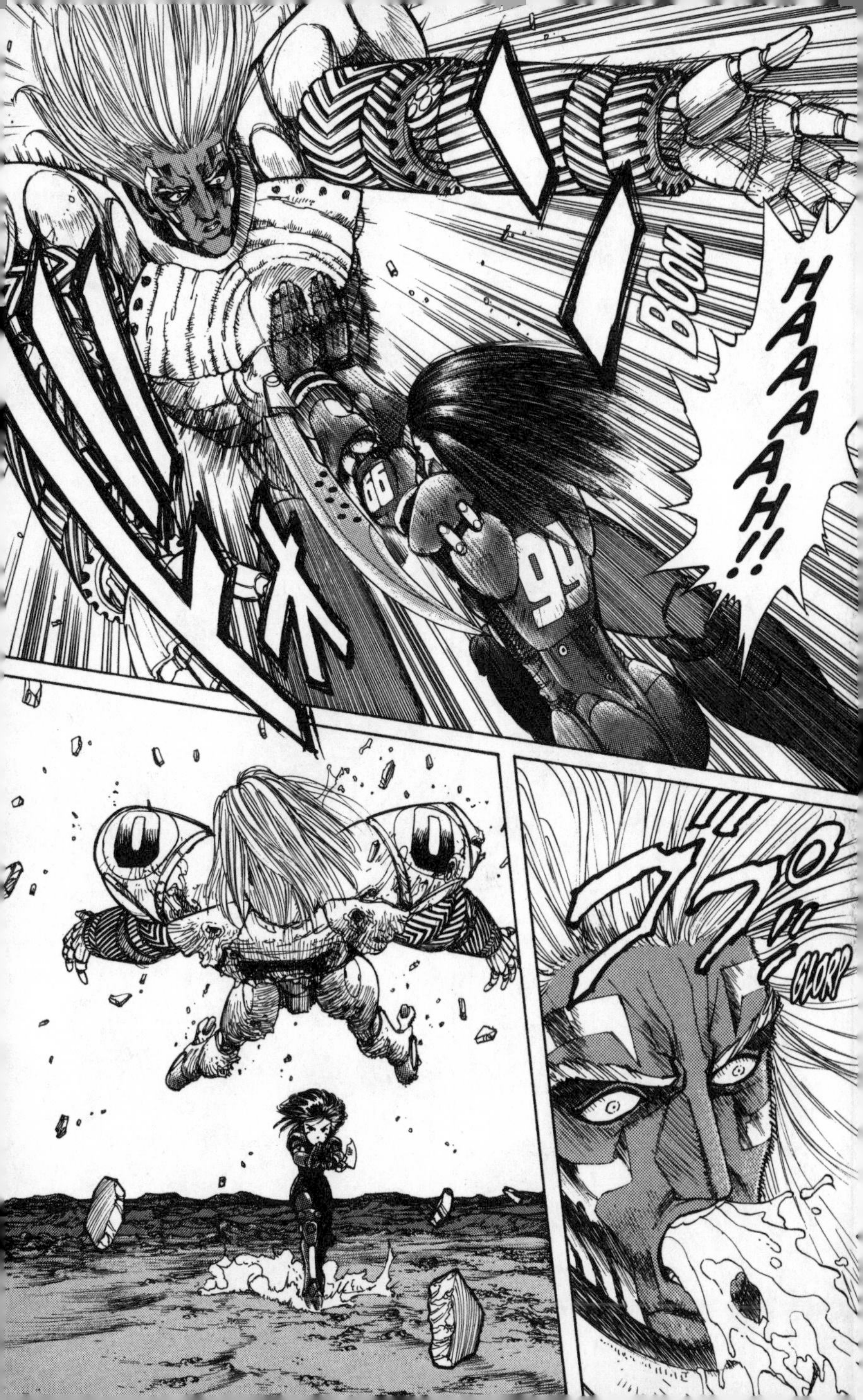
HAAAAAH!!
BOOM
GLORP

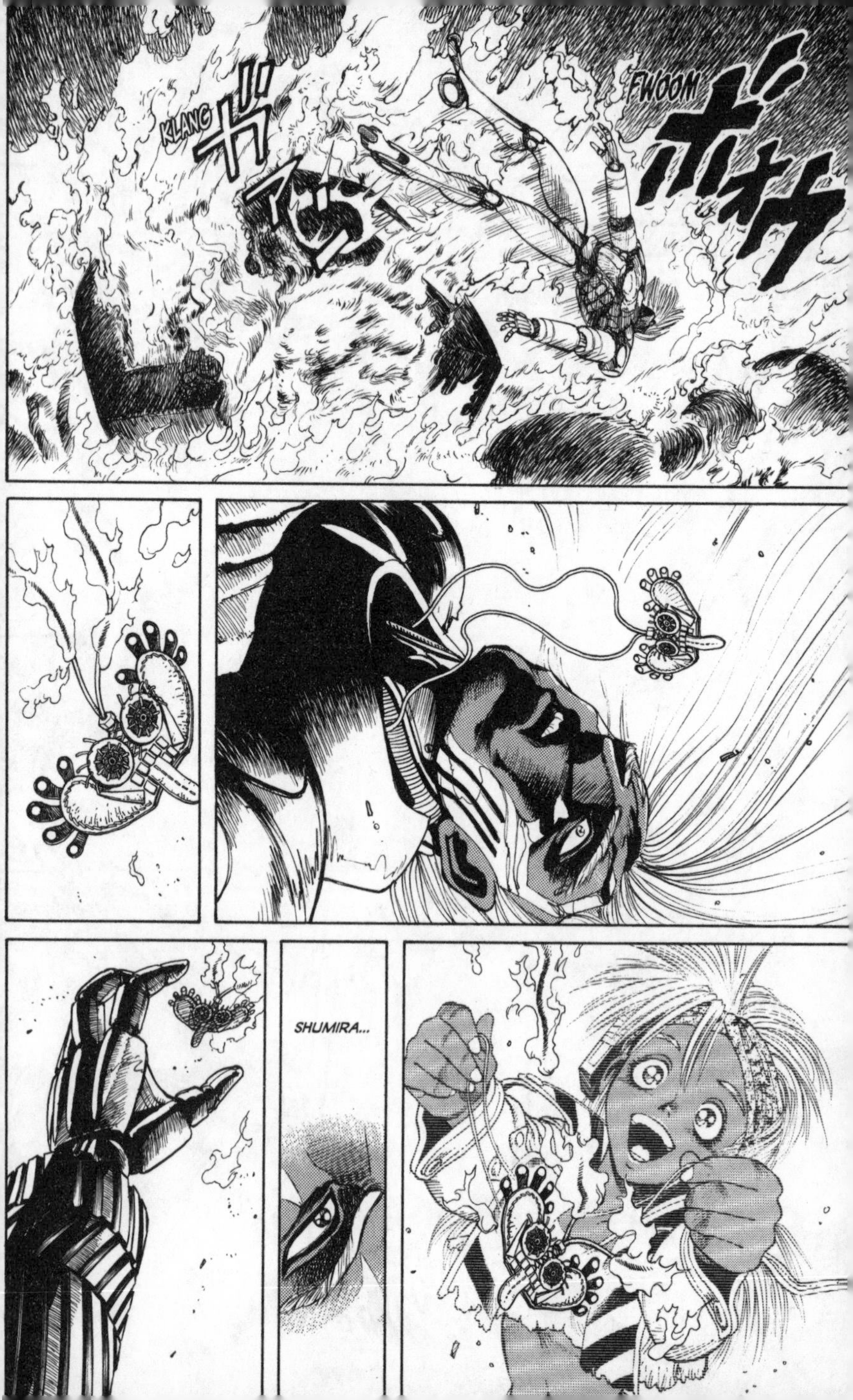
FWOOM
KLANG
SHUMIRA...

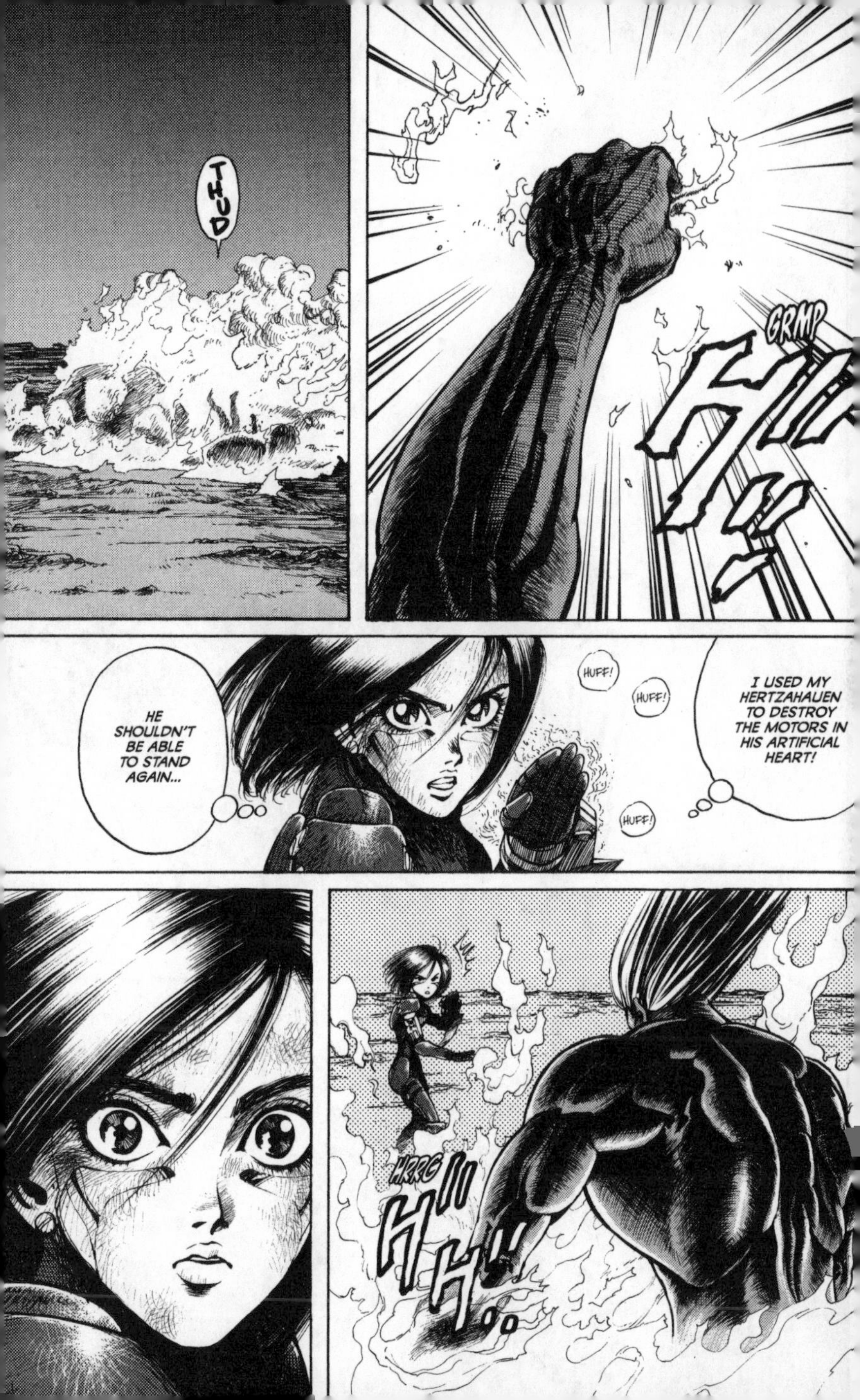
GRMP
THUD
I USED MY HERTZAHAUEN TO DESTROY THE MOTORS IN HIS ARTIFICIAL HEART!
HUFF!
HUFF!
HE SHOULDN'T BE ABLE TO STAND AGAIN...
HUFF!
HRRG

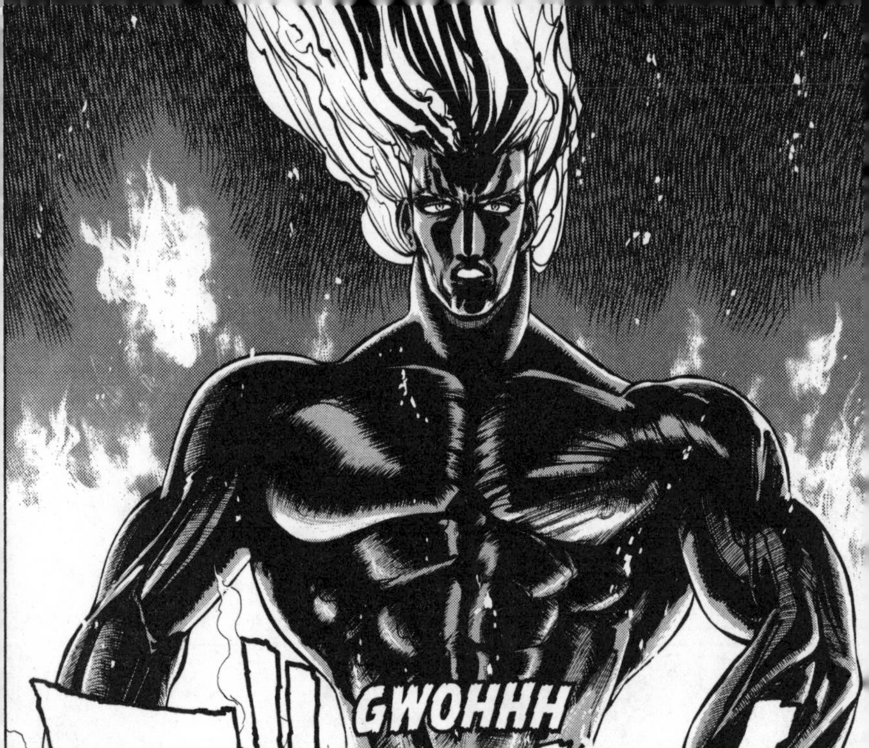
GWOHHH
ゴオオオ
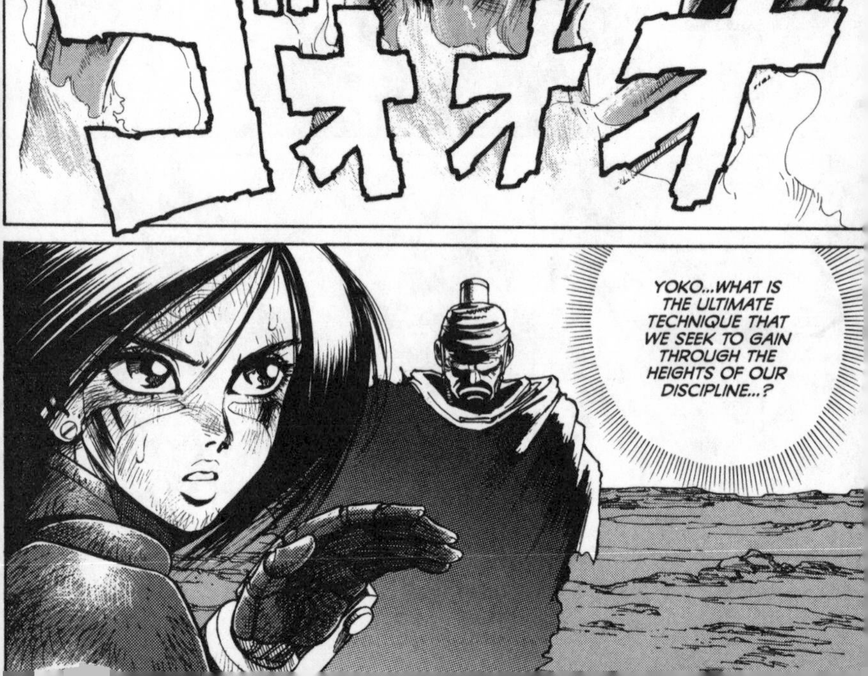
YOKO...WHAT IS THE ULTIMATE TECHNIQUE THAT WE SEEK TO GAIN THROUGH THE HEIGHTS OF OUR DISCIPLINE...?

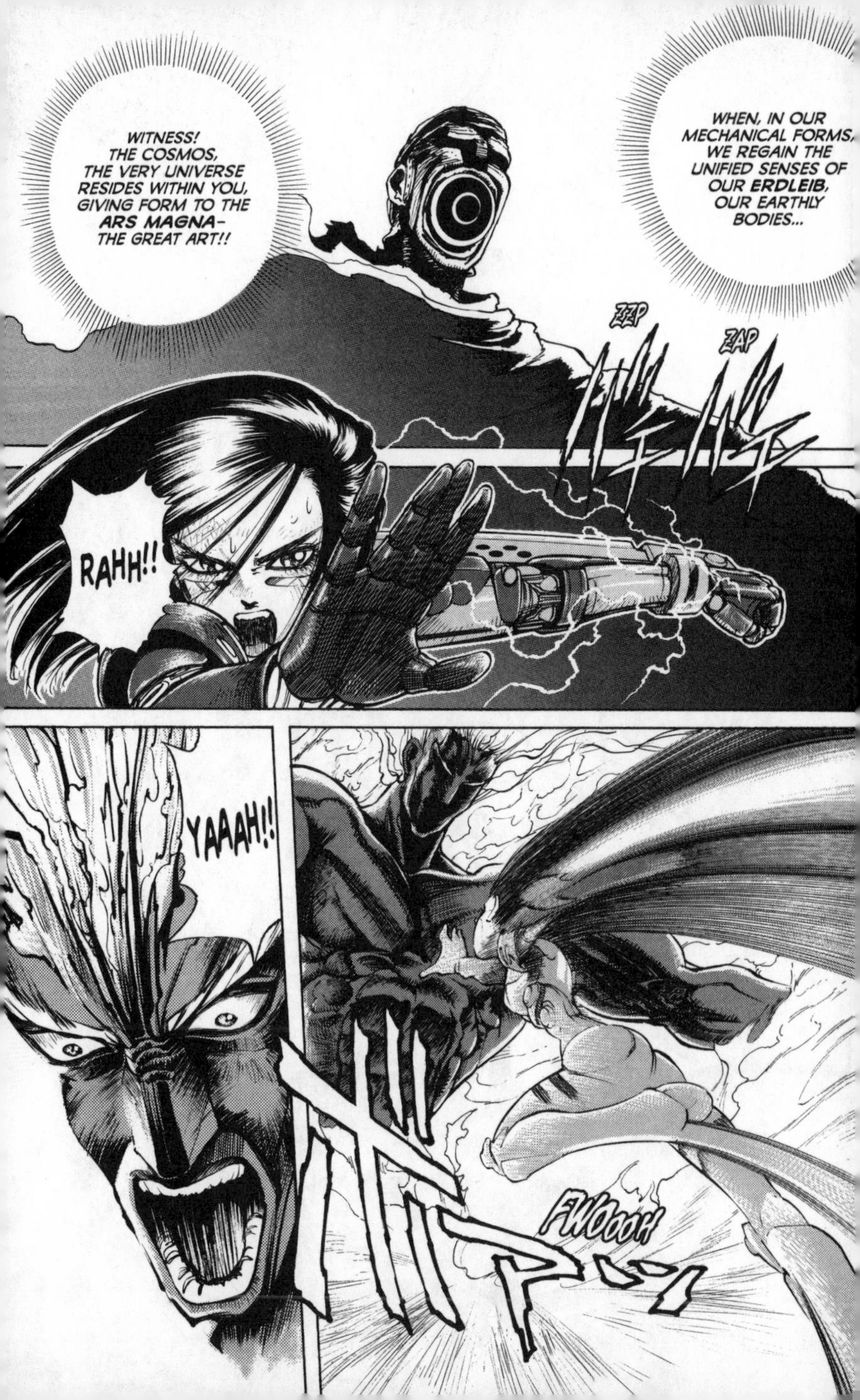
WHEN, IN OUR MECHANICAL FORMS, WE REGAIN THE UNIFIED SENSES OF OUR **ERDLEIB**, OUR EARTHLY BODIES...
WITNESS! THE COSMOS, THE VERY UNIVERSE RESIDES WITHIN YOU, GIVING FORM TO THE **ARS MAGNA**– THE GREAT ART!!
ZAP
ZZZP
RAHH!!
FWOOOH
YAAAH!!

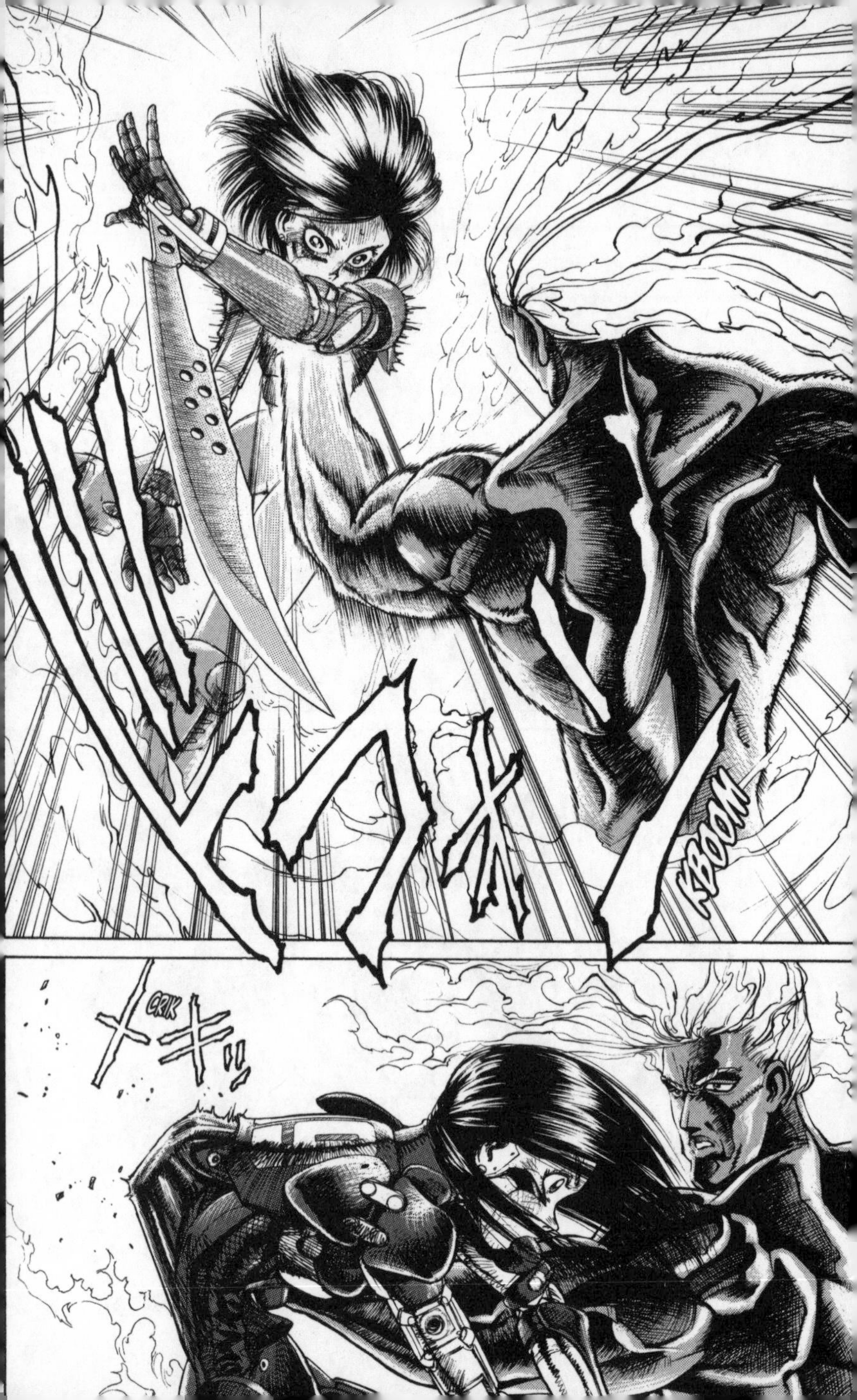
KBOOM
CRIK

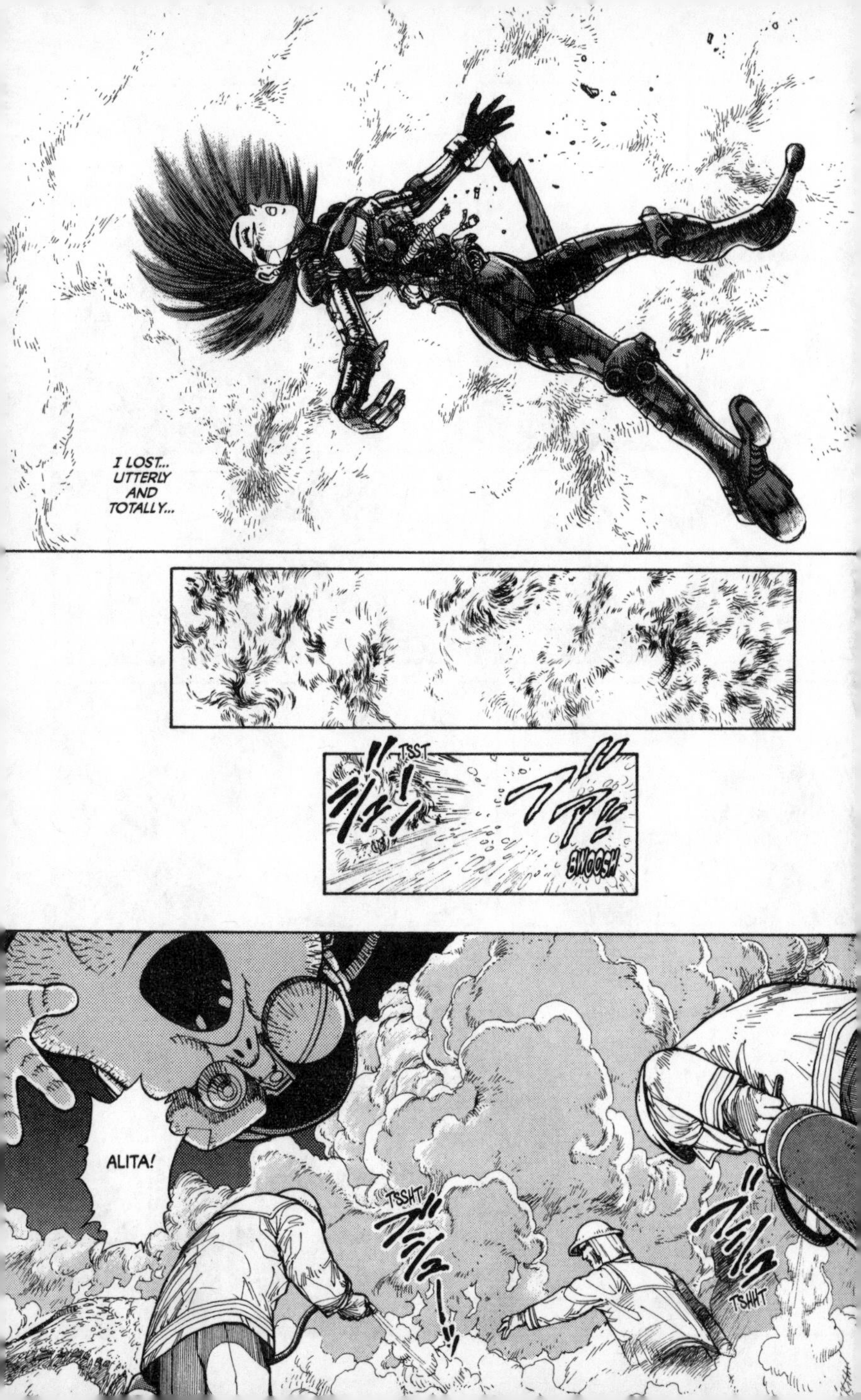
I LOST... UTTERLY AND TOTALLY...
TSST
BWOOSH
TSHHT
TSSHT
ALITA!

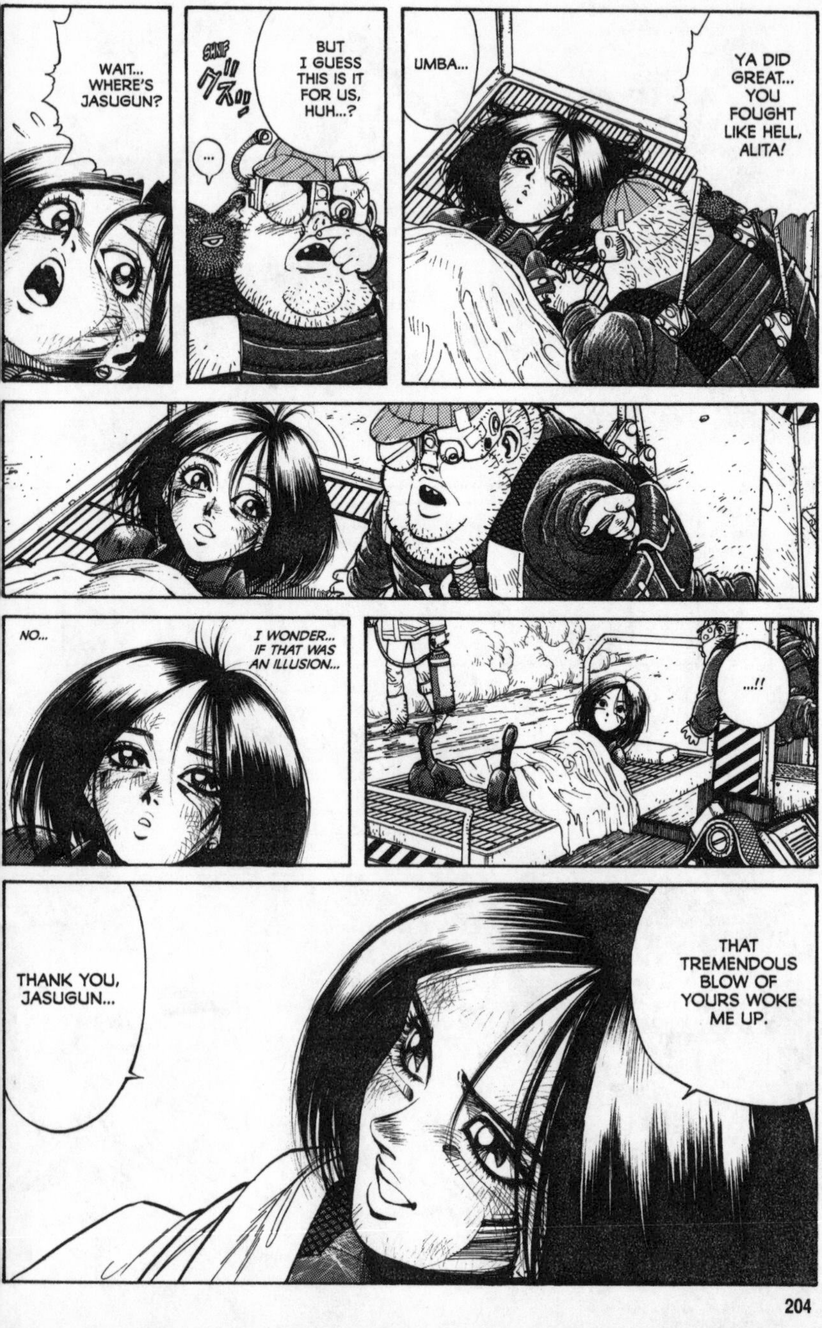
YA DID GREAT... YOU FOUGHT LIKE HELL, ALITA!
UMBA...
BUT I GUESS THIS IS IT FOR US, HUH...?
SNIF
グスッ
...
WAIT... WHERE'S JASUGUN?
...!!
I WONDER... IF THAT WAS AN ILLUSION...
NO...
THAT TREMENDOUS BLOW OF YOURS WOKE ME UP.
THANK YOU, JASUGUN...

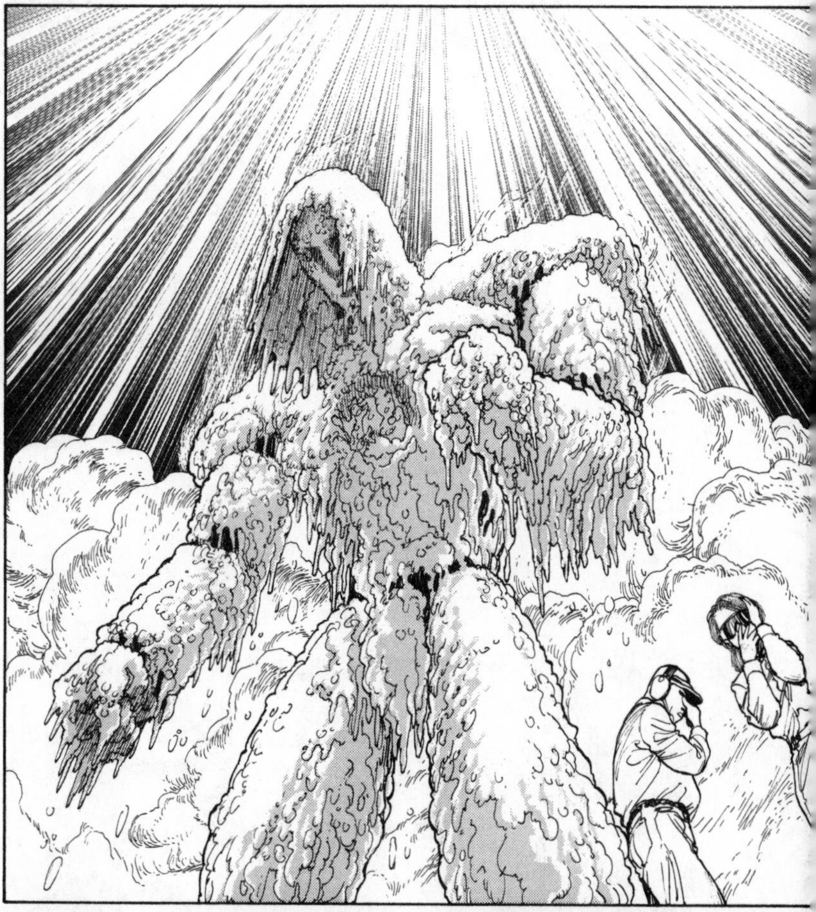

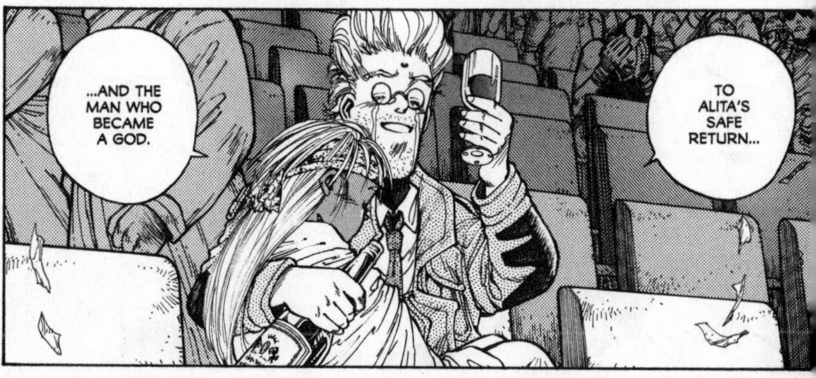
TO ALITA'S SAFE RETURN...
...AND THE MAN WHO BECAME A GOD.

How Cyborgs Work

EXPLAINED!

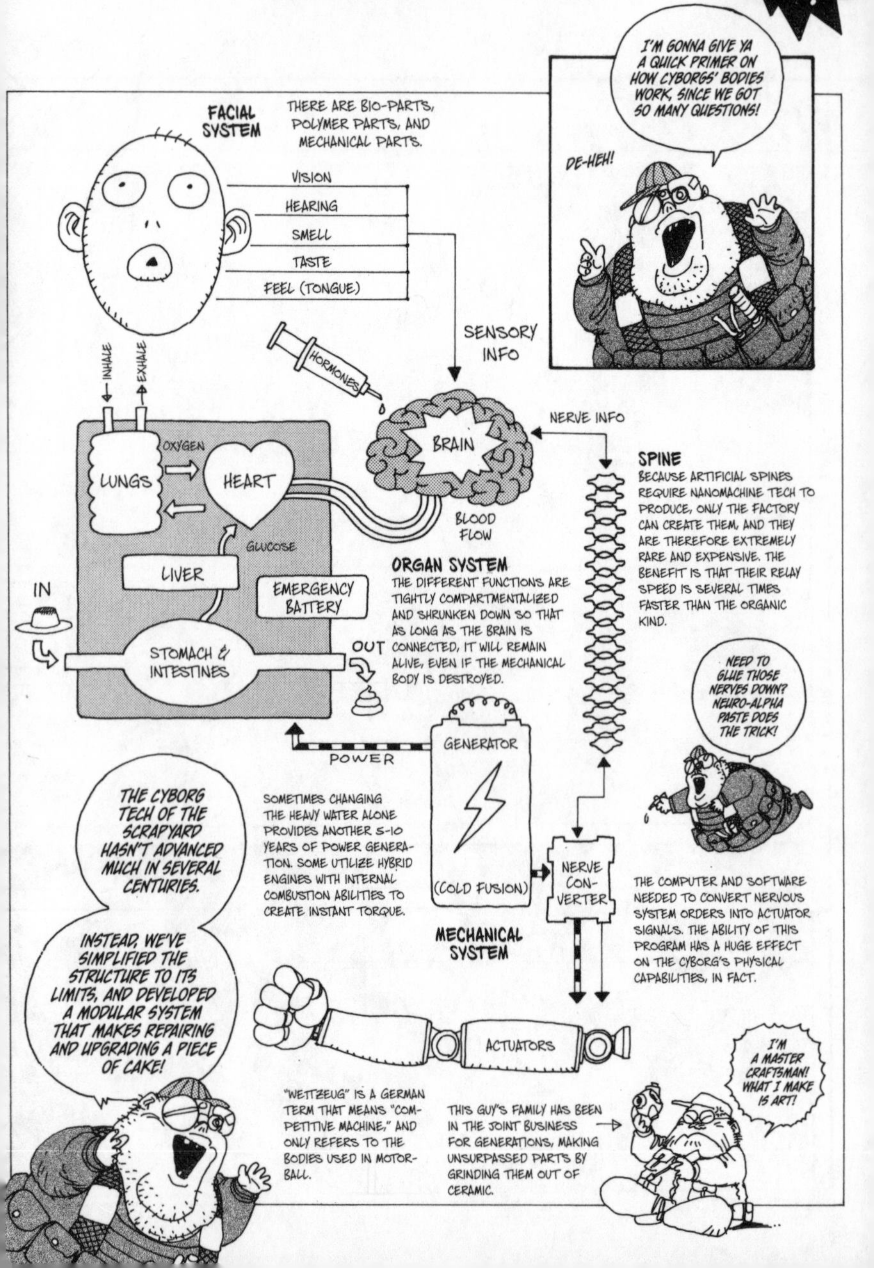
I'M GONNA GIVE YA A QUICK PRIMER ON HOW CYBORGS' BODIES WORK, SINCE WE GOT SO MANY QUESTIONS!
DE-HEH!
FACIAL SYSTEM
THERE ARE BIO-PARTS, POLYMER PARTS, AND MECHANICAL PARTS.
VISION
HEARING
SMELL
TASTE
FEEL (TONGUE)
SENSORY INFO
INHALE
EXHALE
HORMONES
BRAIN
NERVE INFO
OXYGEN
LUNGS
HEART
BLOOD FLOW
GLUCOSE
LIVER
EMERGENCY BATTERY
IN
STOMACH & INTESTINES
OUT
ORGAN SYSTEM
THE DIFFERENT FUNCTIONS ARE TIGHTLY COMPARTMENTALIZED AND SHRUNKEN DOWN SO THAT AS LONG AS THE BRAIN IS CONNECTED, IT WILL REMAIN ALIVE, EVEN IF THE MECHANICAL BODY IS DESTROYED.
SPINE
BECAUSE ARTIFICIAL SPINES REQUIRE NANOMACHINE TECH TO PRODUCE, ONLY THE FACTORY CAN CREATE THEM, AND THEY ARE THEREFORE EXTREMELY RARE AND EXPENSIVE. THE BENEFIT IS THAT THEIR RELAY SPEED IS SEVERAL TIMES FASTER THAN THE ORGANIC KIND.
NEED TO GLUE THOSE NERVES DOWN? NEURO-ALPHA PASTE DOES THE TRICK!
POWER
GENERATOR
(COLD FUSION)
NERVE CON-VERTER
SOMETIMES CHANGING THE HEAVY WATER ALONE PROVIDES ANOTHER 5-10 YEARS OF POWER GENERATION. SOME UTILIZE HYBRID ENGINES WITH INTERNAL COMBUSTION ABILITIES TO CREATE INSTANT TORQUE.
MECHANICAL SYSTEM
THE COMPUTER AND SOFTWARE NEEDED TO CONVERT NERVOUS SYSTEM ORDERS INTO ACTUATOR SIGNALS. THE ABILITY OF THIS PROGRAM HAS A HUGE EFFECT ON THE CYBORG'S PHYSICAL CAPABILITIES, IN FACT.
THE CYBORG TECH OF THE SCRAPYARD HASN'T ADVANCED MUCH IN SEVERAL CENTURIES.
INSTEAD, WE'VE SIMPLIFIED THE STRUCTURE TO ITS LIMITS, AND DEVELOPED A MODULAR SYSTEM THAT MAKES REPAIRING AND UPGRADING A PIECE OF CAKE!
ACTUATORS
I'M A MASTER CRAFTSMAN! WHAT I MAKE IS ART!
"WETTZEUG" IS A GERMAN TERM THAT MEANS "COMPETITIVE MACHINE," AND ONLY REFERS TO THE BODIES USED IN MOTORBALL.
THIS GUY'S FAMILY HAS BEEN IN THE JOINT BUSINESS FOR GENERATIONS, MAKING UNSURPASSED PARTS BY GRINDING THEM OUT OF CERAMIC.

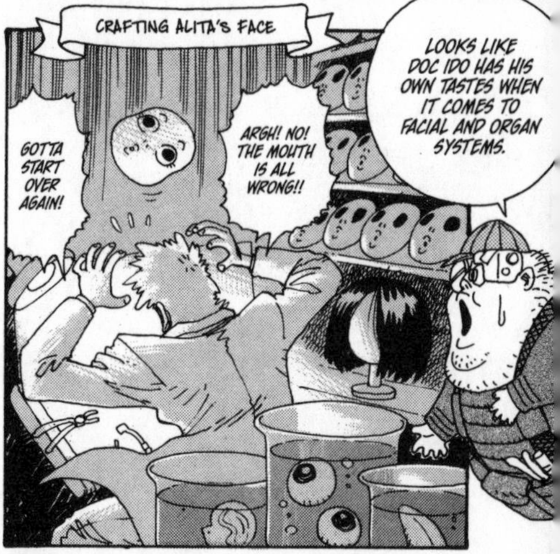
CRAFTING ALITA'S FACE
LOOKS LIKE DOC IDO HAS HIS OWN TASTES WHEN IT COMES TO FACIAL AND ORGAN SYSTEMS.
ARGH! NO! THE MOUTH IS ALL WRONG!!
GOTTA START OVER AGAIN!

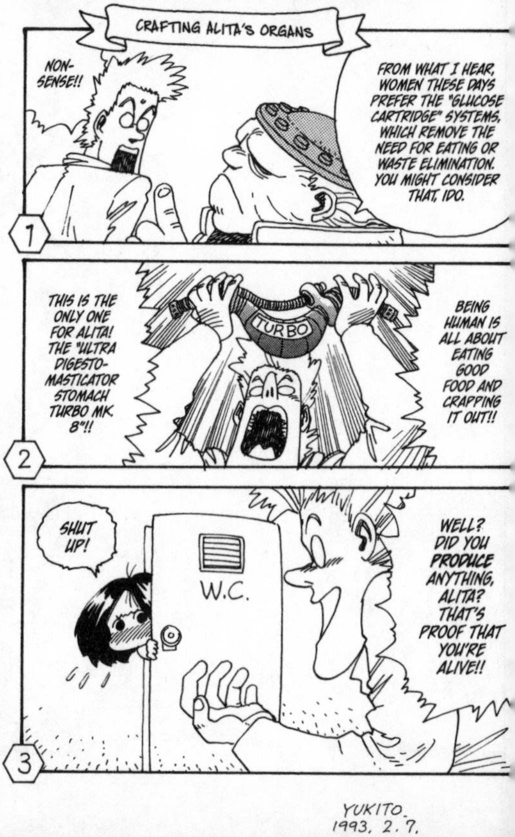
CRAFTING ALITA'S ORGANS
FROM WHAT I HEAR, WOMEN THESE DAYS PREFER THE "GLUCOSE CARTRIDGE" SYSTEMS, WHICH REMOVE THE NEED FOR EATING OR WASTE ELIMINATION. YOU MIGHT CONSIDER THAT, IDO.
NON-SENSE!!
1
BEING HUMAN IS ALL ABOUT EATING GOOD FOOD AND CRAPPING IT OUT!!
TURBO
THIS IS THE ONLY ONE FOR ALITA! THE "ULTRA DIGESTO-MASTICATOR STOMACH TURBO MK. 8"!!
2
WELL? DID YOU PRODUCE ANYTHING, ALITA? THAT'S PROOF THAT YOU'RE ALIVE!!
W.C.
SHUT UP!
3

YUKITO
1993. 2. 7.

THE BIRTH OF A SCRAPYARD CITIZEN!

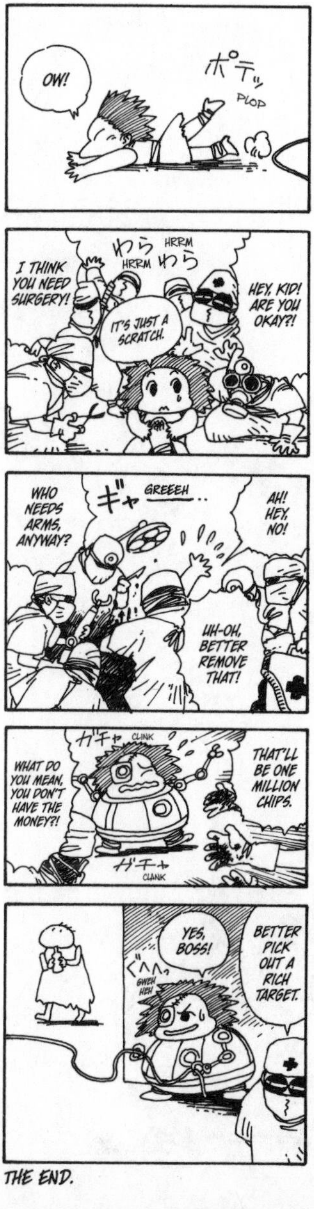
ポテッ
PLOP
OW!
HEY, KID! ARE YOU OKAY?!
わら
HRRM
HRRM
わら
IT'S JUST A SCRATCH.
I THINK YOU NEED SURGERY!
AH! HEY, NO!
ギャ
GREEEH..
WHO NEEDS ARMS, ANYWAY?
UH-OH, BETTER REMOVE THAT!
THAT'LL BE ONE MILLION CHIPS.
ガチャ
CLINK
WHAT DO YOU MEAN, YOU DON'T HAVE THE MONEY?!
ガチャ
CLANK
BETTER PICK OUT A RICH TARGET.
YES, BOSS!
ぐへへ
GWEH HEH

THE END.

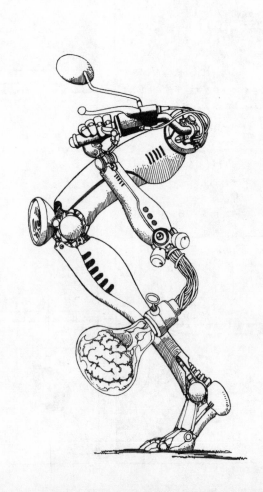

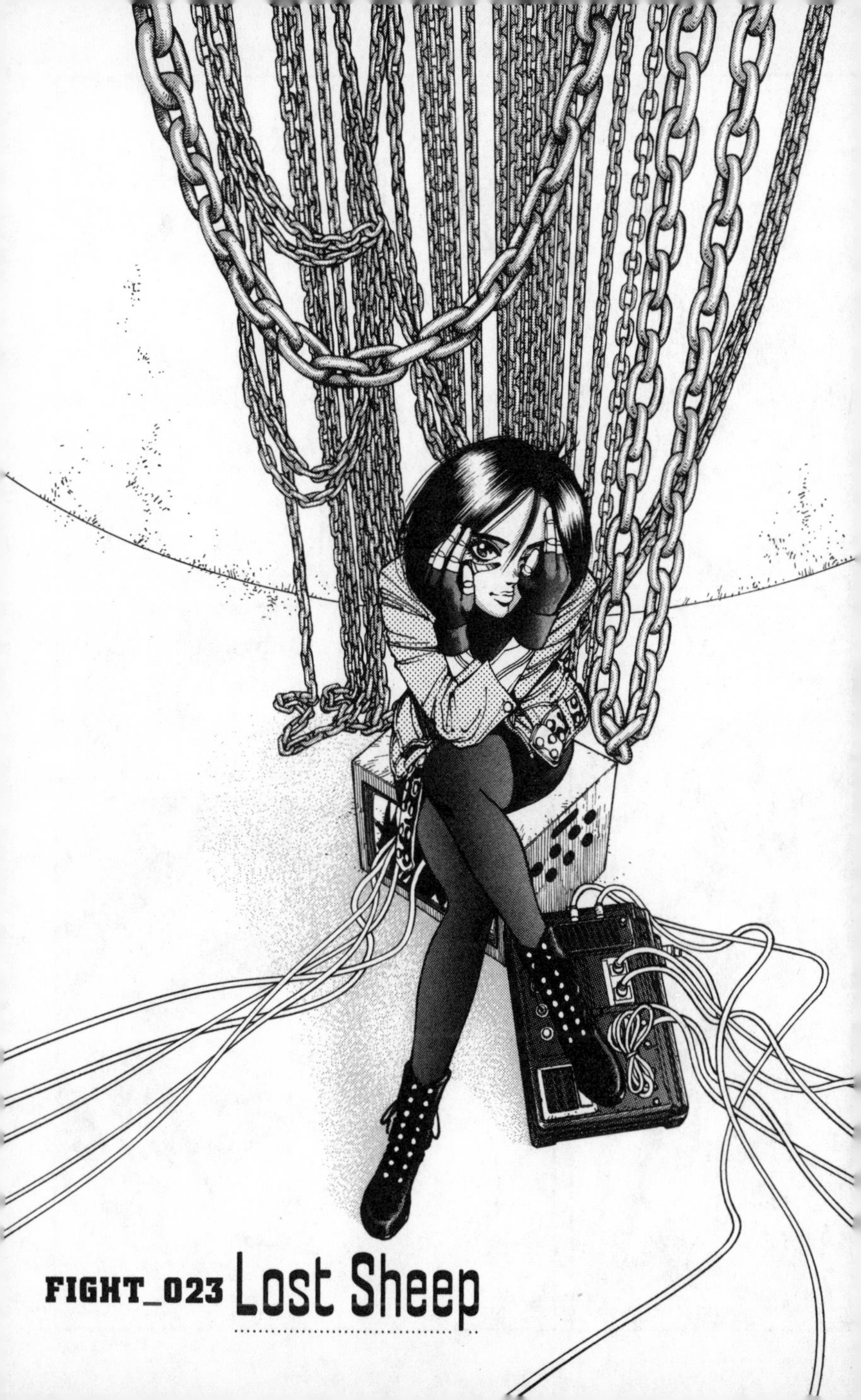

FIGHT_023 Lost Sheep

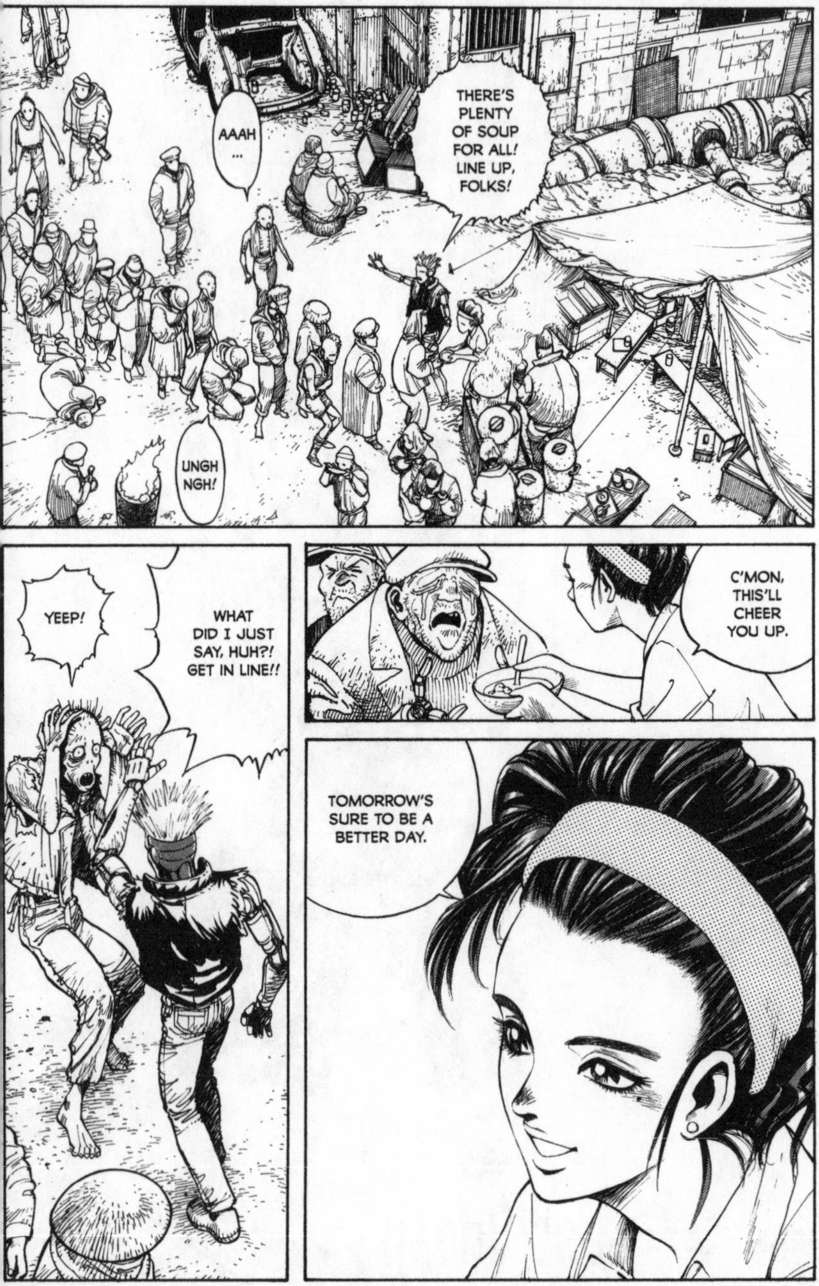
THERE'S PLENTY OF SOUP FOR ALL! LINE UP, FOLKS!
AAAH ...
UNGH NGH!
C'MON, THIS'LL CHEER YOU UP.
TOMORROW'S SURE TO BE A BETTER DAY.
WHAT DID I JUST SAY, HUH?! GET IN LINE!!
YEEP!

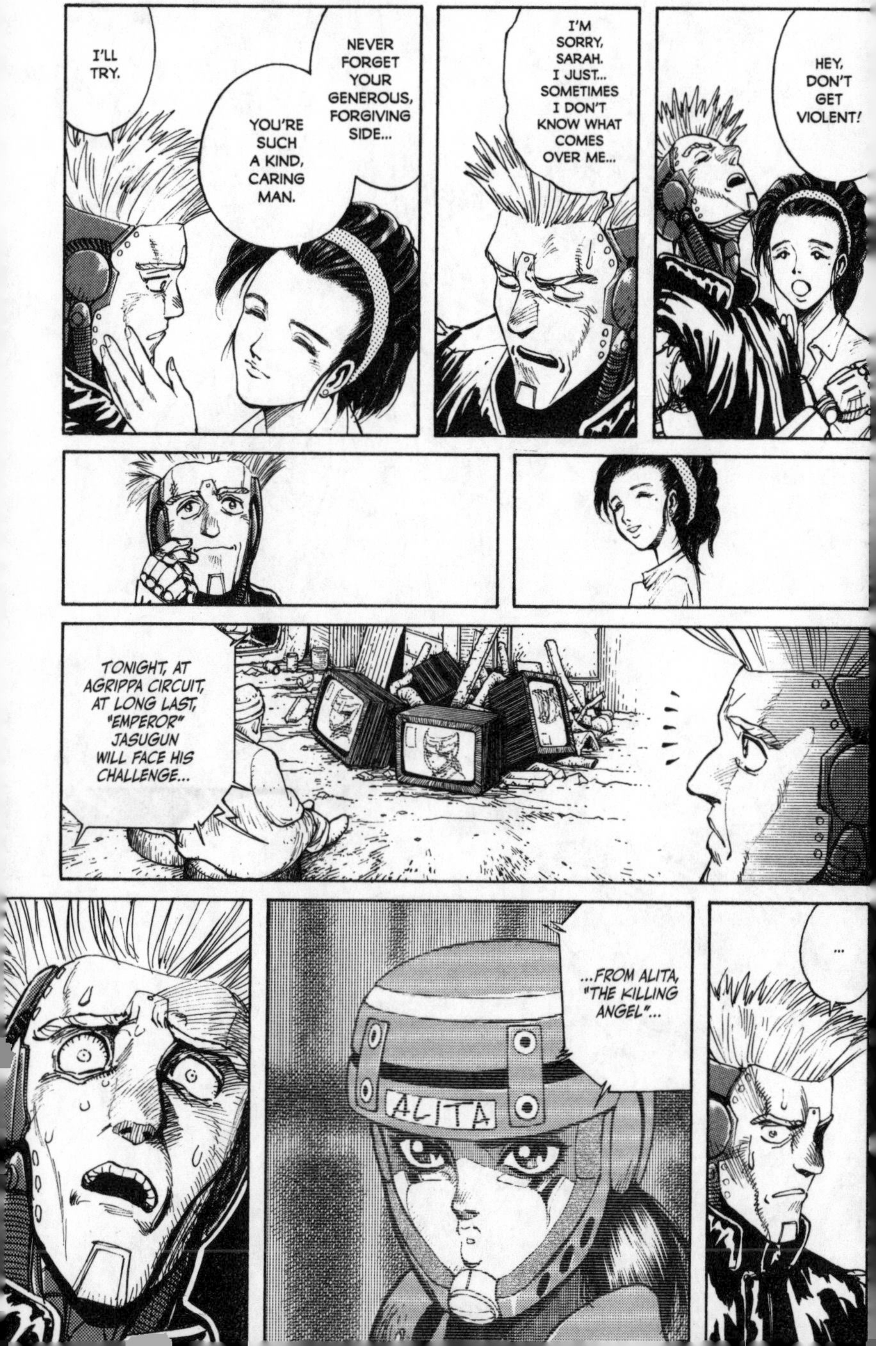
HEY, DON'T GET VIOLENT!
I'M SORRY, SARAH. I JUST... SOMETIMES I DON'T KNOW WHAT COMES OVER ME...
NEVER FORGET YOUR GENEROUS, FORGIVING SIDE...
YOU'RE SUCH A KIND, CARING MAN.
I'LL TRY.
TONIGHT, AT AGRIPPA CIRCUIT, AT LONG LAST, "EMPEROR" JASUGUN WILL FACE HIS CHALLENGE...
...
...FROM ALITA, "THE KILLING ANGEL"...
ALITA

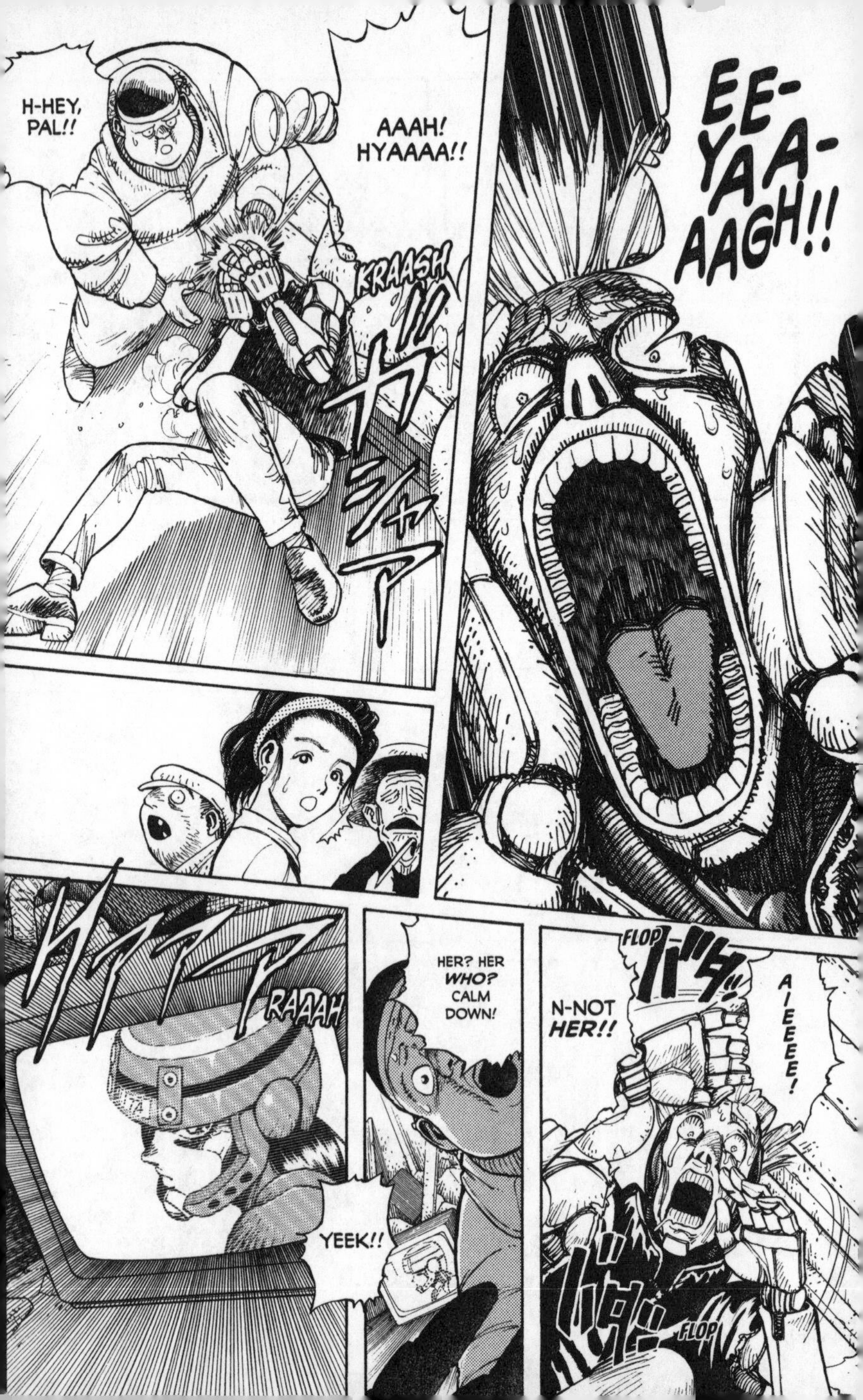
EE-YAA-AAGH!!
AAAH! HYAAAA!!
H-HEY, PAL!!
KRAASH
FLOP
AIEEEE!
N-NOT HER!!
FLOP
HER? HER WHO? CALM DOWN!
YEEK!!
RAAAH

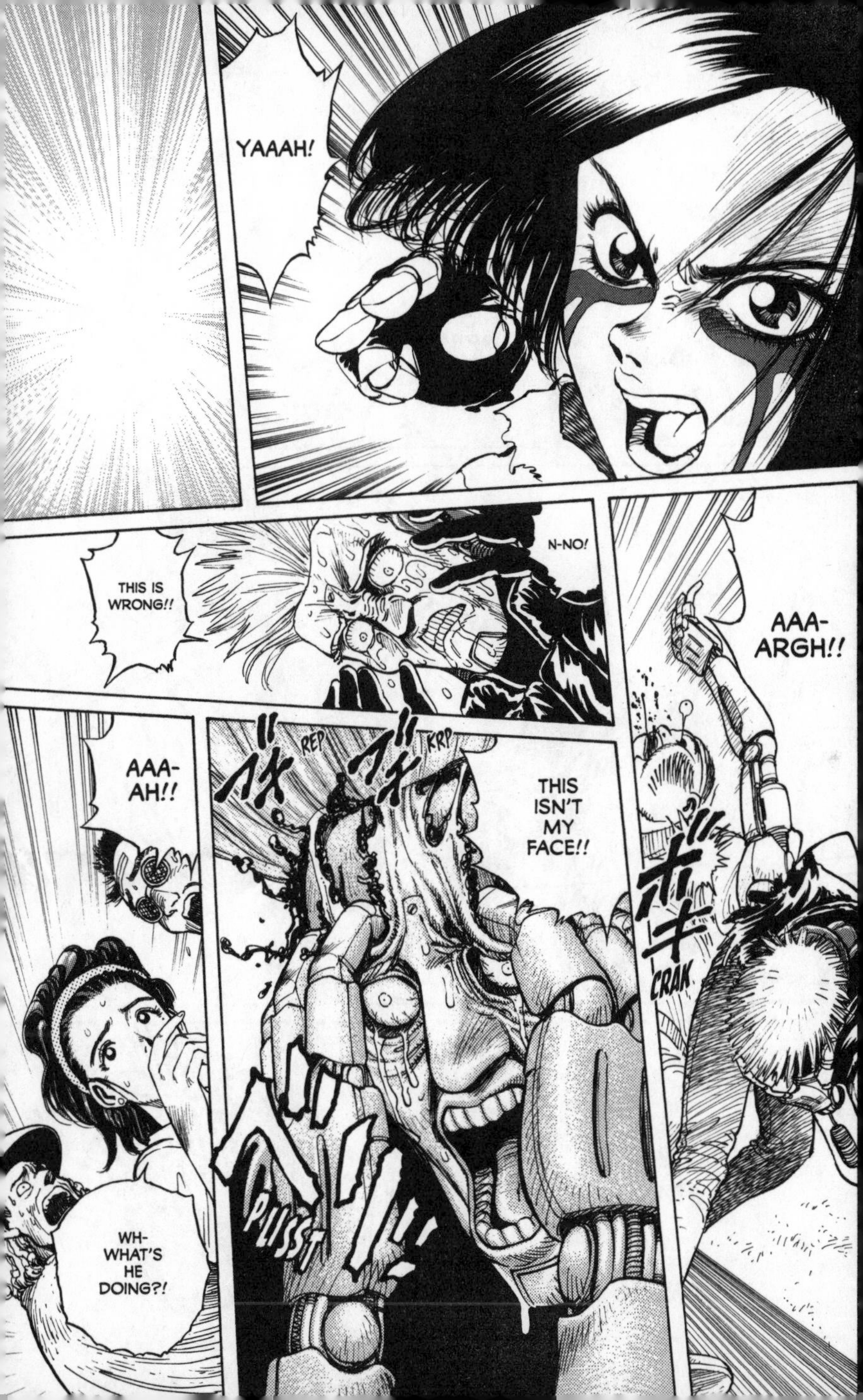
YAAAH!
AAA-ARGH!!
CRAK
N-NO!
THIS IS WRONG!!
REP
KRP
THIS ISN'T MY FACE!!
PLISSST
AAA-AH!!
WH-WHAT'S HE DOING?!

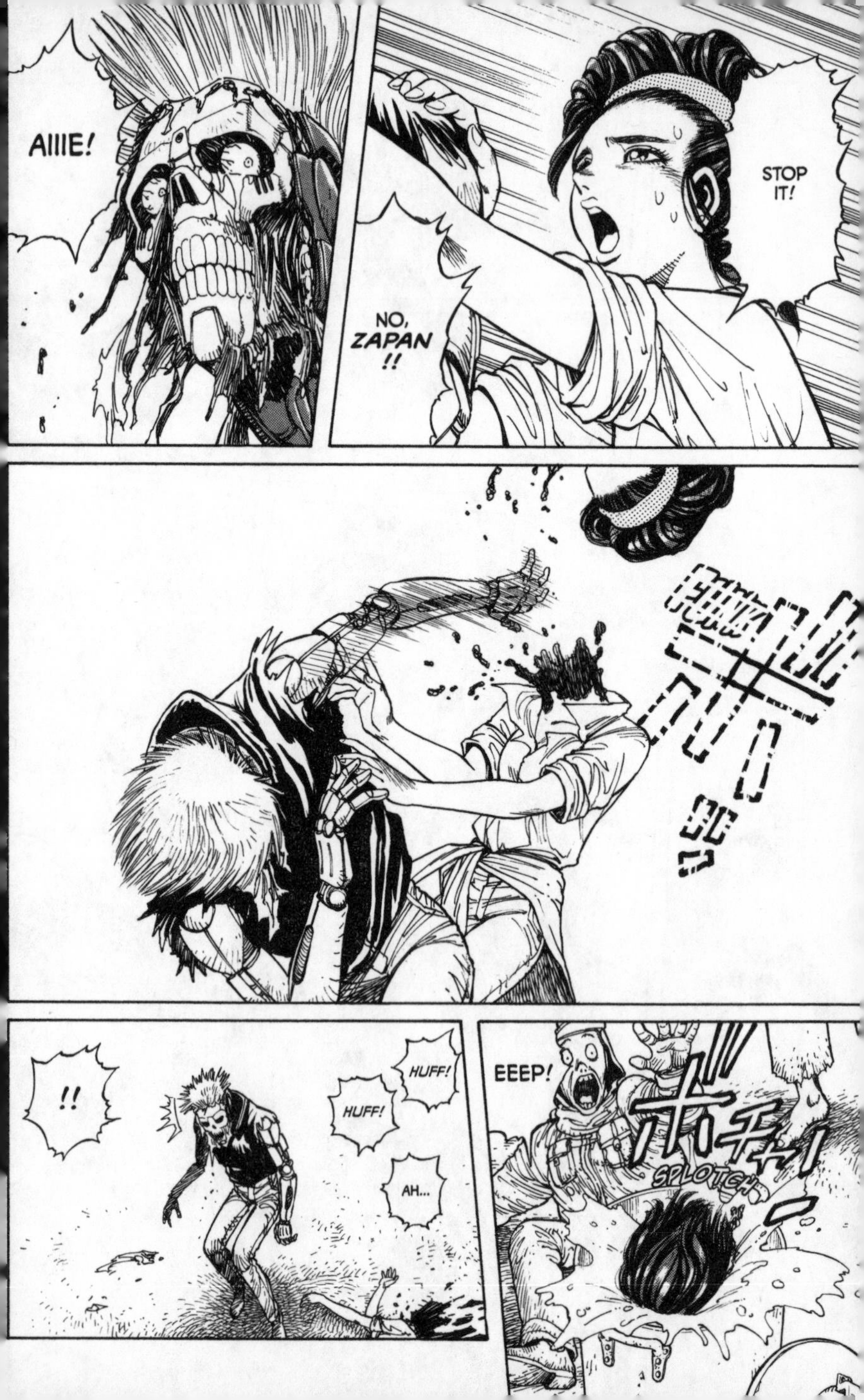
STOP IT!
NO, ZAPAN!!
AIIIE!
EEEP!
SPLOTCH
HUFF!
HUFF!
!!
AH...

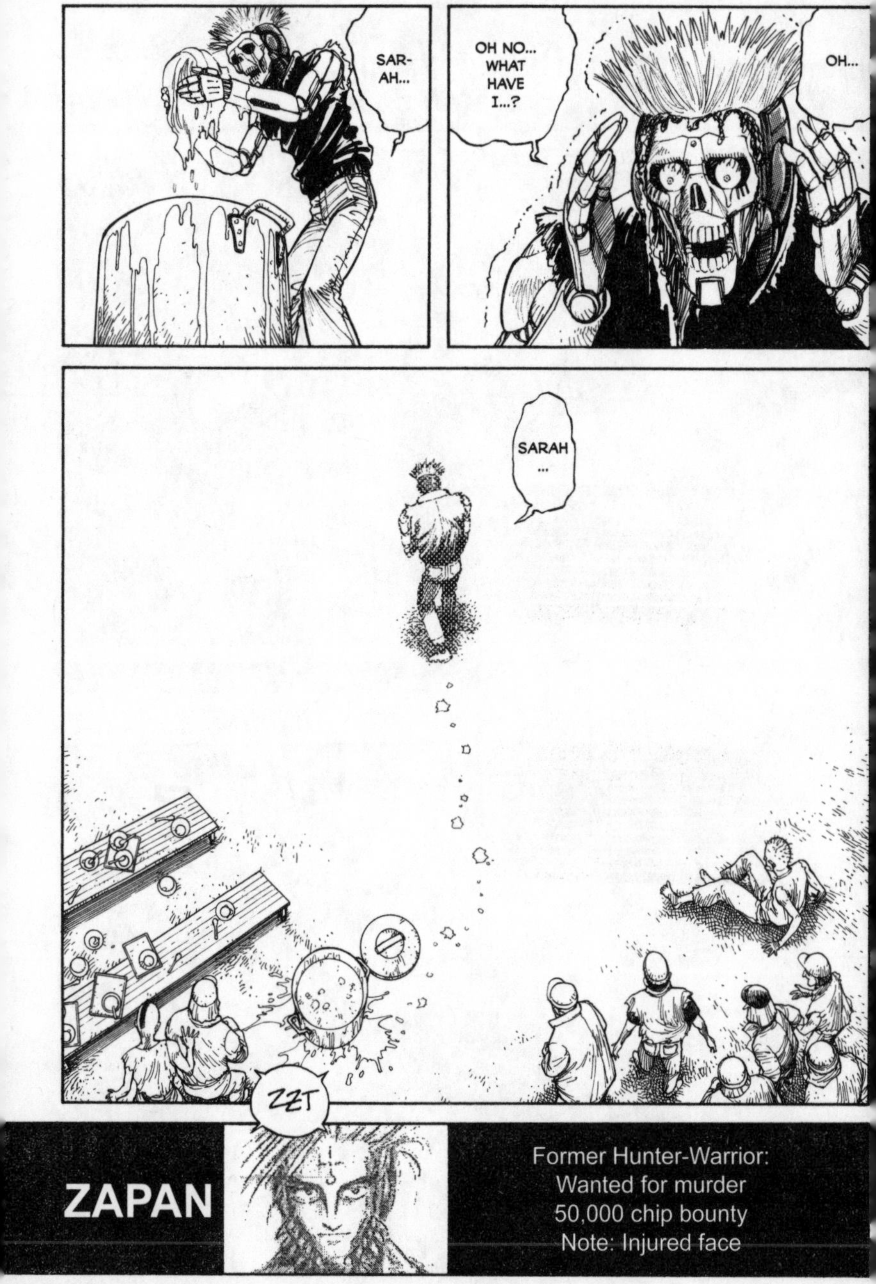
OH...
OH NO... WHAT HAVE I...?
SAR-AH...
SARAH ...
ZZT
ZAPAN
Former Hunter-Warrior:
Wanted for murder
50,000 chip bounty
Note: Injured face

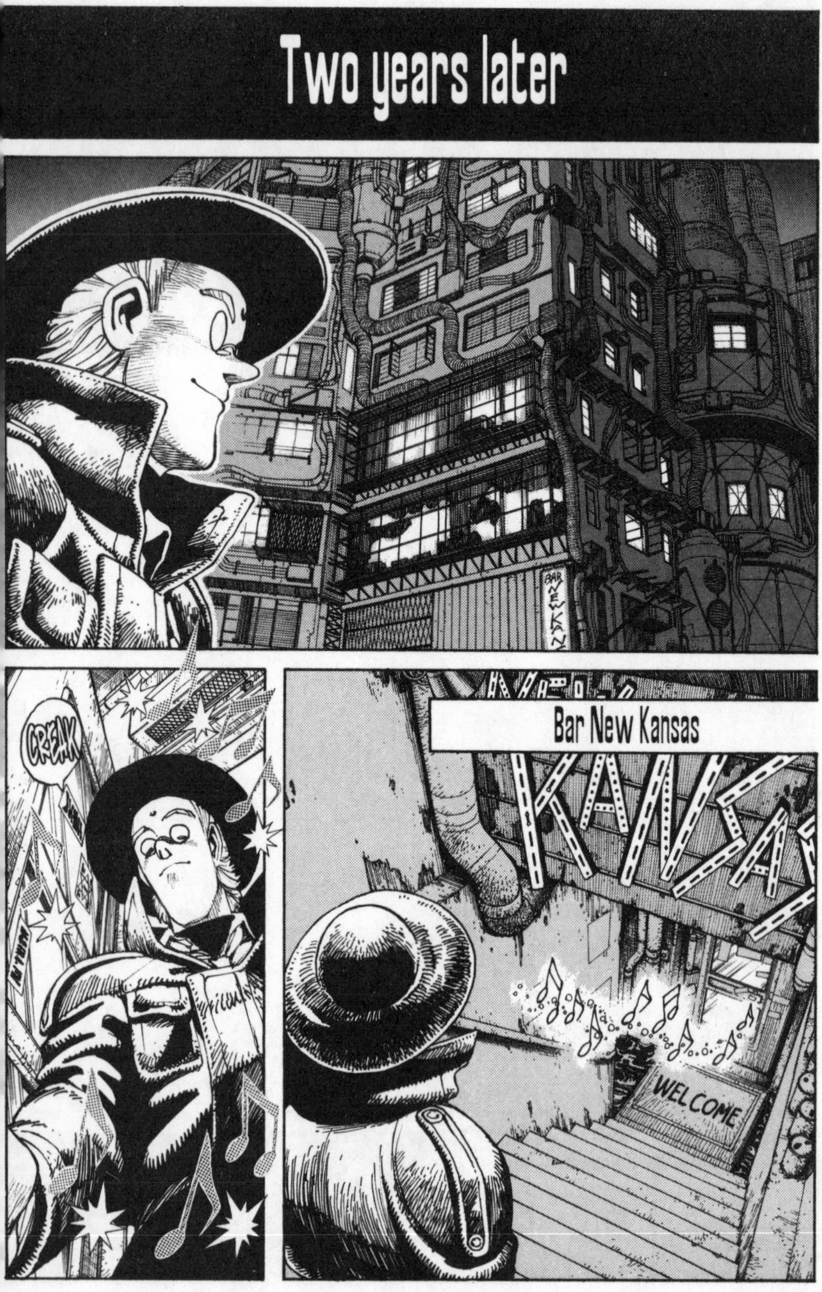
Two years later
Bar New Kansas
WELCOME
CREAK

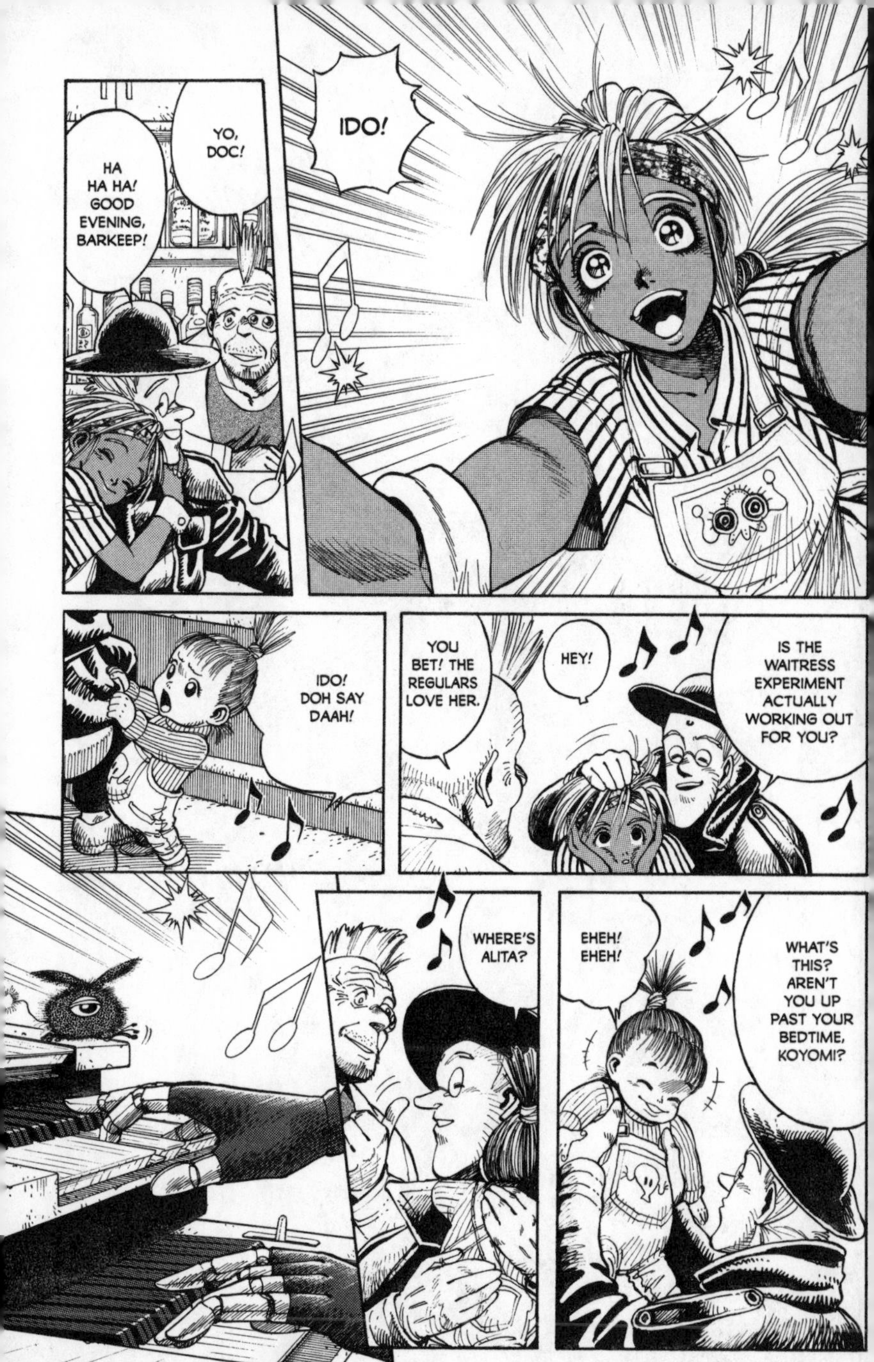
IDO!
YO, DOC!
HA HA HA! GOOD EVENING, BARKEEP!
IS THE WAITRESS EXPERIMENT ACTUALLY WORKING OUT FOR YOU?
HEY!
YOU BET! THE REGULARS LOVE HER.
IDO! DOH SAY DAAH!
WHAT'S THIS? AREN'T YOU UP PAST YOUR BEDTIME, KOYOMI?
EHEH! EHEH!
WHERE'S ALITA?

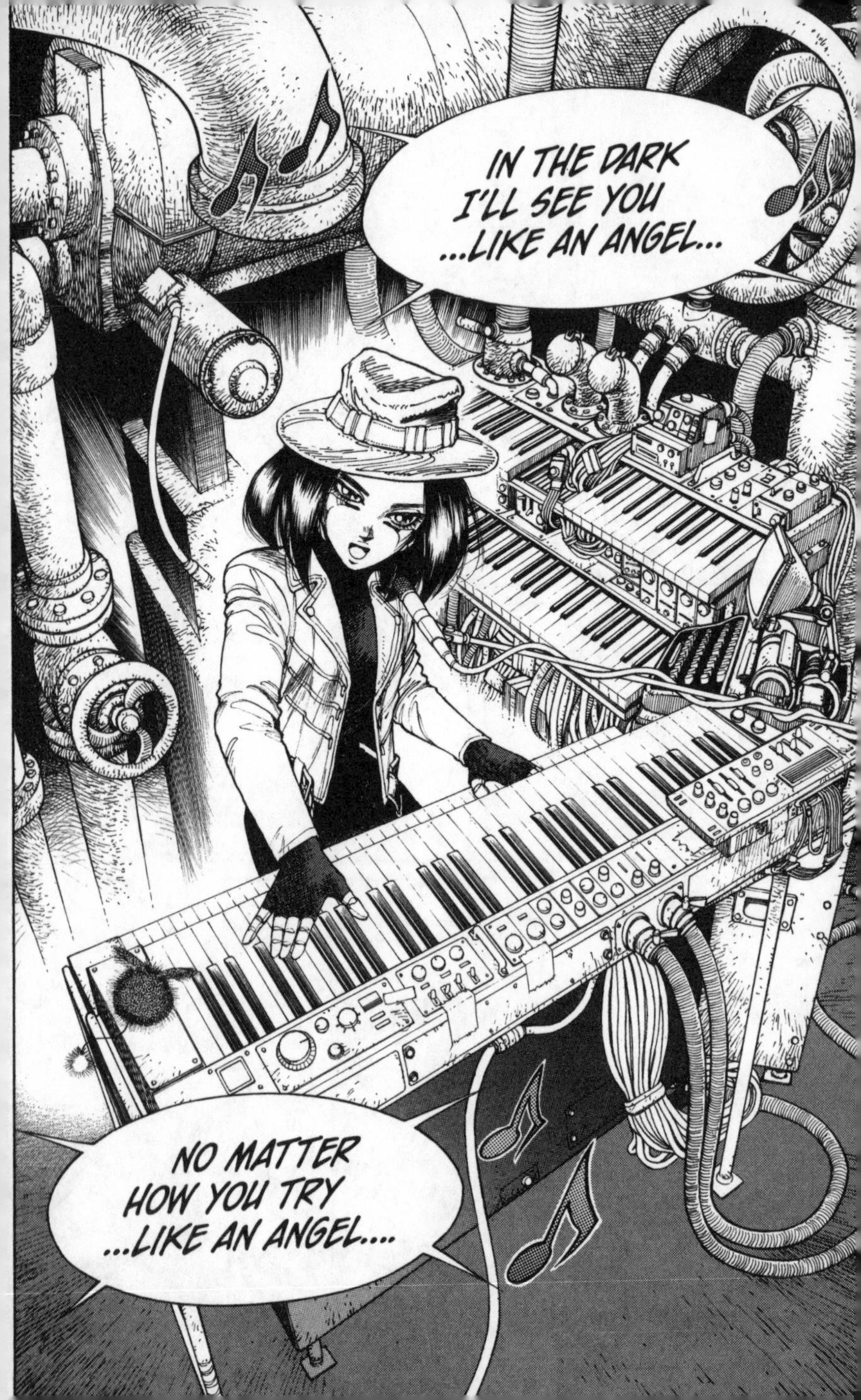
IN THE DARK I'LL SEE YOU ...LIKE AN ANGEL...
NO MATTER HOW YOU TRY ...LIKE AN ANGEL....

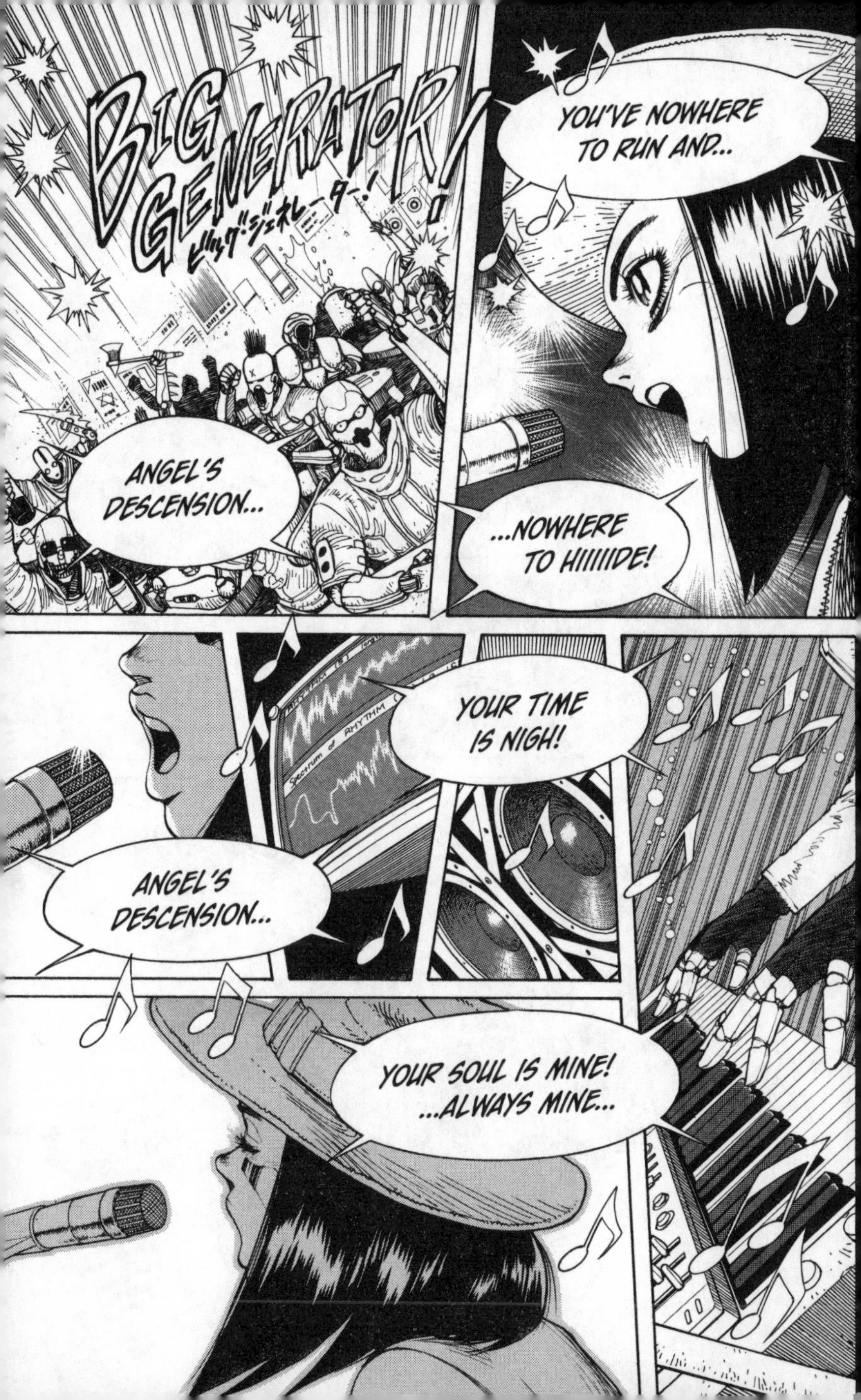
YOU'VE NOWHERE TO RUN AND...
...NOWHERE TO HIIIIIDE!
BIG GENERATOR!
ビッグジェネレーター！
ANGEL'S DESCENSION...
YOUR TIME IS NIGH!
ANGEL'S DESCENSION...
YOUR SOUL IS MINE! ...ALWAYS MINE...

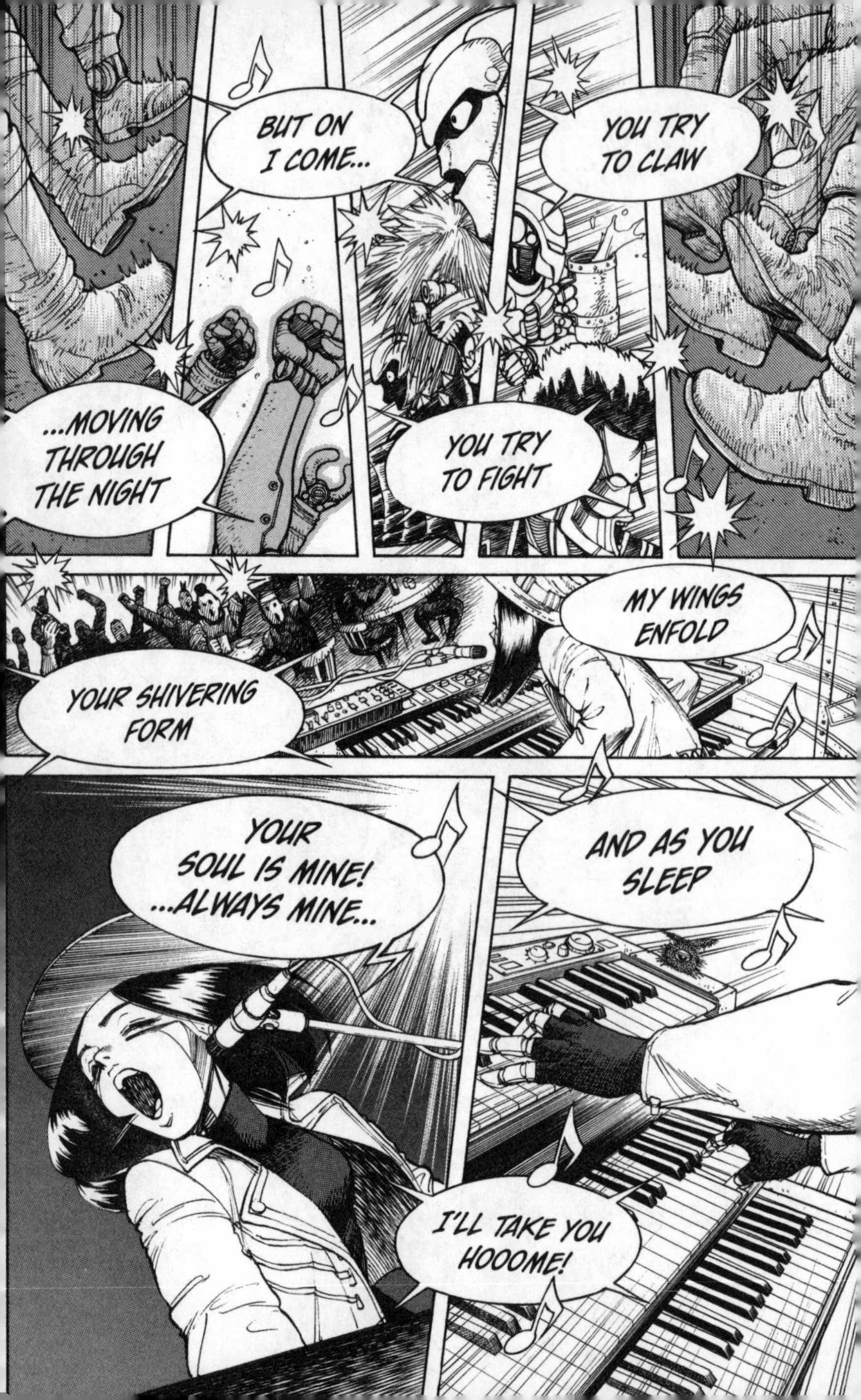
YOU TRY TO CLAW
YOU TRY TO FIGHT
BUT ON I COME...
...MOVING THROUGH THE NIGHT
MY WINGS ENFOLD
YOUR SHIVERING FORM
AND AS YOU SLEEP
I'LL TAKE YOU HOOOME!
YOUR SOUL IS MINE! ...ALWAYS MINE...

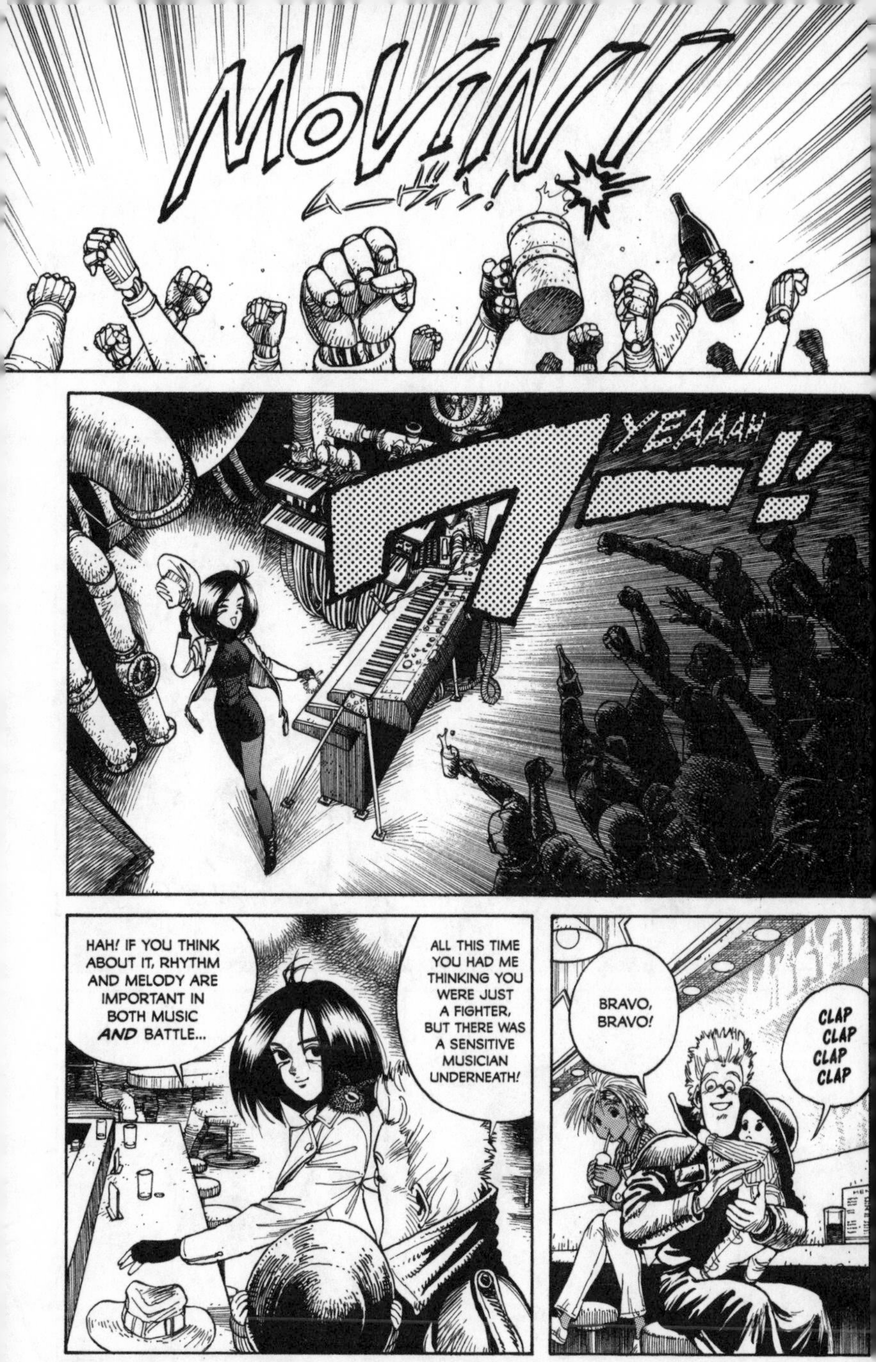
MoViN!
ムーヴィン!
YEAAAH!!
BRAVO, BRAVO!
CLAP CLAP CLAP CLAP
ALL THIS TIME YOU HAD ME THINKING YOU WERE JUST A FIGHTER, BUT THERE WAS A SENSITIVE MUSICIAN UNDERNEATH!
HAH! IF YOU THINK ABOUT IT, RHYTHM AND MELODY ARE IMPORTANT IN BOTH MUSIC *AND* BATTLE...

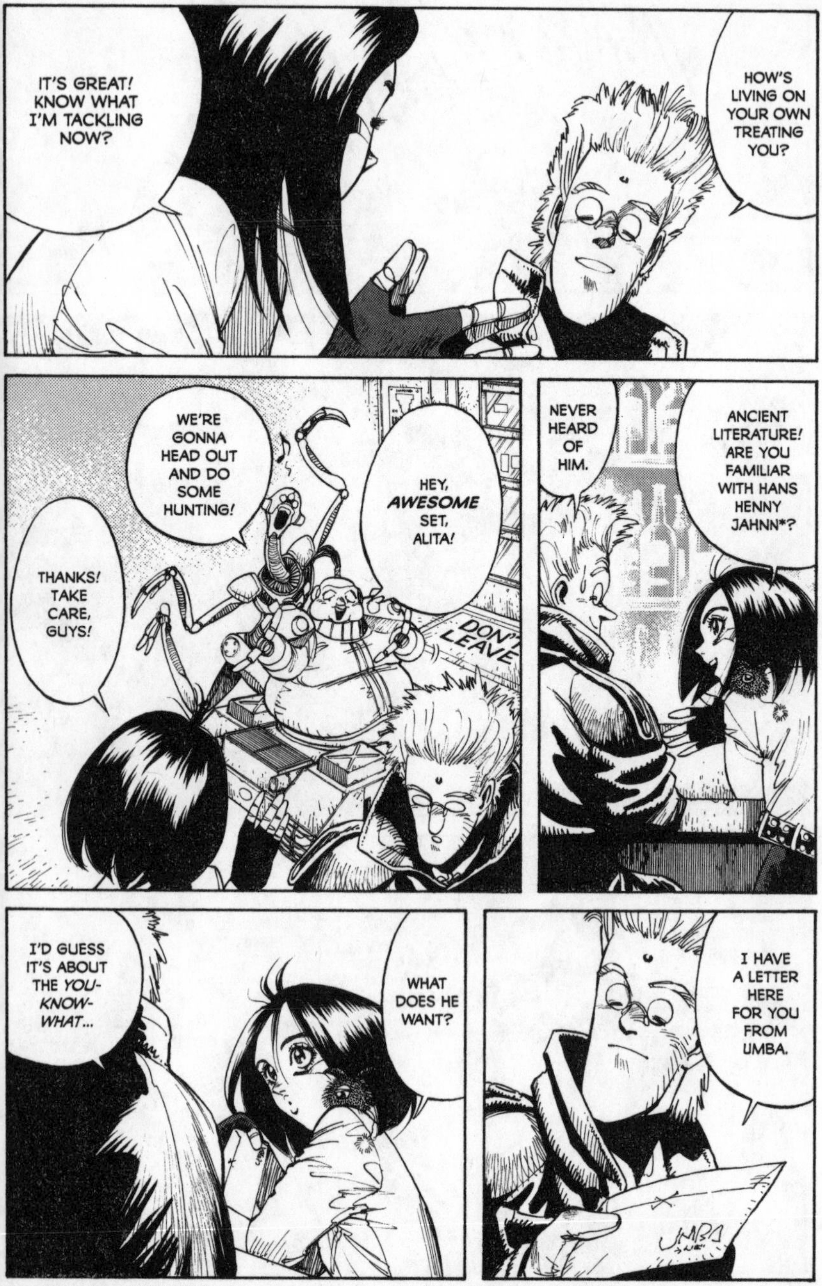
HOW'S LIVING ON YOUR OWN TREATING YOU?
IT'S GREAT! KNOW WHAT I'M TACKLING NOW?
ANCIENT LITERATURE! ARE YOU FAMILIAR WITH HANS HENNY JAHNN*?
NEVER HEARD OF HIM.
HEY, *AWESOME* SET, ALITA!
WE'RE GONNA HEAD OUT AND DO SOME HUNTING!
DON'T LEAVE
THANKS! TAKE CARE, GUYS!
I HAVE A LETTER HERE FOR YOU FROM UMBA.
UMBA
WHAT DOES HE WANT?
I'D GUESS IT'S ABOUT THE *YOU-KNOW-WHAT*...

***Hans Henny Jahnn:** 1894-1959. The "great unknown German playwright." His signature work is *Thirteen Uncanny Stories.*

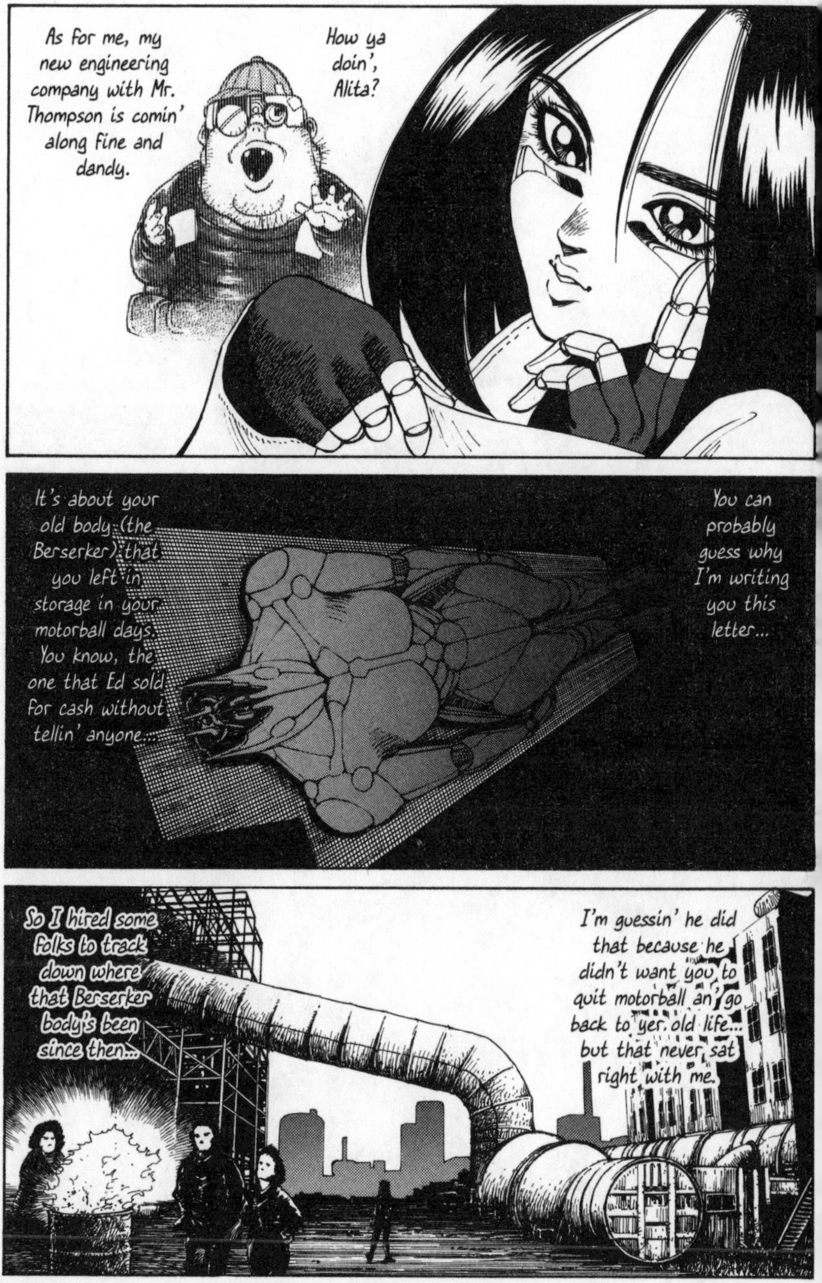
How ya doin', Alita?
As for me, my new engineering company with Mr. Thompson is comin' along fine and dandy.
You can probably guess why I'm writing you this letter...
It's about your old body (the Berserker) that you left in storage in your motorball days. You know, the one that Ed sold for cash without tellin' anyone...
I'm guessin' he did that because he didn't want you to quit motorball an' go back to yer old life... but that never sat right with me.
So I hired some folks to track down where that Berserker body's been since then...

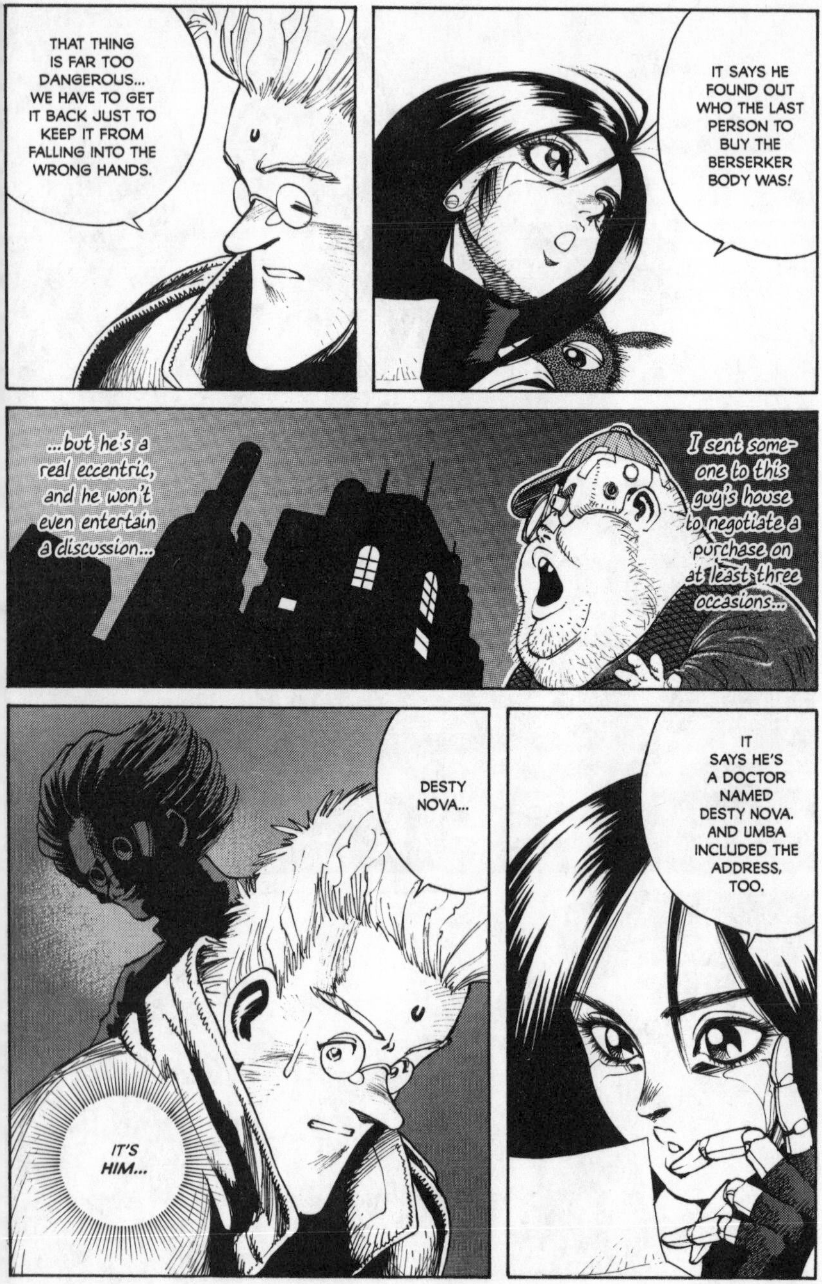
IT SAYS HE FOUND OUT WHO THE LAST PERSON TO BUY THE BERSERKER BODY WAS!
THAT THING IS FAR TOO DANGEROUS... WE HAVE TO GET IT BACK JUST TO KEEP IT FROM FALLING INTO THE WRONG HANDS.
I sent someone to this guy's house to negotiate a purchase on at least three occasions...
...but he's a real eccentric, and he won't even entertain a discussion...
IT SAYS HE'S A DOCTOR NAMED DESTY NOVA. AND UMBA INCLUDED THE ADDRESS, TOO.
DESTY NOVA...
IT'S HIM...

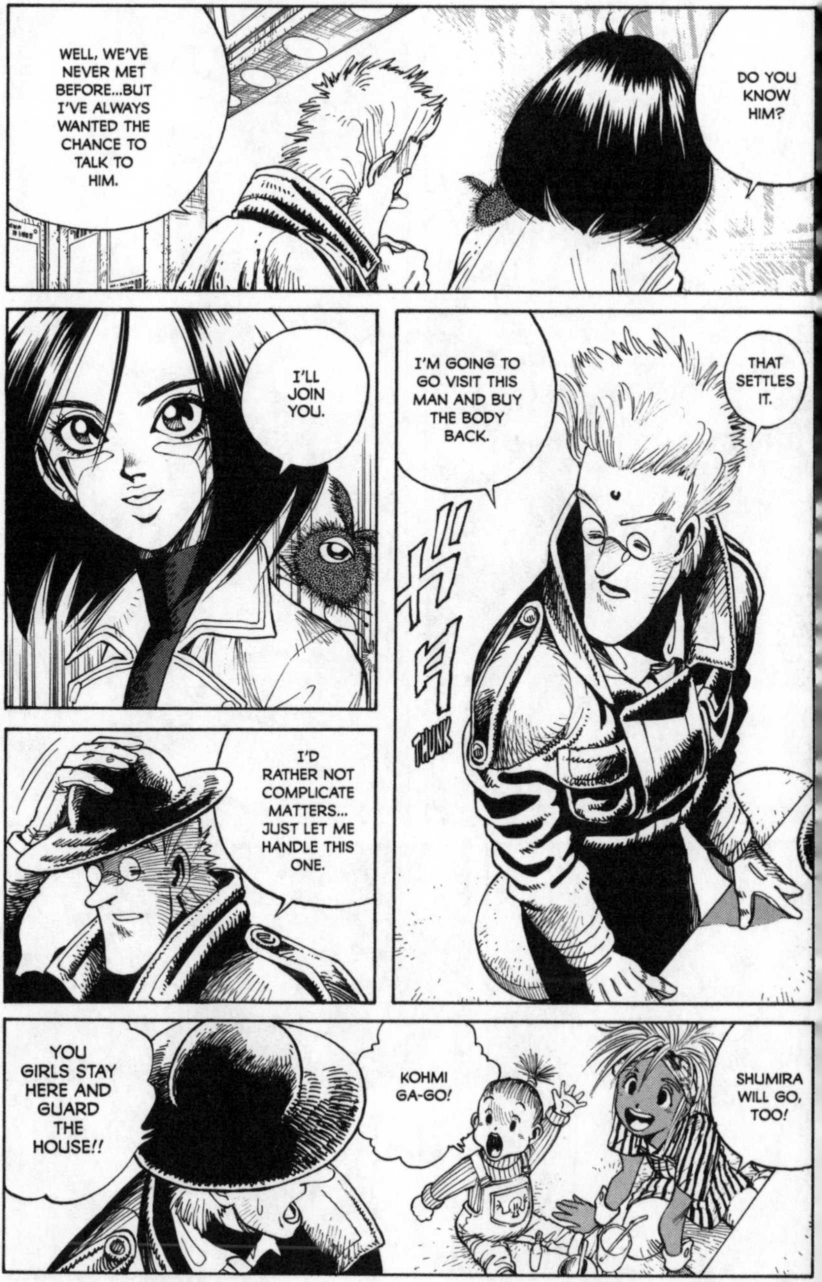
DO YOU KNOW HIM?
WELL, WE'VE NEVER MET BEFORE...BUT I'VE ALWAYS WANTED THE CHANCE TO TALK TO HIM.
THAT SETTLES IT.
I'M GOING TO GO VISIT THIS MAN AND BUY THE BODY BACK.
THUNK
I'LL JOIN YOU.
I'D RATHER NOT COMPLICATE MATTERS... JUST LET ME HANDLE THIS ONE.
SHUMIRA WILL GO, TOO!
KOHMI GA-GO!
YOU GIRLS STAY HERE AND GUARD THE HOUSE!!

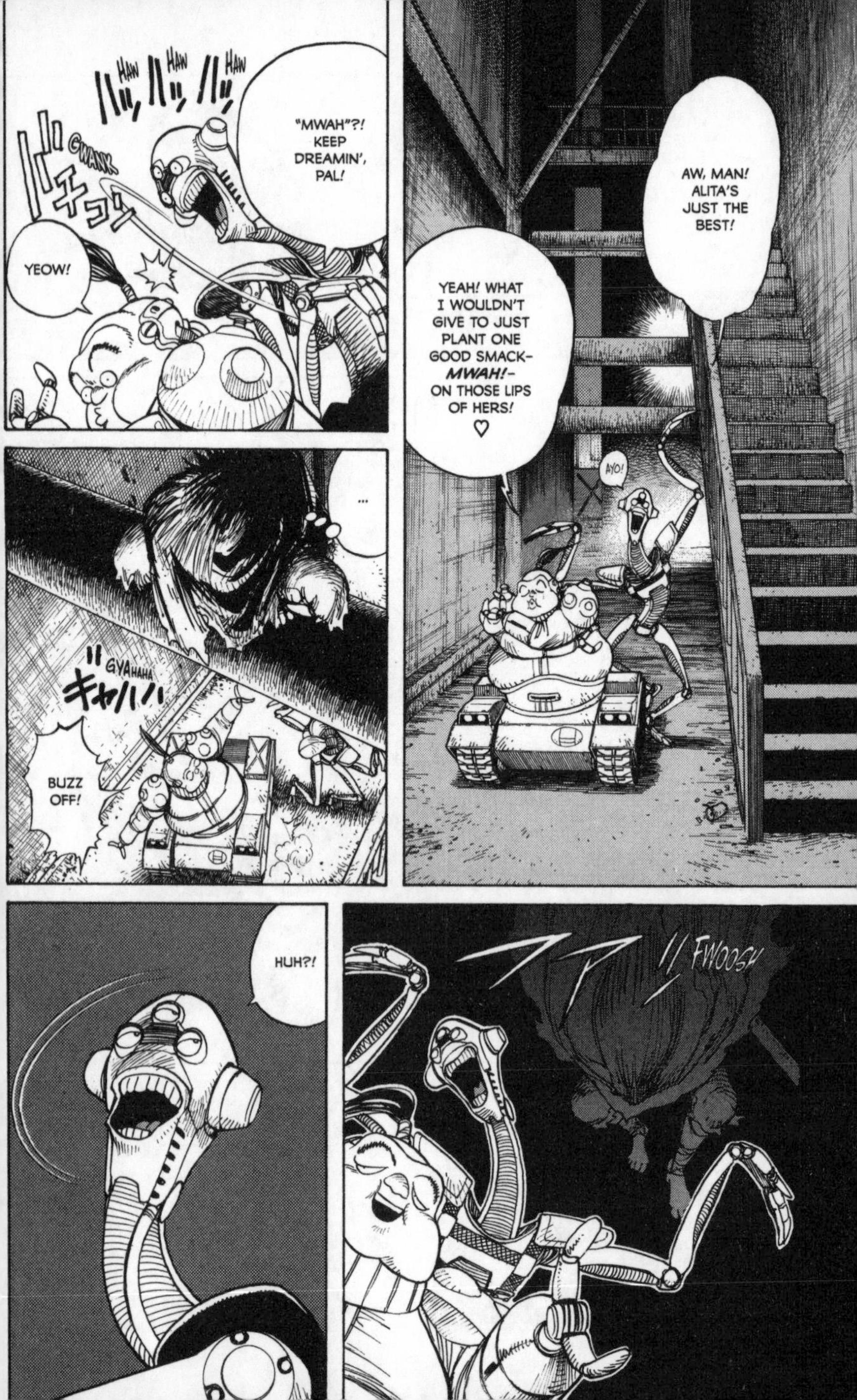
AW, MAN! ALITA'S JUST THE BEST!
YEAH! WHAT I WOULDN'T GIVE TO JUST PLANT ONE GOOD SMACK- *MWAH!*- ON THOSE LIPS OF HERS! ♡
AYO!
"MWAH"?! KEEP DREAMIN', PAL!
HAW HAW HAW
GWANK
YEOW!
...
GYAHAHA
BUZZ OFF!
FWOOSH
HUH?!

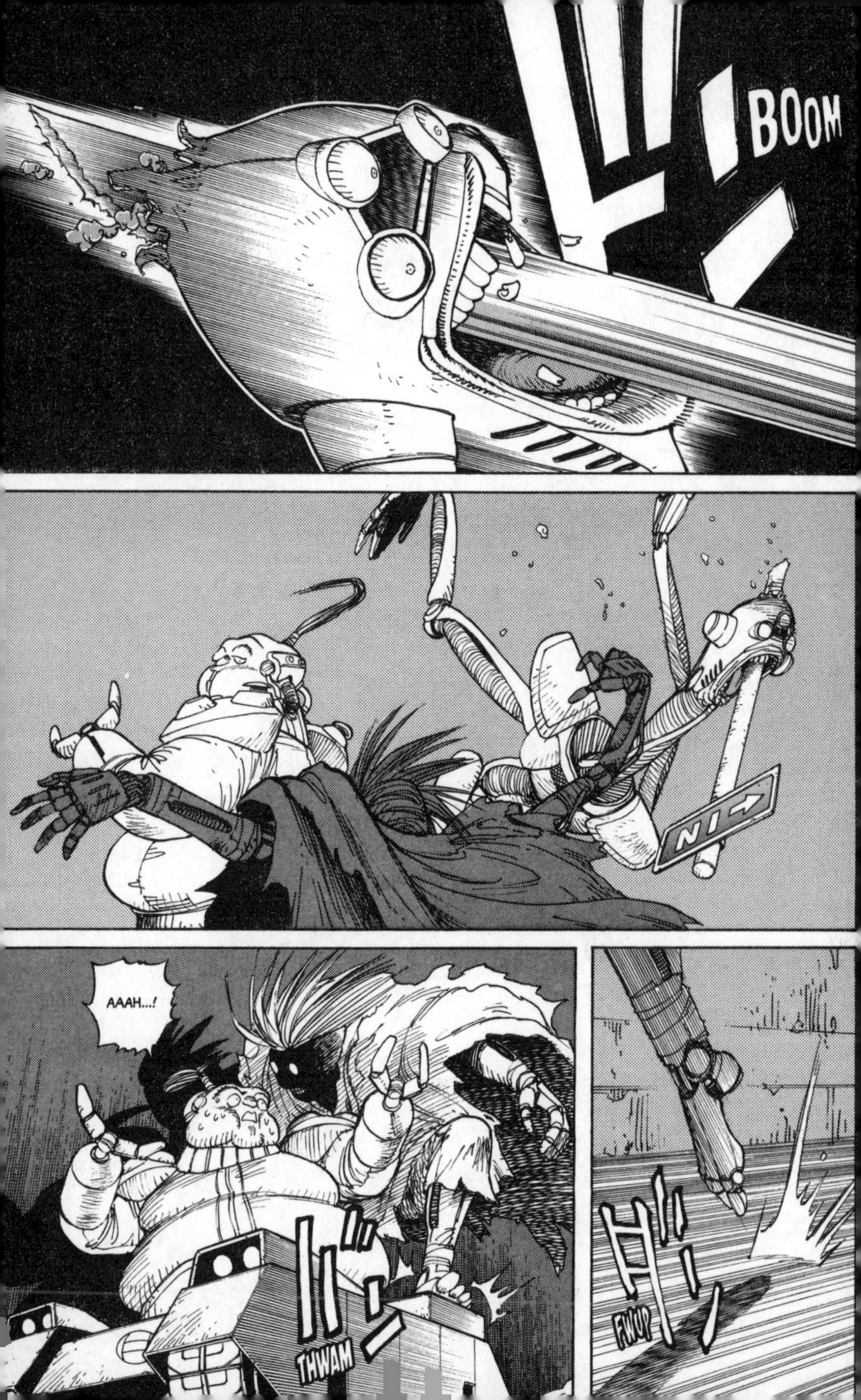
BOOM
FWOP
AAAH...!
THWAM

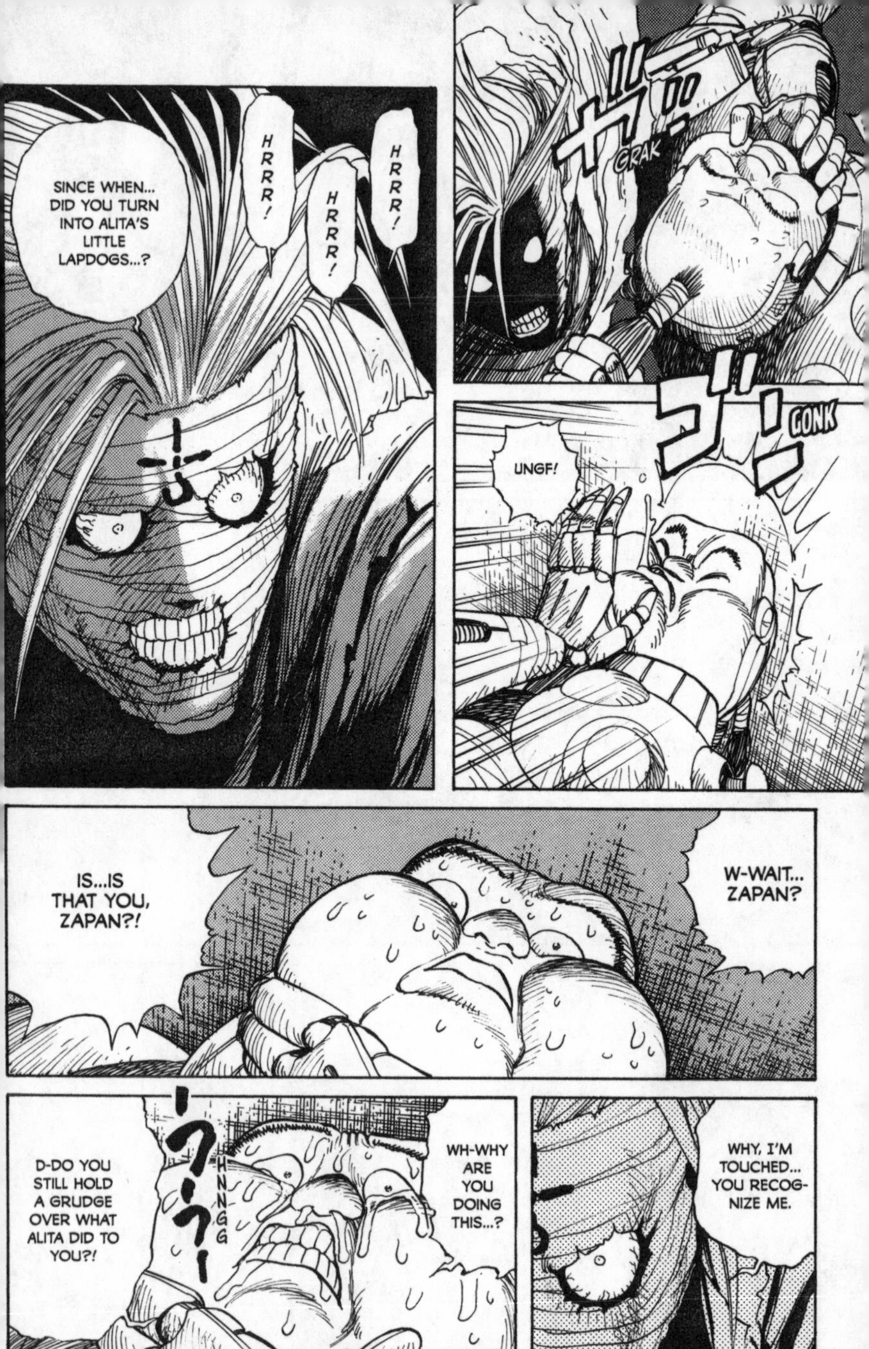
GRAK
GONK
UNGF!
HRRR!
HRRR!
HRRR!
SINCE WHEN... DID YOU TURN INTO ALITA'S LITTLE LAPDOGS...?
W-WAIT... ZAPAN?
IS...IS THAT YOU, ZAPAN?!
WHY, I'M TOUCHED... YOU RECOGNIZE ME.
WH-WHY ARE YOU DOING THIS...?
HNNGG
D-DO YOU STILL HOLD A GRUDGE OVER WHAT ALITA DID TO YOU?!

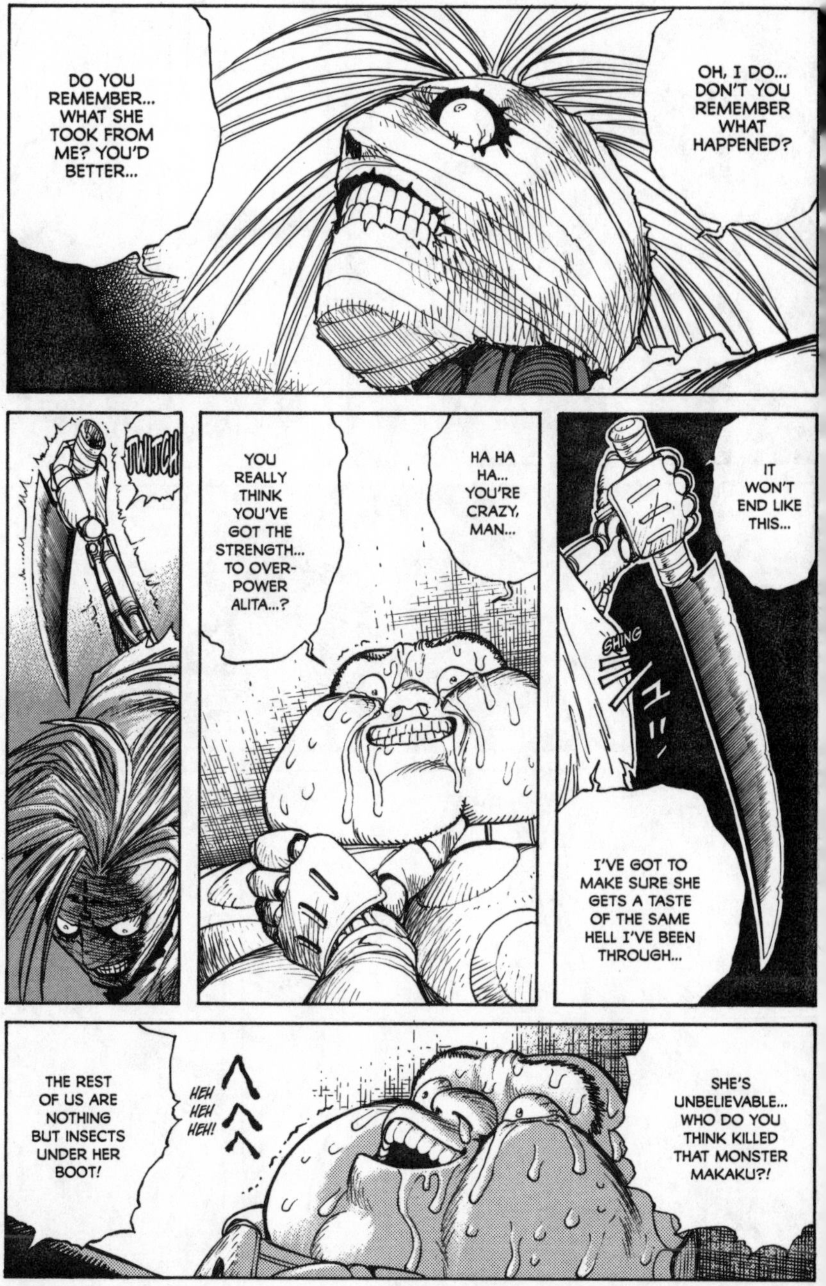
OH, I DO... DON'T YOU REMEMBER WHAT HAPPENED?
DO YOU REMEMBER... WHAT SHE TOOK FROM ME? YOU'D BETTER...
IT WON'T END LIKE THIS...
SHING
I'VE GOT TO MAKE SURE SHE GETS A TASTE OF THE SAME HELL I'VE BEEN THROUGH...
HA HA HA... YOU'RE CRAZY, MAN...
YOU REALLY THINK YOU'VE GOT THE STRENGTH... TO OVER-POWER ALITA...?
TWITCH
SHE'S UNBELIEVABLE... WHO DO YOU THINK KILLED THAT MONSTER MAKAKU?!
HEH HEH HEH!
THE REST OF US ARE NOTHING BUT INSECTS UNDER HER BOOT!

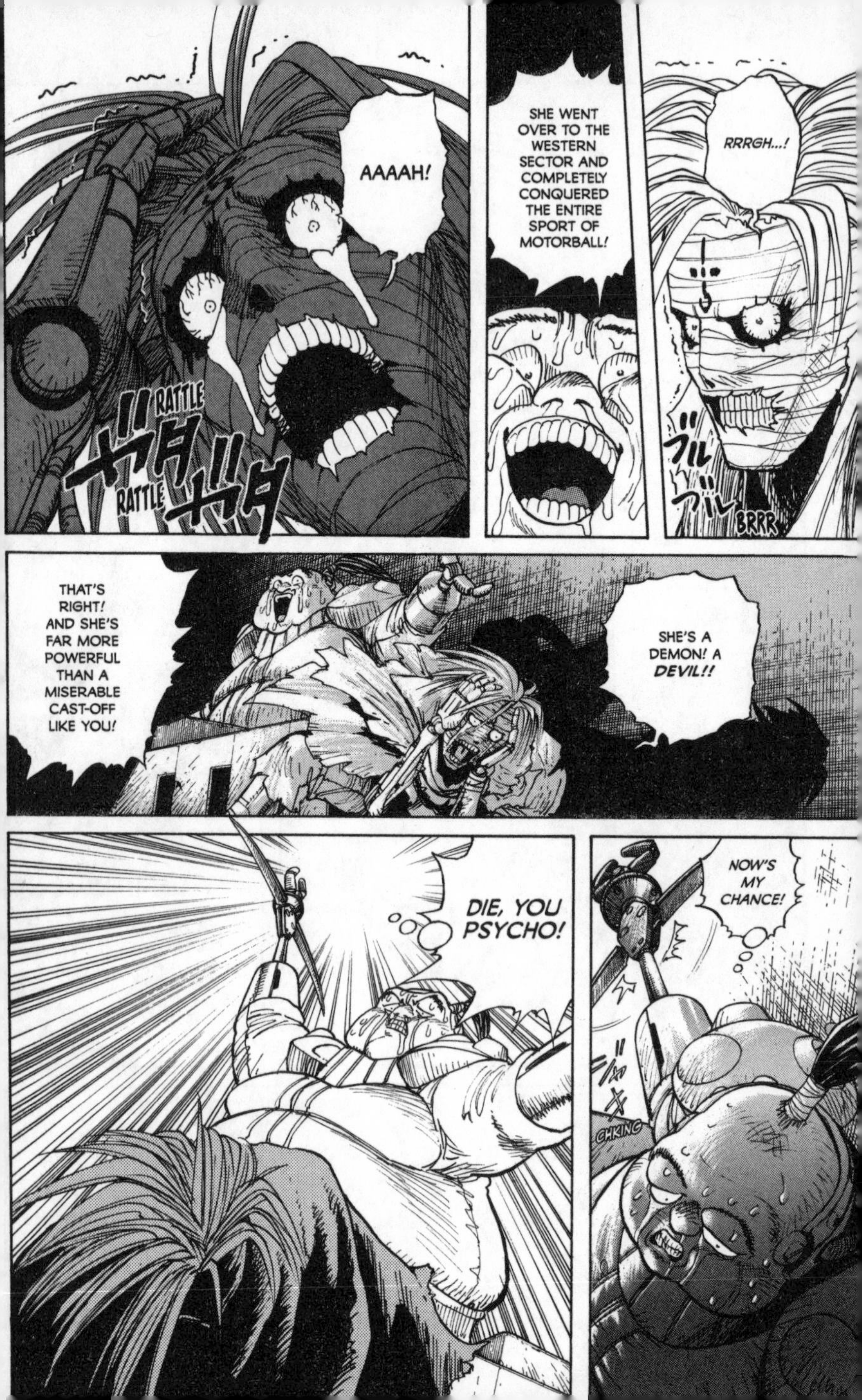
RRRGH...!
BRRR
SHE WENT OVER TO THE WESTERN SECTOR AND COMPLETELY CONQUERED THE ENTIRE SPORT OF MOTORBALL!
AAAAH!
RATTLE
RATTLE
SHE'S A DEMON! A DEVIL!!
THAT'S RIGHT! AND SHE'S FAR MORE POWERFUL THAN A MISERABLE CAST-OFF LIKE YOU!
NOW'S MY CHANCE!
CHKING
DIE, YOU PSYCHO!

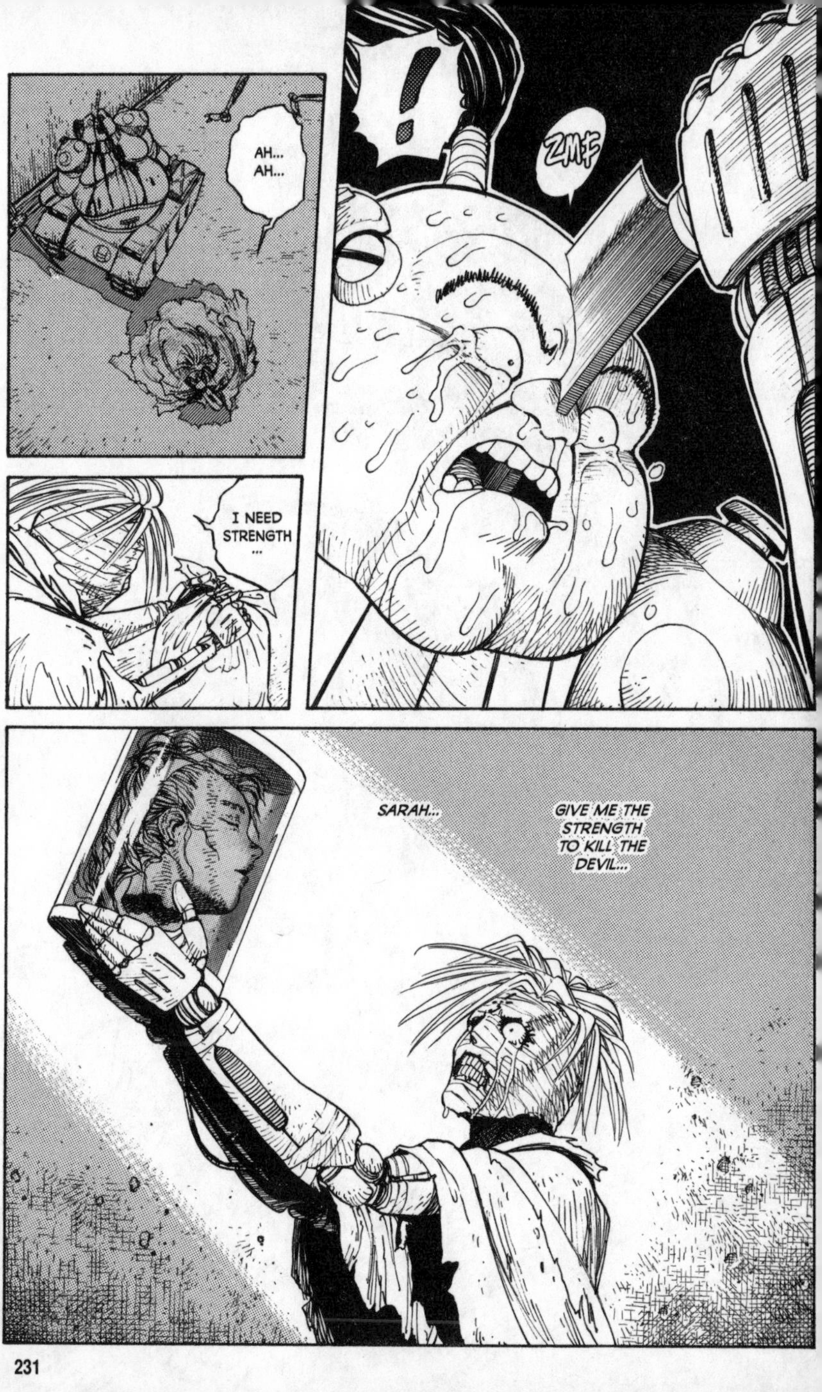
!
ZMF
AH... AH...
I NEED STRENGTH ...
GIVE ME THE STRENGTH TO KILL THE DEVIL...
SARAH...

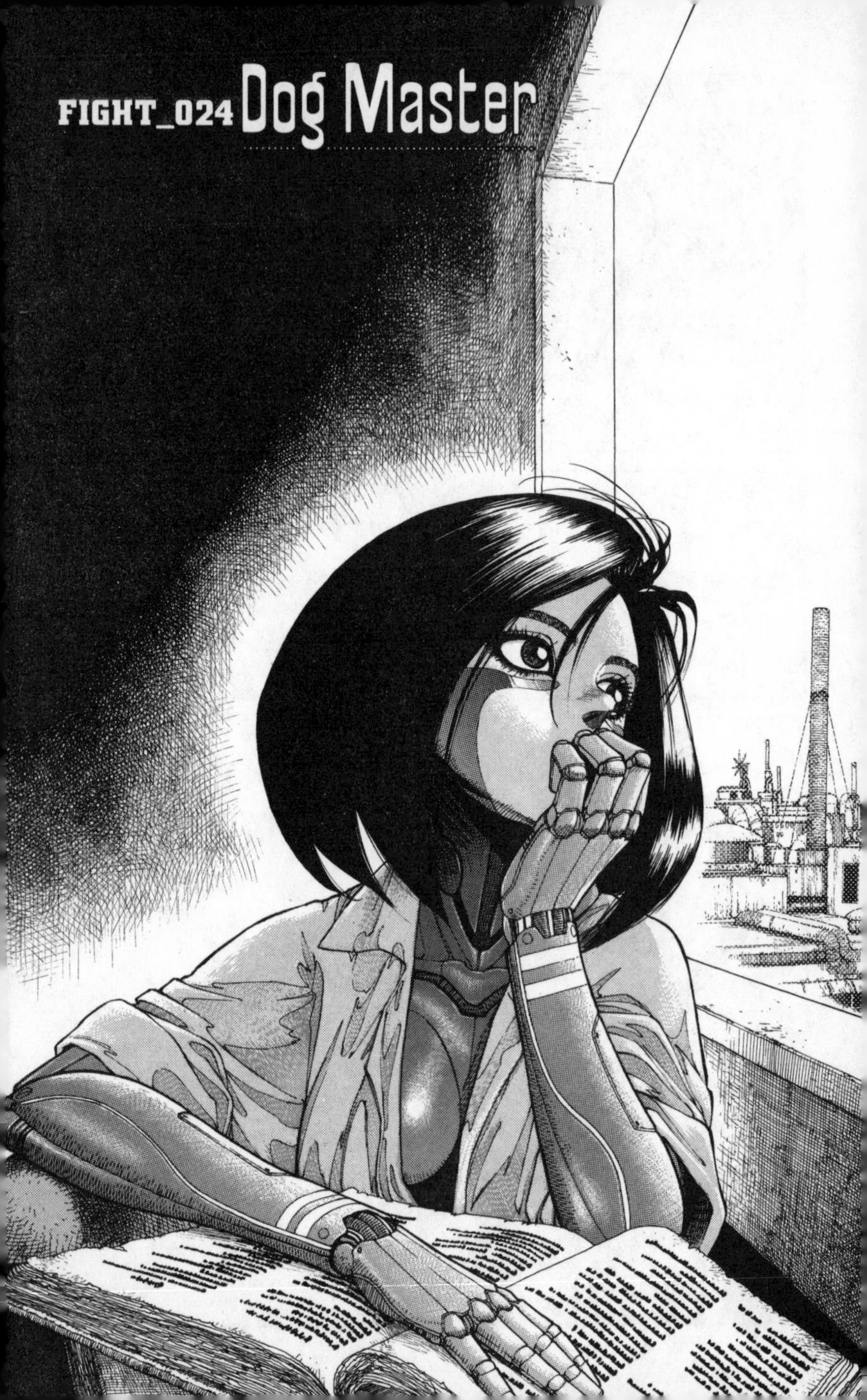
FIGHT_024 Dog Master

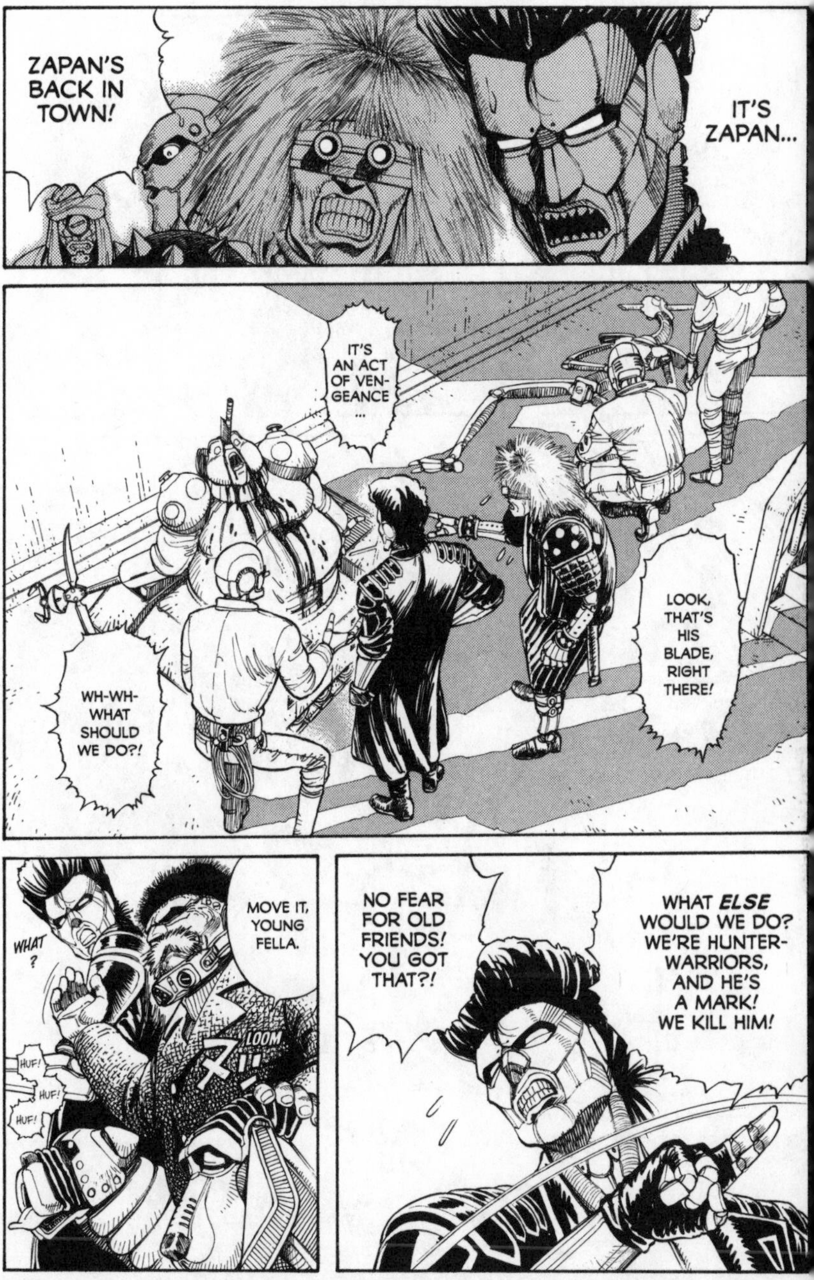
IT'S ZAPAN...
ZAPAN'S BACK IN TOWN!
IT'S AN ACT OF VEN- GEANCE ...
LOOK, THAT'S HIS BLADE, RIGHT THERE!
WH-WH-WHAT SHOULD WE DO?!
WHAT *ELSE* WOULD WE DO? WE'RE HUNTER-WARRIORS, AND HE'S A MARK! WE KILL HIM!
NO FEAR FOR OLD FRIENDS! YOU GOT THAT?!
MOVE IT, YOUNG FELLA.
WHAT ?
LOOM
HUF!
HUF!
HUF!

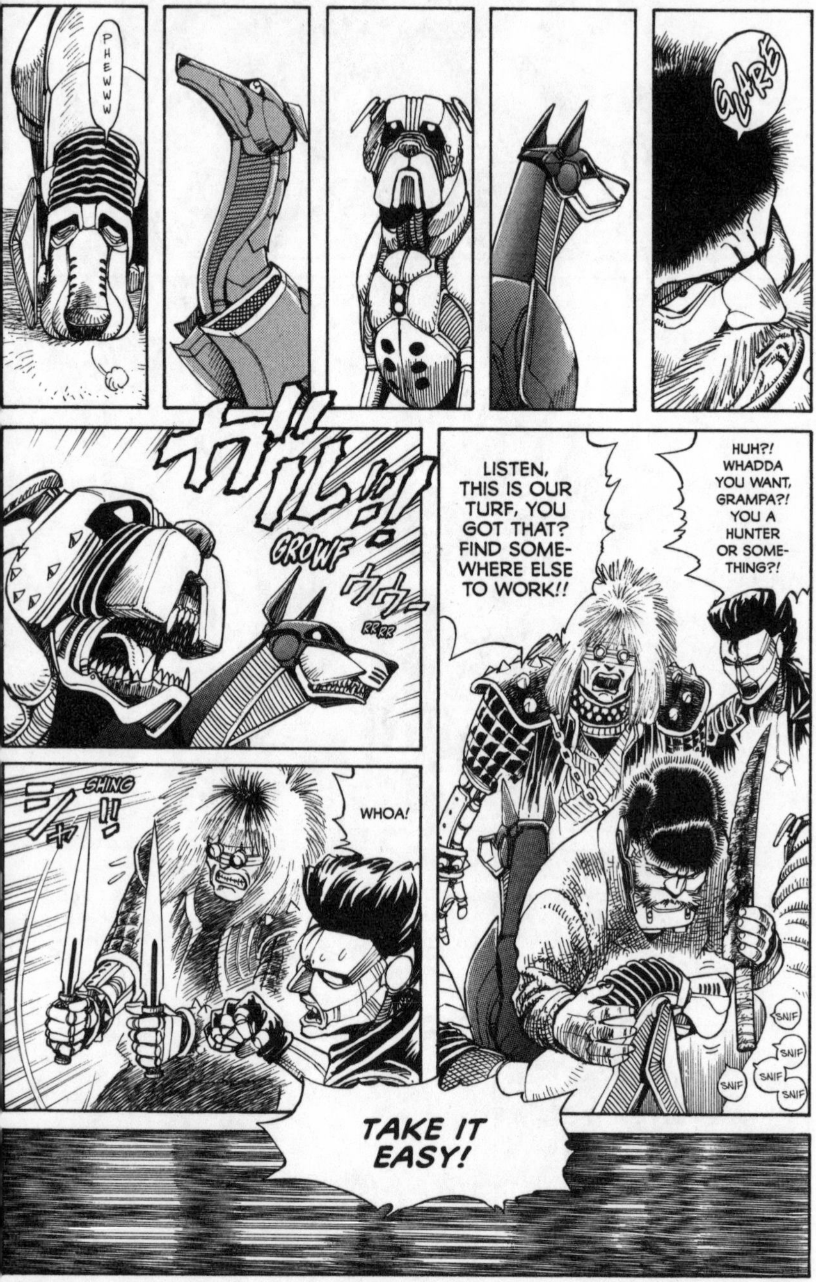
GLARE
PHEWWW
HUH?! WHADDA YOU WANT, GRAMPA?! YOU A HUNTER OR SOMETHING?!
LISTEN, THIS IS OUR TURF, YOU GOT THAT? FIND SOME-WHERE ELSE TO WORK!!
SNIF
SNIF
SNIF
SNIF
SNIF
GROWF
RRRR
WHOA!
SHING
TAKE IT EASY!

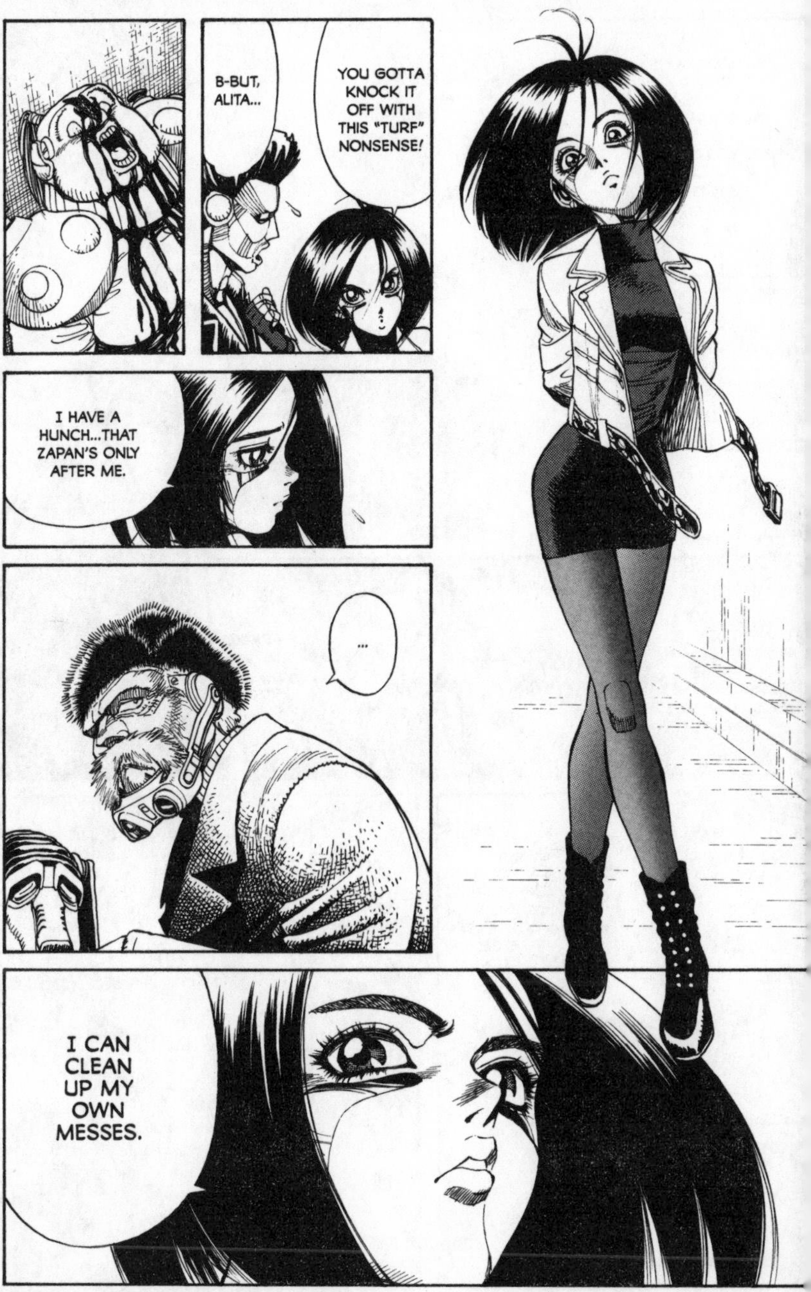
YOU GOTTA KNOCK IT OFF WITH THIS "TURF" NONSENSE!
B-BUT, ALITA...
I HAVE A HUNCH...THAT ZAPAN'S ONLY AFTER ME.
...
I CAN CLEAN UP MY OWN MESSES.

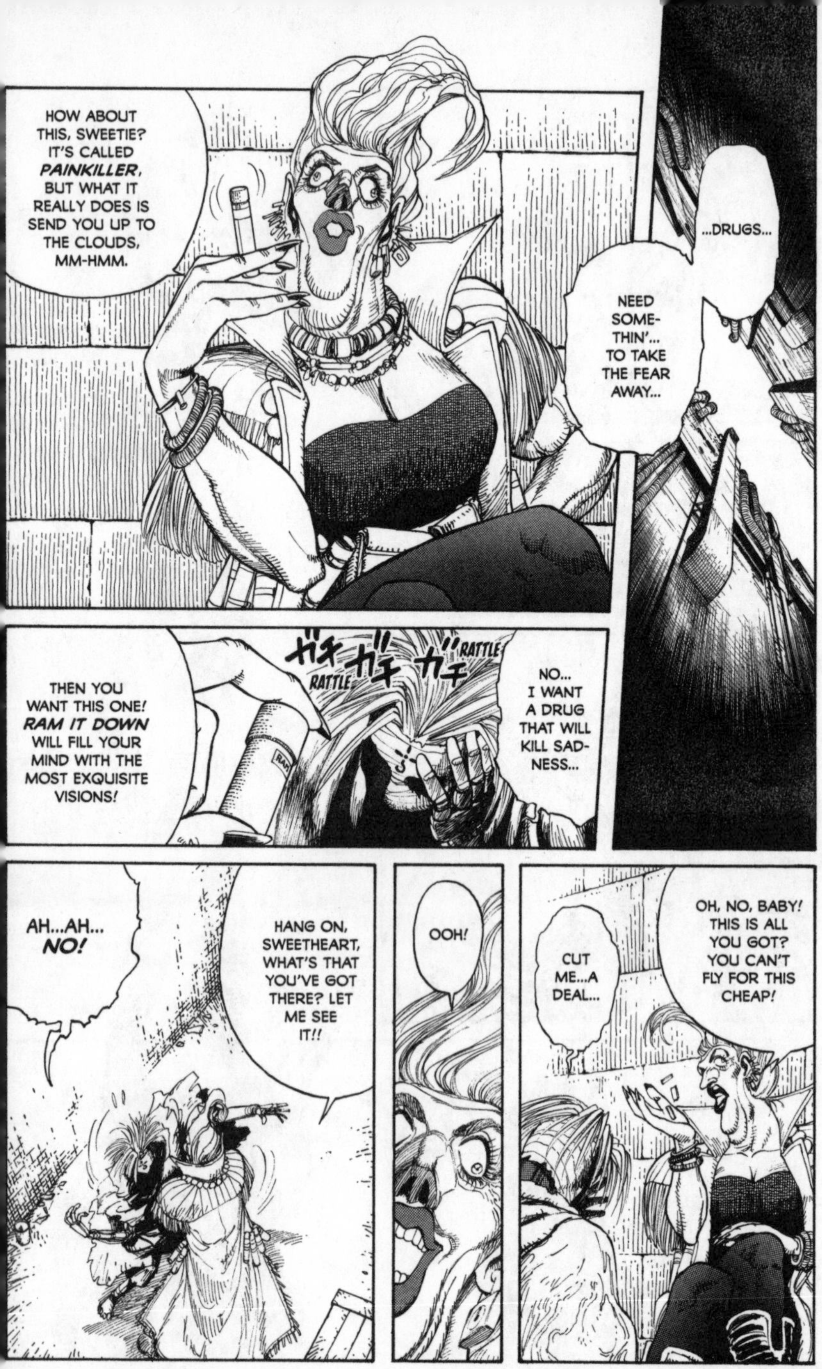
...DRUGS...
NEED SOME-THIN'... TO TAKE THE FEAR AWAY...
HOW ABOUT THIS, SWEETIE? IT'S CALLED ***PAINKILLER***, BUT WHAT IT REALLY DOES IS SEND YOU UP TO THE CLOUDS, MM-HMM.
NO... I WANT A DRUG THAT WILL KILL SAD-NESS...
RATTLE
ガチ
ガチ
ガチ
RATTLE
THEN YOU WANT THIS ONE! ***RAM IT DOWN*** WILL FILL YOUR MIND WITH THE MOST EXQUISITE VISIONS!
OH, NO, BABY! THIS IS ALL YOU GOT? YOU CAN'T FLY FOR THIS CHEAP!
CUT ME...A DEAL...
OOH!
HANG ON, SWEETHEART, WHAT'S THAT YOU'VE GOT THERE? LET ME SEE IT!!
AH...AH... ***NO!***

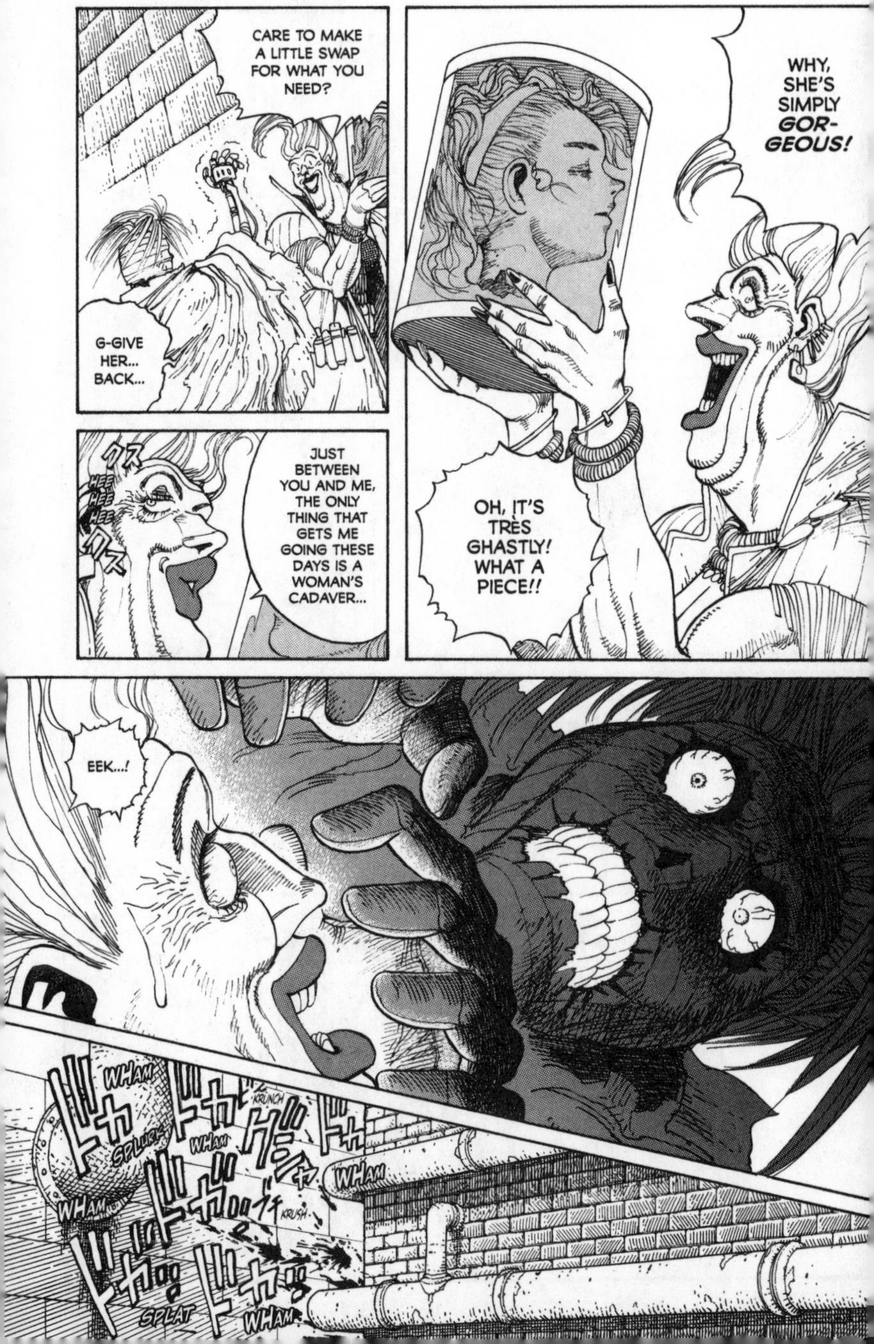
WHY, SHE'S SIMPLY GORGEOUS!
OH, IT'S TRÈS GHASTLY! WHAT A PIECE!!
CARE TO MAKE A LITTLE SWAP FOR WHAT YOU NEED?
G-GIVE HER... BACK...
HEE HEE HEE
JUST BETWEEN YOU AND ME, THE ONLY THING THAT GETS ME GOING THESE DAYS IS A WOMAN'S CADAVER...
EEK...!
WHAM
KRUNCH
SPLURK
WHAM
WHAM
WHAM
KRUSH
SPLAT
WHAM

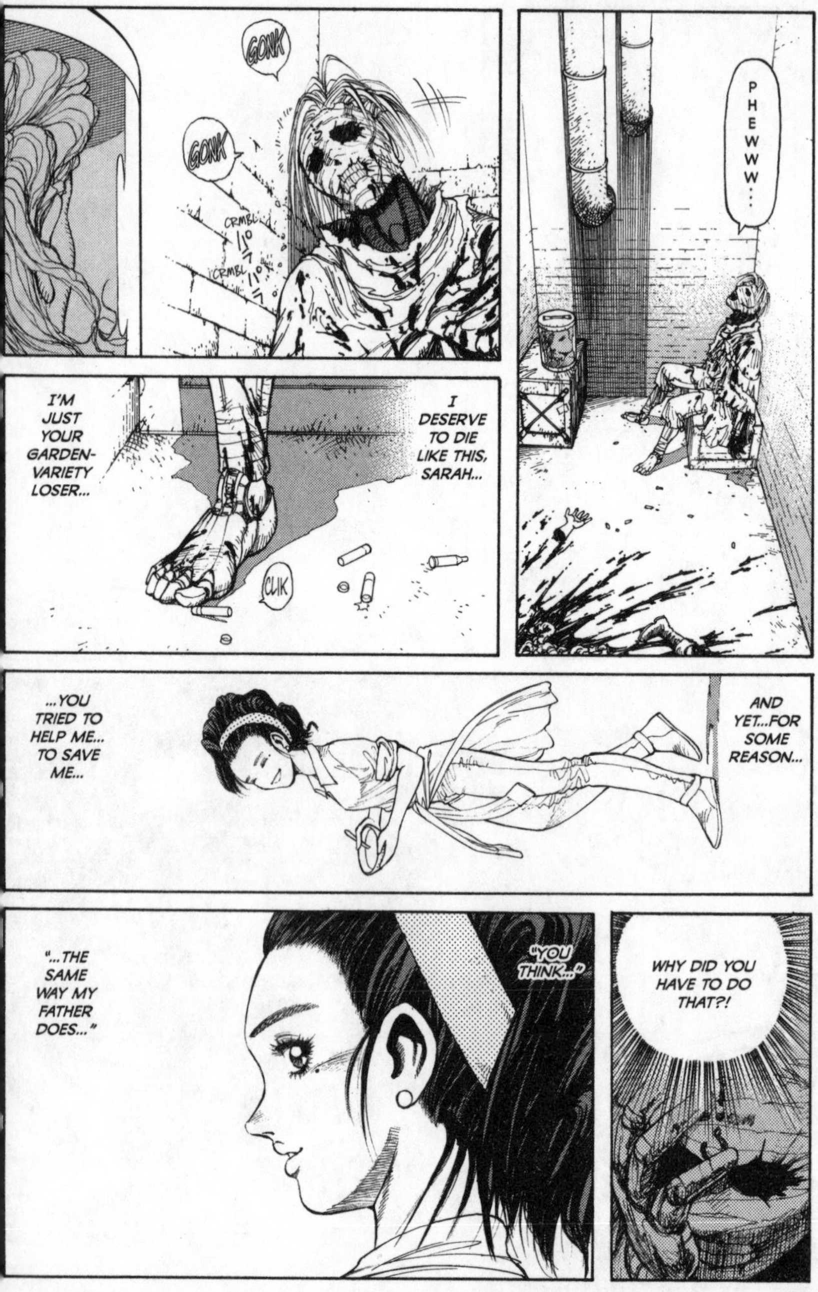
PHEWWW...
GONK
GONK
CRMBL
CRMBL
I DESERVE TO DIE LIKE THIS, SARAH...
I'M JUST YOUR GARDEN-VARIETY LOSER...
CLIK
AND YET...FOR SOME REASON...
...YOU TRIED TO HELP ME... TO SAVE ME...
WHY DID YOU HAVE TO DO THAT?!
"YOU THINK..."
"...THE SAME WAY MY FATHER DOES..."

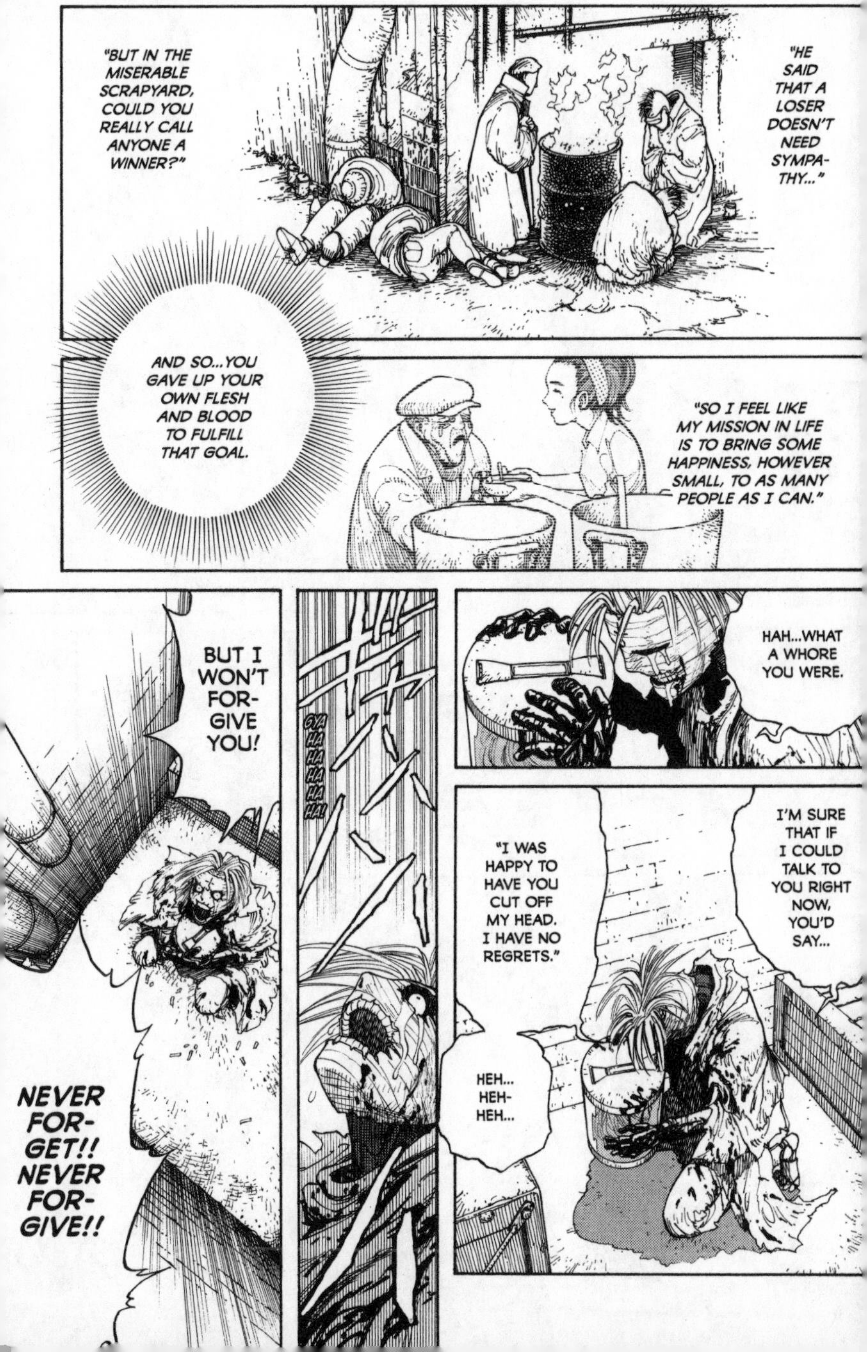
"HE SAID THAT A LOSER DOESN'T NEED SYMPA-THY..."
"BUT IN THE MISERABLE SCRAPYARD, COULD YOU REALLY CALL ANYONE A WINNER?"
"SO I FEEL LIKE MY MISSION IN LIFE IS TO BRING SOME HAPPINESS, HOWEVER SMALL, TO AS MANY PEOPLE AS I CAN."
AND SO...YOU GAVE UP YOUR OWN FLESH AND BLOOD TO FULFILL THAT GOAL.
HAH...WHAT A WHORE YOU WERE.
I'M SURE THAT IF I COULD TALK TO YOU RIGHT NOW, YOU'D SAY...
"I WAS HAPPY TO HAVE YOU CUT OFF MY HEAD. I HAVE NO REGRETS."
HEH... HEH-HEH...
GYA HA HA HA HA HA!
BUT I WON'T FOR-GIVE YOU!
NEVER FOR-GET!! NEVER FOR-GIVE!!

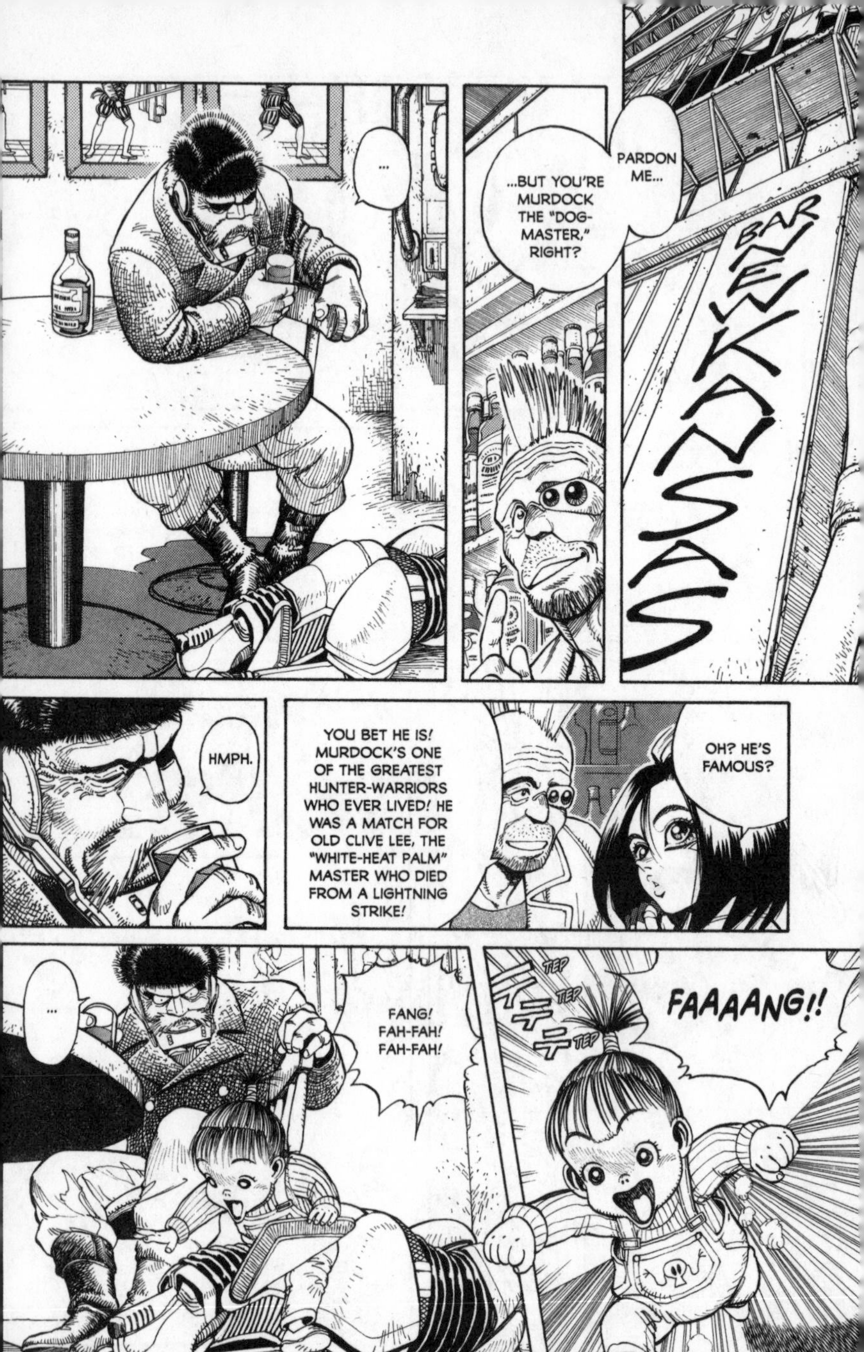
BAR NEW KANSAS
PARDON ME...
...BUT YOU'RE MURDOCK THE "DOG-MASTER," RIGHT?
...
OH? HE'S FAMOUS?
YOU BET HE IS! MURDOCK'S ONE OF THE GREATEST HUNTER-WARRIORS WHO EVER LIVED! HE WAS A MATCH FOR OLD CLIVE LEE, THE "WHITE-HEAT PALM" MASTER WHO DIED FROM A LIGHTNING STRIKE!
HMPH.
TEP TEP TEP
FAAAANG!!
FANG! FAH-FAH! FAH-FAH!
...

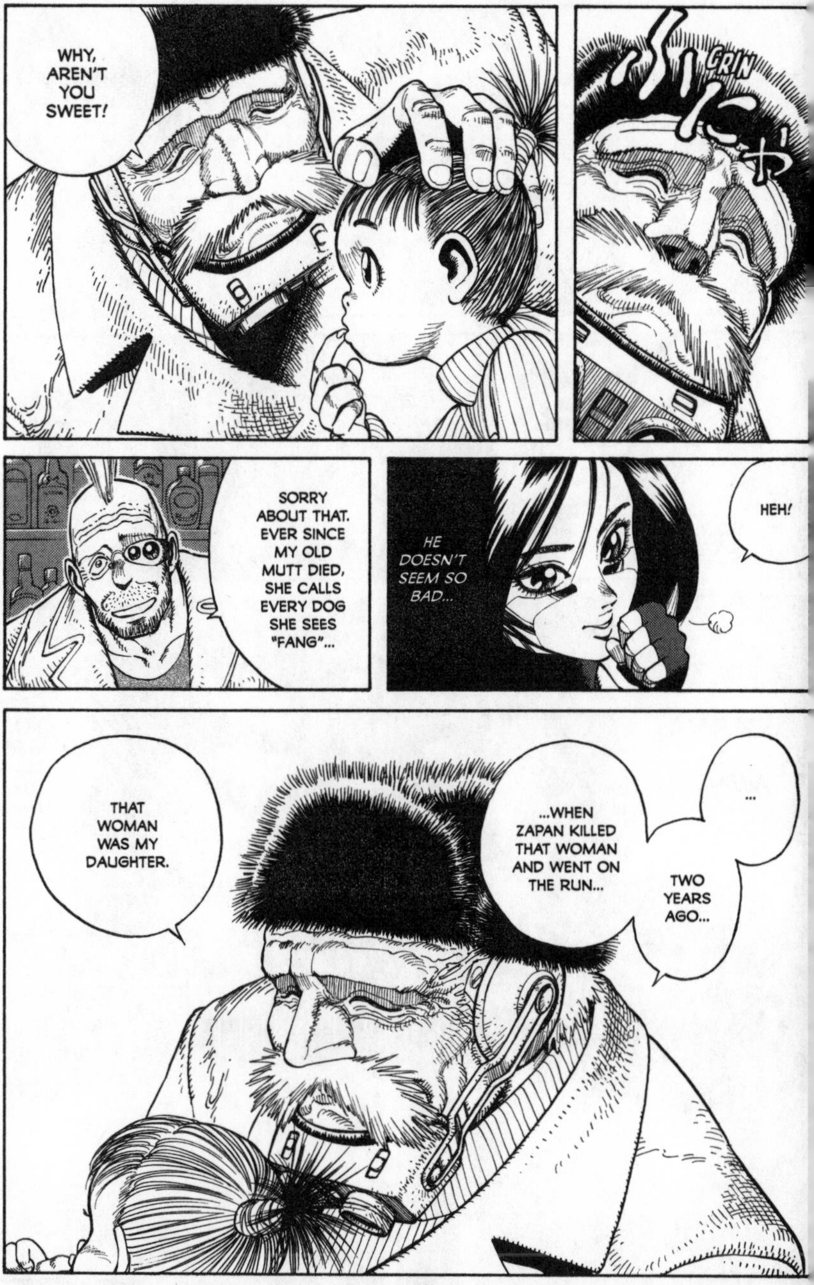
ふにゃ
GRIN
WHY, AREN'T YOU SWEET!
HEH!
HE DOESN'T SEEM SO BAD...
SORRY ABOUT THAT. EVER SINCE MY OLD MUTT DIED, SHE CALLS EVERY DOG SHE SEES "FANG"...
...
TWO YEARS AGO...
...WHEN ZAPAN KILLED THAT WOMAN AND WENT ON THE RUN...
THAT WOMAN WAS MY DAUGHTER.

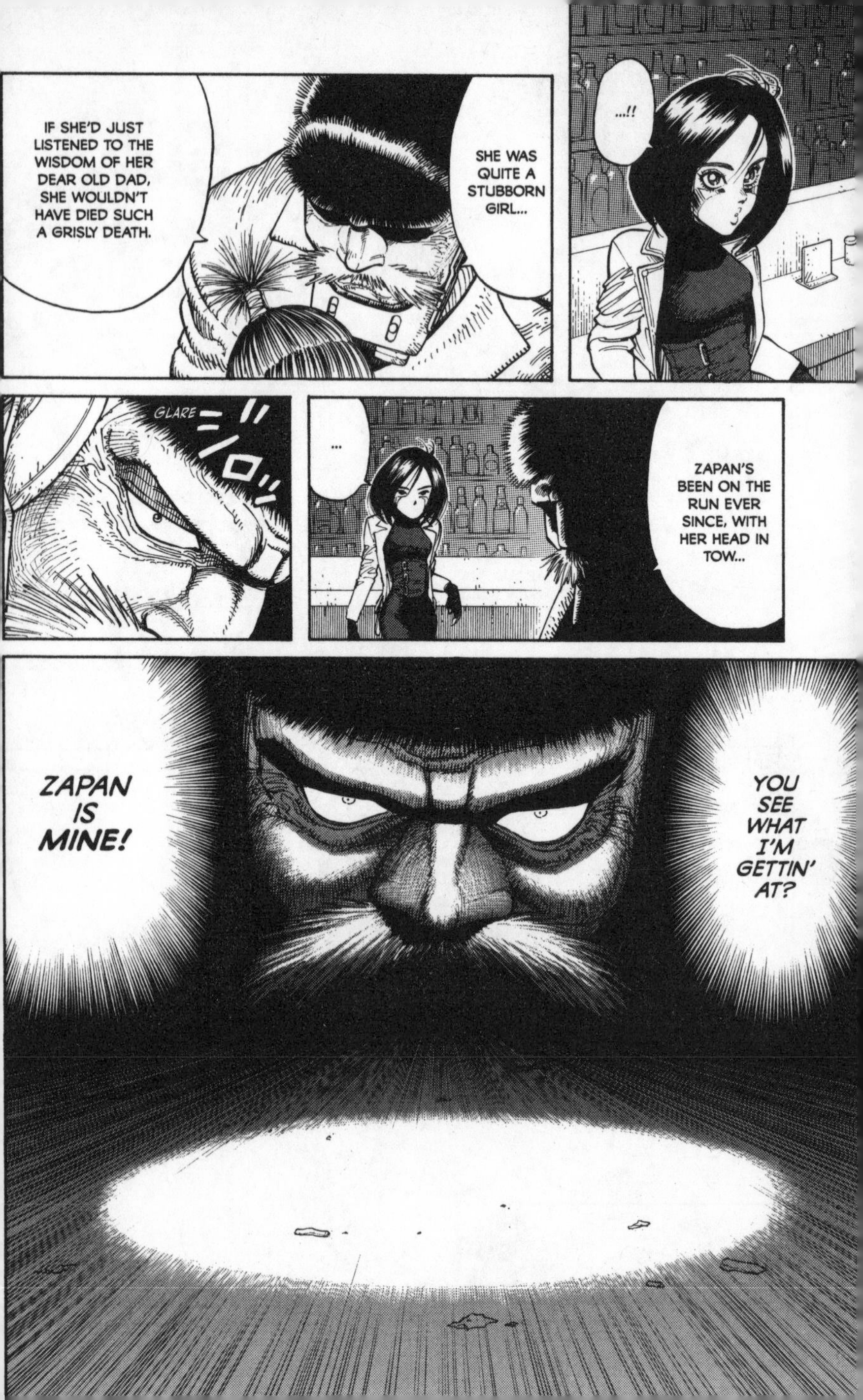
...!!
SHE WAS QUITE A STUBBORN GIRL...
IF SHE'D JUST LISTENED TO THE WISDOM OF HER DEAR OLD DAD, SHE WOULDN'T HAVE DIED SUCH A GRISLY DEATH.
ZAPAN'S BEEN ON THE RUN EVER SINCE, WITH HER HEAD IN TOW...
...
GLARE
YOU SEE WHAT I'M GETTIN' AT?
ZAPAN IS MINE!

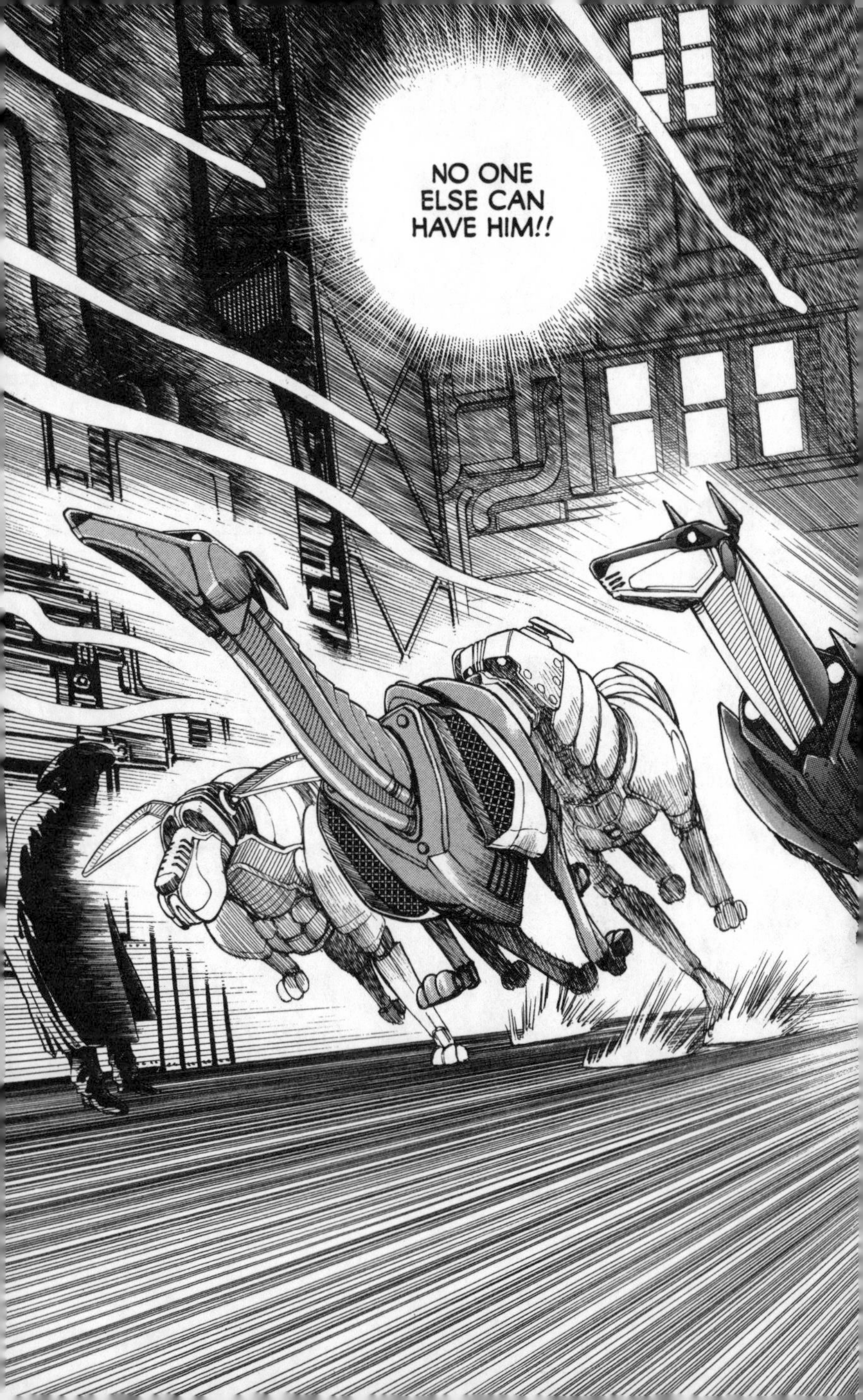
NO ONE ELSE CAN HAVE HIM!!

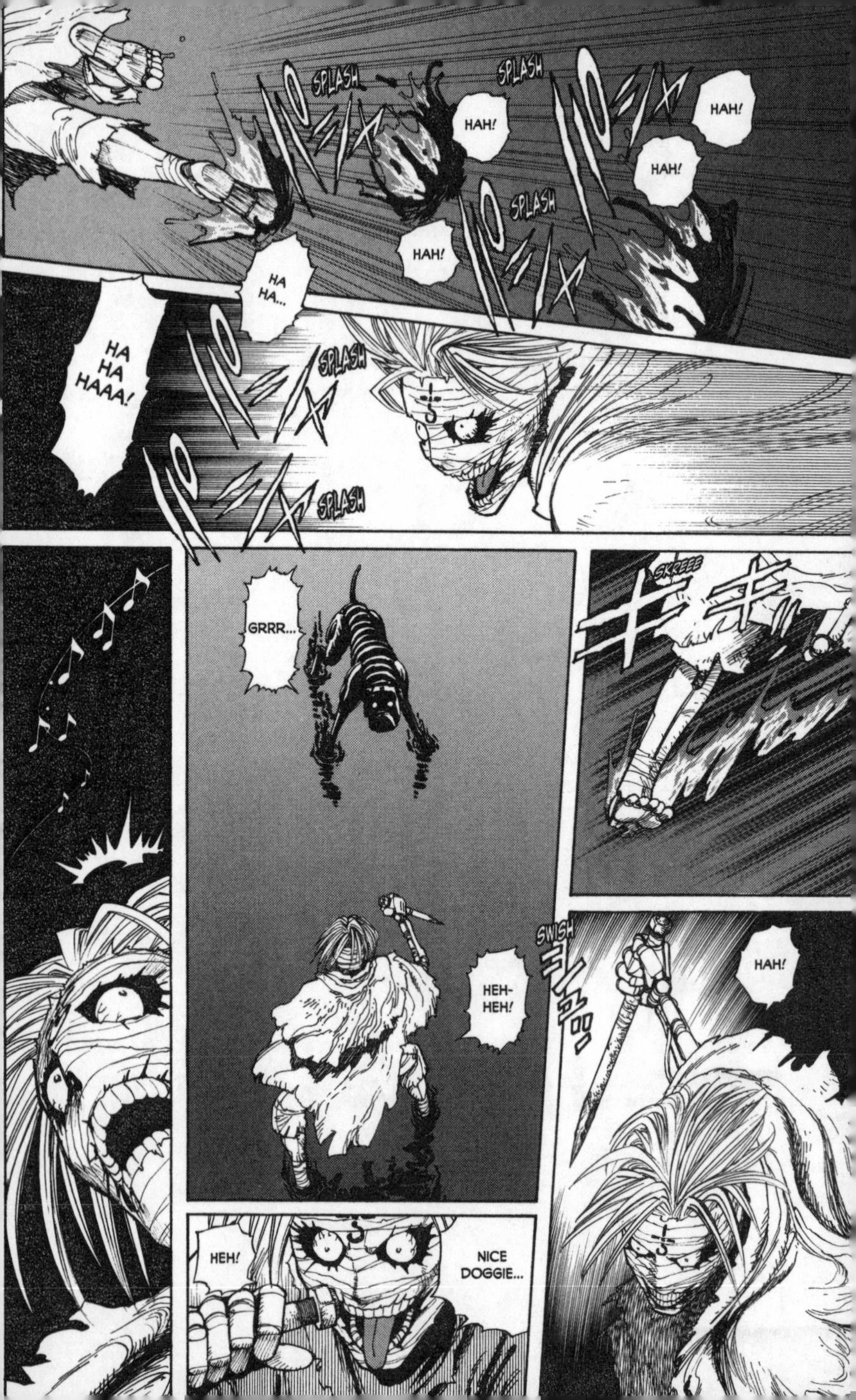
HAH!
HAH!
SPLASH
HAH!
SPLASH
HAH!
SPLASH
HA HA...
SPLASH
HA HA HAAA!
SPLASH
SKREEE
HAH!
SWISH
GRRR...
HEH-HEH!
NICE DOGGIE...
HEH!

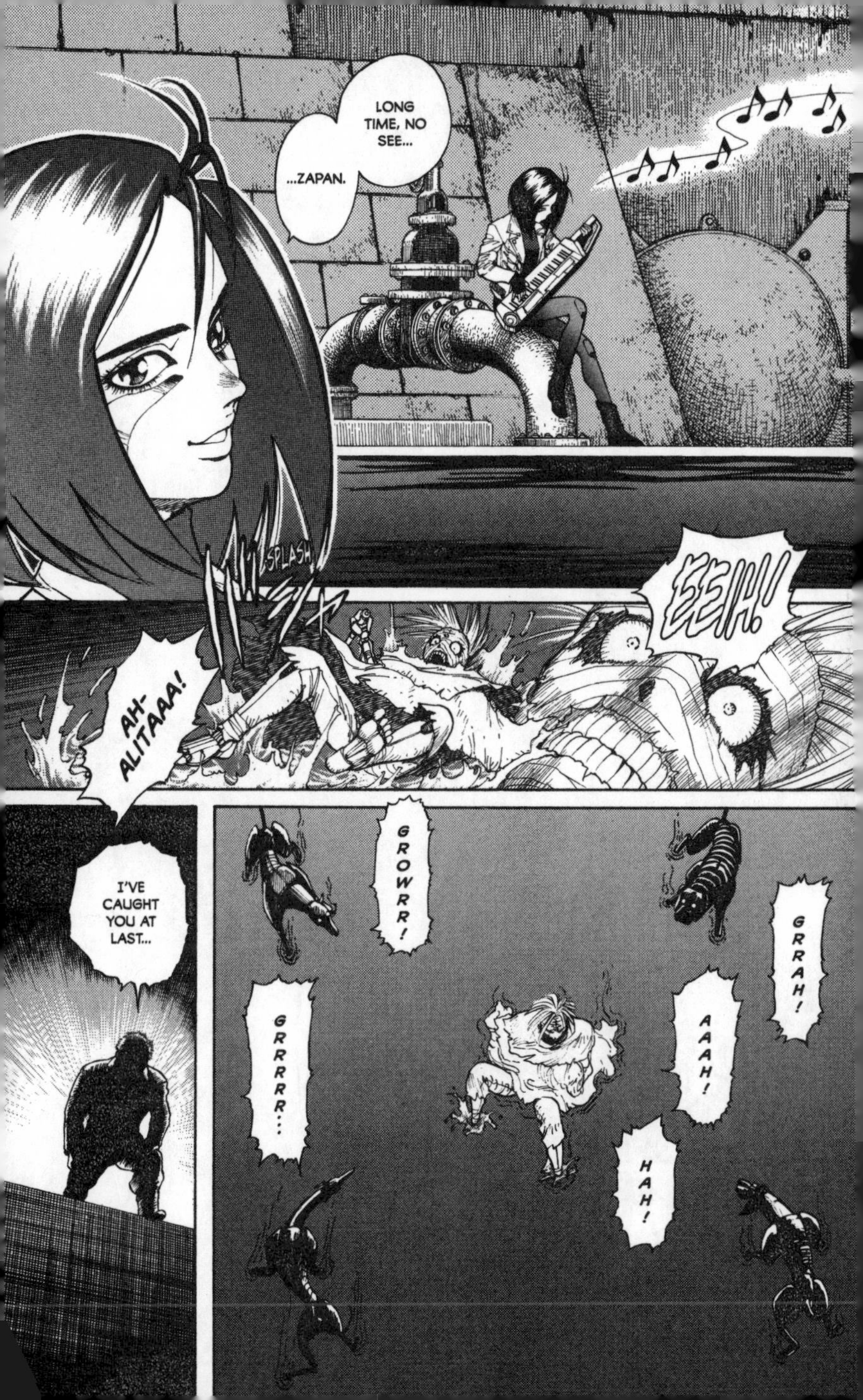

LONG TIME, NO SEE...
...ZAPAN.
EEIH!
SPLASH
AH-ALITAAA!
GRRAH!
GROWRR!
AAAH!
GRRRRR...
HAH!
I'VE CAUGHT YOU AT LAST...

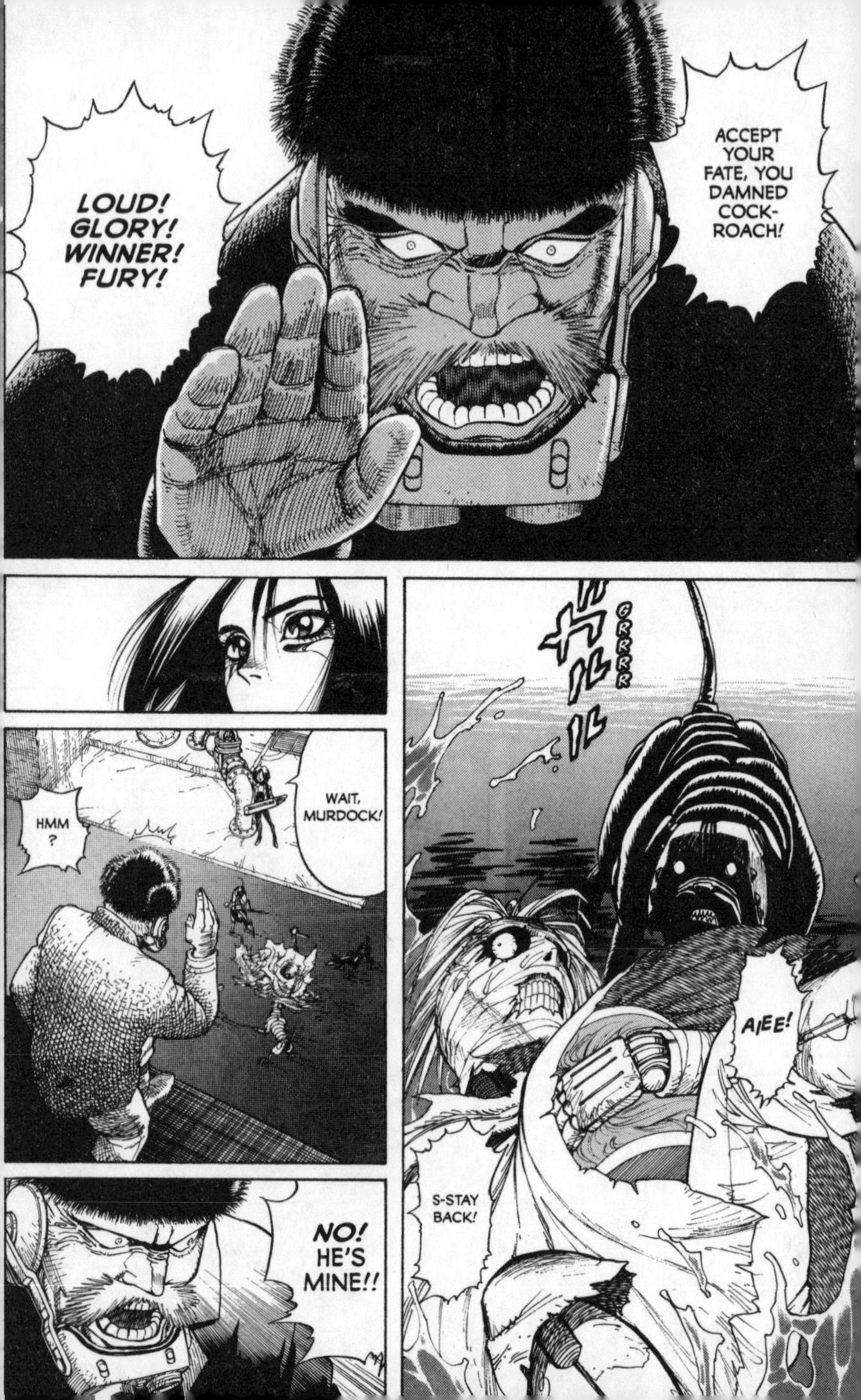
ACCEPT YOUR FATE, YOU DAMNED COCK-ROACH!
LOUD! GLORY! WINNER! FURY!
GRRRR
AIEE!
S-STAY BACK!
WAIT, MURDOCK!
HMM ?
NO! HE'S MINE!!

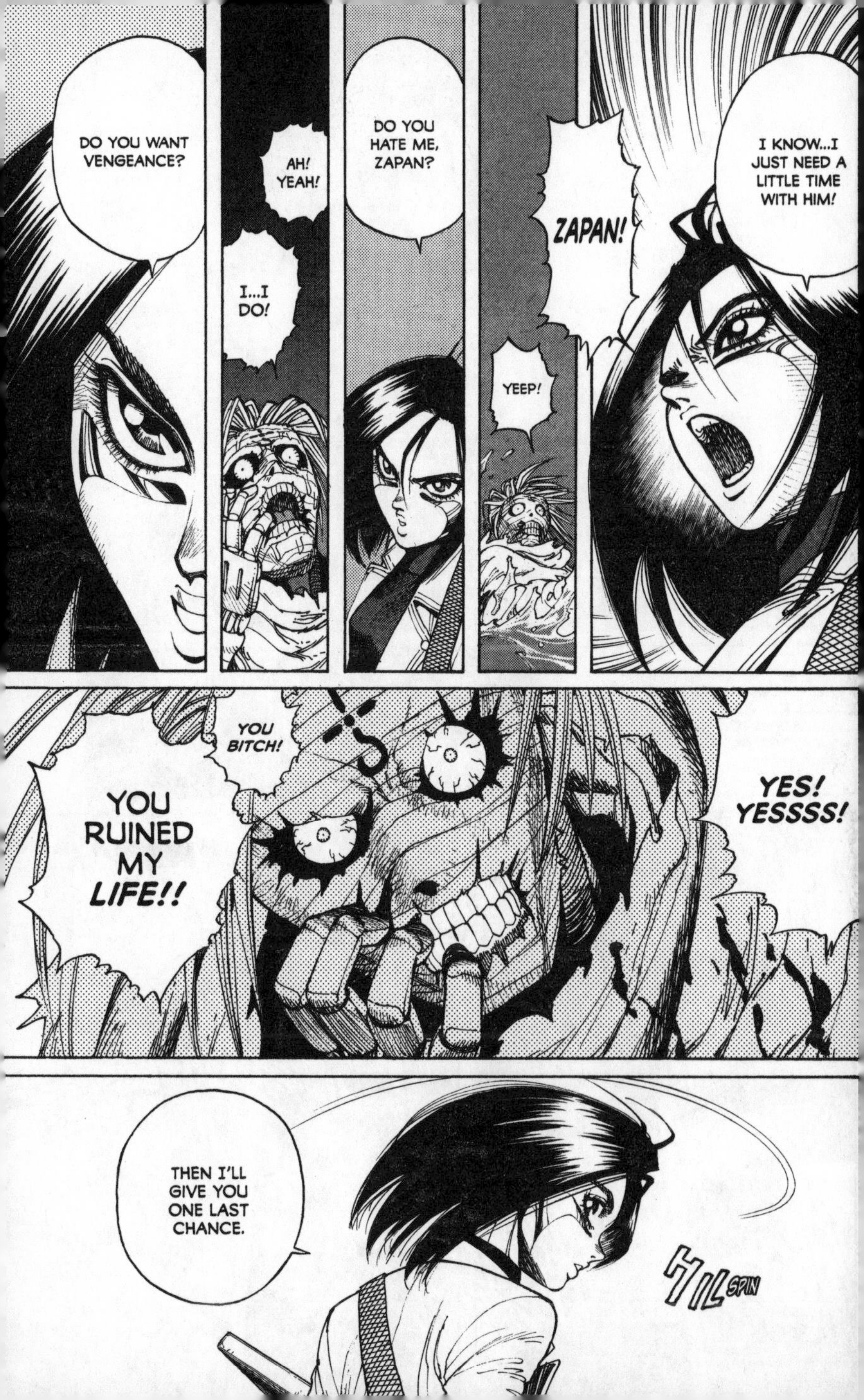
I KNOW...I JUST NEED A LITTLE TIME WITH HIM!
ZAPAN!
YEEP!
DO YOU HATE ME, ZAPAN?
AH! YEAH!
I...I DO!
DO YOU WANT VENGEANCE?
YES! YESSSS!
YOU BITCH!
YOU RUINED MY LIFE!!
THEN I'LL GIVE YOU ONE LAST CHANCE.
SPIN

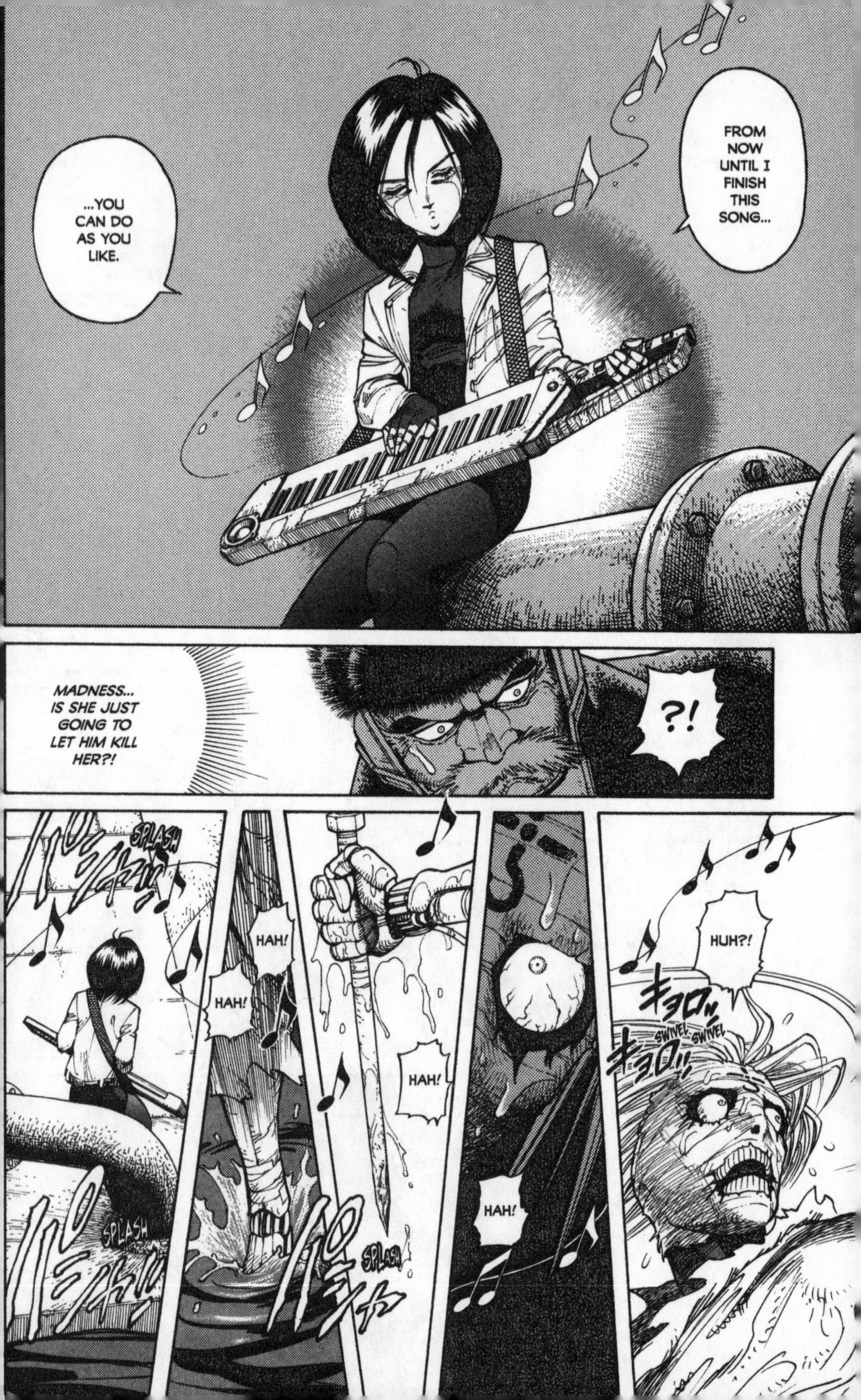
FROM NOW UNTIL I FINISH THIS SONG...
...YOU CAN DO AS YOU LIKE.
?!
MADNESS... IS SHE JUST GOING TO LET HIM KILL HER?!
HUH?!
キョロッ SWIVEL
キョロッ SWIVEL
HAH!
HAH!
SPLASH
HAH!
HAH!
SPLASH
SPLASH

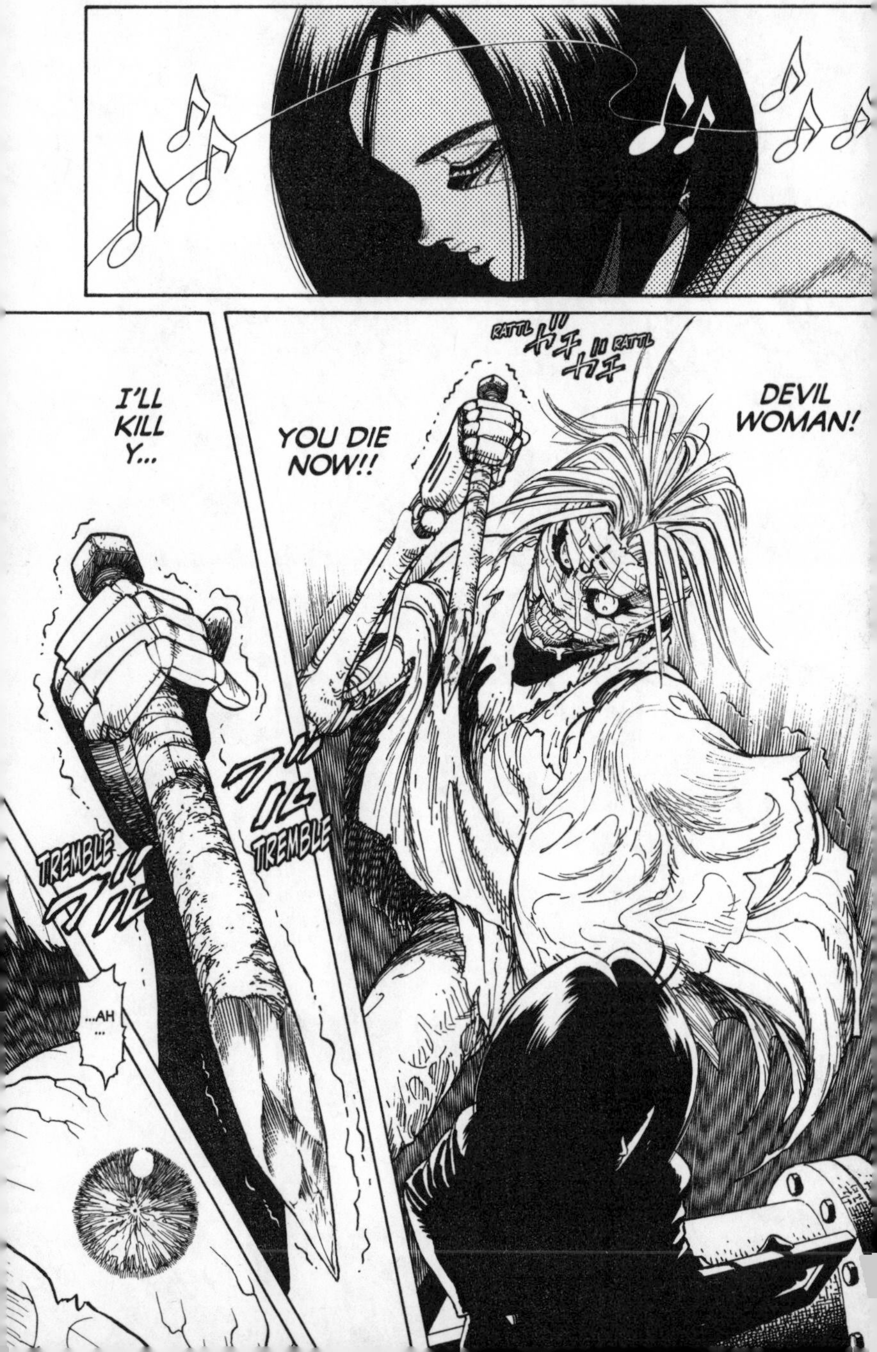

RATTL RATTL
DEVIL WOMAN!
YOU DIE NOW!!
TREMBLE
I'LL KILL Y...
TREMBLE
...AH ...

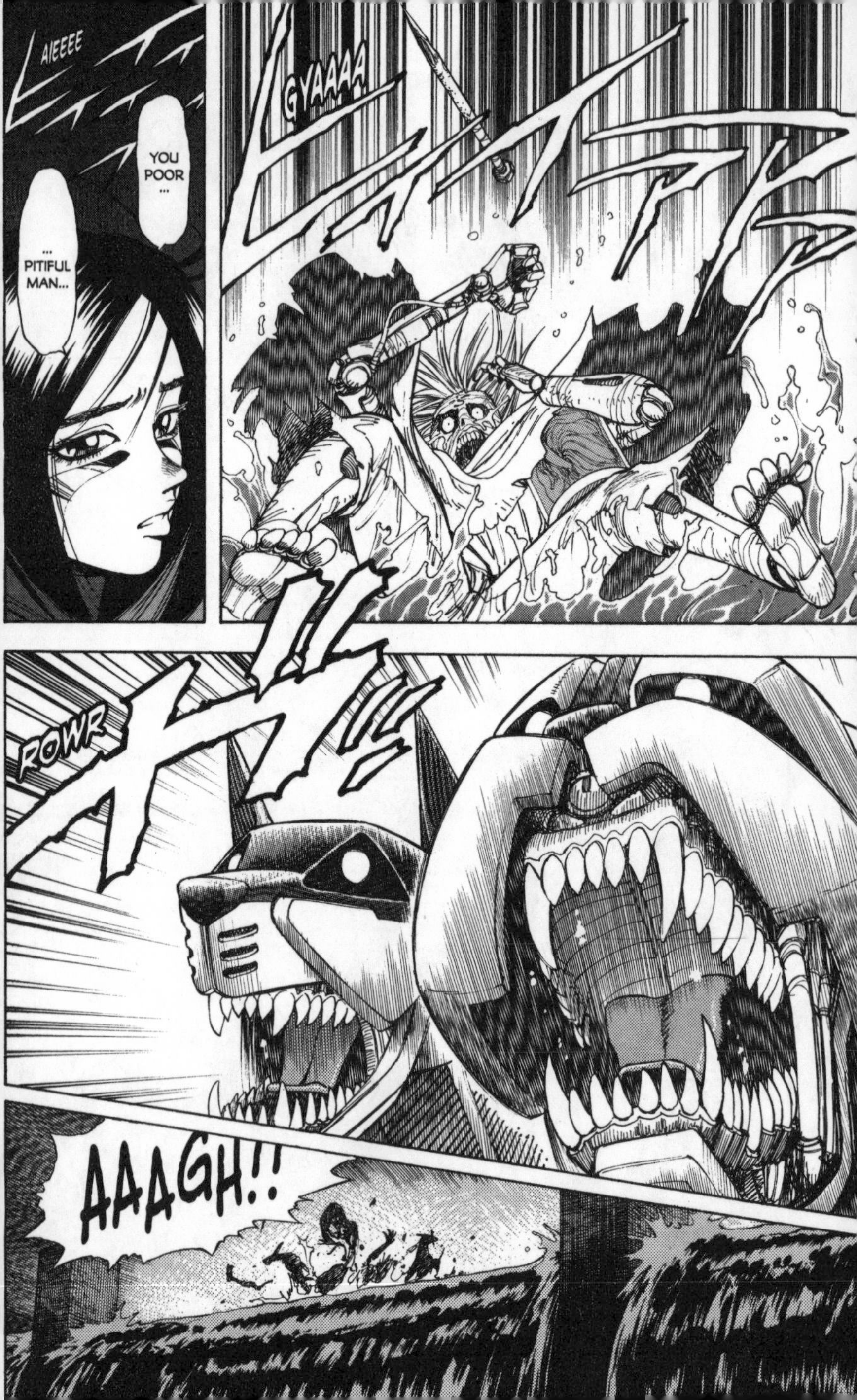
GYAAAA
AIEEEE
YOU POOR ...
... PITIFUL MAN...
ROWR
AAAGH!!

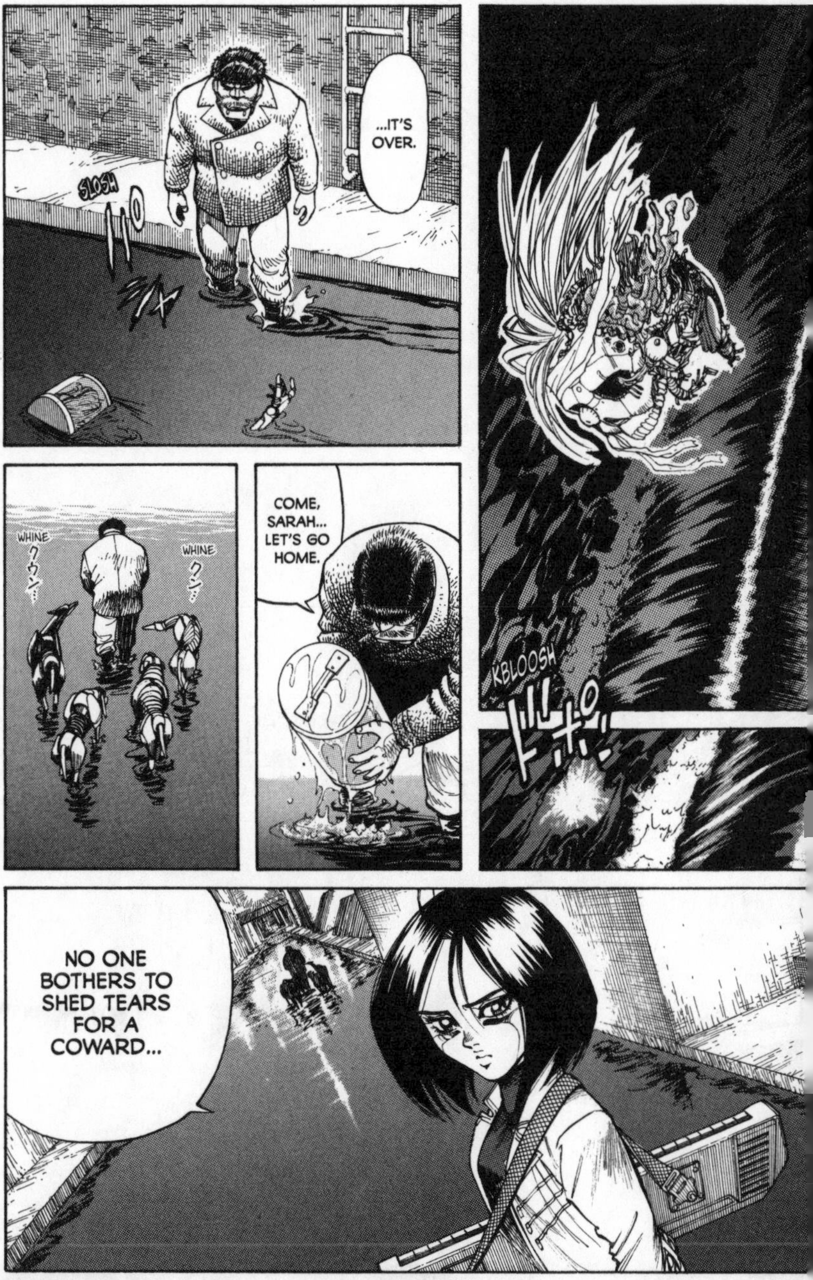
KBLOOSH
...IT'S OVER.
SLOSH
COME, SARAH... LET'S GO HOME.
WHINE
WHINE
NO ONE BOTHERS TO SHED TEARS FOR A COWARD...

LOUD

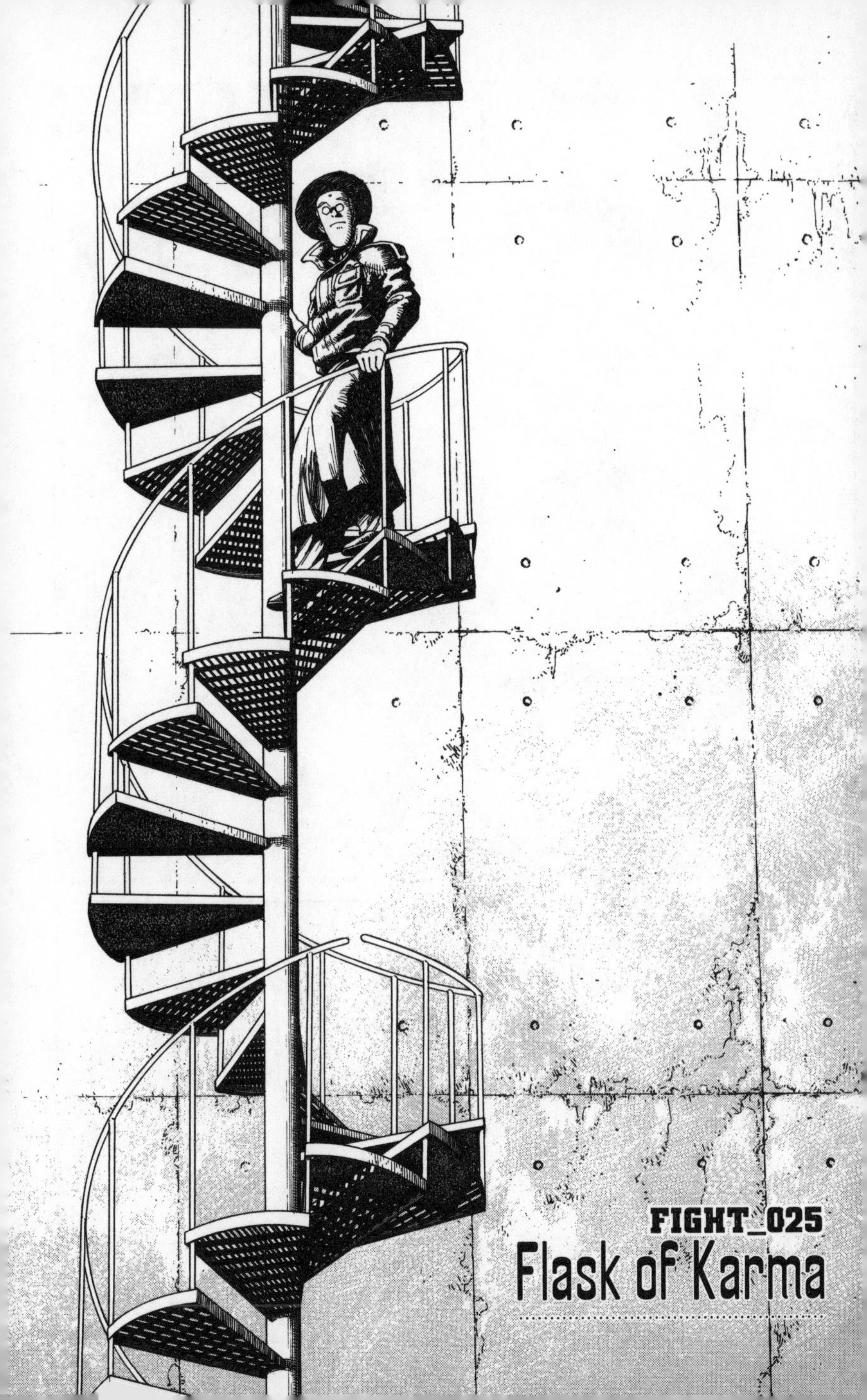

FIGHT_025
Flask of Karma

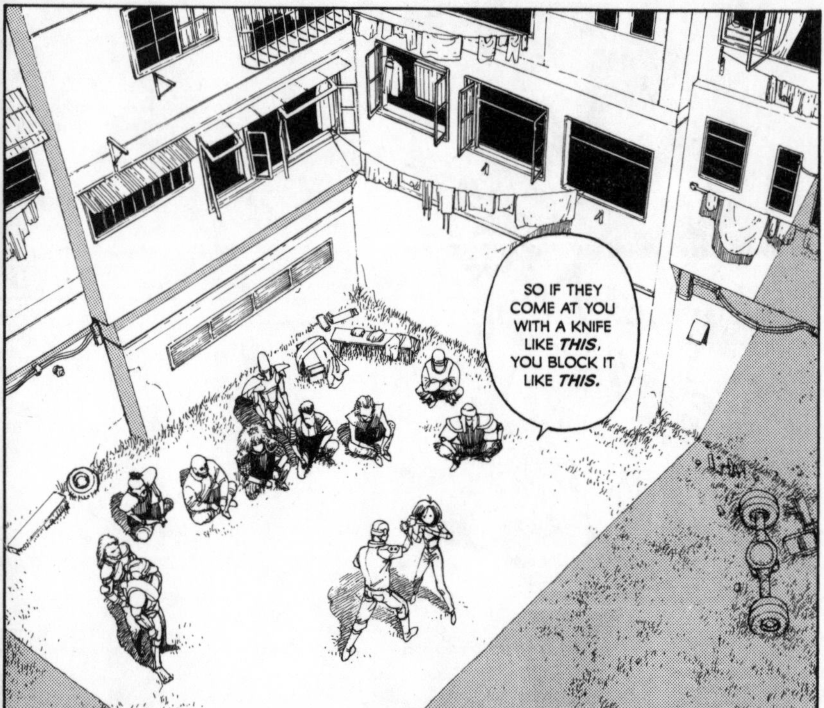
SO IF THEY COME AT YOU WITH A KNIFE LIKE *THIS*, YOU BLOCK IT LIKE *THIS*.
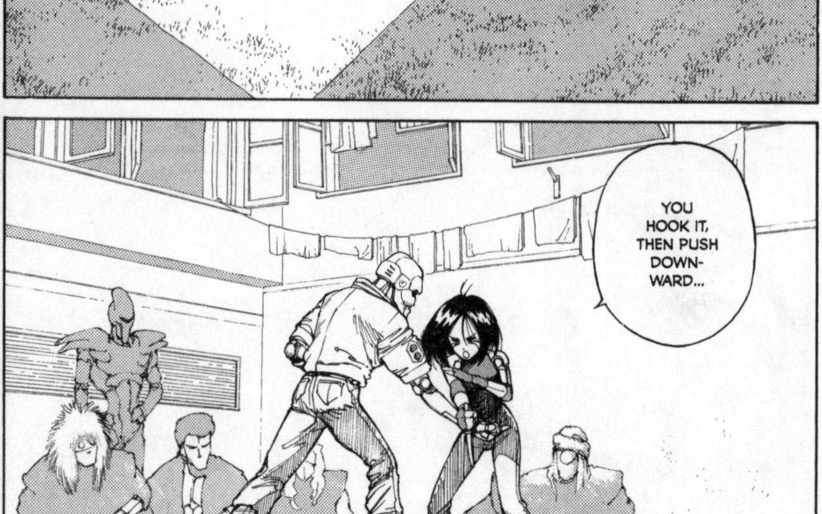
YOU HOOK IT, THEN PUSH DOWN-WARD...

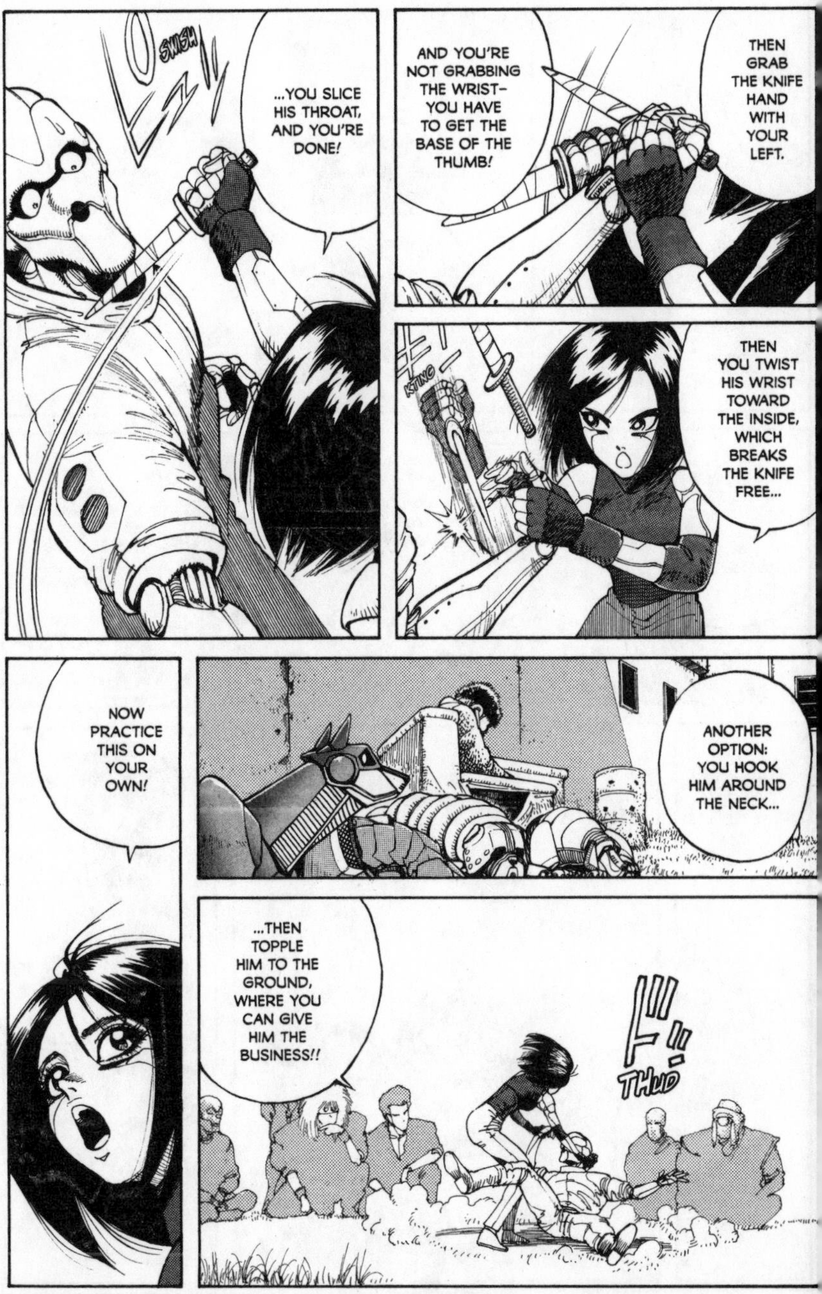
THEN GRAB THE KNIFE HAND WITH YOUR LEFT.
AND YOU'RE NOT GRABBING THE WRIST- YOU HAVE TO GET THE BASE OF THE THUMB!
KTING
THEN YOU TWIST HIS WRIST TOWARD THE INSIDE, WHICH BREAKS THE KNIFE FREE...
SWISH
...YOU SLICE HIS THROAT, AND YOU'RE DONE!
ANOTHER OPTION: YOU HOOK HIM AROUND THE NECK...
THUD
...THEN TOPPLE HIM TO THE GROUND, WHERE YOU CAN GIVE HIM THE BUSINESS!!
NOW PRACTICE THIS ON YOUR OWN!

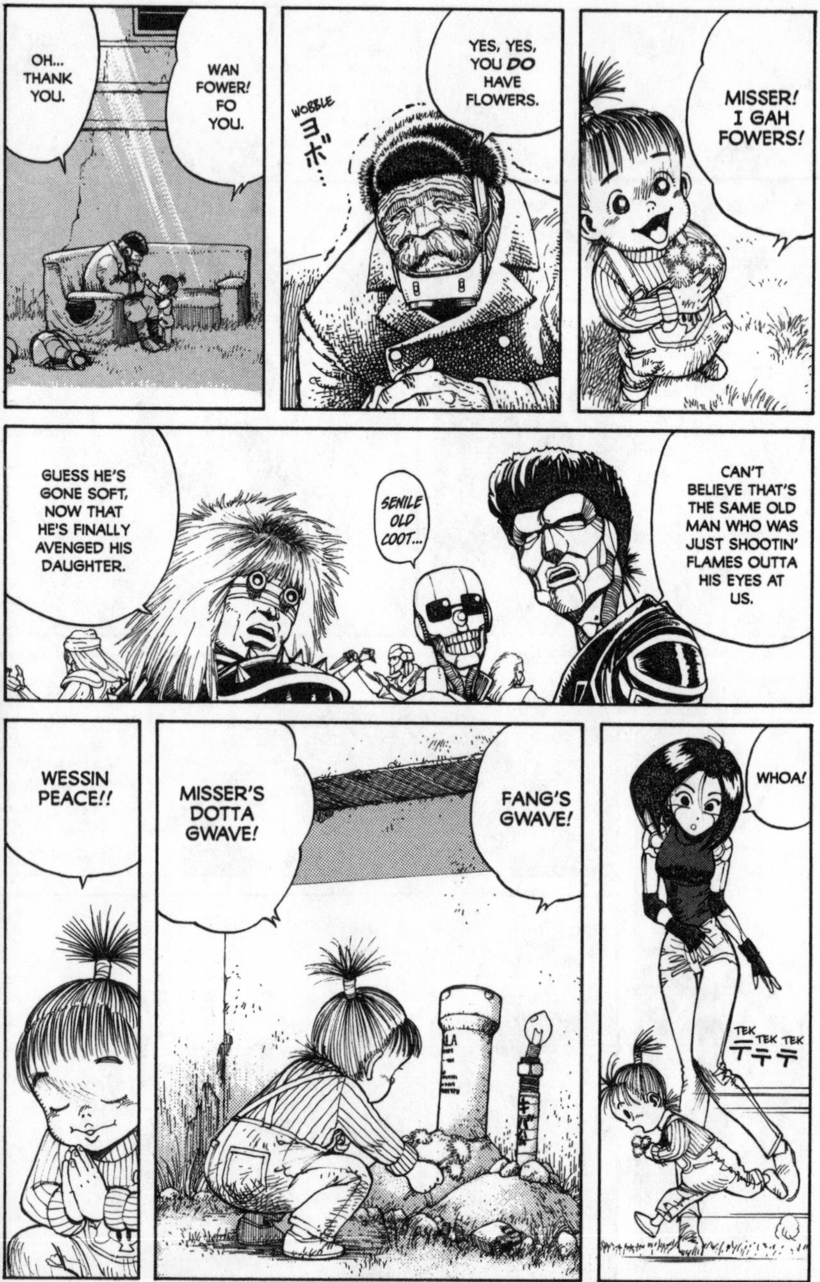
MISSER! I GAH FOWERS!
WOBBLE
ヨボ…
YES, YES, YOU *DO* HAVE FLOWERS.
WAN FOWER! FO YOU.
OH... THANK YOU.
CAN'T BELIEVE THAT'S THE SAME OLD MAN WHO WAS JUST SHOOTIN' FLAMES OUTTA HIS EYES AT US.
SENILE OLD COOT...
GUESS HE'S GONE SOFT, NOW THAT HE'S FINALLY AVENGED HIS DAUGHTER.
WHOA!
TEK TEK TEK
テテテ
FANG'S GWAVE!
MISSER'S DOTTA GWAVE!
WESSIN PEACE!!

Marker: Fang

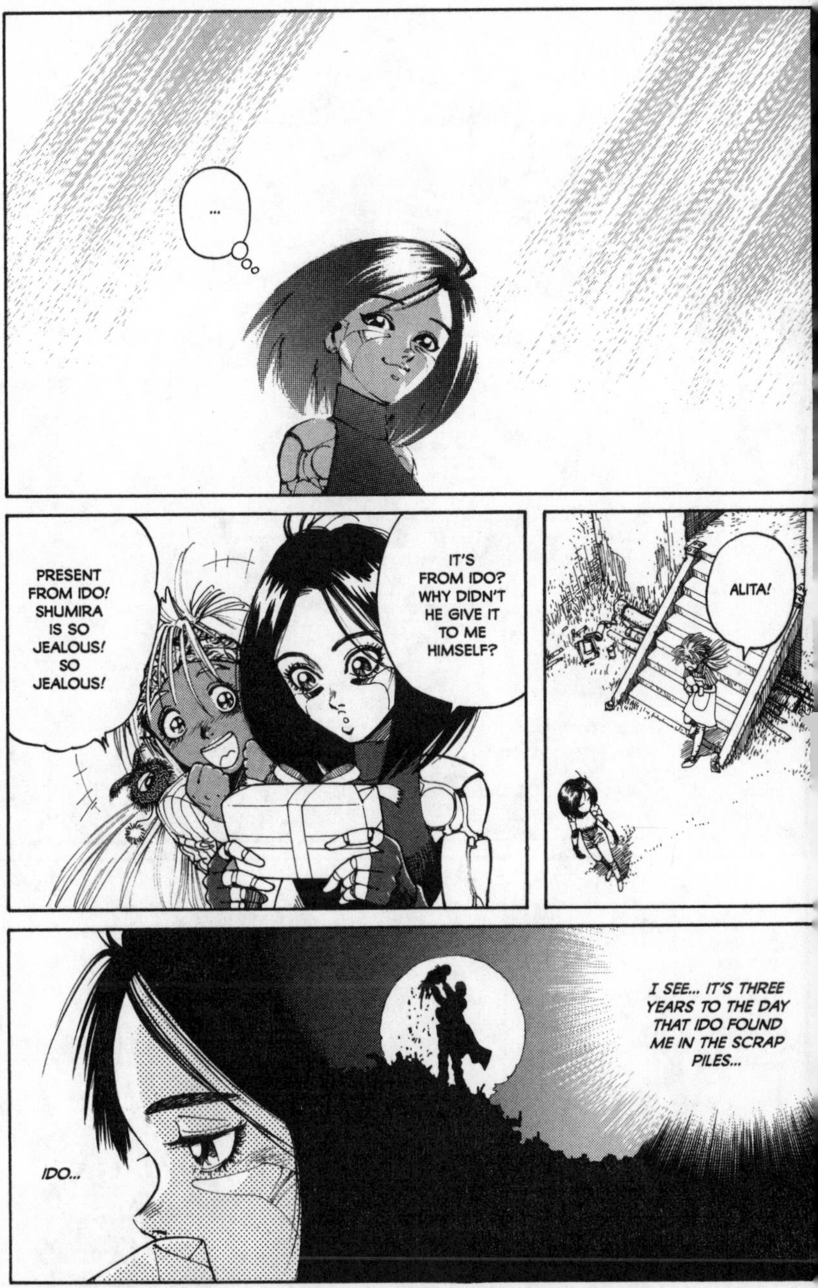
...
ALITA!
IT'S FROM IDO? WHY DIDN'T HE GIVE IT TO ME HIMSELF?
PRESENT FROM IDO! SHUMIRA IS SO JEALOUS! SO JEALOUS!
I SEE... IT'S THREE YEARS TO THE DAY THAT IDO FOUND ME IN THE SCRAP PILES...
IDO...

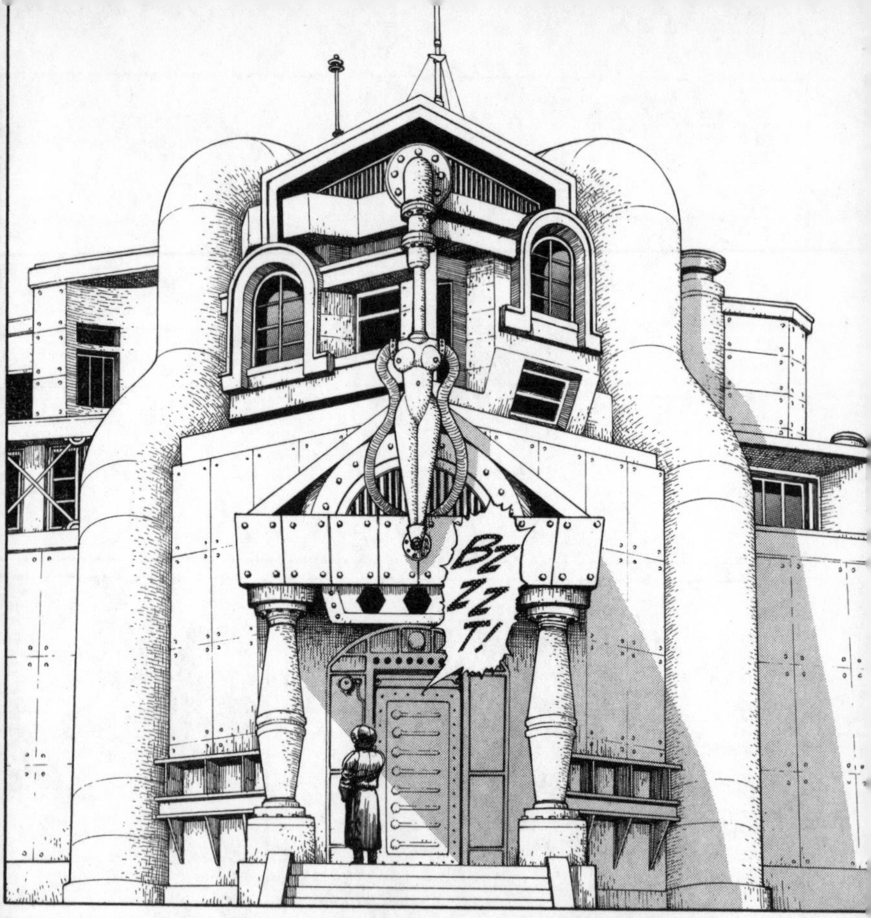
BZZZT!

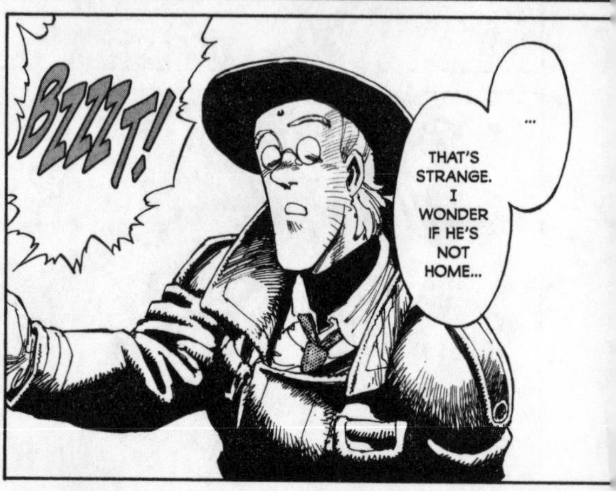
BZZZT!
... THAT'S STRANGE. I WONDER IF HE'S NOT HOME...

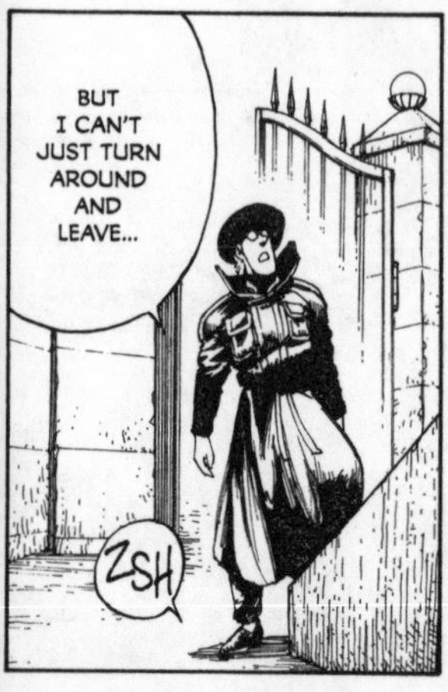
BUT I CAN'T JUST TURN AROUND AND LEAVE...
ZSH

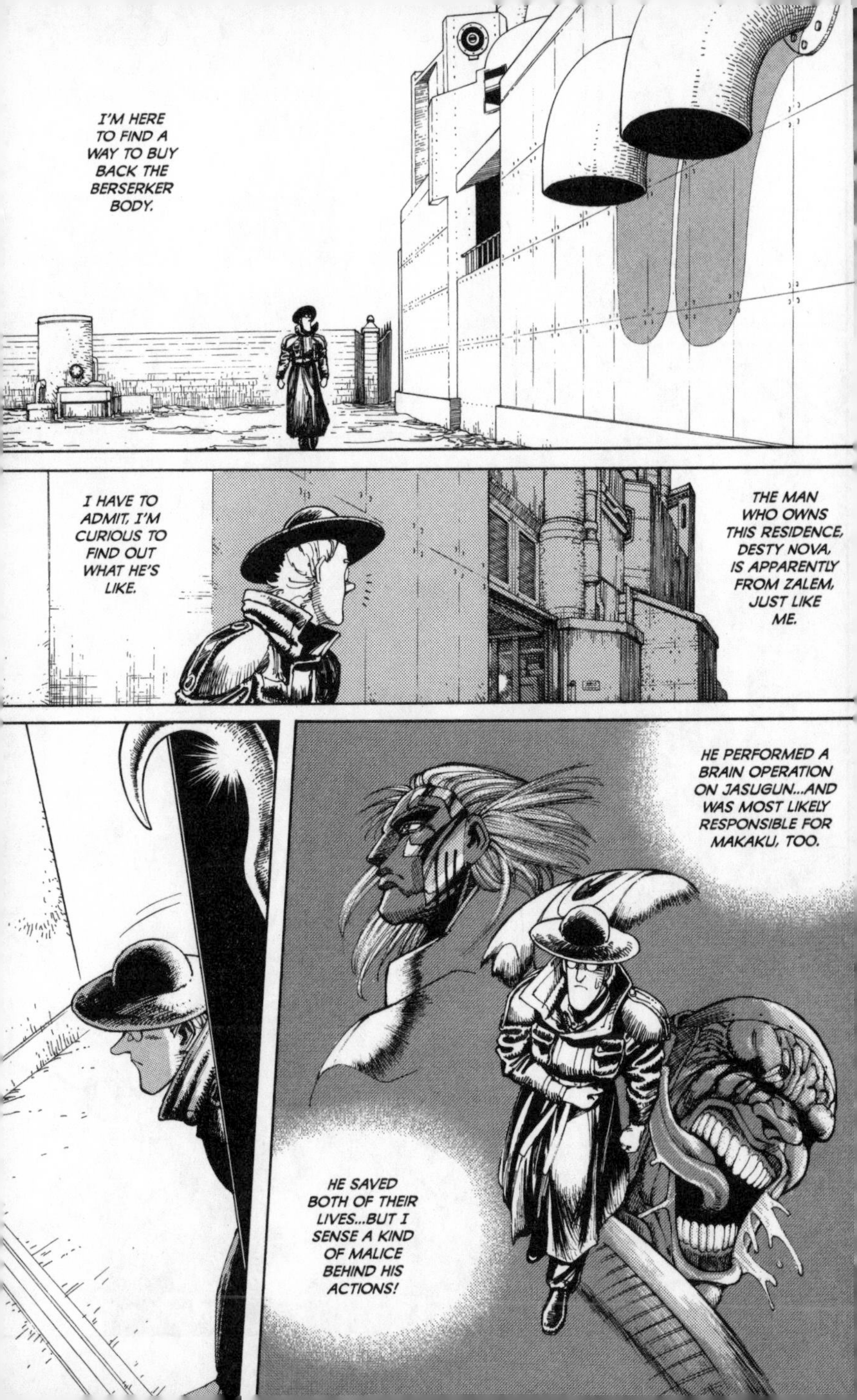
I'M HERE TO FIND A WAY TO BUY BACK THE BERSERKER BODY.
THE MAN WHO OWNS THIS RESIDENCE, DESTY NOVA, IS APPARENTLY FROM ZALEM, JUST LIKE ME.
I HAVE TO ADMIT, I'M CURIOUS TO FIND OUT WHAT HE'S LIKE.
HE PERFORMED A BRAIN OPERATION ON JASUGUN...AND WAS MOST LIKELY RESPONSIBLE FOR MAKAKU, TOO.
HE SAVED BOTH OF THEIR LIVES...BUT I SENSE A KIND OF MALICE BEHIND HIS ACTIONS!

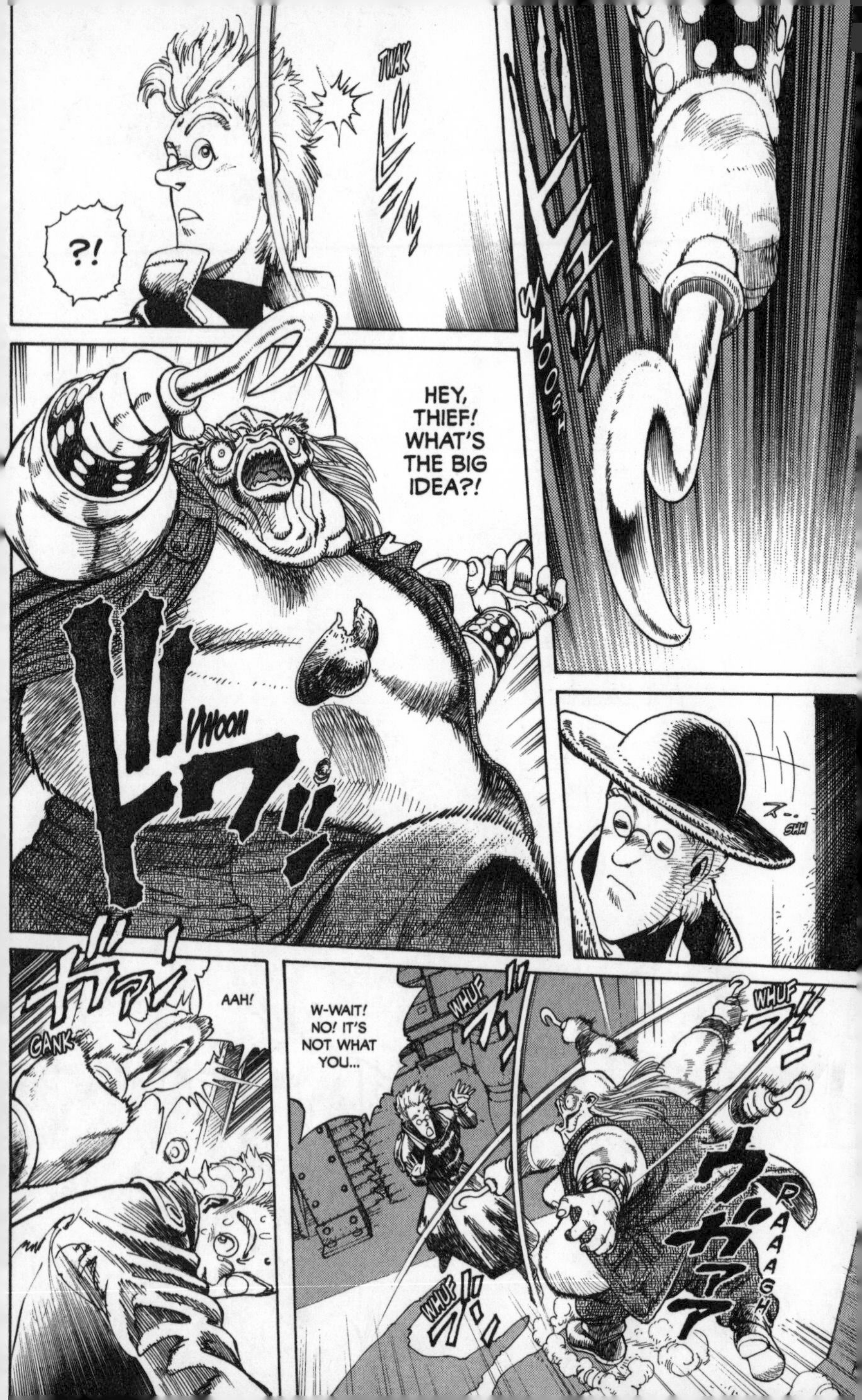
WHOOOSH
TWAK
?!
HEY, THIEF! WHAT'S THE BIG IDEA?!
VHOOM
SHH
WHUF
WHUF
W-WAIT! NO! IT'S NOT WHAT YOU...
RAAAGH
WHUF
AAH!
CANK

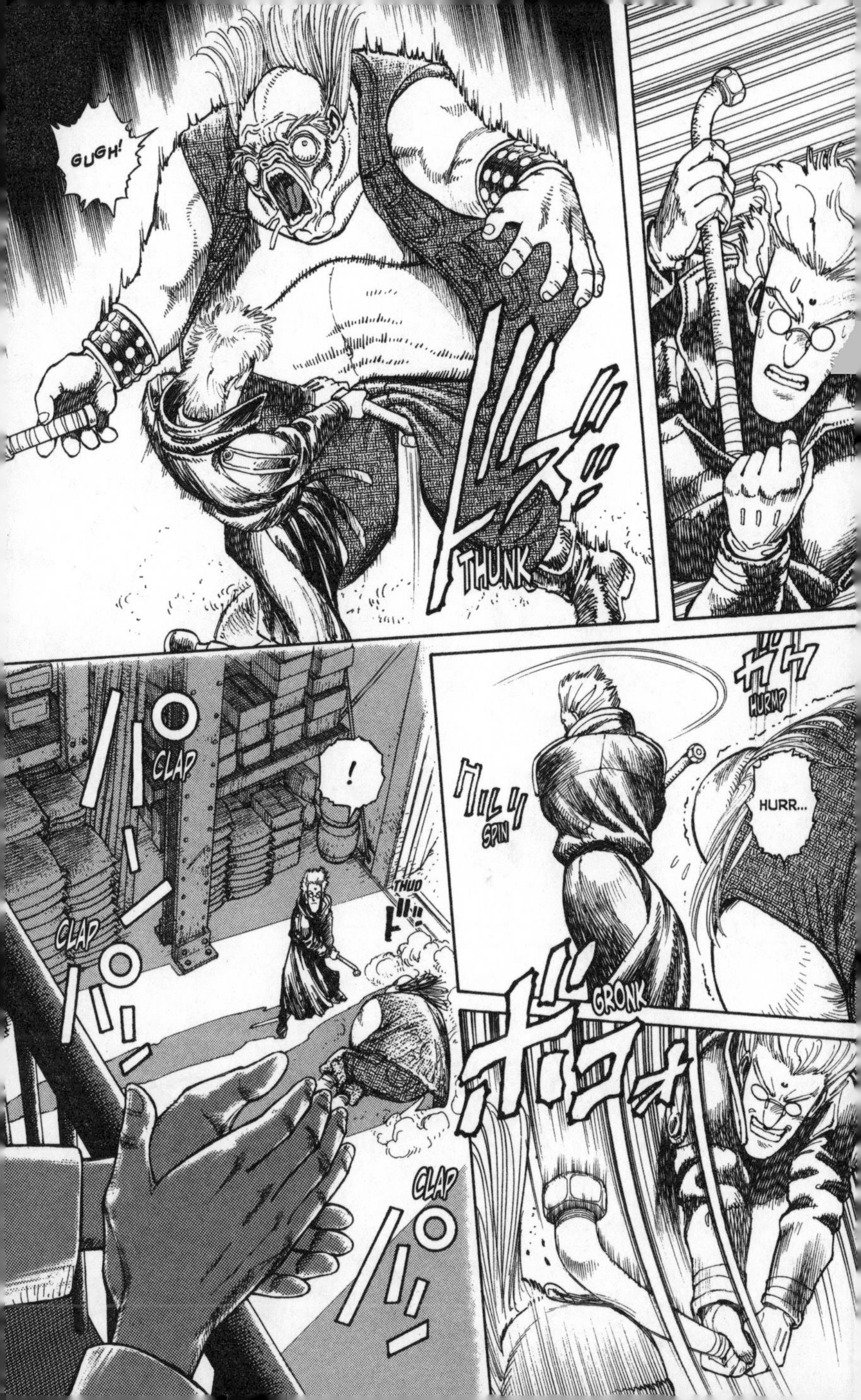
GUGH!
THUNK
HURMP
HURR...
SPIN
GRONK
!
CLAP
THUD
CLAP
CLAP

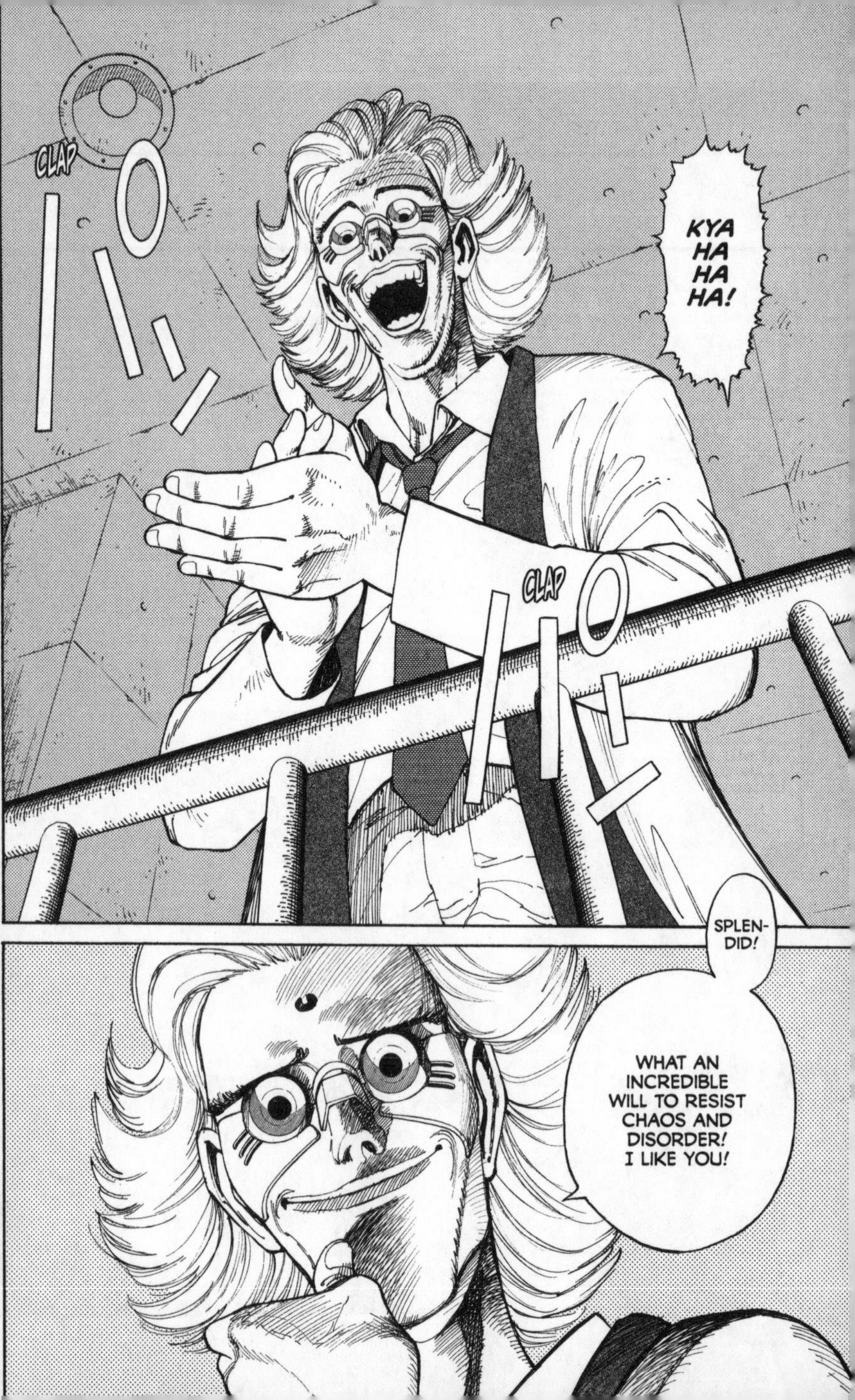
KYA HA HA HA!
CLAP
CLAP
SPLEN-DID!
WHAT AN INCREDIBLE WILL TO RESIST CHAOS AND DISORDER! I LIKE YOU!

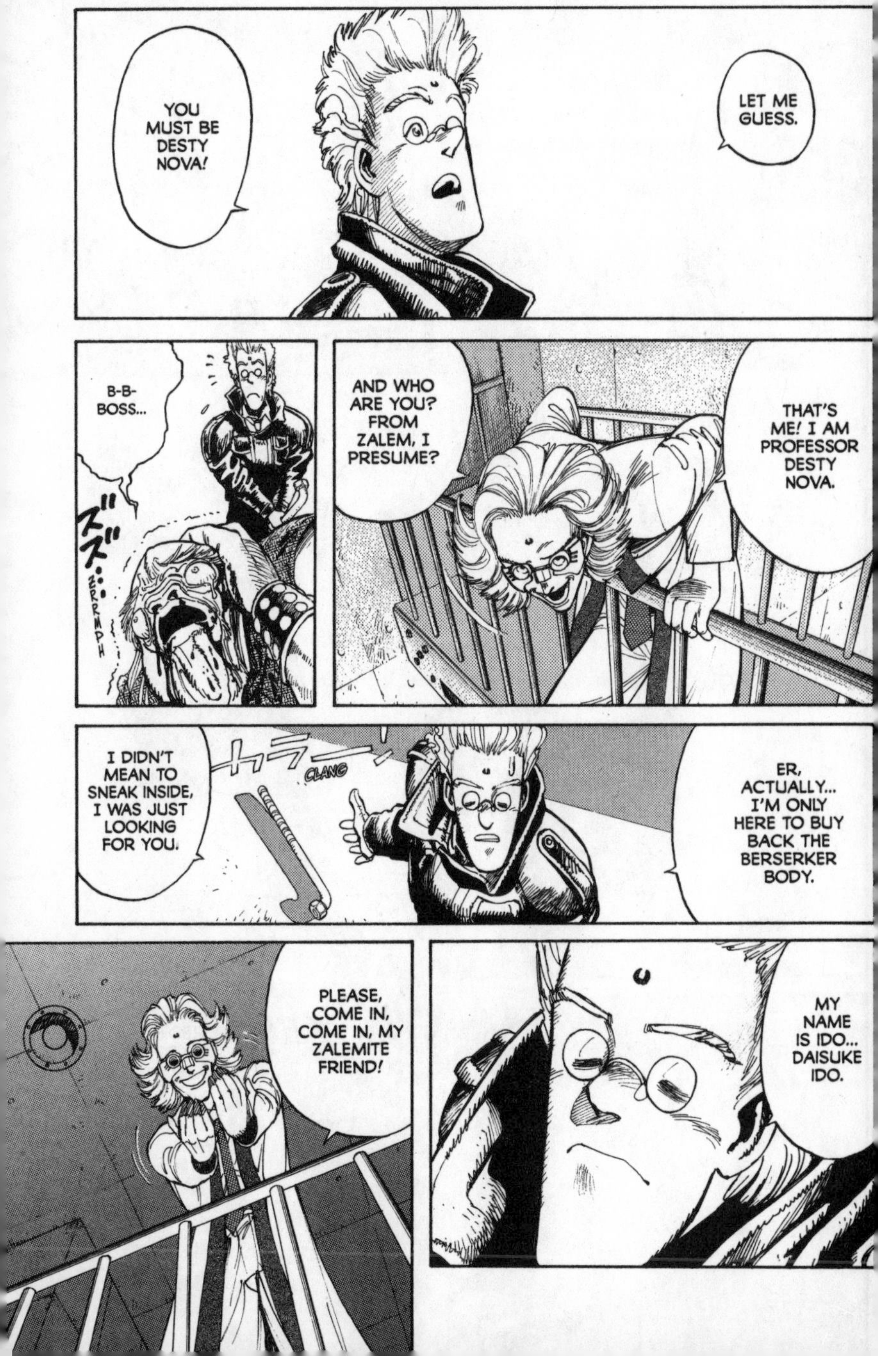
LET ME GUESS.
YOU MUST BE DESTY NOVA!
THAT'S ME! I AM PROFESSOR DESTY NOVA.
AND WHO ARE YOU? FROM ZALEM, I PRESUME?
B-B-BOSS...
ZERRMPH
ER, ACTUALLY... I'M ONLY HERE TO BUY BACK THE BERSERKER BODY.
CLANG
I DIDN'T MEAN TO SNEAK INSIDE, I WAS JUST LOOKING FOR YOU.
MY NAME IS IDO... DAISUKE IDO.
PLEASE, COME IN, COME IN, MY ZALEMITE FRIEND!

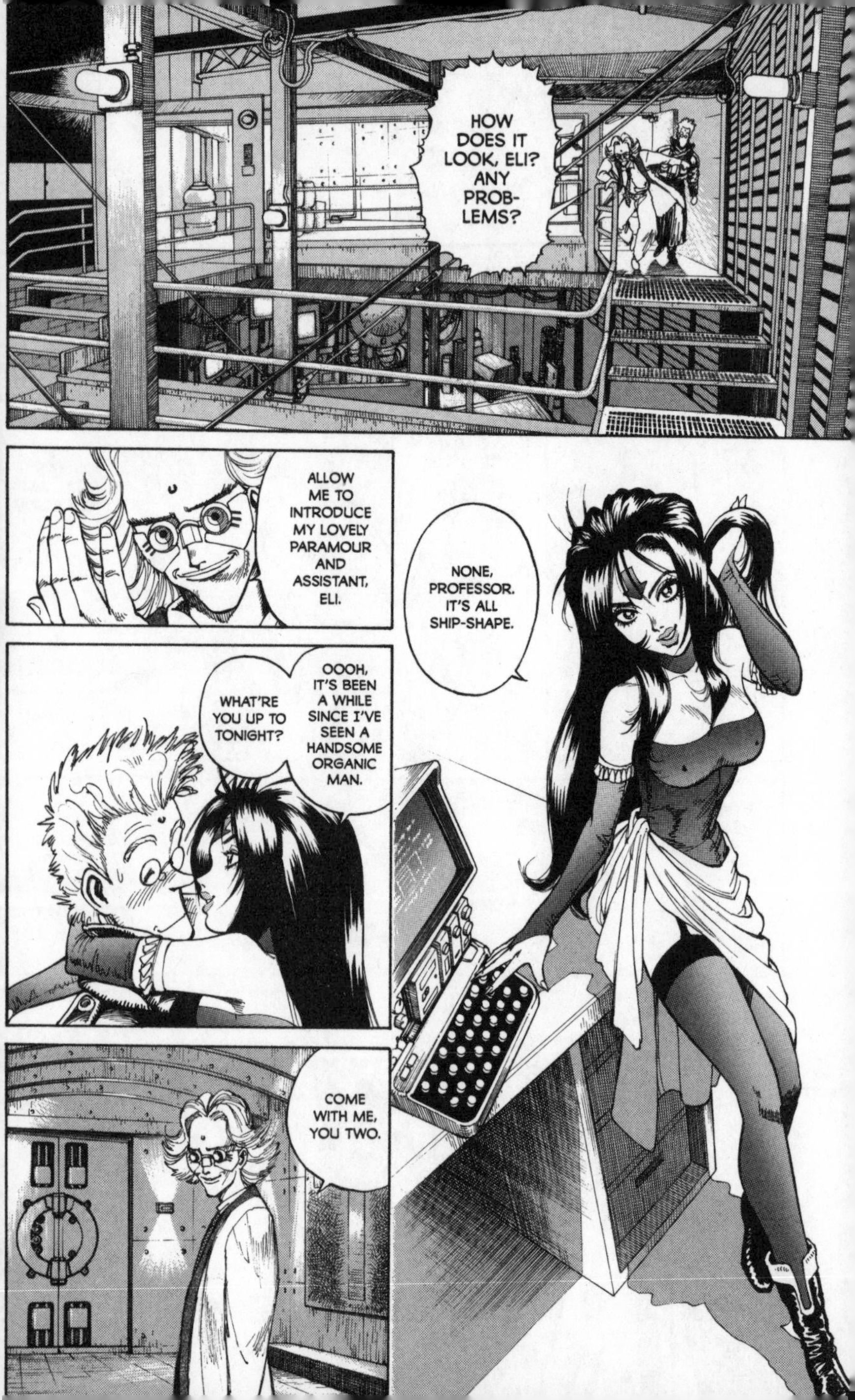
HOW DOES IT LOOK, ELI? ANY PROB-LEMS?
NONE, PROFESSOR. IT'S ALL SHIP-SHAPE.
ALLOW ME TO INTRODUCE MY LOVELY PARAMOUR AND ASSISTANT, ELI.
OOOH, IT'S BEEN A WHILE SINCE I'VE SEEN A HANDSOME ORGANIC MAN.
WHAT'RE YOU UP TO TONIGHT?
COME WITH ME, YOU TWO.

AWOOO

RAHHH

KYA HA HA!
SURPRISED?
I DON'T
BLAME YOU.
THESE ARE ALL
FAILURES.

WH-
WHAT'S
THIS?!

THEY'RE...
THEY'RE
INSANE.

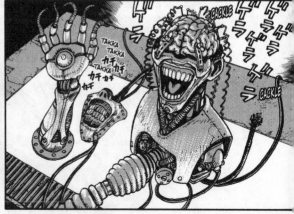

CACKLE

TAKKA
TAKKA

CACKLE

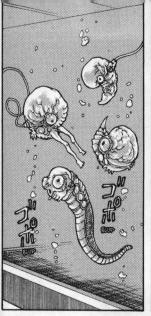

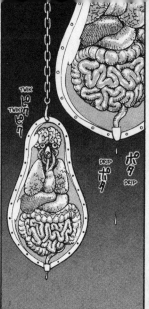

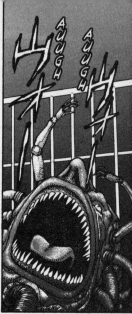

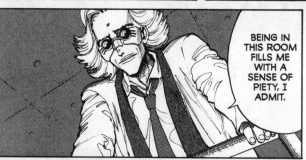

AUGGH
AUGGH
ポタ DRIP
ポタ DRIP
ピク TWIK
ピク TWIK
ゴポ BLUP
ゴポ BLUP
BEING IN THIS ROOM FILLS ME WITH A SENSE OF PIETY, I ADMIT.
EVERYTHING ONE MIGHT FIND ON THE SURFACE IS HERE–LOVE, HATRED, OPEN LUST, AND UNDENIABLE MADNESS...
WH-WHAT IS THE TRUE PURPOSE OF YOUR RESEARCH, PROFESSOR NOVA?!

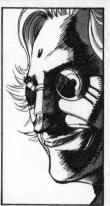

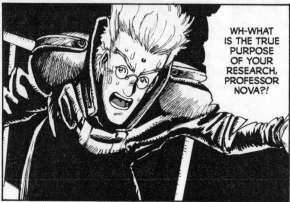

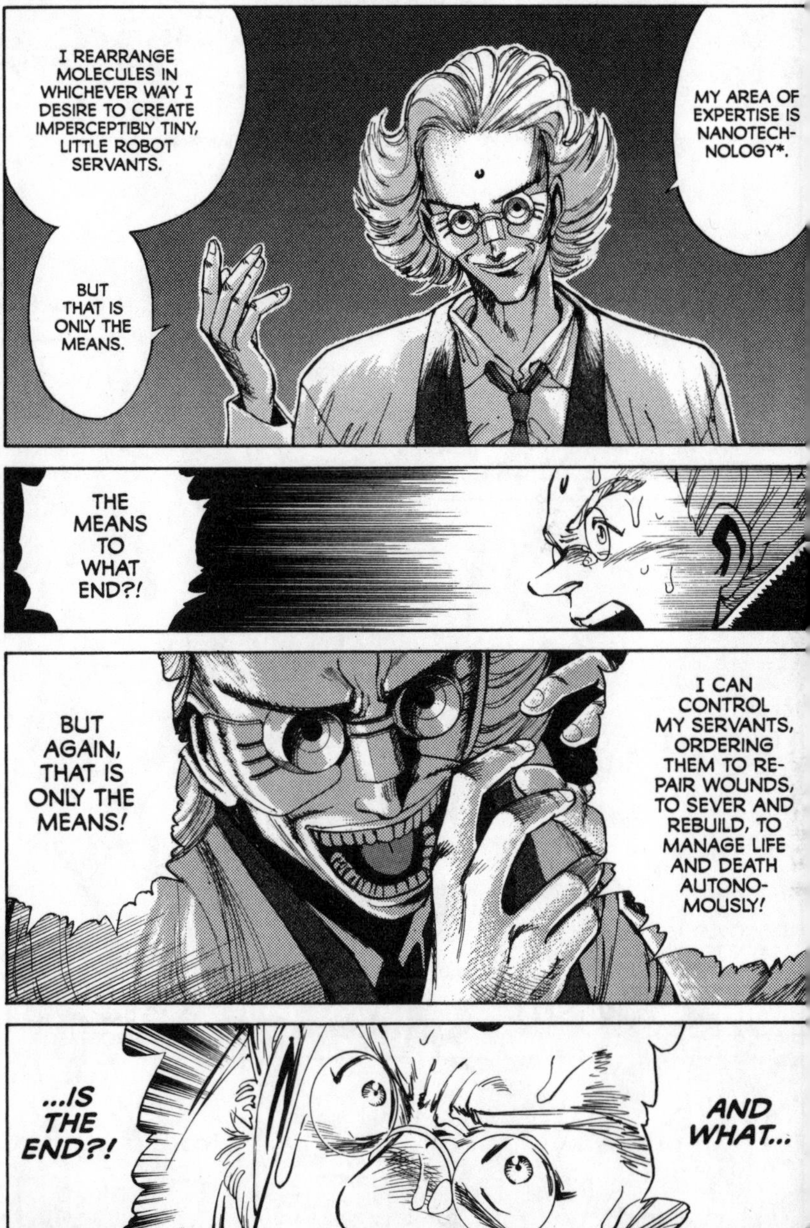
MY AREA OF EXPERTISE IS NANOTECH-NOLOGY*.
I REARRANGE MOLECULES IN WHICHEVER WAY I DESIRE TO CREATE IMPERCEPTIBLY TINY, LITTLE ROBOT SERVANTS.
BUT THAT IS ONLY THE MEANS.
THE MEANS TO WHAT END?!
I CAN CONTROL MY SERVANTS, ORDERING THEM TO RE-PAIR WOUNDS, TO SEVER AND REBUILD, TO MANAGE LIFE AND DEATH AUTONO-MOUSLY!
BUT AGAIN, THAT IS ONLY THE MEANS!
AND WHAT...
...IS THE END?!

***Nanotechnology:** A nanomachine (hypothetically speaking) is named for being one nanometer in size, which is one billionth of a meter. The name was coined by Eric Drexler in 1986.

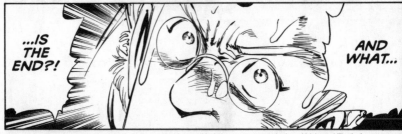

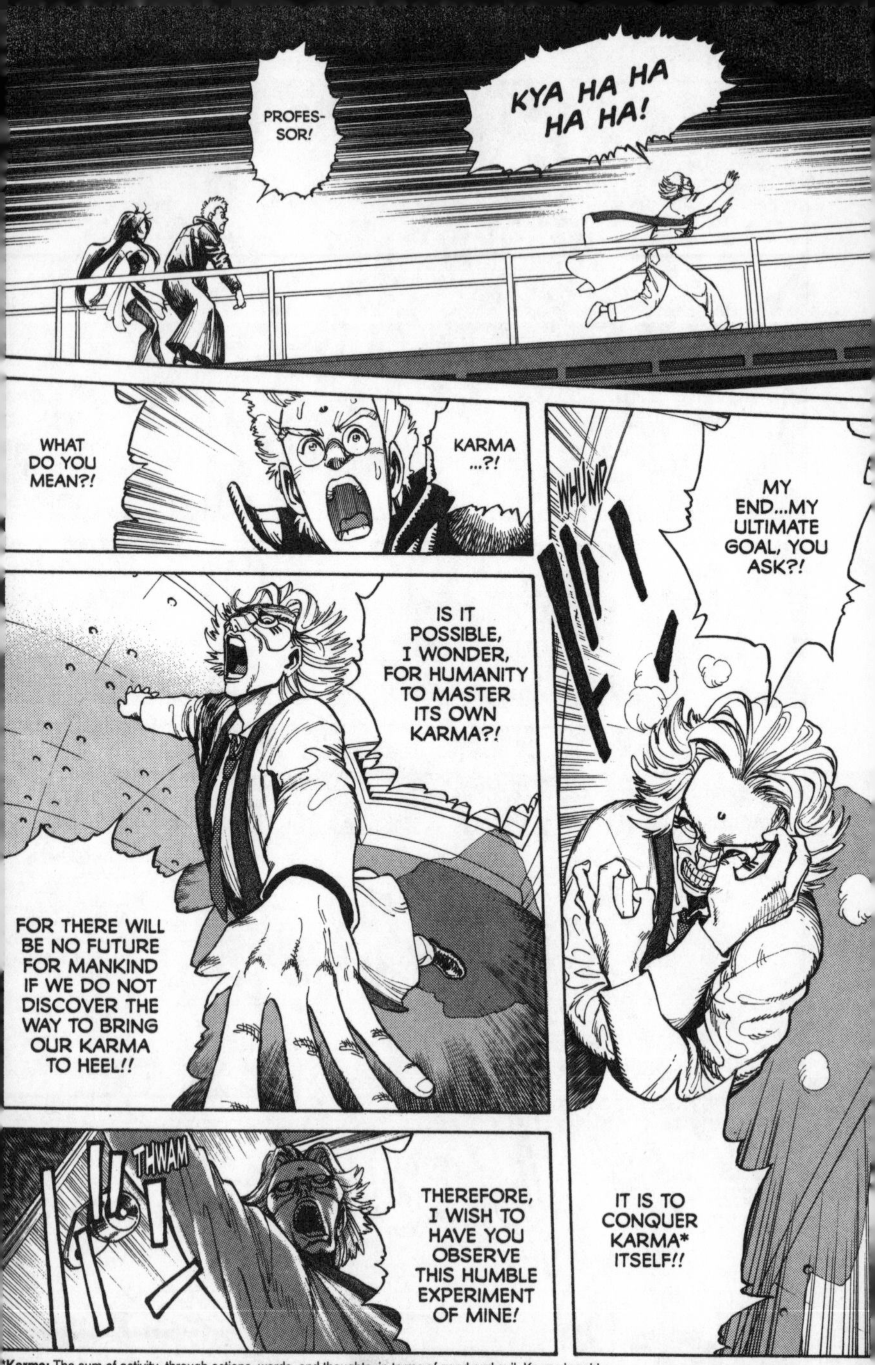
KYA HA HA HA HA!
PROFES-SOR!
WHUMP
MY END...MY ULTIMATE GOAL, YOU ASK?!
IT IS TO CONQUER KARMA* ITSELF!!
KARMA ...?!
WHAT DO YOU MEAN?!
IS IT POSSIBLE, I WONDER, FOR HUMANITY TO MASTER ITS OWN KARMA?!
FOR THERE WILL BE NO FUTURE FOR MANKIND IF WE DO NOT DISCOVER THE WAY TO BRING OUR KARMA TO HEEL!!
THWAM
THEREFORE, I WISH TO HAVE YOU OBSERVE THIS HUMBLE EXPERIMENT OF MINE!

***Karma:** The sum of activity, through actions, words, and thoughts, in terms of good and evil. Karma is said to influence the outcome of the events of one's life. The term is from Sanskrit, and means "action" or "deed."

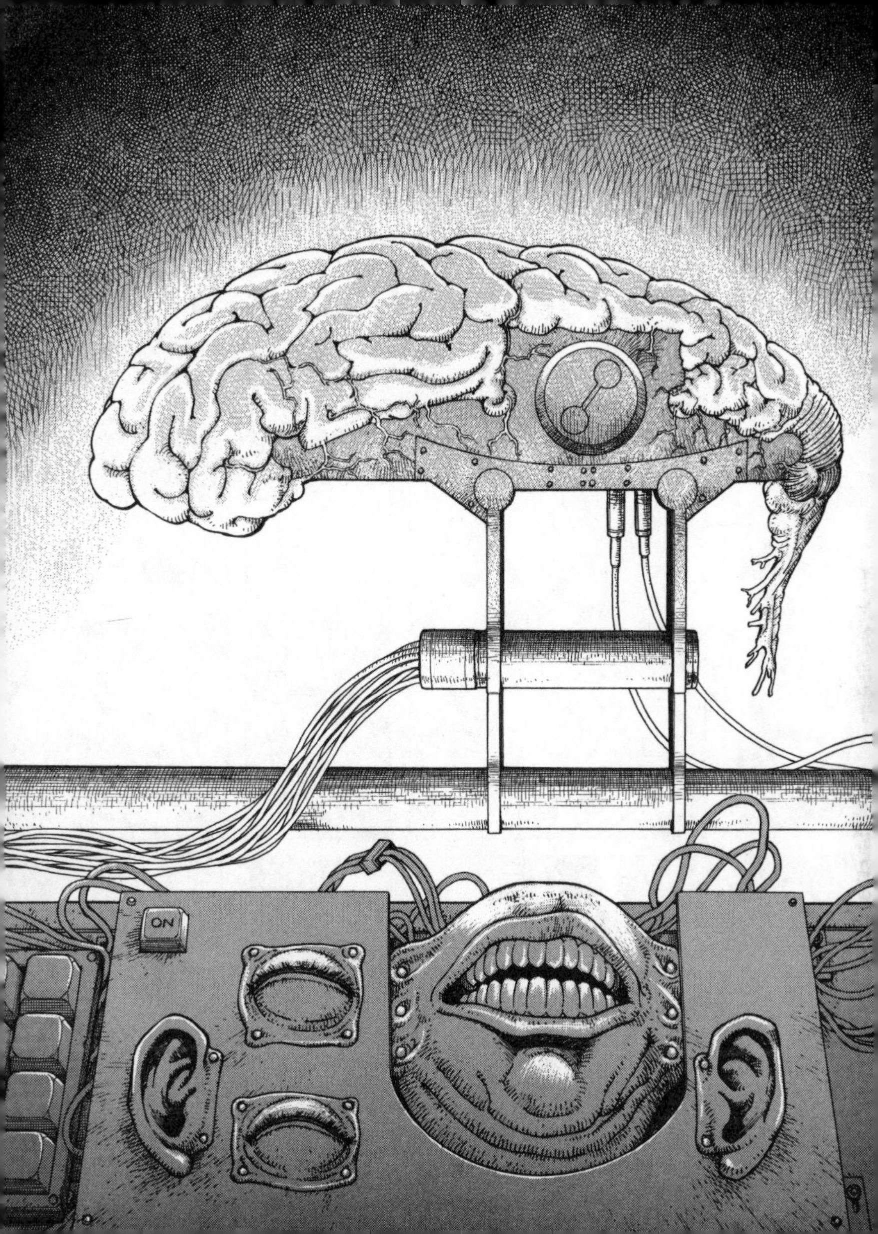
ON

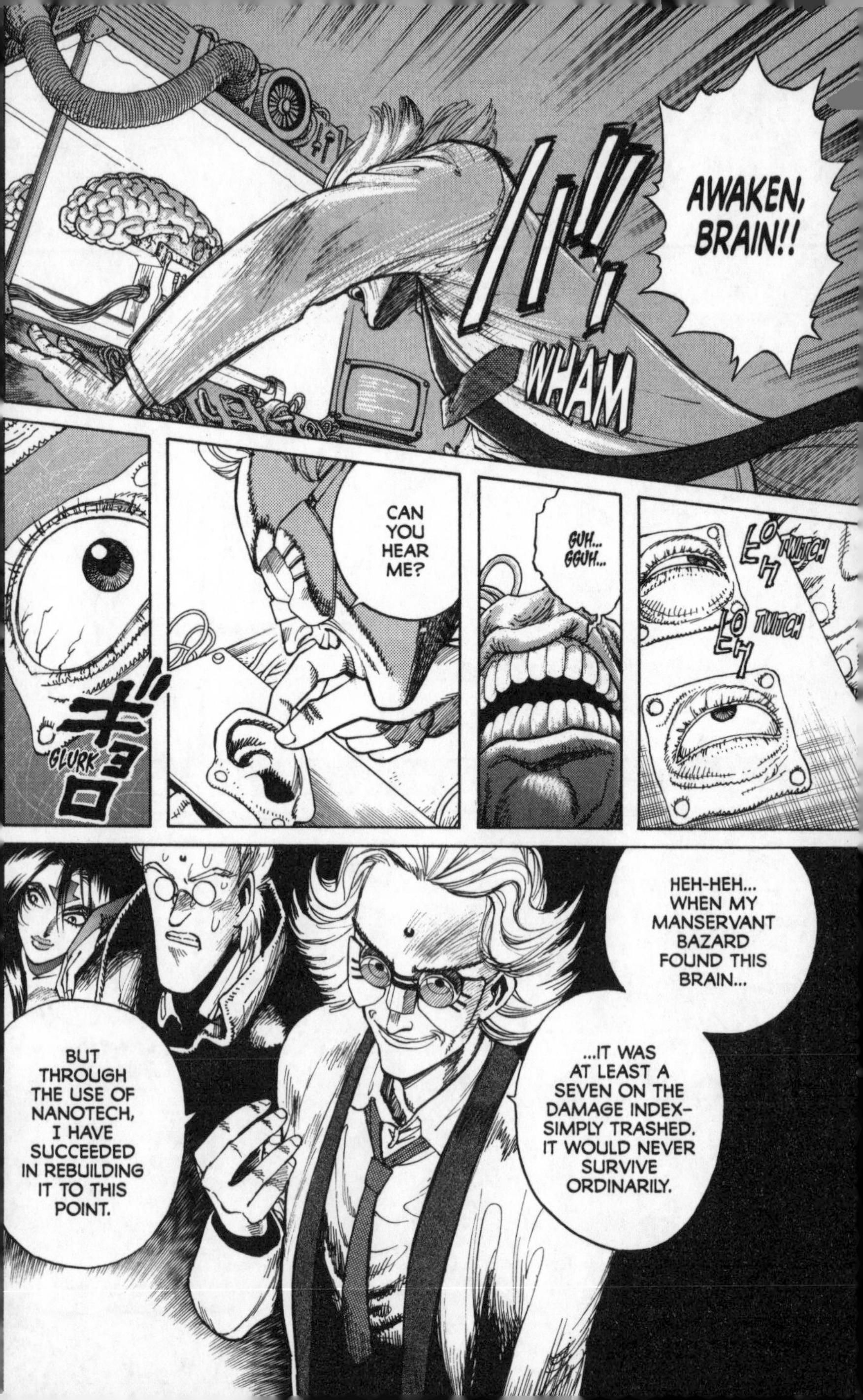

AWAKEN, BRAIN!!
WHAM
ピク
TWITCH
ピク
TWITCH
GUH... GGUH...
CAN YOU HEAR ME?
ギョロ
GLURK
HEH-HEH... WHEN MY MANSERVANT BAZARD FOUND THIS BRAIN...
...IT WAS AT LEAST A SEVEN ON THE DAMAGE INDEX–SIMPLY TRASHED. IT WOULD NEVER SURVIVE ORDINARILY.
BUT THROUGH THE USE OF NANOTECH, I HAVE SUCCEEDED IN REBUILDING IT TO THIS POINT.

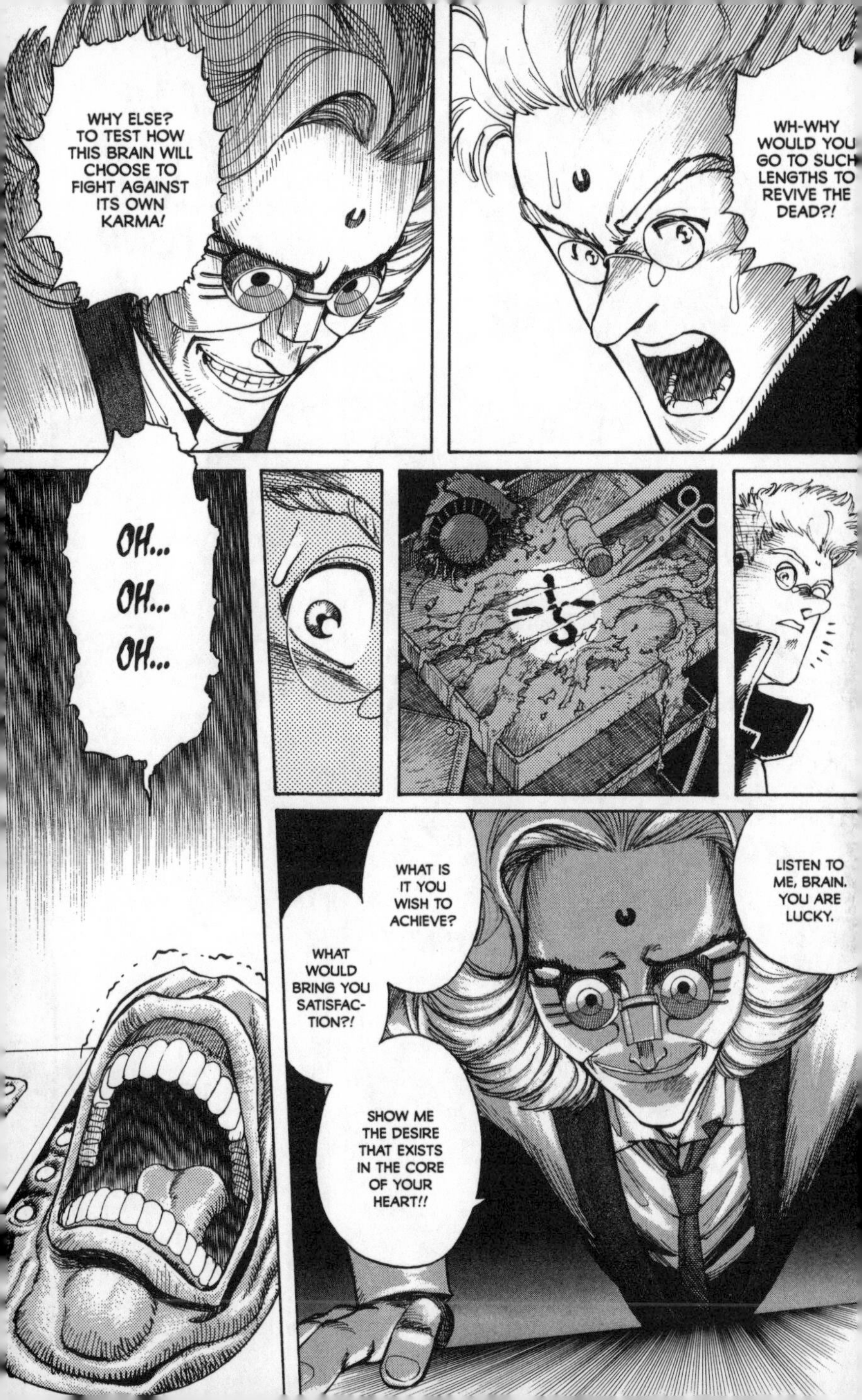
WH-WHY WOULD YOU GO TO SUCH LENGTHS TO REVIVE THE DEAD?!
WHY ELSE? TO TEST HOW THIS BRAIN WILL CHOOSE TO FIGHT AGAINST ITS OWN KARMA!
LISTEN TO ME, BRAIN. YOU ARE LUCKY.
WHAT IS IT YOU WISH TO ACHIEVE?
WHAT WOULD BRING YOU SATISFACTION?!
SHOW ME THE DESIRE THAT EXISTS IN THE CORE OF YOUR HEART!!
OH... OH... OH...

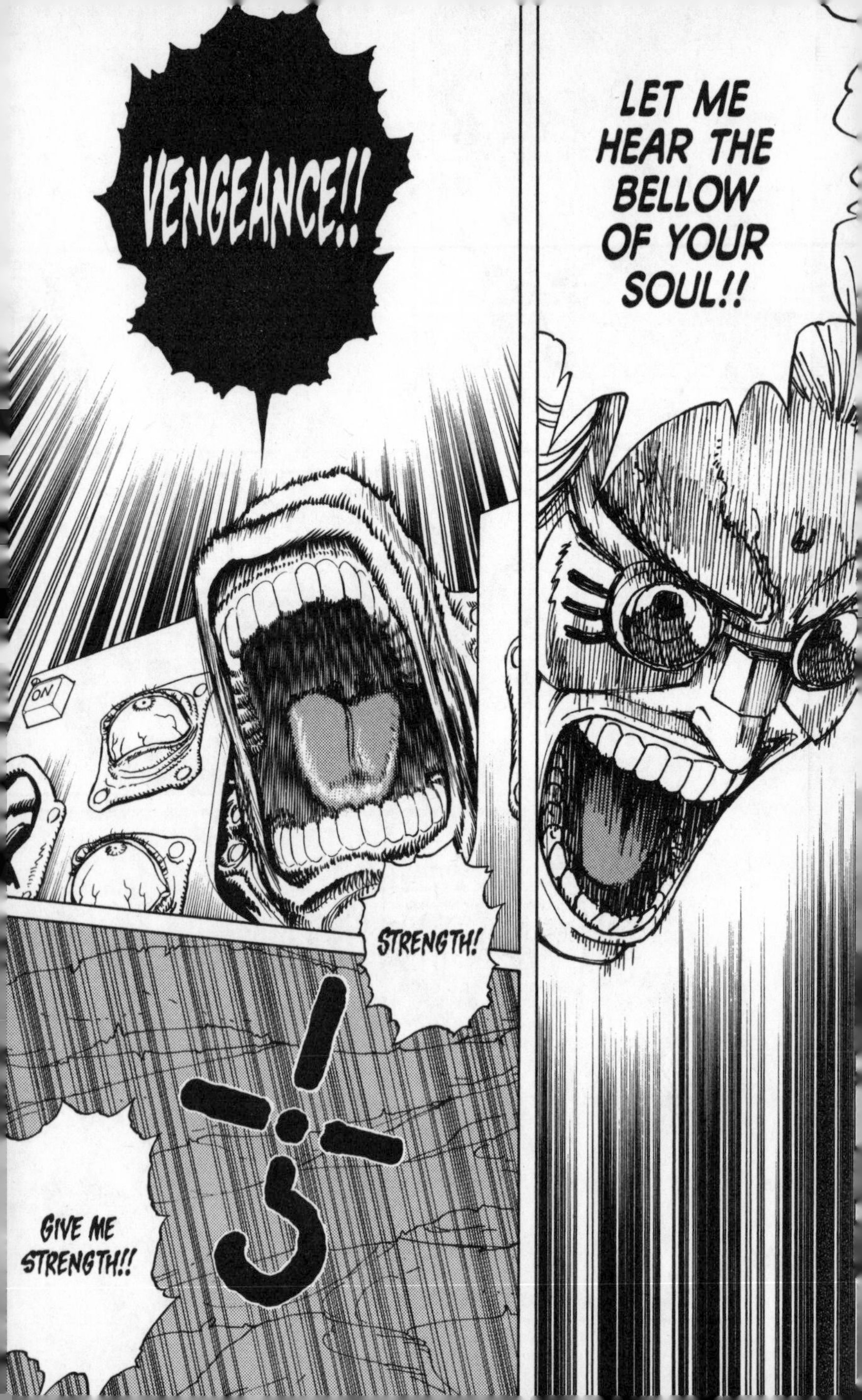
LET ME HEAR THE BELLOW OF YOUR SOUL!!
VENGEANCE!!
STRENGTH!
GIVE ME STRENGTH!!

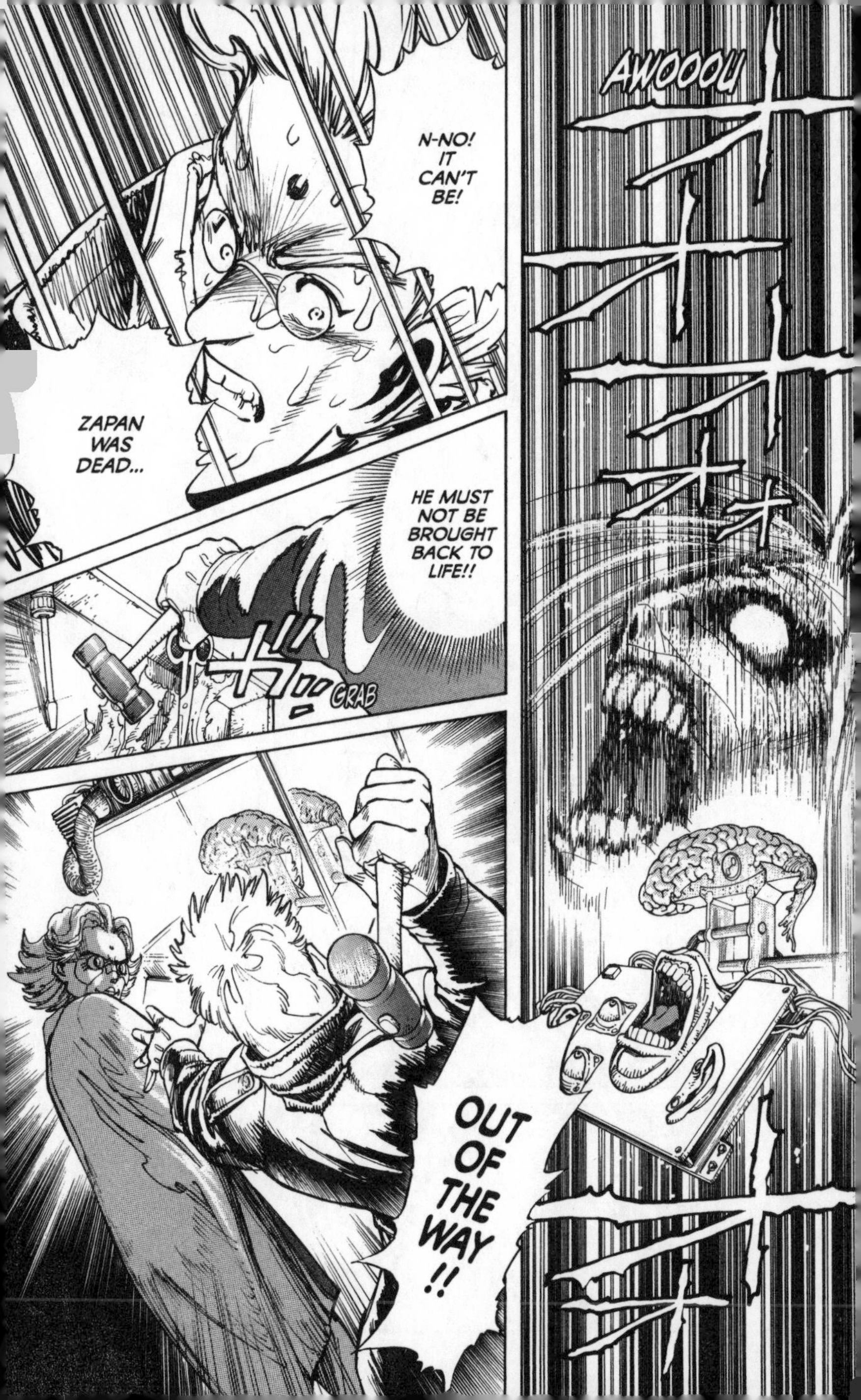
AWOOOU
N-NO! IT CAN'T BE!
ZAPAN WAS DEAD...
HE MUST NOT BE BROUGHT BACK TO LIFE!!
GRAB
OUT OF THE WAY!!

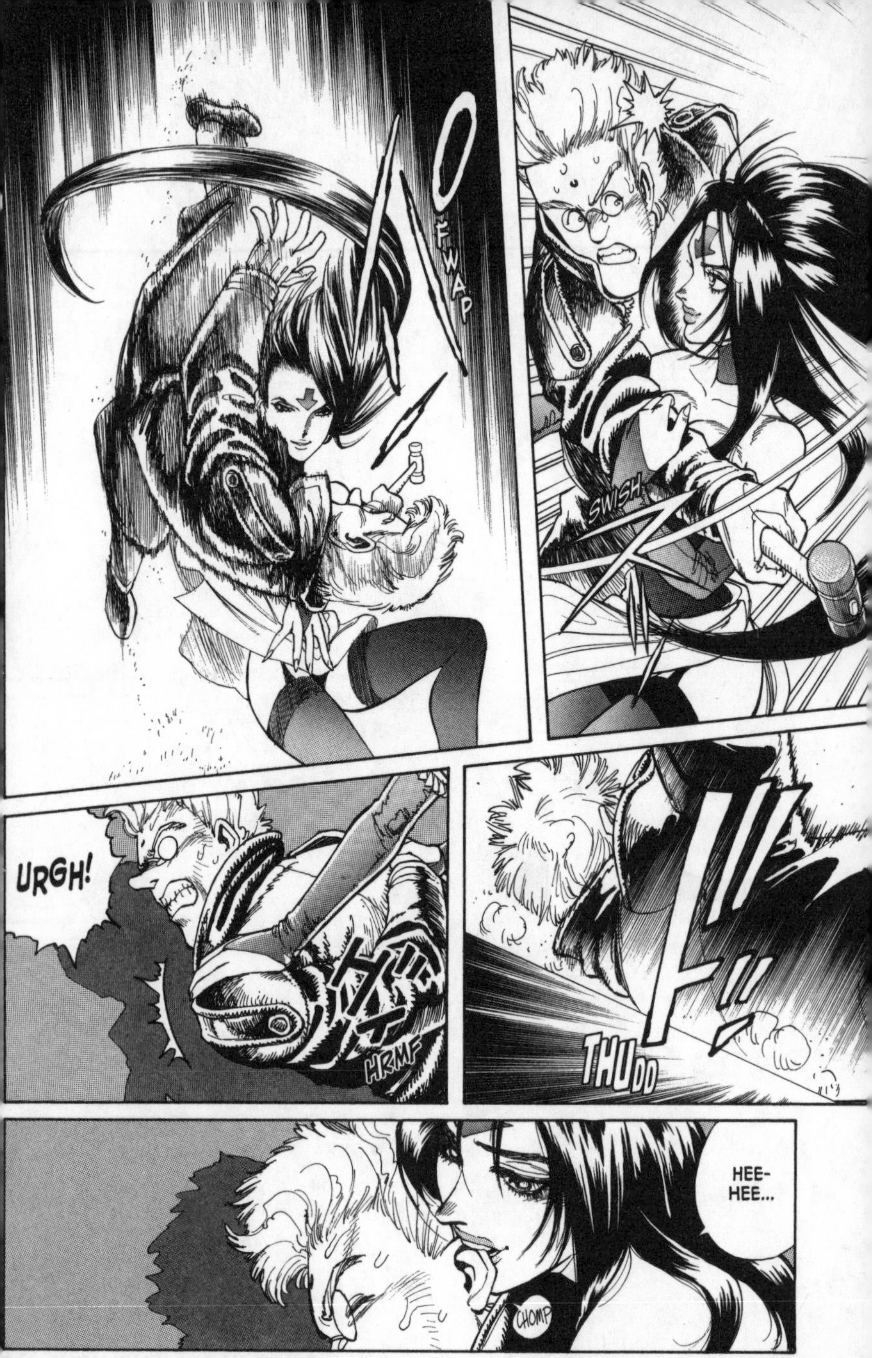
SWISH
FWAP
THUDD
URGH!
HRMF
HEE-HEE...
CHOMP

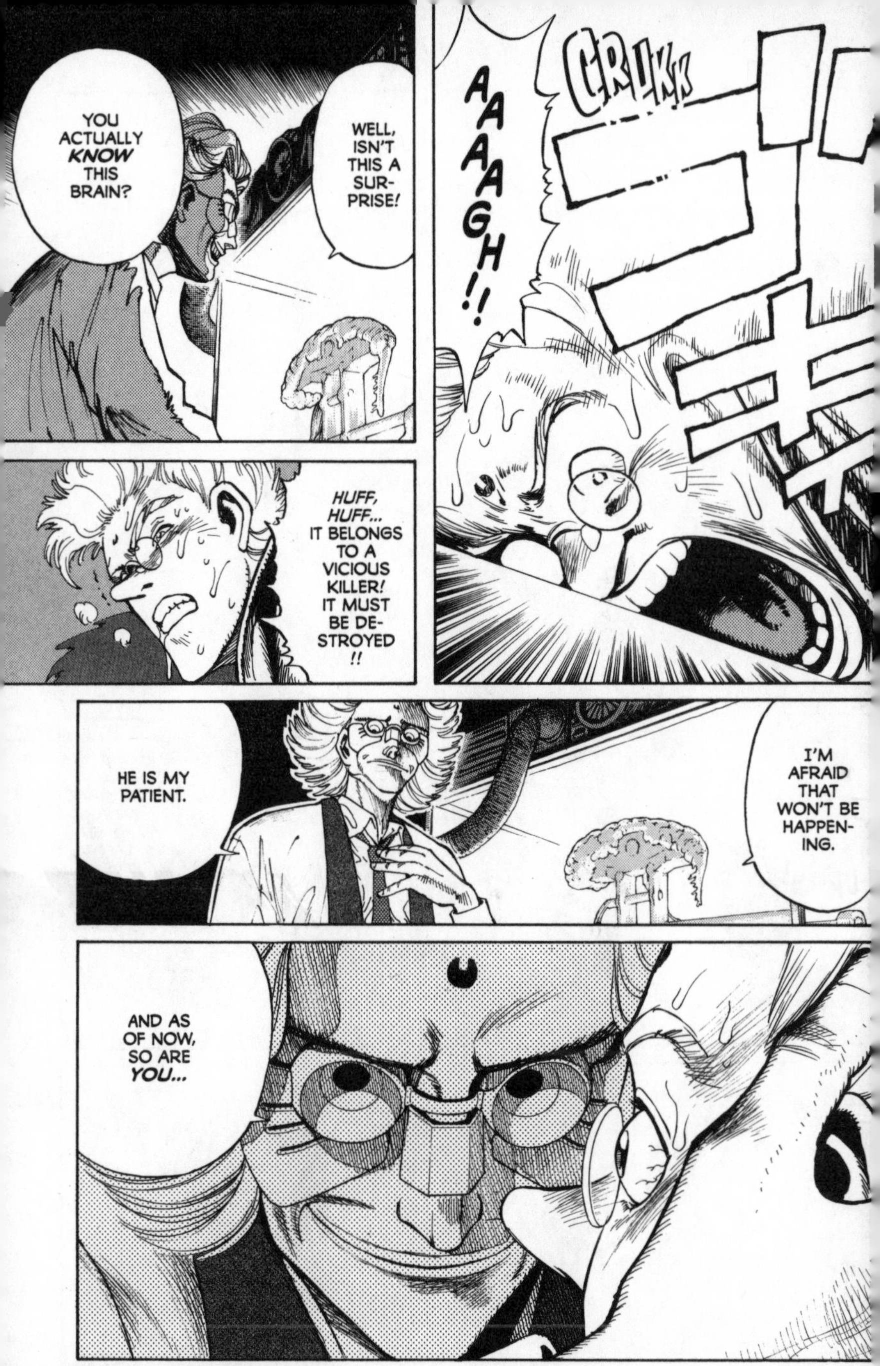
AAAAAGH!!
CRUKK
YOU ACTUALLY ***KNOW*** THIS BRAIN?
WELL, ISN'T THIS A SURPRISE!
HUFF, HUFF... IT BELONGS TO A VICIOUS KILLER! IT MUST BE DESTROYED!!
I'M AFRAID THAT WON'T BE HAPPENING.
HE IS MY PATIENT.
AND AS OF NOW, SO ARE ***YOU...***

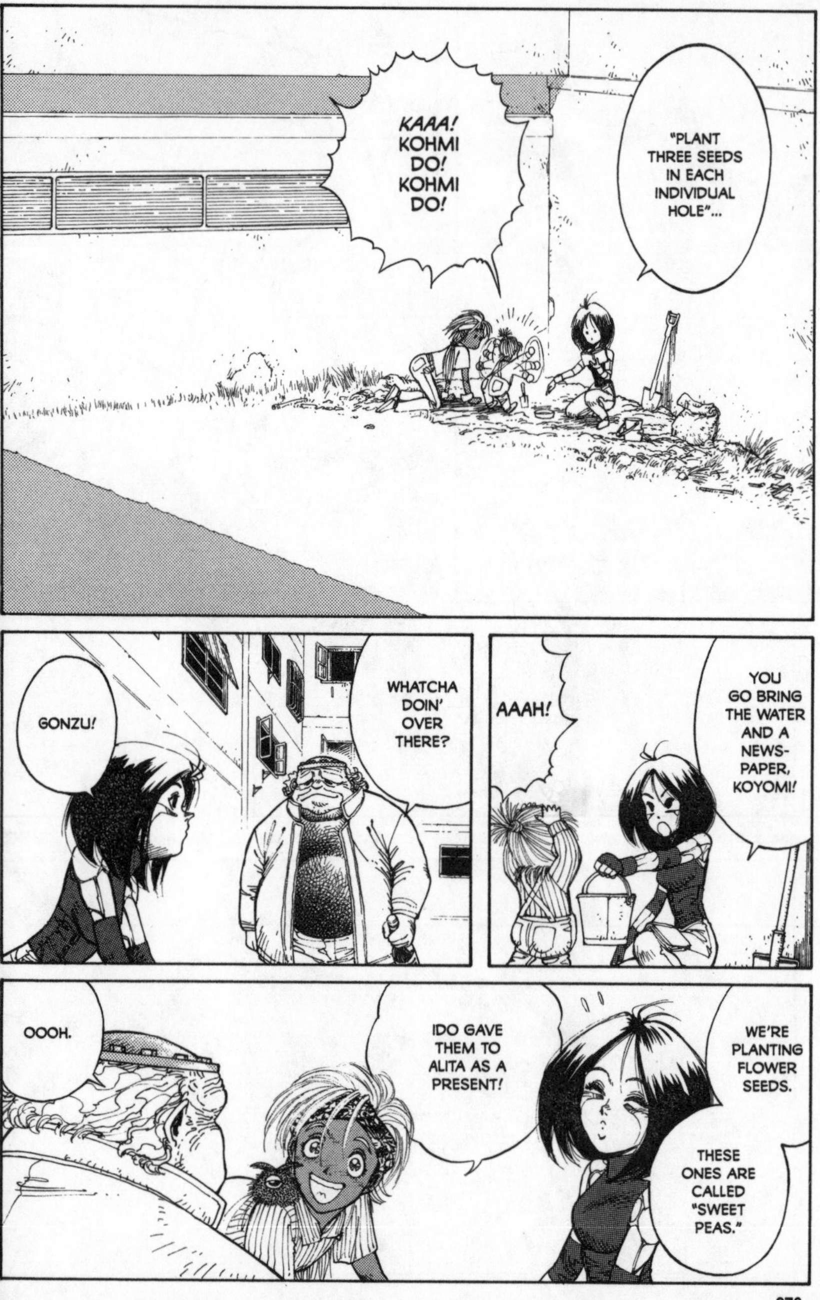
"PLANT THREE SEEDS IN EACH INDIVIDUAL HOLE"...
KAAA! KOHMI DO! KOHMI DO!
YOU GO BRING THE WATER AND A NEWS-PAPER, KOYOMI!
AAAH!
WHATCHA DOIN' OVER THERE?
GONZU!
WE'RE PLANTING FLOWER SEEDS.
THESE ONES ARE CALLED "SWEET PEAS."
IDO GAVE THEM TO ALITA AS A PRESENT!
OOOH.

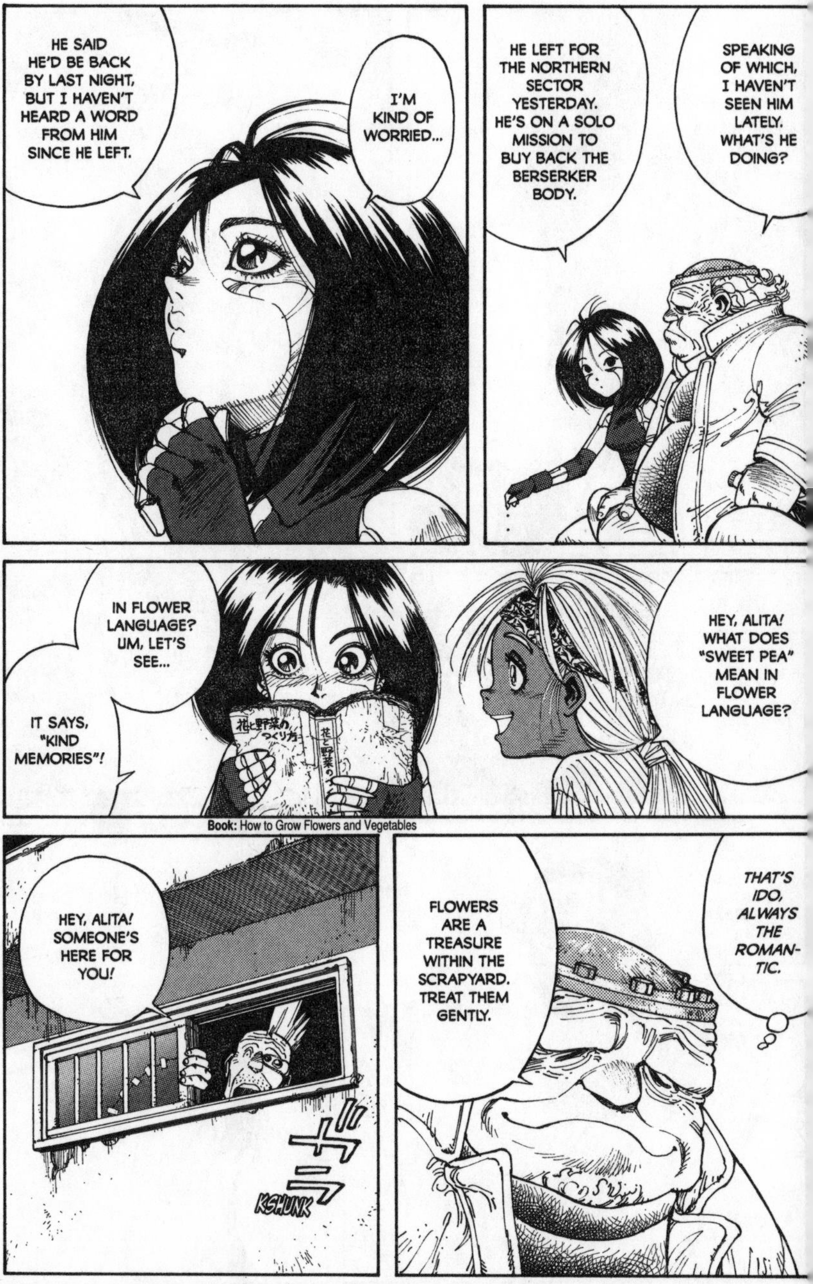
SPEAKING OF WHICH, I HAVEN'T SEEN HIM LATELY. WHAT'S HE DOING?
HE LEFT FOR THE NORTHERN SECTOR YESTERDAY. HE'S ON A SOLO MISSION TO BUY BACK THE BERSERKER BODY.
I'M KIND OF WORRIED...
HE SAID HE'D BE BACK BY LAST NIGHT, BUT I HAVEN'T HEARD A WORD FROM HIM SINCE HE LEFT.
HEY, ALITA! WHAT DOES "SWEET PEA" MEAN IN FLOWER LANGUAGE?
IN FLOWER LANGUAGE? UM, LET'S SEE...
IT SAYS, "KIND MEMORIES"!
Book: How to Grow Flowers and Vegetables
THAT'S IDO, ALWAYS THE ROMANTIC.
FLOWERS ARE A TREASURE WITHIN THE SCRAPYARD. TREAT THEM GENTLY.
HEY, ALITA! SOMEONE'S HERE FOR YOU!
KSHUNK

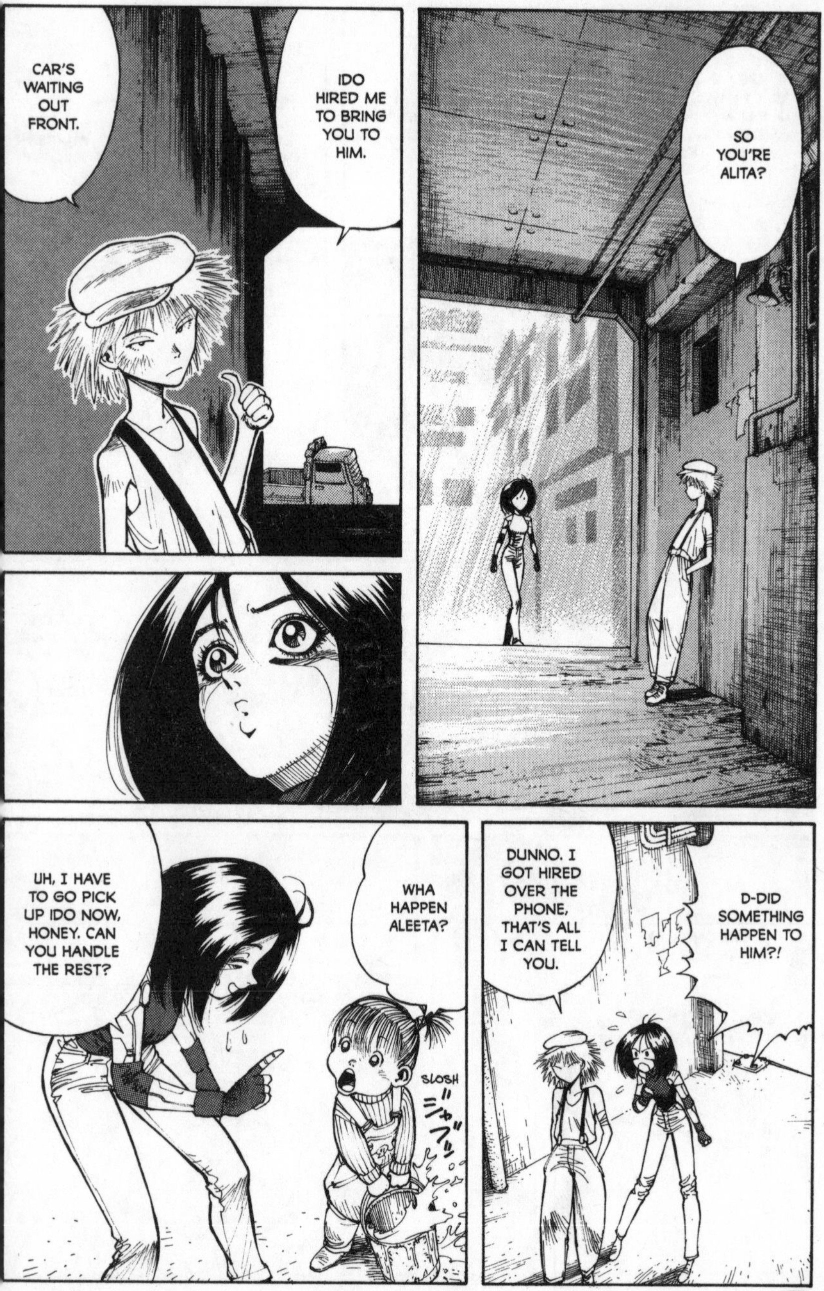
SO YOU'RE ALITA?
IDO HIRED ME TO BRING YOU TO HIM.
CAR'S WAITING OUT FRONT.
D-DID SOMETHING HAPPEN TO HIM?!
DUNNO. I GOT HIRED OVER THE PHONE, THAT'S ALL I CAN TELL YOU.
WHA HAPPEN ALEETA?
UH, I HAVE TO GO PICK UP IDO NOW, HONEY. CAN YOU HANDLE THE REST?
SLOSH

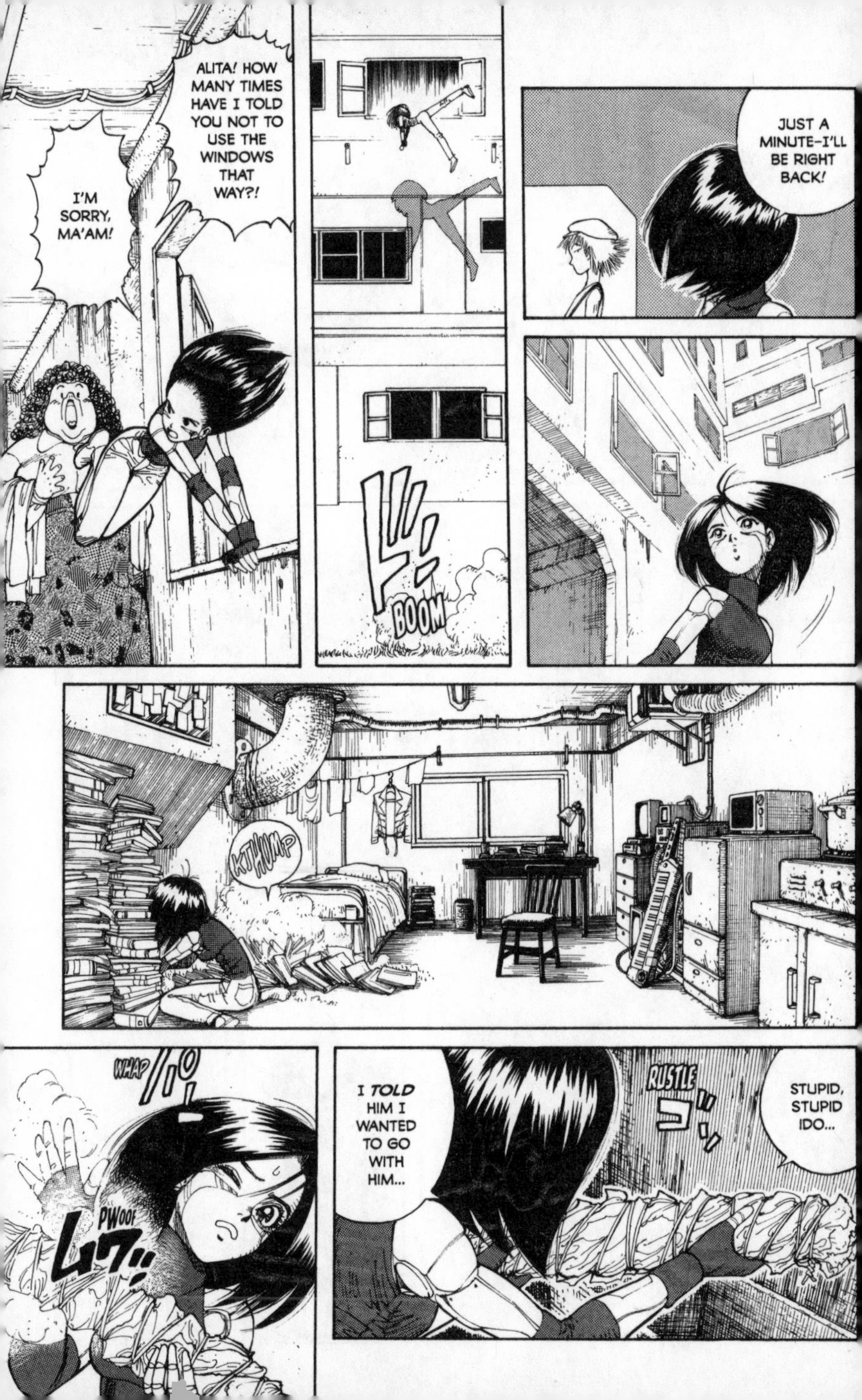
JUST A MINUTE–I'LL BE RIGHT BACK!
BOOM
ALITA! HOW MANY TIMES HAVE I TOLD YOU NOT TO USE THE WINDOWS THAT WAY?!
I'M SORRY, MA'AM!
KTHUMP
STUPID, STUPID IDO...
RUSTLE
I *TOLD* HIM I WANTED TO GO WITH HIM...
WHAP
PWOOF

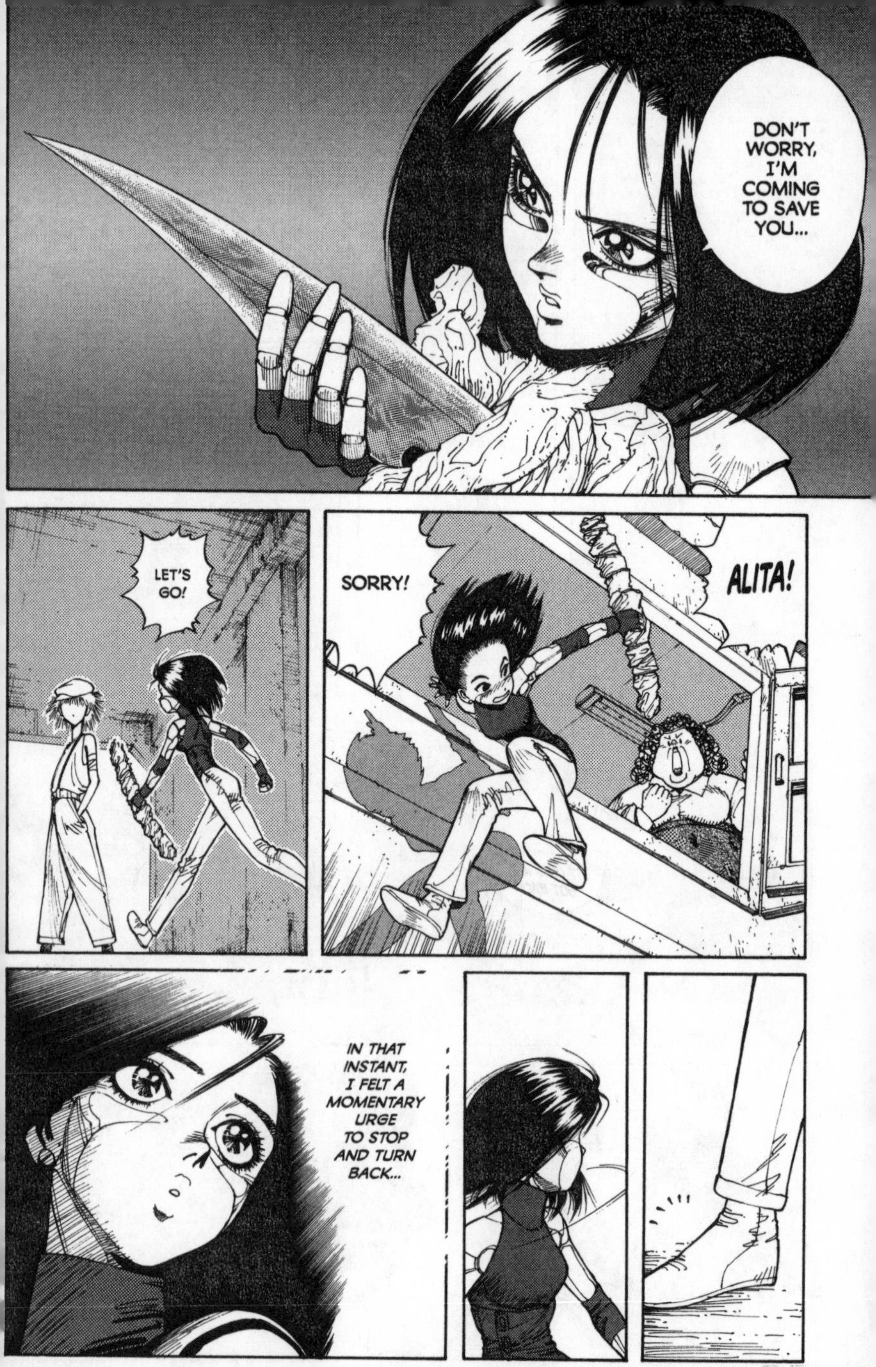
DON'T WORRY, I'M COMING TO SAVE YOU...
ALITA!
SORRY!
LET'S GO!
IN THAT INSTANT, I FELT A MOMENTARY URGE TO STOP AND TURN BACK...

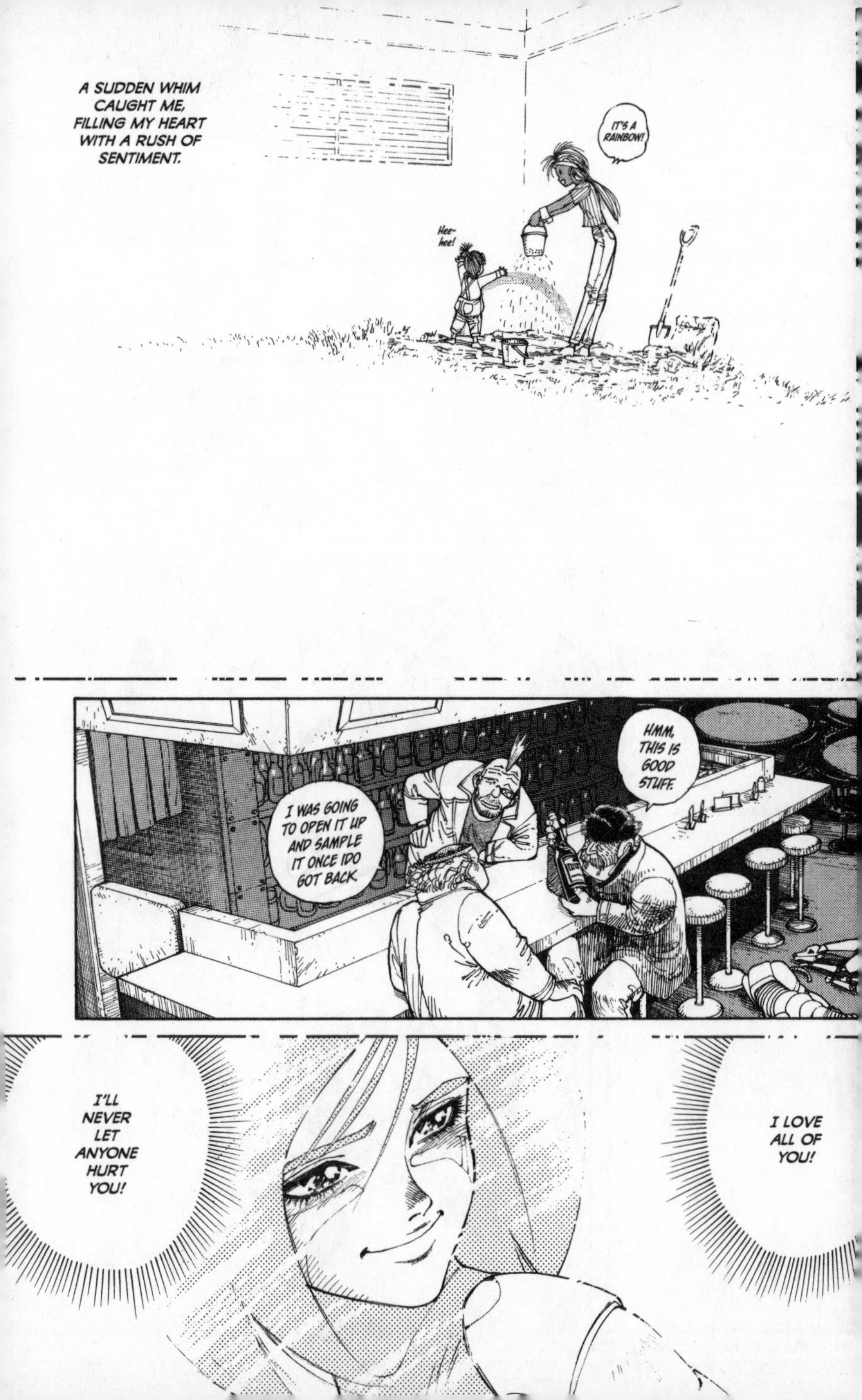
IT'S A RAINBOW!
Hee-hee!
A SUDDEN WHIM CAUGHT ME, FILLING MY HEART WITH A RUSH OF SENTIMENT.
HMM, THIS IS GOOD STUFF.
I WAS GOING TO OPEN IT UP AND SAMPLE IT ONCE IDO GOT BACK.
I LOVE ALL OF YOU!
I'LL NEVER LET ANYONE HURT YOU!

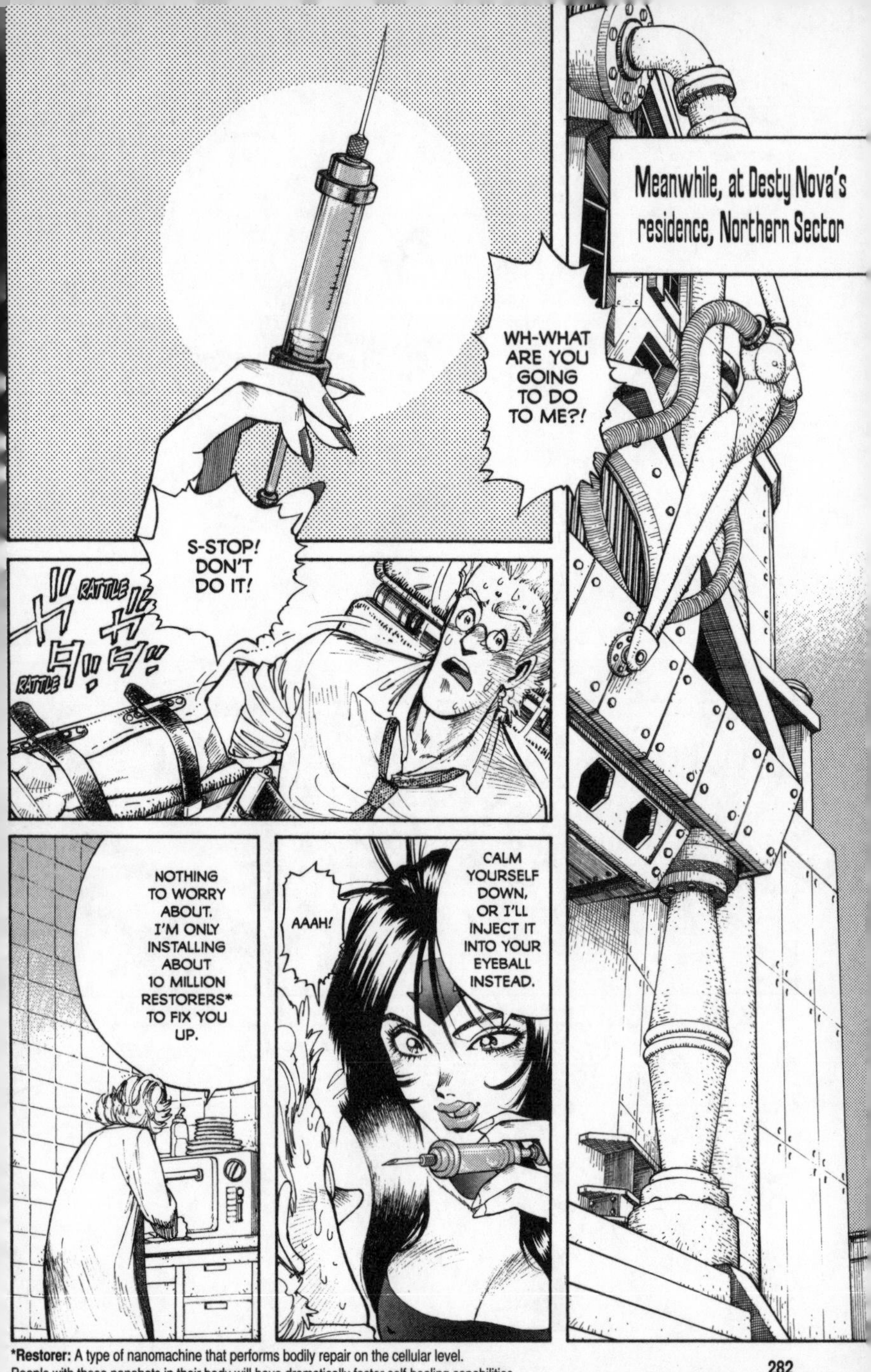
Meanwhile, at Desty Nova's residence, Northern Sector
WH-WHAT ARE YOU GOING TO DO TO ME?!
S-STOP! DON'T DO IT!
RATTLE
RATTLE
CALM YOURSELF DOWN, OR I'LL INJECT IT INTO YOUR EYEBALL INSTEAD.
AAAH!
NOTHING TO WORRY ABOUT. I'M ONLY INSTALLING ABOUT 10 MILLION RESTORERS* TO FIX YOU UP.

***Restorer:** A type of nanomachine that performs bodily repair on the cellular level. People with these nanobots in their body will have dramatically faster self-healing capabilities.

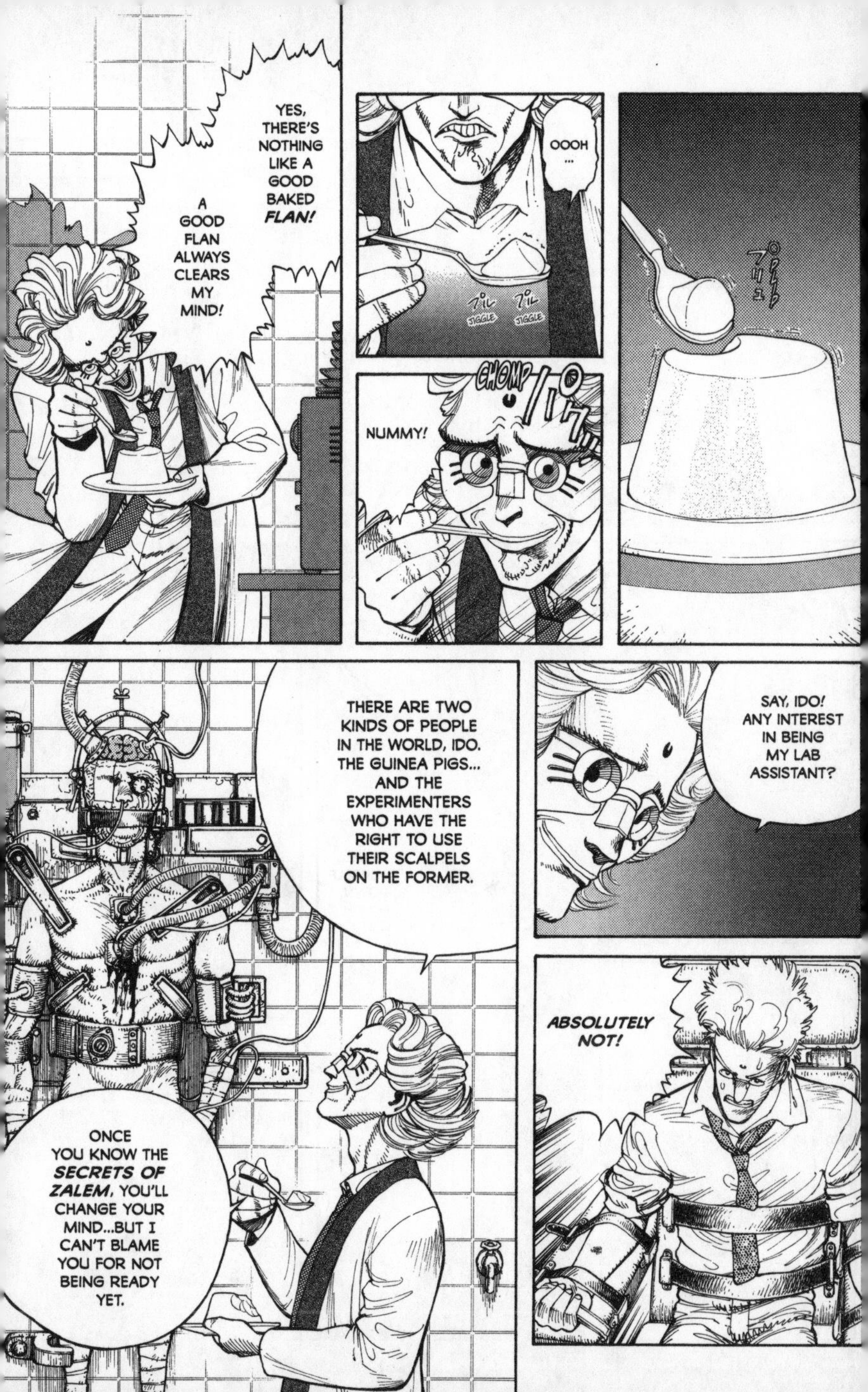
OOOH ...
JIGGLE
JIGGLE
CHOMP
NUMMY!
YES, THERE'S NOTHING LIKE A GOOD BAKED FLAN!
A GOOD FLAN ALWAYS CLEARS MY MIND!
SAY, IDO! ANY INTEREST IN BEING MY LAB ASSISTANT?
ABSOLUTELY NOT!
THERE ARE TWO KINDS OF PEOPLE IN THE WORLD, IDO. THE GUINEA PIGS... AND THE EXPERIMENTERS WHO HAVE THE RIGHT TO USE THEIR SCALPELS ON THE FORMER.
ONCE YOU KNOW THE SECRETS OF ZALEM, YOU'LL CHANGE YOUR MIND...BUT I CAN'T BLAME YOU FOR NOT BEING READY YET.

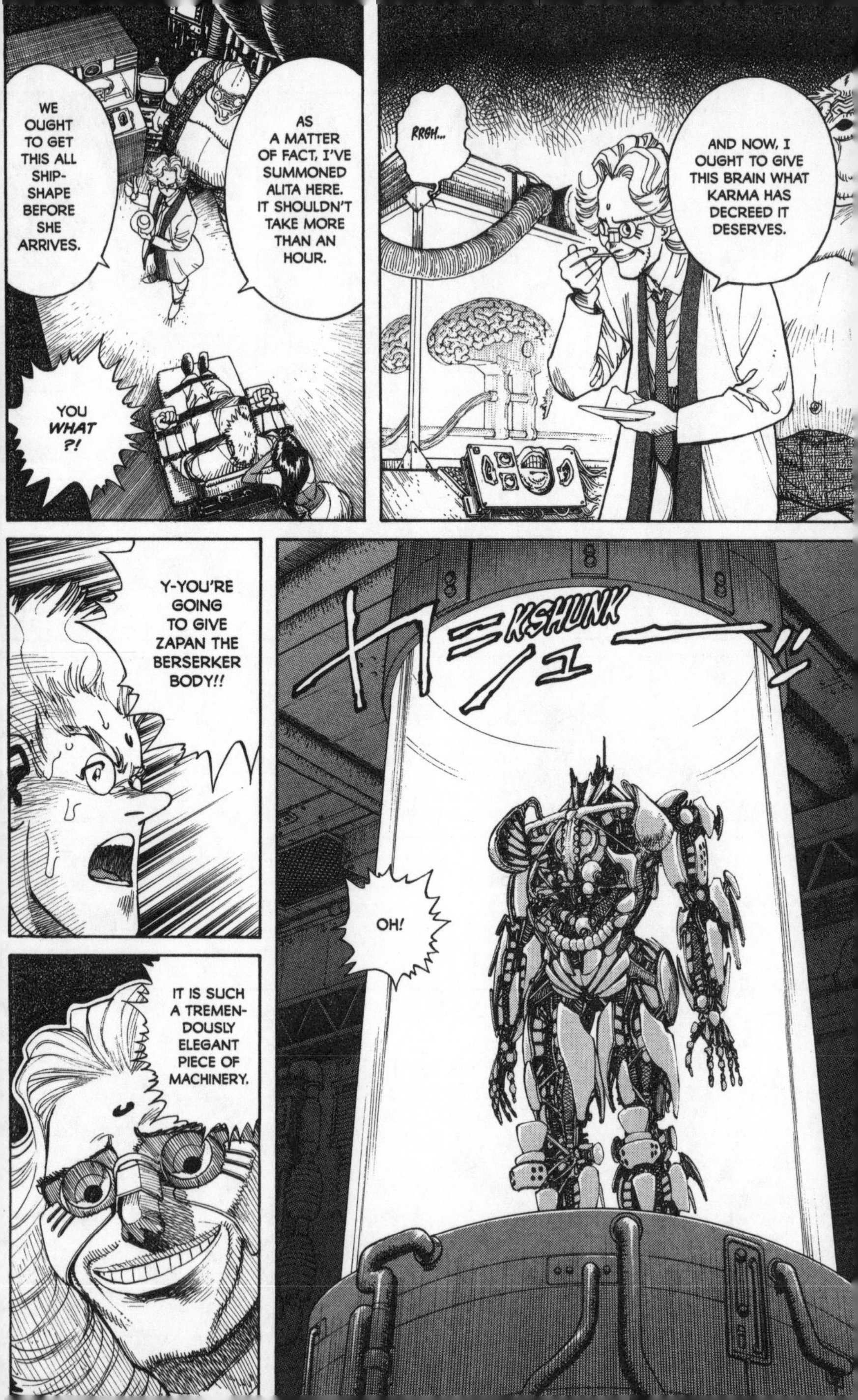
RRGH...
AND NOW, I OUGHT TO GIVE THIS BRAIN WHAT KARMA HAS DECREED IT DESERVES.
AS A MATTER OF FACT, I'VE SUMMONED ALITA HERE. IT SHOULDN'T TAKE MORE THAN AN HOUR.
WE OUGHT TO GET THIS ALL SHIP-SHAPE BEFORE SHE ARRIVES.
YOU *WHAT* ?!
KSHUNK
OH!
Y-YOU'RE GOING TO GIVE ZAPAN THE BERSERKER BODY!!
IT IS SUCH A TREMEN-DOUSLY ELEGANT PIECE OF MACHINERY.

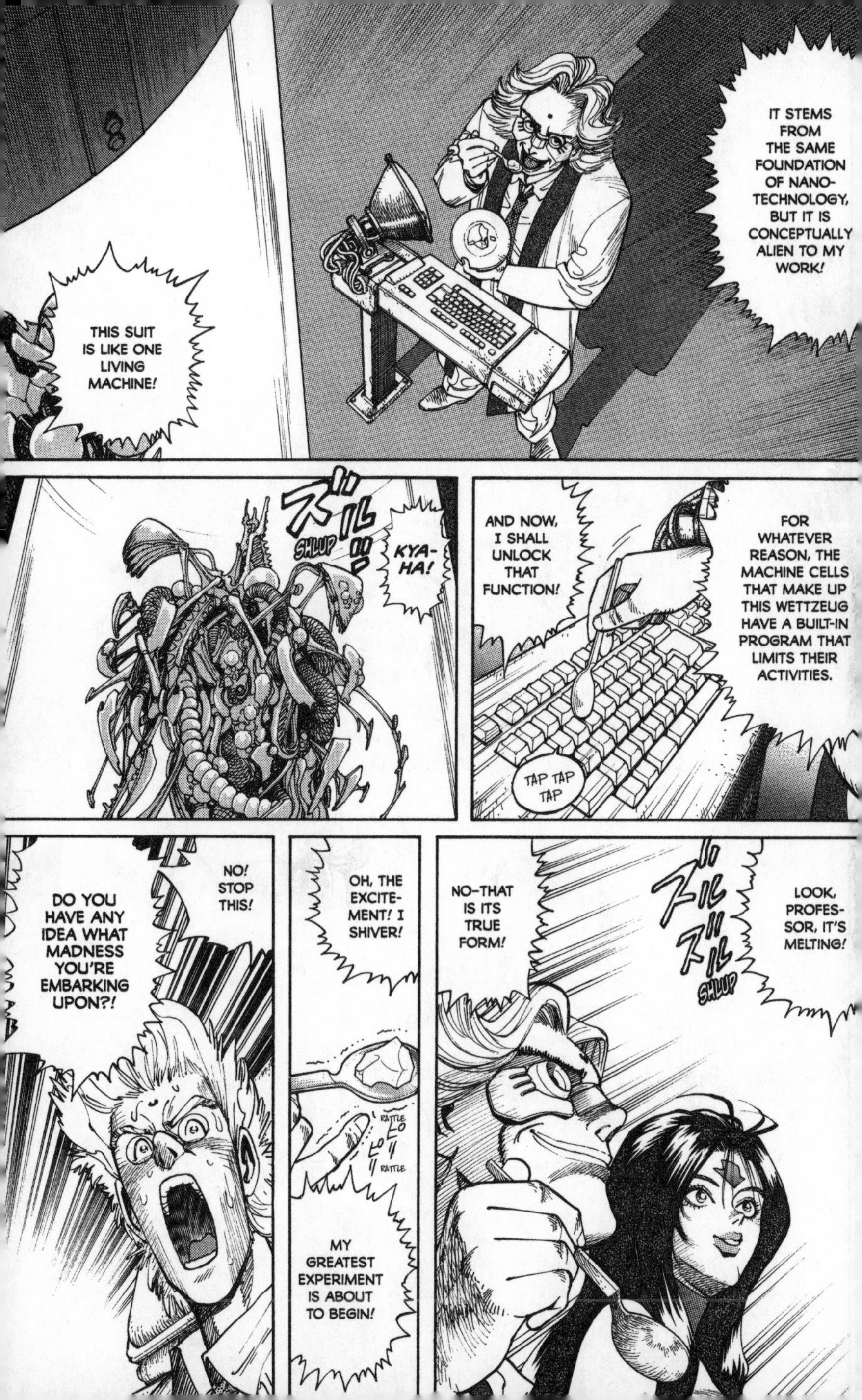
IT STEMS FROM THE SAME FOUNDATION OF NANO-TECHNOLOGY, BUT IT IS CONCEPTUALLY ALIEN TO MY WORK!
THIS SUIT IS LIKE ONE LIVING MACHINE!
FOR WHATEVER REASON, THE MACHINE CELLS THAT MAKE UP THIS WETTZEUG HAVE A BUILT-IN PROGRAM THAT LIMITS THEIR ACTIVITIES.
AND NOW, I SHALL UNLOCK THAT FUNCTION!
TAP TAP TAP
SHLUP
KYA-HA!
LOOK, PROFES-SOR, IT'S MELTING!
SHLUP
NO—THAT IS ITS TRUE FORM!
OH, THE EXCITE-MENT! I SHIVER!
RATTLE
RATTLE
MY GREATEST EXPERIMENT IS ABOUT TO BEGIN!
NO! STOP THIS!
DO YOU HAVE ANY IDEA WHAT MADNESS YOU'RE EMBARKING UPON?!

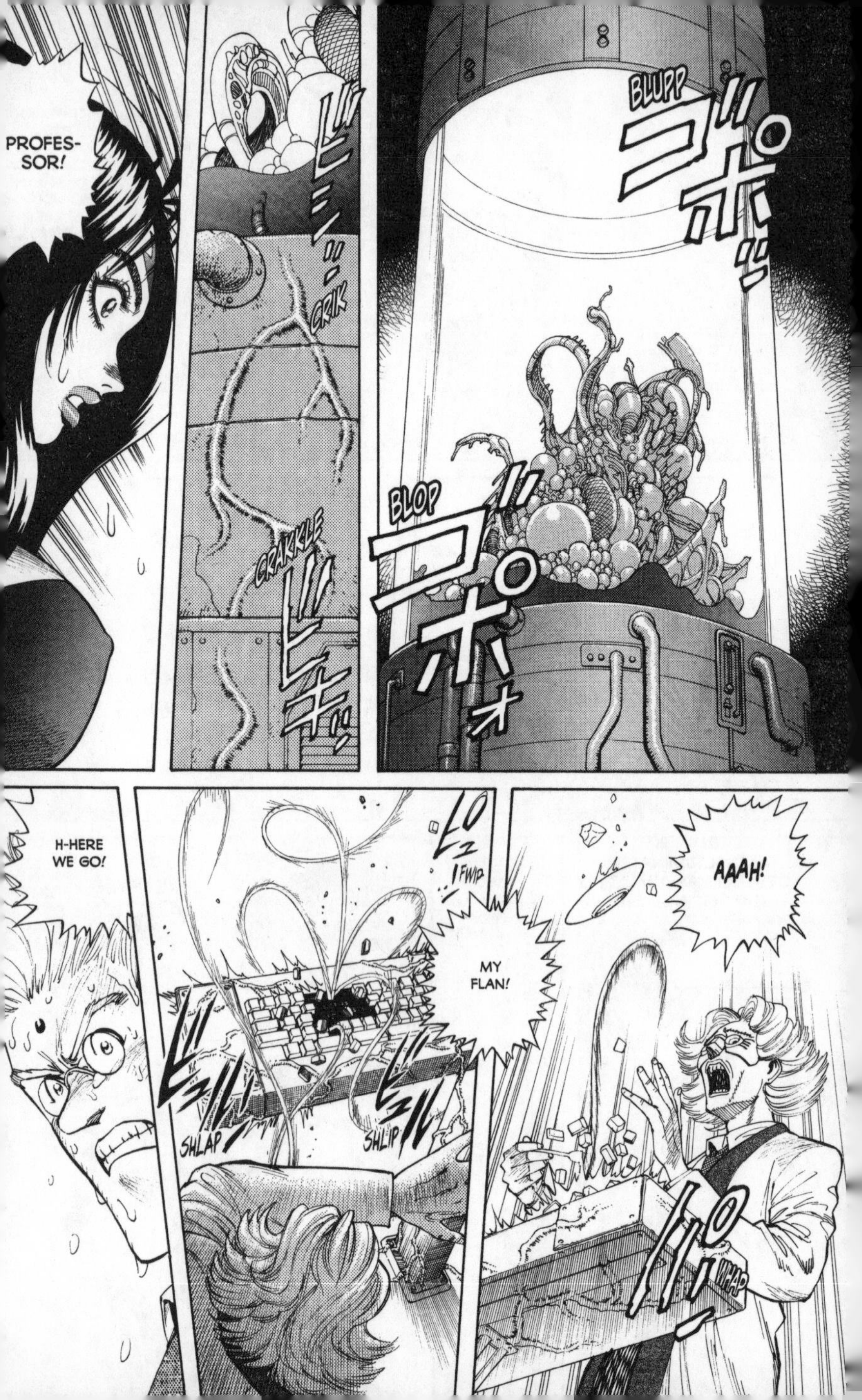
BLUPP
BLOP
CRIK
CRAKKLE
PROFES-SOR!
AAAH!
WHAP
FWIP
MY FLAN!
SHLIP
SHLAP
H-HERE WE GO!

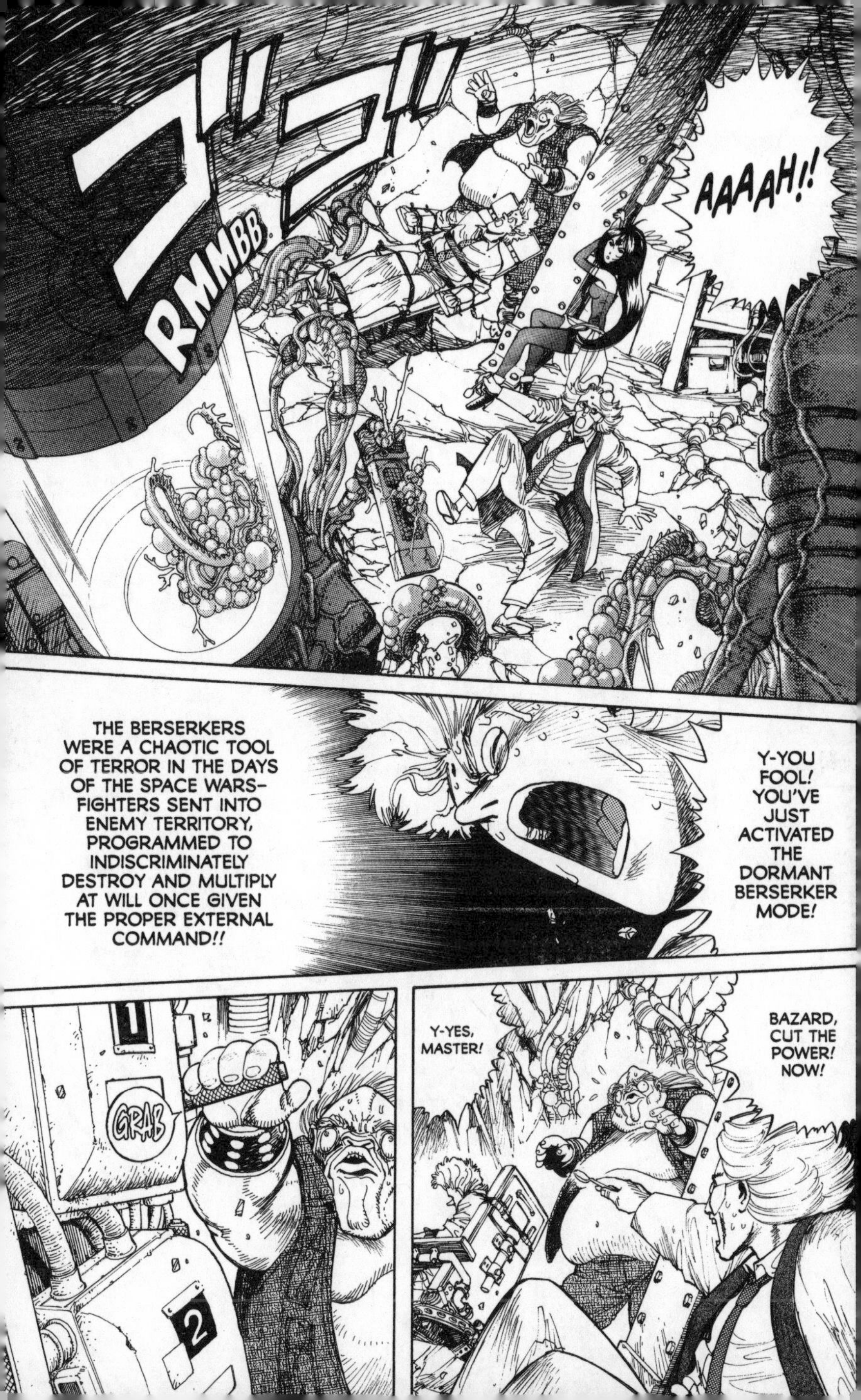
AAAAH!!
RMMBB
Y-YOU FOOL! YOU'VE JUST ACTIVATED THE DORMANT BERSERKER MODE!
THE BERSERKERS WERE A CHAOTIC TOOL OF TERROR IN THE DAYS OF THE SPACE WARS–FIGHTERS SENT INTO ENEMY TERRITORY, PROGRAMMED TO INDISCRIMINATELY DESTROY AND MULTIPLY AT WILL ONCE GIVEN THE PROPER EXTERNAL COMMAND!!
BAZARD, CUT THE POWER! NOW!
Y-YES, MASTER!
GRAB
1
2

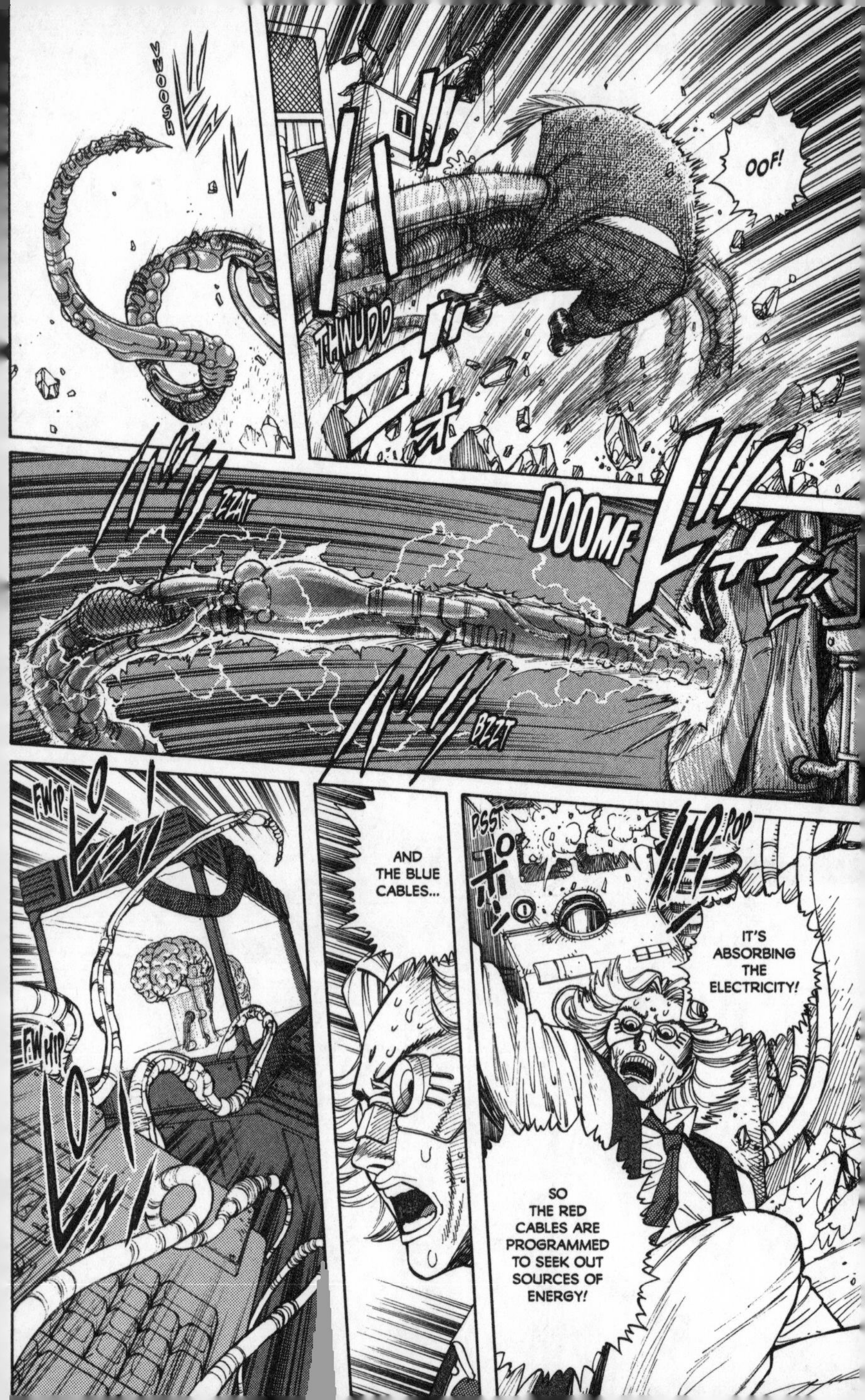
OOF!
THWUDD
VWOOSH
DOOMF
ZZZAT
BZZAT
POP
PSST
IT'S ABSORBING THE ELECTRICITY!
SO THE RED CABLES ARE PROGRAMMED TO SEEK OUT SOURCES OF ENERGY!
AND THE BLUE CABLES...
FWIP
FWHIP

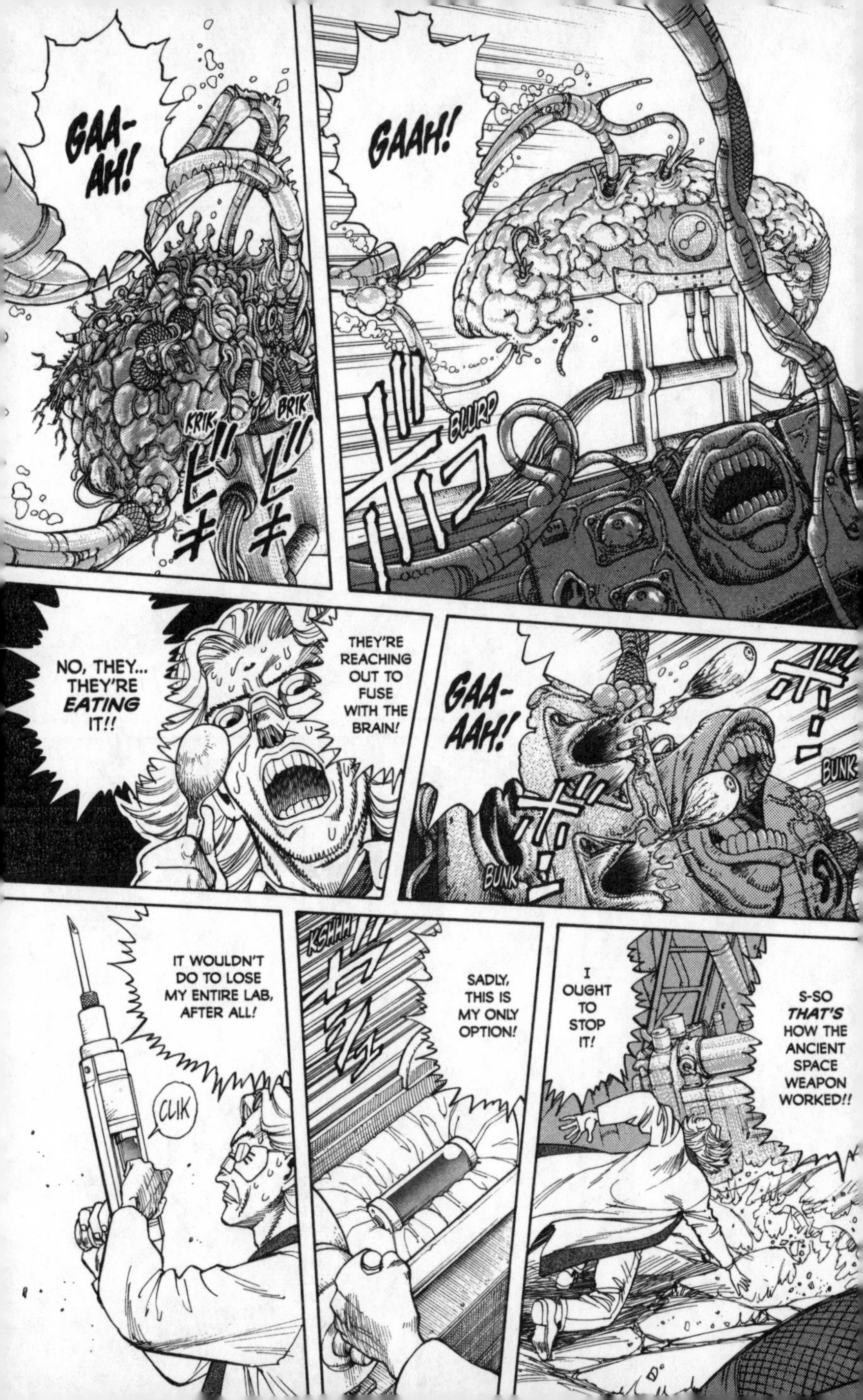
GAAH!
BLURP
GAA-AH!
KRIK
BRIK
GAA-AAH!
BUNK
BUNK
THEY'RE REACHING OUT TO FUSE WITH THE BRAIN!
NO, THEY... THEY'RE *EATING* IT!!
S-SO *THAT'S* HOW THE ANCIENT SPACE WEAPON WORKED!!
I OUGHT TO STOP IT!
KSHHH
SADLY, THIS IS MY ONLY OPTION!
IT WOULDN'T DO TO LOSE MY ENTIRE LAB, AFTER ALL!
CLIK

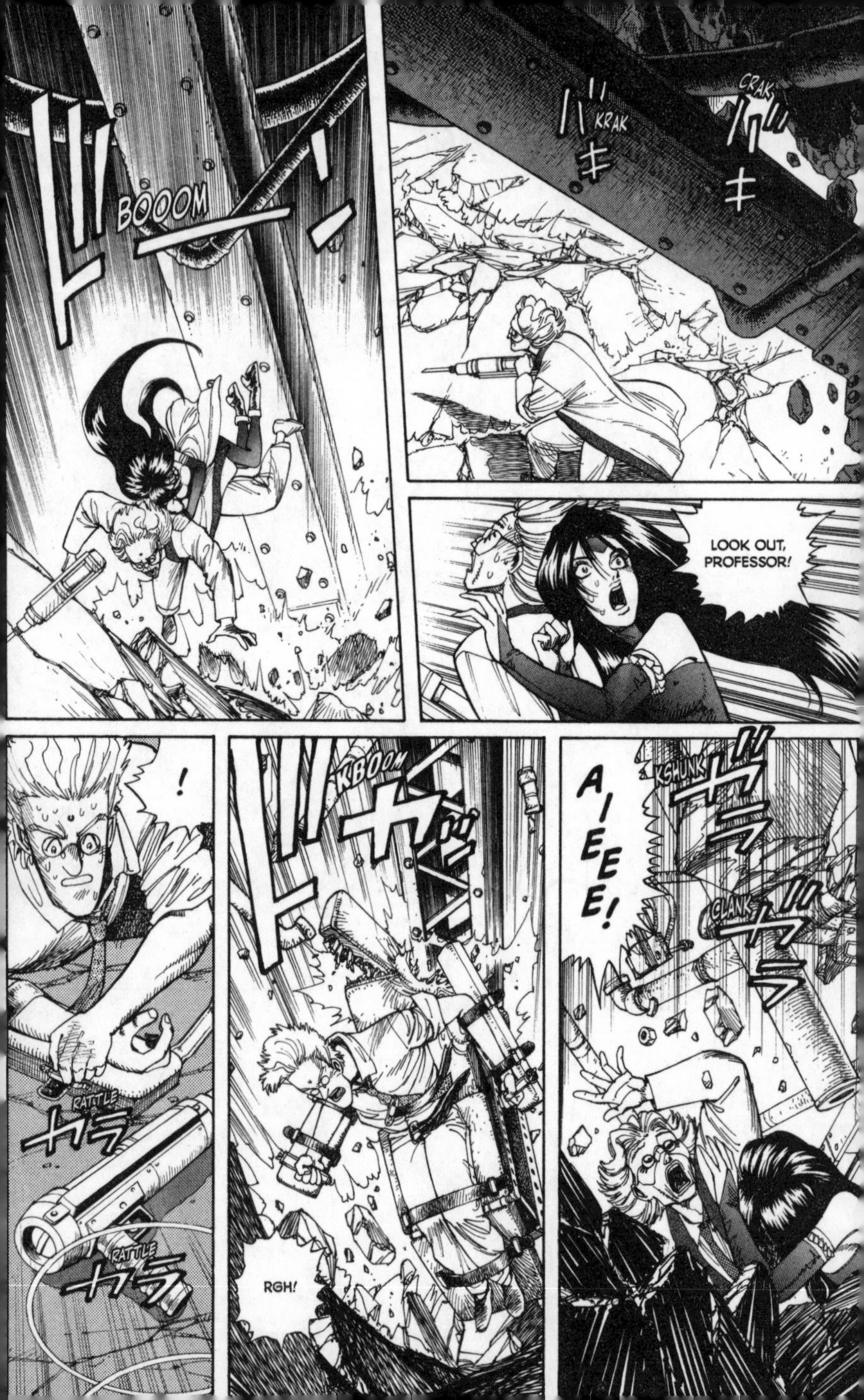
KRAK
CRAK
LOOK OUT, PROFESSOR!
BOOOM
KSHUNK
CLANK
AIEEEE!
KBOOM
RGH!
!
RATTLE
RATTLE

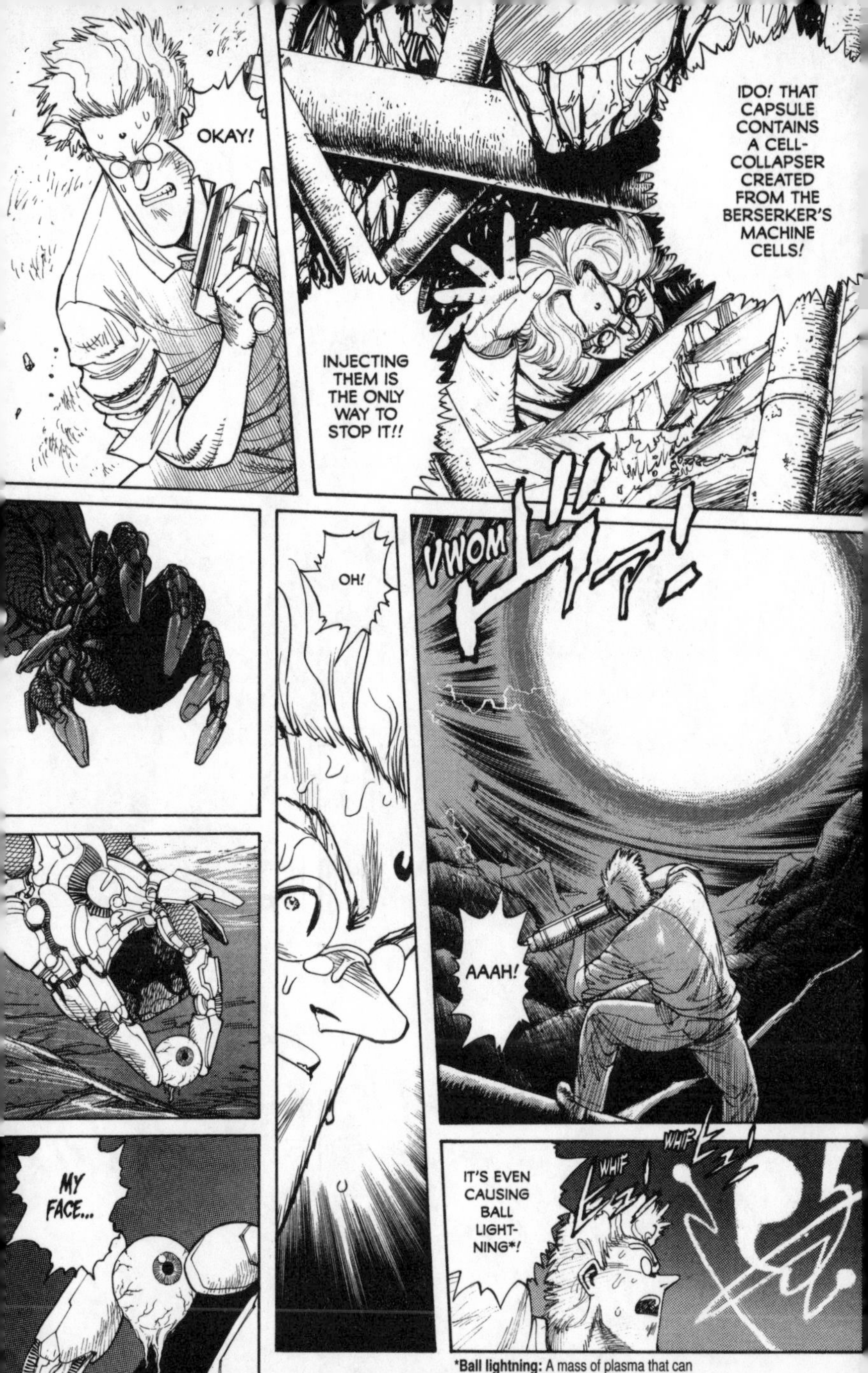
IDO! THAT CAPSULE CONTAINS A CELL-COLLAPSER CREATED FROM THE BERSERKER'S MACHINE CELLS!
INJECTING THEM IS THE ONLY WAY TO STOP IT!!
OKAY!
VWOM
AAAH!
IT'S EVEN CAUSING BALL LIGHT-NING*!
WHIF
WHIF
OH!
MY FACE...

***Ball lightning:** A mass of plasma that can form naturally in midair during thunderstorms.

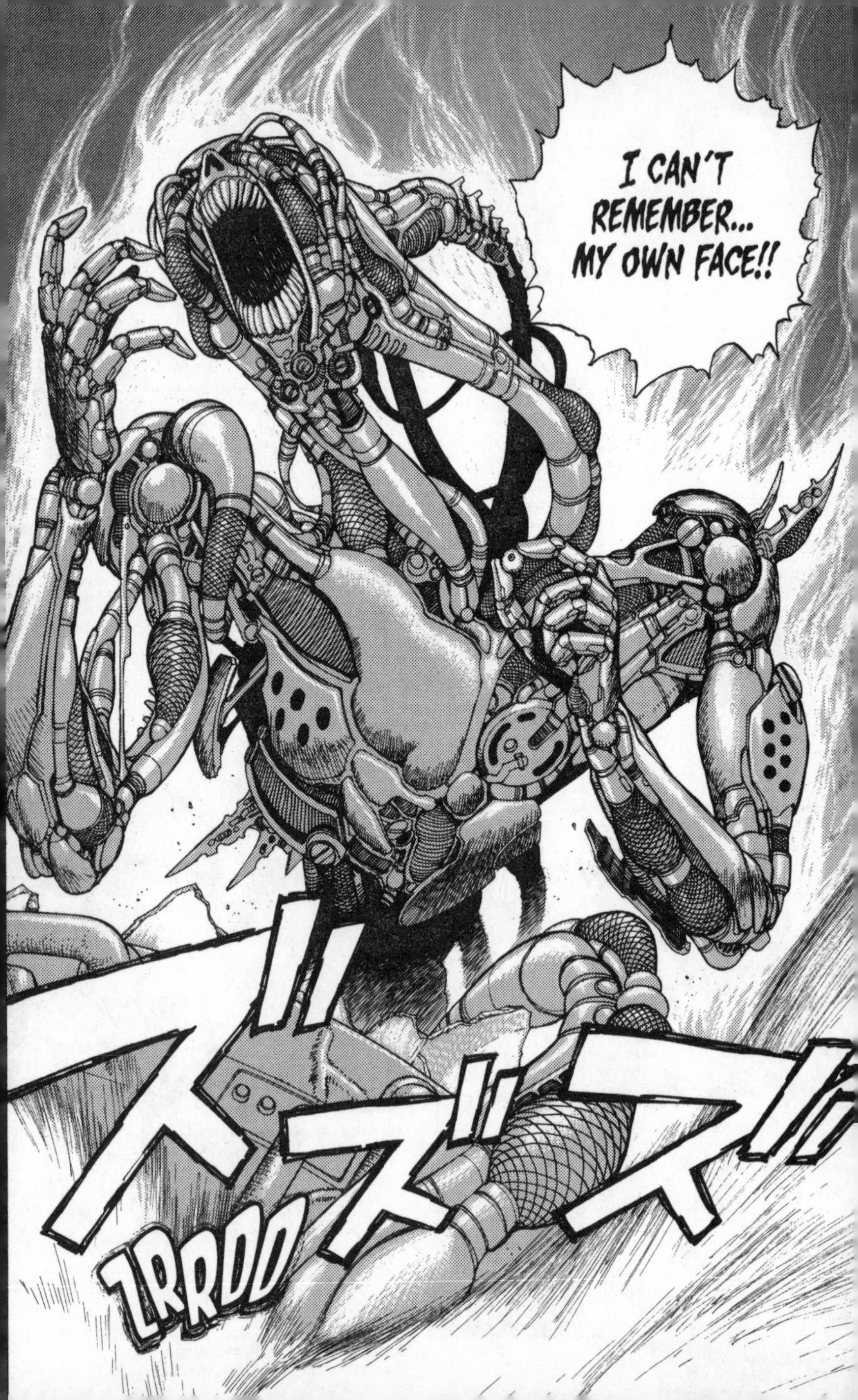
I CAN'T REMEMBER... MY OWN FACE!!
ZRROO

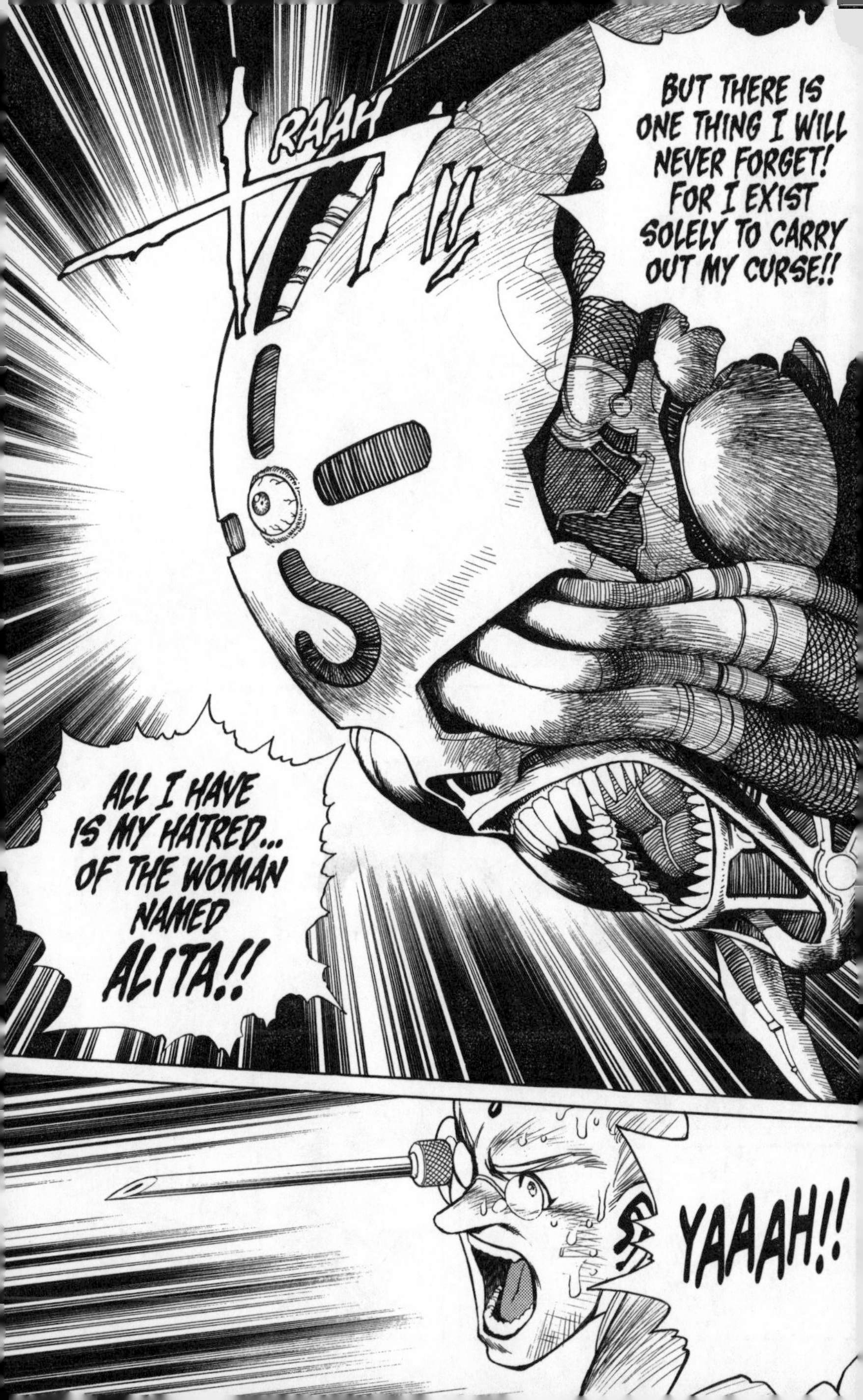
BUT THERE IS ONE THING I WILL NEVER FORGET! FOR I EXIST SOLELY TO CARRY OUT MY CURSE!!
RAAH
ALL I HAVE IS MY HATRED... OF THE WOMAN NAMED ALITA!!
YAAAH!!

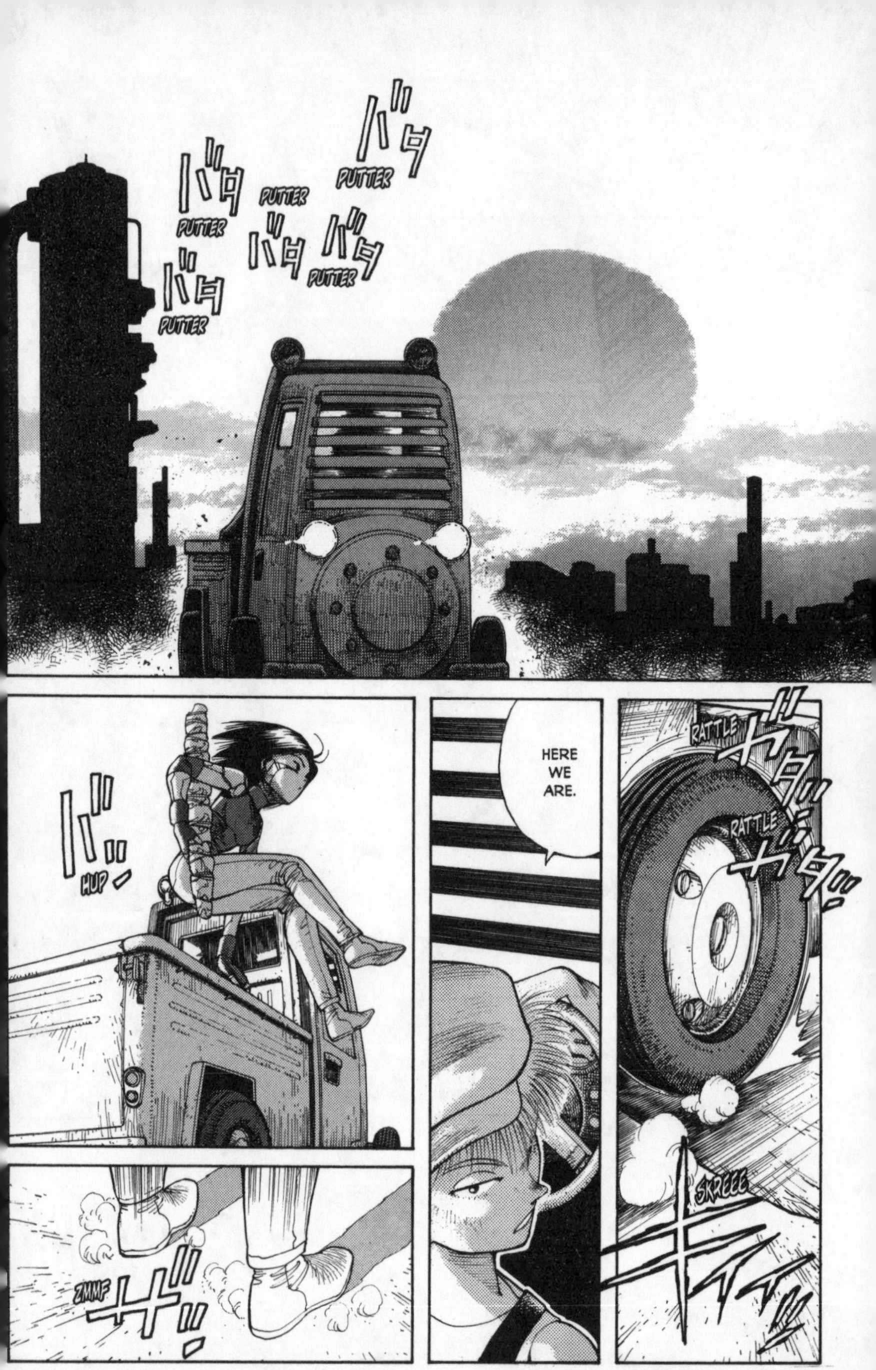

バタ
PUTTER
バタ
PUTTER
バタ
PUTTER
バタ
PUTTER
バタ
PUTTER
RATTLE
ガタ
RATTLE
ガタ
SKREEE
キィィ
HERE WE ARE.
HUP
バッ
ZMMF
ザッ

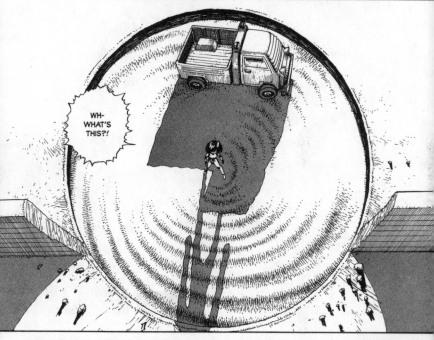

WH-WHAT'S THIS?!

IT'S BEEN MELTED AWAY INTO GLASS...

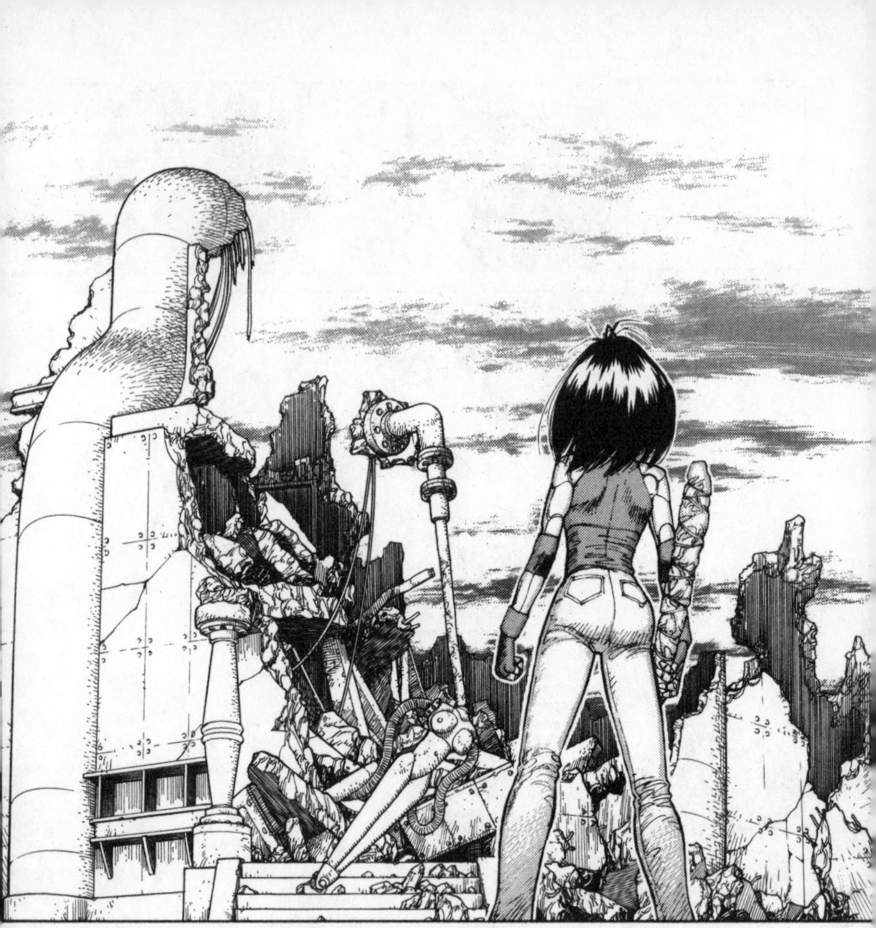

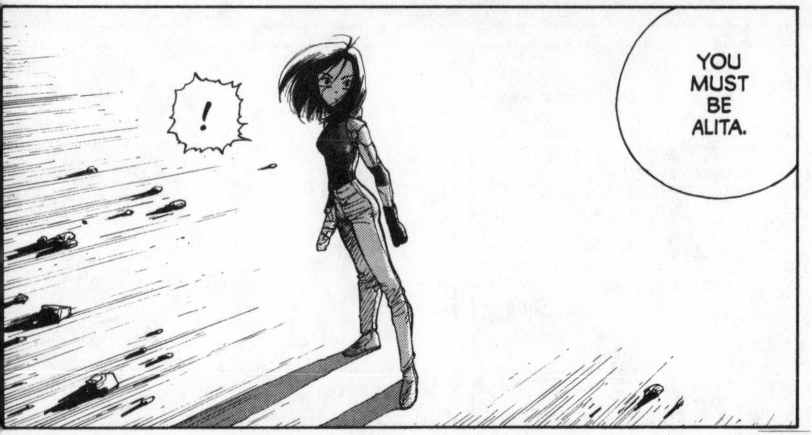
YOU MUST BE ALITA.
!

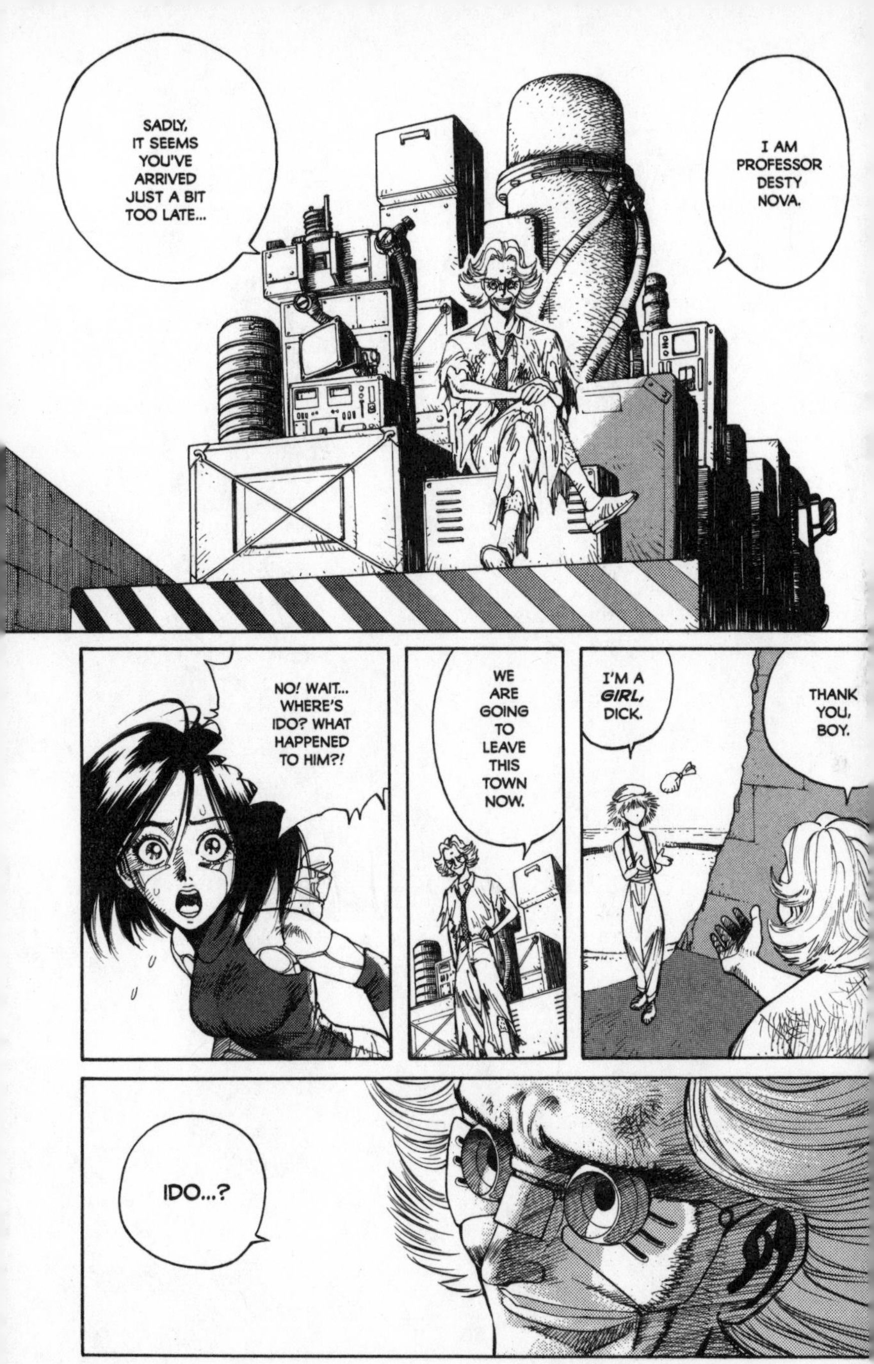
I AM PROFESSOR DESTY NOVA.
SADLY, IT SEEMS YOU'VE ARRIVED JUST A BIT TOO LATE...
THANK YOU, BOY.
I'M A *GIRL,* DICK.
WE ARE GOING TO LEAVE THIS TOWN NOW.
NO! WAIT... WHERE'S IDO? WHAT HAPPENED TO HIM?!
IDO...?

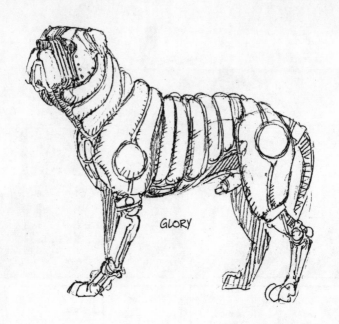

GLORY

Computer Tarot, page 3

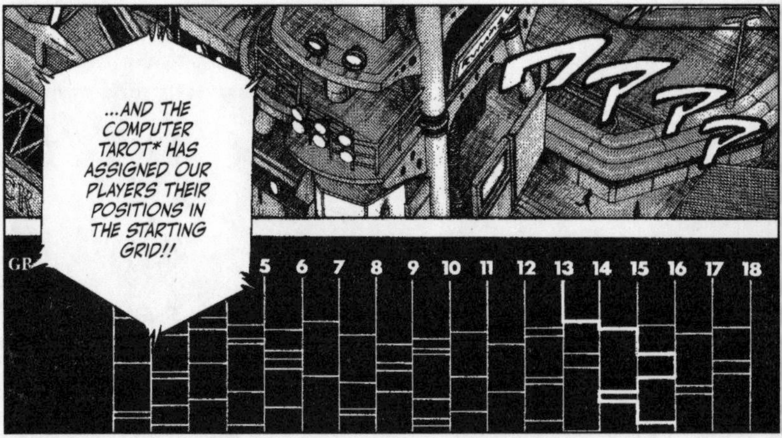
...AND THE COMPUTER TAROT* HAS ASSIGNED OUR PLAYERS THEIR POSITIONS IN THE STARTING GRID!!
5 6 7 8 9 10 11 12 13 14 15 16 17 18

While this term is meant to conjure images of tarot cards, the actual grid as depicted is a kind of "random" drawing method called *amidakuji* in Japanese. In *amidakuji*, contestants pick their columns and then trace them along the randomized legs toward the other end of the column, taking each possible side path along the way. It's an alternative to drawing straws, or rock-paper-scissors.

Gunjian, page 19

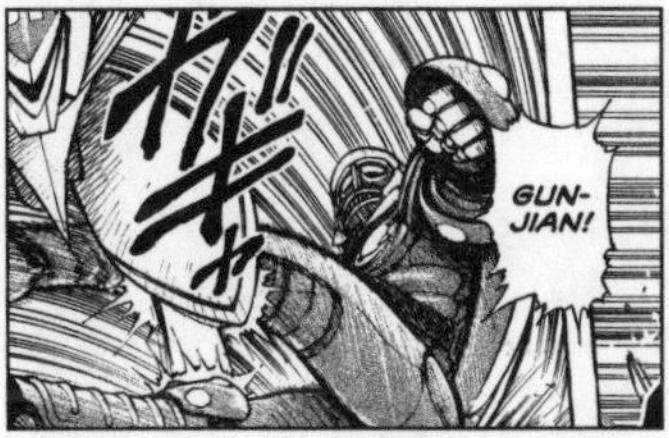
GUN-JIAN!

A Chinese term that means "spin slice."

Bandal Chagi, page 36

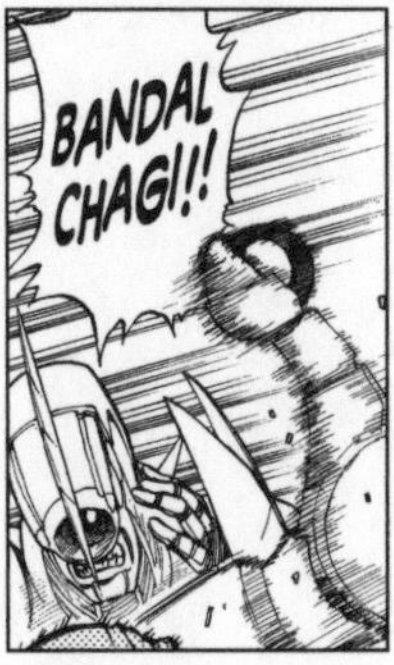
BANDAL CHAGI!!

An actual kick technique in taekwondo that means "crescent kick."

Digongtui, page 43

A derivation of the digong from Aydakatti's style (digongquan), meaning "great earth," plus "kick" or "leg."

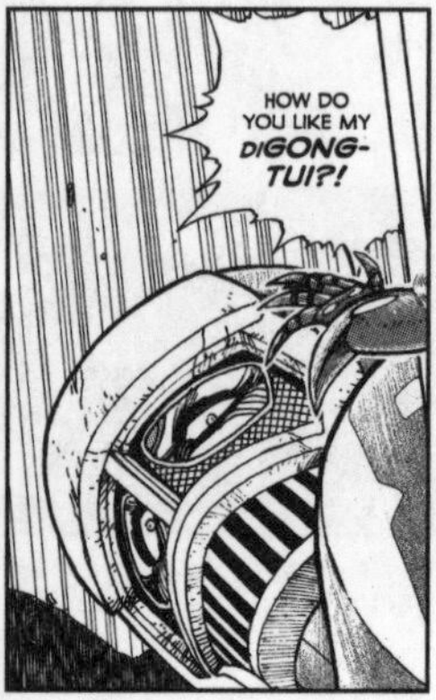
HOW DO YOU LIKE MY DIGONG-TUI?!

Aufzett Stossen, page 51

A German-derived attack name that is intended to mean "overhead angle kick."

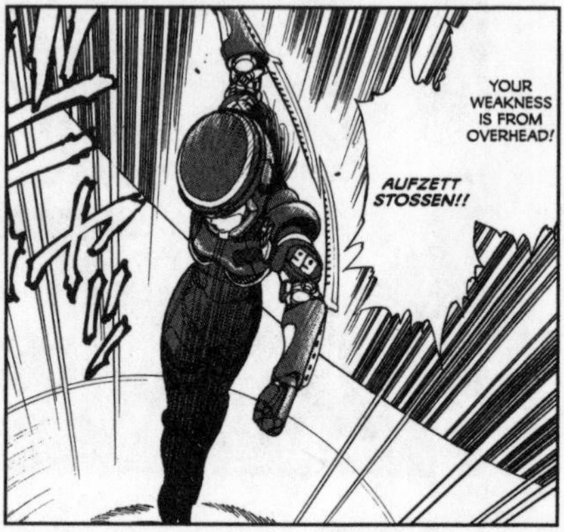
YOUR WEAKNESS IS FROM OVERHEAD!
AUFZETT STOSSEN!!

Kimujina, page 130

The kanji provided for Kimji's full name (Kimujina) mean "machine badger."

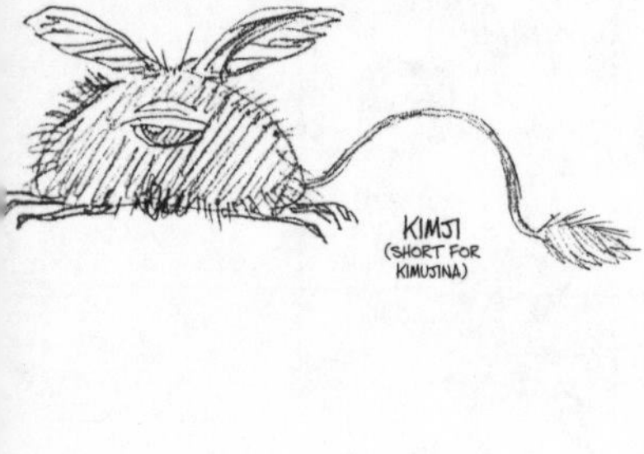
KIMJI (SHORT FOR KIMUJINA)

Geheimnis, page 174

The German word for "secret." In this case it refers to the secret teachings of Panzer Kunst.

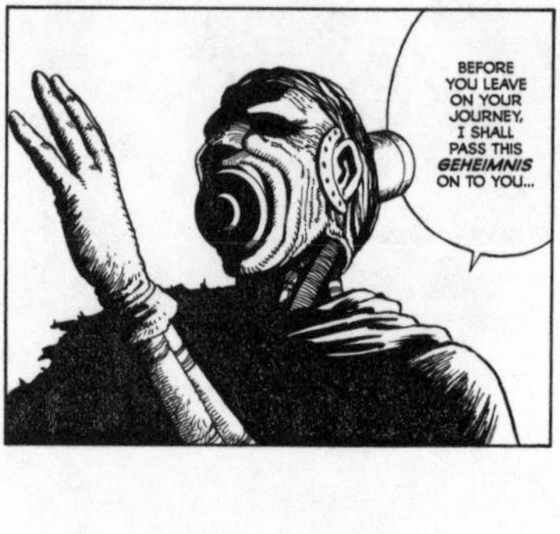
BEFORE YOU LEAVE ON YOUR JOURNEY, I SHALL PASS THIS GEHEIMNIS ON TO YOU...

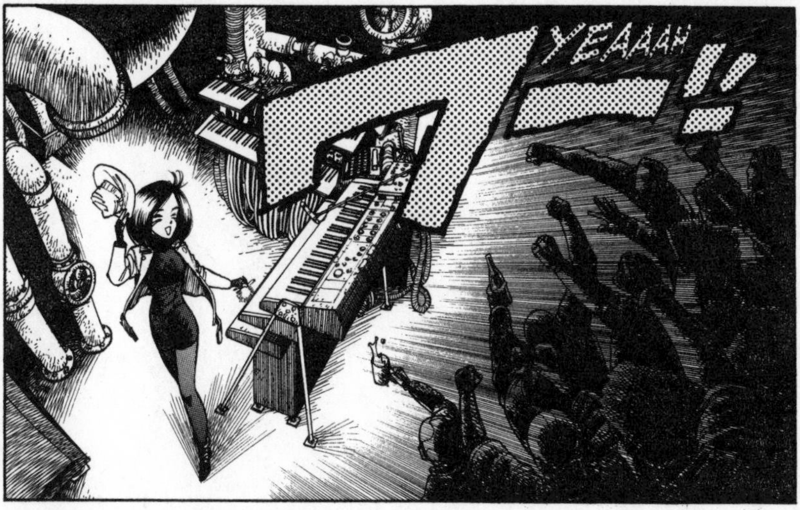
YEAAAH!!

Big Generator, page 221

The lyrics to Alita's song in this scene come from the original English adaptation of the Battle Angel Alita manga by Fred Burke and Toshifumi Yoshida for Viz Media in 1998, and are printed as such in the latest edition of the manga in Japan. However, in the initial 1993 Japanese release, she was singing the lyrics (with proper attribution) to the Yes song "Big Generator." Some remnants of this can be seen in the crowd chants, which are left in their untouched state like all of the sound effects in this edition.

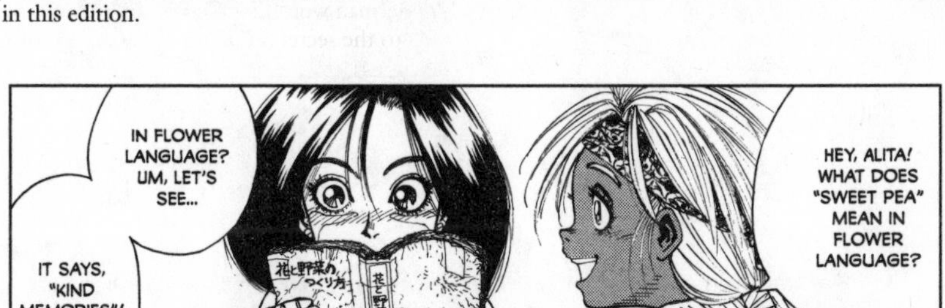
HEY, ALITA! WHAT DOES "SWEET PEA" MEAN IN FLOWER LANGUAGE?
IN FLOWER LANGUAGE? UM, LET'S SEE...
花と野菜のつくり方
IT SAYS, "KIND MEMORIES"!

Flower language, page 277

Originally called *hanakotoba* in Japanese, flower language is a way to communicate meaning through flowers. In the West, this can be called "the language of flowers" or "florigraphy." In Japan, *hanakotoba* as a concept is fairly common, so it often comes up in media like manga and anime.

PERFECT WORLD

Rie Aruga

A TOUCHING NEW SERIES ABOUT LOVE AND COPING WITH DISABILITY

An office party reunites Tsugumi with her high school crush Itsuki. He's realized his dream of becoming an architect, but along the way, he experienced a spinal injury that put him in a wheelchair. Now Tsugumi's rekindled feelings will butt up against prejudices she never considered — and Itsuki will have to decide if he's ready to let someone into his heart...

"Depicts with great delicacy and courage the difficulties some with disabilities experience getting involved in romantic relationships... Rie Aruga refuses to romanticize, pushing her heroine to face the reality of disability. She invites her readers to the same tasks of empathy, knowledge and recognition."
—Slate.fr

"An important entry [in manga romance]... The emotional core of both plot and characters indicates thoughtfulness... [Aruga's] research is readily apparent in the text and artwork, making this feel like a real story."
—Anime News Network

KC KODANSHA COMICS

A SMART, NEW ROMANTIC COMEDY FOR FANS OF *SHORTCAKE CAKE* AND *TERRACE HOUSE*!

Living-Room Matsunaga-san © Keiko Iwashita / Kodansha Ltd.

A romance manga starring high school girl Meeko, who learns to live on her own in a boarding house whose living room is home to the odd (but handsome) Matsunaga-san. She begins to adjust to her new life away from her parents, but Meeko soon learns that no matter how far away from home she is, she's still a young girl at heart — especially when she finds herself falling for Matsunaga-san.

Battle Angel Alita Paperback volume 3 is a work of fiction. Names, characters, places, and incidents are the products of the author's imagination or are used fictitiously. Any resemblance to actual events, locales, or persons, living or dead, is entirely coincidental.

A Kodansha Comics Trade Paperback Original
Battle Angel Alita Paperback volume 3 copyright © 2016 Yukito Kishiro
English translation copyright © 2021 Yukito Kishiro

All rights reserved.

Published in the United States by Kodansha Comics, an imprint of
Kodansha USA Publishing, LLC, New York.

Publication rights for this English edition arranged through
Kodansha Ltd., Tokyo.

First published in Japan in 2016 by Kodansha Ltd., Tokyo,
as *Battle Angel Alita* volume 2.

ISBN 978-1-64651-259-1

Printed in the United States of America.

www.kodansha.us

1st Printing
Translation: Stephen Paul
Lettering: Scott O. Brown, Evan Hayden
Editing: Ajani Oloye, Alejandro Arbona
Kodansha Comics edition cover design by Phil Balsman

Publisher: Kiichiro Sugawara

Director of publishing services: Ben Applegate
Associate director of operations: Stephen Pakula
Publishing services managing editors: Madison Salters, Alanna Ruse
Production managers: Emi Lotto, Angela Zurlo
Logo © Kodansha USA Publishing, LLC